Participants in the
Battle of the Little Big Horn

Participants in the Battle of the Little Big Horn

A Biographical Dictionary of Sioux, Cheyenne and United States Military Personnel

FREDERIC C. WAGNER III

McFarland & Company, Inc., Publishers

Jefferson, North Carolina, and London

LIBRARY OF CONGRESS CATALOGUING-IN-PUBLICATION DATA

Wagner, Frederic C., 1940–
Participants in the Battle of the Little Big Horn : a biographical
dictionary of Sioux, Cheyenne and United States military personnel /
Frederic C. Wagner III.
p.   cm.
Includes bibliographical references and index.

ISBN 978-0-7864-6289-6
illustrated case binding : 50# alkaline paper ∞

1. Little Bighorn, Battle of the, Mont., 1876.
2. Little Bighorn, Battle of the, Mont., 1876 — Biography — Dictionaries.
3. United States, Army. Cavalry Regiment, 7th — Biography — Dictionaries.
4. Dakota Indians — Biography — Dictionaries.
5. Cheyenne Indians — Biography — Dictionaries.
I. Title.
E83.876.W23   2011   973.8'2 — dc22   2011013179

British Library cataloguing data are available

Front cover: *The Battle of Little Big Horn* (© 2011 The Granger
Collection); foreground border © 2011 Shutterstock

Manufactured in the United States of America

McFarland & Company, Inc., Publishers
Box 611, Jefferson, North Carolina 28640
www.mcfarlandpub.com

To my wife, Lisa,
with whom all things are possible

Table of Contents

Abbreviations

1SG — First sergeant

3C — Third Cavalry

5I — Fifth Infantry

6I — Sixth Infantry

BG — Brigadier General

BSM — Blacksmith

Bvt — Brevet

C — Cheyenne.

CBHMA — Custer Battlefield Historical & Museum Association

CO — Commanding Officer

CPL — Corporal

CPT — Captain

D.T. — Dakota Territory

DOR — Date of rank

DOW — Died of wounds

E/7I, etc. — Unit designation (here, Company E, Seventh Infantry)

EM — Enlisted men or man

FAL — Fort Abraham Lincoln

FAR — Farrier

GO — General Order(s)

GAC — George Armstrong Custer

KIA — Killed in action

LBHA — Little Big Horn Associates

LSH — Last Stand Hill

LTC — Lieutenant Colonel

M.T. — Montana Territory (as distinct from MT, the modern state abbreviation)

MH — Medal of Honor

MTC — Medicine Tail Coulee

PRD — Powder River Depot (also called Yellowstone Depot)

RCOI — Reno Court of Inquiry (the event, and *italicized*, the book title)

SAD — Saddler

TDY — Temporary duty

TMP — Trumpeter (the cavalry used "trumpets"; the infantry used "bugles")

USMA — United States Military Academy

W.T. — Wyoming Territory

WAG — Wagoner

WIA — Wounded in action

Preface and Acknowledgments

This work was never meant to be published, at least not initially. It started out as a series of notes, haphazard at best, but always growing, new information always being added, anecdotes, rumors, stories and old wives' tales eagerly sought after and sometimes received. I never thought it would be complete — still don't — but somehow, through the accumulation of new books and data, I managed to come as close as I think possible in discovering who, exactly, was at the Little Big Horn on the side of the military.

There are few events in the history of our Republic as contentious as those that unfolded on June 25 and 26, 1876, two hot summer days in the dusty, inhospitable hills of what we now call Montana. By the time June 27 rolled around, the American army had suffered the most ignominious defeat in its history, a defeat unrivaled to this day, regardless of the numbers involved. It was made all the more embarrassing by the fact that a magnificent regiment of United States cavalry was brought to its knees by a seemingly undisciplined horde of what we liked, in those days, quite undeservedly, to call savages.

Maybe the only certainty surrounding the battle of the Little Big Horn is that Lieutenant Colonel George Armstrong Custer — considered a modern, true American hero in his day because of his Civil War exploits — and a couple of his brothers, died there. There are those who dispute the body counts, the methods of death, the number of soldiers in the fight, and every other item of minutiæ imaginable. Needless to say, if we cannot agree on the number of soldiers, civilian scouts, government employees, and ordinary civilians who were there, what chance do we have of agreeing on the number of Indians?

What follows here is an attempt to clarify some of the uncertainty involving the battle's participants, and while I originally strived to clear up murky waters, I fear I am only adding to the confusion, the uncertainty, and even the vitriol of disagreement. While it seems the organizational structure of the military is quite straightforward, that rather closed society has its own peculiar way of shipping men hither-and-yon, and confusing even the most organized of minds. It was no different in 1876 than it is today, and some troopers were attached, detached, sick, deserting, straggling, and in one form or another struggling with their mortality for a couple of days. To add to the confusion, some of the soldiers later obfuscated their roles in the battle. By the time the last one died seventy-five years later, it was even less clear what had really happened.

The rosters and short biographies found within these pages are broken into several sections. Section I begins with a brief history of the Seventh Cavalry from its inception in 1866, to the fateful campaign ten years later, and is then organized alphabetically by individual, containing the names of the soldiers of the regiment who were present June 25 and June 26, 1876, on the field of battle, and those who were on the campaign, but were assigned to support functions along the way.

While there are some minor exceptions, generally only those men of the regiment who were on the Great Sioux Campaign are listed, i.e., those who departed Fort Abraham Lincoln on May 17, 1876. These exceptions, however, appeared on the regimental returns, so I am loath to exclude them. (A note of caution is necessary here. A number of enlisted men joined the army under assumed names or aliases. For consistency's sake, they are listed by the name used in the army's "returns." The name listed may not necessarily have been the man's real name, but the real name — if known — is included in parentheses.)

Every attempt — within reason — has been made to assure accuracy. Not only have historians been solicited and published works consulted, but also the actual regimental returns for the months of May, June, and July 1876, have been gone through to correct discrepancies. These so-called "returns" were the documents prepared by company first sergeants and the regimental sergeant major that indicated the whereabouts of every individual assigned to the regiment during that period, and were submitted through military channels to the Adjutant General's office. Where those men were before, or what happened to them after, is of little concern for this study; we are primarily interested in the two days of the battle.

Section II lists — alphabetically by a specific *category* this time — those individuals who accompanied the Seventh, serving in one capacity or another, such as scouts, civilian mule packers, guides, interpreters, reporters, and messengers (all of whom fought and some of whom died), and it also includes a number of Indian scouts who accompanied the forty-day campaign — much as Seventh Cavalry troopers who were on the campaign but were assigned elsewhere — but had departed the column for other duties or for various reasons. These men are included only for the sake of clarity, because in a number of cases, there is dispute over their presence or non-presence at the battle, brought about by the already confusing situation regarding their names: they are all Indians, and their Anglicized names can be confusing because many of them had multiple names. Some were called by their phonetically-spelled Indian names while others shared a name with a different individual. Because of the nature of record-keeping at the time, complete information — even birth and death dates — is often not available.

Section III is unique. It contains one of the most comprehensive sets of Indian names ever assembled — almost fifteen hundred men, women, and children — who were in the village along the banks of the Little Big Horn River at the time of the battle. It is compiled from a number of sources — vetted sources — and as far as I am concerned, is far from complete, as we define that word — or shall it ever be. It contains biographical sketches, and as should be apparent, indicates only presence, not necessarily participation in the actual fighting. Also apparent is the tenuousness of several entries, indicated by the symbol " ."

Beyond the main sections are appendices. These are included for a number of reasons. The biographies of the troopers show their unit designation. An appendix shows who else was in that unit. Also shown is a place of birth. An appendix shows how many others were from that country or that state. As one can imagine, language was a problem for the army of 1876. Did it have an effect at the battle? There is confusion over just how experienced a regiment the Seventh Cavalry really was. An appendix clears that up. What's a claybank or a dun? Is a gray a gray or is it a white? Or *is* there a white? Check the appendix for horses; they too were at the battle and played a significant role. If one of the Indians listed fought the Custer column, but not Major Marcus Reno's command, who else was with that man?

Check an appendix; it is there. And while Custer's Chief-of-Scouts, Second Lieutenant Charles Albert Varnum once bemoaned, "There were more Indians than I ever saw before. I had seen immense numbers ... and knew there was a very large village," *I* bemoan the fact that as of this writing we can be reasonably certain of the names of only some 185 Indians up against Custer, and 106 battling Reno, his harried subordinate.

For simplicity and easier reading, the entire work is organized in an entry format, with some minor paragraphing where appropriate. I have tried to use as few abbreviations as possible, though I have kept many of the obvious. I find this a more no-nonsense approach, and it eliminates a lot of extraneous verbiage while keeping things relatively simple. All three sections are organized in a similar fashion, with place and date of birth, place and date of death, as well as cause of death, if known, listed first. When necessary, there may be notes within that entry to clarify it further. In the case of military personnel, the individual's specific unit, rank, and assignment on June 25 comes next, followed by personal appearance and related information; then enlistment data, schooling, and military experience. Additional entries are added for those with larger stories to tell. Section II is similar, though the dubiety regarding some personnel has forced me to take more license than I would like. As for the Indians in Section III, they are organized in much the same way: name, tribal affiliation, dates of birth and death, all followed by whatever else we know of them.

There are no footnotes for individual entries, though I have included source references throughout and wherever I thought necessary. In some cases, organizations such as the Little Big Horn Associates (LBHA) or the Custer Battlefield Historical & Museum Association (CBHMA) are the primary source for the information. In others, the sources are well-known authors and historians in the field. Though some information has proven to be obscure, there is *some* documentation, however hazy, with every name, be it a mere handwritten entry on a 110-year-old census form or a yellowed article in a by-gone newspaper.

It has become impossible for me to remember the names of friends and acquaintances who have helped in one way or another, simply because I never expected these "notes" to see the light of day. This is also not meant to replace any existing work, for there is not enough research for me ever to make that claim. I tend to doubt anyone will ever be able to out-do the magnificent work of Roger L. Williams in his book, *Military Register of Custer's Last Command,* a *sine qua non* for those who want to know the details of the military careers of the battle participants under the aegis of George Armstrong Custer. I used that book as a fact-checker in not just a few of these entries. In addition, I will never claim to be the authority on the Sioux Indians involved in this epic battle that my late friend Ephriam D. Dickson III is, and whose generosity and help has added hundreds of names to my work on the Sioux participants. Without Ephriam's help and his work, this would have remained that original series of notes. The same must be said for my late friend, Michael Nunnally. It always takes more than data to do something like this and Michael provided a great deal of the "more." One of those friends whose brain and beautifully organized work I have cherry-picked to my advantage is Ray Hillyer. The generosity label must also include Billy Markland who lives in Kansas, and a wonderful and brilliant English lady named Elisabeth Kimber, both of whom I have never met, and both of who have opened their heart and mind to so much of my studies of the Little Big Horn. As much as anyone, Dr. Richard Allan Fox, Jr., and his brother Dennis Fox, whether they know it or not, have helped me immeasurably and this work is strewn with references to Richard's work. Also, my dear friends, Frank Bodden,

Michael Reeve, Scott Nelson, Michael Olson, and Gary Lemery have all trekked with me to many of the sites mentioned throughout this work, and Marc Abrams continues to provide me with information through his magnificent collection of period newspaper articles. I must also thank Diane Merkel for the idea and the encouragement of developing my "notes" into this work. It was Diane who first convinced me I had something worthwhile to say and without whose early support I doubt anything would have ever developed. The most credit, however, goes to my lovely wife Lisa, who contributed understanding and love ... not to mention the spurs of advice.

I graduated from Georgetown University and as an alumnus I am always on the lookout for fellow alumni, past and present. I found several men of the Seventh who fought in the battle and who were associated in one fashion or another with the college. One fought and died side-by-side with George Custer: Second Lieutenant William Van Wyke Reily, a handsome, dashing young officer with George Yates' Company F — the "Band-Box Troop." The intrepid Doctor Henry Porter, a civilian contract surgeon, who proved to be one of the bravest of them all, and who battled on Reno Hill as much to save lives, as so many others strove to take them. Doc Porter graduated from Georgetown Medical. Captain Tom McDougall's nephew, the Rev. David H. Buel, S. J., became a president of the university and McDougall's funeral was held in the then-new Dahlgren Chapel, a beautiful little church on campus that I know so well. My thanks to both Maura Seale, the Georgetown University Lauinger Library research and instruction librarian, and Lynn Conway, the archivist, Special Collections of the library, who provided me with a number of documents pertaining to these men, as well as another, Captain Thomas French of Company M.

What I have attempted to do here is to give life to some of the men — white and red and black — and the Indian women who witnessed this monumental event in American history. I have tried to add more than just data, facts of birth and death and military service. Where I found a story, I tried to attach it to a name, I tried to give us all a little more than abbreviations or a name on a wall or a monument or a slab of marble or granite. We all deserve that, but many times it is not included in the single line history grants most people. Unfortunately, there are too many single lines, even in here.

While I mentioned earlier that this work is far from complete, it is hopeless to think it will ever be. As one will find out, estimates of the number of Indians encamped along the Little Big Horn that day vary wildly, from less than 1,000 warriors to more than 8,000. Both figures are incorrect, the true number being somewhere in between. The best we can hope for is to add as lore tells us ... or to correct, as fact shows us.

Introduction

Many people see the Battle of the Little Big Horn as the death of George Armstrong Custer and the complete destruction of the Seventh United States Cavalry. That is incorrect, and I am pleased to tell the reader that the Seventh Cavalry at least is alive and well. What *is* true is that the companies of the regiment that accompanied General Custer himself were in fact wiped out to a man. The entire battle, however, was considerably more spread out and a lot larger and longer than the segment involving Custer.

Some few minutes after noon on June 25, 1876, Custer divided his twelve-company regiment into four parts. One part — or battalion, in military parlance — consisting of three companies, roughly 18 percent of the command, was sent off on a scout to the left of the general direction the rest of the regiment would march. This battalion consisted of lettered companies D, H, and K (117 officers, men, and a scout), and was commanded by the Seventh's senior captain, Frederick William Benteen. Another portion consisted of a single company — Captain Tom McDougall's Company B, along with seven men drawn from the other eleven companies (143 officers and men, including five or siz civilian packers; 22 percent of the command) — that accompanied and drove approximately 175 mules carrying equipment, food, and ammunition. The remaining eight companies were divided into two unequal parts, three companies — A, G, and M (170 officers and men, including thirty-two scouts; 26 percent) — under the command of the regiment's sole major, Marcus Albert Reno, while Custer himself took the last five (225 men, total [34 percent], also further subdivided, but of no relevance here).*

Once the division was complete and orders issued, the Custer and Reno segments moved down the valley of a small creek (subsequently named for Major Reno), for some ten miles and at considerable speed. The campaign was already forty days old and the object of the troops' attention — the non-treaty Indians of the Sioux and Cheyenne nations (also known as the "winter roamers") — were finally discovered and were about to be punished for not adhering to the U.S. government's latest policy of reporting to their respective reservations when so ordered. Part of Custer's rush was the fact that these Indians were always known to scatter when confronted by strong, organized military forces, and Custer had received several indications that surprise had been lost. That would spell disaster for the campaign and would do nothing to enhance the reputations

*It should be understood that this division of command took place about fifteen miles from the village and not all these men were in the battle or remained with their assigned units. A number of the scouts with Reno, for example, never crossed the Little Big Horn; messengers were sent and wound up with other commands; stragglers fell out and wound up elsewhere, etc.

of America's hero and his superiors. As Custer and Reno approached the Little Big Horn River, they noticed considerable activity in the valley beyond: running Indians, massive pony herds, men on the move ... more activity than they wanted to see. Custer immediately formulated orders and sped Reno on his way: he was to cross the Little Big Horn, and proceed down the valley (north), to drive all before him, bringing the Indians to battle. Custer promised to support him and Reno understood the support was to be by a follow-up of his own initial confrontation, Custer directly behind him. It did not happen that way and thus began the controversy that has swirled around these events for more than 130 years.

As Reno was crossing the river, one of his interpreters, an experienced frontiersman whom Reno disliked intensely — Frederic Francis Gerard — was told by his Arikara (Ree) scouts that the Sioux were not running, but were in fact coming out to confront the advancing cavalry. This was unheard of. The report got back to Custer, who halted in his approach to the river, and reassessed the situation. This news could mean one thing only: a screen set up to protect and cover the scattering of the village. In other words, disaster and failure. In the decision that cost him and 209 of his men (including two brothers, a brother-in-law, and a nephew) their lives, George Custer turned to the right and mounted the steep hills that formed the eastern, or right, bank of the river.

In the meantime, Reno completed his move downriver, but when suddenly confronted by a ravine full of unmounted Indians and a sky full of dust and smoke obscuring a good deal of his visibility, the major wisely dismounted his men and formed skirmish lines to confront and advance on his enemy. Custer, meanwhile, continued his move north, stopping briefly to view Reno's progress in the valley. He then went on in an attempt to further assess his options, his foe, and to discover their progress in fleeing. In all likelihood, he figured if he could get ahead of the retreating families,

he could drive his command through them, killing and creating havoc, and forcing the warriors into a piecemeal defense, a posture Custer was sure he could defeat.

The problem, however, was that these Indians were going nowhere this day despite the families' plight, and there were considerably more of them than George Custer or his soldiers ever bargained for. In fact, there would be indications that this was the largest aggregate encampment of American Indians ever assembled. In addition, the action was now coming so fast and furiously and was over such great distances, that Custer's battalions became separated by too much terrain and fell out of mutual support, a fatal mistake in divided military actions. Benteen was sent for and ordered to gather the pack train, but instead of joining Custer, fell across a fully routed Reno, who had been driven out of the valley, across the river, and up the bluffs in between Custer's command and the hustling Benteen, all the while suffering horrible casualties. Rather than leave the defeated soldiers and their wounded to the howling masses (estimated at some 900 warriors) in the valley below, Benteen halted and gathered all about him, making sure he understood the situation and the necessity for getting the pack train up, and then, with ammunition distributed and the wounded properly arranged, the command moved toward Custer. In the eyes of many, this delay — plus his acerbic personality and dislike of George Custer — has condemned Fred Benteen to the purgatory of history, blamed for Custer's demise and never to be forgiven. That determination, of course, is sheer nonsense — as those who served with Captain Benteen would eventually tell us — for Custer brought about his own end.

Meanwhile, Custer's move north was discovered by other Indians and many in the valley left to confront this new threat. Unfortunately for our hero, the majority of the available Indians had not even gotten into the fracas with Reno, but they were now headed to cut off Custer and his 209 men. It is this part of the battle we know little if anything about; it is this part of the battle no white soldier survived and we have only the fractured testimony of Indian participants to ponder and discuss. Often, when seen within their own particular sphere of action, the Indian testimonies allow us to make *some* coherent judgments of how the final hour and forty minutes or so of George Custer's life unfolded, but these judgments are mostly theories, so we can only apply anecdotal evidence and the empiricism of archaeological findings in trying to set up our postulations. What is known or at least believed by one school of thought — this writer's included — is that the Custer portion of the fighting began fairly slowly and involved few mounted Indians in the actual combat, horsemen only closing in at the ends of the fight's several stages.

As Custer continued his move north to get below the fleeing "refugees," he divided his five companies again, leaving the dashing, Irish-born Captain Myles Keogh behind with three companies — Keogh's own I, along with L (commanded by Custer's brother-in-law, Lieutenant Jim Calhoun), and C (brother Tom Custer's command, but handled by Lieutenant Henry Moore Harrington, as Tom was assisting George). Ostensibly, Keogh was to act as a reserve, protect Custer's rear as the latter moved north, and await Benteen's arrival with the idea of then following Custer, linking up, and the whole group crossing the river and attacking. As Custer reconnoitered north to find a suitable crossing, Keogh was coming under increasing pressure as Indians forded the river between his command and the Reno-Benteen contingent more than three miles away. To ease the pressure, Keogh sent Harrington into a coulee to rout out Indians who had been firing arrows into the air and down onto the troops and their horses.

This marked the beginning of the debacle. Harrington went either too far or he dismounted — or both — but in either case as the Indians melted away through the sheer force of a thirty-eight-man cavalry charge, they regrouped and utterly overwhelmed the young lieutenant and his men. Survivors ran — both on foot and on horseback — to the nearest high ground where the carnage continued. Those who managed to survive that mini-maelstrom continued running toward what they perceived as a modicum of safety — the soldiers of Company L, who had been trying to provide covering fire during the onslaught. The panicked C Company men — fewer and fewer — continued through L and into Keogh's own Company I. The emboldened Indians now swarmed over Calhoun and L, killing the valiant officer, and surrounding the remainder of Keogh's command.

To the north, Custer had found his crossing point and the farthest extent of the Indian retreat, and was heading back toward a rendezvous with Keogh. He reached a ridgeline (where today's visitors' center now stands in the Little Big Horn National Park) and waited ... not terribly long, for he was beginning to come under pressure as well. Once again, he divided his now-meager force into two separate commands, sending Captain George Yates and Company F into a shallow basin to head off Indians infiltrating up a deep ravine (in modern parlance, Deep Ravine). This now put thirty-eight soldiers at the top of a head-cut, along with forty-nine on a ridge, to confront a significant portion of the Sioux and Cheyenne nations. The pressure became so severe that Custer's contingent was overrun and forced to the high ground where the monument stands today. Yates and his men soon joined them. And other than a feeble attempt at a possible breakout by the famed Gray Horse Troop — Lieutenant Algernon Smith's Company E — that is where they died.

When Crazy Horse and his followers finished with Custer, they headed toward Reno and Benteen. Those two much maligned officers, had in the meantime, begun a slow, methodical move north (toting wounded), but when suddenly confronted by the thundering, howling hordes leaving the Custer battlefield, they quickly retreated to the high ground they had left. For the remainder of that day (from about 5:30 PM until dark, 9 PM) and continuing throughout the next (June 26) until some time in the afternoon, men on both sides continued to fight and continued to die. The regiment took 655 officers, men, scouts, and civilians — white, red, and one black — into the fray, and lost 268, some from each group and some taking as long as four months to die … 41 percent dead!

No one knows how many Indians lost their lives, but we can account for at least 63 in this study. We can probably add the two wives and three children of the famous Hunkpapa Sioux battle chief, Gall, to that total, and heaven only knows how many Indians were wounded and may have died. While the Battle of the Little Big Horn marked the pinnacle of the Indians' military prowess, it also marked the death knell of their way of life, for the U.S. government renewed its effort with ever-increasing force and vigor to compel compliance with the unwritten policies of Manifest Destiny. Four hundred thirty-six days after the battle, the great Sioux leader, Crazy Horse, lay dead, the victim of a soldier's bayonet … while in captivity. And like so much of the Battle of the Little Big Horn, the secret of where that magnificent Indian reposes is buried with him, just as the secrets of what really happened that day lie buried with the men who fought and died there.

The Seventh Cavalry

Under the act of July 28, 1866, the designation and organization of regiments by which the military peace establishment is increased and fixed will be as follows. The provisions of this order are in accordance with the conditions of the Army on, and are of effect from, the 21st day of September 1866. The two additional regiments of Cavalry, composes of white men, will be the Seventh and Eighth Regiment of Cavalry.

— War Department GO 56, August 1, 1866,
War Department GO 92, Sept. 1–Dec. 22, 1866.

Origin and Organization of the Seventh Cavalry

It is important to understand the circumstances and tenor of the times surrounding the formation of arguably the most famous cavalry regiment in United States history. What follows is a brief synopsis of its ten-year history leading up to the events of May and June 1876.

In May 1865, as the Civil War was ending, there were 1,034,000 volunteers in the army. By November, more than 800,000 had been released. In addition to its old mission of patrolling America's vast frontier, the army now had to occupy the conquered Southern states and maintain a show of force along the Mexican border, but by the end of the year, the regular army numbered only 38,545. To meet growing needs, Congress — in July of the same year — authorized the reorganization of the army's nineteen regular infantry regiments into forty-five regiments of ten companies each. The cavalry service, with six regiments, was enlarged to ten, each with twelve companies. Post-war army strength was set at 57,000.

The Seventh U.S. Cavalry Regiment was officially created on July 28, 1866, and Andrew Jackson Smith, an able and experienced Indian fighter and an old frontier veteran and successful commander against the likes of Nathan Bedford Forest and John Bell Hood during the War — and who also now commanded the District of the Upper Arkansas — was assigned as the regiment's first colonel. Lieutenant Colonel George Armstrong Custer — "boy" general and another famous Civil War commander — was appointed the regiment's second-in-command, but because of Smith's additional duties, became the de facto commanding officer. The Seventh Cavalry began organizing at Fort Riley, Kansas, in August 1866, and by December the unit's organization was complete. About half the men who joined initially were foreign, many from Germany and Ireland (not a lot different than ten years later at the Little Big Horn: 30 percent), and a great number of the new recruits could barely speak English. By the end of 1866, the regiment consisted of some fifteen officers and 963 enlisted personnel.

During the Civil War, volunteers took over the duties of the regular army in the Indian territories. They were more brutal and less understanding than the regulars and by the war's end the Indian problem was getting worse. Another Civil War hero, General Winfield Scott Hancock, now commanding the Department of Missouri, was sent to do something about the latest series of reported depredations.

In early 1867, George Custer took the Seventh from Fort Riley, Kansas, to Fort Harker and then to Fort Larned. The first confrontation with the Sioux and Cheyenne took place at encampments on the north fork of the Pawnee River about thirty miles west of Larned. Attempts at negotiations had come to naught and the Indians fled with Custer in pursuit. Custer then marched north to the Smoky Hill River, east to Fort Hays, and finally arrived in camp at Big Creek on April 19, 1867. The first series of complaints against the over-zealous commander began to occur around this time, with criticism for over-marching his tired horses and men, all the while Custer learning it was more difficult to catch the Indians than to fight them. At the same time, the command was rife with desertions, but rather than blame the rigors of soldiering or his own personal foibles, Custer blamed the poor morale on insufficient and bad rations, brought on by fraud by dishonest contractors. Regardless of the accusations or recriminations, by June 1 the regiment was on the move once again. Companies A, D, E, H, K, and M left Fort Hays and the Smoky Hill route and marched to the Platte, while companies B, C, F, G, I, and L were detailed to other Kansas posts.

Custer proceeded from Hays to Fort McPherson, Nebraska, and from there to a camp on the Republican River near present-day Benkelman, where he remained from June 22 to 28. More problems had arisen when on June 8, 1867, the second in command, Major Wickliffe Cooper, committed suicide. (Captain Frederick Benteen — one of the senior company commanders in the regiment — called Cooper a "most gallant soldier during the war," and blamed Custer for his death [Carroll, *The Benteen-Goldin Letters,* p. 250; February 12, 1896], even though Cooper was a notorious alcoholic and all indications pointed to a booze-induced self-murder.)

During this time, there were several skirmishes. On the morning of June 24, 1867 — in George Custer's first actual fight with Plains Indians — the Seventh's camp was attacked. A chase after a band of Sioux under Pawnee Killer ensued when the Indians tried to stampede the soldiers' horses. Then, two days later the Sioux attacked a wagon train led by lieutenants Sam Robbins and William Winer Cooke, ten miles south of present-day Edson, Kansas. It was a fifteen-mile running fight that lasted more than three hours, and it was one of the few times Indians attacked and circled a wagon train. In another skirmish the same day, Captain Albert Barnitz suffered eleven casualties some one and one half miles northwest of Fort Wallace.

On July 5–6, Custer camped at the Riverside [stage coach] Station on the South Platte in Colorado, and on July 12 — heading back to Fort Wallace — he found the remains of Lieutenant Lyman Kidder and eleven soldiers near the north bank of Beaver Creek. The campaign ended the following day.

Because of some of his more *outré* shenanigans, Custer was ordered arrested by General Hancock and subsequently court-martialed for his conduct on the campaign — primarily for leaving the command, but also for having deserters shot. He was found guilty in November 1867, and suspended from rank and command for one year. George and Libbie Custer headed back to Monroe, Michigan, and Major Joel Elliott became field commander of the Seventh Cavalry during Custer's Michigan sojourn.

On September 7, 1868, General Alfred Sully, the new commander of the District of the Upper Arkansas, led an expedition hoping to draw raiding Cheyenne, Kiowa, Arapaho, and Comanche away from settlements. He led nine companies of the Seventh under Elliott, and parts of the Third Infantry across the Arkansas River toward the Cimarron. There were several confrontations with Indians, one in which Sully almost lost his wagon train. This attempt ended on September 13, and Sully returned to Fort Dodge. In yet another effort to quell the depredations, General Phil Sheridan, commander of the Department of the Missouri, decided on a winter campaign and since Sully had failed, Sheridan looked for a new commander. He offered Benteen the job, but he refused, and so Custer was recalled, returning to Fort Hays by September 30.

(It was also about this time when Custer decided to "color the horses," i.e., each company would have its own distinctly colored horses. First Sergeant John Ryan claimed the "coloring of horses" occurred during the "Winter Campaign" [before the Washita battle] when the regiment reached their camp on Medicine Lodge Creek [Barnard, *Ten Years with Custer*, p. 68]. Troop commanders, in order of rank, selected the horses they wanted. Some — captains Benteen and Barnitz in particular — thought this was a ridiculous idea with no merit whatsoever.)

The winter campaign began on November 12, 1868, with eleven companies of the regiment (Company L remained at Fort Lyon), three companies of the Third Infantry, one company of the Fifth Infantry, one company of the Thirty-eighth Infantry, and 450 wagons loaded with forage and supplies. On November 27, fifty Cheyenne lodges — the village of the Cheyenne "peace" chief, Black Kettle — were spotted on the Washita River. Ironically, Black Kettle camped his village farther away from the more warlike Cheyenne, precisely because he did not want a repeat of the notorious Sand Creek imbroglio. The infantry remained at Camp Supply and Custer divided his

cavalry into four battalions: Major Elliott took G, H, and M companies and was to swing around the hills north of the camp and attack from the northeast. Captain William Thompson (oldest officer in the regiment at fifty-four) would take B and F companies in from the south; Captain Myers would take E and I and go to the right, coming down the river from the southwest; and Custer would take A, C, D and K, plus a sharpshooter unit led by Lieutenant Cooke, cross the river and come in from the west. About seven hundred troops were involved. Before the attack, Thompson said to Custer, "'General, suppose we find more Indians than we can handle, etc.' Custer said gruffly, 'Hell, all I am afraid of we won't find half enough. There are not Indians enough in the country to whip the Seventh Cavalry'" (Foley, "Walter Camp & Ben Clark," *Custer and His Times, Book Five*, p. 117). The scout, Ben Clark, rode alongside Custer; Custer would allow no one to get ahead of him (Foley, p. 118). Clark said the village consisted of about sixty lodges (Sheridan's report claimed fifty-one [Foley, p. 124]).

Lieutenant Edward Godfrey was assigned to capture the Indians' pony herd. He took a platoon and proceeded downriver, and from the crest of a high bluff discovered more villages in the valley and warriors preparing to come to Black Kettle's aid. Godfrey headed back to warn Custer, fighting off Indians along the way (Stewart, *Custer's Luck*, p. 164).

While it was a rout for the Indians, the Seventh did not come away unscathed. Captain Louis McLane Hamilton — the grandson of Alexander Hamilton and Louis McLane, Secretary of State and of Treasury under Andrew Jackson — was killed; Captain Albert T. Siders Barnitz was severely wounded in the abdomen, and while he lived for many years thereafter, he was never the same as a soldier, retiring on disability in December 1870. After the destruction of Black Kettle's village, Major Elliott took some seventeen men, plus the regimental sergeant major, Walter Kennedy, and chased escaping Indians. No one knew what happened precisely, but they were all killed, including Elliott and the sergeant major. Indians from the camps Godfrey had seen downriver — estimates of the numbers ranging from 1,200 to 1,500 — then began arriving, forcing Custer to fall back to the north, returning to Camp Supply on December 1. Custer and Sheridan returned to the battlefield some eleven days later, finding the bodies of Elliott and Kennedy, along with fifteen other enlisted men. The remainder of the 1868–1869 winter was spent between Fort Cobb and the Seventh's camp on Medicine Bluff Creek, near present-day Fort Sill. Custer continued rounding up Arapaho, Kiowa, and Cheyenne in what was to prove his most successful campaign.

In 1869, Colonel Samuel D. Sturgis assumed command of the Seventh. That year and the next, the regiment was scattered in a number of different posts performing numerous duties. In 1869, five U.S.M.A. graduates joined the regiment: lieutenants Rea, Porter (who was to die at the Little Big Horn), Craycroft, Braden, and Aspinwall. In 1871, the Seventh's tour in the Department of Dakota ended and its companies were scattered to various posts in the Department of the South, primarily to round up and clean out the Ku Klux Klan.

In May 1873, the entire command — save companies D and I — marched for Fort Rice on the Missouri River to accompany Colonel David S. Stanley on an expedition to guide engineering surveyors for the Northern Pacific Railroad. In August, along the Yellowstone River above the Tongue River, the regiment had its first Indian fight in several years. The Sioux — probably Rain-in-the-Face — killed the regimental veterinarian, Dr. John Honsinger, and the sutler, Augustus Baliran. Then on August 11, near the mouth of the Bighorn River, 1,000 Sioux attacked 450 of Custer's cavalrymen. The regiment's best shot was Private Frank Tuttle of E Company and Custer

had him pick off three warriors. The Indians maneuvered Tuttle into a crossfire, however, and killed him, the only soldier death in the battle. After more wasted firing, Custer and his troopers charged the Indians, dispersing them. The regiment returned to Fort Lincoln on September 21.

In June 1874, Custer led ten companies of the regiment, two companies of infantry, and sundry scouts and scientists to "explore" the Black Hills, "explore" being a time-honored euphemism for the search for gold. Then on September 29, six companies were reassigned to the Department of the Gulf. From May to September 1875, companies A, E, and H were stationed near Fort Randall on the Missouri River and were engaged in ejecting miners and other unauthorized persons from the Black Hills. Soon the regiment received its orders for the fateful Spring–Summer Campaign. The various companies received their marching orders and by early May 1876, the entire Seventh Cavalry was gathered at Fort Lincoln. It was the nation's centennial year.

"In the decade since its activation the Seventh Cavalry had acquired a reputation as the most experienced and capable mounted regiment in the armed forces, but it had also developed internal dissension; by 1876 there was more than the usual amount of jealousy and bickering among its officers" (Stewart, *Custer's Luck,* p. 166). Despite the personality issues, a sometimes lack of proper training, and some poor horses, the Seventh Cavalry remained the best in the service. In August 1876, less than two months after its mauling at the Little Big Horn, the Seventh Cavalry was watched by an officer in the Fifth Cavalry, as it moved in an informal parade. He wrote: "Each company as it comes forward opens out like a fan, and a sheaf of skirmishers is launched to the front. Something in the snap and style of the whole movement stamps them at once; no need of waving guidon and stirring call to identify them. I recognize the Seventh Cavalry at a glance..." (Stewart, *Custer's Luck,* p. 177, quoting Captain Charles King in Roe's *Custer's Last Battle,* p. 39).

Note — In 1876, army regulations prescribed minimum and maximum physical requirements for cavalrymen. The minimum height was set at 5'5" and the maximum weight at 155 pounds. As will be seen, there were exceptions in the Seventh Cavalry.

Soldiers at the Little Big Horn

Abbotts, PVT Harry— b. NYC, 1853–d. unknown. Company E, private. Hazel eyes, dark hair, dark complexion; 5'9¼" tall. Enlisted 8 Oct 1875. Extra duty as hospital attendant with Reno since 17 May 1876. Michno claims he remained at Fort Abraham Lincoln during the campaign and was a hospital orderly there, but this is incorrect, as the June Returns do not have him listed in that position or at that location. Vern Smalley carries him as DeWolf's attendant. Resided in Parkersburg, WV, after his discharge.

Abrams, PVT William G.— b. Baltimore, MD, 1 Dec 1840–d. Sioux City, IA, 28 May 1901. Company L, private. Black or blue eyes, dark or brown hair, dark or fair complexion; 5'9¼" to 5'10" tall — sounds like two different people! Enlisted 30 Sep 1863 in Hartford, CT. Wounded at Bristol Station, VA, on 14 Oct 1863; mustered out 18 Oct 1865. Enlisted 29 Aug 1866. Deserted 14 Jan 1867; surrendered and restored. Appointed first sergeant 1 Nov 1870; enlisted 1 Sep 1871 in Seventh Cavalry (as a private). John Burkman — George Custer's striker — claimed Abrams was not at the fight, but further research shows Abrams was with the pack train. Married Elizabeth Adelphine Smith Marine, 6 Nov 1881, Sioux City. Died at 713 West 14th Street, Sioux City. Buried in Floyd Cemetery. His brother, George, served in the Confederate Army.

Ackerman, PVT Charles— b. Baden, Germany, 5 Sep 1848–d. Fort Snelling, MN, 6 Apr 1930. Company K, private. Hazel eyes, brown hair, fair complexion; 5'7¾–8½" tall. Enlisted 9 Sep 1875. Remained at the Powder River Depot. Presence confirmed on June Returns. Married Ephresina Peterson 21 Feb 1881. Children: Lucretia Marie Josephine; Hattie Louise and Julia Amanda (twins). Served in Spanish-American War. Buried in Forest Cemetery, St. Paul, MN.

Ackison, PVT David— b. Troy, NY, Jan 1852–d. unknown. Company E, private. Gray eyes, brown hair, fair complexion; 5'5 or 5'6½" tall. Enlisted 1

Oct 1873. Discharged in 1878. On steamer *Far West,* sick with consumption. June Returns state he had been sent back to Fort Lincoln.

Adams, PVT George E.— b. Minersville, PA, Jul 1846–d. 25 Jun 1876, killed at the Little Big Horn. Company L, private. Blue eyes, light hair, fair complexion; 5'8½" tall. Enlisted 18 Oct 1869 and discharged 19 Dec 1872; reenlisted 27 Jan 1874. Listed number 192 in "June Returns, Alterations … Killed in action." In all likelihood he was killed on Calhoun Hill, though the possibility exists he was one of those killed during the panic through the Keogh Sector. No remains found during the 1984–1985 archaeological work match his description.

Adams, PVT Jacob— b. Stark County, OH, 25 Jun 1852–d. Vincennes, IN, 13 May 1934. Company H, private. Brown eyes, brown hair, fair complexion; 5'8" tall. Enlisted 13 Apr 1873. Assigned to the pack train. Along with LT Frank Gibson, helped bury LT McIntosh. Illiterate. Buried in Mount Calvary Catholic Cemetery, Vincennes, IN. Survived by two sons, two daughters, two sisters, and two brothers.

Adams, William A. *see* **Teeman, CPL William**

Akers, CPL James— b. Kings County, Ireland, 1851–d. Washington, D.C., 3 Aug 1881. Company G, corporal. Hazel eyes, auburn hair, fair or dark complexion; 5'6" tall, 135 pounds. Enlisted 4 Dec 1874. Promoted to sergeant 25 Jun 1876. PVT Theodore Goldin claimed Akers was not at the battle [Carroll, *The Benteen-Goldin Letters,* p. 50], but this is incorrect. Not listed as "absent" on June Returns, indicating he was with his unit and probably involved in the valley fighting with Reno. Later cited by Benteen for conspicuous gallantry against the Nez Percé, 13 Sep 1877, at Cañon Creek, M.T.

Alberts, PVT James H.— b. Woodstock, IL, 1847–d. killed in the Snake Creek fight of the Nez Percé War of 1877. Company D, private. Blue eyes, brown hair, fair complexion; 5'5¾" tall. Enlisted 24 Sep 1875. Recommended for medal for conspicuous gallantry at LBH fight on Reno Hill.

Alcott, SGT Samuel— b. Allegheny, PA, 1851–d. Toronto, Canada, 24 Mar 1926. Company A, sergeant. Brown eyes, black hair, dark complexion; 5'6" tall. Enlisted 10 Jan 1872. Remained at Powder River Depot. Presence confirmed on June Returns. Resided at 419 Shaw Street, Toronto. Attended dedication of the Custer monument in Monroe, MI, 4 Jun 1910. Buried in Lot E 1/2 224, Section A, Park Lawn Cemetery, Toronto. Survived by widow, Agnes, and son, Aldridge.

Allan (or Allen), **PVT Alfred (Fred) Ernest**— b. Melton Mowbray, Leicestershire, England, 14 Aug 1847–d. 25 Jun 1876, killed at the Little Big Horn. Company C, private. Brown eyes, black hair, dark complexion; 5'8⅛" tall. Had been in the army since 3 Oct 1873. Civilian occupation was a watchmaker. In the C Company charge off Battle Ridge/Calhoun Hill, but body was never identified. May have died in Calhoun Coulee, Finley/Finckle Ridge, the Keogh Sector, or possibly even Last Stand Hill. Listed number 23 in "June Returns, Alterations … Killed in action."

Aller, PVT Charles— b. Prussia, 1847–d. unknown. Company A, private. Blue eyes, brown hair, fair complexion; 5'7¾" tall. Enlisted on 9 Dec 1874. Deserted on 24 Apr 1877; surrendered and confined. Escaped from Fort Sanders, W.T., on 23 Oct 1877, and never apprehended. No known record exists of his participation in the battle, other than his presence with his unit during the valley fighting and subsequent defense of Reno Hill.

Anderson, PVT Charles L.— b. Albion, NY, 1845 (same town as LT Henry Moore Harrington)–d. unknown. Company C, private. Dark hair, gray eyes, dark complexion; 5'8¼" tall. Had been a sailor. With the Seventh Cavalry less than one year. Enlisted 15 Sep 1875. Remained at the Powder River Depot. Deserted from the depot, 20 Jun 1876; never apprehended. The June Returns do not list any Company C personnel at Powder River, so this is consistent with desertion.

Anderson, Thomas *see* **Murphy, PVT Thomas**

Andrews, PVT William— b. Prussia, 1843–d. 25 Jun 1876, killed at the Little Big Horn. Company L, private. Blue eyes, brown or dark hair, fair complexion; 5'6½" tall. Enlisted 19 Dec 1865 to 19 Dec 1868; enlisted 21 May 1869 and re-upped 21 May 1875. In all likelihood he was killed on Calhoun Hill, though the possibility exists he was one of those killed during the panic through the Keogh Sector. No remains found during the 1984–1985 archaeological work match his description. Listed number 194 in "June Returns, Alterations … Killed in action."

Angst, Solomon *see* **Meier, PVT John H.**

Armstrong, PVT John E.— b. Philadelphia, PA, 4 Nov 1836–d. 25 Jun 1876, killed at the Little Big Horn. Company A, private. Blue eyes, light brown hair, fair complexion; 5'8¾" tall. Enlisted 25 Aug 1865, Sixth Cavalry; discharged 25 Aug 1868. Enlisted 7 Jul 1869, First Cavalry. Discharged 7 Jul 1874. Enlisted 2 Apr 1875, Seventh Cavalry. Killed in the valley, his headless body found near the in-

terpreter's, Isaiah Dorman. One of twenty men — one officer, three scouts, sixteen enlisted men — left in the timber in the valley bottoms. Bruce Liddic claims he was one of those who wound up staying in the timber and then refusing to leave when everyone else left. His scorched head was purportedly found in the lower part of the Indian village and identified by Myles Moylan. Headless remains found on 25 May 1926, were thought to be his and were buried at Garryowen, MT, as an unknown soldier. Listed number 4 in "June Returns, Alterations … Killed in action."

Arndt, PVT Otto— b. Bavaria, Germany, 25 Jan 1844–d. at the Presidio, San Francisco, CA, 6 Feb 1917. Headquarters: band. Private. Remained at Powder River Depot. Presence confirmed on June Returns.

Ascough, PVT John B.— b. Philadelphia, PA, 1844–d. Columbus, OH, 4 Dec 1903. Company D, private. Brown eyes, dark hair, ruddy complexion; 5'9¼" tall. Enlisted from 1 Sep 1861 to 8 Sep 1864 in 23rd PA Infantry. Wounded at Cold Harbor during the Civil War. Enlisted 3 Sep 1873. Rode with his unit in Benteen's battalion, and fought on Reno Hill.

Assadaly, PVT Anthony— b. Prussia, 1842–d. 25 Jun 1876, killed at the Little Big Horn. Company L, private. Blue eyes, dark hair, fair complexion; listed as 5'7" tall (1865) and 5'3" tall (1873). Illiterate. Enlisted 23 Jun 1865 to 22 Jun 1868, Third Cavalry. Enlisted 21 Jul 1868; re-upped 21 Jul 1873. At the lower height, his description would be consistent with the bone fragments found at Marker 105 on Last Stand Hill. If correct, this would indicate Assadaly fled Calhoun Hill as it was overrun and escaped through the maelstrom of the Keogh Sector. Listed number 193 in "June Returns, Alterations … Killed in action."

Atcheson, PVT Thomas— b. County Antrim, Ireland, 1838–d. 25 Jun 1876, killed at the Little Big Horn. Company F, private. Hazel eyes, dark hair, dark complexion; 5'5¼" tall. First enlisted on 21 Aug 1866. Enlisted again on 2 Aug 1871. Bone fragments found at Marker 105 on Last Stand Hill would be consistent with his reported age and height. Most men killed at this location were believed to have been from F Company. Several others fit this description, as well. Listed number 98 in "June Returns, Alterations … Killed in action."

August, Solomon *see* **Meier, PVT John H.**

Babcock, PVT Elmer— b. Pharsalia, NY, 10 Jun 1856–d. 25 Jun 1876, killed at the Little Big Horn. Company L, private. Brown eyes, dark hair, dark complexion; 5'6½" tall. Enlisted 21 Sep 1875. In

1985, the battlefield excavation around Marker 128, an isolated marker behind Greasy Grass Ridge, revealed the remains of a soldier estimated to have been 22 years old and about 5'6" tall. The remains were that of a male, between 19 and 22 years old, and approximately 5'6¾" tall, with a range of 5'5¾"–5'7⅞". The individual was stocky with well-developed musculature [Scott, *et al., Archaeological Perspectives*, p. 268] and was right-handed. Nine soldiers matched the age and height criteria, including Babcock [Scott et al., *They Died with Custer*, p. 142; Fox, *Archaeology, History and Custer's Last Battle*, p. 156]. The positioning could indicate a very late casualty of the fighting. Listed number 195 in "June Returns, Alterations … Killed in action."

Bailey, BSM PVT Henry Allen—b. Foster, RI, 25 Mar 1852–d. 25 Jun 1876, killed at the Little Big Horn. Company I, private: company blacksmith. Gray eyes, brown hair, fair complexion; 5'7¼" tall. Enlisted 24 Oct 1872. Marker 174, set apart from the rest of Company I in the Keogh sector near the eastern boundary fence of the National Park is possibly where Bailey fell. Richard Fox and Doug Scott feel he tried to get away and "dashed across the ravines and up the final side slope" [Liddic, *Vanishing Victory*, p. 156, footnote 171, citing Schoenberger, Dale T., *End of Custer* (Hancock House, Blaine, WA, 1995), 199]. He fired his pistol into the ground just as an Indian bullet hit him. There are several eyewitness accounts of a single soldier trying to make a getaway and being intercepted by Cheyenne warriors and in one case by Crazy Horse himself. The Oglala warrior Flying Hawk said, "One soldier was running away to the east, but Crazy Horse saw him and jumped on his pony and went after him. He got him about half a mile from the place where the others were lying dead. The smoke was lifted so we could see a little."

Possibly a little more credible were the testimonies from several Cheyenne who claimed to have seen the incident. Big Beaver, a seventeen-year-old Northern Cheyenne said, "A soldier got up and mounted his horse (this was one of Keogh's men, or Sorrel Horse Troop), and rode as fast as he could towards the east. This is the lone marker next to the fence to the east of the Keogh position. Two Cheyenne Indians cut him off and killed him. They then scalped him and hung the scalp on the sagebrush. I went over there and got the gun and some other things, and that was the first gun I ever owned" [Hardorff, *The Custer Battle Casualties, II*, p. 131]. Wooden Leg said the same thing essentially, though his version has the soldier breaking away from the main action on foot. He verifies Big

Beaver's claim of recovering a weapon as well as the scalp-on-the-sagebrush incident. Two Moon[s] alluded to the incident as if he were one of the assassins, otherwise pretty much keeping to the facts presented by Wooden Leg and Big Beaver. He added, "The authorities say the body was never found. That is partly explained by the fact that some bones of men from which the dogs had eaten the flesh were found in the Indian camp" [Hardorff, p. 130].

Bailey's father—Henry Franklin Bailey—was a carriage maker in Springfield, MA. His mother's name was Hannah Boswell Bailey. Listed number 148 in "June Returns, Alterations … Killed in action."

Bailey, SAD PVT John A. (middle initial also seen as an E.)—b. Joe Daviess County, IL, 20 Sep 1847–d. St Paul, MN, 2 Jun 1915. Company B, private: company saddler. Blue eyes, dark hair, dark complexion; 5'11½" tall. Enlisted 31 Aug 1862 in First IA Cavalry; enlisted 1 Jan 1864 to 15 Feb 1866. Enlisted in Seventh Cavalry, 10 Dec 1870, and re-upped 10 Dec 1875. Assisted in LT Hodgson's burial and was in the burial parties on the Custer battlefield. Divorced, then married Margaret Katherine Johnson, 6 Sep 1894 in Chicago. Died from multiple injuries in an elevator accident. Buried in the Post Cemetery, Fort Snelling.

Baker, PVT William H.—b. Golconda, Pope County, IL, 3 Dec 1848 or in 1849–d. 25 Jun 1876, killed at the Little Big Horn. Company E, private. Blue eyes, brown hair, fair complexion; 5'9" tall. Enlisted 1 Sep 1870 to 1 Sep 1875 in Third Artillery. Reenlisted 1 Oct 1875 at Fort Hamilton, NY, in the Seventh Cavalry. While his body was not specifically identified, he may have been one of the unknowns on either the South Skirmish Line or in Deep Ravine. Married Nancy Ellen Broadway 3 Dec 1868 in Golconda. Daughter Minnie J. (b. 14 Oct 1869). Divorced 6 Jun 1871. Listed number 61 in "June Returns, Alterations … Killed in action."

Bancroft, PVT Neil—b. Oswego, NY, November 1845–d. unknown. Company A, private. Gray eyes, fair hair, fair complexion; 5'6¾" tall. Enlisted on 20 Sep 1873. Won the Medal of Honor for bringing water to the wounded on Reno Hill under severe Indian fire. Never actually received the medal and died never knowing he had won it. Also volunteered to go on picket duty with CPL Roy the night of 25 Jun 1876.

Banks, PVT Charles—b. Dublin, Ireland, April 1845–d. Highland Falls, NY, 14 May 1901. Company L, private. Brown eyes, brown hair, fair complexion; 5'5¼" tall. Enlisted 14 Sep 1868 in NYC. Discharged 14 Sep 1873; re-upped 29 Sep 1873.

With the pack train and then fought on Reno Hill. Married Mary Ann Dempsey, 14 May 1885, in Highland Falls, NY; no children. Died at USMA of cerebral apoplexy and paralysis. Buried at Woodlawn Cemetery, Newburgh, NY.

Barnett, PVT Charles Clinton—b. Camden, OH, 7 May 1857–d. Anacortes, WA, 3 Apr 1935. Company G, private. Blue eyes, brown hair, fair complexion; 5'9" tall. Enlisted 25 Mar 1876. Remained at the Powder River Depot. Presence confirmed on June Returns. Survived by widow Etta Gath Barnett.

Barry, PVT John D.—b. Waterford, Ireland, 1849–d. 25 Jun 1876, killed at the Little Big Horn. Company I, private. Gray eyes, dark hair, ruddy complexion; 5'7¾" tall. Enlisted 21 Sep 1875. Body never identified, but in all likelihood he was killed in the Keogh Sector. Listed number 150 in "June Returns, Alterations … Killed in action."

Barry, PVT Peter Orlando—b. Washington, D.C., circa 1845–d. Morgan, MD, 3 Jul 1907. Company B, private. Brown eyes, brown hair, dark complexion; 5'9¼" tall. In the field on the campaign, but on Detached Service. In all likelihood with Commissary Department, Department of Dakota, where he is listed with Terry's HQ.

Barsantee, PVT James F.—b. Boston, MA, 10 Feb 1853–d. Boston, MA, 7 Jul 1941. Company B, private. Hazel eyes, brown hair, fair complexion; 5'5½" tall. Enlisted in the U.S. Navy from 10 Jun 1867 to Feb 1869 and from 18 Apr 1872 to 15 Sep 1875. Enlisted in the Seventh Cavalry on 8 Mar 1876. Kenneth Hammer originally carried him on detached service, but Smalley corrects this and carries him at the battle in the hilltop fight.

Barth, PVT Robert—b. Pforzheim, Baden, Germany, 1850 or 1851–d. 25 Jun 1876, killed at the Little Big Horn. Company E, private. Gray eyes, brown hair, fair complexion; 5'10½" tall. Enlisted 6 Dec 1872 in Albany, NY. Arrived in U.S. in Aug 1869 with brothers Emil and Friedrich. Parents: Conrad (d. 11 Jan 1863) and Katherina Dorothea Barth. Brothers and sisters: Karl (b. 15 Jan 1862), Konrad, George, Emil, Bertha, Berthold, and Friedrich. While his body was not specifically identified, he may have been one of the unknowns on either the South Skirmish Line or in Deep Ravine. Listed number 62 in "June Returns, Alterations … Killed in action."

Bates, PVT Joseph (aka Joseph C. Murphy)—b. Providence, RI, 1837–d. Sturgis, SD; suicide, 13 Sep 1893. Company M, private. Blue eyes, brown hair, fair complexion; 5'10" tall. Mustered in as Joseph C. Murphy, 27 Oct 1863, First MA Cavalry.

Appointed 1SG, then CPT on 6 Jan 1864. Discharged 26 Jun 1865; reenlisted 26 Mar 1866, Seventh Cavalry. Discharged 27 Mar 1869, reenlisted 18 Jul 1870. Bates was M Company's original first sergeant. John Ryan claimed Bates had served in the 2nd Dragoons before the Civil War, then in the 4th MA Cavalry during the war [Barnard, *Ten Years with Custer*, pp. 18–19]. No specific record exists of his participation in the battle, other than his presence with his unit during the valley fighting and subsequent defense of Reno Hill. Committed suicide; despondency. Buried in Bear Butte Cemetery, Sturgis, SD.

Baumbach, PVT Conrad—b. Berlin, Germany, 1840–d. unknown. Headquarters: band. Private. Blue eyes, dark hair, ruddy complexion; 5'6" tall. Remained at Powder River Depot. Presence confirmed on June Returns.

Baumgartner, PVT Louis—b. Baden, Germany, 1853–d. Washington, D.C., in an insane asylum or hospital, 22 May 1895. Company A, private. Brown eyes, brown hair, fair complexion; 5'6½" tall. Enlisted 3 Feb 1872. No specific record exists of his participation in the battle, other than his presence with his unit during the valley fighting and subsequent defense of Reno Hill. Listed as 1SG, Company A, Dec 1877.

Beck, PVT Benjamin—b. Philadelphia, PA, 15 Oct 1852–d. Camden, NJ, 30 Apr 1910. Headquarters: band. Private. Hazel eyes, light brown hair, fair complexion; 5'5¼" tall. Remained at Powder River Depot. Presence confirmed on June Returns.

Bender, SGT Henry—b. Berlin, Germany (Prussia), 1846–d. unknown. Company L, sergeant. Hazel eyes, black hair, dark complexion; 5'9" tall. Enlisted 28 Jan 1873. Discharged 28 Jan 1878. Remained at the Powder River Depot. Presence confirmed on June Returns.

Bennett, PVT James C.—b. Shelby, OH, 1848–d. 5 Jul 1876, of wounds suffered at the Little Big Horn. Company C, private. Gray eyes, dark hair, dark complexion; 5'6¼" tall. First enlisted 23 Jul 1870. With pack train. Wounded (shot in the spine) on 26 Jun 1876, but died of wounds, 3 pm, 5 Jul 1876 on steamer *Far West*. Body carried back to FAL.

Benteen, CPT (Bvt COL, then BG after retirement) **Frederick William** (Nicknamed "White Bird"; also, "Gray Head" by the Kiowa. Many called him "The Old Man")—b. Petersburg, VA, 24 Aug 1834–d. Atlanta, GA, 22 Jun 1898, of a stroke: paralysis and heart disease. Company H: Commanding Officer. One of the three most important personalities of the battle. Appeared to be fairly tall. PVT Charles Windolph described him as being "the finest-looking soldier I had ever seen. He had bright eyes and a ruddy face, and he had a great thatch of iron-gray hair" [Windolph/Hunt, *I Fought with Custer,* p. 4]. Windolph went on: "And I'm proud to have known and fought under Captain Benteen, of 'H.' He was just about the finest soldier and the greatest gentleman I ever knew" [pp. 2–3]. "[G]overned mainly by suggestion" [Hammer]; "...bright pleasant face"; kind, humorous; "iron hand"; "...expressionless agate eyes of a killer" [Connell]. Extraordinarily brave, with at least four brevet promotions. "It was characteristic of this man's leadership that he *led in person;* he was in the forefront of the battle, always" [Graham, *The Custer Myth,* p. 158]. During the Civil War, his expeditionary commander, COL F. M. Cronyn of the Tenth Missouri, said of Benteen: "Major F. W. Benteen, Commanding the Tenth Missouri Cavalry, *was where a leader should be—in the front*—and by his coolness and great tact and skill, did much toward gaining the day" [Graham, *The Custer Myth,* p. 158]. DOR: 28 Jul 1866, along with Keogh, the senior captains on campaign, though Benteen's brevet to colonel on 13 Aug 1868 made him the senior officer.

WIA (slightly) on Reno-Benteen Hill, probably on 26 June. Quite friendly with Keogh and very close with Tom McDougall. Rode a very fast-walking horse named Dick. Benteen was with the Seventh Cavalry from its inception to December 1882, when he was promoted to major and transferred to the Ninth Cavalry.

Son of Theodore Charles (1809–9 Mar 1885) and Caroline Hargrove Benteen (1810–Oct 1841). Family originally from Holland. Immigrated to Baltimore in 18th century. Father moved to Virginia in early 1830's. Moved to St. Louis in 1841. His father cursed Benteen when he declared he would fight for the Union, saying he hoped one of his own kin would kill Frederick William. Theodore Benteen joined the Confederate army and was engaged in blockade running on the inland rivers. Fred maneuvered his command to capture the father's vessel in 1862 and he had his father imprisoned until the end of the war. The father only learned of this well after the war and from his grandson, F. W. Benteen's son, the major who spoke with Graham.

Married Catherine (Kate) Louise Norman (d. 17 Feb 1906) on 7 Jan 1862, in St. Louis. Lost four of their five children to spinal meningitis [Connell]. A son, Fred, survived. Fred Benteen, Jr., by then a major, was interviewed by W. A. Graham in 1924.

Intense dislike of Custer and his clan. "Benteen later claimed that he was always open and aboveboard in his criticism of Custer, that Custer liked him for it, and would have welcomed him as a friend. Benteen declared, however, that he knew the man too well to be friendly with him" [Stewart, *Custer's Luck,* p. 169].

Benteen may have been the most respected officer in the Seventh Cavalry and recognized as the most fearless. Stewart wrote, "Benteen's dominant characteristic seems to have been jealousy of and hostility to almost everybody and everything" [*Custer's Luck,* p. 169].

Colonel W. A. Graham wrote of Benteen, "... his known character and the habit of his entire life refutes the imputation that at any time or in any circumstances he failed in his duty as an officer and a soldier. He fought as he had lived, fearless, uncompromising, and grimly stern. Benteen was one of the best soldiers the United States Army has ever possessed" [*The Story of the Little Big Horn,* pp. 105–106]. "[Benteen], together with Major Reno, had been attacked and charged by Custer's partisans with responsibility for the disaster of June 25, 1876. He had resented and brooded over the injustice of that charge for many years. From his viewpoint, the man who rashly led five companies of his regiment to destruction, and unnecessarily imperiled the rest, because he met death in a heroic setting, had been glorified by propaganda; while he, the man to whom more than to any other, belonged the credit of saving what was left of the regiment, had been slandered and reviled because he had not rescued that man and those who perished with him. He was bitter.... Moreover, Benteen was the product of an era of bitterness and strife; of a time when passions ran high; when enmities built upon stern judgments were carried to the grave and even beyond it... [T]his stalwart soldier of a bygone day."

"I found my model early in Captain Benteen, the idol of the Seventh Cavalry on the upper Missouri in 1877, who governed mainly by suggestion; in all the years I knew him I never once heard him raise his voice to enforce his purpose. He would sit by the open fire at night, his bright pleasant face framed by his snow-white hair, beaming with kindness and humor, and often I watched his every movement, to find out the secret of his quiet steady government, that I might go out and govern likewise.... If he found this kindly manner were misunderstood, then his iron hand would close down quickly, but that was seldom necessary, and then only with newcomers and never twice with the same person" [Hugh Scott, *Some Memories of a Soldier,* p. 454].

Klokner, *The Officer Corps of Custer's Seventh Cavalry,* p. 45: "Benteen's antagonism and intense dislike for Custer is well documented. He had his own peculiarities but was nevertheless supremely courageous and highly respected, even idolized, particularly by his beloved Company H."

Walter Camp wrote: "Benteen was an officer of long and honorable experience, and a fighter of the bulldog type. He was every bit as able … as Custer himself. In battle he was alert and cool, and quick and clear of perception. Like Custer, he could take in a situation instantly, without study, but he was not headlong. This was the difference in the two men. He was not what would be called a dashing man, although when it came to fighting, Benteen was there to stay, even to the last ditch if necessary, but he burned no bridges behind. He possessed the admirable trait of caution, and he took account of reserve.

"…Benteen, the bravest of the brave, was too large a man to be influenced at such a time by considerations of personal enmity [Hardorff, *On the Little Bighorn with Walter Camp,* p. 232].

"In my opinion, could Benteen have but known Custer's predicament he would have taken matters into his hands much earlier than he did and tried to at least direct [away] some of the force of warriors against Custer. It was not until the incompetence of Reno had more fully shown itself and that the fear of a great disaster to the seven companies had been whispered in Benteen's ear by one of his closest friends, a commissioned officer, that Benteen took hold of the whole situation with a firm hand" [p. 233].

While he joined the Seventh at its beginning in 1866, Benteen's first taste of Indian fighting was in August 1868, chasing a mixed band of Cheyenne, Arapaho, and Sioux in Kansas.

Retired for disability, 7 Jul 1888. Resided in Atlanta, GA. Politically, Benteen was a Democrat. Brevetted BG, 27 Feb 1890, for gallant service at LBH and Cañon Creek. Exhumed and re-buried in Arlington National Cemetery, 1902.

In some of his correspondence, Benteen alludes to his so-called "mess" buddies. Among them were CPT Owen Hale (d. 1877); and possibly the following Seventh Cavalry officers: MAJ Elliott (d. 1868); CPT Myers (d. 1871); CPT West (d. 1869); CPT Keogh (d. 1876); CPT Hamilton (d. 1868).

Berwald, PVT Frank— b. Posen, Poland, 3 Dec 1852, though some sources indicate 1850 or 1851– d. Highland Falls, NY, 9 Oct 1936. Company E, private. Gray eyes, brown hair, florid complexion; 5'5¾" tall. Enlisted 25 Jan 1873. Blacksmith by trade. Kenneth Hammer claims he was assigned to the pack train and fought with Reno on the hilltop. Greg Michno agrees as does Williams, citing Berwald's own statement.

Bischoff, PVT Charles H.— b. Bremen, Germany, 23 Sep 1855–d. Baltimore, MD, 14 Feb 1924. Company C, private. Blue eyes, blond hair, fair complexion; 5'4½" tall. Had been in the army several years. Enlisted 23 Nov 1872. Remained at the Powder River Depot. The June Returns do not list any Company C personnel at Powder River, indicating they must have been returned to their unit. Died in a streetcar accident at age 68. Buried in Lot 92 N1/2, Section XXX, London Park Cemetery, Baltimore, MD.

Bishley, PVT P. Henry— b. Chicago, IL, 1841–d. veterans home, Napa County, CA, 18 Mar 1929. Company H, private. Hazel eyes, brown hair, fair complexion; 5'7" tall. Enlisted 6 Oct 1875. WIA in right shoulder while on Reno Hill, 26 June.

Bishop, CPL Alexander B.— b. Brooklyn, NY, 22 Nov 1853–d. Brooklyn, NY, 19 Sep 1935. Company H, corporal. Hazel eyes, light hair, fair complexion; 5'6" tall. Enlisted 15 Apr 1875. WIA in right arm while on Reno Hill. Resided at 310 Clermont Street and 1216 Dean Street, Brooklyn, NY. Buried in Evergreen Cemetery, Brooklyn, NY.

Bishop, PVT Charles H.— b. Washington, D.C., 11 May 1854–d. East St. Louis, MO, 4 Dec 1929. Company H, private. Hazel eyes, light hair, fair complexion; 5'8" tall. Enlisted 15 Apr 1875. Black Hills expedition in 1875, Nez Percé campaign, and Black Hills and Cheyenne campaigns of 1878. WIA in right arm in hilltop fight. Resided in East St. Louis for 38 years. Married Nellie Elizabeth. Buried in Greenwood Cemetery, East St. Louis.

Black, PVT Henry— b. Donegal, Ireland, 1850– d. unknown. Company H, private. Blue eyes, light brown hair, fair complexion; 6'½" tall. Enlisted 13 Nov 1872. WIA in right arm in hilltop fight.

Blair, PVT James C.— b. Camden, NJ, 18 Dec 1850–d. Pittsburgh, PA, 25 Aug 1918. Company K, private. Blue eyes, light brown hair, fair complexion; 5'8¼" tall. Remained at Fort Lincoln for duty, in charge of company property.

Blair, PVT Wilbur F.— b. Lewisburg, PA, 1841– d. Lewisburg, PA, 2 Oct 1891. Company A, private. Hazel eyes, dark hair, ruddy complexion; 5'6" tall. Enlisted 1 Sep 1872. No specific record exists of his participation in the battle, other than his presence with his unit during the valley fighting and subsequent defense of Reno Hill.

Blake, PVT Thomas (Billy)— b. NYC, 1851–d. NYC, 12 Mar 1927. Company A, private. Gray eyes, dark hair, dark complexion; 5'8½" tall. Enlisted 15 Jan 1872. Wounded, probably in the valley fighting during the retreat. Apparently, he was so scared that when the troops started to move off Reno Hill toward Weir Peak in the early evening of 25 Jun 1876, he complained he was too injured to be moved and his disgusted comrades left him behind. Retired as a commissary sergeant. Resided at 94 West 10th Street, NYC.

Blunt, PVT George— b. Baltimore, MD, 1845– d. 22 Nov 1905. Company K, private. Blue eyes, dark hair, sallow complexion; 5'6¾" tall. Enlisted 10 Sep 1866 in Seventh Cavalry; second enlistment 11 Sep 1871. Rode with his unit in Benteen's battalion, and fought on Reno Hill.

Boam, PVT William— b. Manchester, England, 1853–d. unknown. Company B, private. Gray eyes, brown hair, medium complexion; 5'9" tall. Enlisted 22 Dec 1874. Discharged 12 Apr 1877 for disability. Hammer originally carried him on detached service, but Smalley corrects this and carries him at the battle and in the hilltop fight. Lived at 36 Bowery, NYC, after discharge.

Bobo, 1SG L. Edwin— b. Franklin County, OH, 1845–d. 25 Jun 1876, killed at the Little Big Horn. Company C: first sergeant. Hazel eyes, brown hair, 5'6½" tall. Had first enlisted on 23 Dec 1867 and was assigned to the Seventh Cavalry. Participated in the Washita campaign of '68. Body found near Keogh. Had cholera in Aug 1875, but survived. Married Missouri Ann Wycoff on 2 Oct 1872. She eventually re-married to SGT Daniel Kanipe. Bobo and his wife had two children: Charles F. (b. 16 Aug 1873, Fort Rice–d. 1937 in Knoxville, TN); and Frank E. (b. 10 Jun 1875 in D.T.). Bobo's body was identified in the Keogh Sector meaning he had survived the carnage of the Calhoun Coulee and Finley-Finckle Ridge fighting. His descendants survive him, at least one currently living in North Carolina. Listed number 13 in "June Returns, Alterations … Killed in action."

Bockerman, PVT August— b. Elberfeld, Prussia, 1851–d. St. Joseph, MO, 17 Apr 1904. Company A, private. Blue eyes, light hair, light complexion; 5'11" tall. Enlisted 12 Feb 1872. In Yellowstone and Black Hills expeditions. First wife, Rose J., was born in Denmark about 1858. Remained at the Powder River Depot. Presence confirmed on June Returns.

Bohner, TMP Aloys (aka Louis Braun)— b. Baden, Germany, 1828 or 1830–d. Burlington, IA, 27 Jul 1887. Company D: trumpeter. Hazel eyes, brown hair, dark complexion; 5'7¾" tall. Enlisted 19 Dec 1853 in Second Artillery. Deserted and enlisted 11 Aug 1857 in Third Infantry; enlisted as Bohner 21 Jul 1860 to 4 Apr 1863 in U.S. Mounted Rifles. Enlisted 30 Sep 1863 as chief trumpeter, Eighth IA Cavalry. POW at Newman, GA. Enlisted in Seventh Cavalry from 2 Jan 1866 to 2 Jan 1869; re-upped to 22 Dec 1873; and again 12 Jan 1874. Rode with his unit in Benteen's battalion,

and fought on Reno Hill. Remained in the Seventh Cavalry until his discharge in 1879, by which time he was the chief musician in the regimental band.

Bohner, PVT Hugh *see* **Bonner**

Boisen, PVT Christian C.— b. Denmark, 26 May 1846–d. Fort Smith, AR, 21 Jan 1923. Company K, private. Blue eyes, brown hair, fair complexion; 5'6" tall. Enlisted 25 Mar 1873. Rode with his unit in Benteen's battalion, and fought on Reno Hill.

Bones, PVT Hugh *see* **Bonner**

Bonner (also listed as Bohner and Bones), **PVT Hugh**— b. Boston, MA, Dec 1854–d. unknown. Company B, private. Gray eyes, dark hair, dark complexion; 5'7½" tall. Enlisted 18 Mar 1876. Remained at the Powder River Depot. Hammer also lists him at PRD. Deserted 7 Jul 1876, but apprehended on 13 July. Escaped from confinement at FAL, 6 Sep 1876.

Boren, PVT Ansgarius— b. Linkoping, Sweden, 1850–d. unknown. Company B, private. Blue eyes, light hair, light complexion; 5'5¼" tall. Enlisted 12 Feb 1872. Only known to have been with his unit of Reno Hill. Left the army in 1885, "having been accepted as [a] student for the ministry by Academy of New Church," in Philadelphia [Williams, *Military Register of Custer's Last Command*, p. 43].

Bott, PVT George A.— b. Fort Wayne, IN, 1853– d. unknown. Company A, private. Gray eyes, brown hair, fair complexion; 5'7" tall. Enlisted 16 Sep 1875. No specific record exists of his participation in the battle, other than his presence with his unit during the valley fighting and subsequent defense of Reno Hill.

Botzer, SGT Edward— b. Bremerhaven, Germany, 1846–d. 25 Jun 1876, killed at the Little Big Horn during Reno's retreat from the timber. Company G, sergeant: acting first sergeant. Blue eyes, brown hair, fair complexion; 5'6½" tall. Second enlistment 26 Nov 1871. PVT John Lattman, in an interview with Walter Mason Camp, said Botzer was the company quartermaster sergeant and that SGT Alexander Brown was the acting first sergeant at the Little Big Horn [see Liddic/Harbaugh, *Camp on Custer*, p. 76]. There is also some dispute to where he was killed. Several bones—including most of the facial bones—found on the banks of the LBH at Reno's retreat crossing during a 1989 archaeological dig, were almost certainly his, though there was some speculation they might be from PVT Moodie (Company A). Tests indicated the bones were from a 30–40-year-old white male, about 5'7" tall. Subsequent forensic reconstructions indicate the bones were most likely Botzer's. Hammer claimed he was killed at the retreat ford. Married; no children. Listed number 125 in "June Returns, Alterations … Killed in action."

Boyle, PVT James P.— b. County Tyrone, Ireland, 15 Dec 1853–d. Bismarck, ND, 2 Sep 1920. Company G, private. Hazel eyes, auburn hair, ruddy complexion; 5'6⅜" tall. Enlisted 7 Dec 1874 in Boston. WIA in back during hilltop fight, though not listed as wounded in the 30 Jun 1876 Seventh Cavalry returns. Died of hypertension at St. Alexius Hospital. Buried in Lot 8, Row 8, Block A, St. Mary's Cemetery, Bismarck, ND.

Boyle, PVT Owen— b. Waterford, Ireland, 1843–d. 25 Jun 1876, killed at the Little Big Horn. Company E, private. Gray eyes, dark hair, fair complexion; 5'6" tall. Enlistments: 9 Dec 1862 to 25 Jul 1865 in Twelfth MA Artillery; 15 Sep 1866 to 15 Sep 1869 in 35th Infantry; 27 Oct 1869 to 14 Jul 1874 in 22nd Infantry. Enlisted in Seventh Cavalry 19 Dec 1874. While his body was not specifically identified, he may have been one of the unknowns on either the South Skirmish Line or in Deep Ravine. Listed number 63 in "June Returns, Alterations … Killed in action."

Brady, PVT William— b. Pittsburgh, PA, 1848–d. 25 Jun 1876, killed at the Little Big Horn. Company F, private. Blue eyes, brown hair, ruddy complexion; 5'6½" tall. Enlisted 15 Sep 1875. In all likelihood he was killed on Last Stand Hill with his unit. Listed number 102 in "June Returns, Alterations … Killed in action."

Braendle (also listed as Brandel), **PVT William** (aka William Cummings)— b. Würtemburg, Germany, 1 Nov 1855–d. Santa Rosa, CA, 15 Dec 1932. Company C, private. Hazel eyes, brown hair, fair complexion; 5'9¼" tall. Arrived in U.S. in 1871; enlisted 8 Oct 1873. Civilian occupation was a rancher. Remained at the Powder River Depot. The June Returns do not list any Company C personnel at Powder River, indicating they must have been returned to their unit. Resided in California for 30 years and for 22 years at 1342 147th Street, Santa Rosa. Raised prunes and poultry on his five-acre farm. Died of heart disease and buried in San Francisco. Survived by his widow, Anna.

Brainard, PVT George— b. Brooklyn, OH, 1846–d. Cleveland, OH, 20 Nov 1886. Company B, private. Blue eyes, light hair, light complexion; 5'9½" tall. Enlisted on 22 Jan 1872. Discharged 22 Jan 1877. Detached service with Terry's HQ as Terry's orderly.

Brandon, FAR Benjamin (aka Robert Nelson)— b. Hopkinsville, KY, 1831–d. 25 Jun 1876, killed at the Little Big Horn. Company F: company farrier. Hazel eyes, black hair, ruddy complexion; 5'6½" tall. Second enlistment on 1 Nov 1875. At 45 years old, oldest casualty (with Bob-tail Bull) of battle. In all likelihood he was killed on Last Stand Hill with his unit. Listed number 96 in "June Returns, Alterations … Killed in action."

Brant, PVT Abram B. (or Abraham)— b. NYC, 1849–d. Camp Ruhlen, D.T., 4 Oct 1878, accidental gunshot wound. Company D, private. Hazel eyes, light hair, fair complexion; 5'5⅞" tall. Enlisted 27 Sep 1875. Awarded the Medal of Honor for bringing water up to Reno Hill.

Braun (also Baum and Brunn), **PVT Frank**— b. Berne (Bern), Switzerland, 1848–d. FAL, 4 Oct 1876, of wounds suffered at the Little Big Horn. Company M, private. Hazel eyes, fair hair, fair complexion; 5'6¼" tall. Enlisted 23 Sep 1875. Wounded in the face and left thigh on 25 June on Reno Hill. Died 4 Oct 1876 at Fort Lincoln. Buried in the post cemetery, but when the fort was closed, his body was exhumed and re-buried in Custer Battlefield National Cemetery. He was the last man to die of wounds related to the battle directly.

Braun (also Brown), **PVT Franz C.**— b. Aix-la-Chapelle (Aachen), Germany, 1845–d. unknown. Company I, private. Blue eyes, light hair, fair complexion; 5'8½" tall. Enlisted 13 May 1873. Said to have been illiterate. With the packs; fought on Reno Hill.

Braun, Louis *see* **Bohner, Aloys**

Brennan, PVT John— b. County Waterford, Ireland, 1849–d. unknown. Company C, private. Gray eyes, brown hair, 5'5¾" tall. Less than one year service; enlisted 24 Sep 1875, in St. Louis by LT John Thompson. Straggler; horse gave out. Joined Reno on the hilltop. May have dropped out along Reno Creek approach to LBH. Spent more than 500 days over a three-year period in confinement. Dishonorably discharged, 4 Dec 1879.

Bresnahan, PVT Cornelius— b. Mount Auburn, MA, Jul 1852–d. unknown. Company K, private. Hazel eyes, red hair, medium complexion; 5'9" tall. Enlisted 3 Oct 1873. Rode with his unit in Benteen's battalion, and fought on Reno Hill. After his discharge he resided at 40 Reed Street, North Cambridge, MA.

Brightfield, PVT John— b. Dearborn County, IN, 23 Jun 1853–d. 25 Jun 1876, killed at the Little Big Horn. Company C, private. Brown eyes and hair; 5'9¼" tall. Less than one year service; enlisted 7 Oct 1875. In the C Company charge off Battle Ridge-Calhoun Hill, but body was never identified. May have died in Calhoun Coulee, Finley-Finckle Ridge, the Keogh Sector, or possibly even Last Stand Hill. Listed number 24 in "June Returns, Alterations ... Killed in action."

Bringes, FAR John (or Jonathan)— b. Hanover, Germany, 1846–d. unknown. Company A: farrier. Blue eyes, brown hair, ruddy complexion; 5'9" tall. Second enlistment 22 Sep 1871. No specific record exists of his participation in the battle, other than his presence with his unit during the valley fighting and subsequent defense of Reno Hill.

Brinkerhoff, PVT Henry M. (aka Charles Harry Reynolds)— b. Gettysburg, PA, 12 Apr 1854–d. Los Angeles, CA, 4 Feb 1933. Company G, private. Blue eyes, light hair, fair complexion; 5'6" tall. Enlisted 1 Dec 1874. Promoted to CPL 25 Jun 1876. May have served as a Seventh Cavalry QM employee in the Yellowstone and Black Hills expeditions. Cited by Congress for extraordinary bravery during Sioux campaign and for carrying the dispatch to Terry calling for medical aid and reinforcements on the morning of 27 Jun 1876. Married Lulu Garretson, 21 Apr 1902. Buried in Los Angeles National Cemetery.

Briody, CPL John— b. NYC, 1847–d. 25 Jun 1876, killed at the Little Big Horn. Company F, corporal. Blue eyes, brown hair, dark complexion; 5'5" tall. Second enlistment 13 Aug 1872. Briody's body was identified by SGT Daniel Kanipe (C) just north of Deep Ravine on a slight rise. The right leg had been severed and placed under his head. A body found between Deep Ravine and Calhoun Ridge (Marker 257) could have been Briody. During the archaeological excavations of 1984–1985, the placement of the remains found at this marker would have been consistent with such an event. Listed number 95 in "June Returns, Alterations ... Killed in action."

Broadhurst, PVT Joseph F.— b. Philadelphia, PA, 1852–d. 25 Jun 1876, killed at the Little Big Horn. Company I, private. Brown eyes, dark hair, ruddy complexion; 5'5" tall. Enlisted 22 Sep 1873. Body never identified, but in all likelihood he was killed in the Keogh Sector. Listed number 149 in "June Returns, Alterations ... Killed in action."

Brogan, PVT James— b. Pittsburgh, PA, 1849 or 1850–d. 25 Jun 1876, killed at the Little Big Horn. Company E, private. Hazel eyes, brown hair, ruddy complexion; 5'8¼" tall. Second enlistment 1 Apr 1876. While his body was not specifically identified, he may have been one of the unknowns on either the South Skirmish Line or in Deep Ravine. Listed number 64 in "June Returns, Alterations ... Killed in action."

Bromwell, PVT Latrobe— b. Frederick County, MD, 1847–d. Washington, D.C., 29 Apr 1923. Company E, private. Gray or blue eyes, light hair, fair complexion; 5'5¼–6" tall. Mustered in 2nd MD Infantry 2 Jan 1864 and out 15 Jun 1865; enlisted 12 Jul 1870 in Second Cavalry. Discharged 12 Jul 1875 and enlisted 9 Aug 1875 in Seventh Cavalry. Became sick on Rosebud Creek; sent back to PRD where he remained. Was the chief cook at the Training School for Cooks and Bakers at Fort Riley, KS, until he retired in 1909. Bromwell married 1SG Hohmeyer's (E) widow and they moved to 1304 North 9th Street, Washington, D.C.

Brown, SGT Alexander— b. Aberdeen, Scotland, 19 Feb 1844–d. Fort Meade, D.T., 7 Apr 1884. Company G, sergeant. Hazel eyes, black hair, dark complexion; 5'8½" tall. Second enlistment 13 Dec 1871. Assigned to pack train. According to Goldin, after the battle, Brown was made acting first sergeant [Carroll, *The Benteen-Goldin Letters*, p. 41]. In 1877 he acted as sergeant major of a battalion Benteen commanded. Benteen thought he was a good man, but he drank a lot. In the Walter Camp interviews, PVT John Lattman claimed Brown was the acting first sergeant at the battle, but this seems unlikely since he was assigned to the pack train [see Lattman interview, Liddic/Harbaugh, *Camp on Custer*, p. 75].

Brown, PVT Benjamin Franklin— b. Taylor County, KY, 1849–d. 25 Jun 1876, killed at the Little Big Horn. Company F, private. Hazel eyes, light hair, fair complexion; 5'9" tall. Enlisted 12 Mar 1872. In all likelihood he was killed on Last Stand Hill with his unit. Listed number 100 in "June Returns, Alterations ... Killed in action."

Brown, COMMISSARY SGT Charles (real name was Adam Karl Reinwald)— b. Bavaria, 1846–d. unknown, but he probably returned to Germany, dying there. Headquarters: Commissary Sergeant. Hazel eyes, brown hair, ruddy; 5'7½" tall. Enlisted on 4 Oct 1875; deserted 15 Nov 1876. Remained at the PRD, but on detached service, not with the Seventh Cavalry, specifically.

Brown, CPL George C.— b. Baltimore, MD, 1851–d. 25 Jun 1876, killed at the Little Big Horn. Company E, corporal. Brown eyes, brown hair, ruddy complexion; 5'5½" tall. Enlisted on 19 Oct 1872. Body identified in Deep Ravine. Listed number 57 in "June Returns, Alterations ... Killed in action."

Brown, PVT Hiram Erastus (aka Erastus Grover Brown; Hiram Groves)— b. Mount Vernon, OH–d. Watervliet, NY, 20 May 1904. Company F private. Brown eyes, brown hair, fair complexion;

5' 8¼" tall. Daily duty with QM Department and carried in Department HQ. Ferdinand Widmayer said Brown was with pack train, but he may have gotten him confused with either of two other Browns, both of whom were killed during the Custer part of the battle.

Brown, PVT James— b. Queen's County, Ireland, 1853–d. unknown. Company B, private. Blue eyes, black hair, dark complexion; 5' 6½" tall. Enlisted 23 Mar 1876. Remained at the Powder River Depot.

Brown, PVT Joseph— b. Berlin, Prussia, 1844–d. unknown. Company K, private. Blue eyes, light hair, fair complexion; 5'11" tall. Second enlistment 27 Jan 1875. Rode with his unit in Benteen's battalion, and fought on Reno Hill. Lived in Omaha, NE, after discharge.

Brown, PVT Nathan T.— b. Marion County, IN, 1843–d. Cañon Creek, M.T., 13 Sep 1877. Company L, private. Gray eyes, black hair, dark complexion; 5'7" tall. Second enlistment 25 Nov 1874. With the pack train. Killed in Nez Percé War.

Brown, Thomas *see* **Dolan, PVT John**

Brown, PVT William A.— b. Hamburg, Germany, 1842–d. 25 Jun 1876, killed at the Little Big Horn. Company F, private. Blue eyes, brown hair, fair complexion; 5'5" tall. Second enlistment 10 Dec 1872. Body found on west side of LBH, near mouth of MTC. He may have been the one whose horse bolted across river and into Indian camp Liddic says his body was found 250 yards across the river from the Deep *Coulee* crossing (Ford B) [*Vanishing Victory*, p. 164]. See SGT Ogden (E). PVT James M. Rooney (F) identified Brown's body in the village, in all likelihood making Brown the trooper whose horse bolted as Custer and Yates approached Ford B [Hardorff, *On the LBH with Walter Camp*, p. 13, footnote 2]. Listed number 99 in "June Returns, Alterations … Killed in action."

Bruce, PVT Patrick— b. Cork, Ireland, 1844–d. 25 Jun 1876, killed at the Little Big Horn. Company F, private. Blue eyes, brown hair, ruddy complexion; 5'7" tall. Third enlistment 1 May 1876. In all likelihood he was killed on Last Stand Hill with his unit. Listed number 124 in "June Returns, Alterations … Killed in action."

Bucknell, TMP Thomas J.— b. Cincinnati, OH, 1849–d. 25 Jun 1876, killed at the Little Big Horn. Company C: trumpeter. Gray eyes, light hair, 5' 8½" tall. Was in his second enlistment, 23 Sep 1875. In the C Company charge off Battle Ridge-Calhoun Hill, but body was never identified. May have died in Calhoun Coulee, Finley-Finckle

Ridge, the Keogh Sector, or possibly even Last Stand Hill. Listed number 19 in "June Returns, Alterations … Killed in action."

Burdick, PVT Benjamin F.— b. Grafton, NY, 27 Apr 1851 or 1852 (more likely the latter)–d. Kenwood, Albany, NY, 11 Jan 1930. Company A, private. Blue eyes, brown hair, fair complexion; 5' 8¾" tall. Enlisted 13 Jan 1873. Remained at the Powder River Depot. Presence confirmed on June Returns. Wife, Belle, died earlier than Burdick did. Survived by son, Ernest F. Buried in Burewyck Cemetery, Rensselaer, NY.

Burgdorf, PVT Charles— b. Hanover, Germany, 1845–d. unknown. Company K, private. Presence confirmed on June Returns. Blue eyes, fair hair, ruddy complexion; 5' 5¾" tall. Second enlistment 28 Feb 1876. Remained at the Powder River Depot.

Burke, BSM Edmund H.— b. Manchester, England, 1841 or 10 Aug 1843 (on tombstone)–d. Sumner, IA, circa 24 Apr 1925 [Nunnally, "Seventh U.S. Cavalry Trooper Grave Found?" *LBHA Newsletter*, Vol. XLIII, No. 3, Apr 2009]. Company K: company blacksmith. Hazel eyes, black hair, dark complexion; 5' 8½" tall. Third enlistment 14 Dec 1871. In the CBHMA's "Battlefield Dispatch," Summer 2004, Hammer lists Burke's *widow*, Mary, and a child, indicating Burke was killed in the battle. This is incorrect as the entry in Hammer's book shows Burke's discharge on 14 Dec 1876. Buried in Mount Calvary Cemetery, Sumner, IA.

Burke, PVT John (aka Pardee, Oscar F.)— b. Oneida, NY, 1852–d. 25 Jun 1876, killed at the Little Big Horn. Company L, private. Brown eyes, brown hair, dark complexion; 5' 8¾" tall. Enlisted 29 Aug 1873 in U.S. Marine Corps; deserted 28 Sep 1873. Enlisted 29 Sep 1873 in Seventh Cavalry. Body found on Custer Hill (Scott, in one spot, has him as killed on Reno Hill, but this is incorrect). Listed number 196 in "June Returns, Alterations … Killed in action."

Burke, Michael *see* **McDermott, SGT George M.**

Burkhardt, PVT Charles— b. Summerville, OH, 1846–d. Cloutierville, LA, 1888. Company K, private. Hazel eyes, brown hair, dark complexion; 5' 3" tall. Enlisted 7 Sep 1866 in Seventh Cavalry; third enlistment 1 Sep 1871. Assigned to pack train. Smalley says he was LT Godfrey's cook.

Burkman, PVT John W. ("Old Neutriment")— b. Allegheny County, PA (or possibly Germany; death certificate lists Missouri), 10 Jan 1839–d. Billings, MT, 6 Nov 1925; committed suicide. Company L, private. Hazel eyes, dark hair, ruddy complexion; 5'7" tall. Enlisted 16 Aug 1861.

Enlisted from 16 Aug 1870 to 16 Aug 1875. Re-upped 1 Sep 1875. Custer's personal orderly or "striker." Left behind with pack train; was on Reno Hill. In General Sibley's expedition into Dakota in 1863. Yellowstone expedition (1873), Black Hills expedition (1875), and Nez Percé campaign (1877). Resided in Billings, MT, for nearly 30 years. Suicide by gunshot. Buried in Custer Battlefield National Cemetery.

Burlis, PVT Edmond—b. Klingnau, Switzerland, 19 Mar 1848–d. St. Louis, MO, 22 Oct 1924. Headquarters: band. Private. Hazel eyes, dark hair, dark complexion; 5' 6" tall. Remained at Powder River Depot. Presence confirmed on June Returns.

Burnham, PVT Lucien—b. Conkling, NY, 1851–d. 25 Jun 1876, killed at the Little Big Horn. Company F, private. Gray eyes, red hair, ruddy; 5' 8⅝" tall. Enlisted 9 Dec 1872. A lawyer in civilian life. In all likelihood he was killed on Last Stand Hill with his unit. Listed number 101 in "June Returns, Alterations … Killed in action."

Burns, PVT Charles—b. Howard County, IN (one source claims Howard County, MD), 1847–d. unknown. Company B, private. Blue eyes, brown hair, florid complexion; 5' 9" tall. Enlisted 8 Mar 1876. Remained at the Powder River Depot.

Bush, John *see* **Jones, PVT Henry P.**

Bustard, SGT James—b. Donegal, Ireland, 1846–d. 25 Jun 1876, killed at the Little Big Horn; his company was part of Custer's battalions. Company I, sergeant. Hazel eyes, light hair, fair complexion; 5' 6½" tall. Second enlistment 21 Jul 1875. Body found next to Keogh (according to Edgerly), though one report (Kanipe) claimed it was Bustard's horse that bolted into the Indian village. Kanipe was wrong, though Bustard may have been riding SGT DeLacy's horse that day. SGT James Flannagan (D) who identified Bustard's body on 28 Jun 1876, near Keogh's [Hardorff, *On the LBH with Walter Camp*, p. 13, footnote 2], corroborated this. Listed number 142 in "June Returns, Alterations … Killed in action."

Butler, 1SG James—b. Albany, NY, 1842–d. 25 Jun 1876, killed at the Little Big Horn. Company L: first sergeant. Gray eyes, black hair, fair complexion; 5' 5½" tall. CPL Roy (A) described him as "a heavyset man [who] wore side whiskers and had a bald head" [Hardorff, *On the LBH with Walter Camp*, p. 40]. Enlisted from 31 May 1870 to 31 May 1875 in Seventh Cavalry. Re-upped same day. Bruce Liddic claims he was riding the horse of former SGT Milton DeLacy (I) who had deserted [Liddic, *Vanishing Victory*, p. 153], but everything I have on DeLacy says he was with the pack train

and if anyone was riding his horse it was Bustard from the same company. Butler's body was found between *Deep Coulee* and MTC, ¼-mile from Ford B. "Butler's body lay in an isolated location, between Custer Hill and the Reno-Benteen defense site, in or near lower Deep Coulee or the adjacent rise, not far from Medicine Tail Coulee ford" [Brust, Pohanka, Barnard, *Where Custer Fell*, p. 82]. He may have been one of the four riders who bolted from Battle Ridge, back in the direction they had come, trying to escape from the Keogh Sector melee. It appears he got the farthest before being killed. His remains, discovered in 1905, were interred in an unknown grave in Custer Battlefield National Cemetery. Michno [*Lakota Noon*] claims Butler's body was found in Deep Coulee, about 200 yards farther north of Foley's (C). Foley's was found on the low western terminus of Butler Ridge, in the environs of MTC before it empties into the LBH. Michno says Butler's marker was later placed higher up near the spine of the ridge. In *The Mystery of E Troop*, Michno writes that Stanislaus Roy (A) corresponded with Walter Camp between 1909 and 1912. Roy said he was with the main burial parties on 28 Jun 1876, but did not follow any trail down MTC. Instead, he cut straight across to the battlefield. On the way, the first body he passed by was CPL Foley's. Then he came across 1SG Butler, about 200 yards from Foley. From there to the next group of dead on or near Calhoun Hill was quite a distance. The famous Hunkpapa warrior, Gall, said, "There was a soldier on the hill southeast of us still fighting when the battle ended and we had a hard time to kill him. He killed several of our braves. Finally some of the braves crawled up the hill on all sides. Those behind him finally killed him" [Liddic, *Vanishing Victory*, p. 153, from David F. Barry, *Indian Notes on Custer and His Last Battle*, 1947]. Richard Hardorff wrote, "…Dr. James S. Brust rediscovered Butler's kill site, which was originally identified by Gen. Godfrey in 1916, and which location is some 125 yards southwest of the present site of the Butler marker. In years past, Godfrey's Butler site yielded a horse skeleton, several expended cartridges, a horseshoe and a shank portion of a boot, containing a decomposed foot. The rotted leather revealed some faded initials, thought to read 'JD,' but which may well have been the letters 'JB'" [Hardorff, *On the Little Bighorn with Walter Camp*, p. 6, footnote 2]. Wife Mary and two children. Listed number 182 in "June Returns, Alterations … Killed in action."

Butler, PVT James W.—b. Riverton, NJ, 1 Apr 1844 (death certificate lists his birthplace as Limerick, Ireland)–d. Philadelphia, PA, 8 Jun 1924. Company F, private. Blue eyes, auburn hair, ruddy complexion; 5'6" tall. Served in First PA Reserves during Civil War. Second enlistment 18 Sep 1874. Detailed as a wagon train guard and remained at the Powder River Depot. Overfield claims he was detailed for extra duty as a hospital steward with Reno (since 17 May 1876). Overfield may be correct, but only to a point. Buried in Philadelphia National Cemetery.

Caddle, SGT Michael C.— b. Dublin, Ireland, 9 Jun 1844–d. Bismarck, ND, 1 May 1919. Company I, sergeant. Blue eyes, light hair, fair complexion; 5'5½" tall. Enlisted 20 Sep 1864 in Seventh NY Cavalry. Discharged 6 Jun 1865. Enlisted 29 Sep 1873 in Seventh Cavalry. Remained at the Powder River Depot. Presence confirmed on June Returns. Good friends with McIlhargey who was killed at LBH. Was still with Company I when it went to the battlefield in Jul 1877 to re-bury the dead and mark the officers' graves. Resided in North Dakota for 46 years. Married McIlhargey's widow Josephine 15 Dec 1877. Children: Thomas, Mary, Walter, Dorothy Ann, Hugh, Cornelius, and Julia. Buried at Fort Rice Community Cemetery.

Cain, PVT Morris (Maurice)— b. Barkersville, MA, 1853–d. Colville, WA, 13 Aug 1906. Company M, private. Brown eyes, black hair, dark complexion; 5'7" tall. Enlisted 16 Sep 1875. No specific record exists of his participation in the battle, other than his presence with his unit during the valley fighting and subsequent defense of Reno Hill.

Caldwell, PVT William M.— b. PA, 22 Feb 1857–d. Clearfield, PA, 30 Oct 1913. Company B, private. Blue eyes, black hair, fair complexion; 5'7" tall. Enlisted 23 Mar 1876. Remained at the Powder River Depot. Wife's name was Blanche; married 25 Dec 1887. He was buried in Clearfield Cemetery.

Calhoun, 1LT James ("Jimmi")— b. Cincinnati, OH, 24 Aug 1845–d. 25 Jun 1876, killed at the Little Big Horn, part of Custer's command, Keogh's battalion. Company L: Acting CO. TDY from Company C. Brown eyes, light hair, fair complexion; 5'11" tall. DOR: 9 Jan 1871, making him sixth of nine first lieutenants on campaign.

Rode a white horse. Varnum told Walter Camp that the only way Calhoun's body was identified was by the fillings in his teeth. Edgerly claimed Calhoun was not mutilated at all. Both could have been correct as the heat of the days distorted the bodies considerably.

Son of a merchant. Graduated from Mount Pleasant Academy, Sing Sing, NY, 30 Jun 1860, and traveled in Europe during the Civil War. Calhoun's sister, Charlotte, was married to CPT Moylan. Calhoun married Margaret Emma Custer, George and

Tom's sister, in Monroe, MI, 7 Mar 1872. No children. She remarried in 1903. Buried in Fort Leavenworth Cemetery.

Callahan, CPL John J.— b. Salem, MA, 18 Jul 1853–d. 25 Jun 1876, killed at the Little Big Horn, while serving as part of Custer's HQ command. Company K, corporal. Hospital Orderly and Lord's assistant. Gray eyes, dark hair, fair complexion; 5'7" tall. Enlisted 5 Nov 1872. Body found on Custer Hill, though Scott says Callahan was killed on Reno Hill (this is almost surely incorrect). Listed number 179 in "June Returns, Alterations … Killed in action."

Callan, PVT James— b. Glasgow, Scotland, 1848–d. unknown. Company B, private. Gray eyes, dark hair, fair complexion; 5'7" tall. Enlisted 11 Mar 1876. Remained at the Powder River Depot.

Callan, PVT Thomas Joseph— b. Louth, Ireland, 1855–d. Yonkers, NY, 5 Mar 1908. Company B, private. Blue eyes, dark hair, fair complexion; 5'7" tall. Enlisted 10 Mar 1876. Awarded MH for bringing water up to Reno Hill under severe Indian fire. Resided at 125 Downing Street in Yonkers, NY, for 28 years. Buried in Holy Sepulcher Cemetery, Newark, NJ.

Calran, J. J. *see* **Galvan, PVT James J.**

Campbell, PVT Charles A.— b. Boone County, IL, 1844–d. Bismarck, ND, 2 Aug 1906. Company B, private. Hazel eyes, light brown hair, ruddy complexion; 5'8½" tall. Enlisted 22 Jan 1872. Reduced from SGT, 4 Jun 1876. Arrived on Reno Hill with pack train escort and fought there.

Campbell, PVT Charles W.— b. Guthrie County, IA, 1855–d. Fort Bayard, NM, 2 Aug 1906. Company G, private. Blue eyes, light hair, ruddy complexion; 5'5½" tall. Enlisted 3 Apr 1876. Assigned to pack train. WIA in right shoulder attempting to get water for wounded with the first water party. Wife Elizabeth died 4 Apr 1897. Children: Charles M. Sarah H., George T., twins John and Frank, and Mary E. Died of TB.

Campbell, SGT Jeremiah— b. Sangamon County, IL, 11 Feb 1844–d. Decatur, IL, 8 May 1884. Company K, sergeant. Gray eyes, dark hair, fair complexion; 5'7¾–9" tall. Enlisted 28 Oct 1861 in 32nd IL Infantry. Wounded at Bentonville 19 Mar 1865. Shot in the right ear, the bullet coming out of the left side of nose and a gunshot entering right shoulder and coming out below the shoulder blade. Hospitalized in a Confederate hospital. Discharged 16 Sep 1865. Enlisted from 11 Jan 1869 to 11 Jan 1872 in the 4th Artillery. Enlisted 16 Jan 1872 in Seventh Cavalry. Rode with his unit in Benteen's battalion, and fought on Reno Hill. Resided in Bismarck. Struck by a train car and died. Buried in Moweaqua, IL.

Capes, SGT William G.— b. Portland, ME, 1847–d. Pittsburgh, PA. Company M, sergeant. Gray eyes, black hair, ruddy complexion; 5' 9½" tall. Enlisted 30 Dec 1872. Had been acting QM sergeant of the company. Remained at the Powder River Depot. Presence confirmed on June Returns.

Carey (aka Casey, Carry, and Cory), **PVT John J.**— b. Troy, NY, 1851–d. Benton City, WA, 1930, result of a fall. Company B, private. Blue eyes, brown hair, sallow complexion; 5' 5½" tall. Enlisted 25 Oct 1872. With the pack train escort, Company B. Arrived and fought on Reno Hill.

Carey (aka Carney), **SGT Patrick**— b. Tipperary, Ireland, 14 Apr 1828–d. Washington, D.C., 3 Oct 1893. Company M, sergeant. Gray eyes, gray hair, light complexion; 5' 7½" tall. Enlisted from 14 Sep 1866 to 14 Sep 1869, 36th Infantry. Enlisted in the Seventh Cavalry, 22 Mar 1875. WIA in right hip. One of twenty men — one officer, three scouts, sixteen enlisted men — left in the timber in the valley bottoms. May have been one of the M Company flankers who got into the village.

Carmody, PVT Thomas— b. NYC, 1841 or 1842–d. New York City, 13 Aug 1912, of cancer. Company B, private. Blue eyes, brown hair, fair complexion; 5' 4½" tall. Second enlistment 1 Aug 1874. With the pack train escort, Company B. Arrived and fought on Reno Hill.

Carney, PVT James— b. County West Meath, Ireland, 1843–d. 25 Jun 1876, killed at the Little Big Horn. Company F, private. Gray eyes, black hair, dark complexion; 5' 4¼" tall. Second enlistment on 9 Dec 1872. Bone fragments found at Marker 105 on Last Stand Hill would be consistent with his reported age and height. Most men killed at this location were believed to have been from F Company. Several others fit this description, as well. Listed number 103 in "June Returns, Alterations … Killed in action."

Carroll, PVT Joseph— b. NYC, 19 Jan 1847–d. Danville, IL, 23 Dec 1904. Headquarters: band. Private. Blue eyes, brown hair, fair complexion; 4' 8" tall. Enlisted at the age of 13, 11 Jun 1860, with mother's consent. Remained at Powder River Depot. Presence confirmed on June Returns.

Carter, PVT Andrew— b. Lincolnshire, England, 1851–d. unknown. Headquarters: band. Private. Brown eyes, brown hair, ruddy complexion; 5' 6¼" tall. Remained at Powder River Depot. Presence confirmed on June Returns.

Cashan (also spelled Cashen), **SGT William**— b. Glenall, County Queens, Ireland, 1845–d. 25 Jun 1876, killed at the Little Big Horn. Company L, sergeant. Blue eyes, brown hair, fair complexion; 5' 9" tall. Enlisted 7 Jan 1867 in 34th Infantry, then transferred to Sixteenth Infantry. Reenlisted from 7 Jan 1870 to 3 Aug 1872. Third enlistment 17 Dec 1872 in Seventh Cavalry. Could have been killed at the head of Deep Ravine, paired Markers 9 and 10 on the South Skirmish Line. This was the largest and most nearly complete grouping of human remains in the 1984 archaeological excavation. Fragments of skull, ribs, vertebrae, hands, a right foot, both upper arms, both lower arms were found [Scott and Fox, *Archaeological Insights into the Custer Battle*, p. 41]. The bones appeared to be from a single individual, buried face down.

(Note — Cheyenne warriors generally turned their dead victims face down, fearing it was bad luck to leave an enemy facing the sky. He may have been buried as found or merely had dirt thrown on him, as found.) Also found at this site were a single .44-caliber Henry bullet found in the lower chest — upper abdominal region; a single .45-caliber Colt bullet found in the area of the head; eleven buttons, including several trouser buttons; three blouse buttons, two with cloth still attached; three four-hole white-glass shirt buttons; an iron arrowhead; and several cobbles. Bones found there were consistent with his age and height, though several others, including PVT Kavanaugh (L), fit the description, as well. "The individual was over twenty-five years old and about five feet eight inches tall. He was also very robust or well muscled.... Evidently this man was severely mutilated at the time of death" [Scott and Fox, p. 102]. Listed number 183 in "June Returns, Alterations … Killed in action."

Cassella, John *see* **James, PVT John**

Cather, PVT Armantheus D.— b. Shippensburg, PA, 1850–d. 25 Jun 1876, killed at the Little Big Horn. Company F, private. Gray eyes, brown hair, fair complexion; 5' 8½" tall. Enlisted 8 Nov 1872. Extra duty as hospital attendant; may have been helping Dr. Lord for this campaign and would therefore have been killed on Last Stand/Custer Hill or environs. Listed number 104 in "June Returns, Alterations … Killed in action."

Causby, QM SGT Thomas Wellesley— b. Liverpool, England, 9 May 1848 (one source claims 1846)–d. Davenport, IA, 16 Oct 1906. Headquarters: Regimental Quartermaster Sergeant. Blue eyes, fair hair, fair complexion; 5'10¾" tall. Second enlistment on 1 Jan 1872. Remained at Powder River camp. Presence confirmed on June Returns.

Channell, PVT William— b. Dorchester, MA, 1849–d. unknown. Company H, private. Brown eyes, dark hair, dark complexion; 5' 6⅞" tall. Enlisted 27 Sep 1875. Rode with his unit in Benteen's battalion, and fought on Reno Hill. Dishonorably discharged for desertion.

Chapman, PVT William H. (aka William H. Dutton)— b. Glastonbury, CT, 1851 or 1852–d. unknown. Company E, private. Gray eyes, dark hair, ruddy complexion; 5' 9¼" tall. Enlisted 13 Mar 1876. Was transferred from Company B on 1 Jun 1876, in the field, but he is carried here in E all the way through. Remained at the Powder River Depot.

Charley, FAR PVT Vincent (battlefield marker has him listed as Vincent Charles)— b. Lucerne, Switzerland, 1848–d. 25 Jun 1876, killed at the Little Big Horn. Company D, private: company farrier. Hazel eyes, red hair, sandy complexion; 5' 10¼" tall. Enlisted 4 Mar 1871 in Chicago. If one tragedy at the Little Big Horn was worse than another, Vincent Charley's may have been the most tragic of all. Was with CPT Weir when company "advanced" off Reno Hill to find Custer. Wounded in hip and left behind, ¼ mile south of Weir Peaks on the slopes above the ravine. LT Edgerly explained that when he last spoke with Charley, he told him to take cover and he would send back men to get him, but Edgerly and SGT Harrison were closely followed by about 200 Sioux and as they looked back, they saw warriors swarming all over Charley. CPT Weir also forbade Edgerly to go back. Body found with stick rammed down his throat. Liddic writes, "His body was found about 650 feet south of the eastern 'sugarloaf,' a good quarter mile northwest of Sharpshooters' Ridge" [*Vanishing Victory,* p. 126; also see, Liddic/Harbaugh, *Camp on Custer,* p. 97, footnote 204, for a fine description of where Charley was found: "The coulee where Charley was killed runs east and west all the way down to Cedar Coulee. Camp goes on further to state A. N. Grover, the second superintendent of the Custer Battlefield found a body in 1903 exactly where Charley had been buried." Liddic cites Hardorff, *The Custer Battle Casualties,* p. 160]. Smalley wrote that SGT Harrison (D) and PVT Creighton (K) claimed Charley was killed between the eastern and western peaks of Weir Point. After the battle his body was found 260 paces—650 feet—south of Weir Peaks. His marker was placed another ½ mile farther south. Listed number 49 in "June Returns, Alterations … Killed in action."

Cheever, PVT Ami (aka Ami Chreer; also Andrew Hester)— b. Elizabeth, PA, 26 May 1849–d. 25 Jun 1876, killed at the Little Big Horn. Company L,

private. Gray eyes, dark hair, light complexion; 5'11¾" tall. Enlisted in 29th Infantry and stationed in Washington, D.C.; enlisted 21 Sep 1872 in Harrisburg, PA. In all likelihood he was killed on Calhoun Hill, though the possibility exists he was one of those killed during the panic through the Keogh Sector. No remains found during the 1984–1985 archaeological work match his description. Listed number 197 in "June Returns, Alterations … Killed in action."

Chesterwood, Charles *see* **Creighton, PVT John C.**

Clark, PVT Frank— b. Sheldon, VT, Nov 1855–d. unknown. Company B, private. Brown eyes, black hair, dark complexion; 5' 6¼" tall. Enlisted 16 Mar 1876 in Boston. With the pack train escort, Company B. Arrived and fought on Reno Hill.

Clear (also seen listed as Clare), **PVT Elihu F.**— b. Randolph County, IN, 1843–d. 25 Jun 1876, killed at the Little Big Horn after crossing the river during Reno's retreat. Company K, private. Blue eyes, brown hair, dark complexion; 5' 6½" tall. Second enlistment 4 Jan 1872. Orderly to LT Hare, though sometimes misidentified as Doctor DeWolf's orderly. Killed near the edge of the river trying to go up bluffs, at bottom of the bluffs, near Meyer. His battlefield marker has been placed near DeWolf's, high up on the bluffs, but this placement is almost certainly incorrect [see Brust, Pohanka, Barnard, *Where Custer Fell,* pp. 58–59]. Listed number 180 in "June Returns, Alterations … Killed in action."

Clyde, CPL Edward (aka Franklin Rankin)— b. Waukesha, WI, 1846–d. Columbus Barracks, OH, 3 Jan 1895; suicide by gunshot to the head. Company F, corporal. Blue eyes, red hair, ruddy complexion; 5' 10" tall. Deserted from 19th Infantry on 1 Apr 1871. Enlisted 17 Apr 1871 in the Seventh Cavalry. Appointed sergeant 27 Sep 1876. Remained at the Powder River Depot.

Coakley, PVT Patrick (aka Patrick Redican)— b. Kingscourt, Ireland, 1842–d. Washington, D.C., 13 Nov 1881. Company K, private. Hazel eyes, brown hair, fair complexion; 5' 7½" tall. Enlisted 26 Sep 1866 to 26 Dec 1871 in Company M, Seventh Cavalry. Reenlisted 26 Dec 1871. Deserted 12 Mar 1872; surrendered 18 Apr 1872. Originally carried in Hammer as on detached service to Department HQ as orderly for GEN Terry, but Smalley has corrected that to "present at the battle." He was in the hilltop fight with his unit.

Cody, Henry M. *see* **Scollin, CPL Henry M.**

Coleman, CPL Charles— b. Terre Haute, IN, 1851–d. 25 Jun 1876, killed at the Little Big Horn.

Company F, corporal. Blue eyes, dark hair, ruddy complexion; 5' 5¼" tall. Enlisted on 9 Sep 1873. In all likelihood he was killed on Last Stand Hill with his unit. Listed number 93 in "June Returns, Alterations … Killed in action."

Coleman, PVT Thomas W.— b. Troy, NY, 25 Dec 1849–d. Sawtelle, CA, 30 Nov 1921. Company B, private. Gray eyes, brown hair, fair complexion; 5' 5⅛" tall. Enlisted from some time in 1861 in 5th MI Volunteers as an assistant to the surgeon. Enlisted from 4 Jun 1864 to 31 May 1865 in the U.S. Navy. Enlisted 4 Jun 1872 in Seventh Cavalry. In Yellowstone and Black Hills expeditions. Coleman kept a diary of the 1876 campaign and recorded much earlier times than LT Wallace's official times. Claims to have buried LT Hodgson on 27 Jun 1876 east of the LBH under a cedar tree on a knoll overlooking the river. Close — the description appears on the money — but Coleman is not mentioned by McDougall to Walter Camp as being one of those who helped bury Hodgson. Wrote that Custer always intended to cross the LBH at Ford D: "(Custer) ordered 'Reno to charge the village at the upper end and he would go down and ford it at the lower end in order to cut them'" [Liddic, *Vanishing Victory,* p. 147]. Liddic says this had to be second-hand information, at best. Buried in Los Angeles National Cemetery.

Conlan, PVT Thomas— b. Ayrshire, Scotland, Oct 1853–d. unknown. Company D, private. Blue eyes, brown hair, dark complexion; 5' 6¾" tall. Enlisted 18 Sep 1875. Remained at Powder River Depot. Presence confirmed on June Returns.

Connell, TMP John— b. Ogdensburg, NY, 1850–d. unknown. Company B: trumpeter. Blue eyes, brown hair, fair complexion; 5' 7" tall. Enlisted 6 Feb 1872. Remained at Powder River Depot. Scott claims he was on Reno Hill, while Overfield has him listed at PRD. Both Smalley and Hammer say he remained at PRD with an accidental gunshot wound.

Connelly, SGT Patrick (aka Patrick C. White)— b. Enniskellen, County Tipperary, Ireland, 22 Mar 1844–d. Minneapolis, MN, 28 Sep 1909. Company H, sergeant. Blue eyes, brown hair, ruddy complexion; 5' 7–7½" tall. Enlisted 22 Aug 1864, 40th MO Infantry; enlisted 18 Aug 1865 in 6th Cavalry; discharged 18 Aug 1868. Enlisted 11 Sep 1868 in Seventh Cavalry; discharged 11 Sep 1873, but reenlisted 5 Oct 1873. In Black Hills expedition, 1874. WIA in left shoulder during hilltop fight. Married Elizabeth J. Ellis 15 Jun 1882; children: Clare E. and Joseph S. Buried in St. Mary's Cemetery, Minneapolis.

Connor, PVT Andrew— b. Limerick, Ireland, 1842–d. in the government hospice for the insane, Washington, D.C., 14 May 1911. Company A, private. Blue eyes, gray hair, florid complexion; 5' 4¾" tall. Enlisted 8 Nov 1872. One of five who volunteered to go on picket duty with CPL Roy the night of 25 June.

Connor, PVT Edward— b. Clare, Ireland, 1846–d. 25 Jun 1876, killed at the Little Big Horn. Company E, private. Hazel eyes, brown hair, ruddy complexion; 5' 8½" tall. Second enlistment 5 Dec 1872. While his body was not specifically identified, he may have been one of the unknowns on either the South Skirmish Line or in Deep Ravine. Listed number 65 in "June Returns, Alterations … Killed in action."

Connors, PVT Thomas— b. Harlem, NY, 1846–d. 25 Jun 1876, killed at the Little Big Horn. Company I, private. Blue eyes, dark hair, fair complexion; 5' 7½" tall. Second enlistment 20 Aug 1875. Body never identified, but in all likelihood he was killed in the Keogh Sector. Listed number 151 in "June Returns, Alterations … Killed in action."

Considine, SGT Martin— b. Clare, Ireland, 1847–d. 25 Jun 1876, killed at the Little Big Horn during Reno's retreat. Company G, sergeant. Blue eyes, brown hair, fair complexion; 5' 7½" tall. Second enlistment 28 Jan 1875. Killed along the retreat route between the timber and the river. Listed number 126 in "June Returns, Alterations … Killed in action."

Cooke, 1LT (Bvt LTC) William Winer (nicknamed "Handsome Man"; also known to irreverent troopers as "The Queen's Own." The "e" in the surname appears to have been added in the U.S., as the family register lists the name as "Cook.")— b. Mount Pleasant, Brant County, Ontario, Canada, 29 May 1846–d. 25 Jun 1876, killed at the Little Big Horn. Headquarters: Regimental Adjutant. Reportedly 6' 2" tall. Was a supreme athlete and a very fast runner. Cooke and CPT French were considered the best shots in the regiment. DOR: 31 Jul 1867, making him senior 1LT on campaign. Apparently, he was 4th-ranking 1LT in the entire army. Joined the U.S. Army in 1863. Body found near top of Custer Hill, scalped twice, including one of his famous sideburns or Dundrearies, as they were called. Godfrey wrote that along with Reily, Yates, and Smith, Cooke's body was found in the vicinity of George Custer's, but nearer the top of the hill [Godfrey/Graham, *The Custer Myth,* p. 345].

Extremely well liked, especially by the Ree scouts. From Walter Camp: "When I showed [the Ree scout] Soldier picture of Lieutenant Cooke, he kissed it, saying that he was a lovable man, his very breath being nothing but kindness" [Camp/Hammer, *Custer in '76,* p. 191]. Rode a white horse. One of the most efficient and capable officers in the regiment [Stewart, *Custer's Luck,* p. 172]. Extremely close to Custer and a top-rate soldier.

From a prominent and wealthy family. His father was a physician. His mother was Angeline Augusta Winer Cook, and the married surname spelling on her monument reads "Cooke," contrary to the family register. Buried in the Winer family plot, #63, Christ Church Section, Hamilton Cemetery, Hamilton, Ontario.

Cooney (aka Corey), **PVT David**—b. Cork, Ireland, 1848–d. 20 Jul 1876, died of wounds suffered at the Little Big Horn. Company I, private. Gray eyes, dark hair, fair complexion; 5'5¾" tall. Enlisted 16 Dec 1872. With the pack train. WIA, 26 Jun 1876, in the Reno-Benteen hilltop fight. Placed aboard steamer *Far West* and moved to FAL. Died of wounds on 20 Jul 1876.

Cooper, PVT John H.—b. Cork, Ireland, 1847– d. Harris, IA, 1903. Company H, private. Blue eyes, brown hair, dark complexion; 5'5" tall. Enlisted 27 Sep 1873. WIA in right elbow while on Reno Hill. Married about 1895; survived by a son and daughter (of Portland, OR).

Corcoran, PVT Patrick—b. Canada (?), 15 Mar 1844 (at enlistment, he stated he was born in Cattaraugus County, NY)–d. Washington, D.C., 4 Mar 1922. Company K, private. Hazel eyes, brown hair, fair complexion; 5'9½" tall. Enlisted from 27 Jul 1867 to July 1872, in Seventh Cavalry. Enlisted 23 Aug 1872. Served in Yellowstone and Black Hills expeditions. WIA in right shoulder on hilltop.

Corey, David *see* **Cooney, PVT David**

Cowley, PVT Cornelius (aka John Sullivan)—b. Cork, Ireland, 1845–d. Washington, D.C., 6 Aug 1908. Company A, private. Blue eyes, brown hair, fair complexion; 5'8" tall. Enlisted as John Sullivan from Jan to Sep 1865, 24th MA Infantry. Enlisted from 1866 to Sep 1869 in 17th Infantry. Enlisted in U.S. Navy from 1870 to 1874. Enlisted 9 Dec 1874 in Seventh Cavalry. No specific record exists of his participation in the battle, other than his presence with his unit during the valley fighting and subsequent defense of Reno Hill. Died at Government Hospital for the Insane, Washington, D.C. Buried in Lowell, MA.

Cowley, PVT Stephen—b. Sligo, Ireland, 1848– d. unknown. Company D, private. Brown eyes, brown hair, florid complexion; 5'6½" tall. Enlisted 14 Nov 1872. Remained at the Powder River Depot. Presence confirmed on June Returns.

Cox, PVT Thomas—b. Cincinnati, OH, 1844– d. unknown. Company D, private. Blue eyes, dark hair, ruddy complexion; 5'8" tall. Enlisted 22 Sep 1873. Illiterate. Had been a brickmaker. Rode with his unit in Benteen's battalion, and fought on Reno Hill. In the Nez Percé campaign of 1877. Discharged 22 Sep 1878 as a corporal.

Crandall, CPL Charles A.—b. New Milford, CT, 1848–d. NYC, 23 Apr 1885. Company C, corporal. Gray eyes, brown hair, dark complexion; 5'10 ½" tall. Civil War vet. Enlisted from 1 Feb 1864 to 19 Jul 1865 in 5th NY Cavalry; enlisted 9 Dec 1872 in 7th Cavalry. Remained at the Powder River Depot. The June Returns do not list any Company C personnel at Powder River, indicating they must have been returned to their unit.

Crawford, PVT William L.—b. Newfield, NY, 1849–d. at Fort Abraham Lincoln, 20 Aug 1876. Company K, private. Gray eyes, light hair, fair complexion; 5'9½" tall. Enlisted 13 Feb 1875. Remained at the Powder River Depot. Presence confirmed on June Returns. Died of typhoid fever.

Creighton, PVT John C. (aka Charles Chesterwood)—b. Massillon, OH (enlistment register shows his birthplace as Memphis, TN), 4 Mar 1850–d. Tacoma, WA, 30 Jan 1935. Company K, private. Red hair, sandy complexion; 5'5½" tall. Enlisted 6 Jan 1872. In Yellowstone expedition. Rode with his unit in Benteen's battalion, and fought on Reno Hill. Father born in Scotland, mother in Ireland. Married Susan E. Andrews in 1882 at FAL. Attended 50th anniversary of battle in 1926.

Criddle, PVT Christopher—b. New Canton, VA, 1851–d. 25 Jun 1876, killed at the Little Big Horn. Company C, private. Gray eyes, brown hair, dark complexion; 5'8" tall. Less than one year service; enlisted 22 Sep 1875. In the C Company charge off Battle Ridge-Calhoun Hill, but body was never identified. May have died in Calhoun Coulee, Finley-Finckle Ridge, the Keogh Sector, or possibly even Last Stand Hill. Listed number 25 in "June Returns, Alterations … Killed in action."

Crisfield, PVT William B.—b. Kent, England, 1835–d. 25 Jun 1876, killed at the Little Big Horn. Company L, private. Gray eyes, black hair, ruddy complexion; 5'7" tall. Enlisted from 21 Oct 1858 to 20 Oct 1863 in Fourth Cavalry; enlisted from 17 Jan 1870 to 17 Jan 1875; enlisted 1 Feb 1875. In all likelihood he was killed on Calhoun Hill, though the possibility exists he was one of those killed during the panic through the Keogh Sector. No remains found during the 1984–1985 archaeological work match his description. Married Mary

Pauline Blanchstone, 29 Jun 1865. This was his second wife. Children: Edward H., Albert J., and Paul D. Listed number 198 in "June Returns, Alterations … Killed in action."

Criswell, SGT Benjamin C.— b. Cameron, Marshall County, VA (now WV) 9 Feb 1849–d. Eldorado, OK, 17 Oct 1921. Company B, sergeant. Hazel eyes, black hair, dark complexion; 5'6¼" tall; weighed 150 pounds. Enlisted 31 May 1870; discharged 31 May 1875 as first sergeant; reenlisted 23 Feb 1876. Wounded on Reno Hill. Awarded MH for bringing up body of LT Hodgson to Reno Hill and for bringing up ammo. Married first wife, Ella Rose Evans (d. 2 Nov 1898) on 16 Aug 1896; married second wife, Annie Hall Criswell 1 Oct 1902. Children from second marriage: Benjamin Theodore, Charles H., Margaret, Marie, and Bert C.

Criswell, PVT Harry— b. Marshall County, WV, 1855–d. unknown. Company B, private. Dark brown eyes, dark brown hair, fair complexion; 5'7" tall. Enlisted 11 Apr 1876 in Pittsburgh. With the pack train escort, Company B. Arrived and fought on Reno Hill.

Crittenden, 2LT John Jordan— b. Frankfort, KY, 7 Jun 1854–d. 25 Jun 1876, killed at the Little Big Horn. Company L: Acting first lieutenant. TDY to Seventh Cavalry from Company G, 20th Infantry in place of LT Edwin Eckerson. DOR: 15 Oct 1875. Junior officer on campaign. Blind in one eye; glass eye. While hunting on 25 Oct 1875, he exploded a cartridge with a knife and a piece of it hit him in the eye. Killed with Calhoun. Body shot with arrows — including one in his glass eye — and tomahawked. Godfrey wrote that Crittenden's body was found, "on the hill on the extreme left of the line (when facing the river)" [Godfrey/Graham, *The Custer Myth*, p. 345].
Came from a very prominent Kentucky family. His grandfather, John J. Crittenden, was active in state and national politics, and introduced the "Crittenden Compromise" in the Senate to try to avoid the Union from dissolving. It failed and he went home to try to keep Kentucky from seceding. The grandfather's oldest son and John Jordan's uncle, George Bibb Crittenden (b. 20 Mar 1812–d. 1880), had been a lieutenant colonel and had graduated from West Point. He resigned at the outbreak of the Civil War and was appointed a brigadier general in the CSA army. Promoted to major general, he was relieved of his command because of drunkenness. He resigned in Oct 1862. John Jordan's father, Thomas Leonidas Crittenden (b. 15 May 1819–d. 1893), stayed in the Union army and became a brigadier general in Sep 1861. Fought at Shiloh, leading his troops impressively, promoted

to MG, and commanded XXI Corps. His command collapsed at Chickamauga in Sep 1863 and he resigned in Dec 1864. After the war, the brothers were reunited, George serving as state librarian, Thomas as state treasurer before returning to the army. Became a lieutenant colonel. Based on the wishes of his parents, he was buried on battlefield where he fell. Eventually reinterred in LBH National Cemetery.

Crowe, PVT Michael— b. County Cork, Ireland, 1849–d. Fort Yates, D.T., 8 Jun 1883. Company B, private. Gray eyes, brown hair, fair complexion; 5'4½" tall. Enlisted 8 Jul 1867 in NYC in 34th Infantry. Discharged 8 Jul 1870; enlisted 9 Jul 1870 in 7th Cavalry. Wounded in skirmish with Sioux on Yellowstone 4 Aug 1873. With the pack train escort, Company B. Arrived and fought on Reno Hill. Died of heart disease; buried in Post Cemetery and reinterred in Keokuk National Cemetery, IA.

Crowely, John L. *see* **Duggan, PVT John F.**

Crowley, PVT Patrick— b. Bangor, ME, 1854–d. unknown. Company B, private. Gray eyes, brown hair, fair complexion; 5'6¼" tall. Enlisted 14 Dec 1875. With the pack train escort, Company B. Arrived and fought on Reno Hill.

Crump, BSM John— b. Lissendorf, Germany, 1853–d. unknown. Company B: blacksmith. Gray eyes, light hair, fair complexion; 5'7". Enlisted 14 Apr 1876. With the pack train escort, Company B. Arrived and fought on Reno Hill. Deserted 29 Mar 1877 and never apprehended.

Crussy, CPL Melanchton H. (also Cressey, Melanchton, and a number of other variations as well. Sometimes listed as Henry M. **Krusee**)— b. NYC, 5 Oct 1840 (one source claims 1841)–d. Hot Springs, SD, 3 Jun 1925. Company G, corporal. Blue eyes, brown hair, dark complexion; 5'6¼" tall. Enlisted 1 Dec 1875. Promoted to corporal on 25 Jun 1876, though the June Returns still have him listed as a private. Remained at the Powder River Depot. Presence confirmed on June Returns. Wife named Mary O. born in Georgia in 1851. Her father was from Scotland and her mother from Georgia. Children all born in Dakota: Julia, Arthur W., Harry M., and Robert.

Culbertson, SGT Ferdinand A.— b. Pittsburgh, PA, 1845–d. Detroit, MI, 10 Jan 1889. Company A. Gray eyes, brown hair, fair complexion; 5'9¾" tall. First enlisted at 19 in Civil War. Enlisted 1 Feb 1873, Seventh Cavalry. On hilltop with Reno. Helped Reno search for LT Hodgson's body. Highly regarded Civil War veteran. Died at his home at 511 Fourth Avenue, Detroit, of pulmonary consumption. Buried in Woodmere Cemetery.

Cummings, William *see* **Braendle**

Cunningham, CPL Albert Joseph— b. Leeds, England, 1837–d. unknown. Company D, corporal. Blue eyes, dark hair, fair complexion; 5'5" tall. Second enlistment 20 Jan 1872. Remained at Powder River Depot. Presence confirmed on June Returns.

Cunningham, CPL Charles— b. Hudson, NY, 1845–d. unknown, but probably in Washington, D.C., where he resided). Company B, corporal. Gray eyes, light hair, fair complexion; 5'7¼" tall. Enlisted 8 Dec 1874. Promoted to CPL in June 1876. WIA in neck in the hilltop fight. Awarded MH: would not leave firing line even though wounded, fighting all the next day as well.

Curtiss (also seen spelled Curtis), **SGT William A.**— b. Albany, NY, 1846–d. Helena, M.T., 27 Oct 1888. Company F, sergeant. Brown eyes, brown hair, dark complexion; 5'8¼" tall. Enlisted 28 Mar 1867 in First Cavalry. Appointed first sergeant in the Seventh Cavalry, 30 Sep 1876. With pack train. It was Curtiss who reported having lost some personal belongings on the morning of 25 June while the regiment was still in the Davis Creek valley prior to crossing the divide. He was sent back with several men to retrieve the lost items when they came across several Cheyenne warriors. After running them off, Curtiss reported to his commander, CPT Yates, leading Custer to believe the command had been spotted. This incident is sometimes reported as a pack of lost hardtack, but this appears unrealistic. Married John P. Kelly's (F) widow. Died of lung disease.

Custer, LTC (Bvt MG) **George Armstrong** (the Southern Cheyenne called him "Red Nose," after seeing him with a sunburned nose; Crows called him *Ihcke Deikdagua*, meaning "Morning Star Sun" or "Morning Star"; the Sioux—*Pahuska* or *Pehin hanska,* meaning "Hair Long," a name also adopted by the Northern Cheyenne; and the Arikara—*Peoushi* or *Ouches*—called him "Long Hair," as well.)— b. New Rumley, OH, 5 Dec 1839–d. 25 Jun 1876, killed at the Little Big Horn. Headquarters: Acting Commanding Officer, Seventh Cavalry. Thought to be 5'10" to 5'11" tall, reportedly about 180 pounds. West Point entry records indicate he was 5'10" tall, seventeen years old at the time. Blond, blue eyes; thin; right-handed. Rode his favorite horse, Vic (aka Victory [or less likely, Victor; Dandy was the other horse]), a sorrel with blaze face and three white socks. There is some evidence Vic was a mare, but this is in all likelihood incorrect. LT Godfrey claimed the horse had four white socks and rumor had it that Indians with Sitting Bull—moving into Canada—had the horse [Graham, *The Custer Myth,* p. 345]. While he had

a reputation for impetuosity, he greatly resented it. Claimed he always had his head in his books. By the age of 36, Custer's "energy and endurance seemed undiminished by fifteen years of soldiering, a good amount of it spent on campaign…. [H]is hairline was … retreating—and his ruddy, lined face betrayed the hard years spent outside in the elements, but he was still lean and muscled, and strong as an ox" [Donovan, *A Terrible Glory,* p. 90]. From Robbins, James S.; Hart, John P., ed., "Custer: The Goat at West Point and at War," *Custer and His Times, Book Five*: Major General George McClellan thought Custer was "reckless and gallant, 'undeterred by fatigue, unconscious of fear; but his head was always clear in danger, and he always brought me clear and intelligible reports of what he saw when under the heaviest fire. I became much attached to him.'" Custer was, "… charismatic, fun and loyal to a fault" [pages 9 and 17]. CPT James H. Kidd, Sixth MI Cavalry: "Custer was 'brave, but not reckless; self-confident, yet modest; ambitious, regulating his conduct at all times by a high sense of honor and duty; eager for laurels, but scorning to wear them unworthily; ready and willing to act, but regardful of human life; quick in emergencies, cool and self-possessed, his courage was of the highest moral type: his perceptions were intuitions'" [Robbins, p. 16]. Kidd continued: "Custer was a fighting man, through and through, but wary and wily as brave. There was in him an indescribable something—call it caution, call it sagacity, call it the real military instinct—it may have been genius—by whatever name entitled, it nearly always impelled him to do intuitively the right thing" [Robbins, p. 18].

Father, Emanuel Henry Custer (10 Dec 1806–17 Nov 1892) was a blacksmith. Mother was Maria Ward Kirkpatrick (31 May 1807–13 Jun 1882). Parents were married on 14 Apr 1836. GAC had two sisters: a half-sister named Lydia (from Emanuel's first marriage) and a full sister named Margaret Emma (who married LT James Calhoun) and three brothers: Tom, Boston, and Nevin. When he was twelve, Custer was sent to Monroe, MI, to live with his half-sister, Lydia, and her husband, David Reed. He returned to New Rumley when he was sixteen.

Evan Connell quotes Gerard, one of the first to see Custer's dead body: "…found the naked bodies of two soldiers, one across the other, and Custer's naked body in a sitting posture between and leaning against them, his upper right arm along and on the topmost body, his right forearm and hand supporting his head in an inclining posture like one resting or asleep…" [*Sun of the Morning Star,* p. 409]. Most accounts agree with this, though Windolph always swore Custer was still fully clothed. LT James Bradley, who first found the body, said Custer was stripped naked, but not mutilated at all, and lay there as peaceful as though he were asleep [Bradley, *The March of the Montana Column*, pp. 172–173]. Shot twice, once in the left side, below the heart, and once in the left temple. The side wound was probably first and killed him, because that was the one that was bloody. There was also a wound in his right forearm, but that was probably made by the exiting of the bullet in his side. Benteen felt neither wound was made by a .45, so he was in all likelihood killed by a Henry or a Winchester from some distance. Godfrey said Custer was not mutilated at all: "...he laid on his back, his upper arms on the ground, the hands folded or so placed as to cross the body above the stomach.... One hit was in the front of the left temple, and one in the left breast at or near the heart" [Godfrey/Graham, *The Custer Myth*, p. 345]. Godfrey said Custer's body was slightly down the slope — toward the river — from those of Yates, Cooke, Smith, and Reily [Graham, *The Custer Myth*, p. 345]. 1SG John Ryan (M) said all men but Mark Kellogg had been stripped, but Custer was not scalped. Ryan, CPL Harrison Davis, CPL Frank Neely, and PVT James Severs buried both Tom and George at the *foot of the knoll*. They dug a grave about 18" deep and wrapped both bodies in canvas, covering the grave with the basket from an Indian travois, then secured it with stones [Ryan/Barnard, *Ten Years with Custer*, p. 304].

First member of family in America was Paul Küster from Kaldenkirchen in the Rheinland, who left the village of Crefeld in 1684 with his wife, Gertraud, and four children. Settled in Germantown, PA.

Edgar I. Stewart says apparently from a Hessian family and that an article appeared in the *Cheyenne Daily Leader*, 29 Jul 1876, saying that Custer was actually born in Baden, Germany [*Custer's Luck*, p. 167, footnote 10].

Married Elizabeth (Libbie) Clift Bacon (b. Monroe, MI, 3 Apr 1842–d. NYC, 14 Apr 1933) on 9 Feb 1864 in Monroe, MI. Libbie was the daughter of Judge Daniel Stanton Bacon and Sophia Page Bacon. Daniel Bacon was born in upstate NY, near Syracuse and lived there for 24 years before moving to Michigan in 1822. In 1926 Libbie Custer lived at 71 Park Avenue, New York City [Graham, *The Custer Myth*, p. 355].

Appointed lieutenant colonel, Seventh Cavalry, effective 28 Jul 1866, the date the regiment was organized at Fort Riley, KS.

Had two other horses with him during the campaign: Dandy, a bay, brown, or dark brown stallion (possibly a gelding and supposedly his favorite); and Bluegrass, a stallion ridden by Custer's orderly, Burkman. According to Burkman, Custer started off riding Dandy on the morning of 25 June, but switched to Vic [Liddic/Harbaugh, *Camp on Custer*, p. 120]. Had four of his hounds with him as well: Tuck, Swift, Lady, and Kaiser (one source said he also had Bleuch or Blucher with him). According to Godfrey, the dogs were left with the wagon train (PRD) [Godfrey/Graham, *The Custer Myth*, p. 345] and we hear no more of them. Donovan, however — citing Hardorff, *The Custer Battle Casualties, II*, pp. 188–189, says Blucher and Tuck accompanied the column up the Rosebud [*A Terrible Glory*, p. 184, footnote (9) 48]. It appears the Donovan/Hardorff opinion is in error, however, for the Rees virtually agreed that no dogs accompanied the column after it left the PRD [Libby, *The Arikara Narrative*, p. 71, footnote 34].

"Custer carried a Remington Sporting rifle, octagonal barrel; two Bulldog self-cocking, English, white-handled pistols, with a ring in the butt for a lanyard; a hunting knife, in a beaded fringed scabbard; and a canvas cartridge belt. He wore a whitish gray hat, with broad brim and rather low crown, very similar to the Cowboy hat; buck skin suit, with a fringed welt in outer seams of trousers and arms of blouse; the blouse with double-breasted military buttons, lapels generally open; turn-down collar, and fringe on bottom of shirt" [LT Godfrey/Graham, *The Custer Myth*, p. 345]. The Remington was a No. 1 Rolling Block Sporting Rifle with a Soule Tang sight, .50–70 caliber. The octagonal barrel length would be thirty inches long.

Custer, CPT (Bvt MAJ) Thomas Ward (nicknamed "Scar Face") — b. New Rumley, OH, 15 Mar 1845–d. 25 Jun 1876, killed at the Little Big Horn. Company C: Commanding Officer, though probably not leading his command in the battle. Probably "detached" to serve as his brother's titular Aide-de-Camp during the battle. GAC's "right arm" [Willert, *Little Big Horn Diary*, p. 8]. Enlistment records show him as having blue eyes, sandy-colored hair, light complexion, and 5'7" tall. He first enlisted in Company H, 21st Ohio Infantry, 2 Sep 1861, well under the age limit. Officer records of the period did not traditionally include height, but there is indication he was not a very large man, not growing much more from when he was sixteen. Some photographs, however, show he may have been about the same height as his brother George, possibly 5'10" tall. DOR: 2 Dec 1875, seventh-ranking, only ahead of McDougall. The only C Company body identified on Custer Hill. Body horribly mutilated, "perhaps the worse [*sic*] example on the field" [Liddic, *Vanishing Victory*, p. 164] and could only be recognized by the T. W. C. tattoo on his arm. Head smashed in, his whole scalp missing, disemboweled, and shot with dozens of arrows. Body found near GAC, maybe fifteen feet away. His body was found near the top of the knoll, "... a few yards from the General, lying on his face; his features were so pressed out of shape as to be almost beyond recognition; a number of arrows had been shot in his back, several in his head, one I remember, without the shaft, the head bent so that it could hardly be withdrawn; his skull was crushed and nearly all the hair scalped, except a very little on the nape of the neck" [Godfrey/Graham, *The Custer Myth*, p. 345]. 1SG John Ryan of M Company, described his body as follows: "The head was smashed as flat as the palm of one's hand. When we found him, he was lying on his face and hands, split down through the center of his body" [Ryan/Barnard, *Ten Years with Custer*, p. 304]. Buried at Fort Leavenworth National Cemetery. Awarded two Medals of Honor in Civil War. [One of only 19 men ever to be so honored and the only man during the Civil War.]

Dale, HOSPITAL STEWARD Alfred W.—d. some time after Jan 1911. Headquarters: Hospital Steward. Detached service on steamer *Far West*.

Dalious (aka Dallons), **CPL James**—b. Sunbury, PA, 1851–d. 25 Jun 1876, killed at the Little Big Horn. Company A. Brown eyes, dark hair, ruddy complexion; 5'10½" tall. Enlisted 5 Nov 1872 in Toledo, OH. Killed in the valley fight, possibly along the retreat route. Ken Hammer, in *The Battlefield Dispatch*, Winter 2005, says he was killed at the ford, which is possible entirely. Listed number 3 in "June Returns, Alterations ... Killed in action."

Dann, PVT George—b. Elmira, NY, 1852–d. unknown. Company D, private. Blue eyes, light hair, fair complexion; 5'8¾" tall. Enlisted 3 Jun 1873. Rode with his unit in Benteen's battalion, and fought on Reno Hill.

Darcy, James Wilber *see* **Wilber, PVT James**

Darris, PVT John—b. Goshen, NY, 1846–d. 25 Jun 1876, killed at the Little Big Horn. Company E, private. Blue eyes, brown hair, dark complexion; 5'6½" tall. Enlisted from 27 Aug 1861 to 31 May 1865 in First NJ Cavalry. Enlisted in Seventh Cavalry 9 Sep 1875, abandoning his wife and two children to do so. A former farmer. Possibly killed in Deep Coulee, where a skeleton with an arrowhead embedded in its cervical vertebrae and a boot with the initials "JD" was found in the 1920s. Jerome Greene has speculated this could have belonged to John Duggan of Company L, but Michno feels since Company E can definitely be traced to this area, the remains more likely belong to Darris. On

the other hand, there is very strong evidence that the strap could have belonged to 1SG Butler (L), and the faded or worn initials read "JB" rather than "JD." Listed number 66 in "June Returns, Alterations ... Killed in action."

Davenport, PVT William Henry—b. Williamsburg, NY, Jun 1858–d. Flushing, NY, 30 Mar 1934. Company B, private. Blue eyes, light brown hair, fair complexion; 5'9¼" tall. Enlisted 15 Mar 1876 in Boston. With the pack train escort, Company B. Arrived and fought on Reno Hill. Married Jessica C. Turton about 1878. Son: Harry Kirkham Davenport. Resided at 118 Wythe Av, Brooklyn, NY, and 248 Schenck Avenue, Brooklyn, NY, in 1900. Buried in Flushing Cemetery.

Davern, PVT Edward—b. Limerick, Ireland, 1844–d. Washington, D.C., 10 Aug 1896. Company F, private. Gray eyes, brown hair, fair complexion; 5'6¾" tall. Enlisted 12 Aug 1872. (It appears this date may be wrong. At the RCOI of Inquiry held in January and February 1879, he said he had been in the army for 16 years. That would make an enlistment of around 1862 [Nichols, *RCOI*, p. 357], so 1872 is either a mis-reading or Davern was on a third enlistment.) Major Reno's orderly. Had a hand-to-hand fight with an Indian in retreat from the valley. Testified on 29–30 Jan 1879 at Reno Court of Inquiry in Chicago. Resided in Washington, D.C., for three years, 439 7th Street. Died suddenly at 52, heat stroke and asthenia. Buried at Arlington National Cemetery.

Davis, PVT Henry Harrison—b. Bellvernon, VA, 19 or 20 Jan 1846, though one source claims he was born in Fayette City, PA–d. Monessen, PA, 21 May 1918. Company M, private. Brown eyes, sandy hair, fair complexion; 5'6½" tall. Enlisted from 13 Jul 1864 to 9 Nov 1864, 193rd PA Volunteers; enlisted 2 Feb 1865 to 1 Jul 1865; enlisted 21 Dec 1866 to 21 Dec 1871, then on 21 Dec 1871 in Seventh Cavalry. No specific record exists of his participation in the battle, other than his presence with his unit during the valley fighting and subsequent defense of Reno Hill. Helped bury the Custers or at least George Custer (this is confirmed by 1SG Ryan [Barnard, *Ten Years with Custer*, p. 161].) Resided near Standing Rock Agency. Ferdinand Widmayer, a fellow M Company trooper, told Walter Camp that Davis froze to death about 1905. Illiterate.

Davis, PVT William (aka Dawes)—b. Vandalia, IL, 1851–d. 25 Jun 1876, killed at the Little Big Horn. Company E, private. Gray eyes, brown hair, fair complexion; 5'6" tall. Enlisted 19 Dec 1874. While his body was not specifically identified, he may have been one of the unknowns on either the South Skirmish Line or in Deep Ravine. Listed number 67 in "June Returns, Alterations ... Killed in action."

Dawsey, PVT David Edward— b. Belleville, OH, 1851–d. 30 Sep 1877, killed at Snake Creek, M.T. in the Nez Percé War. Company D, private. Gray eyes, sandy hair, sandy complexion; 5' 4½" tall. Enlisted 17 Dec 1872. Rode with his unit in Benteen's battalion, and fought on Reno Hill. Recommended for medal for conspicuous gallantry at LBH fight.

Day, PVT John H.— b. Warren County, IN, Mar 1851–d. Monroe, LA, 13 Jun 1894. Company H, private. Hazel eyes, auburn hair, fair complexion; 5' 7" tall. Enlisted 23 Sep 1873. Rode with his unit in Benteen's battalion, and fought on Reno Hill. Dishonorably discharged for desertion.

Dean, Thomas *see* **O'Neill, PVT Thomas F.**

Deetline (or **Dietlein**), **BSM Frederick**— b. Offenheim-Wittenberg Germany, 1846–d. San Antonio, TX, 13 Dec 1910. Company D: company blacksmith. Slate or gray eyes, brown hair, fair complexion; 5' 9½–11" tall. Enlisted 21 Jul 1870 in 17th Infantry in Baltimore; discharged 21 Jul 1875; enlisted 5 Aug 1875 in Seventh Cavalry. Rode with his unit in Benteen's battalion, and fought on Reno Hill. Awarded MH for voluntarily bringing water up to Reno Hill. Illiterate. Buried in San Antonio National Cemetery.

Deihle, PVT Jacob— b. Würtemburg, Germany, 1853–d. Washington, D.C., 2 Sep 1885. Company A, private. Gray or blue eyes, brown hair, ruddy complexion; 5' 5¾–6½" tall. Enlisted 1 Oct 1875. Wounded; shot in the left cheek on hilltop, 25 June. CPT Moylan's orderly on the 25th.

DeLacy, SGT Milton J.— b. Ulster County, NY, 1847–d. unknown. Company I, sergeant. Blue eyes, red hair, light complexion; 5' 5¾" tall. Second enlistment 13 May 1875. With pack train (Overfield) in charge of company mules.

Delaney, PVT Michael— b. Broome County, NY, 1854–d. Olney, IL, 12 Feb 1884. Company K, private. Blue eyes, brown hair, dark complexion; 5' 8¼" tall. Enlisted 20 May 1875. Remained at the Powder River Depot. Presence confirmed on June Returns. Wounded in right lung in Snake Creek fight, 30 Sep 1877. Married Florence E. Strack, 7 Jul 1883.

Dellienhousen, Edward *see* **Housen, PVT Edward Gustav**

DeRudio, 1LT Charles (Carlo) **Camilius** (aka John de Sylva; "The Count")— b. Belluno, Venetia Province, Austria, 26 Aug 1832–d. Los Angeles, CA, 1 Nov 1910. Company A. Dark eyes, black hair,

dark complexion; 5' 7" tall. A genius for sculpture and a teller of tall tales! DOR: 15 Dec 1875, junior 1LT on campaign. Assigned to the Seventh Cavalry, 14 Jul 1869, in Benteen's H Company. Educated at the Austrian Military Academy. Served on Garibaldi's staff in Italy. The son of Count and Countess Aquila di Rudio. Participated in an assassination attempt on Napoleon III. He was sentenced to death, but the sentence was commuted to life and he was sent to Devil's Island. He *escaped* (fall of 1858) and made his way to England. Emigrated to U.S., arriving in Florida in 1864 and fought in Civil War; 79th NY and 2nd U.S. Colored Infantry. Married Eliza Booth (b. Feb 1840, Nottingham, England–d. 9 Jan 1922), 9 Dec 1855 at Parish Church, Godalming, Surrey. Had four children.

In the summer of 1870, he commanded Company K and escorted a train of settlers in Kansas. They presented him with a saber as a thank you for his protection. In the Yellowstone Expedition of 1873. TDY from Company E. Michno claims he was re-assigned from E to Company A, because his promotion would have made him next in line to command E Company upon McDougall's promotion to captain and transfer to Company B, and GAC did not care for DeRudio. Custer believed him to be a "confirmed grumbler and a natural conspirator ... the inferior of every first lieutenant in this regiment" [Klokner, *The Officer Corps of Custer's...*, p. 58]. Apparently, Reno did not care for him either, but the feeling was mutual, DeRudio eventually making the comment that if it were not for a coward (Reno), they would all have died in the timber at the LBH. Left behind in woods with PVT O'Neill, Gerard, and Billy Jackson after Reno's retreat. Reached Reno Hill with O'Neill about 3 am on 27 June. Benteen referred to him as "Count No-Account."

Took part in the 1877 campaign against the Nez Percé, serving under LT Doane's scouting battalion. Spent virtually his entire army career on frontier duty in New Mexico and the Dakotas.

According to Theodore Goldin, when DeRudio was promoted to captain and given command of E Troop, he managed to get O'Neill transferred to E and made him his first sergeant [Carroll, *The Benteen-Goldin Letters*, p. 23]. Retired in 1896; wholly retired in 1909 after being promoted to major.

Camp at Fort A. Lincoln, D.T.
May 14th 1876
To the Adjutant General of the Army
Washington, D.C.
Sir
Feeling that the manner in which I have been treated by the present Regimental Commander is

unjust and such action having been sanctioned by the Department Commander after the hereto appended request (and to which I have not even received a reply), I would respectfully request that action may be taken on my request to the General of the Army of last April.

During a personal interview with the General Commanding of the Department granted me at my request, the General told me the "he would not answer my communication at present."

I have the honor to inform the General that in order to deprive me of my right, another 1st Lieutenant (Smith) has been temporarily assigned to command my own company ("E") and I have been assigned to Company "A" to which he (Smith) properly belongs.

Hoping that the General of the Army will adjust my lawful claim, by ordering me to assume the command of my own company, I have the honor to be

Very Respectfully
Your Obt Servant
Charles C. DeRudio
1st Lieut 7th Cavalry
Through Regimental Head Quarters

1st Endorsement
Headqrs. 7th Cavalry
Fort A. Lincoln, D.T.
May 14, 1876
Respectfully forwarded.

Lieut. DeRudio is the junior 1st Lieut of this Regiment, having only been promoted to that grade within the past few months. Lieut. Smith, the officer assigned to command the company to which Lieut. DeRudio belongs, has held the grade of 1st Lieut. For several years and is an officer of extensive experience, not only as a company commander but in service against hostile Indians.

Lieut. DeRudio possesses neither the experience nor the ability which can be claimed for Lieut. Smith, nor is he a fit person in my opinion to exercise not only the command of, but to be the only officer present with, a cavalry company, liable to be called upon at any moment to engage in important service against hostile Indians. He is a confirmed grumbler, and asserting to his own confession is a natural conspirator, having once barely averted suffering the death penalty for conspiracy against the life of the sovereign of the land in which he formerly resided. He is, all things considered, the inferior of every first lieutenant in this Regt. As an efficient and subordinate officer.

The transfer of Lieut. DeRudio to "A" Company was made partially at his request and to give two officers to each company.

No better commentary could probably be made upon the value of Lieut. DeRudio's services

as a company officer than to state that the Captain of the company to which Lieut. DeRudio has been assigned, protesting in respectful terms against having Lieut. DeRudio in the company, preferring to perform the entire duty alone.

I would further add that while I regard Lieut. Smith as a most excellent company commander, he was not designated by me to command Lieut. DeRudio's company.

G. A. Custer
Lieut. Colonel 7th Cavalry
Brev. Major Genl. U.S.A.
Comdg. Regiment

Desmond, John *see* **Reagan, PVT Michael**

DeTourreil, PVT Louis— b. Tours, France, 1854– d. unknown. Company B, private. Blue eyes, brown hair, dark complexion; 5'5" tall. Enlisted 3 Apr 1876 in NYC. Remained at the Powder River Depot.

DeVoto, PVT Augustus Louis— b. Genoa, Italy, 27 Feb 1852–d. Tacoma, WA, 23 Nov 1923. Company B, private. Hazel eyes, black hair, dark complexion; 5'9" tall. Enlisted 4 Oct 1873. In Black Hills expedition. With the pack train escort, Company B. Arrived and fought on Reno Hill. Claimed to have helped bury LT Hodgson. Married Teresa Bonetti 29 Nov 1885; children: Amelia, Augustus Jr., Rosa, and Leon. Buried in Calvary Cemetery, Tacoma.

Dewey, PVT George W.— b. Middlebury, VT, 1851–d. unknown. Company H, private. Gray eyes, dark hair, ruddy complexion; 5'6" tall. Enlisted 13 Apr 1873. Rode with his unit in Benteen's battalion, and fought on Reno Hill. Illiterate.

DeWolf, Dr. James Madison— b. Jenningsville (Mehoopany), PA, 14 Jan 1843–d. 25 Jun 1876, killed at the Little Big Horn. Attached to Headquarters for the campaign: acting assistant surgeon (contract surgeon). Detached to Reno's command during the battle. Dark, gray eyes, light hair (balding), 5'8" tall. Civil War enlistee serving with the First PA Artillery. Wounded in 1862. Attended Harvard Medical School after the Civil War, graduating in Jun 1875. Detailed to Reno and killed going up bluffs. Shot in abdomen, in head six times, and face, from above. Wife's name was Fannie J. Apparently, DeWolf was not particularly fond of Reno, though why, we do not know. "…[Major] Reno who commands my wing I cannot like but suppose acquaintance will improve perhaps when we understand each other" [Willert, *Little Big Horn Diary*, p. 7].

Diamond, PVT Edward— b. Stoughton, MA, 11 Jun 1853 or 25 Jun 1854 (both dates have been listed)–d. unknown. Company H, private. Gray eyes, dark hair, ruddy complexion; 5'5¾" tall. Enlisted 18 Sep 1875. Rode with his unit in Benteen's battalion, and fought on Reno Hill.

Dohman (also Dorman or Dohlman), **PVT Anton**— b. Hanover, Germany, 1850–d. 25 Jun 1876, killed at the Little Big Horn. Company F, private. Gray eyes, brown hair, fair complexion; 5'2½" tall. Second enlistment 3 Aug 1871. Body found and identified on Custer Hill, near GAC. Listed number 105 in "June Returns, Alterations … Killed in action."

Dolan, PVT John (aka Thomas Brown)— b. Dublin, Ireland, 14 Apr 1843–d. Fort Myer, VA, 31 Mar 1922. Company M, private. Hazel, gray, or brown eyes, brown or dark hair, dark or ruddy complexion; 5'9½–10" tall. Enlisted 16 Feb 1866, 1st Cavalry. Discharged 15 Feb 1869; reenlisted 13 Mar 1869. Deserted and enlisted in NYC as Thomas Brown, 1 Oct 1873. Reduced from SGT 14 Jun 1876, for engaging in a fistfight with CPT French. Remained at the Powder River Depot. Presence confirmed on June Returns. At PRD awaiting discharge, but enlisted again, 2 Aug 1876. CPL Miles O'Harra was promoted to sergeant to replace him. Married Lena G. Fagan (d. 20 May 1882), 10 Jan 1876; sons John and Dudley. Married Josephine Fisher; son Peter. Buried in Arlington National Cemetery.

Doll, PVT Jacob W.— b. Russel, England, 1849–d. 16 Dec 1905. Company B, private. Brown eyes, black hair, fair complexion; 5'7" tall. Enlisted 21 Mar 1876 in Baltimore. Remained at the Powder River Depot.

Donahoe, SAD John (Jack)— b. Galway, Ireland, 1848–d. San Francisco, CA, heart failure, 16 Dec 1905. Company M: company saddler. Hazel eyes, brown hair, light complexion; 5'3" tall. Second enlistment 20 Oct 1871. No specific record exists of his participation in the battle, other than his presence with his unit during the valley fighting and subsequent defense of Reno Hill.

Donnelly, PVT Timothy— b. Darlington, England, Apr 1854–d. 25 Jun 1876, killed at the Little Big Horn. Company F, private. Blue eyes, dark hair, fair complexion; 5'6" tall. Enlisted 21 Sep 1875. Body identified in Deep Ravine by PVT Dennis Lynch (F). Listed number 106 in "June Returns, Alterations … Killed in action."

Donohue (also spelled Donoughue; also seen as O'Donohue), **PVT John F.**— b. Tipperary, Ireland, 1850–d. Butte, MT, 3 Dec 1924. Company K, private. Hazel eyes, dark hair, medium complexion; 5'9" tall. Enlisted 14 Dec 1872. Donohue wrote in 1888 how he had seen Custer on the bluffs just before the command commenced firing. That would mean he had moved down the valley with Reno's battalion [Saum, Lewis O., "Private John F. O'-Donohue's Reflections on the LBH," *Montana Magazine,* Vol. 50, No. 4, Winter 2000, as cited in Donovan, *A Terrible Glory,* p. 444, footnote (12) 50]. Bill Boyes writes much the same thing: "…Donohue, 'K' Troop but serving with Company 'M'…" [Boyes, "Custer's Battle Plan for 25 June 1876," *Research Review,* Vol. 22, No. 1, Winter, 2008, p. 14; citing W. Kent King, *The Custer Cover-Up,* p. 182; and *Montana Magazine,* Vol. 50, No. 4, Winter 2000, p. 44]. Both the Donovan and Boyes citations appear incorrect, however. There is no evidence showing Donohue served with any unit but his own Company K. Donohue also claimed that Custer gave the orders directly to Reno, but there is little evidence showing Custer communicated with his second-in-command. Even LT Wallace said Custer issued his orders to Reno through LT Cooke.

Dorn (aka Doran), **PVT Richard B.**— b. Bronson, MI, 11 Feb 1853–d. 26 Jun 1876, killed at the Little Big Horn. Company B, private. Gray eyes, dark hair, dark complexion; 5'9" tall. Enlisted 20 Jan 1872 in Chicago. CPT McDougall's orderly. Killed on Reno hill, early morning of 26 June, while waking McDougall. Shot in head. Son of John and Bridget Hanley Dorn. Had two brothers, William and Michael. Civilian occupation: laborer. Father died Nov 1863. Listed number 11 in "June Returns, Alterations … Killed in action."

Dose, TMP Henry C.— b. Holstein, Germany, 1849–d. 25 Jun 1876, killed at the Little Big Horn with Custer's command. Company G: trumpeter. Gray eyes, brown hair, fair complexion; 5'6" tall. Second enlistment: 4 Jan 1870 to 4 Jan 1875 with Third Infantry; then 1 Feb 1875 with Seventh Cavalry. He was one of three orderlies with Custer. Body found on the flats near LBH, between Medicine Tail Coulee and Deep Coulee, possibly killed when Custer and the left wing moved down MTC to Ford B, or later while trying to escape, though that is improbable. Arrows found in his back and sides. Hammer has him being killed in the valley fight, but this is incorrect. Also, Hardorff claimed Dose was found "a short distance above the lower fork of Deep *Ravine* [emphasis added], with arrows shot in his back and sides" [*Hokahey!…,* p. 80]. Married Anna Elizabeth Fettis, a laundress. Two children: Hattie and Charles. Listed number 129 in "June Returns, Alterations … Killed in action."

Dougherty, CPL James— b. Oxford, NJ, 1851–d. Nicholson, PA, of TB, 6 Oct 1884. Company B, corporal. Gray eyes, dark hair, ruddy complexion; 5'7¾" tall. Enlisted 5 Dec 1872. Recommended by CPT McDougall for medal for gallantry, but not awarded the MH.

Downing, PVT Thomas Patrick— b. Limerick, Ireland, 6 May 1856–d. 25 Jun 1876, killed at the Little Big Horn. Company I, private. Blue eyes, sandy hair, florid complexion; 5'8¼" tall. Enlisted 12 Feb 1873. Body never identified, but in all likelihood he was killed in the Keogh Sector. No recorded marriage, though he did have a daughter. Elisabeth Kimber says that he was married and ran away to enlist to escape his wife. She cites Langellier, Cox, and Pohanka, *Myles Keogh: the Life and legend of an "Irish Dragoon" in the Seventh Cavalry,* p. 121. Listed number 152 in "June Returns, Alterations … Killed in action."

Drinan (also spelled Drinnan), **PVT James**— b. Cork, Ireland, 1853–d. 25 Jun 1876, killed at the Little Big Horn. Company A, private. Gray eyes, light brown hair, dark complexion; 5'7⅜" tall. Enlisted 2 Dec 1874 in Boston. Possibly killed on Reno Hill, though Ken Hammer, in *The Battlefield Dispatch,* Winter 2005, lists him as "unknown location." Smalley claims no one saw him killed and his body was never found [*Little Bighorn Mysteries,* p. 15–7]. Listed number 5 in "June Returns, Alterations … Killed in action."

Driscoll, PVT Edward C.— b. Waterford, Ireland, 1850–d. 25 Jun 1876, killed at the Little Big Horn. Company I, private. Hazel eyes, light hair, light complexion; 5'6" tall. Enlisted 19 May 1873. Body found west of the crest of Custer Hill, near that of LT Cooke: "…on the river side of the hogback on ground a little higher up than Cooke" [Michno, *The Mystery of E Troop,* p. 143]. Hardorff wrote, "near the eastern edge of the elevation" [*Lakota Recollections of the Custer Fight,* p. 66, footnote 10]. Listed number 153 in "June Returns, Alterations … Killed in action."

Duggan, PVT John F. (aka Crowely, John L.)— b. Fitchburg, MA, 7 Feb 1849–d. 25 Jun 1876, killed at the Little Big Horn. Company L, private. Gray eyes, dark hair, fair complexion; 5'9½" tall. Enlisted in U.S. Navy; enlisted 24 Sep 1873. May have been killed in Deep Ravine, possibly one of four riders off Custer Ridge. Boot with initials "JD" found in the Deep Coulee area. Liddic speculates he could have been killed while trying to flee east or south toward Reno [*Vanishing Victory,* p. 153]. Also see PVT John Darris (E) and 1SG Butler (L). Listed number 200 in "June Returns, Alterations … Killed in action."

Durselew, PVT Otto— b. Frankfurt, Germany, 1850–d. 30 Sep 1877, killed in action at Snake Creek, M.T. Company A, private. Blue eyes, brown hair, fair complexion; 5'9½" tall. Enlisted 5 Dec 1874 in NYC. Rumored to have been a lieutenant in the Prussian army during the Franco-Prussian War. No specific record exists of his participation in the battle, other than his presence with his unit during the valley fighting and subsequent defense of Reno Hill. Promoted to corporal, 1 Jul 1876. Killed in the Nez Percé War.

Dutton, William H. *see* **Chapman, PVT William H.**

Dwyer, PVT Edmond P.— b. Fairfax County, VA, Dec 1850–d. unknown. Company G, private. Blue eyes, brown hair, fair complexion; 5'5½" tall. Enlisted 14 Apr 1876. No specific record exists of his participation in the battle, other than his presence with his unit during the valley fighting and subsequent defense of Reno Hill.

Dye, PVT William— b. Marietta, OH, 1850–d. 25 Jun 1876, killed at the Little Big Horn. Company L, private. Brown eyes, black hair, fair complexion; 5'9½" tall. Enlisted 23 Sep 1875. In all likelihood he was killed on Calhoun Hill, though the possibility exists he was one of those killed during the panic through the Keogh Sector. No remains found during the 1984–1985 archaeological work match his description. Listed number 199 in "June Returns, Alterations … Killed in action."

Eades, PVT William— b. Dublin, Ireland, 1844–d. near Dickinson, D.T., 12 May 1887. Company F, private. Gray eyes, black hair, fair complexion; 5'7" tall. Detailed to Department QM as mechanic.

Eagan, Thomas P. *see* **Hagan, CPL Thomas P.**

Easley, SGT John Thomas— b. Montgomery County, IL, 1853–d. unknown. Company A. Brown eyes, light hair, fair complexion; 5'8¼" tall. Enlisted on 21 Dec 1874. Deserted on 17 Oct 1876. No specific record exists of his participation in the battle, other than his presence with his unit during the valley fighting and subsequent defense of Reno Hill.

Edgerly, 2LT Winfield Scott (nicknamed "Big Feet")— b. Farmington, NH, 29 May 1846–d. Farmington, NH, 10 Sep 1927. Company D. DOR: 15 Jun 1870, same as Hodgson; senior second lieutenants on campaign. Blue eyes, gray hair; at 6'4", reputedly the tallest man in the regiment. Parents born in Farmington, as well. Graduated from Phillips Exeter Academy, 1864, a classmate of Robert Lincoln, son of the president. Graduated from the U.S. Military Academy. Married Grace Cory Blum (b. Cooperstown, NY, 3 Oct

1857–d. Washington, D.C., 8 Apr 1939) on 27 Oct 1875 in St. Paul, MN. It appears Grace's closest relative was her cousin, a prominent attorney named Edward C. Bailly and when he died, Edgerly's papers went to Bailly's wife, Elizabeth Donovan Bailly. George M. Clark obtained these papers in 1962 [*Scalp Dance,* p. 10]. Winifred, their only child, died at age 3 in 1885 at Fort Leavenworth. Buried in Arlington National Cemetery, Section 3, Grave 3886A. One of the most trustworthy eyewitnesses of the Little Big Horn battle.

Eiseman, PVT George— b. Philadelphia, PA, 16 May 1854–d. 25 Jun 1876, killed at the Little Big Horn. Company C, private. Blue eyes, dark hair; 5' 5¼" tall. In the army since 15 Jan 1872. Had been a brush maker. Not married. In the C Company charge off Battle Ridge-Calhoun Hill, but body was never identified. May have died in Calhoun Coulee, Finley-Finckle Ridge, the Keogh Sector, or possibly even Last Stand Hill. Listed number 26 in "June Returns, Alterations … Killed in action."

Eixenberger, PVT Peter— b. Munich, Bavaria, Germany, 12 Jun 1860, though there is indication the year may have been earlier–d. Sykes, MT, 12 Sep 1917. Headquarters: band. Private. Dark eyes, dark hair, fair complexion; 5' 5½" tall. He enlisted, 15 Nov 1875, at the reported age of 19, making his year of birth 1856. Remained at Powder River Depot. Presence confirmed on June Returns.

Emerich, PVT Jacob (aka Huff)— b. Bavaria, Germany, 22 Oct 1850–d. Danville, IL, 18 Aug 1929. Blue eyes, light hair, fair complexion; 5' 8½" tall. Headquarters: band. Private. Remained at Powder River Depot. Presence confirmed on June Returns.

Engle, PVT Gustave— b. Würtemburg, Germany, 1849–d. 25 Jun 1876, killed at the Little Big Horn. Company C, private. Brown eyes, brown hair; 5' 8" tall. In the army less than one year. Enlisted 27 Sep 1875. In the C Company charge off Battle Ridge-Calhoun Hill, but body was never identified. May have died in Calhoun Coulee, Finley-Finckle Ridge, the Keogh Sector, or possibly even Last Stand Hill. Listed number 27 in "June Returns, Alterations … Killed in action."

Etzler, PVT William— b. Wheeling, WV, 1852–d. unknown. Company L, private. Blue eyes, dark hair, fair complexion; 5' 6½" tall. Enlisted 9 Sep 1873. With the pack train. Married Mary Ann Hackett, 17 Aug 1877.

Farley, PVT Henry James (also listed as Turley and Tenley)— b. Troy, NY, Mar 1851–d. 25 Jun 1876, killed at the Little Big Horn probably during Reno's retreat. Company M, private. Brown eyes, black hair, dark complexion; 5' 4⅛" tall. Enlisted 29 Oct 1872. Killed at foot of bluffs. Body found with his hunting knife driven through his eye. Ken Hammer, in *The Battlefield Dispatch,* Winter 2005, however, says he was killed in the timber. Willert claims the bluffs [*Little Big Horn Diary,* p. 319]. In an article written for the *Hardin, Montana Tribune,* June 22, 1923, 1SG Ryan wrote that as the command reached the timber after riding down the valley, Turley's horse bolted and Ryan last saw him heading toward the Indian village [Graham, *The Custer Myth,* p. 242], thereby giving us a third version. Listed number 235 in "June Returns, Alterations … Killed in action."

Farley, PVT William— b. Ireland, 1850–d. unknown. Company H, private. Blue eyes, dark hair, florid complexion; 5' 7" tall. Enlisted 1 Jun 1875. WIA in left shoulder during hilltop fight.

Farrand, PVT James— b. Washington County, IL, 1839–d. 25 Jun 1876, killed at the Little Big Horn. Company C, private. Dark eyes, black hair, dark complexion; 58" tall. Was in his second enlistment, 10 Nov 1875. In the C Company charge off Battle Ridge-Calhoun Hill, but body was never identified. May have died in Calhoun Coulee, Finley-Finckle Ridge, the Keogh Sector, or possibly even Last Stand Hill. Listed number 28 in "June Returns, Alterations … Killed in action."

Farrar, PVT Morris M.— b. Sidney, Australia, 30 Jul 1846–d. Philadelphia, PA, 9 Apr 1899. Company C, private. Black hair; 5' 8¾" tall. Veteran of the Civil War. Had been with the Seventh Cavalry for more than four years. Straggled from the company, eventually joining Reno on the hilltop. May have dropped out along Reno Creek approach to LBH, possibly the earliest to do so. His horse may have even kept him back as early as the trek up the Rosebud. Smalley writes that he was not a straggler, but does not account for him any other way. Buried at Holy Cross Cemetery, Philadelphia, PA.

Farrell, PVT Richard— b. Dublin, Ireland, 1851–d. 25 Jun 1876, killed at the Little Big Horn. Company E, private. Gray eyes, brown hair, fair complexion; 5' 8¾" tall. Enlisted 29 Sep 1875. Body found in Deep Ravine by Frank Berwald. Listed number 68 in "June Returns, Alterations … Killed in action."

Fay, PVT John J.— b. Chicago, IL, 1852–d. Washington, D.C., 26 Dec 1932. Company D, private. Gray eyes, brown hair, fair complexion; 5' 5" tall. Enlisted some time before Aug 1871, then again 8 Sep 1873. Rode with his unit in Benteen's battalion, and fought on Reno Hill.

Fehler (Feihler), **SGT Henry**— b. Hanover, Germany, 1837–d. Fort Union, NM, of "alcohol poisoning," 15 May 1889. Company A. Blue or gray eyes, light hair, fair complexion; 5′ 7½–8½″ tall. Enlisted 14 Aug 1872. Took over when 1SG Heyn was wounded. Carried company guidon, but threw it away in the timber of the valley fight when he could not control his unruly horse. Fehler was in overall charge of A Company's horses while they were in the timber during the valley fight.

Finckle (also seen spelled Finkle), **SGT George August**— b. Berlin, Germany, 1844–d. 25 Jun 1876, killed at the Little Big Horn. Company C, sergeant. Gray eyes, dark hair, dark complexion; 6′½″ tall. PVT Windolph claimed Finckle was the tallest enlisted man in the regiment. Enlisted on 27 Jan 1872. Reputed to have been a captain in the German army (Windolph to Walter Camp). Killed on Calhoun Ridge near Finley. SGT Kanipe, interviewed by the *Greensboro (NC) Daily Record*, said Finckle rode near Tom Custer and with Mitch Boyer and that his horse played out and he dropped out of the column [Michno, *The Mystery of E Troop*, p. 157]. Apparently he managed to get back with the troop, which leads one to believe C Company *had* to have been one of the units on the Luce/Nye-Cartwright ridges complex, because those companies halted while E and F rode on to Ford B. Only on the ridges could Finckle have managed to catch up. This was the reason Tom Custer chose Kanipe and not Finckle to deliver a message to hurry the packs. Finckle's body was found between SGT Finley and LT Calhoun and like Finley's, was severely mutilated. Listed number 15 in "June Returns, Alterations … Killed in action."

Finley, SGT Jeremiah— b. Tipperary, Ireland, 1841–d. 25 Jun 1876, killed at the Little Big Horn. Company C, sergeant. Gray eyes, brown hair; 5′ 7″ tall. Arrived in U.S. in 1860 at nineteen. Served for four years in the Civil War. Reenlisted on 18 Sep 1868 and assigned to Seventh Cavalry. Veteran of the Union Army. Also a tailor; made Custer's buckskin jacket. His horse was named Carlo. Killed on lower Calhoun Ridge, near southeast border of the reservation. His body was severely mutilated, with twelve arrows sticking in it and was found next to the head of his horse [Liddic, *Vanishing Victory*, p. 150]. Kanipe claimed Finley took the scalp found at the sundance camp and kept it. He had it in his saddlebags when he was killed [Graham, *The Custer Myth*, p. 248; interview in the Greensboro, NC, *Daily Record*, April 27, 1924]. Wife's name was Ellen Anna Elizabeth. They had 3 children: Mary Ellen, William H., and Jeremiah. Listed number 14 in "June Returns, Alterations … Killed in action."

Finnegan, PVT Thomas J.— b. Hillsboro, OH, 1 Sep 1850–d. Leavenworth, KS, 4 Feb 1923. Company F, private. Gray eyes, black hair, fair complexion; 5′ 9¾″ tall. Enlisted 19 Aug 1873. Civilian occupation was a poultry man. Assigned to wagon train at the Powder River Depot. Overfield says he was left with pack train, but this is incorrect.

Fischer (name also seen spelled "Fisher"; aka Charles Hanke; seen as Hinke), **TMP Charles** (nicknamed "Bounce")— b. Breslau, Germany, 1844–d. some time after 1905. Company M: trumpeter. Gray eyes, dark brown hair, fair complexion; 5′ 4½″ tall. Third enlistment 14 Sep 1875. Retired from Second Cavalry on 30 Oct 1905, as first sergeant. 1SG John Ryan claims it was Fischer who aided LT Hodgson by having the lieutenant grab a stirrup while crossing the LBH [Barnard, *Ten Years with Custer*, p. 296], though Willert claims it was PVT William E. Morris. Willert quotes Morris [*Little Big Horn Diary*, p. 319], but PVT Slaper (M) also claims it was Fischer and PVT Davern claimed it was an M Company trumpeter. Fischer could have been Hodgson's first attempt to grab hold, and much of what we have heard from Morris proved to be fiction. Ryan also says he heard of two others with the same distinction. Employed by Walter Sterland in his boarding house in Bismarck.

Fisher, PVT Charles O.— b. Bavaria, 1849–d. West Point, NY, 5 Mar 1898. Company K, private; transferred to H Company, 14 Jun 1876 (effective, 1 July). Gray eyes, dark hair, dark complexion; 5′ 6½″ tall. Enlisted 20 Mar 1876 in Chicago. Remained at the Powder River Depot in charge of CPT Benteen's personal property. Presence confirmed on June Returns.

Fitzgerald, FAR John— b. Staffordshire, England, 1841–d. 7 May 1900. Company C: farrier. Well into his fourth enlistment, 19 Jan 1872. Straggler. Hammer says his horse gave out and he wound up joining Reno's forces on the hilltop. May have dropped out along Reno Creek approach to LBH. The story has its skeptics, though SGT Hanley and PVT McGuire—both with the packs on 25 June—remember Fitzgerald as having been at the LBH. PVT Peter Thompson claims Fitzgerald—along with Watson and Brennan—were in his set of four at the battle. That is first-hand testimony to Fitzgerald's presence [Thompson, "The Experience of a Private Soldier in the Custer Massacre," p. 28]. There was been some skepticism about Fitzgerald's presence at the battle, but the June Returns do not show him on detached service or any other duty that would have precluded his presence on the LBH.

Flannagan, SGT James— b. Innis, County Clare, Ireland, 24 Apr 1839–d. Mandan, ND, 21 Apr 1921.

Company D, sergeant. Blue eyes, brown hair, light complexion; 5'10½" tall. Enlisted from Aug 1863 to Aug 1996 in 11th OH Cavalry. Stationed along the Oregon Trail. Served in Second Cavalry after Civil War. Enlisted in Seventh Cavalry 15 Nov 1871. Recommended for medal for conspicuous gallantry for LBH fight. Identified SGT Bustard's body near Keogh's [Hardorff, *On the LBH with Walter Camp*, p. 13, footnote 2]. Wife Mary, a laundress, died in 1915; survived by daughter Minnie and son William. Buried in Grave 5, Lot 90, Catholic Section, Union Cemetery, Mandan, ND, beside his wife.

Foley, CPL John— b. Salem, MA, 1850–d. 25 Jun 1876, killed at the Little Big Horn. Company C, corporal. Blue eyes, gray hair, ruddy complexion; 5' 8½" tall. Enlisted 18 Sep 1873. Richard Fox says he was killed in MTC environs, possibly while trying to escape. Michno says Foley's body "was found about the place of Yellow Nose's attack, on the low western terminus of Butler Ridge" [*Lakota Noon*, p. 150], though others believe the Yellow Nose incident occurred in a different location. This would place the body in or near MTC before it emptied into Ford B. Hardorff wrote that Foley's "remains lay on a rise north of MTC, nearly 400 yards from the river" [*On the LBH with Walter Camp*, p. 44, footnote 10] and this almost certainly appears correct. CPL Roy (A) was with the main burial parties on 28 Jun 1876, but did not follow any trail down MTC. Instead, he cut straight across to the battlefield. On the way, the first body he passed by was Foley's. Then he came across 1SG Butler (L), about 200 yards from Foley. From there to the next group of dead on or near Calhoun Hill was quite a distance. At the tenth reunion of the battle, organized by COL Herbert J. Slocum, Gall was asked about Foley: "Gall showed them where the lone soldier rode away, pursued by several Indians, and finally shot himself and fell off the horse. It corroborates [Walter Camp's] information about Corpl. Foley, as told me by Turtle Rib. Gall told them this soldier had chevrons on his sleeve" [Camp/Hammer, *Custer in '76*, p. 254]. Listed number 17 in "June Returns, Alterations … Killed in action."

Foley, PVT John— b. Dublin, Ireland, 20 Apr 1839–d. Washington, D.C., 6 Mar 1926. Company K, private. Gray eyes, black hair, dark complexion; 5' 9" tall. Enlisted from 20 Apr 1861 to 19 Aug 1861 in 22nd OH Infantry; enlisted from 29 Aug 1861 to 21 Feb 1863 in First OH Cavalry. Badly wounded at battle of Cedar Mountain. Enlisted 29 Jul 1863 in Second OH Heavy Artillery. Enlisted 11 Aug 1866 in Seventh Cavalry; reenlisted 11 Aug 1871. In Washita, Yellowstone, Black Hills, Sioux, and Nez Percé campaigns. At the Little Big Horn,

he was part of the water party, 26 June. Married; buried in Soldiers' Home National Cemetery.

Folsom, John *see* **Jennys, PVT Alonzo**

Forbes, John Stuart Stuart *see* **Hiley, PVT John S.**

Foster, PVT Samuel James— b. Clay County, KY, 1847–d. lung disease, Manchester, KY, 26 Mar 1884. Company A, private. Black eyes, brown hair, dark complexion; 5' 6½" tall. Enlisted 9 May 1872. No specific record exists of his participation in the battle, other than his presence with his unit during the valley fighting and subsequent defense of Reno Hill. Wounded in right arm, probably on the hilltop. Wife Martha (d. 13 Feb 1941). Children: Nancy M. and Lottie.

Fowler, PVT Isaac— b. Dark County, OH, 15 Sep 1844–d. Union City, IN, 5 Dec 1881. Company C, private. Brown eyes, dark hair, fair complexion; 5' 7¼" tall. Enlisted 21 Aug 1861, 53rd OH Infantry; enlisted 1 Jan 1864 to 26 Jun 1865, and again on 29 Sep 1873. Civil War veteran. With pack train.

Fox, PVT Harvey A.— b. Alexander County, NC, 1848–d. Warm Springs, MT, 28 Mar 1913. Company D, private. Gray eyes, fair hair, fair or sandy complexion; 5' 6" or 7" tall, 160 pounds. Enlisted 27 Jul 1871. Remained at the Powder River Depot. Presence confirmed on June Returns. Married Amelia Monroe Jackson in Dec 1878. She was the half-blood Piegan mother of Robert and Billy Jackson, the "Ree" scouts on the campaign (Billy Jackson fought at the Little Big Horn). Son: Alexander.

Fox, PVT John— b. Buffalo, NY, 3 Jan 1844–d. at the U.S. Soldiers' Home, Washington, D.C., 26 Jan 1932. Company D, private. Blue eyes, dark hair, dark complexion; 5' 8½" tall. Enlisted 24 Sep 1875. Rode with his unit in Benteen's battalion, and fought on Reno Hill. After his enlistment expired, he reenlisted in the First, Second, and Fourth U.S. Infantries until 1897. He retired a sergeant. He was buried on the grounds of the Soldiers' Home.

Frank, PVT William— b. Magdeburg, Prussia, 1836–d. Baltimore, MD, 6 Apr 1880. Company B, private. Hazel eyes, brown hair, light complexion; 5' 8¼" tall. Enlisted from 18 Jun 1865 to 26 Oct 1872 in Second Cavalry. Enlisted from 5 Sep 1873 to 1 Nov 1873 in U.S. Marine Corps. Fifth enlistment 12 Oct 1875. With the pack train escort, Company B. Arrived and fought on Reno Hill. Wife was named Elizabeth. Buried in St. Paul's Cemetery, Baltimore.

Franklin, PVT John W.— b. Providence, RI, 1850–d. unknown. Company A, private. Gray eyes, brown hair, dark complexion; 5' 9" tall. Enlisted 11 Jan 1875. With packs and hilltop fight (Hammer, 1995).

Fredericks, SGT Andrew— b. Bedford County, PA, 1844–d. Fort Totten, D.T., 14 Jan 1881. Company K, sergeant. Hazel eyes, dark hair, light complexion; 5' 3½" tall. Second enlistment 23 Apr 1872. Rode with his unit in Benteen's battalion, and fought on Reno Hill. Died of pneumonia; buried in Custer Battlefield National Cemetery.

French, CPL Henry Eldon— b. Portsmouth, NH, 1849–d. 25 Jun 1876, killed at the Little Big Horn. Company C, corporal. Hazel eyes, brown hair; 5' 6" tall. Enlisted on 22 Jan 1872. In the C Company charge off Battle Ridge-Calhoun Hill. May have died in Calhoun Coulee, Finley-Finckle Ridge (most likely), the Keogh Sector, or possibly even Last Stand Hill. Listed number 16 in "June Returns, Alterations ... Killed in action."

French, CPT Thomas Henry (nickname among EM, "Tucker")— b. Baltimore, MD, 4 or 5 Mar 1843–d. Planter's House, Leavenworth, KS, 27 Mar 1882, probably from the affects of alcohol. Company M: Commanding Officer. Hazel eyes, brown hair, fair complexion; 5' 6" tall. DOR: 26 Mar 1868; fifth-ranking captain on campaign. Appointed 2LT, Tenth Infantry, 18 May 1864. Fought at Petersburg, Weldon RR, and Chappell House, where he was wounded. Brevetted captain. Assigned to Seventh Cavalry 1 Jan 1871.

Along with LT Cooke, considered best shot in regiment. Carried a "Long Tom" infantry rifle, an old Springfield, .50-caliber, breech-loader. His horse had four white stockings. Willert wrote the horse was a gray and quoted 1SG Ryan, saying the animal was "the best buffalo horse in the command" [*Little Big Horn Diary*, p. 402]. This brings into question French's claim of being the "bravest" soldier mentioned in the Red Horse story (see below). The horse was shot in the head while on Reno Hill (26 Jun 1876), but Willert does not say if he died. Company M first sergeant John Ryan claimed every company horse but his own was killed, so this could mean French's as well. A bullet went through French's hat while on Reno Hill.

Both parents had been previously widowed: Thomas French and Ellen Burke Foy. Father born in Spalding, Lincolnshire, England, dying in Baltimore in 1858 of fever. Mother died at 65 on 22 Mar 1888 and buried in Holy Rood Cemetery, Washington, D.C. Enrolled at Georgetown College, Washington, D.C., the Prep Division, on 14 Mar 1853 when he was ten years old. He was placed in the "Second Rudiments," indicating some prior schooling. His name appears in the 1852–

1853 students list, but not the list for the following year.

Extremely brave, even recognized by the Indians at the battle, especially the Sioux chief Red Horse during the Reno rout, though some doubt this story pertains to French. Disliked Reno intensely for what he did and wished that a "friendly" bullet had accomplished what French could not bring himself to do. Heavy drinker, causing him to be court martialed and dismissed from the service. Sentence commuted by President Hayes. Unfortunately, his court-martial prevented him from testifying at the RCOI. Essentially forced to retire, 5 Feb 1880.

Fire destroyed his home in Bismarck, ND (34 North 4th Street) on 20 Feb 1880. Buried in Fort Leavenworth cemetery, but exhumed on 4 Mar 1891 and reinterred in Holy Rood Cemetery, Washington, D.C., Section 23, Lot 257.

"During all this fighting I was near Captain French helping get the guns loaded whenever an empty shell would stick, and this happened to most of the guns as soon as they got hot. Captain French was a crack shot and always carried a 'Long Tom' Infantry rifle. This gun had a ramrod carried under the barrel and I think it was the only ramrod in the whole outfit. Whenever a shell would stick he would recover the gun and either pick it out with his knife or I would push it out with my ramrod. We would then load the gun and return it to it's [*sic*] owner. In doing this Captain French was exposed most of the time but was perfectly cool and for some reason escaped unhurt" [Swanson, *G. A. Custer, His Life and Times,* 134. From a book written by PVT Daniel J. Newell (M), *The Story of the Little Bighorn Campaign of 1876*].

"Capt. Benteen paid him a cryptic compliment, regarding the leadership during the fight, stating, '... *They were all a pack of cowards, Capt. French excluded*'" [Klockner, *The Officer Corps of Custer's Seventh Cavalry,* p. 61, citing the "Benteen-Goldin Papers"].

Gaffney, SGT George— b. Cavan, Ireland, 1846–d. Washington, D.C., at the U.S. Soldiers Home, 22 Nov 1916. Company I, sergeant. Gray eyes, dark hair, dark complexion; 5' 2" tall. Attached to Department HQ, with AAQM in the field, for duty. A Civil War veteran of the 9th MA Infantry. His third enlistment ended on 20 Nov 1881 and he was discharged. During the battle, Gaffney was aboard the steamer *Far West*, serving as assistant quartermaster with LT Nowlan. When Walter Camp interviewed him he lived at 333 Missouri Avenue, NW, Washington, D.C. Never married.

Gallenne (also seen spelled Gallene), **PVT Jean Baptiste Desire**— b. Lorient, France, 1849–d.

Washington, D.C., 12 Feb 1911. Company M, private. Blue eyes, black hair, dark complexion; 5' 5¼" tall. Enlisted 30 Sep 1873. No specific record exists of his participation in the battle, other than his presence with his unit during the valley fighting and subsequent defense of Reno Hill. Lost his left leg in the Snake Creek fight against Chief Joseph and the Nez Percé, 30 Sep 1877. Wife Josephine; children: Amainthe, Gabrielle, Eugenie, Isabell J., Jean H., and Louise. Resided at 814 6th Street, NE, Washington, D.C., for 19 years. Buried in Mount Olivet Cemetery, DC.

Galvan, PVT James J. *(*aka Michael J. Miller; also Calran)–b. Liverpool, England, 16 Nov 1848–d. 25 Jun 1876, killed at the Little Big Horn. Company L, private. Gray eyes, dark hair, dark complexion; 5' 6¾" tall. Enlisted 28 Sep 1875. In all likelihood he was killed on Calhoun Hill, though the possibility exists he was one of those killed during the panic through the Keogh Sector. No remains found during the 1984–1985 archaeological work match his description. Obituary in *New York Times,* 11 Jul 1876. Listed number 202 in "June Returns, Alterations … Killed in action."

Gannon, SGT Peter—b. Manchester, England, 1844–d. Fort Assiniboine, M. T., 12 Jun 1886. Company B, sergeant. Blue eyes, brown hair, light complexion; 5' 6¾" tall. Enlisted 18 Jun 1867 in Seventh Cavalry in Boston. Discharged 18 Jun 1872; reenlisted 16 Jul 1872. Remained at Powder River Depot. Scott claims he was on Reno Hill, while Overfield has him listed at PRD. Hammer also says PRD. Died of TB and is now buried in Custer Battlefield National Cemetery.

Gardiner, PVT John (also William Gardner)–b. Brockville, Ontario, Canada, 2 Feb 1845 (enlistment records of 1870 show birthplace as Hanover, Germany)–d. 25 Jun 1876, killed at the Little Big Horn. Company F, private. Blue eyes, light hair, light complexion; 5' 7" tall. Civilian butcher. Arrived in U.S. in 1860; enlisted from 28 Jul 1862 to 26 Jun 1865 in Fifth NY Artillery. Appointed sergeant on 25 Jun 1863 and later lieutenant. Returned to his family in Buffalo, NY. Enlisted again on 12 Aug 1870 to 12 Aug 1875 in Third Artillery, then on 28 Aug 1875 in NYC and assigned to Seventh Cavalry. In all likelihood he was killed on Last Stand Hill with his unit. Listed number 107 in "June Returns, Alterations … Killed in action."

Gebhart, Jacob Henry *see* **Tanner, PVT James J.**

Gehrmann, PVT Frederick H.— b. Baltimore, MD, 18 Nov 1854–d. Washington, D.C., 10 Dec 1922. Company B, private. Blue eyes, brown hair, ruddy complexion; 5' 9¾" tall. Enlisted 13 Mar 1876. Remained at the Powder River Depot. Both parents born in Germany; became a policeman after leaving army 1 Apr 1886. Resided at 321 Lenworth Place, SW, Washington, D.C. First wife, Mary, died 12 Jan 1910. Children: Harry A.; Frederick, Jr.; Charles A.; Marie C. Second wife, Geneva B. Gehrmann, died 22 Jan 1934. He is buried at Arlington National Cemetery.

Geiger, SGT George H.— b. Cincinnati, 1843–d. Dayton, OH, 23 Jan 1904. Company H, sergeant. Gray eyes, light hair, fair complexion; 5' 4½" tall. Enlisted from 15 Jan 1861 to 11 Aug 1865 in 47th OH Infantry. Enlisted from 29 Nov 1867 to 29 Nov 1872 in Seventh Cavalry, then reupped 18 Dec 1872. Awarded MH for firing and holding an exposed, standing position with Windolph, Mechlin, and Voit, on the brow of Reno Hill, as a diversion while others carried water up from the LBH. Married Augusta Krick, Sep 1889; no children. He was Jewish. Buried in Dayton National Cemetery.

Geist, PVT Frank J.— b. Würzburg, Germany, 16 Feb 1856–d. Minneapolis, MN, 20 Nov 1918. Company G, private. Gray eyes, light hair, fair complexion; 5' 6" tall. Enlisted 14 Apr 1876. Remained at the Powder River Depot. Presence confirmed on June Returns. Friends with PVT Stella (E) in Germany, having gone to school with him there. Survived by widow Ena M. Geist and four sons: Robert, Frank, Walter, and Edward and two daughters Minnie and Elsie. Resided in Minneapolis for 39 years.

George, PVT William Montell— b. Lexington, KY, 1846–d. Powder River, M. T., 3 Jul 1876, as a result of wounds suffered at the Little Big Horn. Company H, private. Blue eyes, light or sandy hair, fair complexion; 5' 9" tall. Enlisted in Merrill's Horse Volunteers, the Second MO Cavalry 7 Sep 1864; mustered out 15 Jun 1865. Enlisted 25 Aug 1866 in Seventh Cavalry; discharged 25 Aug 1871. Enlisted again in Seventh Cavalry 1 May 1875. Wounded on 25 June on Reno Hill, but died of wounds on steamer *Far West,* either on the afternoon of 3 July or early morning, 4 Jul 1876. Buried near Powder River Depot.

Gibbs, PVT William— b. Manchester, England, 28 Jul 1845–d. Napa, CA, 18 Feb 1934. Company K, private. Blue eyes, brown hair, fair complexion; 5' 7¼" tall. Enlisted 15 Dec 1874. At McComb City, MS, for duty, until 15 Apr 1876. At the LBH, he took part in the hilltop fight. Buried in Veterans' Home Cemetery, Yountville, CA.

Gibson, 1LT Francis Marion ("Gibby")—b. Philadelphia, PA, 14 Dec 1847–d. NYC, 17 Jun 1919. Company H. DOR: 11 Jul 1871; seventh-ranking of nine first lieutenants on the campaign. A George Custer favorite, had almost transferred to Company E when Craycroft was sent on detached service. His wife had a bad premonition, however, and much to Gibson's annoyance, talked him out of the transfer. Took command of Company G on Reno Hill, after McIntosh's death. LT "Tosh" McIntosh's brother-in-law. Benteen did not think too highly of him, believing him to be somewhat of a conniver. According to Donovan, however, Gibson was "an ardent admirer and defender of Benteen's..." [*A Terrible Glory,* p. 449, footnote (13) 11]. Participated in the Washita campaign, serving on TDY with Company F. Also went south with the regiment and served on both the Yellowstone and Black Hills campaigns, 1873 and 1874. Was also in the 1877 campaign against the Nez Percé. Remained on frontier duty until Jun 1889. A popular and "lighthearted" officer [Klokner, p. 64]. Married Katherine Garrett. (Date of marriage unknown, but he was married at the time of the campaign.) Had one daughter, Katherine Gibson Fougera. She became an author, writing a book titled *with Custer's Cavalry.* Lived for a time at 80 Pequot Avenue, New London, CT. Buried in Arlington National Cemetery.

Gilbert, PVT John M.—b. Cork, Ireland, 1854–d. unknown. Company A, private. Hazel eyes, brown hair, fair complexion; 5'7" tall. Enlisted 6 Oct 1875. One of five men who volunteered to go on picket duty with CPL Roy the night of 25 June. In the 26 June water party.

Gilbert, CPL William H.—b. Philadelphia, PA, 11 Nov 1851–d. 25 Jun 1876, killed at the Little Big Horn. Company L, corporal. Blue eyes, brown hair, dark complexion; 5'7¾" tall. Enlisted 2 Oct 1873. In all likelihood he was killed on Calhoun Hill, though the possibility exists he was one of those killed during the panic through the Keogh Sector. No remains found during the 1984–1985 archaeological work match his description. Married Mary E. Hevener, 7 Apr 1870. One son, Rudy K. Gilbert. Listed number 187 in "June Returns, Alterations ... Killed in action."

Gillette, PVT David C.—b. Onandaiga County, NY, 1851–d. 25 Jun 1876, killed at the Little Big Horn. Company I, private. Blue eyes, light hair, fair complexion; 5'5" tall. Enlisted 1 Oct 1873. Extra duty as hospital attendant and may have been killed on Custer/Last Stand Hill near Doctor Lord. Listed number 154 in "June Returns, Alterations ... Killed in action."

Glenn, PVT George W. (aka George W. Glease)—b. Boston, MA, 1845–d. Richmond, VA, 18 Sep 1914. Company H, private. Blue eyes, brown hair, ruddy complexion; 5'5" tall. Enlisted in 12th MA Infantry, then in 18th Infantry. Enlisted from 5 Sep 1866 to 5 Sep 1871 in Eighth Cavalry. Reenlisted 17 Nov 1871, but deserted 21 Jul 1875. Enlisted 3 Sep 1875 in Seventh Cavalry. Rode with his unit in Benteen's battalion, and fought on Reno Hill. Deserted again in 1877, but apprehended and dishonorably discharged in 1880. Interviewed by Walter Mason Camp in 1914. Buried in Hampton National Cemetery.

Godfrey, 1LT Edward Settle—b. Kalida, OH, 9 Oct 1843–d. Cookstown, NJ, 1 Apr 1932. Company K: Acting CO. DOR: 1 Feb 1868. Next to Cooke, highest-ranking first lieutenant on the campaign. Fought in the Civil War and graduated from the USMA in 1867. Originally assigned to Company G. Escort duty with the Peace Commission in Oct 1867, then on the Winter–Washita Campaign of 1868. His poor performance to date, had him recommended by COL Sturgis for "review" before the Benzine Boards, but he made it through. Accompanied the regiment to the south, then participated in the Yellowstone Expedition of 1873, including the 11 Aug 1873 fight near Pompey's Pillar. Also in the Black Hills Expedition of 1874. Filled Weir's position as CO, Company D, when Weir died in late 1876. Awarded the MH in 1894 for actions in the Snake Creek (Bear Paw Mountain) fight in 1877, where he was wounded in the hip. Took part in every major action of the Seventh Cavalry from 1867 through Wounded Knee in 1890. Instructor at West Point from 1879 to 1883. Severely injured in a train accident in the 1890s and that kept him out of the field. Served in Cuba in Jan 1899, and the Philippines. Promoted to BG in 1907. He probably put more thoughts about the battle at the LBH on paper than any other participant [Michno]. Godfrey and Hare were roundly praised for their bravery and initiative in covering the move back from Weir Peak.

Apparently, very hard of hearing. Camp called him deaf [Camp/Hammer, *Custer in '76,* p. 70]. Close friends with LT James H. Bradley, Gibbon's Seventh Infantry chief of scouts. He may not have been the "shining light" he was reputed to be. Benteen certainly thought less and less of him over the years, though Benteen confided in him right after the LBH fight. LT Eckerson was with Godfrey at Cedar Creek, M. T., in spring of 1877 when they chased Indians who had robbed the U.S. mail. Apparently, Godfrey failed to pursue them and Benteen claimed Eckerson said Godfrey was a coward [Carroll, *The Benteen-Goldin Letters,* pp. 207–208].

Benteen called him, "…rather an obtuse fellow, and like the traditional Englishman, it takes him a good while to see the nub of a joke" [Carroll, *The Benteen-Goldin Letters,* p. 289]. It seems he was rather humorless, maybe a bit too staid.

Married Mary J. Pocock (d. 22 Feb 1886), 15 Jun 1869, in Harpsville. Had three sons, one daughter. Married Ida De La Mothe Emley, 6 Oct 1892, in Cookstown, NJ. Buried in Arlington National Cemetery.

Golden, PVT Bernard— b. Cavan, Ireland, 1842– d. unknown. Company M, private. Gray eyes, brown hair, ruddy complexion; 5'7" tall. Second enlistment 5 Oct 1875. No specific record exists of his participation in the battle, other than his presence with his unit during the valley fighting and subsequent defense of Reno Hill. Deserted, 18 Dec 1877, from FAL after killing James Weeks in a pistol fight during a poker game.

Golden, PVT Patrick M.— b. Sligo, Ireland, 1849–d. 25 Jun 1876, killed at the Little Big Horn. Company D, private. Blue eyes, brown hair, fair complexion; 5'9¼" tall. Enlisted 22 Jan 1872 in Boston. Killed on Reno hill. Shot four times before a bullet finally struck him in the head while on the D Company line. He was standing at the time, shouting to his friends, "Boys, that is number three, but I'm still here. Number four…" Listed number 50 in "June Returns, Alterations … Killed in action."

Goldin, PVT Theodore W. (born as John Stilwell)— b. Avon Township, Rock County, WI, 29 Jul 1858, making him underaged for the army (he claimed he was born 29 Jul 1855)–d. King, WI, 15 Feb 1935. Company G, private. Claimed to have been attached to Headquarters and sent back with a note to Reno, thereafter serving with his company. There is no proof this claim was valid. Blue eyes, brown hair, fair complexion; 5'7¾" tall. Later documents show his height as 5'10", more consistent with descriptions of him as a "husky young fellow" [Sklenar, "…Goldin: Too Soon Discredited?"]. Enlisted 8 Apr 1876 (in later years Goldin claimed he enlisted in April 1875). Discharged 13 Nov 1877, without honor, when his parents informed the military he enlisted without their consent and he was underage (Goldin lied about this as well, claiming he was discharged on 29 Sep 1879 for disability caused by wounds suffered at the LBH).

Ultimately awarded MH (in 1896) for voluntarily bringing water up from LBH (he was chairman of the state Republican Committee at the time). Of course, wangling a friendship with Benteen probably helped as well. In October 1878, a board awarded honors to survivors of the battle. While it awarded MH to 23 EM, nothing was mentioned of Goldin. Goldin claimed he was called to HQ on 21 Jun 1876, to assist the sergeant major in preparing various orders and records. LT Cooke retained him at HQ as an orderly/messenger [Goldin/Carroll, *The Benteen-Goldin Letters,* p. 59]. There is one story about a G Company trooper found hiding in the bushes, scared "witless," by the Reno/Culbertson party looking for LT Hodgson's body. Culbertson, in his RCOI testimony, mentions finding a G Company trooper in the bushes on the hillside [Nichols, *RCOI,* p. 371]. Some think it was Goldin, who spent the rest of his life making up stories about his role in the fight. Graham once remarked that you could take your choice of which story — of the message — to believe for they "all are priced the same. If you can be satisfied with any one of them, you will have done better than I was able to do."

Possibly served as an orderly to LT Cooke on 25 Jun 1876, but he is carried here with his company since he eventually wound up with his unit. Claimed to have been in the valley fight, but Sklenar seriously doubts it. Sklenar does believe, however, that Goldin served as a messenger and carried a note from Custer to Reno, though it was never delivered. This is a good story and rings true, despite Goldin's prolific lying. The note would have been given to Goldin as Custer's column was moving up Reno Hill and Goldin may have traveled down the valley behind Reno, reaching that command just as it was being routed. This would lend further credence to the hiding-in-the-bushes story. Graham, however, disputes Goldin's "orderly" story, writing that "Old Army" officers like Custer and Cooke would never have selected a raw recruit and entrusted him with any such important message to Reno. Graham also greatly disputes Goldin's farcical claims of being on very close terms with various officers, especially Custer, citing Goldin's claims that he had known Custer since joining the regiment in *1873* [*The Custer Myth,* pp. 274–275]. In addition to this, Graham points out the circumstances on the awarding of MH to Goldin, some 20 years after the fact. He mentions that Goldin was the chairman of the [WI] State Central Committee (the Republican Party) and that the assistant secretary of war was J. B. Doe (of Delavan, WI), also of Wisconsin. "Many of the old time Indian fighters I used to meet around Washington … seemed to know about this particular award, and were inclined to criticize it because of the circumstances under which it was bestowed. Some of them, indeed, ascribed it to political influence rather than to heroic conduct" [*The Custer Myth,* pp. 276–277].

Goldin eventually became a colonel in the WI Army National Guard. One of the primary sources of info about battle, though much of it was clearly fabricated, including his alleged wounds (Graham). Probably similar efforts used to award Goldin the MH were used in changing his discharge. On 3 March 1927 — fifty-one years after the battle — a special act was passed "directing that in the administration of the pension laws Mr. Goldin was to be considered as having been honorably discharged" [Graham, *The Custer Myth,* p. 278]. Married Laura Belle Dunwiddie 23 Feb 1881. Children: Herbert D. Goldin. Buried in Veterans Memorial Cemetery, King, WI.

Gordon, PVT Henry — b. Chatham, England, 1851–d. 25 Jun 1876, killed at the Little Big Horn during Reno's retreat from the timber. Company M, private. Brown eyes, brown hair, fair complexion; 5' 6" tall. Enlisted 5 Dec 1872 in Boston. Killed at foot of bluffs. Shot in the neck. Listed number 229 in "June Returns, Alterations ... Killed in action."

Gordon, PVT Thomas Albin — b. Boston, MA, 9 Dec 1853–d. Chelsea, MA, 21 Dec 1935. Company K, private. Gray eyes, black hair, dark complexion; 5' 6½" tall. Enlisted 26 Sep 1873. Rode with his unit in Benteen's battalion, and fought on Reno Hill. Married Nellie Frances Hurd, 23 Jun 1892 in Newton, MA; son Edwin A. Gordon. Buried in Swan Dale Cemetery, Mendon, MA.

Gorham, John *see* **Quinn, PVT John E.**

Graham, PVT Charles — b. County Tyrone, Ireland, 1837–d. 25 Jun 1876, killed at the Little Big Horn. Company L, private. Blue eyes, brown hair, florid complexion; 5' 6¾" tall. Second enlistment 7 Jul 1872. Body found in Keogh Sector, on a line between Keogh and Calhoun. Listed number 201 in "June Returns, Alterations ... Killed in action."

Graham, PVT Thomas Eaton — b. Alton, OH, 20 Nov 1831–d. Columbus, OH, 17 Feb 1907. Company G, private. Gray eyes, light hair, fair complexion; 5' 6¾" tall. Enlisted from 1848 to 1853 and helped build Fort Laramie. Served in 40th Ohio Infantry in the Civil War. Enlisted the Seventh Cavalry, 4 Nov 1872. No specific record exists of his participation in the battle, other than his presence with his unit during the valley fighting and subsequent defense of Reno Hill. One of the oldest men in the battle. Married with 4 daughters and 3 sons. Buried in VA Military Cemetery, Dayton, OH.

Gray, PVT John R. — b. Troy, NY, 8 Apr 1855–d. Worcester, MA, 30 Apr 1915. Company B, private. Gray eyes, brown hair, fair complexion; 5' 9¾" tall. Enlisted 23 Mar 1876. Remained at the Powder River Depot. Married to Tillie J. Gray. Resided at 105 Plantation Street, Worcester, MA. Buried in East Pepperell, MA.

Gray, PVT William S. — b. New Bedford, MA, 1855–d. unknown. Company G, private. Hazel eyes, brown hair, dark complexion; 5' 6¾" tall, though one source said he was the shortest trooper in the regiment at 5'¾". Enlisted 10 Apr 1876. Remained at the Powder River Depot. Presence confirmed on June Returns.

Grayson, PVT Edward (aka Edward Wilson) — b. Providence, RI, 1837–d. Fort Adams, RI, of dropsy, 24 Mar 1881. Company G, private. Blue eyes, brown hair, light complexion; 5' 5¾" tall. Second enlistment 18 Dec 1872. Originally detailed for HQ fatigue duty, but Smalley lists him at the battle. No specific record exists of his participation in the battle, other than his presence with his unit during the valley fighting and subsequent defense of Reno Hill.

Green, PVT John (aka Henry Gross) — b. Racine, WI, 1850–d. unknown. Company D, private. Gray eyes, light hair, light complexion; 5' 7" tall. Enlisted 5 Feb 1872. Remained at the Powder River Depot. Presence confirmed on June Returns.

Green, PVT Joseph H. — b. Leitrim, Ireland, 8 Aug 1849–d. Washington, D.C., 13 Apr 1922. Company D, private. Blue eyes, brown hair, fair complexion; 5' 5¾" tall. Enlisted 22 Jan 1872. Rode with his unit in Benteen's battalion, and fought on Reno Hill.

Green, PVT Thomas J. — b. Aurora, IL, Jan 1854–d. Springfield, MA, 1906. Company K, private. Blue eyes, dark hair, dark complexion; 5' 6¾" tall. Enlisted 10 Dec 1875. Remained at the Powder River Depot. Presence confirmed on June Returns.

Gregg, PVT William J. — b. Baltimore, MD, 5 Jul 1847–d. Hampton, VA, 10 Dec 1913. Company F, private. Blue eyes, brown hair, fair complexion; 5' 7" tall. Enlisted 21 Jan 1865 to 29 May 1865 in 13th MD Infantry. Enlisted again 20 Aug 1866 in C Company, Seventh Cavalry. Discharged from F Company 21 Dec 1867 as a corporal. Enlisted once more on 11 Nov 1872. With the pack train on Reno Hill. Buried in Hampton National Cemetery, Hampton, VA.

Griesner, PVT Julius — b. Neurode, Germany, circa 1844–d. Fort Lewis, CO, 15 Feb 1882. Headquarters: band. Private. Gray eyes, light hair, fair complexion; 5' 5¾" tall. Remained at Powder River Depot. Presence confirmed on June Returns.

Griffin, PVT Patrick — b. Dingle, County Kerry, Ireland, 1848–d. 25 Jun 1876, killed at the Little

Big Horn. Company C, private. Black eyes, dark hair; ruddy; 5' 9" tall. In the Seventh Cavalry since 16 Oct 1872. In the C Company charge off Battle Ridge–Calhoun Hill, but body was never identified. May have died in Calhoun Coulee, Finley-Finckle Ridge, the Keogh Sector, or possibly even Last Stand Hill. Listed number 29 in "June Returns, Alterations … Killed in action."

Grimes, PVT Andrew— b. Allegheny, PA, circa 1847–d. unknown. Company I, private. Blue eyes, light hair, fair complexion; 5' 9¼" tall. Enlisted, 24 Sep 1875. Remained at Fort Lincoln for duty.

Groesbeck, John H. *see* **Vickory, SGT John H.**

Gross, PVT George H.— b. Germany, 1845–d. 25 Jun 1876, killed at the Little Big Horn. Company I, private. Blue eyes, light hair, fair complexion; 5' 6½" tall. Enlisted 18 Oct 1872. Body never identified, but in all likelihood he was killed in the Keogh Sector. Listed number 155 in "June Returns, Alterations … Killed in action."

Gross, Henry *see* **Green, PVT John**

Groves, Hiram *see* **Brown, PVT Hiram**

Guessbacher (also Geesbacher), **PVT Gabriel**— b. Bavaria, Germany, 1846–d. Warwick, ND, 4 Aug 1916. Company I, private. Light brown hair, brown eyes, ruddy complexion; 5' 5¼" tall. Enlisted 6 Oct 1873. Remained at the Powder River Depot. Presence confirmed on June Returns. Not married.

Haack, PVT Henry— b. York County, PA, 1838–d. Washington D.C., 27 Jul 1881. Company H, private. Black eyes, black hair, dark complexion; 5' 7½" tall. Enlisted 4 Oct 1872. Recommended by Benteen for medal of distinguished gallantry.

Hackett, PVT John— b. Dublin, Ireland, May 1851–d. Fort Sheridan, IL, 25 Feb 1904. Company G, private. Gray eyes, brown hair, fair complexion; 5' 4¼" tall. Enlisted 14 Nov 1872. LT Wallace's orderly. WIA in left arm during hilltop fight. Married Esther Smith 28 Jun 1902. Buried in Post Cemetery, Fort Sheridan, IL.

Hagan (aka Eagan), **CPL Thomas P.**— b. Ireland, 1847 or 1848–d. 25 Jun 1876, killed at the Little Big Horn. Company E, corporal. Gray eyes, sandy hair, light complexion; 5' 5½" tall. Enlisted 12 Sep 1873. Had a half-sister, Ella, who lived in Ireland. While his body was not specifically identified, he may have been one of the unknowns on either the South Skirmish Line or in Deep Ravine. Listed number 55 in "June Returns, Alterations … Killed in action."

Hagemann, CPL Otto— b. Hanover, Germany, 1859–d. 25 Jun 1876, killed at the Little Big Horn during Reno's retreat. Company G, corporal. Brown eyes, brown hair, fair complexion; 5' 9½" tall. Enlisted 2 Oct 1873. Killed near river on east side during Reno's retreat. His remains were found by Roman Rutten, but Rutten did not comment of the condition of the body. The packer, John Frett, apparently counted "seventy-five well-defined wounds on his body, and that his limbs were cut off" [Hardorff, *On the LBH with Walter Camp*, p. 68, footnote 7]. Listed number 128 in "June Returns, Alterations … Killed in action."

Hager (aka Hayer), **PVT John**— b. Buffalo, NY, 1858–d. unknown. Company D, private. Hazel eyes, brown hair, fair to ruddy complexion; 5' 8½" tall. Enlisted 10 Jan 1872. Rode with his unit in Benteen's battalion, and fought on Reno Hill.

Haley, PVT Timothy— b. Cork, Ireland, 26 Dec 1846–d. Washington, D.C., 31 Dec 1913. Company H, private. Blue eyes, brown hair, fair complexion; 5' 6½" tall. Enlisted from 12 Oct 1864 to 22 Jun 1866 in Fourth U.S. Volunteer Infantry. Enlisted from Jan 1867 to Dec 1871 in 17th Infantry; enlisted 15 Jan 1875 in Seventh Cavalry. Rode with his unit in Benteen's battalion, and fought on Reno Hill. Buried in Soldiers' Home National Cemetery.

Hall, PVT John Curtis— b. Lycoming County, PA, 29 Jan 1852–d. Warsaw, IN, 6 Apr 1908. Company D, private. Hazel eyes, brown hair, ruddy complexion; 5'11" tall. Enlisted 9 Dec 1872. Rode with his unit in Benteen's battalion, and fought on Reno Hill. Totally disabled by gunshot wound in left thigh and knee 7 Jan 1888. Wife's name was Mary; one son. Resided on South Indiana Street, Warsaw, IN, for ten or twelve years. Buried in Lakewood Cemetery, Warsaw.

Hamel or Hammel, George *see* **Howell, SAD George**

Hamilton, BSM Andrew— b. Port Glasgow, Scotland, 1849–d. unknown. Company A: blacksmith. Gray eyes, light hair, fair complexion; 5' 6" tall. Enlisted 17 Apr 1872. No specific record exists of his participation in the battle, other than his presence with his unit during the valley fighting and subsequent defense of Reno Hill.

Hamilton, PVT Henry— b. Dexter, NY, 1842–d. 25 Jun 1876, killed at the Little Big Horn. Company L, private. Blue eyes, brown hair, fair complexion; 5' 6¼" tall. Second enlistment 20 Jan 1872. His niece, Susan Kirschermann of Yakima, WA, claimed her uncle ran away from home to be a drummer boy in the Civil War. In all likelihood he was killed on Calhoun Hill, though the possibility exists he was one of those killed during the panic through the Keogh Sector. No remains found during the 1984–1985 archaeological work match his description. Listed number 206 in "June Returns, Alterations … Killed in action."

Hammon, PVT George W.— b. Fulton County, OH, 1852–d. 25 Jun 1876, killed at the Little Big Horn. Company F, private. Blue eyes, dark brown hair, florid complexion; 5' 8" tall. Brother of John E. Hammon of G Company, Seventh Cavalry. Enlisted 9 Sep 1873. Extra duty as hospital attendant on the campaign. While his body was never identified, both his unit and assignment that day leads us to believe he was killed on Custer/Last Stand Hill, somewhere near Dr. Lord. Listed number 108 in "June Returns, Alterations … Killed in action."

Hammon, CPL John E.— b. Lynchburg, OH, 4 Dec 1857–d. Sturgis, SD, 19 Jan 1909. Company G, corporal. Blue eyes, dark brown hair, fair complexion; 5' 7¼" tall. Brother of George W. Hammon, F Company, who was killed with Yates and Custer. Enlisted 1 Sep 1873. Promoted to SGT 25 Jun 1876. No specific record exists of his participation in the battle, other than his presence with his unit during the valley fighting and subsequent defense of Reno Hill. Survived by widow Victoria and 6 children. Buried in Bear Butte Cemetery.

Hanley, SGT Richard P.— b. Boston, MA, 1843–d. Boston, MA, 13 Sep 1923. Company C, sergeant. Blue eyes, dark hair; 5'11½" tall. Was into his fifth enlistment, 18 Sep 1873. With pack train. Awarded MH for recapturing, under heavy enemy fire for twenty minutes and without orders, a stampeding pack mule named Barnum, loaded with ammo. In an interview with Walter Mason Camp, he claims Fitzgerald (C Company) was with the column and straggled back from the vicinity of MTC. Retired as a sergeant. Lived at 23 Green Street, Boston, MA. Also, employed by (lieutenant) Francis Gibson in the Street Department in NYC for a number of years.

Hardden, PVT William— b. NYC, 1850–d. unknown. Company D, private. Gray eyes, sandy hair, dark complexion; 5' 8" tall. Enlisted 27 Jan 1872. Rode with his unit in Benteen's battalion, and fought on Reno Hill.

Hardy, TMP William G. (aka Charles Laurse)— b. Staten Island, NY, 20 Dec 1849–d. San Francisco, CA, 7 Apr 1919. Company A. Trumpeter. Gray eyes, light hair, fair complexion; 5' 6⅜" tall. Enlisted from 26 Jan 1864 to 1 Jun 1866, Fourth Cavalry. Enlisted 15 Dec 1874, Seventh Cavalry. No specific record exists of his participation in the battle, other than his presence with his unit during the valley fighting and subsequent defense of Reno Hill. Wife's name was Alice (d. 26 May 1938). Resided in California for 12 years; 201 1/2 Virginia Street, San Francisco, CA. Died at Letterman General Hospital, Presidio: diabetes, gangrene. Buried in Presidio National Cemetery, New Section, Grave 1133A.

Hare, 2LT Luther Rector— b. Noblesville, IN, 24 Aug 1851–d. Washington, D.C., 22 Dec 1929. Company K. On 24 Jun 1876 Hare was assigned as LT Varnum's assistant to command the scouts. Supposed to have been a fairly big man [see Donovan, *A Terrible Glory*]; baby-faced. DOR: 17 Jun 1874. A junior 2LT, outranking only Sturgis and Reily, as well as the attached LT Crittenden. Family moved to Texas when he was two years old. His father fought for the Confederacy. Graduated from the USMA. Appointed to Company K out of West Point. Took part in the Yellowstone Expedition. Detached to scouts (24 June) and commanded the Crows during the battle. Fought with Reno in bottoms. Put in charge of "led horses" while Reno fought on foot. He moved into the timber, and then made it to Reno Hill. Both Hare and Godfrey were roundly praised for their bravery and initiative in covering the move back from Weir Peak. As good a rider as there was in the regiment. Also fought in the Nez Percé campaign.

Hare was one of the more enigmatic officers in the regiment after the battle and was very close-mouthed regarding the events of those days. He did not want anything to come out that might hurt Libbie Custer, whom he greatly admired even though he was not part of the so-called "Custer Clan." Refused to answer many letters written to him by various authors, soldiers, and historians. He was interviewed by Walter Camp in 1910, and that is surprising. In a September 14, 1895, letter to Theodore Goldin, Benteen wrote, "Hare should have been brevetted for L. B. Horn…" [Carroll, *The Benteen-Goldin Letters,* p. 232], a compliment indeed, especially coming from Fred Benteen.

Fought at Wounded Knee (1890) and in the Philippines during the Spanish-American War. Retired on a disability in 1903. Married Virginia Hancock (niece of GEN Winfield Scott Hancock), 21 Jun 1878. They had three daughters. Buried in Arlington National Cemetery.

Harlfinger, PVT Gustav— b. Baden, Germany, 1847–d. unknown. Company D, private. Hazel eyes, light hair, fair complexion; 5' 6¾" tall. Enlisted 6 Aug 1866; enlisted 7 Sep 1871. Remained at the Powder River Depot. Presence confirmed on June Returns.

Harrington, 2LT Henry Moore— b. Albion, NY, 30 Apr 1849–d. 25 Jun 1876, killed at the Little

Big Horn. Company C. Probably the acting CO of the company as it is assumed that Tom Custer rode as an aide to his brother. DOR: 14 Jun 1872, same as Varnum and Wallace; third-ranking 2LT on campaign behind Hodgson and Edgerly. Graduated from USMA in 1872 with Varnum and Wallace. Body never found. Wore white canvas trousers and a blue blouse. It is said his watch or watchcase (minus the guts) was either found or bought from an Indian. Took part in both the Yellowstone (1873) and Black Hills (1874) expeditions. Bruce Liddic agrees Harrington commanded C Company on 25 Jun 1876 [*Vanishing Victory*, p. 108], as does Donovan [*A Terrible Glory*, p. 218]. Parents were Shelly A. (or William; "Wm." Was engraved in the gold watchcase) and Nancy K. Harrington. Family moved to Coldwater, MI, when Harrington was a youngster. Married Grace Berard, 20 Nov 1872. Daughter of John and Mary Berard of Highland Falls, NY. On leave of absence from 10 Oct 1875 to 9 Mar 1876. At Fort Seward, D.T., 9 Mar 1876 to 17 Apr 1876 when C Company left for Fort Lincoln. Wife disappeared in Dallas in 1885 while visiting her sister, Minnie Matthews, in TX. Found nine days later suffering from amnesia and pneumonia. She was still alive in 1903, and was granted a pension by the U.S. Senate from 18 Feb 1903. Two children: Grace Aileen (b. Fort Lincoln, D.T., 26 Dec 1873) and Harry Berard (b. 26 Sep 1874–d. Fort Rice, 11 Oct 1916). Daughter was postmistress at USMA from Dec 1927. Had been a teacher in Grand Rapids, MI. She attended 60th anniversary ceremony at LBH on 25 Jun 1936. LT Harrington was also survived by a brother, C. D. Harrington of Montpelier, VT.

There is some evidence — more anecdotal than real — suggesting he may have been among the last survivors, and as the battle neared its conclusion, made a break for it. He rode a huge and strong horse — a unique, large sorrel and its identification by some warriors may have made Harrington the "chief" the Indians referred to as "the bravest man they had ever seen" — and breaking through the encirclement, he was pursued by several (7) Indians. One account says he shot himself rather than be captured (Hardorff), though many historians largely discount a Harrington suicide. More than one account has a body being found in a dry lakebed, ravine, or sag, some distance from the battlefield (Hardorff) and some time afterwards. Benteen admitted he could not find Harrington. Moylan and Gibson agreed.

Harrington, PVT Weston — b. Alton, OH, 9 Feb 1855–d. 25 Jun 1876, killed at the Little Big Horn. Company L, private. Brown eyes, brown hair, fair complexion; 5' 8" tall. Enlisted 4 Nov 1872. Son of

Peter (b. 14 Jul 1820–d. 17 Feb 1904) and Mary A. Harrington (b. 10 May 1828–d. 14 Jul 1875). Gravestone in Lot 83, Section 2, Alton Cemetery, Prairie Township, Franklin County, OH. Body found near top of South Skirmish Line below Custer Hill, though the archaeologists, during the 1984–1985 excavation of the Custer field, speculated that it might have been Harrington's remains that were found at Marker 200 in the Keogh Sector. A number of other troopers fit the morphology requirements, however. Listed number 203 in "June Returns, Alterations … Killed in action."

Harris, PVT David W. — b. Indianapolis, IN, 1852–d. sometime after 1908. Company A, private. Blue eyes, brown hair, florid complexion; 5' 6¾" tall. Enlisted 29 Sep 1873. One of five who volunteered to go on picket duty with CPL Roy the night of 25 June. Awarded MH for also volunteering to carry water up to Reno Hill, 26 Jun 1876. Married Mary Duffy 19 Jul 1881 at Fort Meade. Children: John Silas, Willie, and Richard. Resided in Washington, D.C., in 1897 and 1908.

Harris, PVT James — b. Yarmouth, Nova Scotia, Canada, Aug 1854–d. unknown. Company D, private. Gray eyes, dark hair, fair complexion; 5' 6½" tall. Enlisted 21 Sep 1875. Rode with his unit in Benteen's battalion, and fought on Reno Hill.

Harris, PVT William M. — b. Madison County, KY, 1850–d. killed in a gunfight, Berea, KY, 6 Jun 1885. Company D, private. Gray eyes, light hair, fair complexion; 5'10½" tall. Enlisted 25 Aug 1871. Rode with his unit in Benteen's battalion, and fought on Reno Hill. Awarded MH for voluntarily bringing water up to Reno Hill from the LBH.

Harrison, SGT Thomas Wilford — b. Sligo, Ireland, 1849–d. Philadelphia, PA, 25 Dec 1917. Company D, sergeant. Blue eyes, brown hair, fair complexion; 5' 9½" tall. Enlisted from 9 Aug 1866 to 9 Aug 1871 in Seventh Cavalry. Re-upped 10 Aug 1871. In Washita campaign of 1868. Vern Smalley claims he was Edgerly's orderly on 25 Jun 1876. Rode with his unit in Benteen's battalion, and fought on Reno Hill. Recommended for a medal for gallantry in LBH fight. Married Margaret Fargus 11 Jan 1882. Buried in Grave 1, Lot 7, Section 12, Range 2, Holy Cross Cemetery, Philadelphia.

Harrison, CPL William H. — b. Gloucester, MA, 1845–d. 25 Jun 1876, killed at the Little Big Horn. Company L, corporal. Hazel eyes, auburn hair, dark complexion; 5' 7¾" tall. Third enlistment 9 Oct 1875. In all likelihood he was killed on Calhoun Hill, though the possibility exists he was one of those killed during the panic through the

Keogh Sector. No remains found during the 1984–1985 archaeological work match his description. Listed number 185 in "June Returns, Alterations … Killed in action."

Hathersall, PVT James— b. Liverpool, England, 1849–d. 25 Jun 1876, killed at the Little Big Horn. Company C, private. Blue eyes, light hair; 5' 6" tall. Was in his second enlistment, 13 Sep 1875. In the C Company charge off Battle Ridge–Calhoun Hill, but body was never identified. May have died in Calhoun Coulee, Finley-Finckle Ridge, the Keogh Sector, or possibly even LSH. Listed number 30 in "June Returns, Alterations … Killed in action."

Hauggi (also Hange, Hanggie, and Haugge), **PVT Louis**— b. Alsace, Germany, 1851 (it is unclear what part of Alsace he was born in; in 1851, most of the territory was within France, but was annexed by Bismarck as Elsaß— Lothringen in 1871)–d. 25 Jun 1876, killed at the Little Big Horn. Company L, private. Brown eyes, light hair, fair complexion; 5' 7" tall. Enlisted 6 Oct 1873. In all likelihood he was killed on Calhoun Hill, though the possibility exists he was one of those killed during the panic through the Keogh Sector. No remains found during the 1984–1985 archaeological work match his description. Listed number 204 in "June Returns, Alterations … Killed in action."

Heath, FAR William H.— b. Staffordshire, England, 1848–d. 25 Jun 1876, killed at the Little Big Horn. Company L: company farrier. Blue eyes, brown hair, dark complexion; 5' 7¼" tall. Enlisted 9 Oct 1875. In all likelihood he was killed on Calhoun Hill, though the possibility exists he was one of those killed during the panic through the Keogh Sector. No remains found during the 1984–1985 archaeological work match his description. Listed number 190 in "June Returns, Alterations … Killed in action."

Hegner, PVT Francis— b. Berlin, Germany (Prussia), 1843–d. Kenockee Township, MI, 17 Jan 1891. Company F, private. Blue eyes, light hair, fair complexion; 5' 9" tall. Assigned to Department QM as laborer.

Heid, PVT George (also listed as Larry Heid)— b. Bavaria, 1842–d. Fort Totten, D.T., 1 Feb 1887. Company M, private. Gray eyes, dark hair, ruddy complexion; 5' 6¼" tall. Second enlistment 17 Jun 1870. No specific record exists of his participation in the battle, other than his presence with his unit during the valley fighting and subsequent defense of Reno Hill. Buried at Custer Battlefield National Cemetery.

Heim, PVT John— b. St. Louis, MO, 1851 or 1852–d. 25 Jun 1876, killed at the Little Big Horn. Company E, private. Brown eyes, light hair, fair complexion; 5'1" tall. Enlisted 19 Jan 1875. While his body was not specifically identified, he may have been one of the unknowns on either the South Skirmish Line or in Deep Ravine. Listed number 69 in "June Returns, Alterations … Killed in action."

Helmer, TMP Julius— b. Hanover, Germany, 1846–d. 26 Jun 1876, killed at the Little Big Horn, on Reno Hill. Company K: trumpeter. Gray eyes, brown hair, light complexion; 5' 9¾" tall. Third enlistment 10 Jul 1875. Killed on Reno Hill, late in battle. Shot in abdomen. Quite possibly the last one to die in the battle itself, though Hammer claimed he was shot on the evening of the 25th. Was only about a foot from LT Hare when he was shot, LT Godfrey standing quite close, as well. Listed number 181 in "June Returns, Alterations … Killed in action."

Henderson, PVT George W.— b. Hornellsville, NY, 1854–d. unknown. Company G, private. Gray eyes, light hair, ruddy complexion; 5' 7½" tall. Enlisted 2 Mar 1876. Remained at the PRD. Presence confirmed on June Returns.

Henderson, PVT John— b. Cork, Ireland, 1849–d. 25 Jun 1876, killed at the Little Big Horn. Company E, private. Gray eyes, light hair, fair complexion; 5' 7¾" tall. Second enlistment, 22 Sep 1875. While his body was not specifically identified, he may have been one of the unknowns on either the South Skirmish Line or in Deep Ravine. Listed number 71 in "June Returns, Alterations … Killed in action."

Henderson, PVT Sykes— b. Armstrong Country, PA, 1844 or 1845–d. 25 Jun 1876, killed at the Little Big Horn. Company E, private. Brown eyes, brown hair, fair complexion; 5' 8" tall. Second enlistment 3 Dec 1872. Had been reduced in rank from sergeant to private, 20 Mar 1875, though acquitted of a charge of brutally beating a deaf and dumb black man. While his body was not specifically identified, he may have been one of the unknowns on either the South Skirmish Line or in Deep Ravine. Listed number 70 in "June Returns, Alterations … Killed in action."

Hester, Andrew *see* **Cheever, PVT Ami**

Hetesimer, PVT Adam— b. Cincinnati, OH, 1847–d. 25 Jun 1876, killed at the Little Big Horn. Company I, private. Blue eyes, black hair, dark complexion; 5' 7½" tall. Enlisted 6 Oct 1875. Body never identified, but in all likelihood he was killed in the Keogh Sector. Listed number 158 in "June Returns, Alterations … Killed in action."

Hetler, PVT Jacob—b. Mansfield, OH, 2 Aug 1852–d. Greenwich, OH, 22 Feb 1944. Company D, private. Blue eyes, light hair, light complexion; 5' 6" tall. Enlisted 3 Feb 1872. Rode with his unit in Benteen's battalion, and fought on Reno Hill. WIA in left leg on 25 Jun and in the back the following day.

Heyn, 1SG William—b. Bremen, Germany, 12 Jul 1848–d. Washington, D.C., 11 Jun 1910. Company A: first sergeant. Blue eyes, brown hair, fair complexion. 5' 7¾" tall. Enlisted 28 Feb 1867 in Third Cavalry. Discharged 28 Feb 1872 at Benecia Barracks, CA. Enlisted 6 Apr 1872 in NYC in Seventh Cavalry. Wounded in left knee during valley fight. Resided in Washington, D.C., for 30 years. Died of heart disease at 716 P Street, NW. Buried in the Soldiers' Home National Cemetery. From Ephriam Dickson: "Sergeant Heyn noted that he was on the skirmish line with Reno's three companies. He mentioned that he did not fire his weapon very much as he was directing the movements of the soldiers. At some point on the line, his weapon jammed. The shell ejector failed and he borrowed a ramrod in order to get it out. Then the soldiers fell back to the woods, where Sgt Heyn was wounded in the left knee. He noted that there were no commands to leave the woods and scale the hill. 'The men straggled out and started across the flat without any particular command and no bugle being blown, the officers digging spurs into their horses and every man for himself.'"

Hieber, William *see* **Huber, PVT William**

Hiley, PVT John S. (aka Forbes, John Stuart Stuart [double "Stuart" is correct])—b. Rugby, England, 28 May 1849–d. 25 Jun 1876, killed at the Little Big Horn. Company E, private. Hazel eyes, light brown hair, fair complexion; 6' tall. Enlisted 20 Jan 1872 in NYC. Hiley/Forbes was of noble birth, his brother being a baronet. Listed in Foster's *Peerage and Baronetage, 1883.* Apparently left home because of gambling problems and when he enlisted, he used his brother-in-law's last name, Hiley. There is a plaque in St. John's Episcopal Church, West End, Edinburgh, Scotland, in Forbes' memory. Son of Charles Hay Forbes (b. 15 Oct 1806–d. 15 Nov 1859) and Jemina Rebecca MacDonnell Forbes. His father resided in Canaan Park, Edinburgh, Scotland. Mother was the third daughter of Alexander Ranaldson MacDonnell of Glengary. His parents were married 5 Jul 1833. Brothers and sisters: Sir William, 9th Baronet; Rev. Alexander Charles (b. 15 Apr 1837); James Edmund (b. 14 Nov 1851); Elizabeth Jane Stuart; and Henrietta Jemina. While his body was not specifically identified, he may have been one of the unknowns on either the South

Skirmish Line or in Deep Ravine. Listed number 72 in "June Returns, Alterations ... Killed in action."

Hill, 1SG James—b. Edinburgh, Scotland, 15 Aug 1826–d. Wooster, OH, 18 Nov 1906. Company B: first sergeant. Blue eyes, light hair, fair complexion; 5'10" tall. Served nine years in the 71st Highland Light Infantry. Enlisted from 1 Oct 1856 to 3 Oct 1861 in 4th Artillery at Oswego, NY. Fought in Seminole War in Florida; Utah Expedition in 1857; forts Henry and Donaldson, Shiloh, Missionary Ridge in Civil War. Enlisted from 28 Sep 1865 to 1 Jul 1868 in Second Cavalry; 24 Jun 1869 to 24 Jun 1874 in 19th Infantry; 22 Mar 1875 in Seventh Cavalry. Appointed ordnance sergeant, Seventh Cavalry, 20 Jan 1877. With the pack train escort, Company B. Arrived and fought on Reno Hill. One of the oldest men in the battle. Considered utterly fearless. Married Nannie Lowery (b. 1853–d. 1911) in Wooster, OH. Lived on Callowhill Street and Maiden Lane, Wooster, OH, and died there of liver problems. Buried in Lot 1220NE, Section 18, Wooster Cemetery.

Hodgson, 2LT Benjamin "Benny" Hubert (nicknamed by the enlisted men: "Jack of Clubs")—b. Philadelphia, PA, 30 Jun 1848–d. 25 Jun 1876, killed at the Little Big Horn. Company B. Not a big man; fairly short in stature. Served as Reno's adjutant during the battle. DOR: 15 Jun 1870. Hodgson and Edgerly were the senior 2LTs on the campaign. Graduated from USMA in 1870. Joined the regiment in the field in Colorado. Accompanied his unit on reconstruction duty in the south and was on both the Yellowstone Expedition (1873) and the Black Hills Expedition (1874). According to Klokner, Hodgson withdrew his resignation papers for "the thrill of one last campaign" [p. 72]. Other sources claim he was going to be court-martialed for certain infractions and faced dismissal from the service. Killed at the ford, retreating back across river. Body fell at foot of bluffs, then moved to hilltop for burial. May have been buried with SGT O'Harra (M), though Liddic, *Vanishing Victory,* p. 179, writes, "The body of LT Hodgson was finally recovered and buried by a small party on a little knoll 'overlooking the river with a cedar tree at his head.'" Body removed a year later and transported to family. Maybe the most popular officer in the command. A particular favorite of Reno and considered a fierce fighter despite his diminutive size. Close friend of Varnum's. Benteen also thought very highly of him, referring to their relationship as that of "bosom cronies" [Carroll, *The Benteen-Goldin Letters,* p. 285].

SAD John A. Bailey told Walter Camp: "Hodgson's body was found on the bank at the edge of the river. He had been stripped by the Indians before being found on the night of the 26th. His body was buried about 40 or 50 feet up the hill from McDougall's entrenchment under a little bush-like tree, which is no longer there, on the night of June 26" [Liddic/Harbaugh, *Camp on Custer,* pages 81–82. In footnote 166, Liddic mentions that McDougall said three men helped recover Hodgson's body on the night of the 26th: Criswell, Ryan, and Bailey, all of Company B.]. His feet were in the water when he was found. Re-interred in October 1877, in Lot 126, Section 10, Row West #2, space 2 from south line, Laurel Hill Cemetery, Philadelphia, PA.

Hoehn, PVT Max — b. Berlin, Germany, 26 Dec 1854–d. Sturgis, SD, 6 Jan 1911. Company L, private. Gray eyes, light hair, fair complexion; 5' 6¾" tall. Enlisted 4 Oct 1873. In Black Hills expedition. Remained at the Powder River Depot. In charge of regimental records. Presence confirmed on June Returns. Father was born in Mecklenburg, mother in Berlin. Married Annie Lang, 14 Jul 1879. Died of heart disease. Buried in St. Aloysius Cemetery, Sturgis, SD.

Hohmeyer, 1SG Frederick — b. Darmstadt, Germany, 1849–d. 25 Jun 1876, killed at the Little Big Horn. Company, first sergeant. Gray eyes, light hair, dark complexion; 5' 7½" tall. Recent enlistment, his third, 10 May 1875. Probably with the regiment since 1866. Married to Mary (b. about 1842 in Würtemburg, Germany) and had four children: Lizzie (b. 1870, Kansas); William (b. 1872, SC); Lena (b. 1874, D.T.); and Nellie (b. 1876, D.T.). Wife remarried (Latrobe Bromwell) and moved to 1304 9th Street, Washington, D.C. Hohmeyer's body was identified in Deep Ravine by PVT Frank Berwald and CPT McDougall. Hohmeyer's name was stitched on a sock. Listed number 52 in "June Returns, Alterations ... Killed in action."

Holahan, PVT Andrew (also seen spelled Holohan) — b. Kilkenny, Ireland, 1849–d. unknown. Company K, private. Blue eyes, brown hair, ruddy complexion; 5' 7¾" tall. Enlisted 22 Dec 1874. Remained at the Powder River Depot. Presence confirmed on June Returns.

Holcomb, PVT Edward P. — b. Granby, CT, 1845–d. 25 Jun 1876, killed at the Little Big Horn. Company I, private. Black eyes, black hair, dark complexion; 5' 6½" tall. Enlisted 28 Oct 1872. Body never identified, but in all likelihood he was killed in the Keogh Sector. Listed number 156 in "June Returns, Alterations ... Killed in action."

Holden, PVT Henry *(aka James Hurd)* — b. London, England, 1836–d. East Brighton, England, 14 Dec 1905. Company D, private. Gray eyes, light hair, light complexion; 5' 5" tall. Enlisted in the 59th MA Volunteers from 5 Jan 1864 to 30 Jul 1865. Enlisted from 23 Nov 1865 to 23 Nov 1868 in 8th Infantry; enlisted 23 Dec 1868 to 3 Dec 1871; enlisted 9 Jan 1872 in Seventh Cavalry. Awarded MH for voluntarily bringing water up to Reno Hill under galling Indian fire. Returned to England; first wife, Eleanor, died 7 Apr 1894; he then married Frances Ann Launders 17 Nov 1894. Buried in Brighton and Preston Cemetery, Hartington Road, Brighton, England.

Holmstead (also Homstead, Homestead), **PVT Frederick** — b. Copenhagen, Denmark, 1849–d. FAL, 27 Mar 1880. Company A, private. Brown eyes, brown hair, fair complexion; 5' 8¼" tall. Enlisted 6 Nov 1872. Wounded in left wrist. One of twenty men — one officer, three scouts, sixteen enlisted men — left in the timber in the valley bottoms. Eventually made his way up to Reno Hill. Holmstead may have been the A Company trooper who left the timber with Private John Lattman. They had recovered a couple of G Company horses — Lattman had LT McIntosh's — and left the woods, not being able to find the others. In *Camp on Custer,* p. 77, footnote 157, Bruce Liddic speculates that the "A Company trooper" was one of three who fit a description Lattman gave Walter Camp: privates Drinan, McDonald, or Sweetser. He does not mention Holmstead, probably because Lattman said the fellow was about 22 or 23 years of age and Holmstead was 27, yet Holmstead fits the height and hair-color parameters Lattman left us. (The only other A Company man left behind was Armstrong and he was 39 years old, hardly someone who could be mistaken for a 22-year-old lad. Armstrong was killed.) Also, there is no evidence any of the other three had been left behind, yet we know Holmstead was. Failing to reach Reno Hill, they returned to the woods where Lattman reported the A Company man being shot and falling off his horse. Lattman saw no more of him. Holmstead was wounded in the wrist and that could have precipitated the fall from the horse.

Hook, PVT Stanton — b. Coshocton, OH, 1845–d. heart disease, Denver, CO, 8 Oct 1898. Company A, private. Blue eyes, brown hair, fair complexion; 5' 7¾" tall. Enlisted 25 Oct 1863 to 20 Feb 1865 in Ninth OH Cavalry; enlisted in the Seventh Cavalry 12 Oct 1875. No specific record exists of his participation in the battle, other than his presence with his unit during the valley fighting and subsequent defense of Reno Hill. Wife: Martha Jane Hook. Resided at 1254 Champa Street, Denver, CO. Buried in East 1/2, Lot 18, Block 17, Fairmount Cemetery, Denver.

Horn, PVT George— b. Andalusia, Spain, 1844–d. unknown. Company D, private. Dark eyes, dark hair, fair complexion; 5' 6" tall. Enlisted 12 Jan 1872. Rode with his unit in Benteen's battalion, and fought on Reno Hill.

Horn, PVT Marion E.— b. Richmond, IN, 26 Aug 1853–d. 25 Jun 1876, killed at the Little Big Horn. Company I, private. Hazel eyes, brown hair, florid complexion; 5' 6½" tall. Enlisted 18 Nov 1872. Body never identified, but in all likelihood he was killed in the Keogh Sector. Listed number 157 in "June Returns, Alterations … Killed in action."

Horner, PVT Jacob— b. NYC, 6 Oct 1854 (possibly 1855)–d. Bismarck, ND, 21 Sep 1951. Company K, private. Black eyes, black hair, dark complexion; 5' 6" tall. Enlisted 8 Apr 1876. Remained at the Powder River Depot. Presence confirmed on June Returns. Son of Jacob and Anna Mary Richard Horner. Parents arrived Alsace in 1848, but returned in 1857. Jacob Jr. returned to the U.S. when he was fifteen. Last surviving member of the Seventh Cavalry who participated in the Sioux campaign of 1876.

Hose, CPL George— b. Hesse-Kassel, Germany, 29 Apr 1850–d. Lake Nebagamon, WI, 24 Sep 1924. Company K, corporal. Gray eyes, brown hair, dark complexion; 5' 7" tall. Enlisted from 2 Nov 1865 to 2 Nov 1868 in Third Infantry. Enlisted from 24 Dec 1869 to 24 Dec 1874 in Seventh Cavalry. Enlisted 1 Jan 1875. Promoted to SGT 12 Jul 1876. Rode with his unit in Benteen's battalion, and fought on Reno Hill. Also in Nez Percé campaign and fight at Snake Creek 30 Sep 1877. Married Carrie Cole, 4 Dec 1881. Children: Laura B., Elsie B., Marie W., and George C.

Houghtaling, PVT Charles H.— b. Hudson City, NY, 1844–d. Fort Lewis, CO, 14 Aug 1881. Company D, private. Hazel eyes, black hair, dark complexion; 5' 4½" tall. Enlisted from 27 Nov 1868 to 21 Aug 1871; enlisted 8 Sep 1871 in Seventh Cavalry. Promoted to sergeant 1 Jul 1876 for conspicuous bravery during LBH fight. Re-upped 8 Sep 1876. Accidentally killed PVT Joseph Kelley, whose brother was in E Company. Convicted of first-degree manslaughter and discharged 28 Feb 1877. Reenlisted 9 Jun 1880 in the Thirteenth Infantry. Wife died 13 Aug 1876, leaving two children: Andrew and Anna. Died of pleurisy and buried in post cemetery; reinterred in Fort McPherson National Cemetery.

Housen, PVT Edward Gustav (aka Edward Dellienhousen; also seen as Edward Gustaf Dalliehousen)— b. Pittsburgh, PA, 1850, though some sources claim he was born in Frankfurt in modern-day Germany, 14 Feb 1848–d. 25 Jun 1876, killed at the Little Big Horn. Company D, private. Brown eyes, black hair, dark complexion; 5' 8" tall. Enlisted in 33rd Infantry some time prior to Jul 1867 when he deserted. Enlisted in Seventh Cavalry 5 Jul 1872. Water carrier at the battle; possibly killed at the river, though Ken Hammer, in *The Battlefield Dispatch,* Winter 2005, lists him as "unknown location." Vern Smalley claims no one saw him killed and his body was never found [*Little Bighorn Mysteries,* p. 15–7]. Listed number 51 in "June Returns, Alterations … Killed in action." Carried as American-born in demographic studies, Appendix C.

Howard, PVT Frank (aka Henry Pearsal)— b. Brooklyn, NY, 14 Jun 1851 or 1852 (possibly earlier as he enlisted underage)–d. North Troy, NY, 16 Feb 1935. Company F, private. Blue eyes, light hair, fair complexion; 5' 7¾" tall. First enlisted 26 Jun 1866 for three years. At that time he was listed as 5' 4¼", but he was clearly underage. Enlisted 23 Sep 1875. Dishonorably discharged (desertion) at Fort Totten, D.T., 30 Mar 1878. With pack train (Overfield; for additional confirmation, see Williams, *Military Register of Custer's Last Command,* p. 158).

Howell, SAD George (aka Hamel or Hammel)— b. Cold Spring, NY, 1846–d. 25 Jun 1876, killed at the Little Big Horn. Company C: saddler. Gray eyes, dark hair; 5' 5¾" tall. Well into his second enlistment, 4 Dec 1872. In the C Company charge off Battle Ridge–Calhoun Hill, but body was never identified. May have died in Calhoun Coulee, Finley-Finckle Ridge, the Keogh Sector, or possibly even Last Stand Hill. Listed number 21 in "June Returns, Alterations … Killed in action."

Hoyt, PVT Walter— b. Steuben County, NY, 1847–d. Middleborough, KY, 23 Mar 1903. Company K, private. Blue eyes, brown hair, florid complexion; 5' 6¾" tall. Enlisted in 53rd IN Infantry; enlisted 22 Apr 1870 in 16th Infantry. Deserted 16 Sep 1870. Discharged 29 Apr 1875. Enlisted 19 May 1875 in Seventh Cavalry. Remained at the Powder River Depot. Presence confirmed on June Returns.

Huber (also Hieber), **PVT William**— b. Würtemburg, Germany, 1853–d. 25 Jun 1876, killed at the Little Big Horn. Company E, private. Gray eyes, light brown hair, fair complexion; 5' 7" tall. Enlisted 24 Dec 1874 in Cincinnati, OH. Body found in Deep Ravine by PVT Frank Berwald. Listed number 73 in "June Returns, Alterations … Killed in action."

Huff, Jacob *see* **Emerich, PVT Jacob**

Hughes, PVT Francis Thomas— b. Leavenworth, KS, 1854–d. 25 Jun 1876, killed at the Little Big

Horn. Company L, private. Blue eyes, brown hair, light complexion; 5' 7¾" tall. Enlisted 22 May 1875. Married Mary Jane (Mollie) Madden (laundress), 20 Jul 1871. Children: William T., Francis M., and Charles J. Hughes. In what was probably an "interview" via written correspondence, Walter Camp wrote that PVT Roman "Rutten [M] says Francis T. Hughes of Co. L was the last man of 5 cos. Coming down Sundance [Reno] Creek. He had a big black horse which he could not control and could not ride him in the company and so followed behind" [Camp/Hammer, *Custer in '76,* p. 120]. Hughes' body was identified on Custer Hill. Another report had him in a gully off the South Skirmish Line, in all likelihood in Deep Ravine. Foley (K) said he saw Hughes' body near Custer, but he could have been referring to SGT Hughes (K) [Camp/Hammer, *Custer in '76,* p. 147; also, Liddic/Harbaugh, *Camp on Custer,* p. 73, footnote 143]. TMP David McVeigh (A) said he saw this Hughes "at" the gully near the E Company men. Listed number 205 in "June Returns, Alterations … Killed in action."

Hughes, James *see* **Mullen, SGT John**

Hughes, SGT Robert H.— b. Dublin, Ireland, 1840–d. 25 Jun 1876, killed at the Little Big Horn, part of Custer's HQ command. Company K, sergeant. Staff sergeant attached to regimental HQ. One of three Custer orderlies that day (along with Martini and Dose). Carried Custer's flag. Brown eyes, brown hair, fair complexion; 5' 9" tall. Enlisted from 15 Sep 1868 to 14 Sep 1873 in Seventh Cavalry. Reenlisted 1 Oct 1873. Body may have been one of those found with Custer's on Custer Hill, though most reports say he was found in Deep Ravine, possibly at Markers 9 and 10 at the head of the ravine. He was identified by CPT McDougall in that Cemetery Ravine area. Godfrey said he "was killed near the General on the hill" [Godfrey/Graham, *The Custer Myth,* p. 346]. Forensics examination of the remains found at the site indicates "[t]he individual was over twenty-five years old and about five feet eight inches tall. He was also very robust or well muscled…. Evidently this man was severely mutilated at the time of death" [Scott and Fox, *Archaeological Insights into the Custer Battle,* p. 102]. In an undated interview with Walter Mason Camp — probably in the early 1900s — former private August Siefert claimed Hughes carried the regimental standard, but this is, in all likelihood, incorrect. Other sources claim Hughes carried Custer's personal, swallow-tailed standard, a blue and red pennant with white crossed sabers. Wife's name was Annie and they had three children: Maggie, Miles W., and Thomas Hughes.

Listed number 178 in "June Returns, Alterations … Killed in action."

Hughes, PVT Thomas (also Charles Hughes)— b. County Mayo, Ireland, 21 Feb 1845–d. Nashville, TN, 12 Aug 1911. Company H, private. Gray eyes, dark hair, fair complexion; 5' 8" tall. Enlisted 28 Jan 1864 in 13th NY Artillery; discharged 28 Jun 1865. Enlisted from 7 Jul 1866 to 7 Jul 1869 in Second Infantry; enlisted from 30 Jun 1870 to 30 Dec 1877 in Seventh Cavalry. WIA in leg, but not listed as wounded in the returns of the Seventh Cavalry for Jun 1876. Married Ella Maroney 22 Oct 1897. No children. Buried in Nashville National Cemetery.

Hunt, PVT George— b. Boston, MA, 1851–d. unknown. Company D, private. Blue eyes, light brown hair, ruddy complexion; 5' 7" tall. Enlisted 2 Jun 1873. Rode with his unit in Benteen's battalion, and fought on Reno Hill.

Hunt, PVT John— b. Boston, MA, 1835–d. unknown. Company H, private. Blue eyes, auburn hair, ruddy complexion; 5' 5¼" tall. Second enlistment 1 Sep 1871. Rode with his unit in Benteen's battalion, and fought on Reno Hill.

Hunter, PVT Frank— b. Ireland, 1843–d. Washington, D.C., 29 Dec 1899. Company F, private. Gray eyes, light hair, fair complexion; 5' 5½" tall. Enlisted from 17 Aug 1866 to 17 Aug 1871. Reupped 30 Aug 1871. With pack train (Overfield). Hunter was also the subject of an incredible story of him running across Ford B and though the village to Reno Hill, this one told by Dennis Lynch [Camp/Hammer, *Custer in '76,* pp. 139–140]. See Korn. Resided in U.S. Soldiers' Home. Died of acute alcoholism and exposure to cold. Buried in Soldiers' Home National Cemetery. One child, Frank, from first marriage to Bridget Garrity. His second wife, May, died 4 Jan 1922.

Hurd, PVT James (aka James Hood; also Hurel)— b. Jessamine County, KY, 16 May 1850–d. unknown, but probably Harrodsburg, KY, and some time after 1911. Company D, private. Blue eyes, black hair, dark complexion; 5' 6" tall. Enlisted 30 Aug 1871. Rode with his unit in Benteen's battalion, and fought on Reno Hill. Married Georgeann Quinto, 4 Aug 1884; no children.

Hurd, James *see* **Holden, PVT Henry**

Hutchinson, SGT Rufus D.— b. Butlersville, OH, 1850–d. unknown. Company B, sergeant. Blue eyes, light hair, fair complexion; 5'10" tall. Enlisted 25 Sep 1873. Awarded MH for guarding and carrying wounded, for bringing water up to Reno Hill from the LBH, and for directing men, all under heavy enemy fire. The medal was stolen on 4 Jul 1885 in a St. Louis boarding house and a new one was engraved and sent to him.

Hutter, PVT Anton— b. Bavaria, Germany, 1851–d. in a government hospital, 20 Mar 1910. Company E, private. At Washington, D.C., insane asylum from 9 Jun 1872. Hazel eyes, dark hair, fair complexion; 5'10" tall. Enlisted in 1872. Dropped from rolls on 8 Feb 1877, on expiration of service; discharged from hospital 16 Oct 1878.

Ionson (or Jonson), **PVT Emil O.**— b. Kalmar, Sweden, 1853–d. unknown. Company A, private. Dark eyes, light hair, light complexion; 5' 6½" tall. Enlisted 22 Jun 1874. With packs and in the hilltop fight.

Irvine, William *see* **McClurg, PVT William**

James, PVT John (aka John Cassella)— b. Rome, Italy, 1848–d. unknown. Company E, private. Gray eyes, brown hair, dark complexion; 5'7½" tall. Enlisted 13 May 1872. Discharged in 1877 as a corporal. With the pack train and in the Reno Hill fighting.

James, SGT William Batine— b. Pencnwc Farm, in the parish of Dinas (midway between the port of Fishguard and the medieval town of Newport), County of Pembrokeshire, Wales, 3 Mar 1849–d. 25 Jun 1876, killed at the Little Big Horn. Company E, sergeant. Hazel eyes, light hair, light complexion; 5' 9" tall. Enlisted 5 Feb 1872. Civilian occupation was coachman. Promoted to corporal on 27 Jan 1875 and to sergeant on 3 Mar 1876. He was the sixth of nine children and the oldest boy. His parents were John James, a farmer, and Eleanor Batine, married on 2 Mar 1839 at Haverfordwest. The James family had lived in Pembrokeshire for centuries and claimed direct descent from the ancient earls of Ormonde. After their marriage, the James's set up home at Pencnwc where they farmed 80 acres. John James died suddenly in 1863 at the age of 51. Under the terms of the father's will, the various leases and property he owned were liquidated and the proceeds invested in stocks and public bonds of Great Britain to produce an income for Eleanor and the children. One brother and two sisters subsequently died and were buried with the father in Bryn Henllan Cemetery near Dinas Cross. Eleanor lived on in Swansea, South Wales, with her only surviving son, John Clement James, and she died there on 2 Mar 1885 at the age of 73. John, a bachelor, died at Swansea on 17 May 1903 at the age of 52 and was buried with his mother at Bryn Henllan. He was the last in the line of the Pencnwc James's, so the male line of the family died out. Having worked as a builder or carpenter in Nar-

berth, about ten miles east of Haverfordwest, William, fluent in Welsh and probably English, sailed for America in 1870. He wound up in Chicago. One of his great-uncles was a major general in the Indian Army. Another uncle, Francis Batine, was an ensign in the 1st Regiment of Foot. Served in the 1873 Yellowstone Campaign, the 1874 Black Hills Expedition, and in Alabama in 1875 before his company returned to Dakota Territory and its station at Fort Totten. The unit arrived at Abraham Lincoln on 17 Apr 1876 for the campaign against the Sioux. Chances are, he was one of those troopers killed in Deep Ravine. Listed number 54 in "June Returns, Alterations ... Killed in action."

Jennys, PVT Alonzo (aka John Folsom)— b. NYC, 1848–d. unknown, but probably around Mitchell, SD, and some time after 1904. Company K, private. Gray eyes, brown hair, florid complexion; 5'7" tall. Enlisted from Jun 1863 to Jun 1865 in 16th NY Cavalry. Enlisted 12 Jul 1870 to 12 Jul 1875 in 22nd Infantry; enlisted 14 Mar 1876 in Seventh Cavalry. Deserted 18 Apr 1877. Rode with his unit in Benteen's battalion, and fought on Reno Hill. Married Annina Tangle Head in 1877 in Charles Mix County, D.T. Children: Charlie, Peter, Adel, and Jonny.

Johnson, PVT Benjamin (aka Benjamin Johnson Haverstick)— b. Lancaster, PA, Apr 1845 or 1846–d. Lancaster, PA, 15 Nov 1922. Company G, private. Hazel eyes, dark brown hair, dark complexion; 5'5¾" tall. Enlisted 22 Jun 1875. One of twenty men — one officer, three scouts, sixteen enlisted men — left in the timber in the valley bottoms. Eventually made Reno Hill later that afternoon.

Johnson, Francis *see* **Kennedy, PVT Francis Johnson**

Johnson, PVT Samuel— b. Troy, NY, 1851–d. unknown. Company A, private. Brown eyes, brown hair, sallow complexion; 5'5¾" tall. Enlisted 25 Oct 1872. No specific record exists of his participation in the battle, other than his presence with his unit during the valley fighting and subsequent defense of Reno Hill.

Jones, PVT Henry P. (aka John Bush)— b. Lancaster, PA, 8 Nov 1853–d. unknown, but probably in Rosslyn, VA, and after 1921.. Company I, private. Dark eyes, brown hair, dark complexion; 5' 8¼" tall. Enlisted 8 Oct 1873. With pack train (Overfield). After the service he resided in Rosslyn, VA, and was still living there in 1921.

Jones, PVT Julien D.— b. Boston, MA, 1849–d. 26 Jun 1876, killed at the Little Big Horn while on Reno Hill. Company H, private. Gray eyes, dark brown hair, dark complexion; 5' 6½" tall. Enlisted 7 Aug 1871. Shot in the heart while on the H Company line on Reno Hill next to Charles Windolph and near Meador, 26 June. Listed number 139 in "June Returns, Alterations … Killed in action."

Jordan, PVT John— b. Brooklyn, NY, 1844–d. Hartford, CT, 12 Jan 1906. Company C, private. Hazel eyes, black hair; 5' 5¼" tall. In his second enlistment, 28 Nov 1875. Sentenced to loss of $10 for being drunk on duty, Louisville, 31 Aug 1872. With pack train and on Reno Hill. Resided at 362 Windsor Street, Hartford, CT. Buried in Old North Cemetery, Hartford.

Jungesbluth, PVT Julius C.— b. Brunswick, Germany, circa 1843–d. unknown. Headquarters: band. Private. Brown eyes, brown hair, light complexion; 5' 7" tall. Remained at Powder River Depot. Presence confirmed on June Returns.

Kane, PVT William— b. County Kerry, Ireland, 1834–d. Washington, D.C., 2 Nov 1879. Company C, private. Gray eyes, brown hair, fair complexion; 5' 7½" tall. In the Seventh Cavalry for several years; second enlistment, 21 Nov 1872. Had heart disease and was left at the Yellowstone/Powder River depot. Shipped to FAL, sick, on board steamer *Josephine*. Status uncertain.

Kanipe (also seen spelled Knipe), **SGT Daniel Alexander**— b. Marion, SC, 15 Apr 1853–d. Marion, SC, 18 Jul 1926. Company C, sergeant. Hazel eyes, light hair, 5'11" tall. Enlisted 7 Aug 1872 at Lincolnton. Discharged 7 Aug 1877, then reupped the same day. Discharged again, 6 Aug 1882. Participated in the Yellowstone Expedition of 1873 and the Black Hills Expedition of 1874. Married Bobo's widow a year after LBH. Civilian occupation was a farmer. Interviewed by Walter Camp and explained his name was spelled "Kanipe," but enlistment records show he enlisted as "Knipe." Supposedly sent back with message as the Custer battalions were mounting the bluffs overlooking the beginning of the valley fight, though there is some doubt to this and Kanipe may have been shirking. He wound up with pack train.

For a soldier who did not particularly distinguish himself at the LBH, Daniel Kanipe was the subject of more LBH adventures than practically any other man. In addition to his claim that he was sent back by Tom Custer to hurry the packs along, Kanipe also claimed to have spotted some 75–100 Indians on top of the river bluffs and that was the reason George Custer swung his five-company command off to the right instead of following Reno down the valley. Kanipe was also the man who claimed SGT Bustard (I) was the soldier found in the village — which was incorrect — and the author of the story

about SGT Finckle's horse giving out. In addition, Kanipe claimed it was SGT Finley who took and kept the scalp found at the Rosebud sundance site. Also see "Short, PVT Nathan."

Katzenmaier, PVT Jacob— b. Germany, 1852–d. Fort Meade, D.T., 27 Jan 1880. Company G, private. Blue eyes, light brown hair, fair complexion; 5' 8¾" tall. Enlisted 27 Mar 1876. Remained at the Powder River Depot. Presence confirmed on June Returns.

Kavanagh, PVT John (aka James)— b. Roscommon, Ireland, 1850–d. unknown. Company D, private. Gray eyes, brown hair, ruddy complexion; 5' 6" tall. Enlisted 3 Jan 1872. Rode with his unit in Benteen's battalion, and fought on Reno Hill.

Kavanaugh, PVT Charles— b. Pittsburgh, PA, 1840 (1880 census of Fort Meade lists birthplace as NY)–d. Washington, D.C., 14 Feb 1886. Company M, private. Gray eyes, fair hair, dark complexion; 5' 8¾" tall. Enlisted 7 Aug 1867, Seventh Cavalry. Discharged 7 Aug 1872. Reenlisted 13 Sep 1875 in NYC. 1SG Ryan considered Kavanaugh a troublemaker and it was Ryan's harsh punishing of the man that brought about Ryan's court-martial and reduction to private. Apparently, however, Kavanaugh was not so brave at the LBH. Ryan had to roust him out of the Reno-corral and force him back to the line during the fighting on Reno Hill.

Kavanaugh, PVT Thomas G.— b. Dublin, Ireland, 1844–d. 25 Jun 1876, killed at the Little Big Horn. Company L, private. Gray eyes, red hair, ruddy complexion; 5'11¾" tall. Second enlistment 16 Jan 1873. See SGT Cashan: Kavanaugh could have been killed possibly at the head of Deep Ravine, Markers 9 and 10. Bones found there are consistent with his age and height, though several others, including Cashan fit the description. Forensics examination of the remains found at the site indicates "the individual was over twenty-five years old and about five feet eight inches tall. He was also very robust or well muscled…. Evidently this man was severely mutilated at the time of death" [Scott and Fox, *Archaeological Insights into the Custer Battle,* p. 102]. Listed number 207 in "June Returns, Alterations … Killed in action."

Keefe, PVT John J.— b. County Kerry, Ireland, 8 Feb 1855–d. unknown. Company B, private. Blue eyes, brown hair, fair complexion; 5' 5¾" tall. Enlisted 11 Apr 1876. Discharged 9 Feb 1877 for disability (heart disease). Remained at the Powder River Depot.

Keegan, PVT Michael— b. Wexford, Ireland, 1832–d. Chicago, IL, 23 Jul 1900. Company L, private. Blue eyes, light hair, ruddy complexion;

5'6" tall. Enlisted from 3 Jul 1855 to 3 Jul 1860, 2nd Cavalry. Enlisted from 3 Jul 1860 to 19 Jul 1864; then from 19 Jul 1864 to 19 Jul 1867 in Fifth Cavalry. Enlisted from 19 Jul 1867 to 27 Jul 1872 in Seventh Cavalry and again 2 Aug 1872. Discharged 15 Dec 1876. Remained at the Powder River Depot. Presence confirmed on June Returns. Resided in the U.S. Soldiers' Home and National Military Home, Wood, WI. Buried in Calvary Cemetery, Chicago, IL.

Keller, PVT John J.—b. Lancaster, TN, 1846–d. Butte, MT, 8 Feb 1913. Company D, private. Blue eyes, dark hair, ruddy complexion; 5'6¾" tall. Second enlistment 19 Oct 1873, after serving one year in the Civil War. Rode with his unit in Benteen's battalion, and fought on Reno Hill. Also in the Snake Creek fight in Sep 1877. Married; wife (d. 1910) born in Ireland. Resided in Helena for 38 years: 36 East Cutler Street in 1908. Buried in Resurrection Cemetery, Helena.

Kelley, PVT George—b. NYC, 1 Jan 1847–d. Leavenworth, KS, 21 Oct 1922. Company H, private. Hazel eyes, brown hair, light or dark complexion; 5'5" tall. Enlisted 15 Sep 1861 in 91st NY Infantry. Enlisted 17 Dec 1862 in 1st Artillery; discharged 16 Jul 1866. Enlisted from 26 Sep 1866 to 2 Oct 1869; then enlisted 3 Nov 1869 in 22nd Infantry and discharged 3 Nov 1874. Enlisted 16 Apr 1875 in Seventh Cavalry. Rode with his unit in Benteen's battalion, and fought on Reno Hill. Married Octavus Wooley (d. 17 Sep 1875) in 1874. No children.

Kelly, PVT James—b. Boston, MA, 1840–d. unknown. Company H, private. Blue eyes, light hair, florid complexion; 5'4¼" tall. Enlisted 28 Aug 1866 in Seventh Cavalry; deserted 9 Feb 1868, but surrendered more than five years later on 25 Nov 1873. Rode with his unit in Benteen's battalion, and fought on Reno Hill.

Kelly, TMP James—b. Bangor, ME, 1852–d. unknown. Company B: trumpeter. Blue eyes, brown hair, fair complexion; 5'4" tall. Remained at FAL.

Kelly, PVT John P. (also seen listed as Kidey)—b. Easton, PA, 1848–d. 25 Jun 1876, killed at the Little Big Horn. Company F, private. Hazel eyes, light hair, light complexion; 5'6" tall. Enlisted 3 Jan 1867 and again on 3 Jan 1872, in Unionville, SC, by Tom McDougall. Had been a soldier before. Transferred from Company E to Company F, 20 Apr 1876. In all likelihood he was killed on Last Stand Hill with his unit. Survived by wife and 3 children. Widow married SGT Curtiss (F). Ancestor of Joe Kelly from Toms River, NJ (2009). Listed

number 111 in "June Returns, Alterations … Killed in action."

Kelly (or Kelley), **PVT Patrick** (aka Edward H. Kelly)—b. County Mayo, Ireland, 1841–d. 25 Jun 1876, killed at the Little Big Horn. Company I, private. Gray eyes, sandy hair, fair complexion; 5'5" tall. Enlisted from 16 Sep 1866 to 13 Sep 1871 in Seventh Cavalry. Re-upped the same day. Married Ellen Flynn 25 Mar 1873 in Louisville, KY. Two stepchildren: Susan and Ellen. Bone fragments found at Marker 105 on Last Stand Hill would be consistent with his reported age and height, though most men killed at this location were believed to have been from F Company. Several others fit this description, as well. May have been CPT Myles Keogh's striker. Listed number 159 in "June Returns, Alterations … Killed in action."

Kennedy, PVT Francis Johnson (also known as Francis Johnson, the name he enlisted under)—b. Pacific, MO, 12 May 1854 (death certificate lists birthplace as Ireland and birth date as 24 May 1859; this latter date is probably Kennedy's real birth date — and place of birth — as it appears he was an underage enlistee)–d. St. Paul, MN, 9 Jan 1924. Company I, private. Blue eyes, brown hair, dark complexion; 5'7¼" tall. Enlisted 27 Sep 1875. With pack train, fighting on Reno Hill. Married Mary E. Hogan 2 Jul 1882 (d. 16 May 1913). Children: Mary E., Margaret, Anna, John P., Josephine, Elizabeth, Frank T., and Joseph. Resided in St. Paul, MN, for 45 years. He died of cancer at his home, 863 Hague Avenue. Buried Grave 1, Lot 5, Block 25, Section 40, Calvary Cemetery, next to his wife.

Kenney, Jonathan *see* **McKenna, PVT John**

Kenney, 1SG Michael—b. Galway, Ireland, 1849–d. 25 Jun 1876, killed at the Little Big Horn. Company F: first sergeant. Gray eyes, brown hair, fair complexion; 5'7¼" tall. First enlisted in 7th Infantry, 23 Oct 1869, then on 10 Mar 1870 in engineers. Enlisted in 7th Cavalry on 7 Mar 1871, then again on 7 Mar 1876. Body found just below Custer Hill. Listed number 89 in "June Returns, Alterations … Killed in action."

Keogh, CPT (Bvt LTC) **Myles Walter**—b. Orchard House, Leighlinbridge, County Carlow, Ireland, 25 Mar 1840–d. 25 Jun 1876, killed at the Little Big Horn, while commanding one of Custer's two battalions. Company I: Commanding Officer. Thirty-six years old, 6'½" to 6'1½" tall, blue eyes. DOR: 28 Jul 1866, date regiment was formed and the same as Benteen's; the two senior captains on the campaign, though Benteen out-ranked him by virtue of his brevet. Promoted to captain, Seventh Cavalry, 28 Jul 1866, the date the regiment was organized. One of the more remarkable and colorful characters associated with the Little Big Horn.

Keogh's body was found on the east side of Custer/Battle Ridge, with a bunch of others. Godfrey wrote: "Keogh was in a depression just north or below [Calhoun Hill] and on the slope of the ridge that forms the defensive line furthest from the river; the body was stript except the socks, and these had the name cut off; in life he wore a Catholic medal suspended from his neck; it was not removed" [Godfrey/Graham, *The Custer Myth*, p. 345]. Marker 178 on the battlefield is inscribed with Keogh's name and photographic evidence suggests it may be accurately placed. It seems while Keogh was mounted during the battle, a bullet struck him in the leg, breaking it and going through to hit his horse, Comanche. That either threw him or he dismounted and was then rallied around by up to 18 enlisted personnel. There is some evidence his favorite horse was named Paddy, but Keogh did not ride him in the battle, preferring Comanche. Close friends with LT Henry Nowlan and on rather friendly terms with Benteen. Apparently a heavy drinker and described by more than one person—including Libbie Custer—as a "drunken sot." This sobriquet, however, was rather vicious and in all likelihood, not deserved.

A devout Catholic, he served in the Papal Army from 7 Aug 1860–20 Aug 1861. When the army was defeated trying to preserve the Papal States, Keogh was tossed into jail. Repatriated, he was commissioned in the St. Patrick Battalion. With the Irish Zouaves in the Vatican until 20 Feb 1862. Awarded two medals by Pius IX: *Medaglia di Pro Petri Sede* and the *Ordine di San Gregorio* (Cross of the Order of St. Gregory the Great). Arrived in NY, 1 Apr 1862, having been recruited by American agents.

Served with Buford's cavalry brigade: South Mountain, Antietam, Fredericksburg, Chancellorsville, Mine Run, Gettysburg. Participated in more than thirty Civil War engagements, including the last cavalry action of the war, the raid on Salisbury [Kimber]. Was a prisoner of war, briefly [Kimber].

Assistant Inspector General for GEN Sully, 1869.

Despite an almost legendary status within the regiment, Keogh played little part in its earlier field operations, missing the Winter–Washita Campaign. Went south on reconstruction duty, then was on escort duty with the International Boundary Commission in 1873 and 1874. Not particularly close to the Custers, though GAC wrote to Libbie, "I do think him rather absurd, but would rather have him stationed near us than many others" [Klokner, *The Officer Corps of Custer's Seventh Cavalry*, p. 75].

Buried in Fort Hill Cemetery, Auburn, NY,

Throop Martin Lot, on 25 Oct 1877. Survived by one and possibly a second brother and two sisters, all living in Ireland. Brothers: Patrick (oldest) and Tom (d. 15 Aug 1897). Sisters: Margaret and Ellen [Elisabeth Kimber, LBHA]. Ellen "married a John Donahue, and apparently emigrated to Tarrytown, NY ... but appears to have been back in Ireland by 1876. Presumably her husband had died..." [Kimber]. Patrick was—or had been—the coroner of the county and it is uncertain if he was still alive, though contemporary newspapers seemed to imply that he was [Kimber].

Keogh "had become very close to the Martin family of Auburn NY. (Enos Throop Martin...) Two of his closest friends had married into the family: Andrew Alexander (married Evy-Eveline) and Emory Upton (married Emmy-Emmeline). Rumour has it that he himself was engaged to a third sister, Nelly (Cornelia) ... but that's not proven. It may be an after-the-fact rationalisation. But, whatever: he'd asked to be buried in their home town of Auburn, NY; and they—perhaps—went the extra mile by burying him in their family plot in Fort Hill Cemetery. Upton was buried there later, as was Alexander. So Keogh seems to have been accepted as one of the family—for whatever reason" [Kimber].

"A fun fact you'll like, even if it has no relevance: Keogh's grand-niece Margaret was killed while heroically rescuing a wounded Volunteer in the Easter Rising of 1916. (She was a nurse. Some say she was merely caught up accidentally in the fighting, others that she was an active member of the women's revolutionary movement. I'd go for the latter, myself—those Keogh genes....) Nice, eh?" [Kimber].

The following is a letter written by Evy Alexander (Gen. Andrew Alexander's wife) in September 1881. She, Alexander, and their little boy Upton had just made a trip to the battlefield from Fort Custer with Lt. Roe Evy to Nelly, September 17, 1881

> Fort Custer
> Sept. 17th 1881
>
> My dear Nelly,
>
> Yesterday I visited the Custer battle ground— We drove up in our carriage with Upton, & Lt. Roe who was on the bloody field the day after the fight who was the first to know through a crow Indian of the great disaster.
>
> You can imagine the feelings with which I visited that spot, and traced the advance of that fated column from point to point by the silent but significant marks afforded by the stakes driven into the ground wherever a body was found. We could see clearly how Keogh's company had been cut off from the main body, &

surrounded on all sides by Indians, they had all of them died a soldier's death. The cross that marks the spot where he was buried is inscribed

[drawing of the cross:]

Here
fell
COL KEOGH
and
38 men
of I
troop
fighting
with
Sioux
Indians
June 25
1876

[two words crossed out] I looked around upon the smiling valley the river the mountains far away, and thought how his dying glance rested upon it all for the last time, and remembering his oft repeated request — "Do not forget to say a prayer for me sometimes, dear sister" — on that spot where he fell I breathed a prayer for the re-pose of his soul.

Little Upton saw the marks of the spade in the ground where the grave had been opened and said to me — "Have the angels been digging him up?"

I was glad to think his mortal remains no longer rested here, but in that sacred spot where our beloved ones are all gathering.

Yet sad as were my thoughts of our dear Keogh's death — I could not but think — ah! Emory! Your fate was still more to be lamented! You would have envied the soldier who died sword in hand, as you contended not against flesh and blood, but against principalities, against powers, against the rulers of the darkness of this world!

Like our blessed Lord — he saved others, him-self he could not save. But oh grave! Where is thy victory. Christ is able to keep that which is com-mitted to him unto the Last Day! Even so Lord Jesus!

E. M. A. [From Elisabeth Kimber]

Kidey, John *see* **Kelly, PVT John P.**

Kilfoyle, PVT Martin — b. County Clare, Ireland, 1853–d. Washington, D.C., 9 Dec 1894. Company G, private. Blue eyes, light hair, fair complexion; 5'6" tall. Enlisted 4 Dec 1874. Remained at the Powder River Depot. Presence confirmed on June Returns.

Kimm, PVT John G. — b. NYC, 1847 or 1848, though death certificate lists birthplace as Keeblers Cross Roads, TN–d. Johnson City, TN, 28 Jun 1910 (Michno says 1909); Williams lists his date of death as 7 Feb 1909 at the Soldiers' Home in John-

son City. I would tend to go with the Williams date. Company E, private. Gray eyes, black hair, florid complexion; 5'10½" tall. Enlisted from Aug 1864 to Jun 1865 in NY Light Artillery; enlisted from 30 Sep 1865 to 30 Sep 1868 in 2nd Infantry; enlisted 19 Oct 1868 to 2 May 1871 in 12th Infantry, then 1st Cavalry at Benecia Barracks, CA. Dis-charged 19 Oct 1871. Enlisted in 7th Cavalry 18 Jan 1872. With pack train (Overfield), fighting on Reno Hill. Divorced wife Caroline on 1 Aug 1874. Mar-ried Maria Kanna. Children: Elsey, Hazel, John J., Ernestine, Anna, Herman, Mary, and Hamilton. Deserted Maria Aug 1897. Illegally married Lillie Butler. Cause of death was listed as stomach trou-ble. Buried in Mountain Home National Cemetery.

King, CPL George H. — b. Philadelphia, PA, 1848–d. 1 Jul 1876, of wounds suffered at the Little Big Horn battle. Company A, corporal. Hazel eyes, brown hair, fair complexion; 5'10½" tall. Second enlistment 2 Oct 1875. Fought in the valley, then on Reno Hill. Died on the *Far West* at Pease Bot-tom, 1 July or 2 Jul 1876, from a gunshot wound to the abdomen on the evening of 25 June (Smalley says 26 June). Buried on north bank of Yellowstone at mouth of the Big Horn River. Not listed on battle monument. Re-interred in Custer Battlefield National Cemetery.

King, BSM John — b. Basel, Switzerland, 1849–d. 25 Jun 1876, killed at the Little Big Horn. Company C: blacksmith. Gray eyes, brown hair, dark complexion; 5'5¼" tall. Enlisted on 22 Sep 1875, less than one year's service. Not married. Par-ents moved to U.S. when he was very young. In the C Company charge off Battle Ridge–Calhoun Hill, but body was never identified. May have died in Calhoun Coulee, Finley-Finckle Ridge, the Keogh Sector, or possibly even Last Stand Hill. Listed number 22 in "June Returns, Alterations … Killed in action."

Kipp, PVT Fremont — b. Noble Hill, Noble County, OH, 17 Oct 1856–d. Washington, D.C., 16 Jan 1938. Company D, private. Brown eyes, brown hair, dark complexion; 5'8¾" tall. Enlisted 2 Dec 1872 at reported age of 21. Rode with his unit in Benteen's battalion, and fought on Reno Hill. Also fought at Snake Creek in the Nez Percé campaign. Served as drillmaster in Spanish-American War and 2½ years in the Philippines. Resided in Washington, D.C., for 16 years.

Klawitter, PVT Ferdinand — b. Conitz, Berlin, Germany, 19 Jun 1836–d. Max, ND, 17 May 1924. Company B, private. Hammer says he was at FAL as orderly for Mrs. Custer. Overfield claims he was at PRD, which is the only reason he is retained in this list. We accept Hammer, however.

Klein, PVT Gustav (aka Heinrich Klein and Henry Klein)—b. Würtemburg, Germany, 1847–d. 25 Jun 1876, killed at the Little Big Horn. Company F, private. Blue eyes, light hair, fair complexion; 5'7" tall. Enlisted 31 May 1866 in 19th Infantry. Discharged 31 May 1869 and enlisted in 7th Cavalry 15 Mar 1871. Had been 1SG until court-martialed in Feb 1873 for taking four horses and a sleigh against orders from CPT Yates. Current enlistment dated from 16 Mar 1876. Married Appolonia Stark on 13 Jul 1865. They had two boys and two girls: Anton (b. 9 Sep 1867); Catherine (b. 5 Apr 1871); Mathias (b. 14 Sep 1873); and Franziska (b. Feb 1875). His body was found near the foot of Custer Hill, possibly Marker 55. Listed number 109 in "June Returns, Alterations … Killed in action."

Klotzbucher, PVT Henry—b. Baden, Germany, 1848–d. 25 Jun 1876, killed at the Little Big Horn, in the timber as Reno was readying his retreat. Company M, private. CPT French's striker. Brown eyes, brown hair, ruddy complexion; 5'6½" tall. Enlisted 4 Oct 1873. CPT French's striker on 25 June. Mortally wounded in the stomach while in the bottoms, maybe within the timber while mounting. Attended to by Slaper and Neely, but left behind as they figured the wound was fatal. As with Lorentz, he may have been killed by the Cheyenne warriors Turkey Leg, Crooked Nose, and Old Man. Found after the battle; body not mutilated. Listed number 230 in "June Returns, Alterations … Killed in action."

Knauth, PVT Herman (also Krianth)—b. Dammendorf, Prussia, 1838–d. 25 Jun 1876, killed at the Little Big Horn. Company F, private. Blue eyes, light brown hair, fair complexion; 5'8" tall. Civilian occupation was merchant. Enlisted 20 Jan 1872 in Rochester, NY. In all likelihood he was killed on Last Stand Hill with his unit. The results of the archaeological work done at the battlefield during the summers of 1984 and 1985 revealed the following at the paired markers 67 and 68 on Last Stand Hill near the fence enclosing the area. Both human remains and battle related artifacts were found. In addition, there were cobbles; skull fragments (the bones found at this site were of one human and one horse); and vertebrae—with a compressed fracture of lower lumbar—rib, facial bones, hand bone. One of the ribs showed evidence of possible bullet damage. Fragmented facial bones indicate possible postmortem blunt-force damage. The individual was estimated at between 35 and 45 years of age. Five F Company troopers fit within the age parameters, being born between 1831 and 1841 (Note—*This does not mean these bones were from an F Company soldier*): FAR Benjamin Brandon—1831; PVT Thomas Atcheson—1838; PVT Herman Knauth—1838; PVT Sebastian Omling—1838; and PVT George Warren—1840. [See Scott and Fox, *Archaeological Insights into the Custer Battle*; and Scott; Fox; and Connor, *Archaeological Perspectives on the Battle of the Little Bighorn*.] Knauth was listed number 110 in "June Returns, Alterations … Killed in action."

Knecht, PVT Andrew—b. Cincinnati, OH, 12 Apr 1853 or 12 Apr 1852–d. 25 Jun 1876, killed at the Little Big Horn. Company E, private. Hazel eyes, light brown hair, light complexion; 5'6½" tall. Enlisted 22 Sep 1873. He was a butcher in civilian life. Hammer lists him with L Company [clearly wrong] while Michno and Overfield have him in Company E. Smalley corrects Hammer's error. PVT DeVoto (B) saw a dead E Company trooper in Deep Ravine, a man who enlisted about the same time DeVoto did. This was probably Knecht. Listed number 74 in "June Returns, Alterations … Killed in action."

Korn, PVT Gustave—b. Sprallow, Silesia, 1852–d. Wounded Knee, SD, 29 Dec 1890. Company I, private. Straggler; horse gave out, though one version has the horse bolting and being killed near the river during Reno's retreat. Hazel eyes, light hair, light complexion; 5'9¼" tall. Enlisted 17 May 1873. After he lost his horse, Korn managed to join Reno on the hilltop. After the battle, he was the handler for Keogh's horse, Comanche. When Korn was killed at Wounded Knee, Comanche, who apparently grew very fond of the man, seemed to lose all interest in living and died, 6 Nov 1891. Korn was also the subject of one of the Little Big Horn's more outlandish tales. He claimed he was riding down Medicine Tail Coulee with Keogh's battalion when his horse became unmanageable and bolted the length of MTC, across Ford B, and up the valley through the entire Indian village, ultimately landing on Reno Hill. The horse had five bullets in him, but Korn escaped unhurt [Liddic, *Vanishing Victory*, pp. 107–108]. May have been Keogh's orderly that day.

Kramer, TMP William—b. Reading, PA, 1848–d. 25 Jun 1876, killed at the Little Big Horn. Company C: trumpeter. Gray eyes, brown hair, 5'5¾" tall. Less than one year service. Enlisted on 7 Oct 1875. Married; wife's name was Elnora. One child: Orren. Author Vern Smalley claims he *may* have been one of Custer's orderlies, though this seems doubtful, as there is no other evidence for it. In all likelihood he was involved in the C Company charge off Battle Ridge–Calhoun Hill, but body was never identified. May have died in Calhoun Coulee, Finley-Finckle Ridge, the Keogh Sector, or possibly even Last Stand Hill. Listed number 20 in "June Returns, Alterations ... Killed in action."

Kretchmer, PVT Joseph— b. Silesia, Germany, 1833–d. Washington, D.C., 19 Apr 1928. Company D, private. Blue eyes, brown hair, florid complexion; 5' 4" tall. Second enlistment 20 Sep 1872. Rode with his unit in Benteen's battalion, and fought on Reno Hill. WIA in the neck in the hilltop fight.

Krianth, Herman *see* **Knauth, PVT Herman**

Kuehl, PVT Jesse— b. Los Angeles, CA, 1854–d. unknown. Company D, private. Brown eyes, brown hair, dark complexion; 5' 7⅛" tall. Enlisted 9 Oct 1875. Remained at the Powder River Depot. Presence confirmed on June Returns.

Lalor, CPL William— b. Queen's County, Ireland, Jan 1839–d. Ireland, some time after 1912. Company M, corporal. Blue eyes, brown hair, fair complexion; 5' 8" tall. Enlisted from 22 May 1866 to 22 May 1869 in U.S. Engineers; enlisted 29 Sep 1869 in Seventh Cavalry. Re-upped 29 Sep 1875. Promoted to CPL 17 Jun 1876. No specific record exists of his participation in the battle, other than his presence with his unit during the valley fighting and subsequent defense of Reno Hill. Moved back to Ireland and resided in Knockannia, Montrath, Queen's County, Ireland in 1912.

Lange, PVT Henry August— b. Hanover, Germany, 7 Dec 1851 or 17 Dec 1851–d. Chicago, IL, 1 May 1928. Company E, private. Gray eyes, light hair, light complexion; 5' 8" tall. Arrived in U.S. about 1860. Enlisted 6 Jan 1872. With pack train (Overfield). While not listed as wounded, Hammer says he received a pension for "injuries received in the LBH River fight." Married Augusta Herold, 4 Jul 1877. Children: William H., Edward, Fred, Lillie, Mildred, Harry, and Minnie. Resided in Chicago for 35 years. Wife died first; he lived with daughter Minnie at 646 West 119th Street, Chicago, IL. Buried in Mt Hope Cemetery, Worth Township, Cook County, IL.

Lasley, PVT William W.— b. St. Louis County, IL, 19 Nov 1842–d. Washington, D.C., 2 Jul 1924. Company K, private. Blue eyes, brown hair, fair complexion; 5' 7½" tall. Enlisted 17 Oct 1872. Rode with his unit in Benteen's battalion, and fought on Reno Hill. Godfrey considered him and Madden the two best and coolest shots in the company. Married and divorced: Linda.

Lattman, PVT John— b. Zurich, Switzerland, 1848–d. Rapid City, SD, 7 Oct 1913. Company G, private. Gray eyes, auburn hair, ruddy complexion; 5' 6¾" tall. Enlisted 14 Oct 1873. One of twenty men — one officer, three scouts, sixteen enlisted men — left in the timber in the valley bottoms, but

made Reno Hill later that afternoon (see Holmstead entry). Buried in Elk Vale Cemetery, Rapid City, SD.

Lauper, PVT Frank— b. Montgomery, OH, 1852–d. unknown. Company G, private. Blue eyes, light hair, light complexion; 5' 6½" tall. Enlisted 7 Apr 1876. Remained at the Powder River Depot. Presence confirmed on June Returns.

Laurse, Charles *see* **Hardy, William G.**

Lawhorn, PVT Thomas— b. Caldwell County, KY, 1851–d. unknown. Company H, private. Hazel eyes, dark hair, fair complexion; 5' 9" tall. Second enlistment 12 May 1875. Illiterate. Rode with his unit in Benteen's battalion, and fought on Reno Hill.

Lee, PVT Mark E.— b. Castine, ME, 1849–d. unknown. Company I, private. On steamer "Far West." Helped attend to the sick and wounded. Gray eyes, light brown hair, ruddy complexion; 5' 8¼" tall. Enlisted 27 Sep 1875.

Lefler (also seen as Meier Lefler), **PVT Meig**— b. Baden, Germany, 1851–d. in the Army and Navy Hospital, Hot Springs, AR, 21 Jul 1910. Company F, private. Gray eyes, brown hair, fair complexion; 5' 6½" tall. Second enlistment 25 Nov 1871. With the pack train. Fought on Reno Hill. Resided in Presidio hospital in San Francisco, CA.

Lehman, PVT Frederick— b. Berne (Bern), Switzerland, 1848–d. 25 Jun 1876, killed at the Little Big Horn. Company I, private. Blue eyes, light hair, fair complexion; 5' 7½" tall. Enlisted 17 Oct 1871. Body never identified, but in all likelihood he was killed in the Keogh Sector. Listed number 160 in "June Returns, Alterations ... Killed in action."

Lehmann, PVT Henry— b. Berlin, Germany, 1839–d. 25 Jun 1876, killed at the Little Big Horn. Company I, private. Brown eyes, fair hair, fair complexion; 5' 4" tall. Enlisted 11 Nov 1872. Bone fragments found at Marker 105 on Last Stand Hill would be consistent with his reported age and height, though most men killed at this location were believed to have been from F Company. Several others fit this description, as well. Listed number 161 in "June Returns, Alterations ... Killed in action."

Lell, CPL George— b. Hamilton County, OH, 1847–d. 26 or 27 Jun 1876, killed at the Little Big Horn after suffering a wound on 26 June during the hilltop fight. Company H, corporal. Blue eyes, dark hair, dark complexion; 5' 9" tall, or possibly shorter. Enlisted 18 Sep 1873 in Cincinnati. Shot in abdomen/stomach while on the Company H line on hilltop. Died in Reno Hill field hospital, 26 June or possibly early 27 Jun 1876. Listed number 138 in "June Returns, Alterations … Killed in action."

Lepper, PVT Frederick (also Ferdinand Lepper) — b. Hamilton County, OH, 1849–d. unknown. Company L, private. Hazel eyes, brown hair, fair complexion; 5'7¾" tall. Enlisted 12 Nov 1872. Remained at the Powder River Depot, sick. Presence confirmed on June Returns.

Lerock, PVT William H. (also LeRoche) — b. Wayne County, NY, 1850–d. 25 Jun 1876, killed at the Little Big Horn. Company F, private. Hazel eyes, dark hair, fair complexion; 5'5¼" tall. Enlisted 9 Feb 1872 in Buffalo, NY. Body found and identified on Custer Hill. Listed number 112 in "June Returns, Alterations … Killed in action."

Lewis, PVT John — b. Povey County, PA, 1846–d. 25 Jun 1876, killed at the Little Big Horn. Company C, private. Gray eyes, brown hair; 5'8" tall. Well into his 2nd enlistment, 11 Dec 1872. In the C Company charge off Battle Ridge–Calhoun Hill, but body was never identified. May have died in Calhoun Coulee, Finley-Finckle Ridge, the Keogh Sector, or possibly even Last Stand Hill. Listed number 31 in "June Returns, Alterations … Killed in action."

Lewis, PVT Uriah S. — b. Montgomery County, PA, 1852–d. unknown. Company D, private. Blue eyes, brown hair, fair complexion; 5'10" tall. Enlisted 18 Aug 1873. Remained at the Powder River Depot on detached service with band. Presence confirmed on June Returns. Married Amelia H. Buck (d. 9 Oct 1900). Children: George A., Mary B, Grover C., and Lamont D.

Liddiard, PVT Herod T. — b. London, England, 1851–d. 26 or 27 Jun 1876; died of wounds suffered at the Little Big Horn. Company E, private. Blue eyes, light hair, fair complexion; 5'5¼" tall. Enlisted 4 Dec 1872. With pack train. Shot in abdomen on Reno Hill. Died 27 June. Another account has him lying down to take a shot (he was apparently a good shot) and talking with some men. When they noticed he had stopped talking, they saw blood around the rim of his hat. He had been shot in the head. Hammer and Smalley agree with this. Listed number 75 in "June Returns, Alterations … Killed in action."

Liemann (also Luman, Lunden, or Lieman), **PVT Werner L.** — b. Bremen, Germany, 1842–d. 25 Jun 1876, killed at the Little Big Horn. Company F, private. Blue eyes, brown hair, light complexion, 5'5" tall. Enlisted 30 Jan 1873. Body reportedly found on Custer/Last Stand Hill. Bones found at Marker 105 on Custer/Last Stand Hill *may* be his, despite being inscribed, "Algernon Smith." Found

at the excavation site was a complete, mostly articulated left lower arm and hand; numerous other bones: hands and feet; a vertebra; several ribs. Consistent with a single individual. Also found were two four-hole iron trouser buttons, generally associated with those on army trousers for attachment of suspenders and to close the fly; a .45/55 cartridge case found beneath the arm; one .45/55 bullet found near the center of the excavation; five cobbles (stones) associated with those used to hold dirt thrown over the body. The bone fragments are consistent with what is known of Liemann, and are not consistent with what is known of LT Smith. Forensics evidence suggests that the bones are from an individual about 5'7" tall and more than twenty-five years old. "A massive bone growth on the metatarsals suggests that the individual had suffered some sort of injury to his foot which had not healed properly. In all probability this individual walked with a limp…" [Scott and Fox, *Archaeological Insights into the Custer Battle,* p. 101]. The conclusion was reached that the bones could not have belonged to Smith due to his having sustained a crippling injury to his left arm during the Civil War and the absence of such injury in the recovered bones. Listed number 113 in "June Returns, Alterations … Killed in action."

Littlefield, PVT John L. — b. Portland, ME, 1851–d. unknown. Company B, private. Blue eyes, brown hair, fair complexion; 5'10" tall. Enlisted 28 Mar 1876. Remained at the Powder River Depot.

Lloyd, PVT Edward W. — b. Gloucester, England, 1852–d. 25 Jun 1876, killed at the Little Big Horn. Company I, private. Gray eyes, light brown hair, fair complexion; 5'6" tall. Enlisted 30 Sep 1873. Body found in the cluster around Keogh. Listed number 162 in "June Returns, Alterations … Killed in action."

Lobering, PVT Louis — b. Hanover, Germany, 1835–d. 25 Jun 1876, killed at the Little Big Horn. Company L, private. Blue eyes, brown hair, ruddy complexion; 5'6¾" tall. Third enlistment 20 May 1875. In all likelihood he was killed on Calhoun Hill, though the possibility exists he was one of those killed during the panic through the Keogh Sector. No remains found during the 1984–1985 archaeological work match his description. Listed number 208 in "June Returns, Alterations … Killed in action."

Logue, PVT William J. — b. NYC, 4 Jul 1841 (or 1837)–d. Washington, D.C., 25 Jun 1919. Company L, private. Gray eyes, light hair, fair complexion; 5'8½" tall. Enlisted from 2 Dec 1867 to 3 Dec 1872 in Seventh Cavalry; second enlistment 7 Apr

1873. With the pack train. Fought on Reno Hill. Buried in Soldiers' Home National Cemetery.

Lord, 1LT (Dr.) George Edwin— b. Boston, MA, 17 Feb 1846–d. 25 Jun 1876, killed at the Little Big Horn. Headquarters: Assistant Surgeon. Graduated from Bowdoin and Chicago Medical School (now Northwestern University). Apparently killed with Custer. Body found near top of Custer Hill, though Gray says, "twenty feet southwest of Custer's." 2LT Richard E. Thompson, Company K, 6th Infantry, identified Lord's body about twenty feet *southeast* of Custer's. Several years after the battle some archaeological evidence — military buttons worn only by medical personnel — was found that could place Lord's body on the lower South Skirmish Line (also known as the "fugitive line") near Deep Ravine. That location is presently marked by Marker 17.

Sick on the day of the battle, but he insisted on accompanying Custer. Very good friends with Benteen. Brother-in-law of CPT Otho Michaelis, Terry's ordnance chief on the campaign.

Lorentz, PVT George— b. Holstein, Germany, 1851–d. 25 Jun 1876, killed at the Little Big Horn, in Reno's timber, probably as Reno was preparing to charge out of the woods. Company M, private. Assigned as French's orderly. Gray eyes, dark brown hair, fair complexion; 5' 6¾" tall. Enlisted 13 Nov 1872. Killed in woods; shot in the back of the neck and chest, possibly by one of the Cheyenne warriors Turkey Leg, Crooked Nose, or Old Man. Bullet entered the back of his neck and fell out of his mouth. The troops were already mounted and ready to leave the timber [Barnard, *Ten Years with Custer*, p. 293]. Listed number 231 in "June Returns, Alterations ... Killed in action."

Lossee (also Loose or Losse), **PVT William A.**— b. Brewster Station, NY, 1849–d. 25 Jun 1876, killed at the Little Big Horn. Company F, private. Gray eyes, light hair, ruddy complexion; 5' 5½" tall. Enlisted 24 Sep 1875 in NYC. Civilian occupation listed as showman. In all likelihood he was killed on Last Stand Hill with his unit. Listed number 114 in "June Returns, Alterations ... Killed in action."

Loyd, PVT George— b. County Tyrone, Ireland, 1843–d. Fort Riley, KS, 17 Dec 1892, by suicide. Company G, private. Gray eyes, light hair, ruddy complexion; 5' 9" tall. Second enlistment 21 Mar 1869; third, 13 Apr 1874. Promoted to corporal 25 Jun 1876. No specific record exists of his participation in the battle, other than his presence with his unit during the valley fighting and subsequent defense of Reno Hill. Awarded MH for action at Wounded Knee, Dec 1890. Had been in severe pain because of several accidents and some thought the pain caused a mental aberration resulting in the suicide. Was first sergeant of I/7C at time of death.

Lynch, PVT Dennis— b. Cumberland, MD, 22 Feb 1848 (also listed as 22 Feb 1845)–d. Washington, D.C., 13 Oct 1933. Company F, private. Assigned to guard Custer's baggage on the steamer "Far West." Detailed to HQ fatigue party. Gray eyes, brown hair, dark complexion; 5' 5¼" tall. He served previously in the 8th IL Cavalry during the Civil War and fought at the Battle of Brandy Station under CPT George Armstrong Custer. Also fought at Cedar Creek, Winchester, and Yellow Tavern (where J. E. B. Stuart was killed). One of the few Seventh Cavalry enlisted men to have a full war of cavalry experience. Enlisted in the Seventh Cavalry on 3 Aug 1866 in Washington, D.C. His was the first 5-year enlistment in the new regiment. He was in the Washita Campaign (1868), the Yellowstone Expedition (1873), and the Black Hills Expedition (1874). Reenlisted on 3 Mar 1871. Discharged on 3 Aug 1876, but enlisted again before the year was out. In the Nez Percé campaign (1877) and the Milk River campaign in Jan 1881.

Some confusion reigns with this man, however, as he was another of those who made some dubious claims. For the purposes of this study he is carried in Terry's HQ because he was detached before Custer moved up the Rosebud. According to author Jack Pennington, Lynch fought with Reno and would therefore have to have been assigned to the packs or was a straggler. If true, it would change the numbers at the battle by one. (See comment with White Swan.) Michno also says he was with the pack train at the LBH battle, but Hammer has too much ammunition here. Walter Camp wrote that Custer gave Lynch's horse to an unmounted scout, George Herendeen — Lynch complaining — and then ordered Lynch to board the *Far West* and look after Custer's luggage. Years later, Lynch said this saved his life. Lynch himself tells of the White Swan story, but again, in other areas is too contradictory [Camp/Hammer, *Custer in '76*, p. 140; p. 221 and footnote 4]. In 1908 and 1909 he told Camp he did help bury the dead and tend to Keogh's horse, Comanche. He claimed he saw men of the Seventh Infantry carry several bodies out of a deep gully. If the Seventh Infantry was there, then it was certainly possible for Lynch — who had been on the *Far West* — to be there as well, but not as a member of the pack train. Died at Barnes Hospital, U.S. Soldiers' Home and is buried in the Soldiers' Home National Cemetery.

Lynch, PVT Patrick— b. Carrigaholt County Clare, Ireland, 1851–d. unknown, but probably in Douglas City, AK, some time after 1901. Company I, private. Blue eyes, auburn hair, light complexion;

5' 6½" tall. With Department HQ in the field, for duty as orderly for Terry. Special Order 39.

Lyons, PVT Bernard— b. Calway (Galway?), Ireland, 1849–d. 12 Jan 1901. Company F, private. Blue eyes, brown hair, fair complexion; 5' 6⅛" tall. Enlisted 6 Sep 1875. With pack train (Overfield). PVT Pickard claimed he was left back at Fort Lincoln [Hardorff, *On the LBH with Walter Camp*, p. 179], but this seems incorrect.

Lyons, PVT Daniel— b. Brooklyn, NY, 1852–d. unknown. Company K, private. Blue or hazel eyes, brown or black hair, fair complexion; 5' 6⅛–9¼" tall. Enlisted 4 Apr 1876. Remained at the Powder River Depot. Presence confirmed on June Returns.

Madden, SAD Michael P.— b. Galcony, Ireland, 1836–d. Moniteau County, MO, 18 Dec 1883. Company K: company saddler. Gray eyes, dark hair, light complexion; one of the two tallest enlisted men at battle at 6'1½". Smalley writes that he was a huge, intemperate bully [*Little Bighorn Mysteries*, p. 15–9]. First enlistment 1861; enlisted 10 Aug 1866 in Seventh Cavalry. Enlisted again 28 Aug 1871. WIA, in right leg, while trying to get water from the river (26 June). Leg amputated on Reno Hill. Promoted to SGT 12 Jul 1876. Godfrey considered Madden and Lasley the two best and coolest shots in the company. There is a story about Madden — maybe apocryphal — that Dr. Porter gave him whiskey to ease the pain when he was about to amputate Madden's leg. When the operation was over, Madden was reputed to have said, that for another drink Porter could amputate the other leg. He died apparently after a prolonged drinking spree, and it is Madden who is believed to be buried in the Potter's Field Section of the California Cemetery, Moniteau County, Missouri.

Madsen (also Madison), **PVT Christian**— b. Kjertemende, Denmark, Feb 1848–d. 25 Jun 1876, killed at the Little Big Horn. Company F, private. Blue eyes, light hair, fair complexion; 5'11" tall. Enlisted 24 Feb 1872 in Cleveland, OH. Civilian occupation was tanner. In all likelihood he was killed on Last Stand Hill with his unit. Listed number 116 in "June Returns, Alterations … Killed in action."

Mahoney, PVT Bartholomew— b. Bandon, County Cork, Ireland, 1846–d. 25 Jun 1876, killed at the Little Big Horn. Company L, private. Hazel eyes, dark hair, sallow complexion; 5'10" tall. Enlisted 29 Oct 1872. In all likelihood he was killed on Calhoun Hill, though the possibility exists he was one of those killed during the panic through the Keogh Sector. No remains found during the 1984–1985 archaeological work match his descrip-

tion. Listed number 209 in "June Returns, Alterations … Killed in action."

Mahoney, PVT Daniel— b. Cork, Ireland, 1852–d. Washington, D.C., 7 Aug 1885. Company M, private. Gray eyes, brown hair, fair complexion; 5' 9¾" tall. Enlisted 8 Sep 1875 in Boston. No specific record exists of his participation in the battle, other than his presence with his unit during the valley fighting and subsequent defense of Reno Hill.

Mahoney, PVT John J.— b. Cork, Ireland, 31 May 1845–d. Sturgis, SD, 27 Jul 1918. Company C, private. Blue eyes, dark hair; 5'7" tall. In the army less than one year. Enlisted 24 Sep 1875. With packs, fighting on Reno Hill.

Manning, PVT David— b. Dublin, Ireland, 1847–d. NYC, 25 Oct 1910. Company D, private. Gray eyes, sandy hair, florid complexion; 5' 8¼" tall. Enlisted 1 Oct 1873 in Boston. Rode with his unit in Benteen's battalion, and fought on Reno Hill.

Manning, BSM James R.— b. Houston County, GA, 1843–d. 25 Jun 1876, killed at the Little Big Horn. Company F: company blacksmith. Hazel eyes, black hair, dark complexion; 5' 8½" tall. Enlisted on 25 Jan 1873. In all likelihood he was killed on Last Stand Hill with his unit. Listed number 97 in "June Returns, Alterations … Killed in action."

Maroney, SGT Matthew— b. County Clare, Ireland, 1840–d. Washington, D.C., 15 Dec 1880. Company H, sergeant. Blue eyes, brown hair, light complexion; 5' 7½" tall. Enlisted from 22 Aug 1862 in White Plains, NY, to 7 Aug 1865 in Sixth NY Heavy Artillery. Enlisted 4 Jan 1867 in 7th Cavalry, then again 14 Jan 1872. Rode with his unit in Benteen's battalion, and fought on Reno Hill.

Marshall, PVT Jasper— b. Spring Valley, OH, 26 Apr 1852–d. Pleasant Hill, OH, 9 May 1920. Company L, private. Gray eyes, black hair, dark complexion; 5' 5½" tall. Enlisted 22 Sep 1875. With the pack train. WIA in the left foot on Reno Hill.

Marshall, PVT William A.— b. Germany, 21 Jul 1851–d. Washington, D.C., 24 Aug 1892. Company D, private. Gray eyes, light brown hair, fair complexion; 5'7" tall. Enlisted 25 Sep 1875 in Chicago. Rode with his unit in Benteen's battalion, and fought on Reno Hill.

Martin, CPL James— b. County Kildare, Ireland, 1847–d. 25 Jun 1876, killed at the Little Big Horn during Reno's retreat. Company G, corporal. Gray eyes, brown hair, fair complexion; 5'5" tall. Enlisted 6 Feb 1872. Killed near Reno's retreat crossing. The head of a corporal from G Company was found in the Indian village, under a kettle. In all likelihood, it was Martin's. PVT Foley (K) claimed he found a head and it belonged to a corporal from G, but he said it had red hair [Camp/Hammer, *Custer in '76*, p. 147]. Listed number 127 in "June Returns, Alterations ... Killed in action."

Martin, 1SG Michael—b. Dublin, Ireland, 1835–d. killed at Snake Creek, M.T., 5 Oct 1877 in the Nez Percé War. Company D: first sergeant. Gray eyes, fair hair, fair complexion; 5'6½" tall. Enlisted 6 Dec 1867 in Seventh Cavalry; reenlisted 7 Dec 1872. Rode with his unit in Benteen's battalion, and fought on Reno Hill. Killed by a shot in the head on the morning of Chief Joseph's surrender to COL Nelson Miles. Buried in Fort Assiniboine cemetery. Reinterred in Custer Battlefield National Cemetery. Married to Ella Martin; with children.

Martin, PVT William—b. London, England, 1850–d. Fort McPherson, GA, 13 Jan 1900. Company B, private. Blue eyes, brown hair, fair complexion; 5'5¼" tall. Enlisted in 7th Cavalry 4 Sep 1873. Had served earlier and court-martialed in Nov 1869. With the pack train escort, Company B. Arrived and fought on Reno Hill.

Martini (also Martin), **TMP PVT Giovanni** (John)—b. Sola Consalina, Italy, Jan 1853–d. Brooklyn, NY, 24 Dec 1922. Company H: trumpeter; private. Attached to HQ as an orderly-trumpeter for George Custer, but returned to his company with a note for CPT Benteen. Hazel eyes, dark hair, dark complexion; 5'6" tall. Enlisted 1 Jun 1874. A drummer boy in the Italian army, he may have fought the Austrians at Custoza in 1866. Arrived in the U.S. in 1873. One of the more prominent and controversial names associated with the battle of the LBH. Famous for carrying back Adjutant Cooke's note, the last word heard from the Custer column. Long career in the army. Married Julia Higgins, 7 Oct 1879 at St. Raymond's Church, Westchester, NY. Children: sons John Joseph, Frank William, Lawrence Edward, George, and a daughter, Julia. Lived in Brooklyn. His death was probably caused by injuries sustained when he was hit by a beer truck while crossing a street. Buried in Cypress Hills National Cemetery, Brooklyn, NY.

Mask (or Mack), **PVT George Brown**—b. Pittsburgh, PA, Dec 1849–d. 25 Jun 1876, killed at the Little Big Horn. Company B, private. Gray eyes, brown hair, fair complexion; 5'4" tall. Enlisted 15 Nov 1872. Possibly killed in hilltop fight, though Ken Hammer, in *The Battlefield Dispatch*, Winter 2005, lists him as "unknown location." Another report has him being washed away in the LBH.

Vern Smalley claims no one saw him killed and his body was never found [*Little Bighorn Mysteries*, p. 15–7]. That would be consistent with his body being washed away, especially if he was one of the first water carriers on the 25th. The Cheyenne warrior, Wooden Leg, told of shooting a soldier who had come down to the river for water, and while the soldier was in the water, he was set upon by two other Indians who clubbed him to death, dragging his body further downstream. Listed number 12 in "June Returns, Alterations ... Killed in action."

Mason, CPL Henry S.—b. Brownsville, IN, 1847–d. 25 Jun 1876, killed at the Little Big Horn. Company E, corporal. Gray eyes, sandy hair, fair complexion; 5'11¼" tall. In second enlistment, 4 Aug 1875. At one time he had been a sergeant, but was reduced to private for gross neglect of duty, 10 Jul 1874. While his body was not specifically identified, he may have been one of the unknowns on either the South Skirmish Line or in Deep Ravine. Listed number 56 in "June Returns, Alterations ... Killed in action."

Mathey, 1LT Edward Gustave (Edouard Gustave; last name sometimes seen as Mathieu, though the family name was never anything but Mathey; nicknamed the "Bible Thumper")—b. Besançon, France, 27 Oct 1837–d. Denver, CO, 17 Jul 1915. Company M. Detailed to head up the pack train on the 25 June. Black eyes, black hair; dark complexion; 5'9½" tall. DOR: 10 May 1870; fifth-ranking of nine first lieutenants on the campaign. Calhoun—his junior—was appointed ahead of him as Acting CO of L Company. Originally studied for the priesthood. Fought at Stone's River and Chickamauga among many other battles. After joining the Seventh Cavalry (H), he took part in scouting, then transferred to Company A. Was in the Winter–Washita Campaign. Suffering from snow-blindness, he took the packs. Suffered from rheumatism. Not highly thought of by Benteen, though he was a competent officer. Klokner claims he never rose above "mediocrity" [p. 78]. Sturgis tried to have him cashiered in the Benzine Boards, but Custer intervened. Went south with the regiment, then participated in Stanley's Yellowstone Campaign (1873) and the Black Hills Campaign (1874). Also took part in the Nez Percé Campaign and when Owen Hale was killed, Mathey was promoted to captain, Company K. Also in the Northern Cheyenne Campaign (1878) and the Sioux Campaign (1890). He was one of the few officers who had served with the regiment through the culmination of the Plains Indian Wars. Professor of Military Science at Baylor University, 1901–1903, finally retiring with the rank of full colonel.

Varnum referred to him as "not a very literary great, and I do not think he cares to write and possibly expose his grammar to criticism" [Hardorff, *On the LBH with Walter Camp*, p. 75].

Arrived in New Orleans, from Havre, France, in 1845, settling in Corydon, IN, and later at New Albany. Became a citizen in 1859. Married Meda Jones (d. February 19, 1917), on 8 Nov 1871, in Corydon. One daughter, Julia, b. Corydon, IN, 10 Sep 1877. Buried in Arlington National Cemetery.

Maxwell, PVT Thomas E.— b. Allegheny, PA, 1850–d. 25 Jun 1876, killed at the Little Big Horn. Company L, private. Blue eyes, brown hair, ruddy complexion; 5' 5½" tall. Enlisted 27 Dec 1872. In all likelihood he was killed on Calhoun Hill, though the possibility exists he was one of those killed during the panic through the Keogh Sector. No remains found during the 1984–1985 archaeological work match his description. Listed number 210 in "June Returns, Alterations ... Killed in action."

May, Frank *see* **Voit, SAD Otto**

McCabe, PVT John— b. Cavan, Ireland, 1851–d. Washington, D.C., 4 Dec 1891. Company B, private. Brown eyes, brown hair, fair complexion; 5' 8¼" tall. Enlisted from 13 Oct 1870 to 13 Oct 1875 in Eighth Infantry; enlisted 11 Apr 1876 in Seventh Cavalry. With the pack train escort, Company B. Arrived and fought on Reno Hill.

McCarthy, PVT Charles— b. Philadelphia, PA, 1845–d. 25 Jun 1876, killed at the Little Big Horn. Company L, private. Blue eyes, brown hair, dark complexion; 5' 7¼" tall. Second enlistment 30 Sep 1873. Body identified on Custer Hill, which means he was one of the L Company troopers who had managed to escape the maelstrom on Calhoun Hill. Listed number 212 in "June Returns, Alterations ... Killed in action."

McClurg, PVT William (aka William Irvine)— b. Belfast, Ireland, 1854–d. unknown. Company A, private. Blue eyes, brown hair, ruddy complexion; 5' 8" tall. Enlisted 23 Sep 1875. No specific record exists of his participation in the battle, other than his presence with his unit during the valley fighting and subsequent defense of Reno Hill and that he was one of five troopers who volunteered to go on picket duty with CPL Roy the night of 25 June.

McConnell, PVT Wilson— b. New Castle, PA, 28 Jan 1839–d. King, WI, 27 Dec 1906. Company K, private. Gray eyes, light hair, ruddy complexion; 5' 9" tall. Served in 133rd NY Infantry; enlisted from 11 Jan 1865 to 9 Feb 1866 in 90th NY Infantry. Enlisted 3 Jan 1872 in Seventh Cavalry. Rode with

his unit in Benteen's battalion, and fought on Reno Hill. Buried in Veterans' Memorial Cemetery, King, WI.

McCormick, PVT James— b. NYC, 1845–d. unknown. Company M, private. Dark eyes, dark hair, sallow complexion; 5' 6½" tall. Second enlistment 2 Apr 1873. Remained at the Powder River Depot. Presence confirmed on June Returns.

McCormick, PVT Samuel J.— b. County Tyrone, Ireland, 1848–d. Fort Meade, SD, 10 Sep 1908. Company G, private. Gray eyes, brown hair, ruddy complexion; 5' 6½" tall. Enlisted 29 Sep 1873. Gave his horse to LT McIntosh at the beginning of the retreat from the valley fight, while he remained in the woods. One of twenty men — one officer, three scouts, sixteen enlisted men — left in the timber in the valley bottoms. Made it up to Reno Hill with the Herendeen group.

McCue, PVT Martin— b. at sea from Ireland, Nov 1851–d. Washington, D.C., 6 Dec 1923. Company K, private. Gray eyes, brown hair, ruddy complexion; 5' 6½" tall. Enlisted 28 Oct 1872. Rode with his unit in Benteen's battalion, and fought on Reno Hill. Buried in Soldiers' Home National Cemetery.

McCurry, 1SG Joseph— b. Philadelphia, PA, 1850–d. unknown. Company H: first sergeant. Brown eyes, dark hair, ruddy complexion; 5' 7" tall. Enlisted 22 Jan 1872. WIA in left shoulder when he was on Reno Hill, probably on 26 June. Appointed regimental sergeant major, 1 Aug 1876. Resided at 4820 Oliver Street, Philadelphia.

McDermott, SGT George M. (aka Michael Burke)— b. Galway, County Clare, Ireland, 1847–d. killed at Snake Creek, M.T., at the Bear Paw Mountain fight, 30 Sep 1877, in the Nez Percé War. Company A: sergeant. Blue eyes, light hair, fair complexion; 5' 8¼" tall. Enlisted 21 Jan 1870 in NYC. Assigned to 5th Artillery. Deserted 21 Jul 1871. Enlisted as Michael Burke 15 Jan 1872, Seventh Cavalry. He was the first sergeant of Company A when he was killed in 1877. While on Reno Hill he had volunteered to carry a message out to Terry along with some Rees. They were not able to get off the hill. Reinterred in Custer Battlefield National Cemetery.

McDermott, PVT Thomas— b. NYC, 1847–d. after 1923. Company H, private. Gray eyes, black hair, fair complexion; 5' 6¾" tall. Second enlistment 18 May 1872. Rode with his unit in Benteen's battalion, and fought on Reno Hill. Recommended for medal for distinguished gallantry by Benteen. Had a history of deserting and was dishonorably discharged, 21 Jan 1886. Sentenced in a general court-martial to two years confinement at Alcatraz.

McDonald, PVT James— b. Boston, MA, 1853– d. 25 Jun 1876, killed at the Little Big Horn. Company A, private. Gray eyes, brown hair, fair complexion; 5'6" tall. Enlisted 29 Sep 1875. Possibly killed on Reno Hill, though Ken Hammer, in *The Battlefield Dispatch,* Winter 2005, lists him as "unknown location." Smalley claims no one saw him killed and his body was never found [*Little Bighorn Mysteries,* p. 15–7]. Listed number 6 in "June Returns, Alterations … Killed in action."

McDonnell, PVT John— b. NYC, 1844–d. unknown. Company G, private. Blue eyes, auburn hair, fair complexion; 5'9" tall. Enlisted 7 Apr 1873. No specific record exists of his participation in the battle, other than his presence with his unit during the valley fighting and subsequent defense of Reno Hill.

McDonnell, PVT Patrick— b. County Kerry, Ireland, Mar 1852–d. San Antonio, TX, 2 Sep 1922. Company D, private. Gray eyes, dark hair, fair complexion; 5'6" tall. Enlisted 16 Nov 1872. WIA in left leg while fighting on Reno Hill. Buried in Calvary Catholic Cemetery, San Antonio.

McDougall, CPT Thomas Mower (nicknamed "Micky Dougall"; also seen spelled McDougal)— b. Fort Crawford (Prairie-du-Chien), WI, 21 May 1845–d. Echo Lake Farm, near Brandon, VT, 3 Jul 1909. Cause of death was angina pectoris. Company B: Commanding Officer, since Mar 1876. DOR: 15 Dec 1875, eighth- and lowest-ranking CPT on the campaign. Attended St. Mary's Academy in Baltimore, then a military prep academy in New York. Originally an infantry officer with the Fifth U.S. Volunteer Infantry, receiving a commission at the age of 17. Volunteered as A-d-C to General Hawkins in October 1863. Took part in the Vicksburg Campaign and numerous other battles. After the war he got a commission in the infantry and was assigned to Fort Laramie. Fought Indians at Aravipa Canyon, Tonto Point, Point of Mountain, and Rock Springs [Klokner, p. 80]. Promoted to 1LT in 1867. Reassigned to the Seventh Cavalry (E Company) after the reorganization of the army, 31 Dec 1870. In the south on reconstruction duty. Also in the Black Hills Expedition, 1874. Commanded pack train escort on 25 June during LBH. Along with two enlisted men — Ryan and Moore — he buried LT Hodgson. Close friends with Benteen. On scouting duty with Major Lazelle during the Nez Percé Campaign. In May 1888, he went on sick leave, suffering from malaria, and retired on 22 Jul 1890.

Married Alice M. Sheldon (d. Hendersonville, NC, 8 Mar 1920), 21 May 1872, in Spartanburg, SC. His father was a former army doctor, BG (bvt) Charles McDougall, Surgeon, USA. McDougall's funeral was held at Dahlgren Chapel, Georgetown University, 7 Jul 1909. Buried in Arlington National Cemetery. One of McDougall's sisters — Josephine — was married to COL David Hillhouse Buel, who was murdered at Fort Leavenworth while trying to apprehend a deserter when the Seventh Cavalry was stationed there (1870). She later married Buel's brother, Oliver [Kimber]. Her son (McDougall's nephew), David H. Buel, S. J., became the president of Georgetown University and it was there that Tom McDougall's funeral was held.

McEagan, PVT John— b. County Kerry, Ireland, Oct 1847–d. unknown. Company G, private. Gray eyes, brown hair, ruddy complexion; 5'8¾" tall. Enlisted 6 Feb 1872. Assigned to pack train. Reported to have lost his carbine while on march with the packs. Fought on Reno Hill.

McElroy, TMP Thomas (listed elsewhere as McElvay)— b. Neagh, Ireland, 1844 or 1845–d. 25 Jun 1876, killed at the Little Big Horn. Company E: trumpeter. Blue eyes, dark hair, ruddy complexion; 5'5½" tall. Arrived in U.S. in 1863. Served in Civil War and was wounded. Enlisted in First Infantry on 24 May 1870; current enlistment, 3 Jul 1875. While his body was not specifically identified, he may have been one of the unknowns on either the South Skirmish Line or in Deep Ravine. Widow Nora married John Furey, Company E, Seventh Cavalry. One son: Thomas Francis (b. 28 Mar 1874). The son took his stepfather's name. Resided in Monolith, CA. Listed number 59 in "June Returns, Alterations … Killed in action."

McGinniss, PVT John J.— b. Boston, MA, 1849– d. 25 Jun 1876, killed at the Littler Big Horn, probably as the troops were leaving the timber or possibly shortly thereafter, refusing to leave the timber with others. Company G, private. Gray eyes, sandy hair, florid complexion; 5'7¾" tall. Enlisted 2 Dec 1874. In the valley fight. His horse bolted and McGinniss's head was later found on the top of a pole in the village. Since SGT Miles O'Harra is considered the first casualty, McGinniss's plight started probably as the command began its retreat. Quite possibly he was one of the twenty men — one officer, three scouts, sixteen enlisted men — left in the timber in the valley bottoms and as he tried to get out, his he lost control of his horse. Bruce Liddic claims he was one of those who wound up staying in the timber, refusing to leave when everyone else left. Listed number 133 in "June Returns, Alterations … Killed in action."

McGlone, SGT John (possibly also McGlass)— b. Sligo, Ireland, 1844–d. Washington, D.C., 28 Aug 1920. Company M, sergeant. Brown eyes, dark hair, ruddy complexion; 5'9½" tall. Enlisted 18 Dec 1872 in Philadelphia. Promoted to SGT 17 Jun 1876. No specific record exists of his participation in the battle, other than his presence with his unit during the valley fighting and subsequent defense of Reno Hill. May have been also listed by another source as "CPL McGlass," who carried company guidon.

McGonigle, PVT Hugh— b. Philadelphia, PA, Feb 1838–d. Washington, D.C., 16 Nov 1914. Company G, private. Brown eyes, black hair, dark complexion; 5'10" tall. Previously served in the Second Cavalry and in General Service USA. Third enlistment 22 Jul 1872. One of twenty men — one officer, three scouts, sixteen enlisted men — left in the timber in the valley bottoms, but eventually made Reno Hill. According to Fred Gerard, McGonigle was Marcus Reno's stepson [Camp/Hammer, *Custer in '76*, p. 152, footnote 3].

McGucker, TMP John (last name also seen spelled "McCucker," erroneously)— b. Albany, NY, 1836–d. 25 Jun 1876, killed at the Little Big Horn. Company I: trumpeter. Hazel eyes, black hair, ruddy complexion; 5'5" tall. Discharged from Fourth Artillery, 22 Nov 1871. Enlisted 27 Nov 1871; assigned to Seventh Cavalry in May 1875. Bone fragments found at Marker 105 on Last Stand Hill would be consistent with his reported age and height, though most men killed at this location were believed to have been from F Company. Several others fit this description, as well. If not, then he died in the Keogh Sector. Listed number 146 in "June Returns, Alterations ... Killed in action."

McGue, PVT Peter— b. Port Henry, NY, Jul 1847–d. 25 Jun 1876, killed at the Little Big Horn. Company L, private. Brown eyes, black hair, dark complexion; 5'4" tall. Enlisted 23 Dec 1872. In all likelihood he was killed on Calhoun Hill, though the possibility exists he was one of those killed during the panic through the Keogh Sector or even got as far as Last Stand Hill. During the 1984–1985 archaeological digs in the area around Marker 105 (the marker inscribed, "Algernon Smith") on Last Stand Hill a number of artifacts and bone fragments were found. Among them were a complete, mostly articulated left lower arm and hand and numerous other bones: hands and feet; a vertebra; several ribs. The foot bones indicated fracture and infection prior to the battle; and vertebrae damage indicated wounding by stabbing or a metal-tipped arrow. The bones represented a single individual, first thought to be between 20 and 35 years old — later changed to 30–40 years of age — and approximately 5'3" tall, with a range of 5'1¼" to 5'5¼". Three men, not identified elsewhere, fit the height

description, at, or within one inch: PVT Anthony Assadaly, L Company, variously listed as 5'3" or 5'7" tall; PVT Henry Lehmann, I Company, 5'4"; and PVT Peter McGue, L Company, 5'4". Those determined by the archaeologists as fitting the morphological profile were: B. Stafford (E); J. Carney (F); W. Liemann (F); S. Omling (F); T. Acheson (F); P. Kelly (I); H. Lehmann (I); J. McGucker (I); and A. Assadaly (L). In addition to the bone fragments, two four-hole iron trouser buttons, generally associated with those on army trousers to attach suspenders and to close the fly were found; a .45/55 cartridge case was found beneath the arm; a .45/55 bullet was found near the center of the excavation; and five cobbles (stones) associated with those used to hold dirt thrown over the body, were also located at the site [Scott and Fox, *Archaeological Insights into the Custer Battle*; and, Scott; Fox; and Connor, *Archaeological Perspectives on the Battle of the Little Bighorn*]. Listed number 213 in "June Returns, Alterations ... Killed in action."

McGuire (also seen spelled as Maguire), **PVT John B., Jr.**— b. Livermore, Indiana County, PA, 18 Jul 1854–d. Saltsburg, Indiana County, PA, 12 Feb 1932. Company C, private. Brown eyes, brown hair, florid complexion; 5'8" tall. Enlisted 4 Oct 1875; with the Seventh Cavalry less than one year. Attached to pack train. WIA in right arm on Reno Hill. Buried in Area C, Block 3, Grave 22, Livermore Cemetery, Saltsburg, PA.

McGurn, PVT Bernard— b. Newtown, MA, 1851–d. unknown. Company B, private. Blue eyes, brown hair, ruddy complexion; 5'7⅞" tall. Enlisted 23 Mar 1876. Remained at the Powder River Depot.

McHugh, PVT Philip— b. Donegal, Ireland, 1839–d. Allentown, PA, 1 Apr 1910. Company L, private. Hazel eyes, black hair, ruddy complexion; 5'6½" tall. Second enlistment 4 Jun 1874. With the pack train (Overfield); fought on Reno Hill.

McIlhargey (also McEllargey), **PVT Archibald**— b. Antrim, Ireland, 1845–d. 25 Jun 1876, killed at the Little Big Horn. Company I, private. Brown eyes, black hair, dark complexion; 5'5" tall. Enlisted from 19 Nov 1867 to 19 Nov 1872 in Seventh Cavalry. Re-upped on same date. Married; wife's name was Josephine. Two children: Archibald F. and Rosalie. Reno's "striker." He was detailed to Reno, but was sent back as a courier and was killed with Custer. He carried the first message from Reno to Custer reporting that Indians were in front of the command in strong force (Hammer). Body found on Custer Hill. Listed number 163 in "June Returns, Alterations ... Killed in action."

McIntosh, 1LT Donald (nicknamed "The Indian"; also "Tosh")— b. Jasper House, Montréal, Quebec, Canada, 4 Sep 1838. [There is a possible discrepancy with the location of Jasper House. One source claimed it was near present-day Jasper, Alberta, on the Athabasca River, and while that may be correct, McIntosh was certainly born near Montréal.]–d. 25 Jun 1876, killed at the Little Big Horn as Reno retreated from the timber. Company G: Acting CO. DOR: 22 Mar 1870; fourth-ranking 1LT on campaign. Secured a commission to the Seventh Cavalry (M), 17 Aug 1867. An injury kept him from the Winter Campaign of 1868. A courageous officer, extremely well-liked, but on COL Sturgis' list of questionable officers. Managed to survive the Benzine Boards. Deployed to the south with his regiment; also took part in the Yellowstone and Black Hills campaigns (1873 and 1874). Though there are discrepancies in how he was killed, it was certainly in the bottoms, possibly 20 yards from LBH, near Charlie Reynolds. McIntosh's striker, PVT Rapp, was holding his horse, but Rapp took a bullet and died, the horses stampeding. PVT McCormick offered McIntosh his horse. He was probably shot from this horse. His "scalp was torn and cut off from the forehead clear back to the neck" [From an article in the Chicago *Tribune,* 28 Jul 1876, the packer, John Frett, one of the contributors; Graham, *The Custer Myth,* p. 338]. In an article in "Winners of the West," September, 1942, former private George C. Berry (E/7I of Gibbon's command) wrote: "A lieutenant named McIntosh was lying on his face directly in our line of march, and he had on a buckskin shirt with his name written or printed on it" [Graham, p. 365]. Ken Hammer, in *The Battlefield Dispatch,* Winter 2005, says he was killed at the edge of the timber. Horse's name was Puff. Part Indian, part Scottish-Canadian. Born in Canada, into an old trading family. Father was a factor in the Hudson's Bay Company and was killed by Indians when McIntosh was fourteen. Same family as Sir James McIntosh. Mother, Charlotte, was a direct descendent of Red Jacket, a chief of the Six Nations. Married Mary (Molly) Garrett (d. 12 May 1910) on 30 Oct 1866, in Baltimore. Molly's younger sister, Katherine, married LT Francis M. Gibson, H Company, Seventh Cavalry [Goldin/Carroll, *The Benteen-Goldin Letters,* p. 129]. Buried on the battlefield, then reinterred in Fort Leavenworth, then exhumed on 28 Oct 1909 and reinterred in Arlington National Cemetery.

McKay, PVT Edward J.— b. Galway, Ireland, 1854–d. unknown. Company G, private. Blue eyes, black hair, ruddy complexion; 5' 5" tall. Enlisted 12 Apr 1876. Remained at the Powder River Depot. Presence confirmed on June Returns.

McKee, PVT John— b. Meigs County, OH, 1853– d. unknown. Company G, private. Hazel eyes, light hair, fair complexion; 5'10" tall. Enlisted 4 Apr 1876. Remained at the Powder River Depot. Presence confirmed on June Returns.

McKenna, PVT John (aka Jonathan Kenney)— b. Limerick, Ireland, 1843–d. drowned in Ohio River, circa 16 Dec 1888 near Constance, KY. Company E, private. Hazel eyes, dark hair, medium complexion; 5' 8¾" tall. Enlisted 19 Dec 1874. Discharged 18 Dec 1879 as a sergeant. Overfield and Hammer list him with the pack train, but Michno claims he was not at the battle and was not listed on the 30 Jun 1876 muster roll. Witnesses, however, claim he was present at the battle.

McLaughlin, PVT Terrence— b. Harrisburg, PA, 1851–d. unknown. Company B, private. Hazel eyes, brown hair, fair complexion; 5' 6¾" tall. Enlisted 13 Mar 1876 in NYC. With the pack train escort, Company B. Arrived and fought on Reno Hill.

McLaughlin, SGT Thomas F.— b. Philadelphia, PA, 1847–d. Jamestown, Dakota Territory, 3 Mar 1886; it is possible he was admitted to the North Dakota Hospital for the Insane on this date, dying in January 1887. Hammer, Nichols, and Williams, however, all list 3 Mar 1886. Company H, sergeant. Blue eyes, light hair, fair complexion; 5' 4½" tall. Enlisted from 6 Aug 1868 to 6 Aug 1871 in Seventh Cavalry. Re-upped 6 Aug 1871. After his enlistment ran out — according to a Benteen letter to his wife — on 31 Jul 1876, McLaughlin re-upped again from 4 Sep 1876 to 3 Sep 1881, but in the Seventh Infantry, companies A, H, and I. WIA in left arm, undoubtedly on Reno Hill. Wife named Martha. Buried in the hospital cemetery.

McMasters, PVT William— b. Glasgow, Scotland, 1845–d. unknown. Company B, private. Gray eyes, brown hair, ruddy complexion; 5' 6½" tall. Enlisted 14 Dec 1874 in Boston. With the pack train escort, Company B. Arrived and fought on Reno Hill.

McNally, PVT James P.— b. Kildare, Ireland, 1847–d. unknown. Company I, private. Gray eyes, dark hair, ruddy complexion; 6½" tall. Enlisted 12 Nov 1872. With pack train, fighting on Reno Hill.

McNamara, PVT James— b. Rascommon, Ireland, Jul 1848–d. Pittsfield, MA, 24 Jan 1932. Company H, private. Blue eyes, light hair, light complexion; 5' 5" tall. Enlisted 12 Nov 1872. Rode with his unit in Benteen's battalion, and fought on Reno Hill. Married Mary Ainsborough. No children. Buried in St. Mary's Cemetery, Troy.

McPeake, PVT Alexander— b. Canonsburg, PA, Aug 1849–d. unknown. Company L, private. Gray eyes, light hair, fair complexion; 5'7¾" tall. Enlisted 15 Mar 1871. Brother was killed at Spotsylvania Court House. Remained at the Powder River Depot. Presence confirmed on June Returns.

McShane, PVT John— b. Montreal, Quebec, Canada, 1849–d. Fort Lincoln, D.T., 13 Apr 1877. Company I, private. Gray eyes, black hair, dark complexion; 5'6" tall. Enlisted 20 Sep 1875. With pack train. Died of a gunshot wound by the Sergeant of the Guard while confined.

McVay, PVT John— b. Ireland, 1847–d. unknown. Company G, private. Gray eyes, dark hair, dark complexion; 5'8¾" tall. Enlisted 21 Nov 1872. In the valley fight and subsequent retreat to Reno Hill. WIA in left hip on Reno Hill.

McVeigh, TMP David— b. Philadelphia, PA, 1851–d. unknown. Company A. Trumpeter. Blue eyes, light brown hair, fair complexion; 5'7" tall. Enlisted 29 Oct 1872. Smalley wrote that McVeigh was DeRudio's orderly. McVeigh claimed he was Moylan's and DeRudio's horse-holder during the valley fight.

McWilliams, PVT David— b. Edinburgh, Scotland, 1849–d. Fort Meade, D.T., 28 Dec 1881. Company H, private. Blue eyes, brown hair, fair complexion; 5'5½" tall. First enlistment with Seventh Cavalry. Second enlistment 29 Aug 1871. His pistol accidentally discharged as he was mounting his horse (6 Jun 1876), wounding him from the calf down through the right foot. Remained at the Powder River Depot. Carried as "sick." Married: Annie, b. 1846 in Kentucky; son, James.

Meador, PVT Thomas— b. Redford County, VA, 1851–d. 26 Jun 1876, killed at the Little Big Horn while on Reno Hill. Company H, private. Brown eyes, brown hair, ruddy complexion; 5'5¼" tall. Enlisted 19 Jan 1872. Shot in the chest on Company H line on Reno Hill, near PVT Julien Jones, 26 Jun 1876. Listed number 140 in "June Returns, Alterations … Killed in action."

Meadwell, PVT John R. (aka J. R. Meadville)— b. Butler County, PA, 14 Dec 1855 or possibly 1854–d. unknown. Company D, private. Brown eyes, brown hair, fair complexion; 5'7½" tall. Enlisted 13 Sep 1875. Rode with his unit in Benteen's battalion, and fought on Reno Hill. Wounded on 30 Sep 1877 in the Snake Creek fight against Chief Joseph's Nez Percé Indians.

Mechlin (also spelled Meckling), **BSM Henry W. B.**— b. Mount Pleasant, Westmoreland County, PA, 14 Oct 1851–d. Washington, D.C., 10 Apr 1926. Company H: company blacksmith. Gray eyes, dark hair, fair complexion; 5'9¾" tall. Enlisted

5 Aug 1875. Rode with his unit in Benteen's battalion, and fought on Reno Hill. Awarded MH for firing and holding an exposed, standing position with Windolph, Mechlin, and Voit, on the brow of Reno Hill, as a diversion while others carried water up from the LBH. Wife: Ellen E. Mechlin.

Meier, PVT John H. (Nicknamed, "Snopsy"; aka Solomon August, Solomon Angst)— b. Hanover, Germany, 26 Jan 1846–d. Washougal, WA, 12 Jul 1917. Company M, private. Blue eyes, red hair, light complexion; 5'5" tall. Enlisted 6 Sep 1866, Seventh Cavalry. Deserted with no record of apprehension. Enlisted 3 Sep 1873. No specific record exists of his participation in the battle, other than his presence with his unit during the valley fighting and subsequent defense of Reno Hill where he was WIA in back of neck.

Meyer, CPL Albert H.— b. Germany, 1852–d. 25 Jun 1876, killed at the Little Big Horn. Company E, corporal. Blue eyes, light hair, fair complexion; 5'8" tall. Enlisted on 27 Sep 1873. Body found in Deep Ravine and identified by PVT Frank Berwald. Listed number 58 in "June Returns, Alterations … Killed in action."

Meyer, PVT August— b. Hanover, Germany, 1847–d. 25 Jun 1876, killed at the Little Big Horn. Company C, private. Blue eyes, dark hair; 5'6" tall. With the 7th Cavalry less than one year. Enlisted 11 Oct 1875. In the C Company charge off Battle Ridge–Calhoun Hill, but body was never identified. May have died in Calhoun Coulee, Finley-Finckle Ridge, the Keogh Sector, or possibly even Last Stand Hill. Listed number 32 in "June Returns, Alterations … Killed in action."

Meyer (also Mayer, Meier), **PVT Frederick**— b. Delmenhorst, Germany, 1854–d. 25 Jun 1876, killed at the Little Big Horn. Company C, private. Hazel eyes, brown hair; 5'6½" tall. With the Seventh less than one year. Enlisted 24 Dec 1875. He had been a tailor in civilian life. Body never identified, though archaeological work may have placed him at Marker 128, which means he was one of the ones killed during C Company's charge into Calhoun Coulee. Another possibility is Marker 200, near Keogh. Privates Shea and Thadus meet the criteria as well. At Marker 200 (1984 grid location N7126-E2760, in the Keogh area), the following artifacts were found: right cavalry boot, upper section cut away; human bones: lower arm; lower left leg; fingers; toes. Consistent with a single individual of slight build, five feet seven to eight inches tall, and twenty years of age [Scott and Fox, *Archaeological Insights into the Custer Battle*, p. 100]. Listed number 33 in "June Returns, Alterations … Killed in action."

Meyer (also seen spelled Myer and Myers), PVT William D. (nicknamed "Tinker Bill")—b. Pittsburgh, PA, May 1853–d. 25 Jun 1876, killed at the Little Big Horn while scaling the eastern bluffs during Reno's retreat. Company M, private. Blue eyes, light hair, fair complexion; 5' 9½" tall. Enlisted 16 Dec 1875. Killed on his way up the bluffs at the foot of the bluffs, near Clear. Shot in the eye and badly mutilated, though 1SG Ryan claims Meyer was killed (along with Dr. DeWolf, Gordon of M, and Clair [Clear] of K) under troopers' covering fire from the hill and so none of them were scalped. Listed number 232 in "June Returns, Alterations ... Killed in action."

Meyers, SAD John—b. Würtemburg, Germany, 1836–d. Fort Lincoln, M.T., 26 Dec 1877, of wounds suffered in Tongue River battles. Company D: company saddler. Hazel eyes, black hair, ruddy complexion; 5' 7½" tall. Second enlistment 1 Jan 1872. Rode with his unit in Benteen's battalion, and fought on Reno Hill.

Mielke, PVT Max—b. Frankfurt, Germany, 1845–d. killed at Snake Creek, M.T., 30 Sep 1877 in the Nez Percé War. Company K, private. Blue eyes, dark hair, fair complexion; 5'10" tall. Enlisted 27 Mar 1866 in 17th Infantry (re-designated 35th Infantry); discharged 27 Mar 1869. Enlisted 9 Apr 1870 in 10th Infantry; discharged 9 Apr 1875. Enlisted 24 Mar 1876 in Seventh Cavalry. Rode with his unit in Benteen's battalion, and fought on Reno Hill. WIA in left foot in hilltop fight. A sergeant when he died. Married Josephine Rosette 28 Oct 1871 in Brownsville, TX. Daughter, Lilly Josephine born 28 Aug 1872. Buried in Custer Battlefield National Cemetery.

Miller, Charles see Shulte, PVT Frederick

Miller, BSM Henry—b. Baltimore, MD, Dec 1843–d. San Antonio, TX, 30 Dec 1914. Company E: company blacksmith. Blue eyes, brown hair, light complexion; 5' 9" tall. Served in 73rd Ohio Infantry, 3rd Maryland Cavalry, and 8th Cavalry. Also served in the U.S. Navy. Current enlistment 13 Nov 1871. With pack train, though Michno says he could have been at PRD.

Miller, PVT John—b. Philadelphia, PA, 1849–d. 25 Jun 1876, killed at the Little Big Horn. Company L, private. Hazel eyes, brown hair, dark complexion; 5' 8" tall. Second enlistment 4 Sep 1875. In all likelihood he was killed on Calhoun Hill, though the possibility exists he was one of those killed during the panic through the Keogh Sector. No remains found during the 1984–1985 archaeological work match his description. Listed no. 211 in "June Returns, Alterations ... Killed in action."

Miller, Michael J. see Galvan, PVT James J.

Milton, PVT Francis E.—b. Hillsdale, MI, 1853–d. 25 Jun 1876, killed at the Little Big Horn. Company F, private. Blue eyes, light hair, light complexion; 5' 7¼" tall. Enlisted 15 Aug 1871. In all likelihood he was killed on Last Stand Hill with his unit. Listed number 115 in "June Returns, Alterations ... Killed in action."

Milton, PVT Joseph—b. Glasgow, Scotland, 1844–d. 1 Oct 1904. Company F, private. Blue eyes, brown hair, fair complexion; 5' 6½" tall. Second enlistment 1 Jan 1873. Cook for the band. Remained behind at the Powder River Depot.

Mitchell, PVT John Edward—b. Galway, Ireland, 1842–d. 25 Jun 1876, killed at the Little Big Horn. Company I, private. Blue eyes, brown hair, ruddy complexion; 5' 6¼" tall. First enlisted 1 Sep 1866 in Seventh Cavalry and re-upped 14 Sep 1871. Married Catherine Agnes Clemens 28 Apr 1872. Children: Anna, Catherine, and Charles. Detailed to Reno as his cook, but was sent back as a courier and killed with Custer. Body found on Custer Hill. Listed number 164 in "June Returns, Alterations ... Killed in action."

Moller (also seen as Muller), PVT Jan—b. Orsle, Denmark, 13 Sep 1849–d. Deadwood, SD, 23 Feb 1928. Company H, private. Gray eyes, light hair, sandy complexion; 5' 8" tall. Enlisted 15 Jan 1872. Rode with his unit in Benteen's battalion, and fought on Reno Hill. WIA in left thigh while he was on Reno Hill. Married Carolina Anderson (born in Germany). No children from this marriage. Buried in Mount Moriah Cemetery, Deadwood.

Monroe, PVT Joseph—b. Lorraine, France, 1851–d. 25 Jun 1876, killed at the Little Big Horn. Company F, private. Brown eyes, black hair, dark complexion; 5' 6½" tall. Enlisted 14 Sep 1875 in Cincinnati, OH. In all likelihood he was killed on Last Stand Hill with his unit. Listed number 117 in "June Returns, Alterations ... Killed in action."

Moodie, PVT William—b. Edinburgh, Scotland, 1841–d. 25 Jun 1876, killed at the Little Big Horn. Company A, private. Gray eyes, brown hair, florid complexion; 5' 8" tall. Enlisted 15 Dec 1874 in NYC. Thought to have been a dragoon in the British army. Killed west of retreat crossing (see SGT Botzer [G]). Listed number 7 in "June Returns, Alterations ... Killed in action."

Moonie, TMP George A.—b. Boston, MA, 1854 or 1855–d. 25 Jun 1876, killed at the Little Big Horn. Company E: trumpeter. Hazel eyes, dark hair, fair complexion; 5' 6⅜" tall. Enlisted on 18

Mar 1875. Bone fragments found at Marker 128, isolated behind Greasy Grass Ridge, would be consistent with his reported age and height. Men killed at this location were believed to have been from C Company however. Several others fit this description, as well. Both human remains and battle related artifacts were found. Almost a complete burial discovered at this site; the most complete set of human remains recovered during the 1984–1985 archaeological excavations: lower right leg articulated, its foot bones encased in a cavalry boot. Other bones had been re-buried after the flesh had decayed. It was determined to be a male, between 19–22 years old, and approximately 5' 6¾" tall, with a range of 5' 5¾"–5' 7⅛". Individual was stocky with well-developed musculature [Scott, *et al., Archaeological Perspectives,* p. 268]; right-handed. Several men fit the description and the archaeologists listed them as: F. Meier (C); J. Shea (C); J. Thadus (C); N. Short (C); G. Moonie (E); W. Huber (E)—highly doubtful; T. Donnelly (F)—highly doubtful; E. Babcock (L); and F. Hughes (L)—highly doubtful. There was evidence of two gunshot wounds in the chest, one from the right, one from the left. Also, massive blunt-force trauma to the skull at about the time of death: bullet fragment in lower left arm; three parallel cut marks on thighbones and another on collarbone; vertebrae showed congenital defect, probably causing the individual pain when he rode his horse for long periods. Also, blouse and trousers buttons found; underwear cloth; hooks and eyes, probably from his campaign hat. Because of the way the bones were dispersed, the individual had to have been re-buried, probably in 1877 or 1879. Listed number 60 in "June Returns, Alterations … Killed in action."

Moore, PVT Andrew J.—b. Camden, NJ, 1850–d. 26 Jun 1876, killed at the Little Big Horn while on Reno Hill. Company G, private. Blue eyes, dark hair, fair complexion; 5' 8" tall. Enlisted 23 Jan 1872. Shot in kidneys, probably through the back. Died in hospital on Reno Hill on June 26th. One of twenty men — one officer, three scouts, sixteen enlisted men — left in the timber in the valley bottoms, but eventually reaching Reno Hill. Listed number 132 in "June Returns, Alterations … Killed in action."

Moore, PVT Hugh N.—b. Dorchester County, MD, 1843–d. Washington, D.C., 3 Sep 1900. Company M, private. Gray eyes, brown hair, fair complexion; 5' 7½" tall. Enlisted 24 Oct 1872. No specific record exists of his participation in the battle, other than his presence with his unit during the valley fighting and subsequent defense of Reno Hill.

Moore, FAR James F.—b. Hebron, OH, 6 May 1849; one source claimed 1847, but this is probably wrong-d. Union, SC, of consumption, 1 Nov 1894. Company B: farrier. Blue eyes, brown hair, fair complexion; 5' 10" tall. Second enlistment 28 Aug 1871. Along with CPT McDougall and PVT Ryan, recovered LT Hodgson's body on the night of 26 Jun 1876 and helped bury him the following morning [Nichols, *RCOI,* p. 554]. After leaving army he took up a claim on 160 acres between Bismarck and FAL, living there until 1881 when he moved to Union, SC.

Moore, PVT Lansing A.—b. Hoboken, NJ, 12 Sep 1854 (also listed as 12 Sep 1844 and 27 Sep 1846)–d. Rawlins, WY, 27 Jul 1931. Company L, private. Blue eyes, brown hair, ruddy complexion; 5' 8" tall. Enlisted 27 Sep 1875. With the pack train, fighting on Reno Hill. Left home at fourteen. Married Sarah Belcher, 4 Jul 1881, and settled in Sheridan County, W.T. Children: Gertrude Jane Specht (lived in Rawlins); Grace Ann Boersig (Amador, CA); William Riley Moore (Worland, WY); and John Belcher Moore (Amador, CA). Resided in Rawlins for 40 years. Buried in the County Section, Rawlins Cemetery

Morris, CPL George C.—b. Georgetown, DE, 4 Jul 1851–d. 25 Jun 1876, killed at the Little Big Horn. Company I, corporal. Brown eyes, brown hair, fair complexion; 5' 5¾" tall. Enlisted 26 Oct 1872. Body never identified, but in all likelihood he was killed in the Keogh Sector. Listed number 144 in "June Returns, Alterations … Killed in action."

Morris, PVT William Ephraim—b. Boston, MA, 1 May 1854 (it looks like the year should be 1858 or possibly even 1861; Williams claims it was 1858, but even the family is unsure)–d. NYC, 26 Nov 1933. Company M, private. Brown eyes, auburn hair, fair complexion; 5' 7½" tall. Enlisted 22 Sep 1875 in Boston. It appears, however, that Morris lied about his age when he enlisted and may have been only fourteen at the time. His half-brother was Byron (or Bryan) Tarbox and they joined together. His death certificate lists him as 75, but even this may be incorrect.

WIA in left breast while climbing the bluffs. Fractured a bone in his forearm in 1877 in a drunken brawl and was discharged as a "private of worthless character." Became a lawyer and judge in the Bronx, NY (for 21 years; 2nd District). According to Willert, it was Morris who tried to save LT Hodgson by having Hodgson grab onto Morris' stirrup [*Little Big Horn Diary,* p. 319], though he also quotes Slaper as claiming it was TMP Fischer and Davern saying an M Company trumpeter.

Married Arah Abbie, 7 Dec 1879. One child: William E., Jr. Attended 50th anniversary celebration of the LBH fight, 25 Jun 1926. Resided at 69 Park Row, NYC, and 2780 Pond Place, Bronx. Appointed CPT, Company E, 69th Infantry, NYARNG. Buried in Grave 1, Lot 7471, Section 178, Kensico Cemetery, Valhalla, NY.

Morrison, PVT John—b. Zanesville, OH, 1843–d. unknown. Company G, private. Gray eyes, brown hair, ruddy complexion; 5' 8¾" tall. Third enlistment 21 May 1875. No specific record exists of his participation in the battle, other than his presence with his unit during the valley fighting and subsequent defense of Reno Hill. WIA, probably while on Reno Hill.

Morrow, PVT William E.—b. Boston, MA, Oct 1854–d. unknown. Company B, private. Hazel eyes, dark hair, fair complexion; 5' 6¼" tall. Enlisted 24 Mar 1876. Remained at the Powder River Depot.

Moylan, CPT (Bvt MAJ) **Myles** (aka Charles E. Thomas; nicknamed "Aparejo Mickie")—b. Amesbury, MA (one source claims Galway, Ireland), 17 Dec 1838 (or less likely, 1 Dec 1838)–d. San Diego, CA, 11 Dec 1909. Company A: Commanding Officer. Assigned to Reno's battalion during the battle. Gray eyes, black hair, ruddy complexion; 5' 9½" tall. DOR: 1 Mar 1872, sixth-ranking captain on the campaign. Joined the regular army in 1857, and serving under Lewis Merrill, took part in the Utah Campaign. Took part in the battles at Fort Henry, Fort Donalson, and Shiloh. Commissioned a 2LT in the Fifth Cavalry in Feb 1863 (GAC was the unit's 1LT). Fought at Gettysburg, Beverly Ford, and a number of other battles. In Oct 1863, he was arrested for traveling without a pass and dismissed from the service. Enlisting under an assumed name, he received another commission in Jan 1864.

After the Civil War, Moylan joined the Seventh Cavalry as a private, though he quickly became the regiment's first sergeant major. By December 1866, Moylan was in Washington, D.C., taking the exam for officer candidacy. Custer tried to get him a commission, but he failed the test. With Custer's help, he got another chance and passed. Moylan became part of the "Custer Clan." LT Calhoun was his brother-in-law. He was the regiment's adjutant from 1867 to 1870, and ultimately Company A's CO for two decades. Promoted to captain, Company A, 1 Mar 1872. Participated in the Washita campaign, reconstruction duty, the Yellowstone Campaign—was in the 4 Aug 1873 and 11 Aug 1873 battles—and the Black Hills Expedition.

During the RCOI, SGT Culbertson testified that he heard CPT Weir ask Moylan if Custer ever dis-

cussed orders with him. Moylan replied, no, Custer never told him what he was going to do, he just ordered Moylan to tell the company commanders what he wanted [Nichols, *RCOI*, p. 379].

According to PVT Goldin, Moylan was not a particularly popular officer and was thought to have a streak of yellow after his performance at the LBH [Goldin/Carroll, *The Benteen-Goldin Letters*, p. 129]. Moylan was, however, awarded the MH for action at Bear Paw Mountain, 30 Dec 1877, against the Nez Percé, so something must have changed. He was also wounded there.

Spent his career with the Seventh entirely on the frontier, also participating in the fight against the Crows (1887) and the Sioux at Wounded Knee (1890). Moylan was also not a particular favorite of Benteen, apparently spending too much time among the packs during the LBH battle and probably because Moylan was particularly close to George Custer. Goldin later referred to him as "Hard Tack Mick." Benteen: Moylan had been, "pretty well protected from grave danger" [Sklenar, *Research Review*, Vol. 9, No. 1, p. 16]. Benteen: "I didn't know the men of the regiment had such an aversion to Mylie Moylan, but my! How correct they were in so having." Benteen: when Benteen reached Reno Hill, the first thing he saw "was the gallantly mustached captain of Troop A blubbering liked a whipped urchin, tears coursing down his cheeks." Jim Donovan wrote that Moylan was "tough and capable … an able officer but for some reason beyond mere snobbery was not well liked" [*A Terrible Glory*, pp. 60 and 61].

Married Charlotte Calhoun on 22 Oct 1872, in Madison, IN. She was LT Calhoun's sister. She died 29 Mar 1916. No children.

Muering, SAD John—b. St Louis, MO, 1848–d. Fort Wayne, MI, 12 Feb 1902. Company A: saddler. Gray eyes, sandy hair, fair complexion; 5'10" tall. Enlisted 5 Dec 1875. Hammer has him as detached service, but Smalley corrects this and lists him as present at the battle. No specific record exists of his participation in the battle, other than his presence with his unit during the valley fighting and subsequent defense of Reno Hill. Appointed SGT and fought in Snake Creek battle, 30 Sep 1877 against Nez Percé.

Mullen, SGT John (aka James Hughes)—b. Baltimore, MD, 1848–d. San Francisco, CA, 29 Aug 1888. Company L, sergeant. Gray eyes, light hair, fair complexion; 5' 6" tall. Enlisted 29 Jun 1870, First Artillery; deserted 7 Apr 1871; reenlisted as James Hughes, 24 Apr 1871 in Second Cavalry, Fort Wallace, KS. Enlistment cancelled when he surrendered under amnesty. Restored to duty and transferred to Seventh Cavalry. With the pack train, fighting on Reno Hill. Died at the Presidio of respiratory failure. Buried in Section West Side, Grave 221, SF National Cemetery. Survived by his mother, Anna E. Mullen (d. 30 Mar 1903) and invalid sister Mary, who resided at 73 Herron Street, Pittsburgh, PA.

Mullin, PVT Martin — b. Cork, Ireland, 1847–d. unknown. Company C, private. Blue eyes, brown hair; 5'5" tall. First enlisted 3 Jan 1873. Deserted twice and apprehended both times. Attached to pack train. Fought on Reno Hill.

Murphy, Joseph C. *see* **Bates, Joseph**

Murphy, SGT Lawrence — b. Kerry, Ireland, 1849–d. Washington, D.C., 13 Jan 1888 of syphilis. Company E, sergeant. Blue eyes, brown hair, fair complexion; 5'5¾" tall. Enlisted 30 Dec 1871. Douglas Scott claims he was on Reno Hill, but this is probably wrong as all other sources list him at the Powder River Depot.

Murphy, PVT Michael — b. Cork, Ireland, 1838–d. Washington, D.C., 11 Jun 1904. Company K, private. Blue eyes, black hair, fair complexion; 5'3½" tall. Enlisted from 10 Sep 1866 to Sep 1871 in Seventh Cavalry. Enlisted 11 Sep 1871. Rode with his unit in Benteen's battalion, and fought on Reno Hill. Not married. Buried in Soldiers' Home National Cemetery.

Murphy, SGT Robert L. — b. Stanford, NY, 1850–d. killed in train yard accident around 1900 while working as a locomotive engineer in Minneapolis. Company I, sergeant. Brown eyes, brown hair, fair complexion; 5'8¾" tall. With Department HQ in the field, for duty as orderly for GEN Terry. Special Orders 39.

Murphy, PVT Thomas (aka Thomas Anderson) — b. Cork, Ireland, Apr 1853–d. Washington, D.C. Company K, private. Gray eyes, dark hair, fair complexion; 5'9¾" tall. Enlisted 13 Dec 1874. Rode with his unit in Benteen's battalion, and fought on Reno Hill. Buried in Soldiers' Home National Cemetery.

Murray, CPL Henry — b. Boston, MA, 1848–d. Boston, MA, 26 Aug 1909. Company K, corporal. Hazel eyes, dark hair, dark complexion; 5'11" tall. Enlisted from 12 Jul 1866 to 12 Jul 1869 in Fourth Cavalry. Enlisted 4 Nov 1869 to 10 Sep 1870 in 11th Infantry. Enlisted 14 Oct 1875 in Seventh Cavalry. Remained at the Powder River Depot. Presence confirmed on June Returns. Buried in Forest Hills Cemetery.

Murray, SGT Thomas — b. Monaghan, Ireland, 1836–d. Washington, D.C., 4 Aug 1888. Company B, sergeant. Blue eyes, light hair, ruddy comple-

xion; 5'8¼" tall. Enlisted 25 May 1861 in NYC, in 37th NY Infantry. During the Civil War, he was wounded in battle of Williamsburg, 4 May 1862. Enlisted 24 Jul 1863 to 24 Aug 1865 in 13th NY Heavy Artillery. Enlisted 17 Aug 1866 in Seventh Cavalry. WIA on Reno Hill. Awarded MH for bringing up pack train and rations and water under extremely heavy fire. Buried in Soldiers' Home National Cemetery, Section K, Grave 6502.

Myers (also seen as Meyers), **PVT Frank** — b. Quebec, Canada, 1854–d. unknown. Company F, private. Gray eyes, brown hair, dark complexion; 5'8¼" tall. Enlisted 8 Oct 1875 in Cincinnati, OH. Deserted 14 Dec 1876. With the pack train and fought on Reno Hill.

Myers, PVT Frederick William — b. Brunswick, Germany, 1847–d. 5 May 1900. Company I, private. Hazel eyes, dark hair, dark complexion; 5'9¼" tall. Enlisted 17 May 1873. Remained at PRD as teamster. Presence confirmed on June Returns. Married: Emma. Awarded MH for action at White River, SD, 1 Jan 1891.

Nealon (also seen spelled Neelan), **CPL Daniel** — b. Newport, RI, 1849–d. unknown. Company H, corporal. Gray eyes, brown hair, fair complexion; 5'7" tall. Enlisted 9 Feb 1872. Rode with his unit in Benteen's battalion, and fought on Reno Hill. Possibly illiterate, though this is hard to believe for a corporal.

Neely, PVT Frank — b. Collinsville, OH, 1850–d. unknown. Company M, private. Gray eyes, light hair, fair complexion; 5'10" tall. Enlisted 8 Apr 1871. No specific record exists of his participation in the battle, other than his presence with his unit during the valley fighting and subsequent defense of Reno Hill. Helped bury the Custers. Resided near Fort Grant, A. T., after 1890; in San Francisco, CA, in 1902; and near Sheridan, WY, about 1904.

Nees, PVT Edler — b. Ornirhessen, Germany, 1853–d. unknown. Company H, private.
Blue eyes, brown hair, ruddy complexion; 5'7½" tall. Enlisted 7 Sep 1875. Rode with his unit in Benteen's battalion, and fought on Reno Hill.

Nelson, Robert *see* **Brandon, Benjamin**

Newell, PVT Daniel J. — b. Ballinlough, County Rascommon, Ireland, 17 Mar 1847–d. Hot Springs, SD, 23 Sep 1933. Company M, private. Gray eyes, brown hair, dark complexion; 5'7½" tall. Enlisted 8 Oct 1873. WIA in left thigh at the beginning of the retreat from the valley fight; Scollin's bunkmate. Married Mary M. Harlow, 9 Jul 1882. Buried in Bear Butte Cemetery, Sturgis, SD.

Nicholas, PVT Joshua S. — b. London, England, 1850–d. unknown. Company H, private. Blue eyes, light hair, light complexion; 5' 6" tall. Enlisted 2 Feb 1872. Rode with his unit in Benteen's battalion, and fought on Reno Hill.

Nitsche, PVT Ottocar— b. Germany (Prussia), 1851–d. unknown. Company C, private. Blue eyes, light hair, fair complexion; 5' 5¼" tall. Had been with Seventh Cavalry for several years. Enlisted 6 Dec 1872. Ordered to stay behind at Rosebud with Subsistence Department under LT Richard Thompson, Sixth Infantry. Status uncertain.

Niver, Garrett H. *see* **Van Allan, PVT Garrett H.**

Nolan, CPL John— b. Tipperary, Ireland, 1848–d. Newburgh, NY, 17 Jul 1993. Company K, corporal. Blue eyes, brown hair, fair complexion; 5' 7¼" tall. Enlisted 4 Dec 1874 in NYC. Remained at the Powder River Depot. Presence confirmed on June Returns. Married, survived by two children, Edward and Mary. Buried St. Patrick's Cemetery, Newburgh.

Noonan, CPL John (aka Nunan, Minden, McKinney)— b. Fort Wayne, IN, 1846–d. Fort Abraham Lincoln, D.T., 30 Nov 1878 (suicide). Company L, corporal. Blue eyes, dark hair, fair complexion; 5' 7" tall. Enlisted 14 Jan 1872. Remained at the Powder River Depot in charge of the cattle herd. Presence confirmed on June Returns. Subject of a strange story connected with the Seventh Cavalry: he committed suicide FAL, 30 Nov 1878, after his wife died and he found out that his wife — the infamous Mrs. Nash — was actually a man. Noonan was her/his third husband. Shot himself in the company stable. Buried in the FAL Post Cemetery. Reinterred in Custer Battlefield National Cemetery.

Northeg, SGT Olans H.— b. Nannestad, Norway, 1841–d. Fort Meade, D.T., 5 Nov 1882. Company G, sergeant. Gray eyes, fair hair, fair complexion; 5' 9½" tall. Second enlistment 21 Mar 1872. No specific record exists of his participation in the battle, other than his presence with his unit during the valley fighting and subsequent defense of Reno Hill. Died in service. Buried in Post Cemetery, Fort Meade, D.T.

Noshang, PVT Jacob— b. Hamilton County, OH, 1847–d. 25 Jun 1876, killed at the Little Big Horn. Company I, private. Hazel eyes, brown hair, dark complexion; 5' 5¾" tall. Enlisted 23 Jan 1872. Body never identified, but in all likelihood he was killed in the Keogh Sector. Listed number 165 in "June Returns, Alterations ... Killed in action."

Nowlan, 1LT Henry James— b. Corfu, Ionian Islands (at the British garrison), 18 Jun 1837–d. Hot Springs, AR, 10 Nov 1898. Headquarters: regimental quartermaster officer. On detached service as Acting Assistant Quartermaster on General Terry's staff. Graduated from Sandhurst and served as an officer with the British army (Hussars) in the Crimean War. Decorated for gallantry in the siege of Sebastopol, 1854–1855. Also served in the Papal Guard. Came to the U.S. in 1862 and served in the Civil War in the 14th and 18th NY Cavalry. Was a POW at Andersonville for some time, but escaped in early 1865, an unusual occurrence in the Civil War [Kimber]. After the war, he was stationed in New Orleans and participated in the Yorktown Expedition in Texas where he was severely wounded. Joined the Seventh Cavalry (F) in 1866. Promoted to 1LT in Company G, 3 Dec 1866. Appointed regimental commissary and did not take part in field operations during 1867 and 1868. Accompanied the regiment on reconstruction duty in the south. Appointed regimental QM, Mar 1872, and remained in that position for the rest of his time in the Dakotas, though he did take part in the Nez Percé Campaign and the battle of Canyon Creek, 13 Sep 1877. Douglas Scott claims he was with Reno on 25 Jun 1876, though this is certainly incorrect (Hammer places him at PRD). What is certain, however, is that he was at the battlefield on 27 Jun 1876 with Benteen, DeRudio, Bradley, and the H Company detachment.

Promoted to CPT, effective 25 Jun 1876, and replaced Keogh, his good friend. Also accompanied the Sheridan expedition to the battlefield in 1877 as CO, Company I, Seventh Cavalry. Benteen considered him a "coffee-cooler" [Graham, *The Custer Myth*, p. 300], though that appellation appears to be unfair. Nowlan remained on frontier duty for the rest of his career. He died while on leave.

According to LT Godfrey, in the 1877 trip to the battlefield with LTC Michael Sheridan, Nowlan made a point of properly marking the sites of where the officers were buried. "Nowlan told me that he had marked the grave of each officer with a stake driven below the surface of the ground. The name of the officer was written on a slip of paper and put in an empty cartridge shell, and this driven into the top of the stake. He made a sketch of the ground to show the location of the grave of each officer, and he went with Colonel Mike V. Sheridan when the bodies were removed. In some cases part of the bones were somewhat removed from the places of burial, but Capt. Nowlan told me great care was taken in their collection" [Godfrey/Dustin /Graham, *The Custer Myth*, p. 364].

Nugent, PVT William David— b. Grayson County, KY, 5 Nov 1852–d. Coffeyville, KS, 15 Nov 1934. Company A, private. Gray eyes, brown hair, dark complexion; 5' 8½" tall. Enlisted 5 Aug

1872. In the valley and Reno Hill fighting. Wounded while going for water. Liddic writes a great story about Nugent's quest for water on 26 June, and how he dove into the LBH, filling canteens while he was submerged, all the while drinking his fill, bullets pounding the river, then the dirt around him as he scrambled back up the ravine to safety [*Vanishing Victory*, p. 178]. Willert relates the same story [*Little Big Horn Diary*, p. 409]. Married Millie Keller (d. 16 Jan 1885); married Josie Wells (d. 14 Jan 1900), 18 Jul 1889. Children: Myrtle, Mabel G., and Gladys. Farmer for 20 years, residing in Ripley, OK, and RR1, Jefferson, KS, then with daughter in Fawn Township, KS. Buried in Old Parrotte Cemetery near Cushing, OK.

Nursey, SGT Frederick— b. Suffolk, England, Dec 1848–d. 25 Jun 1876, killed at the Little Big Horn. Company F, sergeant. Blue eyes, light hair, fair complexion; 5' 5½" tall. Enlisted 23 Mar 1871; in his second enlistment, 23 Mar 1876. In all likelihood he was killed on Last Stand Hill with his unit. Listed number 90 in "June Returns, Alterations ... Killed in action."

O'Brien, PVT Thomas— b. Limerick, Ireland, 1853–d. Fort Buford, D.T., 15 Sep 1876. Company B, private. Blue eyes, light hair, fair complexion; 5' 5½" tall. Enlisted 31 Mar 1876. Remained at the Powder River Depot. Caught typhoid, then pneumonia set in and he died at post hospital. Buried on post, then reinterred at Custer Battlefield National Cemetery.

O'Bryan, PVT John— b. PA, 1851–d. 25 Jun 1876, killed at the Little Big Horn. Company I, private. Blue eyes, dark brown hair, light complexion; 5' 6½" tall. Enlisted 8 Jun 1873. Body never identified, but in all likelihood he was killed in the Keogh Sector. Listed number 166 in "June Returns, Alterations ... Killed in action."

O'Connell, PVT David J.— b. Cork, Ireland, 1843–d. 25 Jun 1876, killed at the Little Big Horn. Company L, private. Dark eyes, brown hair, ruddy complexion; 5' 7½" tall. Third enlistment 20 May 1874. In all likelihood he was killed on Calhoun Hill, though the possibility exists he was one of those killed during the panic through the Keogh Sector. No remains found during the 1984–1985 archaeological work match his description. Listed number 214 in "June Returns, Alterations ... Killed in action."

O'Connor, PVT Patrick Edward— b. Longford, Ireland, Jul 1851–d. 25 Jun 1876, killed at the Little Big Horn. Company E, private. Blue eyes, light hair, fair complexion; 5' 5½" tall. Enlisted 18 Sep

1873. While his body was not specifically identified, he may have been one of the unknowns on either the South Skirmish Line or in Deep Ravine. Listed number 76 in "June Returns, Alterations ... Killed in action."

Ogden, SGT John S.— b. Newberry, MA, 1845–d. 25 Jun 1876, killed at the Little Big Horn. Company E, sergeant. Gray eyes, light hair, light complexion; 5' 8" tall. In his 2nd enlistment, 15 Nov 1872. Body identified in Deep Ravine and buried near its mouth, near LBH, though Michno says it is possible he was killed near MTC ford. In his narrative in *The Mystery of E Troop*, p. 30, Michno has Ogden as the E Company trooper whose horse bolted across Ford B and into the Cheyenne village. This is wrong, however. It could have been the body of PVT William A. Brown (F). Listed number 53 in "June Returns, Alterations ... Killed in action."

O'Harra (also spelled O'Hara), **SGT Miles F.**— b. Alton, OH, Sep 1851–d. 25 Jun 1876, killed at the Little Big Horn. May have been the first fatality or the first man mortally wounded, dying shortly thereafter. Company M, sergeant. Light hair, gray eyes, ruddy complexion; 5' 8¾" tall. Enlisted 30 Oct 1872. Promoted to SGT only days before the campaign began, replacing SGT John Dolan, who was being discharged. Married, with one daughter. O'Harra had six brothers and sisters and the double "r" in his name was dropped by some members of the family. Possibly killed in woods, though most witnesses said they saw him mortally wounded on the skirmish line. Hammer: shot in chest on the skirmish line; supposedly the first to die. Oddly enough, he was buried on Reno Hill. Smalley corrects Hammer's edition and claims O'Harra died on Reno Hill (clearly not the *first* to die). A mortal wound in the valley, with death on the hill would explain his burial there, though with the helter-skelter retreat from the timber, this is difficult to imagine. Liddic tells the story of PVT Pigford helping O'Harra to a place of safety after he was struck in the chest during the withdrawal from the skirmish line. During an archaeological dig of the Reno-Benteen battlefield in 1958, the remains of three soldiers were unearthed. Almost twenty years later, one of the skulls was sent for facial reconstruction. It matched a picture of O'Harra. Listed number 226 in "June Returns, Alterations ... Killed in action."

O'Mann, PVT William— b. Hamilton County, IN, 14 Jul 1849–d. Fargo, ND, 26 Apr 1901. Company D, private. Brown eyes, brown hair, dark complexion; 5' 8" tall. Enlisted 12 Oct 1875, but had previous service with the Indiana Light Artillery. Rode with his unit in Benteen's battalion, and fought on Reno Hill. Married Barbara Shoe; one son, John B.

Omling, PVT Sebastian (aka Smeling) — b. Windaciler, Bavaria, 1838–d. 25 Jun 1876, killed at the Little Big Horn. Company F, private. Hazel eyes, light hair, fair complexion; 5' 5¼" tall. Enlisted 21 Dec 1871. Civilian occupation: blacksmith. Bone fragments found at Marker 105 on Last Stand Hill would be consistent with his reported age and height. Most men killed at this location were believed to have been from F Company. Several others fit this description, as well. In addition, Omling fits the description forensic work compiled at paired Markers 67 and 68 on Last Stand Hill near the fence enclosing the area. Both human remains and battle related artifacts were found, including cobbles. Bone fragments were found at this site and were of one human and one horse. Skull fragments, vertebrae — with a compressed fracture of lower lumbar — rib, facial bones, hand bone were all uncovered. One of the ribs showed evidence of possible bullet damage. Fragmented facial bones indicate possible postmortem blunt-force damage. The individual was determined to be between 35 and 45 years old. Five F Company troopers fit within the age parameters, being born between 1831 and 1841 (Note — *This does not mean these bones were from an F Company soldier*): FAR Benjamin Brandon — 1831; PVT Thomas Atcheson — 1838; PVT Herman Knauth — 1838; PVT Sebastian Omling — 1838; PVT George Warren — 1840. [Scott and Fox, *Archaeological Insights into the Custer Battle*; and Scott; Fox; and Connor, *Archaeological Perspectives on the Battle of the Little Bighorn*.] Listed number 118 in "June Returns, Alterations ... Killed in action."

O'Neill, PVT Bernard — b. Kilfurboy, Ireland, circa 1841–d. Washington, D.C., 27 Oct 1896. Headquarters: band. Private. Hazel eyes, brown hair, dark complexion; 5' 6" tall. Remained at Powder River Depot. Presence confirmed on June Returns.

O'Neill, PVT John — b. Tipperary, Ireland, 1848–d. Washington, D.C., 2 Mar 1888. Company B, private. Brown eyes, black hair, dark complexion; 5' 6" tall. Enlisted 8 Jan 1872. In Yellowstone and Black Hills expeditions, as well as Nez Percé campaign of 1877. With the pack train escort, Company B. Arrived and fought on Reno Hill. Died of syphilis. Buried in the Soldiers' Home National Cemetery.

O'Neill, PVT Thomas F. *(*aka Thomas Dean)*—* b. Dublin, Ireland, 14 Jan 1846–d. Riverdale, MD, 23 Mar 1914. Company G, private. Blue eyes, black

hair, fair complexion; 5' 8½" tall. Enlisted from 29 Nov 1865 to 29 Nov 1868 in First Artillery. Before that had served in 10th NY Infantry and 12th NY State Militia. Enlisted from 21 Dec 1868 to 21 Dec 1871 in 1st Infantry. Enlisted 17 Jan 1872 in Seventh Cavalry. Deserted 18 Jun 1872, then enlisted as Thomas Dean 15 Jul 1872 in the 18th Infantry. Surrendered and returned to Seventh Cavalry. Served through the years in varying capacities, including first sergeant and instructor. According to Theodore Goldin (G), when DeRudio was promoted to captain and given command of E Troop, DeRudio managed to get O'Neill transferred to E and made him his first sergeant [Carroll, *The Benteen-Goldin Letters*, p. 23].

In the valley fight, but he was one of twenty men who wound up remaining in the timber. Left the woods with LT DeRudio, Gerard, and Billy Jackson. They wound up getting separated, but eventually reached Reno Hill around 3 am of 27 Jun 1876. Smalley writes that O'Neill served as LT McIntosh's cook. Benteen thought very highly of him and considered O'Neill "a cool, level-headed fellow — and tells it plainly *and the same way all the time*—which is a big thing towards convincing one of the truth of a story" [Graham, *The Custer Myth*, p. 300].

Resided at 137 California Street, NW, Washington, D.C., in 1897; and 319 V Street, NE, Washington, D.C. in 1908. Wife's name was Carrie. Buried in Arlington National Cemetery.

Orr, PVT Charles M. — b. Paris, Ontario, Canada, 1847–d. unknown. Company C, private. Blue eyes, brown hair, fair complexion; 5' 9¾" tall. In the army less than one year. Enlisted 24 Sep 1875. Remained at the Powder River Depot. The June Returns do not list any Company C personnel at Powder River, indicating they must have been returned to their unit.

O'Ryan, PVT William — b. Limerick, Ireland, 1854–d. unknown. Company H, private. Blue eyes, sandy hair, ruddy complexion; 5' 7¾" tall. Enlisted 2 Oct 1875. Rode with his unit in Benteen's battalion, and fought on Reno Hill.

O'Toole, PVT Francis — b. County Mayo, Ireland, 1839–d. Washington, D.C., 20 Feb 1914. Company E, private. Blue eyes, brown hair, fair complexion; 5' 9" tall. Enlisted 1872. Detached service to Department HQ (General Terry) as an orderly.

Owens, PVT Eugene — b. Kildare, Ireland, 1848–d. unknown. Company I, private. Blue eyes, brown hair, fair complexion; 5' 7¾" tall. Enlisted 15 Mar 1875. With pack train; fought on Reno Hill.

Pahl, SGT John — b. Bavaria (or possibly Hamburg), 5 Jan 1850–d. Hot Springs, SD, 28 Jan 1924.

Company H, sergeant. Brown eyes, brown hair, fair complexion; 5'6¼" tall. Enlisted in the First Artillery, then on 4 Nov 1872 in the Seventh Cavalry. WIA in right shoulder (back). Recommended for the Medal of Honor by Benteen for conspicuous gallantry during the third charge during the Reno Hill fight. He did not receive it because there was no endorsement from the merit board. Married Anna M. Hafer (6 Oct 1866–4 Jan 1900). Survived by son Albert and three daughters. Buried in Bear Butte Cemetery, Sturgis, SD. "A braver man never lived" [Charles Windolph].

Pardee, Oscar F. *see* **Burke, PVT John**

Parker, PVT John—b. Birmingham, England, 1849–d. 25 Jun 1876, killed at the Little Big Horn. Company I, private. Gray eyes, light hair, light complexion; 5'7" tall. Arrived in NY in 1871; enlisted 3 Feb 1872. Body found near Driscoll's, west of crest of Custer Hill: "...on the river side of the hogback on ground a little higher up than Cooke" [Michno, *The Mystery of E Troop*, p. 143]. Hardorff wrote, "near the eastern edge of the elevation" [*Lakota Recollections of the Custer Fight*, p. 66, footnote 10]. Listed number 167 in "June Returns, Alterations … Killed in action."

Patton, TMP John W.—b. Philadelphia, PA, 1851–d. 25 Jun 1876, killed at the Little Big Horn. Company I: trumpeter. Brown eyes, brown hair, ruddy complexion; 5'3½" tall. Enlisted 21 Oct 1872. Body found in cluster around Keogh, lying over Keogh. In a 1900 interview with Olin N. Wheeler, PVT Francis Johnson Kennedy claimed the only two men he could recognize from Company I were CPL John Wild and a "musician," and those two only because of their size: tall and short. The musician was, in all likelihood, Patton, who was only 5'3½" tall, though Kennedy never said [see Liddic/Harbaugh, *Camp on Custer*, p. 160]. Wild was 5'9¾" tall. Listed number 147 in "June Returns, Alterations … Killed in action."

Pendtle (also seen spelled Pandtle), **PVT Christopher**—b. Bavaria, 15 Jun 1849–d. Gardenville, WA, 4 Jun 1923, of stomach cancer. Company E, private. Brown eyes, light hair, fair complexion; 5'4½" tall. Enlisted 28 Oct 1872. Extra duty as hospital attendant, originally with Dr. Porter. Hammer lists him with Dr. Williams on the *Far West*, since 17 May 1876, but Smalley contradicts that, saying he was at the battle. In a 1912 interview with Hospital Steward Alfred W. Dale, Walter Camp wrote that Dale said Pendtle/Pandtle was detailed with Doc Porter [Liddic/Harbaugh, *Camp on Custer*, p. 106]. Survived by widow Elizabeth and sons John and William, and four daughters, Jane, Elizabeth, Myrtle, and Mary.

Penwell, TMP George B. (also seen as Pennell)— b. Philadelphia, PA, 1848–d. Washington, D.C., 17 Dec 1905. Company K: trumpeter. Gray eyes, brown hair, fair complexion; 5'5" tall. Enlisted from 1 Mar 1866 to 1 Mar 1869 in Seventh Cavalry. Reenlisted in 5th Cavalry 22 Jun 1869, but deserted 20 Jul 1870. Enlisted 16 Jan 1871 in Seventh Cavalry. In Black Hills expedition. Liddic claims he was assigned as Reno's trumpeter on 25 Jun 1876. Smalley says he was Godfrey's orderly. Based on Godfrey's testimony at the RCOI, it seems Liddic is correct. Godfrey said Penwell was sent to him — with *Reno's* compliments — to pull back as quickly as possible from his skirmish line covering the retreat from Weir Peaks [Nichols, *RCOI*, p.485]. Wife was named Martha.

Perkins, SAD Charles—b. York County, ME, 1848–d. 25 Jun 1876, killed at the Little Big Horn. Company L: company saddler. Black eyes, dark hair, dark complexion; 5'10" tall. Enlisted 18 Aug 1875. In all likelihood he was killed on Calhoun Hill, though the possibility exists he was one of those killed during the panic through the Keogh Sector. No remains found during the 1984–1985 archaeological work match his description. Listed number 191 in "June Returns, Alterations … Killed in action."

Petring, PVT Henry—b. Germany, 29 Nov 1853– d. Brooklyn, NY, 7 Oct 1917. Company G, private. Gray eyes, brown hair, florid complexion; 5'6¾" tall. Enlisted 9 Dec 1874. One of twenty men — one officer, three scouts, sixteen enlisted men — left in the timber in the valley bottoms, eventually making Reno Hill later that afternoon. Wounded in the eye and hip, probably while on the hilltop. Arrived in U.S. with his family in 1859. His father's name was Johann Friedrich Petring, which became Frederick Petring, and his mother was named Frederike Luise Pilgrim, which somehow became Julia Pilgrims. Petring resided at 274 and 369 Manhattan Avenue and 195 Stockholm Street, Brooklyn, NY. Buried in Cypress Hills National Cemetery. Survived by widow Louisa whom he married 14 Mar 1881.

Phillips, PVT Edgar—b. Lynn, MA, 1853–d. 25 Jun 1876, killed at the Little Big Horn. Company C, private. Blue eyes, light hair; 5'5¾" tall. In the army less than one year. Enlisted 24 Sep 1875. In the C Company charge off Battle Ridge–Calhoun Hill, but body was never identified. May have died in Calhoun Coulee, Finley-Finckle Ridge, the Keogh Sector, or possibly even Last Stand Hill. Listed number 34 in "June Returns, Alterations … Killed in action."

Phillips, PVT John J.— b. Allegheny County, PA, 1849–d. Pennsylvania, 23 Jul 1896. Company H, private. Blue eyes, light hair, fair complexion; 5'5" tall and weighed 130 pounds. Enlisted 12 Sep 1873. WIA in lower left jaw and both hands in the hilltop fight. Sent to FAL on steamer *Far West*.

Pickard, PVT Edwin H. (first name also seen as Edward and his last name also seen spelled as Pichard, though his enlistment sheet shows him signing as Pickard)— b. Boston, MA, 27 Jan 1854–d. Portland, OR, 30 Jan 1928. Company F, private. Blue eyes, light hair, fair complexion; 5'8" tall. Enlisted 6 Sep 1875. Orderly for CPT Yates on 25 June, then assigned to packs. In the water party on 26 June. James Willert said he was a straggler. It appears as well, that Pickard was another "fame-claimer," a private soldier having a greater role than reality dictated. Son of Edward H. and Charlotte Newton Pickard, both born in MA. Resided for 32 years at 255 Hancock Street and 97 East 79th Street, Portland, OR. Buried in Lincoln Memorial Park, Portland. Survived by his widow, Ethel, whom he had married in Portland.

Pigford, PVT Edward D.— b. West Elizabeth, PA, 11 Jun 1856–d. Lock 3, PA, 16 Dec 1932 (this probably referred to Lock No. 3, on the Monongahela River, south of Pittsburgh). Company M, private. Gray eyes, auburn hair, light complexion; 5'6¾" tall. Enlisted 13 Sep 1875. Claimed to have been WIA in right hip in retreat from valley fight and again on the 26th in the right forearm while on Reno Hill. According to Bruce Liddic, Pigford related a fantastic story about riding— on CPT French's orders — with two other troopers (whose names he conveniently forgot) to the Calhoun Hill vicinity where he watched the final butchering of Calhoun's command. He told this doubtful story to the *Washington Observer* in October 1932 [Liddic, *Vanishing Victory*, p. 133]. Married Frances Brown (d. 1880); married Phoebe Haire in 1882. Children from 2nd marriage: Joseph, Charley, and Sadie. Buried in Richland Cemetery, Dravosberg, PA.

Pilcher, PVT Albert— b. Parkersburg, VA (WV), circa 1848–d. unknown. Company F, private. Blue eyes, dark brown hair, fair complexion; 5'7" tall. Detached Service to Department HQ.

Pinkston, PVT John S.— b. St. Clair County, MI, Jun 1850–d. unknown. Company H, private. Gray eyes, dark hair, fair complexion; 5'7" tall. Enlisted 1 Mar 1872. Rode with his unit in Benteen's battalion, and fought on Reno Hill.

Pitter, PVT Felix James— b. Alesford, Hampshire, England, 1850–d. 25 Jun 1876, killed at the Little Big Horn. Company I, private. Hazel eyes, dark brown hair, fair complexion; 5'6¼" tall. Enlisted 4 Sep 1873. Body never identified, but in all likelihood he was killed in the Keogh Sector. Listed number 168 in "June Returns, Alterations ... Killed in action."

Porter, Dr. Henry Rinaldo— b. New York Mills or Lee Center, NY, 3 or 13 Feb 1848–d. Agra, India, 3 Mar 1903. Blue eyes, light hair, fair complexion; 5'7½" tall. Graduated from Georgetown University School of Medicine in 1872. Served in Arizona with the 5th Cavalry as an acting assistant surgeon, then moved to Bismarck, D.T., where he served with the army at various times. With 5th Cavalry in Apache campaign from 22 Sep 1872 to 25 Apr 1873, including a number of skirmishes and the fight at Muchos Cañon, 26 Sep 1872. Cited by General Crook for "conspicuous gallantry" against the Tonto Apaches, Feb and Mar 1873. Attached to Headquarters for the campaign: Acting Assistant Surgeon (contract surgeon). Detailed to Reno's command during the battle. Based on CPT Moylan's testimony at the RCOI, it seems Porter was DeWolf's assistant. Made it to Reno Hill. Served on contract until 30 Sep 1876. Showed the same bravery at the LBH.

Wife, Charlotte, buried in Westwood Cemetery, Oberlin, OH. Son: Henry (Hallie) Viets Porter; buried in Mansfield Cemetery near Storrs, CT, Spring Hill Road off Highway 195. Porter's two sisters lived in Washington, D.C. Traveled extensively, dying at the Hotel Metropole in Agra, India, of heart disease, while traveling around the world. Buried 4 Mar 1903 in the British Cantonment Cemetery, Agra, India. Hammer lists correspondence to and from Walter Camp dated 1909, so there is obviously some sort of mistake either with the date of the letters or Porter's date of death.

Porter, 1LT James Ezekiel— b. Strong, ME, 2 Feb 1847–d. 25 Jun 1876, killed at the Little Big Horn in the Custer fight. Company I. DOR: 1 Mar 1872. Only DeRudio was a lower-ranking first lieutenant. Originally assigned to Company E. Accompanied the regiment on reconstruction duty in the south. Promoted to 1LT, 1 Mar 1872, Company I. Was with his company on the National Boundary Survey Commission in 1873 and 1874. Body never identified, though his head purportedly found in the village. Wore a buckskin shirt on the day of the battle. This bloodstained shirt, with a bullet hole just below the right shoulder, was found by Dr. Paulding in the abandoned Indian village. Also seeing it: "I found Porter's buckskin blouse in the village ... and from the shot holes in it, he must have had it on and must have been shot from the rear, left side, the bullet coming out on the left breast near the heart" [Godfrey/Graham, *The Custer Myth,* p. 346]. CPT Walter Clifford of Company E, Seventh Infantry was shown Porter's coat with bullet holes in it and his name sewn in the lining. Apparently, Benteen (on 27 Jun 1876) claimed to have seen Porter's body, though he never indicated where. Godfrey disputed Benteen's claim [Liddic, *Vanishing Victory,* p. 156].

USMA classmate of 1LT Braden (L) and 1LT Craycroft (B). Married Eliza Frances Westcott (b. Natick, RI–d. San Jose, CA, 14 Dec 1915), 27 Jul 1869 in Portland, ME. They had two sons, David (b. Chicopee Falls, MA, 13 Oct 1871–d. Idaho, 18 Apr 1903, possibly in a mining accident); and James Francis (b. Fort Lincoln, D.T., 25 Mar 1876–d. Strong, ME, 9 Dec 1876).

Post, PVT George— b. Adrian, MI, 1848–d. 25 Jun 1876, killed at the Little Big Horn. Company I, private. Blue eyes, light hair, ruddy complexion; 5' 7¼" tall. Enlisted from 17 Jul 1866 to 17 Jul 1869 in Fourth Cavalry. Reenlisted in 1870; enlisted in Seventh Cavalry 28 Jun 1875. Body never identified, but in all likelihood he was killed in the Keogh Sector. Married; wife's name was Maggie. No children. Listed number 169 in "June Returns, Alterations … Killed in action."

Proctor (also Procter), **PVT George W.**— b. Manchester, NH, 1850–d. unknown. Company A, private. Gray eyes, brown hair, dark complexion; 5'10¼" tall. Enlisted 15 Jul 1872 in NYC. No specific record exists of his participation in the battle, other than his presence with his unit during the valley fighting and subsequent defense of Reno Hill.

Pym, PVT James— b. Oxfordshire, England, 1852 (this is possibly incorrect; there are some who claim he was born in 1847)–d. Miles City, MT, gunshot wound, 29 Nov 1893. Company B, private. Blue eyes, light hair, fair complexion; 5' 7" tall. Enlisted 11 Dec 1874. WIA in right ankle. Awarded MH for voluntarily bringing water up to Reno Hill from the LBH. Served as city marshal at Lake City, MN, where he married Sarah Underwood, 31 Mar 1888. No children. In 1893 he had been married for five years, but was separated. While unarmed, he was shot in the left side by Alfred Tilton (a 22-year-old cowhand) at the residence of his wife's sister, Mrs. Mary Cronin. He died about a half-hour later. Now buried in Custer County Cemetery, Lot E 1/2 55, Section B. Gravestone inscription reads: "Jas. Pym, Co. B 7th Cavalry." Tolton was captured and sentenced to six years for manslaughter.

Quinn, PVT James— b. Watkins Glen, NY, 1850–d. 25 Jun 1876, killed at the Little Big Horn. Company I, private. Blue eyes, red hair, light complexion; 5' 6" tall. Enlisted 13 Feb 1872. Body never identified, but in all likelihood he was killed in the Keogh Sector. Listed number 170 in "June Returns, Alterations … Killed in action."

Quinn, PVT John E. (aka John Gorham)— b. Hartford, CT, 20 Apr 1852–d. Brookline, MA, 26 Sep 1932. Company D, private. Blue eyes, brown hair, fair complexion; 5' 7¾" tall. Enlisted 19 Jun 1875. Remained at the Powder River Depot. Presence confirmed on June Returns. Wounded in Snake River fight, 30 Sep 1877.

Rafter, SGT John J.— b. Lansingburgh, NY, 20 Jan 1851–d. Leavenworth, KS, 16 Jan 1927. Company K, sergeant. Blue eyes, brown hair, ruddy complexion; 5' 9¼" tall. Enlisted 20 Jan 1872. Assigned to pack train; fought on Reno Hill. Married Mary Madden 17 Feb 1877. Children: John J., Ellen B., Rosalia, Leo R., Norbert, Mary M., Raymond, Leonard L., and Margaret. Resided in Leavenworth, KS, for 50 years. Buried in Mount Calvary Cemetery, Leavenworth.

Ragsdale, PVT John Samuel— b. Elizabethtown, KY, 25 Dec 1850–d. Dayton, OH, 4 Dec 1942. Company A, private. Blue eyes, light hair, fair complexion; 5' 7" tall. Enlisted 23 Jul 1872. Remained at Powder River Depot. Presence confirmed on June Returns. Married Lois Durham 28 Dec 1877; she died 10 Aug 1925. He then married Verna Bell Owen, 14 Jun 1926, but divorced after 1940! Buried in Dayton National Cemetery.

Raichel, PVT Henry W.— b. Hamilton County, OH–d. killed at Snake Creek, M.T., 30 Sep 1877, in the Nez Percé War. Company K, private. Blue eyes, brown hair, florid complexion; 5' 9" tall. Second enlistment 8 Mar 1875. With pack train and in the hilltop fight.

Ramell, TMP William (aka James Wright, Jr.)— b. Staten Island, NY, 25 Dec 1851, though some records show an incorrect date of 1853–d. Bayonne, NJ, 21 Jul 1924. Company H: trumpeter. Brown eyes, dark hair, dark complexion; 5' 3½" tall. Enlisted 1 Jun 1874. Deserted the army on 1 Feb 1877. Rode with his unit in Benteen's battalion, and fought on Reno Hill. WIA in hilltop fight.

Ramsey, PVT Charles— b. Macon, MI, or Mason, MI, 1850–d. unknown. Company I, private. Gray eyes, light hair, dark complexion; 5' 7" tall. Enlisted 26 Jan 1872. With pack train; fought on Reno Hill.

Randall, PVT George F.— b. Northfield, VT, Oct 1853–d. unknown. Company B, private. Blue eyes, light hair, fair complexion; 5' 7⅛" tall. Enlisted 15 Dec 1874. With the pack train escort, Company B. Arrived and fought on Reno Hill.

Randall, PVT William J. (aka William J. Woolslayer)— b. Pittsburgh, PA, 1850–d. Snake Creek,

M.T., 30 Sep 1877; killed in the Nez Percé War. Company D, private. Brown eyes, brown hair, dark complexion; 5' 7¼" tall. Enlisted 15 Sep 1875. Rode with his unit in Benteen's battalion, and fought on Reno Hill.

Rankin, Frank *see* **Clyde, PVT Edward**

Rapp, PVT John—b. Würtemburg, Germany, 1848–d. 25 Jun 1876, killed at the Little Big Horn during Reno's valley fight. Company G, private. Blue eyes, dark hair, dark complexion; 5' 9¾" tall. Enlisted 29 Sep 1873. Acting as McIntosh's orderly or striker and killed in or near timber while acting as a horse holder. Listed number 135 in "June Returns, Alterations ... Killed in action."

Rauter, PVT John—b. Tyrol, Switzerland, 1846–d. 25 Jun 1876, killed at the Little Big Horn. Company C, private. Blue eyes, dark hair, dark complexion; 5' 9¾" tall. Enlisted on 4 Oct 1873. There is a *small* possibility he was killed at the head of Deep Ravine, though no C Company troopers were identified there. Bones found at the paired Markers 9 and 10 on the South Skirmish Line are consistent with his age and height. See also St. John (C) and Stuart (C), and Warren (F). Several others would fit the age and height parameters, as well. This was the largest and most nearly complete grouping of human remains found in the 1984 excavations: fragments of skull, ribs, vertebrae, hands, a right foot, both upper arms, both lower arms. They appeared to be from a single individual with massive head damage and severe cutting across the breastbone. The body had been placed face down. (Note—Cheyenne warriors generally turned their dead victims face down, fearing it was bad luck to leave an enemy facing the sky. He may have been buried as found or merely had dirt thrown on him, as found.) Bone damage indicated blunt-force trauma as well as damage by an arrow or knife and hatchet. Other items found were a .44-caliber Henry bullet found in the lower chest-upper abdominal region; a .45-caliber Colt bullet found in the area of the head; eleven buttons, including several trouser buttons; three blouse buttons, two with cloth still attached; three four-hole white-glass shirt buttons; an iron arrowhead; and several river cobbles used to hold down a tarp or covering of sorts. The bone fragments were consistent with a white male between 30 and 40 years of age; about 5'10½" tall, with a range of 5' 8¾"–6'. Several men fit the description: John Rauter (C); L. St. John (C); Alpheus Stewart (C); G. Warren (F); William Teeman (F)—doubtful; F. Varden (I)—not possible, however; William Reed (I); W. Cashan (L); and T. Kavanaugh (L) [Scott and Fox, *Archaeological Insights into the Custer Battle*; and, Scott; Fox; and

Connor, *Archaeological Perspectives on the Battle of the Little Bighorn*]. Listed number 35 in "June Returns, Alterations ... Killed in action."

Rawlins, Richard *see* **Rollins, PVT Richard**

Reagan (also seen spelled Ragan), **PVT Michael** (aka John Desmond)—b. Queenstown (Cobh), Ireland, 19 Oct 1845–d. Columbia Falls, MT, 1917. Company K, private. Hazel eyes, dark brown hair, fair complexion; 5'7–7¾"tall. Enlisted as John Desmond 15 Oct 1864 to 15 Jul 1865 in 31st ME Infantry (he had run away from home). Mustered out because of a concealed minority enlistment. Enlisted 8 Nov 1873 in Seventh Cavalry. Remained at the Powder River Depot. Presence confirmed on June Returns. Never married.

Redican, Patrick *see* **Coakley, PVT Patrick**

Reed, PVT John A.—b. Chester County, PA, Jan 1846–d. Fort Sisseton, SD, 21 Jul 1897. Company G, private. Gray eyes, brown hair, fair complexion; 5'7" tall. Enlisted 6 Apr 1871; discharged 18 Apr 1876, then reenlisted 18 Apr 1876. No specific record exists of his participation in the battle, other than his presence with his unit during the valley fighting and subsequent defense of Reno Hill. Buried in Custer Battlefield National Cemetery.

Reed, PVT William—b. Baltimore, MD, 1843–d. 25 Jun 1876, killed at the Little Big Horn. Company I, private. Gray eyes, light hair, light complexion; 5' 9¾"tall. Second enlistment 2 Jan 1872. Bones found at paired Markers 9 and 10 at the head of Deep Ravine, are consistent with his age and height, though it is doubtful it was he. [See Rauter, above.] Listed number 171 in "June Returns, Alterations ... Killed in action."

Rees, PVT William Henry—b. Washington, PA, 1848–d. 25 Jun 1876, killed at the Little Big Horn. Company E, private. Gray eyes, sandy hair, fair complexion; one of tallest men in the battle, at 6'1". Enlisted 5 Dec 1872. Son of John and Catherine Rees, married 15 Mar 1843. Father, a farmer, served in Company C, 188th PA Volunteers in the Civil War. Body identified in Deep Ravine by PVT Francis O'Toole (E). Listed number 77 in "June Returns, Alterations ... Killed in action."

Reese, PVT William (aka Ruse)—b. Philadelphia, PA, 1846–d. unknown. Company E, private. Blue eyes, light hair, fair complexion; 5'10" tall. Enlisted 27 Sep 1873. Ken Hammer claims he fought on Reno hill. Probably a straggler from his unit, though Michno says he may have been at PRD.

Reeves, PVT Francis M.—b. Bluffton, IN, 1847–d. Washington, D.C., 4 Sep 1902. Company A, private. Gray eyes, light hair, florid complexion;

5' 5¾"tall. Enlisted from 25 Jul 1861 to 9 Jul 1865 in Seventh IL Volunteers. Captured and paroled as a Confederate prisoner of war at Vicksburg. Enlisted in Seventh Cavalry 17 Oct 1875. Fought in the valley battle and wounded left side and thigh after leaving the timber. Managed to reach Reno Hill.

Reibold, PVT Christian— b. Buffalo, NY, 1850– d. 25 Jun 1876, killed at the Little Big Horn. Company L, private. Gray eyes, light hair, light complexion; 5' 6" tall. Enlisted 1 Aug 1871. In all likelihood he was killed on Calhoun Hill, though the possibility exists he was one of those killed during the panic through the Keogh Sector. No remains found during the 1984–1985 archaeological work match his description. Listed number 215 in "June Returns, Alterations … Killed in action."

Reid, PVT Elwyn S.— b. Greene, NY, May 1845– d. Fort D. A. Russell, WY, heart failure, 20 Aug 1895. Company D, private. Hazel eyes, brown hair, dark complexion; 5'10" tall. Enlisted 26 Oct 1872. Rode with his unit in Benteen's battalion, and fought on Reno Hill.

Reiley, PVT Michael— b. Dunmore, Luzerne County, PA, 1851–d. unknown, but after 1897. Company F, private. Gray eyes, light brown hair, fair complexion; 5' 8⅞" tall. Enlisted 6 Nov 1872. With the pack train; fought on Reno Hill.

Reilly, PVT Michael J.— b. Longford, Ireland, 1851–d. unknown. Company K, private. Hazel eyes, dark hair, dark complexion; 5' 6¼" tall. Second enlistment 8 Jun 1875. Remained at the Powder River Depot. Presence confirmed on June Returns.

Reily (also seen spelled Reilly, Riley, and Reilley), **2LT William Van Wyck**— b. Washington, D.C., 12 Dec 1853–d. 25 Jun 1876, killed at the Little Big Horn. Company F. TDY from Company E; assigned to E/7C, 26 Jan 1876. DOR: 15 Oct 1875. A handsome, dashing young man, he was the most junior (non-attached) officer in the command (Jack Crittenden was junior, but he was attached from the 20th Infantry).

Attended Georgetown College (Washington, D.C.) and the United States Naval Academy (dismissed). While at Georgetown, he spent two years at school in Dresden, Germany. Reily entered Georgetown at age ten. Brian Pohanka described it as a Catholic prep school, but in reality, the "prep" school was part of the college until the 1890s, sharing the same buildings and spaces. Reily's father was a naval officer who died when the USS *Porpoise* was lost in the China Sea, 21 Sep 1854, nine months after "Willie" was born. Mother married COL L. M. Johnson (d. Mar 1872) on 11 Jul 1861.

Body found on Custer Hill. One source claims he was still learning how to ride a horse, but that seems incorrect as his family owned horses and it appears logical that Reily was well versed in the art [Kelly]. Along with Yates, Cooke, and Smith, his body was found in the vicinity of George Custer's, but nearer the top of the hill [Godfrey/Graham, *The Custer Myth*, p. 345]. Remains exhumed in 1877 and reinterred in Mount Olivet Cemetery, Washington, D.C., Lot 2 West, Section R37, 3 Aug 1877. There was a poignant story regarding Reily's mother and a ring her son wore. The ring was surprisingly found and recovered from a Northern Cheyenne warrior who had surrendered at Fort Robinson some two years after the battle. Reily's mother wrote a letter to the Commissioner of Indian Affairs: "My dear sir, may I beg your interest in trying to recover the ring worn by my son, Lieutenant William V. W. Reilly, Seventh Cavalry, U.S. A., sacrificed with Custer, June 25, 1876." The ring was returned [Swanson, *G. A. Custer, His Life and Times*, p. 113]. (An interesting side-note here: is the spelling of Reily's name really with a double "L," or is that a transposition error? His school records are consistent with the use of a single "L.")

Reily's obituary read: "Wm. B. [*sic*] W. Reily, a student here for four years, leaving in Third Humanities in 1867–8, was a Second Lieutenant under General Custer, and was killed in the recent massacre of Custer's command by the Sioux. He was a young half-brother of day-scholar here, Harry M. Johnson" [Georgetown College Archives, *College Journal*, Aug–Oct 1876, Vol. V, No. 1].

Reno, MAJ (Bvt BG) **Marcus Albert** (Rees called him "Man With the Dark Face," his visage usually sun-and wind-burned)— b. Carrollton, IL, 15 Nov 1834–d. Washington, D.C., 30 Mar 1889, after operation for cancer. Buried in Mount Olivet Cemetery, but finally reinterred in LBH National Cemetery on 9 Sep 1967, after his records were corrected (changed) in 1967 to reflect an honorable discharge. A review by the Judge Advocate General concluded he had been improperly dismissed from the service. Headquarters. Commanded a battalion — companies A, G, and M —at the Little Big Horn. Reno was one of the three leading figures involved in the battle and the one who has suffered the most derision from critics of all stripes. Involved in the valley and timber fights, as well as the hilltop fights on 25 and 26 Jun 1876. Short and somewhat stout. Served on frontier duty in the northwest. Participated in numerous Civil War campaigns and battles: the Peninsula, Malvern Hill, Gaines' Mill, Antietam, Kelly's Ford, Trevillian Station, and Sheridan's Shenandoah Valley campaign. Brevetted several times for gallantry.

Appointed major, Seventh Cavalry on 26 Dec

1868 following the death of MAJ Alfred Gibbs. Initially greeted with enthusiasm by Custer, who referred to him as a "good friend" [Donovan, *A Terrible Glory*, p. 93]. Over time, this changed dramatically. Served on scouting duty in Kansas and Colorado and accompanied the regiment on reconstruction duty in the south. Praised for his services against the KKK. In Aug 1872, assigned to New York on the Board of Small Arms. Commanded the escorts on the Northern Boundary Survey Commission.

Parents were James Reno (b. 7 Sep 1801–d. 11 Jan 1849) and Charlotte Hinton Reno (b. 1799–d. 25 Jun 1848). Married Mary Hannah Ross of Harrisburg, PA, 1 Jul 1863. She died 10 Jul 1874 at the age of 30. Son, Robert Ross Reno, b. Apr 1864 (married Ittie Kinney, daughter of Colonel George S. Kinney of Nashville). Reno was the great-grandnephew of Philippe François Renault who came to the U.S. with Lafayette. Renault was awarded for his service to the country with huge tracts of land worth an almost unimaginable fortune, especially in the latter 19th century. Reno's wife was the daughter of Robert Ross, the founder of a glass works and one of the largest banks in Harrisburg, PA. She was also the niece of Senator Don Cameron's wife, related to the founder of the Louisville *Courier Journal* newspaper.

Appointed to the U.S. Military Academy by Senator Stephen A. Douglas. Graduated in 1857, two years after he should have graduated. Poor record there: 20th in class of 38.

At the Court of Inquiry — begun at Reno's insistence, 13 Jan 1879, at the Palmer House in Chicago — he stated he held no animosity towards Custer, but had "no confidence in [Custer's] ability as a soldier." At the same inquiry, LT Carlo DeRudio said Reno had a reputation as a first-rate "drill-master," with a good voice to command.

Court-martialed in Feb 1877 and on 24 Nov 1879 at Fort Meade, D.T., for conduct unbecoming an officer, though Klokner intimates the first court-martial was sought by the army for Reno's "accountability for the defeat" [p. 91]. In that trial, "testimony against him brought to light his intense dislike for Custer" [p. 91]. Dismissed from service on 1 Apr 1880, but discharge changed to honorable in 1967.

Resided in Harrisburg, PA; NYC; and Washington, D.C. He worked last as a clerk in the Bureau of Pensions, Washington, D.C.

Reno did not like George Custer. "In Reno's view, Custer was a sham, a vainglorious popinjay, a poor excuse for an officer" [Willert, *Little Big Horn Diary*, p. 212]. Reno simply shook off Custer's reprimand for the Rosebud recon. This certainly coincided with Benteen's view of the man. Reno

also did not care for Fred Gerard and had once fired him from FAL for stealing government property.

"I judge that Reno (as one of his 'skippers' later told me) became rattled, but he did not stampede, and saved his command by pushing up the bluffs. That the battalion *did* stampede I concede, but our people (i.e. the Indians) had 'put the fear of God' into the men. Reno's record in the War between the States refutes any accusation of cowardice; but he was ignorant of Indian methods of fighting and made a convenient 'goat.'" (Frank H. Huston in a March 1925, letter to W. A. Graham [Graham, *The Custer Myth,* p. 80].)

Benteen was certainly not a fan of Reno's, more than once saying he had very little to do with the man. He seemed, however, very fair and did not want to see Reno needlessly vilified for his actions at the LBH. He wrote Goldin on February 20, 1896, that as "poor a soldier as Reno was, he was a long way ahead of Merrill." He also wrote, "Reno was a far better soldier than Sturgis, and that isn't much praise" [Carroll, *The Benteen-Goldin Letters,* p. 275].

Reynolds, Charles Harry *see* **Brinkerhoff, PVT Henry M.**

Ricketts, WAG Joseph K. (nicknamed "Buckeye") — b. Morrow, Warren County, OH, 27 Feb 1850–d. Dayton, OH, 26 Feb 1909. Company M: company wagoner. Blue eyes, dark hair, ruddy complexion; 5' 9" tall. Enlisted 16 Jan 1873. Remained at the Powder River Depot in charge of the mule train. Presence confirmed on June Returns. Resided in Morrow, OH, and 20 Helena Court, 526 Albany Street, and 450 South Broadway, Dayton, OH. Married Alice Williams, 25 Sep 1884; son Bryan. Buried in Greencastle Cemetery.

Riley, SGT James T. (middle initial also seen as F.; last name also spelled Reilly) — b. Baltimore, MD, 1845–d. Baltimore, MD, 21 Nov 1880. Company E, sergeant. Blue eyes, brown hair, fair complexion; 5'11" tall. First enlisted on 10 Aug 1866. This was his second five-year enlistment. With pack train (Overfield); fought on Reno Hill and WIA in back and left leg. Discharged 11 Aug 1876 upon expiration of service.

Rivers, FAR John — b. Westchester, NY, 1834–d. unknown. Company I: company farrier. Gray eyes, dark hair, dark complexion; 5' 9" tall. Enlisted 11 Sep 1871. Remained at the Powder River Depot. Presence confirmed on June Returns.

Rix, PVT Edward — b. Lowell, MA, Aug 1850–d. 25 Jun 1876, killed at the Little Big Horn. Company C, private. Gray eyes, brown hair; 5' 5¾" tall. Enlisted 1 Oct 1873. In the C Company charge off Battle Ridge–Calhoun Hill, but body was never identified. May have died in Calhoun Coulee, Finley-Finckle Ridge, the Keogh Sector, or possibly even Last Stand Hill. Listed number 36 in "June Returns, Alterations … Killed in action."

Robb, PVT Eldorado J. — b. Warren County, KY, 1850–d. unknown. Company G, private. Hazel eyes, brown hair, ruddy complexion; 5' 9¾" tall. Enlisted 8 Jan 1872. No specific record exists of his participation in the battle, other than his presence with his unit during the valley fighting and subsequent defense of Reno Hill.

Robers, PVT Jonathan — b. Surrey County, NC, 1851–d. unknown, but after 1893. Company K, private. Blue eyes, brown hair, fair complexion; 5' 8" tall. Enlisted 14 Dec 1872. With pack train; fought on Reno Hill. Resided at Painted Robe, MT, about 1891, and at Fort Custer and Crow Agency in 1892.

Roberts, PVT Henry — b. London, England, Feb 1850–d. 25 Jun 1876, killed at the Little Big Horn. Company L, private. Blue eyes, light hair, light complexion; 5' 9" tall. Enlisted 11 Nov 1872. In all likelihood he was killed on Calhoun Hill, though the possibility exists he was one of those killed during the panic through the Keogh Sector. No remains found during the 1984–1985 archaeological work match his description. Listed number 216 in "June Returns, Alterations … Killed in action."

Robinson, PVT William E. — b. Down, Ireland, 1842–d. Seattle, WA, 4 Feb 1928. Company M, private. Detached to Department HQ. Blue eyes, dark brown hair, fair complexion; 5' 9" tall. Enlisted 30 Sep 1873. Special Orders 44 (27 May 1876) detailed him to assist Dr. Clark — on Terry's staff — and he remained with Clark during the remainder of the campaign. I carry him on Terry's staff. He was probably at the Yellowstone (Powder River) Depot at the time of the battle, though Williams feels he may have been assisting Dr. Porter on Reno Hill. This is in all likelihood incorrect.

Rogers, PVT Benjamin F. — b. Madison County, KY, 1847–d. 25 Jun 1876, killed at the Little Big Horn, probably while he was on Reno Hill. Company G, private. Blue eyes, light hair, ruddy complexion; 5'10" tall. Enlisted 5 Jan 1872. (Rogers and Robb may have known one another before joining the service: both were from Kentucky, enlisting three days apart; and both enlisted in Louisville.) Possibly killed on Reno Hill, but no location is certain. Smalley claims no one saw him killed and his body was never found [*Little Bighorn Mysteries,* p. 15–7]. Listed number 134 in "June Returns, Alterations … Killed in action."

Rogers, PVT Walter B. — b. Washington, PA, 1847–d. 25 Jun 1876, killed at the Little Big Horn. Company L, private. Brown eyes, dark hair, medium complexion; 5' 8¼" tall. Enlisted 6 Jun 1873. In all likelihood he was killed on Calhoun Hill, though the possibility exists he was one of those killed during the panic through the Keogh Sector. No remains found during the 1984–1985 archaeological work match his description. Married; wife's name was Emma. Listed number 217 in "June Returns, Alterations … Killed in action."

Rollins (aka Rawlins), **PVT Richard** — b. Breckenridge County, KY, 1849–d. 25 Jun 1876, killed at the Little Big Horn. Company A, private. Blue eyes, brown hair, fair complexion; 5'10¾" tall. Enlisted 26 Nov 1872. Company barber. Ken Hammer, in *The Battlefield Dispatch,* Winter 2005, lists his death as "unknown location." Smalley claims no one saw him killed and his body was never found [*Little Bighorn Mysteries,* p. 15–7]. Listed number 8 in "June Returns, Alterations … Killed in action."

Rood, PVT Edward — b. Tiago County, NY, 1848–d. 25 Jun 1876, killed at the Little Big Horn. Company E, private. Hazel eyes, black hair, dark complexion; 5' 7" tall. Enlisted 19 Sep 1873. While his body was not specifically identified, he may have been one of the unknowns on either the South Skirmish Line or in Deep Ravine. Listed number 78 in "June Returns, Alterations … Killed in action."

Rooney, PVT James M. — b. NYC, 1848–d. Yankton, SD, 5 Aug 1918. Company F, private. Blue eyes, brown hair, dark complexion; 5' 8¼" tall. Enlisted 3 Dec 1867 in NYC in Co. F, Seventh Cavalry. Reenlisted 3 Dec 1872. With pack train (Overfield) and fought on Reno Hill. With the water party on 26 June (Hammer). Discharged 3 Dec 1877 as a sergeant. Resided in Bismarck until 28 Jun 1878. Served in QMD, Fort Meade, SD in 1908. Resided in Bixby, SD, in 1910. Admitted to Yankton State Hospital in July 1911. Cause of death listed as carcinoma of the lip. Buried in Grave 593, Yankton State Hospital Cemetery (South Dakota Human Services Center).

Rose, PVT Peter E. — b. Rockford, IL, 1852–d. unknown. Company L, private. Brown eyes, black hair, dark complexion; 5' 9" tall. Enlisted 28 Sep 1875. With the pack train; fought on Reno Hill.

Rossbury, PVT John W. — b. Rochester, NY, 1849–d. 25 Jun 1876, killed at the Little Big Horn. Company I, private. Hazel eyes, dark hair, fair complexion; 5' 6½" tall. Enlisted 26 Jan 1872. Body never identified, but in all likelihood he was killed in the Keogh Sector. Listed number 172 in "June Returns, Alterations … Killed in action."

Roth, PVT Francis—b. Frankfurt, Germany, 1846–d. Snake Creek, M.T., 30 Sep 1877, killed in the Nez Percé War. Company K, private. Gray eyes, brown hair, fair complexion; 5' 7" tall. Second enlistment 30 Mar 1876. Remained at the Powder River Depot. Presence confirmed on June Returns. Survived by his widow. Buried in Custer Battlefield National Cemetery.

Rott, SGT Louis—b. Bavaria, Germany, 1848–d. unknown. Company K, sergeant. Brown eyes, black hair, dark complexion; 5' 9" tall. Second enlistment 17 Jan 1875. Rode with his unit in Benteen's battalion, and fought on Reno Hill.

Rowland, PVT Robert—b. Warsaw, Poland, 1843–d. Dakota Territory, 15 Apr 1879. Company G, private. Brown eyes, brown hair, ruddy complexion; 5' 8" tall. Enlisted 7 Apr 1876. Remained at the Powder River Depot. Presence confirmed on June Returns. Died at mouth of the Cannonball River in a boat. May have been suicide since he was found with a gunshot wound to the head. Dead for three or four days when found. He was probably disconsolate, having deserted and realizing his arrest was imminent.

Roy (aka Ray), **CPL Stanislaus**—b. France, 12 Nov 1846–d. Columbus Barracks, OH, 10 Feb 1913, of cancer. Company A. Brown eyes, brown hair, light complexion; 5' 5¼" tall. Enlisted 20 Nov 1869 in Seventh Cavalry. Served on both the Yellowstone and Black Hills expeditions. Re-upped 19 Jan 1875. Awarded MH for voluntarily bringing water up to Reno Hill from the LBH. Was with main burial parties on 28 Jun 1876 and corresponded with Walter Camp from 1909 to 1912. Resided at 523 West Park Av., Piqua, OH. Attended the dedication of the Custer monument at Monroe, MI, 4 Jun 1910. Buried in Grave A-183, Government Lot, Section 51, Greenlawn Cemetery, Columbus, OH.

Rudden, PVT Patrick—b. Newark, NJ, 1853–d. 25 Jun 1876, killed at the Little Big Horn. Company F, private. Blue eyes, brown hair, dark complexion; 5' 5⅞" tall. Enlisted 24 Sep 1875. In all likelihood he was killed on Last Stand Hill with his unit. Listed number 119 in "June Returns, Alterations … Killed in action."

Rudolph, PVT George A.—b. Meuterheim, Germany, 24 Feb 1854–d. Eddyville, NY, 4 Dec 1924. Headquarters: band. Private. Blue eyes, brown hair, fair complexion; 5' 4½" tall. Remained at Powder River Depot. Presence confirmed on June Returns.

Russell, PVT James Henry—b. Corpus Christi, TX, Jan 1852–d. 25 Jun 1876, killed at the Little Big Horn. Company C, private. Gray eyes, brown hair; 5' 5" tall. Enlisted 11 Sep 1873. Had been a schoolteacher. Father was a member of the first Florida legislature and a major in the CSA army. In the C Company charge off Battle Ridge–Calhoun Hill, but body was never identified. May have died in Calhoun Coulee, Finley-Finckle Ridge, the Keogh Sector, or possibly even Last Stand Hill. Listed number 37 in "June Returns, Alterations … Killed in action."

Russell, SGT Thomas—b. Oxford, IN, 1848–d. at the Letterman Hospital, Presidio, San Francisco, CA, 28 May 1926. Company D, sergeant. Brown eyes, dark hair, dark complexion; 5' 4" tall. Enlisted 5 Aug 1872. Promoted to SGT, 6 Jun 1876. Rode with his unit in Benteen's battalion, and fought on Reno Hill.

Rutten, PVT Roman (aka Roman Ruttenauer; also listed as Rutler, Rullin, and Bolten)—b. Baden, Germany, 13 Aug 1846–d. Leavenworth, KS, 16 Apr 1925. Company M, private. Brown eyes, light brown hair, ruddy complexion; 5' 6¼" tall. Enlisted from 7 Nov 1866 to 7 Nov 1871 in 8th Cavalry. Enlisted in Seventh Cavalry 17 Jul 1872. WIA in right shoulder, probably during the fighting on Reno Hill. A tailor in civilian life. Wife named Kate (Catherine), from PA. Children were: Emma, Anna, Amor, Rudolph, Verena, and Killian. Buried in Fort Leavenworth National Cemetery.

Ryan, CPL Daniel—b. Syracuse, NY, 1851–d. 25 Jun 1876, killed at the Little Big Horn. Company C, corporal. Gray eyes, dark hair, 5' 7¼" tall. Enlisted 18 Dec 1872. In the C Company charge off Battle Ridge–Calhoun Hill, but body was never identified. May have died in Calhoun Coulee, Finley-Finckle Ridge, the Keogh Sector, or possibly even Last Stand Hill. Listed number 18 in "June Returns, Alterations … Killed in action."

Ryan, 1SG John [M] (origin of middle initial is uncertain and not from birth; Barnard indicates it may have been taken from unit designation and added to his name in later years)—b. West Newton, MA, 25 Aug 1845–d. West Newton, MA, 14 Oct 1926, heart attack. Company M: first sergeant. Gray eyes, sometimes considered blue; auburn hair, sometimes seen as brown; fair complexion turned ruddy after years on the frontier; 5' 6" (as a teen) to 5' 7½" tall; as much as 193 pounds in later years. Enlisted from 13 Dec 1861 to 19 Dec 1864 in 28th MA Vol. Infantry. Wounded three times at Ream's Station, near Petersburg, VA, 25 Aug 1864, during Civil War. Discharged 19 Dec 1864. Enlisted from 30 Jan 1865 to 16 Jul 1865 in

61st MA Infantry. Enlisted 23 Nov 1866 in Seventh Cavalry. When his hitch was up — 23 Nov 1871 — he returned home to MA, but reenlisted shortly thereafter, 21 Dec 1871. Court-martialed and reduced to private — 23 Apr 1876. CPT French then proceeded to make him acting QM sergeant, replacing Capes, who took over as acting first sergeant. As soon as M Company arrived at Fort Lincoln, French told MAJ Reno and Adjutant Cooke he wanted Ryan promoted back to first sergeant, telling them of the circumstances. They agreed. Ryan was promoted, effective 9 May 1876.

In charge of burying GAC and his brother Tom. He was assisted by: PVT Harrison Davis (M); PVT Frank Neely (M); and PVT James W. Severs (M). Apparently a very fine soldier.

Parents from Tipperary, Ireland: Edward (d. 12 Jan 1894) and Hanorah (d. Feb 1859; also spelled, Hannora) Ryan. Became a policeman in West Newton, MA, after leaving army on 19 Dec 1876. Lived at 29 Auburndale Ave. (originally Emerald Avenue), West Newton, where he was born. Died in that house. Married to Mary Jane O'Donnell, 13 Oct 1881. She was committed to Worcester, Mass., Insane Hospital by 1900, and died, institutionalized, 9 Apr 1926. Children: Mary Alice (b. 2 Sep 1886); John Edward (b. 7 Jul 1888); Helen Elizabeth (b. 15 Apr 1890); and Gertrude Anna (b. 7 Jan 1892). Attended Seventh Cavalry reunion at Canandaigua, NY, on 21–22 Aug 1907, and dedication of the Custer monument in Monroe, MI, 4 Jun 1910. Too sick to attend 50th anniversary. Buried in Section 7, Lot 673, Calvary Cemetery, Waltham, MA.

Ryan, PVT Stephen L. — b. Ireland, 1839–d. Bismarck, D.T., 18 Apr 1885. Company B, private. Blue eyes, brown hair, fair complexion; 5' 6" tall. Enlisted from 17 Nov 1865 to 17 Nov 1868 in Third Infantry. Enlisted from 26 Nov 1869 to 26 Nov 1874 in Seventh Cavalry. Reenlisted 1 Dec 1874. Along with Moore and CPT McDougall, buried LT Hodgson's body on the morning of the 27 June, after retrieving it the previous evening [Nichols, *RCOI*, p. 554]. Wife's name was Bessie. Ryan died of Bright's disease. Buried St. Mary's Cemetery, Bismarck.

Ryder, PVT Hobart — b. NYC, 1846–d. possible suicide, Wheeling, WV. Company M, private. Gray eyes, dark brown hair, fair complexion; 5' 7½" tall. Enlisted 15 Sep 1873. Detailed as a nurse or surgeon's orderly at the Powder River Depot. Not certain who he worked for, but his appearance on Reno Hill makes it obvious it had to have been Doc Porter. In both the valley and hilltop fights. Roman Rutten told Walter Camp that Ryder committed suicide in Wheeling, WV.

Rye, PVT William W. — b. Pike County, GA, 1849–d. unknown. Company M, private. Gray eyes, brown hair, fair complexion; 5' 8½" tall. Enlisted 9 Oct 1875. No specific record exists of his participation in the battle, other than his presence with his unit during the valley fighting and subsequent defense of Reno Hill.

Sadler, PVT William — b. Frankfurt, Germany, 10 Feb 1855–d. Bismarck, ND, 12 Nov 1921. Company D, private. Gray eyes, light hair, fair complexion; 5'7" tall. Enlisted 9 Aug 1875. Remained at the Powder River Depot. Presence confirmed on June Returns. Hammer says he was assigned to guard the wagon train at PRD.

Sager, PVT Hiram Wallace — b. Westport, NY, 27 Nov 1850–d. Spokane, WA, 21 Dec 1907. Company B, private. Blue eyes, brown hair, ruddy complexion; 5'10" tall. Enlisted 26 Oct 1870. With the pack train escort, Company B. Arrived and fought on Reno Hill. Married Margaret Ann Easton 8 Dec 1880. Left army 8 Apr 1883, and eventually moved to Mound City, D.T. where Margaret taught school. Children: Edgar Roy, Laura Wallace, Bessie Ethel, Bertha Agnes, Paul Easton, and Hollis Walter. Appointed sheriff of Campbell County. On the staff of first governor of SD. Moved to Spokane after living in SD for 16 years. Buried in Greenwood Cemetery.

St. John, PVT Ludwick — b. Columbia, MO, 3 Mar 1848–d. 25 Jun 1876, killed at the Little Big Horn. Company C, private. Gray eyes, brown hair; 5' 9" tall. Civil War vet. Enlisted at age of 13 in 1861. Had been with Seventh Cavalry for several years. Possibly killed at head of Deep Ravine, though doubtful. See Rauter (C). Listed number 43 in "June Returns, Alterations ... Killed in action."

Sanders, PVT Charles — b. Altenburg, Saxony, Germany, 8 May 1842; one source claims 1843–d. Lincoln, NE, 29 Aug 1915. Company D, private. Hazel eyes, dark hair, dark complexion; 5'10½" tall. Third enlistment 26 Jan 1872. Recommended for a medal for conspicuous gallantry at the LBH fight. Was Weir's orderly on 25 Jun 1876, riding with him to Weir Peak. Several years after the battle, Edgerly wrote that he had never seen a cooler man under fire than Sanders. Edgerly stood in amazement as Indian bullets whizzed all around Sanders while he laughed, joking about how bad their marksmanship was.

Saunders, PVT Richard D. — b. Yarmouth, Nova Scotia, 1853–d. 25 Jun 1876, killed at the Little Big Horn. Company F, private. Blue eyes, brown hair, dark complexion; 5' 9⅜" tall. Enlisted 16 Aug

1875 in Boston. In all likelihood he was killed on Last Stand Hill with his unit. Listed number 120 in "June Returns, Alterations ... Killed in action."

Schele (also Schoole), **PVT Henry**— b. Hanover, Germany, 1843–d. 25 Jun 1876, killed at the Little Big Horn. Company E, private. Blue eyes, light hair, fair complexion; 5'6" tall. Second enlistment, 19 Dec 1872. While his body was not specifically identified, he may have been one of the unknowns on either the South Skirmish Line or in Deep Ravine. Listed number 79 in "June Returns, Alterations ... Killed in action."

Schlafer, PVT Christian— b. Cincinnati, OH, 1847–d. Cincinnati, OH, 11 Feb 1905. Company K, private. Gray eyes, light hair, fair complexion; 5'5¾" tall. Enlisted from 30 Jan 1865 to 7 Sep 1865 in 192nd OH Infantry. Enlisted 2 Oct 1868 to 2 Oct 1873 in Fifth Cavalry. Third enlistment on 24 Mar 1875 in Seventh Cavalry. Rode with his unit in Benteen's battalion, and fought on Reno Hill. Not married. Buried in Walnut Hills Cemetery, Cincinnati.

Schleiffarth, PVT Paul— b. Berlin, Germany, 1839–d. Fort Thomas, KY, of chronic dysentery, 19 Nov 1896. Company F, private. Gray eyes, brown hair, fair complexion; 5'6½" tall. Enlisted 15 Dec 1871. Extra duty with Commissary and Subsistence Department. He was on the steamer *Far West* at the mouth of the Rosebud.

Schleiper, SAD Claus— b. Wipperode, Hesse-Kassel, Germany, 1837–d. unknown, but possibly in NYC. Company F: company saddler. Brown eyes, dark hair, light complexion; 5'9¾" tall. Enlisted from 17 Dec 1866 to 17 Dec 1871; joined Seventh Cavalry 22 Jan 1867; reenlisted 17 Dec 1871. Overfield says he was with the pack train, but there is little support for that. Most other sources claim he was sick and remained behind at the Powder River Depot. This latter choice makes the most sense. Resided at 72 Watts Street, NYC.

Schmidt, PVT Charles— b. Würtemburg, Germany, 1849–d. 25 Jun 1876, killed at the Little Big Horn. Company L, private. Brown eyes, brown hair, fair complexion; 5'8½" tall. Enlisted 14 Nov 1872. In all likelihood he was killed on Calhoun Hill, though the possibility exists he was one of those killed during the panic through the Keogh Sector. No remains found during the 1984–1985 archaeological work match his description. Listed number 218 in "June Returns, Alterations ... Killed in action."

Schwerer, PVT John— b. Germany, 1841–d. Wood, WI, 17 Dec 1913. Company K, private. Brown eyes, dark hair, fair complexion; 5'5¾" tall.

Enlisted from 23 Jun 1864 to 17 Jul 1865 in Seventh NJ Infantry. Enlisted 2 Nov 1872 in Seventh Cavalry. Rode with his unit in Benteen's battalion, and fought on Reno Hill. Not married. Buried in Wood National Cemetery, Wood [Milwaukee], WI.

Scollin (or Scullin), **CPL Henry M.** (his real name was Cody)— b. Nashua, NH, 1851–d. 25 Jun 1876, killed at the Little Big Horn. Company M, corporal. Blue eyes, dark hair, medium complexion; 5'7" tall. Enlisted 24 Sep 1873. Enlisted as Henry "Scollin" so his father would not know of it. Killed on bottoms during retreat; body found between timber and the river, badly mutilated, right leg severed from body. Scott says at foot of bluffs, which seems more accurate. Newell's bunkmate. Smalley lists him as a private. Listed number 227 in "June Returns, Alterations ... Killed in action."

Scott, PVT Charles— b. Scotland, 1851–d. 25 Jun 1876, killed at the Little Big Horn. Company L, private. Blue eyes, brown hair, fair complexion; 5'9" tall. Enlisted 20 Nov 1873. In all likelihood he was killed on Calhoun Hill, though the possibility exists he was one of those killed during the panic through the Keogh Sector. No remains found during the 1984–1985 archaeological work match his description. Listed number 219 in "June Returns, Alterations ... Killed in action."

Scott, PVT George D.— b. Lancaster County, KY, 1850–d. unknown. Company D, private. Blue eyes, brown hair, fair complexion; 5'8" tall. Enlisted 7 Sep 1871. Rode with his unit in Benteen's battalion, and fought on Reno Hill. Awarded MH for voluntarily bringing water up to Reno Hill, but apparently he never received it. Medal discovered in the office of a Washington, D.C., attorney who claimed to not know how it got there. It was sent to the War Department, but no record of Scott's address was found [Williams, *Military Register of Custer's Last Command*, p. 268].

Seafferman, PVT Henry— b. Strasburg, Germany, 1839–d. 25 Jun 1876, killed at the Little Big Horn during Reno's retreat. Company G, private. Hazel eyes, brown hair, florid complexion; 5'7½" tall. Enlisted from 11 Aug 1860 to 1 Jul 1864 in Second Cavalry. Enlisted from 1 Jul 1864 to 1 Jul 1867 in Fifth Cavalry (the Second had been redesignated the Fifth by act of Congress). Enlisted 5 Jul 1867 in Seventh Cavalry. Reenlisted 11 Jul 1872. A real veteran cavalryman! Killed along Reno's retreat route from the timber, though Ken Hammer, in *The Battlefield Dispatch,* Winter 2005, says he was killed *in* the timber. Listed number 136 in "June Returns, Alterations ... Killed in action."

Seamans, PVT John— b. New London, NH, Jan 1854–d. unknown. Company M, private. Blue eyes, brown hair, fair complexion; 5'9" tall. Enlisted 21 Sep 1875. No specific record exists of his participation in the battle, other than his presence with his unit during the valley fighting and subsequent defense of Reno Hill.

Seayers, PVT Thomas— b. Pikesville, Canada, 1854–d. unknown. Company A, private. Brown eyes, brown hair, dark complexion; 5'5¾" tall. Enlisted 10 Sep 1875. No specific record exists of his participation in the battle, other than his presence with his unit during the valley fighting and subsequent defense of Reno Hill.

Seibelder (also Siebelder), **PVT Anton**— b. Lichtenwold, Germany, 25 Feb 1828 (death certificate lists Holland as his birthplace)–d. Washington, D.C., 17 Oct 1913. Company A, private. Blue eyes, brown hair, fair complexion; 5'10" tall. Second enlistment 2 Apr 1872. It was Seibelder who carried an utterly exhausted LT Charles Varnum — asleep — down into the hospital area on Reno Hill on the morning of 26 Jun 1876. Resided in Washington, D.C., for 21 years at 3206 Georgia Ave, NW. Buried in the Soldiers' Home National Cemetery.

Seiler, CPL John— b. Bavaria, 1850–d. 25 Jun 1876, killed at the Little Big Horn. Company L, corporal. Gray eyes, light hair, fair complexion; 5'8" tall. Enlisted 12 Feb 1872. In all likelihood he was killed on Calhoun Hill, though the possibility exists he was one of those killed during the panic through the Keogh Sector. No remains found during the 1984–1985 archaeological work match his description. Listed number 186 in "June Returns, Alterations ... Killed in action."

Selby, SAD Crawford— b. Ashland County, OH, 5 Jun 1845–d. 25 Jun 1876, killed at the Little Big Horn, probably during Reno's retreat. Company G: company saddler. Gray eyes, light brown hair, fair complexion; 5'5½" tall. Enlisted 21 Jun 1875. Married Mary Elizabeth Beck, 10 Nov 1864; divorced 30 Dec 1874. Ken Hammer, in *The Battlefield Dispatch,* Winter 2005, lists his death as being in an "unknown location." Smalley claims no one saw him killed and his body was never found [*Little Bighorn Mysteries,* p. 15–7], however, he had to have been killed during Reno's retreat from the timber. Listed number 131 in "June Returns, Alterations ... Killed in action."

Senn, PVT Robert— b. Zurich, Switzerland, 1848–d. unknown. Company M, private. Blue eyes, brown hair, fair complexion; 5'7¼" tall. Enlisted 23 Sep 1875. No specific record exists of his participation in the battle, other than his presence with his unit during the valley fighting and subsequent defense of Reno Hill.

Severs, PVT James W. (nicknamed "Crazy Jim")— b. Wayne County, NY, Oct 1851–d. Rock Springs, WY, 1912. Company M, private. Blue eyes, light brown hair, fair complexion; 5'5¾" tall. Enlisted 12 Nov 1872. No specific record exists of his participation in the battle, other than his presence with his unit during the valley fighting and subsequent defense of Reno Hill. Helped bury Custers. Illiterate. Never married.

Severs, PVT Samuel— b. St. Louis, MO, 1854–d. El Dorado, OK, 5 Sep 1919. Company H, private. Black eyes, black hair, dark complexion; 5'6" tall. Enlisted 16 Feb 1875. WIA in both thighs in hilltop fight. Sent to FAL aboard steamer "Far West."

Shade, PVT Samuel S.— b. Jonestown, PA, 1847–d. 25 Jun 1876, killed at the Little Big Horn; in Custer's command. Company C, private. Blue eyes, light hair; 5'8¾" tall. In the army less than one year. Enlisted 3 Aug 1875. He had been a schoolteacher in civilian life. In the C Company charge off Battle Ridge–Calhoun Hill, but body was never identified. May have died in Calhoun Coulee, Finley-Finckle Ridge, the Keogh Sector, or possibly even Last Stand Hill. Listed number 38 in "June Returns, Alterations ... Killed in action."

Shanahan, PVT John— b. Youghal, Ireland, Jul 1853–d. unknown. Company G, private. Blue eyes, brown hair, fair complexion; 5'7" tall. Enlisted 9 Dec 1874. Remained at the Powder River Depot. Presence confirmed on June Returns. Lived in Mandan, ND, after leaving army, 8 Dec 1879.

Sharrow, SGM William Hunter— b. York, England, 1843; claimed he was born at sea-d. 25 Jun 1876, killed at the Little Big Horn. Headquarters: Regimental Sergeant Major. Blue eyes, light brown hair, light complexion; 5'7 or 8" tall. Originally enlisted in service on 21 Mar 1865 in Second Cavalry. Discharged 21 Mar 1868. Enlisted 12 Aug 1869 in Seventh Cavalry. Appointed SGM 16 Apr 1872 replacing Joseph B. Furgeson. Enlisted again 10 Sep 1874. Killed with Custer; body found north of Custer Hill, farthest north on the battlefield, opposite the present parking lot on the east side of the service entrance road. Listed number 1 in "June Returns, Alterations ... Killed in action."

Shauer, PVT John— b. Bavaria, Germany, 1851, though more likely, 26 May 1852–d. Seattle, WA, 7 Jul 1924. Company K, private. Gray eyes, dark hair, sallow complexion; 5'8" tall. Enlisted 21 Nov 1872. Rode with his unit in Benteen's battalion, and fought on Reno Hill. Attended 40th anniversary of LBH fight.

Shea, PVT Daniel— b. County Cork, Ireland, 1852–d. Little Rock, AR, of typhoid fever, 24 Jul 1882. Company B, private. Blue eyes, brown hair, fair complexion; 5′ 7¼″ tall. Enlisted 11 Dec 1874 in NYC. With the pack train escort, Company B. Arrived and fought on Reno Hill.

Shea, PVT Jeremiah— b. London, England, March 1854 (or possibly as early as 1850)–d. 25 Jun 1876, killed at the Little Big Horn. Company C, private. Gray eyes, brown hair, ruddy; 5′ 6¼″ tall. In the army less than one year. Enlisted 6 Sep 1875 in Boston. In civilian life, Shea had been an ostler (or hostler), someone employed to take care of the horses of those staying at an inn. Body never identified, though archaeological work may have him at Marker 128, which means he was one of the first ones killed during C Company's charge into Calhoun Coulee. Another possibility is Marker 200, near Keogh. Meyer (C) and Thadus (C) meet the criteria as well. At Marker 200 (1984 grid location N7126-E2760, in the Keogh area), the following artifacts were found: right cavalry boot, upper section cut away; human bones: lower arm; lower left leg; fingers; toes. Consistent with a single individual of slight build, five feet seven to eight inches tall, and twenty years of age [Scott and Fox, *Archaeological Insights into The Custer Battle*, p. 100]. That appears a little taller and a little younger than Shea, but within a tolerable range. Listed number 39 in "June Returns, Alterations … Killed in action."

Mother's name was Ellen Shea. London census records of 1861 show a Jeremiah Shea, whose mother's name was Ellen, listed as eleven years old. If this was the same person, it would indicate a birth date of *circa* 1850 rather than our reputed 1854 [e-mail dated 20 Jan 2010, from Peter G. Russell, Custer Association of Great Britain], and while no means definitive, it highlights the vagaries of 19th-century American military enlistment data.

Sherborne, PVT Thomas— b. Hampshire, England, 1841–d. at the Soldiers Home, Washington, D.C., 19 Aug 1910. Headquarters: band. Private. Hazel eyes, brown hair, dark complexion; 5′ 7″ tall. Remained at Powder River Depot. Presence confirmed on June Returns.

Shields, SAD William M.— b. Vincennes, IN, 1841 or 1842–d. Fort Sill, OK, 6 Sep 1887 or 1888. Company E: company saddler. Gray eyes, brown hair, fair complexion; 5′ 8″ tall. Served in Civil War as 1SG, Illinois Volunteers. Mustered out as a major. Third enlistment 29 Sep 1874. Eventually served as 1SG, E Company, Seventh Cavalry. Probably a straggler at the battle. WIA in the buttocks on Reno Hill. Buried in Post Cemetery, Fort Sill,

OK. Greg Michno says he was at PRD, but this is probably incorrect, especially considering his wound.

Short, PVT Nathan— b. Lehigh County, PA, 1854 (Hardorff says that the Register of Enlistment shows Short's birthplace as London, England)–d. 25 Jun 1876, killed at the Little Big Horn. Company C, private. Gray eyes, brown hair; 5′ 7″ tall; fair or ruddy complexion. With the Seventh Cavalry less than one year. Enlisted 9 Oct 1875. Pre-enlistment occupation listed as a laborer. Was made the company carpenter. Richard Fox says it was possible his body was the one found, miles away, on Rosebud Creek (Scott and Hammer agree, though Smalley does not). May have been a messenger sent back to Terry when the right wing was on Luce Ridge [see Fox, *Archaeology, History, and Custer's Last Battle,* footnote 18–112, p. 378]. Generally acknowledged to have been wearing a light-colored hat with "C7" and crossed sabers *drawn* on the front. The fact that the body found along the Rosebud was thought to be Short's, was that SGT Daniel Kanipe claimed the equipment— which he never saw—was marked with the number, "50," Short's number within C Company. PVT Frank Sniffen (M) told Walter Camp in 1913, that the body belonged to a C Company trooper named Warner and that the men all spoke about it the night the body was found. In either case, the tale has been largely discredited by simple fact that the remains appeared to be considerably older than two months.

Short's age and height specifications are also consistent with the remains discovered at Marker 128 behind Greasy Grass Ridge. Both human remains and battle related artifacts were found there. Almost a complete burial discovered at this site; the most complete set of human remains recovered during the 1984–1985 archaeological excavations. The bones included the lower right leg articulated, its foot bones encased in a cavalry boot. Other bones had been re-buried after the flesh had decayed. The remains were consistent with those of a male between 19 and 22 years old, and approximately 5′ 6¾″ tall, with a range of 5′ 5¾″–5′ 7⅞″. The individual was stocky with well-developed musculature [Scott, *et al., Archaeological Perspectives,* p. 268] and right-handed. The following fit the description: F. Meier (C); J. Shea (C); J. Thadus (C); N. Short (C); G. Moonie (E); W. Huber (E)—highly doubtful; T. Donnelly (F)—highly doubtful; E. Babcock (L); F. Hughes (L)—highly doubtful. There was evidence of two gunshot wounds in the chest, one from the right, one from the left. Also, massive blunt-force trauma to the skull at about the time of death and a bullet fragment was found in the lower left arm. Three parallel cut marks were on the thighbones and another on collarbone. Vertebrae showed congenital defect, probably causing the individual pain when he rode his horse for long periods. Blouse and trousers buttons found; underwear cloth; hooks and eyes, probably from his campaign hat. Because of the way the bones were dispersed, the individual had to have been reburied, probably in 1877 or 1879. Short was listed number 40 in "June Returns, Alterations ... Killed in action."

Shulte, PVT Frederick (aka Charles Miller and Frederick Shutte) — b. Rohden, Prussia, 1846–d. unknown. Company F, private. Blue eyes, brown hair, fair complexion; 5′5¼″ tall. Enlisted 10 Sep 1867 in Second Cavalry. Deserted 2 Aug 1868. Enlisted as Charles Miller 27 Mar 1871 in Seventh Cavalry. Pardoned. Assigned to wagon train at the Powder River Depot. Overfield says he was assigned to *pack* train, but again, this appears confused with the wagons at PRD. In *The Battlefield Dispatch,* dated Winter 2004, Hammer writes, "He came from the Rosebud with ... Terry's column on June 22," indicating he was most certainly not with Custer's pack train.

Sicfous, PVT Francis W. — b. Clarion County, PA, 1852–d. 25 Jun 1876, killed at the Little Big Horn. Company F, private. Gray eyes, light hair, fair complexion; 5′5″ tall. Enlisted 4 Oct 1875. In all likelihood he was killed on Last Stand Hill with his unit. Listed number 121 in "June Returns, Alterations ... Killed in action."

Siefert (also seen as Seifert and Siefort), **PVT August B.** — b. Darmstadt, Hesse, Germany, 26 Jul 1850–d. Highland Park, IL, 20 Jan 1921. One source claims he died on February 25, 1904, but this seems to be an error. Siefert was interviewed by Walter Mason Camp and Camp's interviews began in 1908. Company K, private. Gray eyes, brown hair, light complexion; 5′5″ tall. Arrived in U.S. in 1865. Second enlistment 16 Jan 1875. Rode with his unit in Benteen's battalion, and fought on Reno Hill. Retired as a first sergeant after Spanish-American War. Married: Mary; son: Benjamin. He outlived them both. Buried in Post Cemetery, Fort Sheridan.

Siemon, BSM Charles — b. Copenhagen, Denmark, 1843–d. 25 Jun 1876, killed at the Little Big Horn. Company L: company blacksmith. Gray eyes, brown hair, dark complexion; 5′7½″ tall. Second enlistment 19 Jul 1872. In all likelihood he was killed on Calhoun Hill, though the possibility exists he was one of those killed during the panic through the Keogh Sector. No remains found during the 1984–1985 archaeological work match his descrip-

tion. Listed number 189 in "June Returns, Alterations ... Killed in action."

Siemonson, PVT Bent — b. Milwaukee, WI, Nov 1851–d. 25 Jun 1876, killed at the Little Big Horn. Company L, private. Blue eyes, light hair, light complexion; 5′5½″ tall. Enlisted 6 Feb 1872. In all likelihood he was killed on Calhoun Hill, though the possibility exists he was one of those killed during the panic through the Keogh Sector. No remains found during the 1984–1985 archaeological work match his description. Listed number 221 in "June Returns, Alterations ... Killed in action."

Simons, PVT Patrick — b. Sligo, Ireland, 1854–d. unknown. Company B, private. Gray eyes, brown hair, ruddy complexion; 5′7¼″ tall. Enlisted 14 Mar 1876. Remained at the Powder River Depot.

Sims (also Sems), **PVT John J.** — b. Johnson County, IL, 1852–d. unknown. Company D, private. Blue eyes, brown hair, dark complexion; 5′7¾″ tall. Enlisted 1 Oct 1875. Remained at the Powder River Depot. Presence confirmed on June Returns.

Sivertson (also spelled Sievertsen and Seivertsen), **PVT John** (nicknamed "Big Fritz") — b. Jensen, Norway, 10 Dec 1841–d. Washington, D.C., 30 Aug 1925. Company M, private. Blue eyes, sandy hair, fair complexion; 5′10″ or 11″ tall. Enlisted 19 Jun 1873. One of twenty men — one officer, three scouts, sixteen enlisted men — left in the timber in the valley bottoms, eventually making Reno Hill. Served in Yellowstone and Black Hills expeditions, as well as Nez Percé campaign of 1877.

In 1994, the remains of a horse were discovered along the retreat route used by some of Reno's men. Personal items bearing the initials "JS" and found in the intact saddlebags, supposedly established that it was Sivertson's horse and equipment. Also discovered in the saddlebags were 50 rounds of .45/70 ammunition, but like everything else concerned with this battle, there is doubt surrounding the claim it was Sivertson's. Sivertsen told Walter Camp that he retrieved his horse some time after the battle and that the animal was unhurt. The horse skull discovered in 1994 contained a .44-caliber bullet. According to an article by Sandy Barnard in the 1996 *Greasy Grass* journal, the "discoveries included: various saddle parts; an 1874 mess kit; an 1872 spoon, knife and fork; an 1874 tin cup; a canteen; a curry comb; spectacles; a harmonica; and about 50 rounds of .45/55-caliber cartridges [not .45/70s], .45 Colt and .45 Schofield ammunition." Jason Pitsch — formerly a local landowner and artifact collector, and the author, Glen Swanson — tied the horse's remains and gear to Sivertsen because according to Pitsch the toothbrush had the initials "J. S." on it. There were, however, four other troopers with the initials "J. S." who fought in the valley that day: John Sullivan (A), John Small (G), and James Severs and John Seamans, both of Company M. While Sivertson, Small, Severs, and Seamens all survived the battle, Sullivan was killed, his "unmolested remains ... found on the bottom of a washout which entered the river a short distance north of the retreat ford. The identification was established by the number on Sullivan's pistol and on his carbine which were found with the body according to Sgt. Samuel Alcott" [Hardorff, *On the LBH with Walter Camp,* p. 181, footnote 2]. This description matches perfectly the area where the horse's remains were discovered, in all likelihood making it Sullivan's.

Slaper, PVT William C. — b. Cincinnati, OH, 23 Nov 1854–d. Sawtelle, CA, 13 Nov 1931. Company M, private. Blue eyes, brown hair, fair complexion; 5' 8½" tall. Enlisted 10 Sep 1875. No specific record exists of his participation in the battle, other than his presence with his unit during the valley fighting and subsequent defense of Reno Hill. Wife was named Sarah, but no children. Buried in Los Angeles National Cemetery.

Small, PVT John R. — b. Baltimore, MD, 1834 (U.S. Navy enlistment records of 7 Jan 1867, indicate he was born in 1845)–d. Baltimore, MD, 13 May 1883. Company G, private. Gray eyes, dark hair, fair complexion; 5' 7½" tall. Enlisted 5 Mar 1873. No specific record exists of his participation in the battle, other than his presence with his unit during the valley fighting and subsequent defense of Reno Hill.

Smallwood, PVT William — b. Jonesville, IN, 1852–d. 25 Jun 1876, killed at the Little Big Horn. Company E, private. Brown eyes, brown hair, dark complexion; 5' 8½" tall. Enlisted 18 Dec 1874. While his body was not specifically identified, he may have been one of the unknowns on either the South Skirmish Line or in Deep Ravine. Listed number 80 in "June Returns, Alterations ... Killed in action."

Smeling, Sebastian *see* **Omling, PVT Sebastian**

Smith, PVT Albert A. — b. Queens County, NY, 1838 or 1839–d. 25 Jun 1876, killed at the Little Big Horn. Company E, private. Gray eyes, brown hair, fair complexion; 5' 5¾" tall. Enlisted 1 Jan 1873. While his body was not specifically identified, he may have been one of the unknowns on either the South Skirmish Line or in Deep Ravine. Listed number 81 in "June Returns, Alterations ... Killed in action."

Smith, 1LT (Bvt MAJ) Algernon Emory ("Fresh" Smith) — b. Newport, NY, 17 Sep 1842–d. 25 Jun 1876, killed at the Little Big Horn. Company E: Acting Commander. TDY from Company A. DOR: 5 Dec 1868; third-ranking 1LT on campaign, behind Cooke and Godfrey. The only E Company body identified on Custer Hill, near the crest. Marker 105 is inscribed with his name, though the bone fragments found there are consistent with Company F private, Werner L. Liemann, and are not consistent with what is known of Smith. Forensics evidence suggests that the bones are from an individual about five feet seven inches tall and more than twenty-five years old. "A massive bone growth on the metatarsals suggests that the individual had suffered some sort of injury to his foot which had not healed properly. In all probability this individual walked with a limp..." [Scott and Fox, *Archaeological Insights into the Custer Battle,* p. 101]. The conclusion was reached that the bones could not have belonged to Smith due to his having sustained a crippling injury to his left arm during the Civil War and the absence of such injury in the recovered bones. LT Edward S. Godfrey (K) wrote that along with Reily, Cooke, and Yates, Smith's body was found in the vicinity of George Custer's, but nearer the top of the hill than Custer's [Godfrey/Graham, *The Custer Myth,* p. 345].

Attended Hamilton College in NY. Fought at Fort Wagner, Drewry's (or Drury's) Bluff, and Petersburg. Served as A-d-C to General Alfred Terry and on the staffs of Sully, Ord, and Ames. Severely wounded in an assault of Fort Fisher, Jan 1865; shot up so badly he could not raise his left arm above the shoulder.

Appointed second lieutenant, Seventh Cavalry (F), Aug 1867, joining the regiment in November. Took part in the Sully Expedition and at the Washita. COL Sturgis thought less of him, professionally, than most others, though he was generally well-liked and a member of the "Custer Clan." Very able and experienced. Had served as regimental QM, but relieved because of some questionable practices. Survived the Benzine Boards and transferred to Company A. Took part in the southern reconstruction period, the Yellowstone Expedition and the 11 Aug 1873 battle near Pompey's Pillars, and the Black Hills Expedition of 1874. He got his nickname, "Fresh," because there was at the time another officer with the Seventh named H. W. "Salty" Smith, a former merchant seaman. Married Henrietta (Nettie) B. Bowen (d. 4 Apr 1903) on 10 Oct 1867 at her home in Newport, NY. Originally buried at the LBH, but exhumed in 1877 and reinterred in Fort Leavenworth National Cemetery.

Smith, PVT Frederick (real name was Christian Methfessel) — b. Muhlhausen, Germany, 1846–d.

Muhlhausen, Germany, 18 Aug 1905. Company K, private. Blue eyes, dark brown hair, florid complexion; 5'10½" tall. Enlisted 7 Mar 1876. Remained at the Powder River Depot. Presence confirmed on June Returns. Resided in Reinbeck, IA, until 1901.

Smith, PVT George E.— b. Kennebunk, ME, 1850–d. 25 Jun 1876, killed at the Little Big Horn. Company M, private. Gray eyes, brown hair, fair complexion; 5'6½" tall. Enlisted 6 Sep 1875 in Boston. Killed in flats. Connell says his horse bolted and he was carried or dragged into Indian village where he was butchered, his head put on a stake (Armstrong [A]?). Hammer backs this up with quotes. Willert agrees. Body never found. Scott says his horse bolted near timber, so this may all be correct. Also noted found on skirmish line and at edge of timber (this is obviously doubtful). Listed number 233 in "June Returns, Alterations … Killed in action."

Smith, PVT Henry G.— b. Lake County, IN, 1849–d. unknown. Company D, private. Gray eyes, brown hair, dark complexion; 5'9" tall. Enlisted 8 Sep 1875. Rode with his unit in Benteen's battalion, and fought on Reno Hill. Deserted while on leave, 19 Feb 1877.

Smith, PVT James (1st)— b. Tipperary, Ireland, 1842–d. 25 Jun 1876, killed at the Little Big Horn. Company E, private. Hazel eyes, brown hair, ruddy complexion; 5'6" tall. Enlisted 31 Jul 1861 in the GMS, USA. Joined Company F, Seventh Cavalry 10 Sep 1866; re-upped 1 Aug 1869 and 20 May 1874. While his body was not specifically identified, he may have been one of the unknowns on either the South Skirmish Line or in Deep Ravine. Listed number 82 in "June Returns, Alterations … Killed in action."

Smith, PVT James (2nd)— b. Lynn, MA, 1847–d. 25 Jun 1876, killed at the Little Big Horn. Company E, private. Hazel eyes, black hair, dark complexion; 5'4½" tall. Enlisted 1 Dec 1874. While his body was not specifically identified, he may have been one of the unknowns on either the South Skirmish Line or in Deep Ravine. Listed number 88 in "June Returns, Alterations … Killed in action."

Smith, PVT William Earl— b. Rouses Point, NY, 3 Aug 1853–d. South Deerfield, MA, 10 May 1918. Company D, private. Gray eyes, dark hair, dark complexion; 5'5½" tall. Enlisted 13 Sep 1875. Rode with his unit in Benteen's battalion, and fought on Reno Hill. Married Cora Arvetta Dailey 21 Apr 1886; children: Alice Vivian, Maude Evelyn, Gladys Eola, and Clarice Roselyn. Buried in Grave 1, Lot 016, Section 1, Brookside Cemetery, Deerfield.

Smith, CPL William M.— b. Trenton, NJ, 1852–d. Philadelphia, PA, 4 Jan 1921. Company B, corporal. Blue eyes, dark hair, ruddy complexion; 5'5½" tall. Enlisted 11 Jul 1872. With the pack train escort, Company B. Arrived and fought on Reno Hill. WIA in right arm in hilltop fight. Cremated and buried in Wenonah, NJ.

Sniffen, PVT Frank W.— b. NYC, 12 Sep 1857–d. Fort Oglethorpe, GA, 17 Apr 1931. Company M, private. Blue eyes, light hair, fair complexion; 5'7" tall. Enlisted 1 Sep 1875. Carried company colors in valley fight. Made it to Reno Hill. Divorced his first wife Katherine Solmon about 1902 in San Francisco; married Margaret McCarthy 8 Aug 1910. Buried in Chattanooga National Cemetery.

Snow, PVT Andrew— b. Sorel, Quebec, Canada, 1853–d. 25 Jun 1876, killed at the Little Big Horn. Company L, private. Hazel eyes, black hair, ruddy complexion; 5'5⅛" tall. Enlisted 24 Sep 1875. In all likelihood he was killed on Calhoun Hill, though the possibility exists he was one of those killed during the panic through the Keogh Sector. No remains found during the 1984–1985 archaeological work match his description. Listed number 220 in "June Returns, Alterations … Killed in action."

Spencer, FAR Abel Bennett— b. Plainville, Rock County, WI, 11 Jul 1844 or, according to one source, 1845–d. unknown. Company E: company farrier. Hazel eyes, dark hair, dark complexion; 5'7¾" tall. Enlisted 18 Jan 1872. With packs (Hammer), but Michno says PRD. With the packs is more likely. Had been a farmer. Lived in Chicago more than 30 years.

Spinner, PVT Philipp— b. Baden, Germany, Aug 1846–d. suicide, Camp Douglas, WI, 12 Aug 1895. Company B, private. Gray eyes, light brown hair, fair to ruddy complexion; 5'4½ to 6½" tall. Enlisted 12 Dec 1870 in Seventh Cavalry. Re-upped 12 Dec 1875. With the pack train escort, Company B. Arrived and fought on Reno Hill. Never married. Committed suicide by shooting himself.

Stafford, PVT Benjamin F.— b. Boston, MA, 1846–d. 25 Jun 1876, killed at the Little Big Horn. Company E, private. Brown eyes, black hair, fair complexion; 5'5¼" tall. Enlisted 8 Oct 1873. Bone fragments found at Marker 105 on Last Stand Hill would be consistent with his reported age and height, though most men killed at this location were believed to have been from F Company. Several others fit this description, as well. Listed number 83 in "June Returns, Alterations … Killed in action."

Stanley, PVT Edward— b. Boston, MA, 1850–d. 25 Jun 1876, killed at the Little Big Horn, probably during Reno's retreat. Company G, private. Blue eyes, brown hair, fair complexion; 5'9⅜" tall. Enlisted 22 Nov 1875. Ken Hammer, in *The Battlefield Dispatch,* Winter 2005, lists his death as occurring in an "unknown location." Smalley claims no one saw him killed and his body was never found [*Little Bighorn Mysteries,* p. 15–7]. In all likelihood, he was killed during the retreat from the timber. Listed number 137 in "June Returns, Alterations … Killed in action."

Staples, CPL Samuel Frederick— b. Worcester, MA, 1849–d. 25 Jun 1876, killed at the Little Big Horn. Company I, corporal. Brown eyes, dark hair, dark complexion; 5'6½" tall. Enlisted 9 Jan 1872. Body never identified, but in all likelihood he was killed in the Keogh Sector. Married to Annie C. Staples. They had one daughter. Listed number 145 in "June Returns, Alterations … Killed in action."

Stark, WAG Frank (also seen spelled Starck)— b. Bavaria, 1849–d. St. Louis, MO, 13 May 1907. Company C: wagoner. Hazel eyes, brown hair, fair complexion; 5'7½" tall. Was in his second enlistment, 7 Sep 1875. Remained at the Powder River Depot. The June Returns do not list any Company C personnel at Powder River, indicating they must have been returned to their unit.

Stein, VET SURG Carl A. (also seen as Charles A. Stein)— b. Prussia (Germany)–d. St. Paul, MN, 19 Oct 1891. Headquarters: Regimental veterinary surgeon. Appointed to Seventh Cavalry on 7 Jul 1875. Joined regiment in Mar 1876, resigned 1 Sep 1876. Studied veterinary medicine at Military Veterinary School, Berlin. Served in 1st Prussian Dragoons Regiment. Remained at Powder River camp.

Steinker, FAR John R. (last name also seen spelled Steintker, though that seems more a typo than the correct spelling)— b. Hanover, Germany, 1835–d. FAL, M.T., 28 Nov 1876; committed suicide using opium. Company K: company farrier. Brown eyes, dark hair, ruddy complexion; 5'11½" tall. Second enlistment 30 Nov 1872. Rode with his unit in Benteen's battalion, and fought on Reno Hill. Buried in Custer Battlefield National Cemetery.

Stella, PVT Alexander (aka Stern)— b. Athens, Greece, 1853–d. 25 Jun 1876, killed at the Little Big Horn. Company E, private. Brown eyes, black hair, dark complexion; 5'6" tall. Enlisted 1 Dec 1874. "Frank Geist told Walter Camp that Stella attended school with him in Germany and his name was Stern" [Hammer, *Men with Custer,* p. 332]. While his body was not specifically identified, he may have been one of the unknowns on either the South Skirmish Line or in Deep Ravine. Listed

number 84 in "June Returns, Alterations … Killed in action."

Stephens, PVT George Wesley— b. Madison, IN, 1852–d. Kansas City, MO, 19 Mar 1887. Company G, private. Brown eyes, black hair, dark complexion; 5'8½" tall. Enlisted 4 Apr 1876. Remained at the Powder River Depot. Presence confirmed on June Returns. Illiterate. Married Mary Elizabeth Jett 21 Aug 1882. Children: Mary Etta, Jennie Bessie, and Nancy Druzella.

Sterland, PVT Walter Scott— b. Chesterfield, England, 16 Apr 1851–d. Bismarck, ND, 27 Apr 1922. Company M, private. Blue eyes, light hair, fair complexion; 5'5½" tall. Enlisted 18 Nov 1872. Remained at the Powder River Depot. Presence confirmed on June Returns. Served in South Carolina, the Yellowstone expedition, and the Black Hills expedition. While at PRD, he served as Terry's butcher and came up to the Big Horn camp from the Rosebud on the *Far West* on 22 Jun 1876. Resided in Bismarck from 1879 to 1885, then Dickinson, then Gladstone, ND, for 28 years. Resided near Glendive, MT, in 1910; then Dickinson from 1911. Visited his home in England in 1910. Survived by widow Ella and son Arthur W. Sterland. Buried in Dickinson City Cemetery.

Stevenson, PVT Thomas W. (or J.; nicknamed "Reddy")— b. County Fermanagh, Ireland, 1848–d. Minneapolis, MN, 29 Jan 1898. Company G, private. Blue eyes, red hair, ruddy complexion; 5'5¾" tall. Second enlistment 19 Jul 1875. Goldin claimed he was not at the battle [Carroll, *The Benteen-Goldin Letters,* p. 50], but cites no proof. Stevenson had served in the Seventh Infantry and was seen by some of those men as they approached Reno Hill on 27 June. Survived by widow and sons.

Stivers, PVT Thomas W.— b. Madison County, KY, Jul 1850–d. killed in a gunfight near Richmond, KY, 28 Jun 1877. Company D, private. Blue eyes, dark brown hair, fair complexion; 5'5" tall. Enlisted 16 Sep 1871. Rode with his unit in Benteen's battalion, and fought on Reno Hill. Awarded MH for voluntarily bringing water up to Reno Hill from the LBH River.

Stoffel, PVT Henry— b. Philadelphia, PA, 1850–d. unknown. Company L, private. Blue eyes, light hair, fair complexion; 5'9" tall. Enlisted 22 Jan 1872. With the pack train. Fought on Reno Hill.

Stout, PVT Edward— b. Calhoun, MO, 1841–d. unknown. Company B, private. Brown eyes, brown hair, light complexion; 5'11" tall. Second enlistment 25 Jan 1875. With the pack train escort, Company B. Arrived and fought on Reno Hill. In Black Hills expedition.

Stowers, PVT Thomas James (aka James Thomas)— b. Bucks County, PA, 3 Dec 1848–d. Baxter, TN, 25 Jul 1933. Company B, private. Blue or hazel eyes, light or sandy hair, fair complexion; 5'5" to 5'7" tall. Enlisted 3 Sep 1864 in 119th PA Infantry. Discharged 28 Jun 1865. Enlisted 1 Dec 1874. With the pack train escort, Company B. Arrived and fought on Reno Hill. Buried at Odd Fellows Cemetery, Baxter, TN.

Stratton, PVT Frank— b. Nottingham, England, 1848–d. unknown. Company M, private. Hazel eyes, brown hair, fair complexion; 5'5½" tall. Enlisted 18 Sep 1875. No specific record exists of his participation in the battle, other than his presence with his unit during the valley fighting and subsequent defense of Reno Hill.

Streing (also Stressinger and Stringer), **CPL Frederick**— b. Ripley County, IN, 24 Jun 1852–d. 25 Jun 1876, killed at the Little Big Horn. Company M, corporal. Gray eyes, light hair, fair complexion; 5'5¼" tall. Enlisted 19 Oct 1872. Killed at edge of timber in the valley fight, probably during the retreat. Listed number 228 in "June Returns, Alterations ... Killed in action."

Strode, PVT Elijah T.— b. Monroe County, KY, Mar 1851–d. Sturgis, D.T., 14 Feb 1881; shot in Tom Miller's saloon by Thomas Whalen of H Company. He fell over dead as he was heading out the back door. A judge and sheriff were witnesses and still the jury did not believe it was murder and there was a hung jury. A second trial was held with the same results. Company A, private. Brown eyes, brown hair, fair complexion; 5'9¾" tall. Enlisted 15 Oct 1872. LT Charles Varnum's orderly. In the valley fight. Wounded in right ankle, probably on Reno Hill. Buried in post cemetery, Fort Meade, D.T.

Stuart, PVT Alpheus— b. NYC, 1842–d. 25 Jun 1876, killed at the Little Big Horn. Company C, private. Gray eyes, dark hair; 5'10 or 11½" tall. Was on his second enlistment, 20 Sep 1875. Possibly killed at head of Deep Ravine, though doubtful. Listed number 41 in "June Returns, Alterations ... Killed in action."

Stungewitz, PVT Ygnatz— b. Kovno, Russia, 1847 (One source claimed the city was spelled "Kuuno." *Kuuno* may be today's Kunow, now located in Poland, but that does not seem to be the correct city of birth. With the constantly changing borders in that part of Europe, cities were known by several names depending on the country they were currently part of. For example, *Kovno* was Polish, but when Stungewitz was born, it was part of the Russian Empire. When the city became part of Lithuania, it was known as *Kaunas*. *Wilno*, nearby, was

still Polish, but prior to 1917 it was part of Russia — therefore, *Vilna*. When it was Lithuanian it was called *Vilnius*.)–d. 25 Jun 1876, killed at the Little Big Horn. Company C, private. Blue eyes, light hair; 5'8½" tall. With the Seventh Cavalry for a few years, enlisting on 15 Sep 1873. Body identified apparently on Custer Hill, near Boston Custer, near foot of hill. Listed number 42 in "June Returns, Alterations ... Killed in action."

Sturgis, 2LT James (Jack) **Garland**— b. Albuquerque, NM, 24 Jan 1854–d. 25 Jun 1876, killed at the Little Big Horn. Company E. TDY from Company M, assigned there to replace Alexander. DOR: 16 Jun 1875; second lowest-ranking non-attached officer on campaign, next to Reily. Youngest officer in the Seventh Cavalry, son of the regimental CO. Less than a year out of West Point, joining the regiment in Oct 1875. Body purportedly found on the South Skirmish Line, though there are some doubts to that. CPT Walter Clifford of Company E, Seventh Infantry — among others — saw Sturgis' bloodstained underclothes in a tepee in the abandoned village. Apparently, his spurs were found there as well. Today, his gravestone is Marker 48, set in Cemetery Ravine along the South Skirmish Line, almost assuredly spurious, though it does not mean he was not killed somewhere nearby. On December 29, 1931, Theodore Goldin wrote a letter to Albert W. Johnson stating he had seen a grave marked with Sturgis' name, "...well down the hillside toward the river..." [Carroll, *The Benteen-Goldin Letters*, p. 34]. Bruce Liddic wrote that the lone horseman who tried running away to the north from the South Skirmish Line environs might have been Sturgis.

Sullivan, PVT Daniel— b. Cork, Ireland, 1852–d. Ardagilla, Skibbereen, Ireland, 25 Jun 1931. Company G, private. Blue eyes, dark hair, medium complexion; 5'8" tall. Enlisted 8 Dec 1874 in Boston. Remained at the Powder River Depot. Presence confirmed on June Returns. Survived by his widow Margaret and his son Daniel.

Sullivan, John *see* **Cowley, PVT Cornelius**

Sullivan, PVT John— b. Dublin, Ireland, 1851–d. 25 Jun 1876, killed at the Little Big Horn. Company A, private. Gray eyes, brown hair, medium complexion; 5'6⅛" tall. Enlisted 7 Dec 1874. Horse bolted during retreat from valley fight. His body was found in or at the edge of the LBH. "Sullivan's unmolested remains were found on the bottom of a washout which entered the river a short distance north of the retreat ford. The identification was established by the number on Sullivan's pistol and on his carbine which were found with the body according to Sgt. Samuel Alcott" [Hardorff, *On the*

LBH with Walter Camp, p. 181, footnote 2]. [See the Sivertson entry, above.] Listed number 9 in "June Returns, Alterations … Killed in action."

Sullivan, PVT Timothy—b. Chelsea, MA, 1844– d. Washington, D.C., 10 Jan 1903. Company L, private. Hazel eyes, brown hair, dark complexion; 5′ 4½″ tall. Second enlistment 17 Sep 1875. With the pack train. Fought on Reno Hill.

Summers, PVT David—b. Pettis County, MO, 1848–d. 25 Jun 1876, killed at the Little Big Horn, in the timber. Company M, private. Blue eyes, sandy hair, ruddy complexion; 5′ 8½″ tall. Second enlistment 13 May 1876. Killed in timber; body found badly mutilated. Listed number 234 in "June Returns, Alterations … Killed in action."

Sweeney, PVT John W.—b. Marion County, MO, 1846–d. near Graefensburg, KY, 14 Apr 1884. Company F, private. Gray eyes, light hair, fair complexion; 5′ 8½″ tall. Second enlistment 4 Jan 1872. Listed in hilltop fight, though he may have been with packs. In all likelihood, however, he was a straggler.

Sweetser, PVT Thomas P. (aka Switzer)—b. Reading, MA, 1850–d. 25 Jun 1876, killed at the Little Big Horn. Company A, private. Blue eyes, brown hair, dark complexion; 5′ 7¾″ tall. Enlisted 8 Sep 1875. Killed during the retreat from the timber. Body never found and Hammer, in *The Battlefield Dispatch,* Winter 2005, lists him as "unknown location." Smalley claims no one saw him killed and his body was never found [*Little Bighorn Mysteries,* p. 15–7]. Listed number 10 in "June Returns, Alterations … Killed in action."

Symms, PVT Darwin L.—b. Montreal, Quebec, Canada, 1852–d. 25 Jun 1876, killed at the Little Big Horn. Company I, private. Blue eyes, light hair, fair complexion; 5′ 9″ tall. Enlisted 25 Aug 1875. Body never identified, but in all likelihood he was killed in the Keogh Sector. Married Isabell Smith 17 Aug 1872; no children. Listed number 173 in "June Returns, Alterations … Killed in action."

Tanner, PVT James J. (aka Jacob Henry Gebhart)—b. Altoona, PA, 1849–d. 27 Jun 1876, killed at the Little Big Horn, dying of wounds suffered in one of the Benteen charges the previous day. Company M, private. Brown eyes, black hair, dark complexion; 5′ 7¾″ tall. Enlisted 18 Sep 1875. Wounded in Benteen's charge on Reno Hill. Died 27 June in field hospital on Reno Hill. Buried in same grave as Voight. There are some accounts that have him killed at the river—on 26 June—attempting to get water [Marquis, *Wooden Leg,* p. 260]. Wooden Leg's description is pretty vivid,

lending some credibility to the story, though Wooden Leg probably ran the water-gathering and Benteen's charge events together. 1SG Ryan said Tanner was mortally wounded in Benteen's charge and he and three others gather the wounded man up and brought him to the hospital area where he died "in about five minutes" [Barnard, *Ten Years with Custer,* p. 300]. Ryan's word is pretty definitive. Listed number 237 in "June Returns, Alterations … Killed in action."

Tarbox, PVT Byron (also seen as Bryan) **L.**—b. Brooksville, ME, 1852–d. 25 Jun 1876, killed at the Little Big Horn. Company L, private. Gray eyes, dark hair, fair complexion; 5′ 6¼″ tall. Enlisted 22 Sep 1875. In all likelihood he was killed on Calhoun Hill, though the possibility exists he was one of those killed during the panic through the Keogh Sector. No remains found during the 1984–1985 archaeological work match his description. Listed number 222 in "June Returns, Alterations … Killed in action."

Taube, PVT Emil—b. Damerau, Germany, 18 Nov 1847–d. Eddy, TX, 12 Feb 1917. Company K, private. Hazel eyes, black hair, dark complexion; 5′ 5½″ tall. Enlisted 21 Mar 1876. Remained at the Powder River Depot. Presence confirmed on June Returns. Married Mollie Huber, 13 Sep 1882. Children: Emil, Bettie, Adolph, and Selma. Buried in Shiloh Cemetery, Troy, TX.

Taylor, BSM Walter O.—b. Scituate, RI, 5 Jul 1844 (birth date also seen listed as 1854 which seems more reasonable)–d. Rockland, MA, 26 Jan 1931. Company G: company blacksmith. Gray eyes, light hair, fair complexion; 5′ 6¾″ tall. Enlisted 22 Nov 1875. Fought in the valley fight. One of twenty men—one officer, three scouts, sixteen enlisted men—left in the timber in the valley bottoms, eventually making Reno Hill later that afternoon. Survived by widow Emma M. King Taylor and daughter Sarah. Buried in Northville Cemetery, East Bridgewater, MA.

Taylor, PVT William Othneil—b. Canandaigua, NY, 18 Feb 1855–d. Orange, MA, 19 Feb 1923. Company A, private. Gray eyes, light hair, fair complexion; 5′ 6¾″ tall. Enlisted 22 Nov 1875. An A Company horse-holder in the timber during the valley fight. Wrote a book about the battle many years later. Resided near Whitman, MA, and at 831 Beech St, Rockland, MA. Buried in Northville Cemetery, East Bridgewater, MA.

Teeman (Tieman), **CPL William** (aka William A. Adams)—b. Denmark, 1846–d. 25 Jun 1876, killed at the Little Big Horn. Company F, corporal. Gray eyes, light brown hair, fair to dark complexion;

5'9" tall. Enlisted on 30 Sep 1867; deserted from second enlistment, then enlisted as William A. Adams on 27 Aug 1872 at a listed age of 23, and from Buffalo, NY. Granted amnesty and restored to duty. Killed on Custer Hill, his body found near Klein's, near foot of the hill. Possibly Marker 56. Listed number 94 in "June Returns, Alterations ... Killed in action."

Tenley, Henry *see* **Farley, PVT Henry James**

Tessier, PVT Edmond D. — b. Montreal, Quebec, Canada, 1847–d. 25 Jun 1876, killed at the Little Big Horn. Company L, private. Hazel eyes, dark hair, dark complexion; 5'7½" tall. Second enlistment 26 Nov 1871. In all likelihood he was killed on Calhoun Hill, though the possibility exists he was one of those killed during the panic through the Keogh Sector. No remains found during the 1984–1985 archaeological work match his description. Listed number 223 in "June Returns, Alterations ... Killed in action."

Thadus, PVT John — b. Guilford County, NC, 1854–d. 25 Jun 1876, killed at the Little Big Horn. Company C, private. Black eyes, dark hair, dark complexion; 5'6¼" tall. In the army less than one year. Enlisted 17 Aug 1875. Had been a farmer in civilian life. Body never identified, though in all likelihood, his was the body found buried at Marker 128 in the upper reaches of Calhoun Coulee, which means he was one of the men killed during C Company's charge into the coulee. Another possibility is Marker 200, near Keogh. Meyer (C) and Shea (C) meet the criteria as well. At Marker 200 (1984 grid location N7126-E2760, in the Keogh area), the following artifacts were found: right cavalry boot, upper section cut away; human bones: lower arm; lower left leg; fingers; toes. Consistent with a single individual of slight build, five feet seven to eight inches tall, and twenty years of age [Scott and Fox, *Archaeological Insights into the Custer Battle,* p. 100].

An article published June 25, 2008, in *The News & Record* of Greensboro reported on Thadus' death on the battlefield.

There is some controversy as to whether or not "Thadus" was this man's real name. Peter G. Russell of the Custer Association of Great Britain claims no one named Thadus shows up in any records for Guilford County, N. C., and in fact, the name does not appear in any census records across the country in either 1851 or 1861. Listed number 44 in "June Returns, Alterations ... Killed in action."

Thomas, James *see* **Stowers, PVT Thomas James**

Thompson, PVT Peter — b. Markinch, Fife, Scotland, 28 Dec 1854 (in a letter dated March 15, 1974,

Frank E. Vyzralek, Archivist at the State Historical Society of North Dakota, claimed Thompson was born in Fifishire, Scotland, December 28, 1856. Thompson claimed the same thing. Thompson tombstone carries a birth date of December 28, 1848 (courtesy of William W. Boyes, Jr.)–d. Hot Springs, SD, 3 Dec 1928. Company C, private. Brown eyes, brown hair, ruddy; 5'8¾" tall. In the service for less than one year: enlisted 21 Sep 1875, in Pittsburgh, by LT Thomas Gregg. Arrived in the U.S. with parents in 1865. They went to Banksville, PA. Thompson then moved to Indiana County, PA, where he was living when he enlisted. Horse gave out in Medicine Tail Coulee and he and Watson eventually found their way back to Reno on the hill. In one of the more legendary — and farfetched — stories associated with the Little Big Horn, Thompson claimed both he and Watson hid for a while in the Medicine Tail ford area, opposite the end of the village. During this miasmic adventure he saw George Custer all alone at the river and one of the Ree or Crow scouts in the village, hauling out an Indian woman. WIA — shot through the hand as he was voluntarily bringing water back up to Reno Hill from the LBH. He made more trips despite the remonstrance of his sergeant. Awarded MH. He could very well have been one of the two stragglers reported by the Ree scouts, Soldier, White Eagle, and Bull. Discharged at Fort Meade, D.T., in 1880.

Note: "...Private Peter Thompson, Company C, was most certainly not born on 28 December 1848 even though this precise date is boldly inscribed on his tombstone and continues to be universally quoted...." — Peter Russell.

Worked for Homestake Mining after the army. Became a wealthy and successful rancher in the Little Missouri country below Alzada, MT, establishing a superb reputation.

Thornberry, PVT Levi — b. Marietta, OH, 1853–d. Watertown, OH, 27 May 1902. Company M, private. Blue eyes, brown hair, dark complexion; 5'6¼" tall. Enlisted 20 Sep 1875. No specific record exists of his participation in the battle, other than his presence with his unit during the valley fighting and subsequent defense of Reno Hill.

Thorpe, PVT Rollins L. — b. NYC, 1854; Williams says, 6 Nov 1859–d. unknown. Company M, private. Gray eyes, dark brown hair, dark complexion; 5'7½" tall. Enlisted 7 Sep 1875, claiming to be 21 years old, which would explain the 1854 birth date. No specific record exists of his participation in the battle, other than his presence with his unit during the valley fighting and subsequent defense of Reno Hill.

Tinkham, PVT Henry L.—b. Montpelier, VT, Nov 1854–d. unknown. Company B, private. Blue eyes, brown hair, fair complexion; 5'8¾" tall. Enlisted 30 Mar 1876. Remained at the Powder River Depot.

Tolan, PVT Frank—b. Malone, NY, May 1854–d. unknown. Company D, private. Gray eyes, brown hair, fair complexion; 5'8" tall. Enlisted 31 Aug 1875. Rode with his unit in Benteen's battalion, and fought on Reno Hill. Awarded MH for voluntarily carrying water back up to Reno Hill from the LBH.

Torrey, PVT William A. (also Tarr)—b. Weymouth, MA Jul 1850–d. 25 Jun 1876, killed at the Little Big Horn. Company E, private. Gray eyes, light hair, fair complexion; 5'4½" tall. Enlisted 12 Nov 1872. While his body was not specifically identified, he may have been one of the unknowns on either the South Skirmish Line or in Deep Ravine. Listed number 85 in "June Returns, Alterations … Killed in action."

Tritten, SAD SGT John G.—b. Canton Bern, Switzerland, 8 Oct 1846–d. Dayton, OH, 12 Dec 1918. Headquarters: Regimental Saddler Sergeant. Blue eyes, light hair, light complexion; 5'7" tall. First enlisted on 6 Aug 1866. Remained at Powder River camp. Presence confirmed on June Returns.

Troy, PVT James E.—b. Richmond, MA, 1849–d. 25 Jun 1876, killed at the Little Big Horn. Company I, private. Gray eyes, brown hair, dark complexion; 5'5¼" tall. Enlisted 30 Dec 1871. Body never identified, but in all likelihood he was killed in the Keogh Sector. Listed number 174 in "June Returns, Alterations … Killed in action."

Trumble, PVT William—b. Iowa, 1852–d. unknown. Company B, private. Gray eyes, brown hair, florid complexion; 5'8" tall. Enlisted 9 Sep 1873. On 26 Jan 1889, he enlisted for the fourth time, this time at Fort Sill in the Eighth Cavalry. Fought in the valley and on Reno Hill. LT Hodgson's orderly on 25 Jun 1876. Illiterate and not married.

Tulo, PVT Joseph—b. Rand, France, 1852–d. unknown. Company G, private. Gray eyes, brown hair, fair complexion; 5'8½" tall. Enlisted 7 Mar 1876. Remained at the Powder River Depot. Presence confirmed on June Returns.

Turley, Henry *see* **Farley, PVT Henry James**

Tweed, PVT Thomas S.—b. North Liberty, OH, 1853–d. 25 Jun 1876, killed at the Little Big Horn. Company L, private. Gray eyes, brown hair, fair complexion; 5'5¼" tall. Enlisted 1 Sep 1875. Body found on Custer Hill, fifty yards up from Boston Custer, split up the crotch, shot with arrows in both eyes. Listed number 224 in "June Returns, Alterations … Killed in action."

Van Allen, PVT Garrett H. (aka Garrett H. Niver; first name also seen spelled Gerrit)—b. Bethlehem, NY, 1 Feb 1846 (enlistment register shows birthplace as New Brunswick, NJ)–d. 25 Jun 1876, killed at the Little Big Horn. Company C, private. Blue eyes, black hair; 5'7" tall. Had been in the service for a few years; enlisted 2 Oct 1873. Previous occupation was farmer. His mother remarried and took the name Niver. One of the older privates at the battle. In the C Company charge off Battle Ridge–Calhoun Hill, but body was never identified. May have died in Calhoun Coulee, Finley-Finckle Ridge, the Keogh Sector, or possibly even Last Stand Hill. Not married. There is a monument dedicated to him in the Elmwood Cemetery, Bethlehem, NY, showing his name as Niver. Listed number 45 in "June Returns, Alterations … Killed in action."

Van Bramer, PVT Charles—b. Canterbury, NH, Sep 1850–d. 25 Jun 1876, killed at the Little Big Horn. Company I, private. Gray eyes, dark hair, dark complexion; 5'9½" tall. Enlisted 3 Jan 1872. Body never identified, but in all likelihood he was killed in the Keogh Sector. Listed number 175 in "June Returns, Alterations … Killed in action."

Van Pelt, PVT William E.—b. NYC, 1848–d. Staten Island, NY, 20 Nov 1895. Company K, private. Blue eyes, brown hair, fair complexion; 5'7" tall. Enlisted 13 Jan 1876. Remained at the Powder River Depot. Presence confirmed on June Returns.

Van Sant, PVT Cornelius (also Vaugant)—b. Cincinnati, OH, May 1850–d. 25 Jun 1876, killed at the Little Big Horn. Company E, private. Blue eyes, brown hair, fair complexion; 5'7¼" tall. Enlisted 5 Sep 1872. While his body was not specifically identified, he may have been one of the unknowns on either the South Skirmish Line or in Deep Ravine. Listed number 86 in "June Returns, Alterations … Killed in action."

Varden, 1SG Frank E.—b. Yarmouth, ME, 1845–d. 25 Jun 1876, killed at the Little Big Horn during the Custer fighting. Company I: first sergeant. Blue eyes, brown hair, light complexion; 5'10" tall. Served in 11th ME Infantry, 24 Sep 1861 to 23 Nov 1864. Enlisted 15 Dec 1866 and assigned to Seventh Cavalry. Re-upped 26 May 1872. Body found in the cluster around CPT Keogh. Listed number 141 in "June Returns, Alterations … Killed in action."

Varner, PVT Thomas B.—b. Franklin County, MO, 1853–d. unknown. Company M, private. Blue eyes, brown hair, fair complexion; 5'8¼" tall.

Enlisted 24 Aug 1875. In the valley fight and the fighting on Reno Hill. WIA in the right ear on Reno Hill. Sent to FAL on steamer *Far West*.

Varnum, 2LT Charles Albert (Indians nicknamed him "Pointed Face" or "Peak Face") — b. Troy, NY, 21 Jun 1849 – d. San Francisco, CA, 26 Feb 1936. Buried in San Francisco National Cemetery. Company A. Detached and assigned as Chief-of-Scouts for the campaign. DOR: 14 Jun 1872. USMA classmate of Harrington and Wallace; roommate of Wallace. Varnum and Wallace were very close friends. Varnum was also very close to Benny Hodgson. Finished 17th out of 57 in his class, and behind Wallace. Son of John Varnum and Nancy E. Green. Unusually large family residing near Dracut, MA. The first Varnum to come to this country was George, who came to Ipswich, MA, with wife and two children in 1635. Originally Welsh, but by mid–19th century, almost entirely English stock. Varnum had two sisters and two brothers. One sister was Mary E. Varnum (b. 22 Apr 1847). Two Varnum generals during American Revolution, uncles of Varnum's great-grandfather, Prescott Varnum. Charles moved to Dracut when he was two and grew up there. Varnum's father was a Union Army officer and ended the Civil War in Florida, his family moving to Pensacola in 1866.

Joined Company A, replacing Frank Gibson. Took part in the Yellowstone Expedition of 1873, including both the 4 Aug 1873 and 11 Aug 1873 engagements, where he greatly impressed Custer. Was also in the Black Hills Expedition, then went south with his company, returning to the Dakotas in May 1875.

Rode a Kentucky thoroughbred at the battle. Wounded in both legs during hilltop fight, 26 June. After the battle, he was promoted to 1LT, Company C, replacing Jim Calhoun. Appointed regimental QM, Nov 1876. Took part in the Nez Percé Campaign, 1877, and was at Canyon Creek, 13 Sep 1877. Longest surviving officer of the Little Bighorn battle. Commanded H Company by or in 1889; Windolph was his first sergeant. Promoted to captain, Company B, 22 Jul 1890, and was in the Sioux Campaign, 1890. Awarded MH for action at White Clay Creek in 1890. Served in Cuba and the Philippines.

Wife, Mary Alice; daughter, Georgia or Georgie. Fred Benteen felt Varnum, Hare, Wallace, and Godfrey should have been brevetted for their performance at the LBH; no one else. "Varnum [was] referred to by fellow cavalryman and friend Frederick Benteen as a soldier 'of magnificent courage'" [Klockner, *The Officer Corps of Custer's Seventh Cavalry*, p. 105].

At the RCOI, when asked about the morale of the men by the time they reached Reno Hill, Varnum replied, "It is difficult for me to state anything about that because for a long time before that I had not served with the command and knew but a few men even of my own company. I had been detached and absent a long time" [Nichols, *Reno Court of Inquiry*, p. 153]. Was one of Custer's favorite lieutenants, though there is no evidence the two were particularly close.

Vaugant, Cornelius *see* **Van Sant, PVT Cornelius**

Vetter, PVT Johann Michael — b. Hessen, Germany, 23 Dec 1853 (22 years old; lied about his age at enlistment, claiming he was two years older) – d. 25 Jun 1876, killed at the Little Big Horn. Company L, private. Blue eyes, light hair, fair complexion; 5'9¼" tall. Enlisted 4 Oct 1875. Arrived in Pittsburgh in 1869 at age 17. In all likelihood he was killed on Calhoun Hill, though the possibility exists he was one of those killed during the panic through the Keogh Sector. No remains found during the 1984–1985 archaeological work match his description. Listed number 225 in "June Returns, Alterations … Killed in action."

Vickory, SGT John H. (also Vickery, Vockroy, Victor, and Vickyard; aka Groesbeck) — b. Toronto, Canada, Jul 1847 – d. 25 Jun 1876, killed at the Little Big Horn. Company F, sergeant. Blue eyes, brown hair, dark complexion; 5'10" tall. Enlisted 23 Nov 1862 in Fourteenth NY Heavy Artillery. Deserted 23 Apr 1864 and enlisted in 2nd MA Cavalry as John Vickory, 10 May 1864 to 2 Jul 1865. Enlisted in Seventh Cavalry 31 Jul 1866. His father died in Oswego, NY, 19 Feb 1887. Killed on Custer Hill; body found with George Custer's. There are some writers who say Vickory was one of two personal flag-bearers for Custer (SGT Hughes [K] being the other). Vickory was, however, the regimental standard bearer. That banner was not carried into the battle, but remained furled in its case and was carried in the pack train. There are some who believe Custer ordered a five or six-man scout out of CPT Yates' F Company to proceed his advance as he moved up the bluffs along the river. Being freed of his duties as the standard-bearer, Vickory could very well have led this small foray, though this must remain sheer conjecture. Listed number 91 in "June Returns, Alterations … Killed in action."

Vinatieri, CHIEF MUSICIAN Felix Villiet — b. Turin, Italy, 1834 – d. Yankton, SD, 5 or 15 Dec 1891. Headquarters: Regimental Bandmaster. Remained at PRD. Presence confirmed on June Returns. 5'2" tall. Discharged from Army six months after the battle. Composed and arranged music, conducted an orchestra, and traveled with various shows, including Ringling Bros and Barnum and Bailey circuses. He had been a bandleader of the Queen's Guard of Spagnis in Italy. Custer heard him in Yankton — probably in 1873 — and convinced him to join the Seventh Cavalry as Chief Musician. By 1875, however, their relationship had so deteriorated that Vinatieri applied to be released. His application was denied [Donovan, *A Terrible Glory,* p. 87]. Married; 8 children.

His great-great-grandson — Adam Vinatieri — was/is the place-kicker for the New England Patriots and Indianapolis Colts professional football teams.

Voigt (also seen spelled as Voyte, Voight, Voyt), **PVT Henry Carl** — b. Hanover, Germany, 1855 – d. 26 Jun 1876, killed at the Little Big Horn. Company M, private. Blue eyes, brown hair, fair complexion; 5' 5½" tall. Enlisted 1 Oct 1873. Had been a baker; enlisted 1 Oct 1873. Shot in the head on Reno Hill. Windolph says he was a horse-holder on the hill and when he saw Voigt lying dead on the evening of the 25th or early morning of the 26th, he was still holding the reins of four horses. 1SG Ryan wrote that when CPT French's horse was shot, Voigt saw him staggering and ran to bring him away from the other horses so he wouldn't get hurt even more. This was when Voigt got shot. Buried in same grave as Tanner. The regimental returns carry him as dying on 26 June. Listed number 236 in "June Returns, Alterations … Killed in action."

Voit, SAD Otto *(aka Frank May)* — b. Baden, Germany, 1845 – d. Louisville, KY, 1 Jun 1906. Company H: company saddler. Hazel or brown eyes, dark brown hair, fair or dark complexion; 5' 4" tall. Enlisted 1 Dec 1864 in the 13th Infantry. Deserted and enlisted as Frank May, 21 Dec 1866, in Seventh Cavalry. Re-upped 21 Dec 1871 and pardoned. Reenlisted 9 Oct 1875. WIA on Reno Hill. Awarded MH for holding a diversionary position with Geiger, Mechlin, and Windolph on the brow of Reno Hill, drawing Indian fire while others got water from the LBH. Fred Benteen called Voit, "One of the most faithful soldiers I have ever had in my company." And, "An excellent soldier and a trustworthy man."

Von Arnim, PVT Julius — b. Prussia, 1838 – d. unknown. Company C, private. Brown eyes, dark hair, dark complexion; 5' 3¾" tall. In the service for several years; second enlistment 16 Aug 1871. Detached to band at the Powder River Depot. The June Returns do not list any Company C personnel at Powder River, indicating they must have returned to their unit. There may be a connection with von Arnim to the aristocratic Junker family

of the former Prussian Estates. If so, he had several famous descendants — from one branch of the family — rise to the rank of general officer in the German army of World War II, namely Major General Fritz von Arnim, an artillery officer; Major General Harry von Arnim, a cavalry officer; Lieutenant General Hans-Heinrich Sixt von Arnim, who was captured at Stalingrad, eventually dying in a Soviet POW camp; and most famous of all, Colonel General Hans-Jürgen Theodor "Dieter" von Arnim, described by author Paul Carell as "one of the last knights of the Old School." This last von Arnim surrendered to the British army on 12 May 1943, ending the legend of the *Afrika Korps.*

Voss, CTMP Henry — b. Hanover, Germany, 1849 (there is some indication that Voss may have been born in Gestemunde, Holland. In a Williams footnote, it appears that a trooper who had served with Voss in the Fifth Cavalry claimed Voss was from Holland [Williams, *Military Register of Custer's Last Command,* p. 299, footnote 13] – d. 25 Jun 1876, killed at the Little Big Horn. Headquarters: Regimental Chief Trumpeter. Blue eyes, light hair, fair complexion; 5' 8¾" tall. First enlistment was 1 Jun 1866, in Company G, Fifth Cavalry. Third enlistment on 18 Jan 1875. Greg Michno claims Voss was a Company E man. Richard Fox says Voss' body was found with GAC on Custer Hill, twelve feet from LT Cooke, though other reports have him on the ridge towards the river and further down than Kellogg, maybe a mile from the battlefield. PVT Glenn of Company H reported seeing Voss' and Kellogg's bodies "near the river," while PVT Siefert reported seeing Voss near Custer. Being found near Custer makes sense — he was the regimental trumpeter, after all. Listed number 2 in "June Returns, Alterations … Killed in action."

Only known relative in the U.S. was George C. Voss of 711 Hazel Street, Atlantic, IA.

Walker, PVT George P. (aka George P. Weldon) — b. Providence, RI, 1852 – d. 25 Jun 1876, killed at the Little Big Horn. Company E, private. Gray eyes, brown hair, florid complexion; 5' 6½" tall. Enlisted 12 Dec 1874. While his body was not specifically identified, he may have been one of the unknowns on either the South Skirmish Line or in Deep Ravine. Listed number 87 in "June Returns, Alterations … Killed in action."

Walker, PVT Robert — b. Boston, MA, 1853 – d. unknown. Company C, private. Brown eyes, black hair, dark complexion; 5' 7¼" tall. In the service for less than one year. Enlisted 20 Aug 1875. Remained at the Powder River Depot. The June Returns do not list Company C personnel at Powder River, indicating they must have been returned to their unit.

Wallace, 2LT George Daniel (nicknamed and called primarily "Nick," "Long Soldier," or "Tony Soldier")—b. York County, SC, 29 Jun 1849–d. killed in action at Wounded Knee, SD, 29 Dec 1890. Company G. DOR: 14 Jun 1872, same as Harrington and Varnum. Graduated from the USMA with Varnum and Harrington. Supposed to have been between 6'3" and 6'4" tall, probably only slightly shorter than Edgerly. Acting Engineer Officer for the campaign: the itinerist or regimental recorder with the column. Appointed regimental adjutant after the battle. Joined the 7th Cavalry (G) in the south, replacing T. J. March. Participated in the Yellowstone (1873) and Black Hills (1874) expeditions. Took part in the Nez Percé Campaign in Benteen's battalion and was at the battle of Canyon Creek, 13 Sep 1877. Promoted to captain, Company L, 23 Sep 1885, and served in Kansas, Montana, and Missouri.

Very close friend and roommate of Varnum. Father was a congressman from SC, Alexander Stewart Wallace (b. 30 Dec 1810–d. 27 Jun 1893). Mother was Nancy Lee Ratchford. Wallace married Caroline (Carrie) Otis, 6 Oct 1882, in St. Paul, MN. She died in Bronxville, NY, 9 Apr 1942. Son, Otis Alexander, b. 12 Sep 1889. Wallace was killed — shot in the head and abdomen — 29 Dec 1890, at Wounded Knee while leading a dismounted charge. He was the last of the officers who served under George Custer to die in battle. Buried in Yorkville, SC.

Wallace, PVT John W.—b. Salem, IN, Dec 1849–d. unknown. Company G, private. Blue eyes, auburn hair, florid complexion; 5'9" tall. Enlisted 1 Nov 1872. Promoted to CPL 25 Jun 1876. Fought in the valley battle, then on Reno Hill. He chased a warrior back across the LBH, killed him, and scalped him, waving the scalp around when he returned to Reno Hill.

Wallace, PVT Richard A.—b. Boston, MA, 1852–d. Big Horn River, M.T., 25 Jul 1876; drowned while crossing river to go on picket duty. Company B, private. Gray eyes, dark hair, sallow complexion; 5'7½" tall. Enlisted 7 Dec 1874. With the pack train escort, Company B. Arrived and fought on Reno Hill.

Walsh, TMP Frederick—b. Carlisle, PA, 1851–d. 25 Jun 1876, killed at the Little Big Horn. Company L: trumpeter. Hazel eyes, brown hair, dark complexion; 5'7" tall. Enlisted 1 Dec 1872. In all likelihood he was killed on Calhoun Hill, though the possibility exists he was one of those killed during the panic through the Keogh Sector. No remains found during the 1984–1985 archaeological work match his description. Listed number

188 in "June Returns, Alterations ... Killed in action."

Walsh, PVT Thomas—b. County Roscommon, Ireland, 1842–d. Washington, D.C., date unknown. Company F, private. Gray eyes, brown hair, dark complexion; 5'4½" tall. Enlisted 21 Sep 1875. Remained at the Powder River Depot. Discharged for disability at Fort Totten, D.T., 12 Apr 1880.

Walter, PVT Aloyse Louis—b. Willien, France, or more likely, Willer, Alsace, France, 1834–d. unknown. Company H, private. Hazel eyes, brown hair, fair complexion; 5'7" tall. Enlisted from 25 Jul 1851 to 25 Jul 1856 in Fifth Infantry. Enlisted 29 Sep 1856 in First Cavalry; deserted, then discharged 25 Jan 1862. Enlisted from 25 Jun 1862 to 15 Nov 1864; from 13 Oct 1865 to 13 Oct 1868; from 6 Jan 1869 to 6 Jan 1874; and finally on 1 Mar 1875 in Seventh Cavalry. Remained at the Powder River Depot. Presence confirmed on June Returns.

Warner, PVT Oscar T. (also listed as Warren and Oscar L. Warner)—b. Berne, IN, 1840–d. 25 Jun 1876, killed at the Little Big Horn. Company C, private. Blue eyes, brown hair; 5'5¾" tall. Civil War vet, enlisting from 22 Oct 1861 to 22 Oct 1864, Company H, Third NY Infantry. Enlisted in the Seventh Cavalry on 8 Oct 1875. Married. Wife's name was Sarah. In the C Company charge off Battle Ridge–Calhoun Hill, but body was never identified. May have died in Calhoun Coulee, Finley-Finckle Ridge, the Keogh Sector, or possibly even Last Stand Hill. In August 1876, while General Terry was moving up the Rosebud, a dead soldier and horse were found near the stream. PVT Frank W. Sniffen (M) claimed the body was identified as that of Oscar T. Warner of C Company. Sniffen said Warner's name was in his hat, but he did not see the actual remains [Liddic/Harbaugh, *Camp on Custer,* pages 86–87, and footnote 183, page 87]. The unfortunate soldier in this story is usually thought to be Nathan Short, so this was a completely new twist. In either case — Short or Warner — the tale has been discredited by most. Listed number 46 in "June Returns, Alterations ... Killed in action."

Warren, SGT Amos B.—b. Brooklyn, NY, Jun 1849–d. 25 Jun 1876, killed at the Little Big Horn. Company L, sergeant. Hazel eyes, brown hair, dark complexion; 5'10" tall. Enlisted 13 Sep 1873. Obviously in charge of part of the L Company skirmish line atop Calhoun Hill. His body was never identified, so in all likelihood he died there, though the possibility exists he may have fled to the Keogh Sector or even as far as Last Stand Hill. Listed number 184 in "June Returns, Alterations ... Killed in action."

Warren (also Wanew), **PVT George A.**— b. Gibson County, IN, 1840–d. 25 Jun 1876, killed at the Little Big Horn. Company F, private. Hazel eyes, brown hair, fair complexion; 5' 9½" tall. Enlisted 7 Sep 1875 in St. Louis at 32 to 36 years old, depending on enlistment records. Could have been killed at the head of Deep Ravine, Markers 9 and 10 (near 7). Bones discovered there suggest his age and height. Other soldiers fit the description, but through a process of elimination, Warren is probably the man. Listed number 123 in "June Returns, Alterations ... Killed in action."

Wasmus, PVT Ernest Emil— b. Brunswick, Germany, 1847–d. unknown. Company K, private. Brown eyes, brown hair, fair complexion; 5' 8¾" tall. Enlisted 17 Dec 1874. Rode with his unit in Benteen's battalion, and fought on Reno Hill. Married, Beulah J. Wasmus.

Watson, PVT James— b. Hudson, NY, 1850–d. unknown (possibly in Grand Rapids, MI). Company C, private. Blue eyes, brown hair; 5' 6½" tall. With the Seventh Cavalry less than one year. Enlisted 10 Sep 1875, in Cincinnati, by LT Patrick Cusack. Straggler. His horse gave out and he waited for the pack train, eventually making his way to Reno on the hill. Walter Camp wrote in an April 4, 1923, letter to Kanipe, that Camp had met William Slaper (M) who told him "he remembers distinctly that on the evening of June 25, 1876, Watson came in with the rear guard, under McDougall, leading his horse, and explained that his horse had played out some distance back ... and that he had waited until the rear guard came along and then walked with it, leading his played-out horse. Slaper says Watson never at that time, or any other time, told him of being with Thompson" [Hardorff, *On the LBH with Walter Camp*, p. 166–167].

Way, TMP Thomas N.— b. Chester County, PA, 1847–d. 25 Jun 1876, killed at the Little Big Horn. Company F: trumpeter. Hazel eyes, dark hair, dark complexion; 5' 7" tall. Enlisted from 5 Jun 1866 to 5 Jun 1869 in Fifth Cavalry. Second enlistment 11 Jul 1875. In all likelihood he was killed on Last Stand Hill with his unit. Listed number 122 in "June Returns, Alterations ... Killed in action." Married: Rebecca A. Way. No children.

Weaver, PVT George (nicknamed, "Cully")— b. Lancaster, PA, 1843–d. Fort Meade, D.T., 14 Oct 1886. Company M, private. Blue eyes, brown hair, florid complexion; 5' 7" tall. Second enlistment 15 Mar 1876. No specific record exists of his participation in the battle, other than his presence with his unit during the valley fighting and subsequent defense of Reno Hill. Illiterate.

Weaver, TMP Henry C.— b. Philadelphia, PA, 1842–d. unknown. Company M: trumpeter. Gray eyes, dark hair, ruddy complexion; 5' 4¾" tall. Second enlistment 1 May 1875. It is quite possible Weaver was one of the ten M Company troopers assigned as a skirmish line to scout the banks of the LBH River as Reno made his charge down the valley. From there, Weaver and pals would have made it into the Indian village, setting fire to several tepees. One of twenty men — one officer, three scouts, sixteen enlisted men — left in the timber in the valley bottoms, eventually making Reno Hill later that afternoon.

Weaver, PVT Howard H.— b. Willimantic, CT, Jan 1851–d. Scotland, CT, 2 Dec 1884. Company A, private. Gray eyes, auburn hair, ruddy complexion; 5' 5¾" tall. Enlisted 4 Nov 1872. No specific record exists of his participation in the battle, other than his presence with his unit during the valley fighting and subsequent defense of Reno Hill.

Weeks, PVT James— b. Halifax, Nova Scotia, Jun 1854–d. Crow Agency, M.T., 26 Aug 1877. Company M, private. Blue eyes, brown hair, fair complexion; 5' 9⅞" tall. Enlisted 23 Aug 1875. No specific record exists of his participation in the battle, other than his presence with his unit during the valley fighting and subsequent defense of Reno Hill. Killed by a pistol shot in a fight with Bernard Golden.

Weihe, SGT Henry Charles (aka Charles White)— b. Saxony, Germany, 16 Sep 1847–d. Fort Meade, SD, 23 Oct 1906. Company M, sergeant. Gray eyes, brown hair, fair complexion; 5' 3¾" tall. Enlisted from 6 Nov 1867 to 6 Nov 1870, Seventeenth Infantry. Enlisted 8 Mar 1871 in Seventh Cavalry; re-upped 8 Mar 1876. One of twenty men — one officer, three scouts, sixteen enlisted men — left in the timber in the valley bottoms; came up to hill later. May have been one of the M Company flankers who rode through the timber area and got into the village. WIA in right arm, probably on Reno Hill. Replaced Ryan as company first sergeant, Dec 1876, when Ryan was discharged. Married Sarah Wells (d. 23 Oct 1887), widow of FAR Benj. Wells, on 14 Sep 1884. Married Jennie W. [Weihe], 29 Jul 1889. Homesteaded near Fort Meade, SD. Resided in Sturgis for 28 years. Buried in Post Cemetery, Fort Meade, as Charles White.

Weir, CPT (Bvt LTC) Thomas Benton— b. Nashville, OH, 28 Sep 1838 (or possibly 28 Nov 1838)–d. Governors Island, NY, 9 Dec 1876, 38 years old; not battle related. Smalley says it was from alcoholism. Company D: Commanding Officer. Gray eyes, brown hair, light complexion;

6' tall. DOR: 31 Jul 1867, making Weir the fourth-ranking captain. Regimental returns from Harker list him there on 27 Aug 1867. Entered military service on 27 Aug 1861 with Third Michigan Cavalry. Served through all enlisted ranks. Appointed 2LT, 13 Oct 1861. Served in battles of New Madrid, Corinth, Farmington, Iuka, Coffeeville, and 2nd battle of Corinth. Taken prisoner by the Confederates on 26 Jun 1862, released on 8 Jan 1863. Served as Acting Assistant Inspector General on staff of MG G. A. Custer. Fought at New Madrid and Corinth. Captured Jun 1862, but released, Jan 1863. Brevetted MAJ and LTC on 31 Jul 1867 for his action during the Civil War against Nathan Bedford Forrest on 1 Dec 1863.

Attended school in Albion, MI, and graduated from University of Michigan in Jun 1861. Appointed first lieutenant, Seventh Cavalry on 28 Jul 1866, the date the regiment was organized, endorsed by Custer, of whom he became a close confidant; fiercely loyal to Custer and very close to both him and Libbie. Some said he and Libbie were *too* close. Considered part of the "Custer Clan." Took part in the Winter Campaign of 1868. Survived by sister, Mrs. Samuel Brown, Greenville, MS. Very engaging personality. Rode a beautiful horse named Jake. Health deteriorated from the fatigue and exposure of the campaign and he was assigned to Cavalry Recruiting Office in New York City (Burton Mansion on Hudson Street). Supposedly died of pneumonia, but others claimed it was melancholia and congestion of the brain [Connell]. Weir was a very heavy drinker, probably an alcoholic. Originally buried on Governors Island. Reinterred in Cypress Hills National Cemetery.

Weiss, PVT Markus— b. Caban, Hungary, Sep 1846–d. Fort Meade, D.T., 15 Nov 1879. Company G, private. Gray eyes, brown hair, fair complexion; 5' 8" tall. Enlisted on 17 Aug 1866, deserted 20 May 1869. Surrendered on 31 Oct 1873 under Presidential Proclamation and restored to duty. Reenlisted 27 Feb 1876. One of twenty men — one officer, three scouts, sixteen enlisted men — left in the timber in the valley bottoms when Reno retreated, eventually reaching Reno Hill with Herendeen. Died of a skull fracture in accident, when a bank of earth caved in on him during construction of guardhouse, stable, and saddler shop at Fort Meade.

Welch, PVT Charles H.— b. NYC, 16 Mar 1845–d. LaSalle, CO, 22 Jun 1915. Company D, private. Gray eyes, brown hair, fair complexion; 5' 7¾" tall. Enlisted 3 Jun 1873. Awarded MH for voluntarily bringing water back up to Reno Hill from the LBH. Wounded in the Snake Creek fight, 30 Sep 1877. Parents were from Ireland. His father joined

a group going to the California gold fields and never returned.

Weldon, George P. *see* **Walker, PVT George P.**

Wells, FAR Benjamin J.— b. Sangamon, IL, 1843–d. 25 Jun 1876, killed at the Little Big Horn during Reno's retreat. Company G: company farrier. Blue eyes, fair hair, fair complexion; 5' 6½" tall. Enlisted from 28 Nov 1866 to 28 Nov 1871 in Seventh Cavalry; enlisted again 5 Dec 1871. Widow's name was Sarah. One child: Charles W. Wells. Apparently killed when his horse — Wild Bill — bolted into Indians while crossing ford during Reno's retreat or possibly south of retreat line (Hammer). Listed number 130 in "June Returns, Alterations … Killed in action."

Wetzel, CPL Adam— b. St. Louis, MO, 9 Oct 1846–d. Bozeman, MT, 20 Mar 1909. Company B, corporal. Blue eyes, sandy hair, fair complexion; 5' 7" tall. Enlisted from 6 Sep 1862 to 20 Jun 1865, Ninth MO Cavalry. Enlisted from 12 Jun 1867 to 28 Jun 1872 and on 5 Jul 1872 in Seventh Cavalry. With the pack train escort, Company B. Arrived and fought on Reno Hill. Resided in Montana for 23 years. Buried in the Catholic Cemetery, Bozeman, MT.

Whaley, PVT William B.— b. Harrison County, KY, 1849–d. 25 Jun 1876, killed at the Little Big Horn. Company I, private. Brown eyes, dark hair, florid complexion; 5' 6" tall. Enlisted 24 Sep 1873. Body never identified, but in all likelihood he was killed in the Keogh Sector. Listed number 176 in "June Returns, Alterations … Killed in action."

Whisten, PVT John Valentine— b. NYC, 14 Feb 1852–d. Oakland, CA, 20 Nov 1912. Company M, private. Blue eyes, light hair, fair complexion; 5' 5½" tall. Enlisted 22 Sep 1873. No specific record exists of his participation in the battle, other than his presence with his unit during the valley fighting and subsequent defense of Reno Hill. Also participated in the Boxer Rebellion in China and the Spanish-American War, making him very much a part of American military history. Married Sarah T. Doriss. Children: Arthur A. and William E.

Whitaker, PVT Alfred— b. New Orleans, LA, 1847–d. Kansas City, MO, of tuberculosis, 10 Feb 1887. Company C, private. Blue eyes, dark hair; 5' 6" tall. Had been with Seventh Cavalry almost three years; enlisted 26 Sep 1873. Attached to pack train. WIA in the hilltop fighting.

White, Patrick C. *see* **Connelly, SGT Patrick**

Whitlow, PVT William— b. Cavendish, VT, 1845–d. Snake Creek, M.T., 30 Sep 1877, killed in the Nez Percé War. Company K, private. Black eyes, black hair, dark complexion; 5'5" tall. Enlisted 10 Dec 1872. Rode with his unit in Benteen's battalion, and fought on Reno Hill. Buried in Custer Battlefield National Cemetery.

Whytefield, WAG Albert— b. Sandusky, OH, 1846–d. unknown. Company K: company saddler. Blue eyes, light hair, fair complexion; 5'4½" tall. Enlisted 10 Sep 1866 in Seventh Cavalry. Deserted. Remained at the Powder River Depot. Presence confirmed on June Returns.

Widmayer, PVT Ferdinand— b. Würtemburg, Germany, 1849–d. Riverton, NJ, 18 Sep 1913. Company M, private. Blue eyes, brown hair, fair complexion; 5'5" tall. Enlisted 26 Sep 1873. Remained at the Powder River Depot. Presence confirmed on June Returns. Married; wife's name was Hedwig. Resided at 2529 South 8th Street, Philadelphia, and 733 Highland Street, Palmyra, NJ. Buried in Methodist Cemetery, Palmyra, NJ.

Wiedman, PVT Charles Theodore— b. Boston, MA, 28 May 1855–d. Oatman, AZ, 15 May 1921. Company M, private. Gray eyes, brown hair, dark complexion; 5'9¾" tall. Enlisted 23 Sep 1875. No specific record exists of his participation in the battle, other than his presence with his unit during the valley fighting and subsequent defense of Reno Hill where he was WIA in left leg on Reno Hill. Married Florence Marston, 19 Aug 1882. Divorced March 1908 in Butte, MT. Married Charlotte Simpson, 28 Mar 1912.

Wight, PVT Edwin B.— b. Casco, ME, 25 Dec 1851–d. Togus, ME, 19 Mar 1917. Company B, private. Blue eyes, brown hair, ruddy complexion; 5'8½" tall. Enlisted 29 Mar 1876; discharged 28 Mar 1881. Remained at the Powder River Depot. Wounded in Nez Percé campaign in 1877. Married Clarry T. Husey (d. 29 Jun 1885). He then married Abbie J. Gamell, 1 Nov 1886. Children from second marriage: Cassie O. and Lester E. Divorced and married Alia E. Roberts, 12 Apr 1906.

Wilber, PVT James (aka James Wilber Darcy)— b. Baltimore, MD, 1849 (death certificate lists birthplace as Ireland)–d. Washington, D.C., 13 Jul 1920. Company M, private. Hazel eyes, light hair, fair complexion; 5'8¾" tall. Served in U.S. Navy. Enlisted 8 Sep 1875. In the valley fighting and WIA on Reno Hill or while with the water party on 26 June. Partially paralyzed. Discharged 1 Nov 1876 for disability.

Wild, CPL John— b. Buffalo, NY, Dec 1849–d. 25 Jun 1876, killed at the Little Big Horn. Company I, corporal. Hazel eyes, brown hair, fair complexion; 5'9¾" tall. Enlisted 21 May 1873 in Chicago. Survived by his mother Catherine and his widow Annie Dawson. Body found in cluster around Keogh. There is speculation — apparently confirmed by some photographic analyses — that he was killed at Marker 199, but bones found there indicate a much younger man, no older than nineteen, and possibly as young as 15 or 17, and probably about 5'7½" tall [Scott, Fox, Connor, *Archaeological Perspectives on the Battle of the Little Bighorn*, pp. 65–69]. Some skull fragments were found there as well as several buttons. A short distance north of the marker, the archaeologists found an articulated arm with all the bones from the shoulder down. Some thirty cm's away were found a scattering of bones from the opposite hand. Found between these bones were a tailbone, four more buttons, and two five-cent pieces. Wild's name on his original wooden marker may have led to an apocryphal story of the "Wild I" nickname for Keogh's command. In a 1900 interview with Olin N. Wheeler, PVT Francis Johnson Kennedy claimed the only two men he could recognize from Company I were Wild and a "musician," and those two only because of their size: tall and short. The musician was, in all likelihood, TMP John W. Patton, who was only 5'3½" tall, though Kennedy never said [see Liddic/Harbaugh, *Camp on Custer*, p. 160]. Listed number 143 in "June Returns, Alterations … Killed in action."

Wilkinson, SGT John R.— b. Salem, NY, Aug 1847–d. 25 Jun 1876, killed at the Little Big Horn. Company F, sergeant. Gray eyes, dark brown hair, florid complexion; 5'7¾" tall. Enlisted on 5 Jan 1872. In all likelihood he was killed on Last Stand Hill with his unit. Married Anna B. Howard on 18 Nov 1875. Listed number 92 in "June Returns, Alterations … Killed in action."

Williams, PVT Charles H.— b. Delaware County, PA, 1849–d. unknown. Company M, private. Blue eyes, brown hair, fair complexion; 5'5" tall. Enlisted from 11 Aug 1870 to 15 Jul 1875 in Twenty-Second Infantry. Enlisted 3 Aug 1875. No specific record exists of his participation in the battle, other than his presence with his unit during the valley fighting and subsequent defense of Reno Hill. Lived in Leavenworth City, KS.

Williams, PVT William C.— b. Wheeling, VA, 28 Mar 1856–d. Norfolk, VA, 22 May 1919. Company H, private. Gray eyes, light hair, fair complexion; 5'10" tall. Enlisted 27 Sep 1873. WIA in left leg, but not listed among the wounded on the Returns for Jun 1876. Williams was the one of the men who inscribed a rock near camp in the Little Missouri Badlands: "W. C. Williams, Co. H, 7 Cavalry." It is still visible today. Survived by widow Martha. Buried IOOF Cemetery, New Vienna,

OH. His dress coat and helmet are displayed at Little Big Horn National Monument.

Williamson, PVT Pasavan — b. Petersburg, OH, 1847–d. Fort Leavenworth, KS, probably some time between 1877 and 1881. Company G, private. Blue eyes, brown hair, light complexion; 5' 9¾" tall. Enlisted 18 Apr 1876. Remained at the Powder River Depot. Presence confirmed on June Returns. Died in Leavenworth prison, apparent suicide.

Wilson, Edward *see* **Grayson, PVT Edward**

Wilson, PVT George A. — b. Madison County, OH, 1839–d. unknown. Company K, private. Black eyes, dark hair, dark complexion; 5' 7¾" tall. Second enlistment 2 Oct 1871. Remained at the Powder River Depot. Presence confirmed on June Returns.

Windolph, PVT Charles A. (aka Wrangel or Wrangell; nicknamed "Dutchy" and "Sauerkraut"; sometimes called "Heinie") — b. Bergen, Germany, 9 Dec 1851–d. Lead, SD, 11 Mar 1950 at age of 98, the last white survivor of the battle itself (Horner, K Company, outlived him, but Horner was at the Powder River Depot). Company H, private. Brown eyes, brown hair, dark complexion; 5' 6" tall. Enlisted 12 Nov 1871 in Second Infantry. Deserted 18 Jul 1872 and enlisted in Seventh Cavalry 23 Jul 1872 as Charles Wrangel[1]. Company shoemaker and tailor. Awarded MH for holding a diversionary position, while standing with Geiger, Mechlin, and Voit on the brow of Reno Hill, drawing Indian fire as others got water from the LBH. Benteen promoted him to sergeant, on 26 June. WIA in the buttocks. Promoted by Benteen to first sergeant in 1880. Varnum's first sergeant in H Company in 1889 [Goldin/Carroll, *The Benteen-Goldin Letters*, p. 110], though Windolph himself disputes this, saying he served only until 1883 when his "sweetheart" told him it was her or the army. He chose the girl [*I Fought with Custer*, p. 114].

Father's name was Joseph, and mother's was Adolphina. Joseph was a master shoemaker. Fled to Sweden in 1870 to escape compulsory military service and the Franco-Prussian War. When Windolph got to New York, he got a job in a shoe shop on Avenue A, then after a few weeks, he was employed by a bootmaker in Hoboken. Married Mathilda Ludlow, 16 Aug 1884. Children: Mary, Robert, and Irene. Author/historian James Willert interviewed Windolph's son, Robert, in Lead, SD, May 1967. Attended 50th and 60th anniversaries of the battle. Buried in Black Hills National Cemetery.

Winney, 1SG DeWitt — b. Saratoga, NY, 1845–d. 26 Jun 1876, killed at the Little Big Horn while on Reno Hill. Company K: first sergeant. Gray eyes, brown hair, dark complexion; 5' 4½" tall. Enlisted 6 Nov 1872 in NYC. Shot in forehead; found on right of Company K line on Reno Hill. Lying about six feet from LT Hare when he was killed. Helmer was on the other side of Hare. LT Godfrey said he was standing right there when Winney and Helmer were shot. Listed number 177 in "June Returns, Alterations … Killed in action."

Witt, PVT Henry N. B. — b. Cincinnati, OH, 10 Dec 1852 (death certificate lists Denmark as his birthplace)–d. Santa Monica, CA, 5 Aug 1929. Company K, private. Blue eyes, brown hair, fair complexion; 5' 9" tall. Enlisted 9 Dec 1875. Remained at the Powder River Depot. Presence confirmed on June Returns. Survived by his widow, Mildred M. Witt.

Woods, PVT Aaron L. — b. Philadelphia, PA, 1852–d. Philadelphia, PA, 26 Mar 1902. Company B, private. Brown eyes, dark hair, ruddy complexion; 5' 7½" tall. Enlisted 2 Sep 1873. With the pack train escort, Company B. Arrived and fought on Reno Hill. Woods had no middle name, but used the initial "L" in memory of a friend, Lee, who was killed while in the service. Married Elizabeth (Lizzie) Moore 4 Oct 1880. Children: Florence Eleanor, Ethel Elizabeth, and Emily Jane Weir Woods. Buried in Mount Moriah Cemetery, Philadelphia.

Woolslayer, William J. *see* **Randall, PVT William J.**

Wright, PVT Willis B. — b. Osktheloosa, IA, 7 Jun 1859–d. 25 Jun 1876, killed at Little Big Horn. Company C, private. Blue eyes, brown hair, ruddy; 5' 6½" tall. Lied about his age when enlisting; really only seventeen years old when he died. Youngest casualty of the battle (based on enlistment records). Had been with Seventh Cavalry less than one year; enlisted 25 Aug 1875. Body thought to have been found on Custer Hill, though Scott and Fox speculate through bone analysis (height and age) that it *may* be Wright at Marker 199 (near Keogh). Wright is the only person with Custer's command — other than Autie Reed — whose age and stature meet the forensic analysis. Listed number 47 in "June Returns, Alterations … Killed in action."

Wylie, CPL George Washington — b. New Orleans, LA, 28 Feb 1848–d. Kansas City, MO, 13 Mar 1931. Company D, corporal. Blue eyes, light hair, fair complexion; 5' 8¼" tall. Enlisted from 16 Oct 1867 to 15 Jul 1870 in Sixth Cavalry; enlisted 17 Mar 1873 in Seventh Cavalry. Rode with his unit in Benteen's battalion, and fought on Reno Hill.

Married Jessie R. Rockhold 14 Feb 1895. Son: Cortez V. Wylie. Buried in Fort Leavenworth National Cemetery.

Wyman, PVT Henry— b. Woburn, MA, 1840–d. 25 Jun 1876, killed at the Little Big Horn. Company C, private. Brown eyes, dark hair; 5' 6¼" tall. Had served in the U.S. Navy. Enlisted in the army 22 Aug 1873. In the C Company charge off Battle Ridge–Calhoun Hill, but body was never identified. May have died in Calhoun Coulee, Finley-Finckle Ridge, the Keogh Sector, or possibly even Last Stand Hill. Listed number 48 in "June Returns, Alterations … Killed in action."

Wynn, PVT James— b. Dublin, Ireland, 1836–d. Fort Yates, ND, 21 Mar 1892. Company D, private. Gray eyes, gray hair, ruddy complexion; 5'5" tall. Apparently, he was rather heavy. Enlisted from 1861 to 1865 in First CO Cavalry. Enlisted 1 Mar 1868 in Seventh Cavalry. Enlisted 12 Mar 1873. Rode with his unit in Benteen's battalion, and fought on Reno Hill. Rode a quiet old horse, blind in one eye. Married Ella Ahern in NYC in 1852. No children.

Yates, CPT (Bvt LTC) George Wilhelmus Mancius— b. Albany, NY, 26 Feb 1843–d. 25 Jun 1876, killed at the Little Big Horn. Company F: Commanding Officer. Thirty-three years old; 6' tall. DOR: 12 Jun 1867; accepted appointment 19 Aug 1867. Third-ranking captain behind Benteen and Keogh. Came from an influential and prominent New York family. Took part in battles at Bull Run, Seven Days, Beverly Ford, Antietam, Fredericksburg, Chancellorsville. He met George Custer while recovering from wounds suffered at Fredericksburg and they became fast friends. Served with Custer at Gettysburg. Brevetted major 13 Mar 1865. Brevetted lieutenant colonel for conspicuous gallantry at Beverly Ford, Fredericksburg, and Gettysburg. George Custer helped Yates get into the Seventh Cavalry (F). On escort duty of the Indian Peace Commission, summer 1867. Took part in the Sully Expedition, 1868, and the Winter Campaign of 1868. Accompanied the regiment to the south and took part in both the Yellowstone (1873) and Black Hills expeditions (1874).

One account says his body was found near the foot of Custer Hill, although Godfrey says differently. Godfrey wrote that along with Reily, Cooke, and Smith, Yates' body was found in the vicinity of George Custer's, but nearer the top of the hill than Custer's [Godfrey/Graham, *The Custer Myth*, p. 345]. His gauntlets were found in the abandoned Sioux village.

Married Lucretia Beaumont Irwin, 5 Jan 1865; divorced in St. Louis, 31 Jan 1867. Married Annie Gibson Roberts (of Carlisle, PA) on 12 Feb 1872 in NYC. She died 9 Dec 1914, following a subway accident in NYC. They had three children: George Livingston (b. Louisville, KY, 11 Dec 1872); Bessie Violet (b. Fort Lincoln, 25 Sep 1874); and Milnor Roberts (b. Fort Lincoln, 27 Nov 1875). Buried Fort Leavenworth National Cemetery.

Civilians, Quartermaster Employees, and Scouts

Civilians and Quartermaster Employees

Bloody Knife— b. Hunkpapa Reservation, D.T., 1837–d. 25 Jun 1876, killed at the Little Big Horn, in the timber. QM employee. Custer's personal scout, detailed to Reno for the battle. Copper complexion, 5'7" tall. Looked more Spanish than Indian, with a long aquiline nose and thin lips. Original date of enlistment was 1 May 1868. His mother was a Ree, but father was Sioux, and contrary to normal practice, lived with father's family. Not well liked by Sioux as a child, hated as an adult. Insolent and surly toward whites, especially Custer, who put up with his moods. Married: She Owl. One child: Stay Overnight.

Killed in woods; shot in head. Young Hawk claimed that after the battle a white man came up to him and several other Rees and asked them if a scalp he was carrying on a stick was from a Sioux. The hair was laced with gray and the Rees claimed it had to have been Bloody Knife's. Bloody Knife was the only Ree scout with a government-issued saddle [Libby, *The Arikara Narrative*, p. 127].

Boyer (sometimes spelled "Bouyer"), **Michel** (first name sometimes listed as Minton. More commonly called "Mitch"; aka "Chopper"; "Two Bodies"; or *Kar-paysh* or *Ca Pay* or *Ka-Pesh*; also probably "Man-With-[or Wearing-]A-Calfskin-Vest.")— b. 1837, making him 38 or 39 at time of battle (this, according to records, though he claimed to be about two years younger)–d. 25 Jun 1876, killed at the Little Big Horn, fighting with Custer's command. QM employee. Assigned From Gibbon, 10 Jun 1876, for Reno's scout, and again on 22 Jun 1876.

Mixed-blood French and Sioux. Spoke fluent Dakota and Crow as well as English. Probably about 5'5" tall. Smoked a pipe. Wore a vest made of calfskin, tanned with the hair on [Camp/Hammer, *Custer in '76*, p. 241]. Mother was a full Santee Sioux; father, Jean (John) Baptiste Boyer, was a French-Canadian trapper, killed by Indians some time before 1871. Hammer claims the father's name was Vital and that he was a blacksmith killed in 1863 at Fort Laramie while trapping, but this is wrong. Gray points out the confusion with the name "Vital" (from a Vital Beauvais, which they pronounced "*boo-vay*"). Gray is certainly correct here. His research has the father being killed some time between Nov 1867 and Apr 1871. His best guess is late 1867. Boyer was a quiet-spoken, diffident man, who spoke in an almost hesitating way. Looked Indian, but dressed like a white man. It was claimed Sitting Bull offered a bounty of 100 horses for Boyer's scalp [Stewart, *Custer's Luck*, p. 105]. COL John Gibbon said Boyer was the only half-blood he knew who could give proper distances, in miles, with any degree of accuracy [Stewart, *Custer's Luck*, p. 105]. Gray considered him the best guide/scout since Jim Bridger; he was a protégé of Bridger. "…[A] keen instinct … an open, adaptable, perceptive, and understanding mind" [Gray, *Custer's Last Campaign*, p. 21]. Married a full-blood Crow named Magpie Outdoors (Mary, to whites) in fall of 1869. Had a daughter, also named Mary, within a year. Had two more children: Thomas and James. His wife "…proved to be a fine wife and mother, big-hearted, loyal, generous, and respected among her people…" [Gray, *Custer's Last Campaign*, p. 89]. His wife eventually married Mitch's best friend, Tom LeForgé, some time after both Mitch was killed and Tom's wife, Cherry, died. Had been to the Crow's Nest with LT Varnum.

According to archaeologist Richard Fox, his

facial bones were the ones found near the middle of the South Skirmish Line (paired Markers 33 and 34), just below the crest of a ridge forming the north side of the primary drainage area of Deep Ravine. They indicate that is where he died. Bones are also consistent with his age, 35–45. Bone fragments included skull fragments; finger; coccyx. Consistent with the bones of a single individual. Also found were a .50/70 bullet; a lead bullet fragment; lead shot; a boot heel and boot nails; a rubber poncho button; three, 4-hole iron trouser buttons; one mother-of-pearl shirt button; a cedar stake fragment; and some cobbles. The pearl button is consistent with buttons found on the bib-front of a "fireman's" shirt known to have been worn by Custer and other officers [Scott and Fox, *Archaeological Insights into The Custer Battle,* pp. 92–93]. Forensics evidence suggests the individual may have had a deformed finger and may have been a pipe-smoker because of the wear on recovered left-side teeth. "[A] boot heel was found five feet five inches from the skull fragments. The distance between the fragments and the boot heel may approximate the man's height. The skull fragments suggest that the head was crushed about the time of death" [p. 102]. Other reports have Boyer in Deep Ravine, at the mouth of the ravine, in the LBH at MTC, between Custer and Reno, and lastly, several miles north of the battlefield. Also on Reno's scout and may have been the cause of Reno moving to the Rosebud.

Custer, Boston— b. New Rumley, OH, 31 Oct 1848–d. 25 Jun 1876, killed at the Little Big Horn, riding with the headquarters command. QM employee. Employed as a scout and civilian forage master at $100 a month, though this amount may be questionable. Had worked in this capacity since the 1874 Black Hills Expedition. Younger brother of George and Tom Custer; 27 years old. Dressed similar to his brothers.

Body found near foot of Custer Hill, near Armstrong Reed, and about 100 yards down from GAC (Edgerly). Shot several times and somewhat mutilated (Moylan). Body was perhaps 100 yards below the monument (Godfrey). "[H]is body was found about 200 yards from 'Custer Hill,' between that and the LBH, at the foot of the ridge that runs up from the river, and as it were, forms the lower boundary of the battlefield. The body was stript except his white cotton socks and they had the name cut off" [Godfrey/Graham, *The Custer Myth,* p. 345]. Body dug up in summer of 1877 by CPT Henry Nowlan and reinterred in Monroe, MI.

Dorman (Walter Camp said he had also seen the name written as Darman and Darwin), **Isaiah** (aka Teat; some of the Rees referred to him as Isa)— b.

circa 1830–d. 25 Jun 1876, killed at the Little Big Horn during Reno's retreat from the timber. QM employee. Interpreter for the Dakota scouts. Detailed to Reno. Dorman was the only black man in the battle. Very big and very dark-skinned. One source said he was an escaped slave or freedman, probably born in the 1830's, Alabama, Louisiana, Mississippi region. Another has him from New Orleans [Donovan, *A Terrible Glory,* p. 119]. No record of him until after the Civil War. Theodore Goldin wrote that it was thought Dorman's father was from Jamaica and his mother was an Indian squaw [Carroll, *The Benteen-Goldin Letters,* pp. 40–41]. Several male slaves belonging to the D'Orman family of Louisiana and Alabama during the 1840s were reported to have escaped; one of them was named Isaiah [Connell, *Son of the Morning Star,* p. 26]. Married to a Lakota-Teton/Hunkpapa Sioux squaw named Visible, though more than one source says she was a Dakota-Santee or Eastern Sioux. They had two children: Baptiste and Pierre. Another source says they had none [Donovan, *A Terrible Glory,* p. 119].

A "man of considerable intelligence and a man who enjoyed the respect and confidence of the soldiers in spite of his color" [Camp/Hammer, *Custer in '76,* p. 224, footnote 12]. Detailed out of Fort Rice where he was employed as an interpreter. Killed in bottoms on edge of woods. His badly mutilated body found near that of Charlie Reynolds. It was rumored he was killed by a Sioux woman — Her Eagle Robe (aka Moving Robe Woman). Moving Robe's brother was Deeds, who was killed before Reno crossed the LBH at Ford A. That would explain some of the horrific savagery taken against Dorman. Connell claimed the Sioux took their time in killing him and did so with particular relish, filling his coffee cup with his blood. Michno says when his horse went down, Dorman made his stand on one knee, firing away as the Indians fired back and continuously struck him with war clubs. He was found with "pistol balls in his legs, skin stripped from his body, and a kettle of his own blood sitting by his head … an iron picket pin … thrust through his testicles, pinning him to the ground … the interpreter's penis … cut off and stuffed in his mouth" [Michno, *Lakota Noon,* p. 88]. George Custer's striker, PVT John Burkman, said much the same thing, though not phrased as delicately as Michno. Dorman was killed not far from Reynolds, about 30 feet apart. Hardorff, in *Lakota Recollections,* p. 102, footnote 7, describes where Dorman fell as being in the midst of a prairie dog town, some 100 yards "southeast of the stretch of timber" that housed Reno's command for a short while. Herendeen watched from the timber as Indians kept shooting Dorman while squaws pounded him with stone hammers [Camp/Hammer, *Custer in '76,* pp. 223–224]. Goldin also said Dorman's body was not far from Reynolds,' a bit to the south and east of Reynolds [Carroll, *The Benteen-Goldin Letters,* p. 39]. The Oglala warrior, Eagle Elk, claimed he saw Moving Robe aim a pistol at Dorman while he was sitting on the ground. The first time she pulled the trigger, the gun misfired, but the second time she was successful, killing him.

Gerard (also seen spelled as Girard), **Frederic Francis** (nicknamed "Fast Bull" or "Swift Buffalo"; many Rees called him "Seven Yanktons")— b. St. Louis, MO, 14 Nov 1829–d. St. Cloud, MN, 30 Jan 1913. QM employee. Interpreter for Arikara (Ree) scouts. Detailed to Reno. Blue eyes, fair hair. Forty-six years old at the time of the battle, making him one of the oldest participants. Enlisted for the job on 12 May 1876.

French ancestry. Educated at Xavier College where he spent four years. Went up the Missouri with Honore Picotte 28 Sep 1848, then worked for American Fur Company at Fort Pierre, SD. Went to Fort Berthold in 1855. On Christmas Day 1863, six hundred Yankton Sioux attacked the fort. Gerard — with seventeen others (or even more)— held them off all day, until Assiniboines drove them off. Gerard then held the fort by himself for ten days, ready to blow it up if the Sioux returned.

Owned a farm at Mandan and was always on the lookout for the Sioux who had vowed to kill him because of his stout defense of Berthold. On 6 Jul 1872, he was hired on as post interpreter at FAL. In 1873 he saved (former CSA general) Thomas Rosser — Custer's close, USMA friend — and a surveying party from being cut off by hostiles.

At the time of the Reno Court of Inquiry (Jan 1879), Gerard was married to a white woman. One author claimed he was married to a Ree, and Gerard — at the RCOI —first said he had been, but corrected it the following day. Jim Donovan in *A Terrible Glory,* says he was married to a Ree and had three half-breed daughters that he sent to a Benedictine school in St. Joseph, MN [pp. 118–119].

It seems neither Reno nor Gerard cared for one another. Reno had him dismissed from his position at FAL on May 6, 1876, telling him he could hire three teamsters for what he was paying Gerard. Rode a black stallion at the LBH. Gerard was close friends with Charlie Reynolds. In all likelihood, it was Gerard's warning of Indians moving up the valley — rather than retreating — that caused Custer to veer to the right, mounting the bluffs on his way to the northern end of the encampment. This movement was contrary to Reno's belief of promised support and has led to more than 130 years of heated debate and recriminations [see Wag-

ner, "Frederic Francis Gerard, A Questionable Cause and an Unforeseen Effect," *Research Review,* Vol. 21, No. 1, Winter 2007, p. 13].

At the Little Big Horn battle, after Reno's retreat from the timber, Gerard was left behind in woods with LT DeRudio, PVT O'Neill, and scout Billy Jackson, making Reno Hill some time before midnight of 26 Jun 1876. In the early morning, before dawn, 26 Jun 1876, LT DeRudio, PVT O'Neill, Gerard, and Billy Jackson tried to cross the river to reach Reno's command on the bluffs. Gerard, superstitious apparently, said a prayer to the Indians' Great Spirit and tossed his watch in the river as a token, all this hoping to find a suitable crossing point. He later denied the incident, claiming he lost the watch and instead threw his rifle into the river, trying to get it out of his way [Willert, *Little Big Horn Diary,* pp. 392–393]. Eventually became an ad agent for Pillsbury Corporation in Minneapolis.

The writer Fred Dustin felt about Gerard much the same as Reno did: "Dustin had no use for the testimonies of Frederic F. Gerard — questioned the validity of all of them" [Willert, *Little Big Horn Diary,* footnote, p. 441]. Other than the watch incident — more of an embarrassment than anything else — there is little, if any, evidence substantiating Dustin's claim or opinion.

Herendeen (name also seen as "Herendon," "Herndon," "Hunbein," and "Haynden"), **George B.**— b. Parkman Township, Geauga County, OH, 28 Nov 1846–d. Harlem, MT, 17 Jun 1918. QM employee. Only scout not enlisted in army, despite his QM designation. Assigned from Gibbon to Seventh Cavalry 22 Jun 1876. Rode with Reno in the valley fight. Trapped in woods, but eventually got out that afternoon, guiding eleven soldiers with him. Also served as a scout in the 1877 Nez Percé campaign. Civil War veteran. Went west after the war and wound up in Denver in 1868. Probably worked as a cowboy in New Mexico and reached Montana by 1869. Joined the Custer column on 22 Jun 1876. Buried in Harlem, MT, cemetery.

Kellogg, Marcus Henry (Mark)— b. Brighton, Ontario, Canada, 31 Mar 1833–d. 25 Jun 1876, killed at the Little Big Horn, in all likelihood while riding with the headquarters command. Civilian newspaper reporter. Wrote for both the *Bismarck Tribune* and the *New York Herald.* The editor of the *Tribune* was Clement Lounsberry and it was Lounsberry who was supposed to go on the expedition; but when Lounsberry's wife became ill, he sent Kellogg as his place.

Body tentatively identified on flats near river, below Cemetery Ridge, about ½ to ¾ miles from Custer Ridge. 2LT Richard E. Thompson, Company K, Sixth Infantry, identified Kellogg's body about 100 yards from the LBH on a side hill. Michno [*The Mystery of E Troop*, p. 178] says, "Continuing up the valley, which then became an open grassy slope [COL Gibbon] found one body, which was identified as … Kellogg…. [O]ther accounts report that Mark Kellogg was found near the junction of the north and south forks of Deep Ravine." Two other writers, Michael Moore and Michael Donahue, also using Gibbon's account, say Gibbon "found Kellogg's body in a ravine just west of the present cemetery grounds." Godfrey claimed Kellogg lay between the monument and Autie Reed and Boston Custer. PVT Glenn said that when Benteen went to Custer Hill on 27 Jun 1876, he went up "Crazy Horse Gully" (Deep Ravine). The body nearest the river was CTMP Voss and near Voss was Kellogg. Both were within a stone's throw of the river. COL Gibbon said Kellogg was found on his back, the body in an advanced state of decomposition. He had been scalped and one ear was cut off. He was not stripped. LT Mathey said he buried Kellogg on the 29th and that he was the last one buried. His body lay near a ravine between Custer and the river.

Buried at Custer Battlefield National Cemetery. He was a widower — his wife had died in 1868 — and he had two children: Cora Sue and Martha Grace. His wife's name was Martha Robinson. She is buried at the Oak Grove Cemetery, La Crosse, WI. Kellogg was in some financial trouble apparently and wanted to get to the Black Hills to make his "fortune."

Reed, Harry Armstrong "Autie" (also seen referred to, incorrectly, as "Arthur" Reed; last name sometimes seen spelled "Reid," also incorrect) — b. Monroe, MI, 27 Apr 1858–d. 25 Jun 1876, killed at the Little Big Horn while riding with the headquarters command. Nephew of George, Tom, and Boston Custer. Had been signed on as a "herder." Body found near Boston Custer at foot of the hill about 100 yards from GAC. Shot in the body. Still had most of his clothes. Body dug up in the summer of 1877 by CPT Henry Nowlan and reinterred in Monroe, MI. Son of David and Lydia Ann Reed, GAC's favorite half-sister.

Reynolds, Charles Alexander (aka "Lucky Man"; "Lucky Hunter"; "Hunter-Who-Never-Goes-Out-For-Nothing"; or "Lonesome Charlie") — b. Stevensburg, Hardin County, KY, 20 Mar 1842 (Connell says Warren County, IL, on the same date)–d. 25 Jun 1876, killed at the Little Big Horn, during Reno's retreat from the timber. QM employee: scout/guide. Large, dark blue eyes; 5'8" tall; stocky build; baby-faced. Did not drink (generally) or smoke. Very shy in front of females. Had been in

Crow's Nest with LT Varnum. Killed near LT McIntosh at the edge of the timber while attempting to help Dr. Porter. Shot through the heart. Some accounts have him being killed while crossing the LBH, but these are almost surely incorrect. Dr. Porter accounts for Reynolds' death and Ken Hammer, in *The Battlefield Dispatch*, Winter 2005, says he was killed at the beginning of the retreat, which would tie in with "at the edge of the timber." "[O]ne of the truly outstanding white civilian scouts of America's frontier years…" [Willert, *Little Big Horn Diary*, p. 214]. According to PVT Peter Thompson (C), Reynolds' "mount was invariably a grey mule" ["The Experience of a Private Soldier in the Custer Massacre," p. 11]. Particular favorite of George and Libbie Custer. Told Libbie Custer he was born a gentleman. Family traced back to colonial Virginia. Father was a physician. Reynolds attended Abingdon College.

Civilian Packers

Kenneth Hammer claims there were as many as twelve civilian packers with the pack train and therefore at the battle itself. While this appears to make some sense — one packer for each company — chances are Hammer is incorrect. Most other accounts claim only six, naming just four or five for certain. At the Reno Court of Inquiry in January–February 1879, Packer Frett claimed there were only five or six; packer Churchill said six or seven; LT Edward Mathey said four or five, obviously indicating no one knew for certain. The best guess may be five and they are indicated by an asterisk (*).

* **Alexander, William** — b. England, 1838–d. Washington, D.C., 6 Feb 1922. Resided in the Soldier's Home in Washington D.C. Presence at the battle confirmed by R. C. Hillyer, "Which They Had Captured All," *Research Review*, Winter 2007, Vol. 21, No. 1.

* **Churchill, Benjamin Franklin**

Edwards, George — Not listed in Camp's work.

Flint, Moses E.

* **Frett, John** — Had a serious argument with Reno on the hilltop, where Reno threatened to shoot him. Claimed Reno had been drinking.

Lainplough, John (also seen spelled Lamplough) — d. Brunsville, MT, 8 Feb 1881, result of a wagon accident.

Lawless, William — b. Clair, Ireland

Loeser, Christian— Died some time after 1911.

* **Mann, Frank C.**—d. 26 Jun 1876, killed at the Little Big Horn in the hilltop fight in Company A's sector, 26 Jun 1876. Shot between the eyes or in temple.

McBratney, Henry (Harry) T.

Moore, Edward L.

* **Wagoner** (also spelled Wagner), **John C.**—b. NY, 1836–d. St. Paul, MN, 5 May 1899. Chief packer. WIA in head.

Enlisted Scouts

Crow Scouts

All were originally with COL John Gibbon's Montana Command.

Curley (aka *Shi-shia*; also, *Shuh shee ohsh*; sometimes referred to as Curly Head by the Rees, but there was also a Ree with the same name, usually seen spelled differently, i.e., "Curly")—b. Little Rosebud Creek, M.T., 1858–d. Crow Agency, MT, 21 May 1923, of pneumonia. Had been at the Crow's Nest with Varnum. Rode with Custer; left column early. Claimed to have watched battle from a distance, though this is hardly credible. Said he was the only survivor and the last one to leave the column and survive. Buried in LBH National Cemetery.

Goes Ahead (aka Child of the Stars; The First One; One Ahead; the Rees called him Comes Leading, or Man With Fur Belt; *Bah-suk-ush; Basuk-ose; Ma-suck-cosh; Baksu-hush-hahis*)—b. Platte River, 1852 (though some sources say either 1851 or 1859)–d. Crow Agency, MT, 31 May 1919. Had been at the Crow's Nest with Varnum. With Custer, leaving him when command was in Cedar Coulee. Joined hilltop fight. His father was Many Sisters and his mother was Her Door. There was a story among the Crow tribe that it was Goes Ahead who killed the young Sioux boy, Deeds, the first Indian fatality at the Little Big Horn.

Hairy Moccasin (*Esup-ewyahes*; possibly Comes Leading rather than Goes Ahead, above [Heski, p. 22], though this does not seem correct)—b. circa 1854–d. Lodge Grass, MT, 9 Oct 1922. A Mountain Crow. Had been at the Crow's Nest with Varnum. With Custer. Left him in Cedar Coulee. Joined hilltop fight.

Half Yellow Face (aka Paints-Half-His-Face-Yellow; Son of Little Face; *Ise-Chusa-Shida;* or a variation, *Iss-too-sah-shee-dah*. The Ree scout, Young Hawk, claimed Half Yellow Face was his friend and referred to him as "Big Belly," the same name applied to White Man Runs Him; Red Star also referred to him as "Big Belly." PVT Peter Thompson said he was also called "Two Bloody Hands," though we do not know how Thompson would know this [see, Thompson, "The Experience of a Private Soldier in the Custer Massacre," p. 33])— b. Montana, probably in the 1810's–d. Montana, 1879. There is considerable debate over the exact year of Half Yellow Face's birth. Roger L. Williams lists it as "circa 1835," but this appears much too late as anecdotal evidence suggests he was in his sixties at the time of the battle. As proof, Williams cites comments by Pretty Shield (b. circa 1856), Half Yellow Face's niece, saying the father and daughter lived next to one another and the father was born circa 1828, "Presumably, Half Yellow Face was a younger brother" [Williams, *Military Register of Custer's Last Command,* pp. 329 and 341, footnote 74]. There appears to be little justification, however, for the "younger brother" claim, Williams offering no additional proof. While Williams' data may be correct, the claims of contemporaries might seem to out-weigh modern presumptions. Husky; big build; considered handsome.

Half Yellow Face was the Crow leader. He was probably in his sixties at the time of the battle. Rode with Custer on the night of June 24–25, up Davis Creek. Was *not* with Varnum at the Crow's Nest. By a mistake, he wound up with Reno. Fought on skirmish line with White Swan and a group of four Rees led by Young Hawk. Remained in the LBH valley until he and White Swan were able to join Reno on the hill.

White Man Runs Him (some of the Rees called him Big Belly; *aka*, White Buffalo That Turns Around; Crow Who Talks Gros Ventre; *Mahritah-thee-dah-ka-roosh; Ma-esta-she-coo-roosh*)— b. circa 1856–1858–d. Lodge Grass, MT, 2 Jun 1929. Had been at the Crow's Nest with Varnum. With Custer, but left. Joined hilltop fight. Buried in LBH National Cemetery. In Graham's *The Custer Myth* [p. 15], White Man Runs Him claimed he was one of the "oldest" scouts and did most of the advance scouting.

White Swan (aka Strikes Enemy; Fighting Lion; *Mee-nah-tsee-us;* or a variation *Me-lar-cheash*)— b. Montana, 1851–d. Crow Agency, MT, 11 or 12 Aug 1904. Interred at the Little Big Horn National Cemetery. Probably the principal Crow warrior of the six scouts [Smalley, *More Little Bighorn Mysteries,* p. 1–7]. Had been at the Crow's Nest with Varnum. Went with Reno in error. Fought on the skirmish line. John Gray claimed he made Reno Hill after being wounded and trapped in the woods. WIA severely, in right wrist and thigh, receiving multiple wounds while crossing the LBH in retreat. PVT Lynch of F Company said White Swan had been wounded five or six times. PVT Siefert said the same thing. Reputed to have been deaf or partially so.

Arikara Scouts

The Arikara were called Rees, for short. LT Charles A. Varnum, Chief-of-Scouts, claimed he took only 24 scouts with him up the Rosebud. He specifically mentioned the Jackson brothers and Billy Cross. At a later date, Varnum wrote that the number was 25, but enlistment and discharge records show he was wrong about Robert Jackson.

Black Fox (*Chil-ira-two-ca-tis*; also, *Chewa-koo-katit*) — b. circa 1847 (twenty-nine years old at the time of the battle). Still alive in 1896. Black eyes, black hair, copper complexion; 5' 7" tall. Had been at the Crow's Nest with LT Varnum. Arrived in LBH area; met pack train, then backtracked down Rosebud. Black Fox is the source of considerable debate. Ree accounts agree that he overtook and joined the rear guard (Gray breaks down the Rees into two groups: horse herders [10 +] and rear guard) at the mouth of the Rosebud in the morning of 27 Jun 1876. He had two horses, his own and a Sioux pony given him by the three Crows some time before 4 pm, 25 Jun 1876. At around 2 pm, 28 Jun 1876, this group of eleven Rees — including Billy Cross — arrived at MAJ Moore's PRD and informed him of the fight. According to Gray, this meant Black Fox did not leave Reno Hill until around 10 am on 26 Jun 1876. The author Jack Pennington on the other hand, says that according to Red Star, Black Fox met Curley — who had left Custer around 1:40 pm, Pennington's time — near Ford A in the afternoon of 25 Jun 1876, *neither* having been on Reno Hill [Pennington's time of 1:40 pm would be too early, though not by a lot]. Other than Curley not having been on Reno Hill, Pennington's argument makes eminent sense. They then went back to where Curley knew there was some hardtack because they were hungry. They left the battle scene before the other Rees. Curley decided to leave, but Black Fox returned to the command, probably arriving near Reno Hill toward nightfall of 25 June. He moved closer to Reno Hill in the morning of the 26th, saw Reno surrounded and left. Both Billy Cross and Black Fox wore handkerchiefs tied about their heads, and it was most likely Black Fox riding a new pony that was seen by George Wylie during the Weir advance [Smalley, *Little Bighorn Mysteries,* p. A6–6].

Bob-tail Bull (*Hocus-ta-ris; Hucus-ta-nix*) [SGT] — b. 1831–d. 25 Jun 1876, killed at the Little Big Horn. Black eyes, black hair, copper complexion; 5'11" tall. Enlisted as a sergeant and wore the attendant stripes on his uniform blouse. First leader of the Ree scouts. With Custer at Crow's Nest. Along with FAR Brandon (Company F), oldest killed at battle, 45 years old. A lot of confusion surrounds his death. Hammer has him killed near the river [*The Battlefield Dispatch,* Winter 2005]. Others have him killed either in bottoms or on east bank of river and even on the left side of the skirmish line as it moved towards timber. Red Feather and Kicking Bear could have killed him during Reno's dash out of the timber. Michno has two Ree scouts being clubbed and stabbed on the east side of the river, after Reno's retreat, which ties in not only with Hammer, but with other versions as well. Hardorff felt Bob-tail Bull fell just prior to Little Brave [*Hokahey!... p. 47*]. Wooden Leg and several others killed one of them, possibly Little Brave. Wooden Leg also cites an incident where the Cheyenne warrior, Whirlwind, killed and was killed by, a war bonnet-wearing Indian scout in the flats on the east side of the river [Marquis, *Wooden Leg,* p. 224]. The Sioux warrior, Eagle Elk, confirms one of the accounts. This latter incident with Whirlwind could have been Bob-tail Bull. Married to Bear Woman (d. Jul 1876), with one or three children, depending on the source [Williams claims three].

Boy Chief (aka Black Calf; *Hanue-ca-tis; Ani-Kadit*) — b. 1857–d. Armstrong, ND, 4 Jun 1922. Black eyes, black hair, copper complexion; 5' 6" tall. After crossing LBH, moved to the right to capture Sioux ponies with Strikes Two and Red Star, and drive them back across river. Fired at in error by the trailing troops of Custer's command as they reached the top of the bluffs. Horse wounded. Left in charge of ponies; made hill but left the battlefield.

Bull (aka Bellow; *Hocus; Nkos*) — b. 1856. Black eyes, black hair, copper complexion; 5' 8" tall. Had been in Crow's Nest with LT Varnum. Straggler; made hill. Smalley writes that Strikes Two said Bull was one of two Rees assigned to the packs (Pretty Face being the other), but goes on to cite evidence proving Bull was not with the packs that day [*More Little Bighorn Mysteries,* p. 5–1]. Never crossed the LBH. Joined six scouts including Soldier, Stab, and White Eagle, who captured the Sioux ponies and helped guard herd. Left the battlefield with other Rees.

Bull Stands in Water (aka Bull in the Water; Bull in Water; *Hocus-ty-arit*) — b. 1847. Still alive in 1893; lived at Fort Berthold. Black eyes, black hair, copper complexion; 5'11" tall. Apparently never crossed the LBH, but was left in charge of ponies during Reno's charge. Made hill. Helped guard pony herd, then left the battlefield with others. Was with the main column when Varnum was at the Crow's Nest.

Cross, William (Billy) (half-breed Two Kettle Sioux, but carried as a Ree; aka *E-esk; Ieska; Scolla.* The scout/guide/interpreter, John Bruguier — who knew Cross — claimed he was a half-breed Minneconjou) — b. 1854 – d. Fort Peck Reservation, near Culbertson, MT, Jul 1894, in an accident. Brown eyes, black hair, copper complexion; 5'6" tall. Left Custer's column before it was engaged, joining the pack train. Made Reno Hill, then left with other Rees. Probably crossed the LBH and helped herd and guard ponies. Was not in the valley fight, though he always told the scout, John Bruguier, that he was. "Billy Cross was with the pack train. Both he and Black Fox wore handkerchiefs tied about their heads, and it was most likely Black Fox riding a new pony that was seen by George Wylie during the Weir advance" [Smalley, *Little Bighorn Mysteries,* p. A6–6]. There is also an odd story of someone (CPL Wylie [D]) seeing him coming back *to* Weir Point from farther north, in the direction of the Custer field. Hardorff, however, says Cross preceded the Reno advance to Weir Point and it was on his return when Wylie saw him [*On The Little Bighorn With Walter Camp,* p. 43, footnote 8]. Smalley disputes this, claiming Wylie mistook Cross for Black Fox [*More Little Bighorn Mysteries,* p. 5–2].

Curly Head (aka Hair; Curly Hair; *Pich-ga-ri-wee*) — b. 1856. Black eyes, black hair, copper complexion; 5'6" tall. Originally thought to be on detached service, carrying messages from Rosebud Creek to Yellowstone from 22 Jun 1876 on and Walter Mason Camp lists him as such, but Smalley has him present at the battle. He was probably still used to try to carry messages out. Listed by Willert as one of four Rees (Foolish Bear, Howling Wolf, and Running Wolf) who left Terry's camp on the Rosebud, 22 Jun 1876, to deliver dispatches to MAJ Moore at PRD. They supposedly arrived on 24 Jun 1876 [*Little Big Horn Diary,* p. 483]. This is confirmed in the *Arikara Narrative.* Red Star, however, claimed Curly Head was left behind at PRD [Libby, *The Arikara Narrative,* p. 74]. To support Red Star's story, it should be noted that nothing is mentioned by anyone else about this particular Curly having been at the battle. Listed in the Fort Berthold census, 1900.

Forked Horn (aka Crooked Horn, Rough Horn; *Arri-chitt*) — b. in the Dakota Territory, either in

1815 or 1839, it is uncertain – d. 1894. Black eyes, black hair, copper complexion; 5'10" tall. Sometimes reported to be Young Hawk's father, but this could be incorrect (see Libby, *The Arikara Narrative,* pp. 114–115; then p. 193). Had been on Reno recon. Had been in Crow's Nest with LT Varnum. Fought on the left side of Reno's skirmish line. Trapped on east bank; made it to Reno Hill around 5 pm. In the group trying to carry a message out. One source says the right side of the line; see Young Hawk.

Good Face (*aka,* Pretty Face; Bear Good Face; Share; *Sea-ri; Skaré*) — b. 1855. Black eyes, black hair, copper complexion; 5'4" tall. With packs, then rode ahead. Scott says he was the only scout assigned to the packs. This is supported by the *Arikara Narrative* excerpt in Graham, *The Custer Myth,* page 31. Stewart claimed the same thing [*Custer's Luck,* p. 281]. Joined the six scouts who had captured the Sioux ponies on the hilltop. Left the battlefield with other Rees.

Goose (*Co-sk; Co-et; Goht; Maga*) — b. 1855. Black eyes, black hair, copper complexion; 5'8" tall. Soldier's nephew. On the skirmish line; trapped on east bank. Made Reno Hill. WIA, in the hand.

Howling Wolf — b. 1854. Black eyes, black hair, copper complexion; 5'6" tall. Originally thought to have been on detached service carrying mail from Rosebud to Yellowstone Depot and this is how Camp carries him, but Smalley lists him among the Rees present at the battle site, detailed to carry messages. Listed by Willert as one of four Rees (Curley Head, Foolish Bear, and Running Wolf) who left Terry's camp on the Rosebud, 22 Jun 1876, to deliver dispatches to MAJ Moore at PRD. They supposedly arrived on 24 Jun 1876 [*Little Big Horn Diary,* p. 483]. This is confirmed in the *Arikara Narrative.* Red Star, however, claimed he was left behind at PRD [Libby, *The Arikara Narrative,* p. 74].

Jackson, William (Billy) — b. Red River Portage, LaPreary, Canada, 1860 (also reported as Fort Benton, M.T.; also possibly in 1856) – d. Cutbank Creek, Blackfoot Reservation, 30 or 31 Dec 1899. Quarter-blood Pikuni Blackfoot, but considered and carried as a Ree. Brown eyes, black hair, dark complexion; 5'6" tall. Brother of Robert "Bob" Jackson. Left in timber with LT DeRudio and Gerard as Reno retreated from the valley. There is a story in Liddic's *Vanishing Victory,* p. 75, when Reno's command was in the timber LT Wallace asked CPT Moylan if there was any chance of getting a messenger through to Custer. Apparently Billy Jackson was standing nearby and Moylan asked him if he could get out. Jackson replied, "No one man could get through alive." At the Reno Court of Inquiry in 1879, Wallace testified that this occurred shortly after the skirmish line advanced to its final halt (its right flank on the river bend). Wallace looked back and did not see Custer as expected. He asked Moylan and the two officers asked Jackson. This was also the first time Wallace had noticed Indians to the rear. After being left behind in the timber, Jackson finally made Reno Hill sometime before midnight the next day, 26 Jun 1876. Early on 27 Jun 1876, he was given a message to take to General Terry. He rode north and came upon Custer's battlefield, eventually claiming to be the first man to see the field (ahead of Gibbon's scout, LT James Bradley).

He returned to the battlefield in 1878 with the COL Miles expedition and COL Sturgis' wife, Mamie, who was looking for her son, LT James Sturgis.

Little Brave (aka Little Soldier and Stub; also, Bear's Trail [Hardorff]; also, reputedly called Little Whirlwind; *Naha-cus-chu Reposch; Na-hocus-chisee-pustch*. The Sioux knew him as Buffalo Cloud) — b. 1849 or 1850–d. 25 Jun 1876, killed at the Little Big Horn. Black eyes, black hair, copper complexion; 5' 7" tall. With Custer on trip to Crow's Nest. Fought on Reno's skirmish line in the valley. Libbie Custer said he was killed near the ford, from a wound in the right shoulder. Another account says on east bank of LBH. Ken Hammer, in *The Battlefield Dispatch,* Winter 2005, says he was "likely killed west of river." Some Indian accounts say near some trees that were chopped down, left of the line of retreat. Michno has two Ree scouts being clubbed and stabbed on the east side of the river, after Reno's retreat, one of them in the flats. This ties in with Hammer. Wooden Leg and several others killed one of them, possibly Little Brave. Wooden Leg also cites an incident where the Cheyenne warrior, Whirlwind, killed and was killed by, a war bonnet-wearing Indian scout [*rather odd!*] on the east side of the river [Marquis, *Wooden Leg,* p. 224]. The Sioux warrior Eagle Elk confirms one account. The incident with Whirlwind could have been Bob-tail Bull. Stewart wrote that Little Brave was, "generally supposed to have been killed just below Reno's crossing and on the left bank [the west side] of the river" [*Custer's Luck,* p. 375]. The Ree scout Red Bear said he saw Little Brave crossing the LBH during the retreat. Red Bear saw that the scout was wounded under his right shoulder, blood soaking his white shirt [Libby, *The Arikara Narrative,* pp. 126–127]. The accounts of his death being on the west side of the river are, in all likelihood, incorrect, for there is enough Lakota evidence to the contrary. Little

Brave, fearless and respected by the Sioux (he spoke some Lakota), probably died shortly after Bob-tail Bull and, like his tribesman, on the east side of the Little Big Horn. Married.

Little Sioux (aka One Wolf, Sioux; *Sen-nen-urt; Sen-nen-net; Senaru Art*) — b. Fort Clark, D.T., 1857 [Libby, *The Arikara Narrative,* p. 191]; other sources list his date of birth between 1854 and 1856–d. Nishu, ND, 31 Aug 1933. Dark eyes, black hair, copper complexion; 5' 7" tall. A nephew of Bloody Knife and Stabbed. Father was Small Brave, a Dakota; mother was Young Holy Woman, a Ree. After crossing LBH, went right, after Sioux ponies; drove them to Reno Hill. Left the battlefield with other Rees. Claimed to have seen Forked Horn and Black Fox in front of Reno's skirmish line [Libby, *The Arikara Narrative,* p. 150].

One Feather (aka *Hacui-tis*) — b. in the spring of 1832, though possibly late 1831. Black eyes, black hair, copper complexion; 5' 7" tall. His father was Blue Bird (d.-of cholera at Fort Clark, summer 1851); his mother was Young White Girl (d.-of cholera at Fort Clark, summer 1851). After crossing LBH, went after Sioux ponies. Made it to Reno Hill. Left the battlefield with other Rees. Had been on Reno recon.

Red Bear (aka Handsome Elk [his early name]; Good Elk; *Wan-nee*) — b. Fort Clark, D.T., Sep 1853 (one source claimed he was born in 1849 though this is near impossible if his mother was born in 1837)–d. Nishu, ND, 7 May 1934. Had been assigned to the Reno recon, but did not make it because his horse gave out. Had been in Crow's Nest with LT Varnum. Fought on skirmish line, then trapped on east bank. Made Reno Hill, where he joined the six scouts who had captured the Sioux ponies. Left the battlefield with other Rees. According to Willert, Red Bear was with the main column and *not* with Varnum at the Crow's Nest [*Little Big Horn Diary,* p. 253]. Presence verified by Little Sioux in Camp/Hammer, *Custer in '76,* p. 181; however, Red Star claimed he was left behind at PRD [Libby, *The Arikara Narrative,* p. 73]. His father was Red Bear or Red Man (b. among the Pawnee in 1793–d. killed in the Fort Lincoln fight, 1872). His mother was White Corn (b. 1837).

Red Foolish Bear (*aka,* Foolish Red Bear; Crooked Foot; *Coonough-sen-gauch*) — b. 1848. Originally thought by Hammer to have carried dispatches between Rosebud and Yellowstone, and was listed as sick at Yellowstone camp on 25 June. Smalley has corrected this, however, and he is now listed as having crossed the LBH with Reno's command and participating in the valley fight as well as the hilltop battle. He must have been the one with Varnum at the Crow's Nest. It is also pretty certain that he tried to carry a message from the hilltop, but was forced back. In *Custer in '76,* Camp lists him as remaining with the command throughout the battle [see Smalley, *More Little Bighorn Mysteries,* p. 1–8].

Red Star (aka Strikes the Bear or Strike Bear [he was given the name Red Star *after* the Sioux campaign]; White Calf; *Ani Daka; Coonough-ta-cha; Coonough-ticho*) — b. 1854 or 1858 at Fort Clark, D.T.–d. Ree, ND, 7 Jun 1929. Had been in Crow's Nest with LT Varnum, then with Custer in Crow's Nest. Brought Varnum's message to Custer. After crossing the LBH, went to right to capture a herd of Sioux ponies and drive them to the hilltop. Left the battlefield with other Rees. Name changed to Red Star some time after the LBH. Red Star's father was also named Red Star (b. 1828–d. 1860 or early 1861). His mother was Woman Goes into Every House (b. 1831–d. killed with her 5-year old daughter by Sioux in the Arikara village near Berthold).

Red Wolf (aka Bush; Brush; Red Brush; *Na-pa-run-ough; Napa-ran-nogh*) — b. 1847 or 1849–d. circa 1916. Black eyes, black hair, copper complexion; 5'6" tall. Straggler; made hill, never crossing the LBH. Helped guard pony herd. Left the battlefield with other Rees.

Running Wolf (aka Wolf Runs) — b. Fort Clark, D.T., winter, 1855–1856, but probably in Dec 1855–d. Elbowoods, ND, 13 Mar 1936. Black eyes, black hair, copper complexion; 5'3" tall. Originally thought by Hammer to have traveled with the command up the Rosebud on 22 Jun 1876, then sent back with mail. Camp has him listed this way in *Custer in '76.* Hammer also claimed he was only a dispatch rider and not with Terry's column as a scout. Smalley says he was a dispatch rider, but was present at the battle, nonetheless. Listed by Willert as one of four Rees (Curley Head, Howling Wolf, and Foolish Bear) who left Terry's camp on the Rosebud, 22 Jun 1876, to deliver dispatches to MAJ Moore at PRD. They supposedly arrived on 24 Jun 1876 [*Little Big Horn Diary,* p. 483]. This is confirmed in the *Arikara Narrative.* Red Star, however, claimed he was left behind at PRD [Libby, *The Arikara Narrative,* p. 74]. His father was Gun Pointing to Breast and his mother was Chief Woman Village.

Rushing Bull (aka Spotted Horn Cloud, Running Bull, and Charging Bull; *Watoksha; Watokshu; Hocus-ne-ginn; Hocus-pa-cut-rer*; also possibly called Little Crow) — b. circa 1831–d. unknown. Black eyes, black hair, copper complexion; 5'6" tall. Approximately 5'9" tall. Straggler; made Reno Hill. Did not cross the Little Big Horn. Probably helped guard pony herd. Left the battlefield with other Rees. (See the Dakota scout Whole Buffalo [below] for name clarification.)

Soldier (*Kananch; Kanauch; Hoo-nanch; Hkoo-eh; Kun-atch; Heunatch*) [CPL] — b. late fall, 1831–d. 7 May 1921. Black eyes, black hair, copper complexion; 5'6" tall. A corporal and the second leader of the Ree scouts. Goose's uncle. Father was Bear's Arm (1767–1837); mother was Assiniboine Woman (1787–1837). Both parents died of smallpox. Straggler (his pony gave out). Eventually made it to Reno Hill. Helped guard pony herd. Left the battlefield with other Rees.

Stab (Stabbed; *Ca-wars*) [CPL] — b. circa 1831–d. killed by a Sioux Indian while hunting in the Little Missouri badlands, 1882. Black eyes, black hair, dark complexion; 5'6" tall. A corporal and one of the older Rees. Something of a medicine man or spiritual leader. Detailed to scout with Benteen (Hammer). Then he rejoined Soldier. Gray claimed he was a straggler who arrived at Reno Hill, which, if he joined Soldier, was probably true. Helped guard pony herd. Left the battlefield with other Rees. May have carried some sort of message to Benteen. Soldier claimed to have talked with Stab who told him that [Camp/Hammer, *Custer in '76,* p. 188]. An uncle of Little Sioux.

Strikes the Lodge (*Tay-kee-chee; Tay Ku Chi*) — b. Dakota Territory, 1847–d. unknown. Black eyes, black hair, copper complexion; 5'9" tall. Had been in Crow's Nest with LT Varnum. Straggler; made hill. Probably helped guard the pony herd. Left the battlefield with other Rees.

Strike[s] Two (*Ti-ta-wa-ri-cho; Tata-ree-chi; Sita-ka-visha*) — b. Fort Clark Village, D.T., 1844 or 1847–d. Elbowoods, ND, 8 Sep 1922. First scout to reach the "lone tepee" on the march down Reno Creek. He was the one reported to have struck the lodge with his riding crop. After crossing LBH, he went after Sioux ponies; made Reno Hill. Left the battlefield with other Rees. Father was Arikara Chief (d. Fort Berthold, 1901); mother was Young Woman Village (d. cholera, circa 1851).

White Eagle (*Na-ta-sta-ca; Nota-staka*) — b. circa 1849–1851–d. unknown. Black eyes, black hair, copper complexion; 5'4" tall. Straggler; pony gave out. Made Reno hill; helped guard pony herd. Left the battlefield with other Rees.

Young Hawk (aka Striped Horn [early]; then Crazy Head; *Ach-ta-wi-si-henune; Achta-wisi-hum; Neku-ta-wisi; Hani;* when he was thirteen, his father named him Young Hawk after a very brave uncle. There is also the possibility that Young Hawk was the Ree scout the Sioux called Buffalo Cloud. In the interviews of the Minneconjou warrior, White Bull, he referred to a Ree by this name, who was responsible for the deaths of Swift Bear and White Eagle) — b. in the winter village of the Arikara just below Mannhaven, D.T., spring, 1859 – d. Elbowoods, ND, 16 Jan 1915. Son of either Horns in Front or Forked Horn [see Libby, *The Arikara Narrative*, p. 114, then p. 193]. Black eyes, black hair, dark complexion; 5' 6" tall. His mother was Red Corn Silk Woman (1835–1911). On left side of skirmish line (Gray) between Goose and Half Yellow Face. Trapped on the east bank of the LBH, but made Reno Hill after the packs had arrived. In the group that tried to send a message, but was forced back. Had been on the Reno reconnaissance. With Forked Horn, made first contact with Gibbon after the battle. A favorite of Custer; used to cook the general's meat for him when they killed fresh game. Some sources have him with a group (four Rees and two Crows) on the right side of the skirmish line. There is some anecdotal evidence that it may have been Young Hawk who killed the Hunkpapa warriors, White Bull and Swift Bear. The death of White Eagle — an Oglala — may also be linked to Young Hawk's feats of valor, though in all likelihood this latter slaying may have been by either Bob-tail Bull or Little Brave, both of whom perished in the fighting.

Dakota Scouts

Caroo (aka Bear Running in the Timber; Bear Come Out; Comes the Bear; and Bear Going in the Woods; also, "Old Caddoo") — b. 1825 or 1835, it is unclear which–d. FAL, killed in a drunken brawl over an Indian woman, 8 Jun 1878. Blackfeet Sioux. Married to an Arikara woman. Made Reno Hill. Had been on Reno recon. With Reno, but did not cross the LBH. Joined the six scouts and helped guard the pony herd. Served as rear guard for captured Sioux ponies on the return to the PRD. Left the battlefield.

Left Hand (*Chat-ka*) [Note: Also listed in Section III] — b. 1829–d. 25 Jun 1876, killed at the Little Big Horn. Reputedly, he fought at the LBH, but not for the soldiers. Left Hand and Scabby (Barking) Wolf left for FAL during the snowstorm of 1–2 Jun 1876 and he was discharged on 9 Jun 1876. He then rejoined his people in time for the battle. His body and his dead horse were found in the Indian village after the fighting was over. "They [several Rees] went on to the Dakota camp and found the body of a dead Dakota lying on a tanned buffalo hide. Young Hawk recognized this warrior as one who had been a scout at Fort Lincoln, *Chat-ka*. He had on a white shirt, the shoulders were painted green, and on his forehead, painted in red, was the sign of a secret society" [Libby, *The Arikara Narrative*, p. 109].

In the typical drama that so often trails certain names associated with this campaign, Roger Williams makes no allowance for Left Hand being a Sioux and claims the name showed up on the post returns for June 1876, the man reenlisting on 10 June 1876, and then being discharged 10 Dec 1876. If this is correct, then there had to have been *two* Left Hands, one a Ree and one a Dakota.

Ma-tok-sha (aka Bear Waiting; Bear-Come-Out, though this may be problematic and may have been confused with *Caroo*, above; Carrier; Round Wooden Cloud; possibly Ring Cloud [see Whole Buffalo, below, for the confusion; also, Smalley, *More Little Bighorn Mysteries*, p. 5–5], though his age works against him from a Walter Camp interview; *Watoksha*) — b. 1827. Possibly a Blackfeet Sioux if he is indeed also Ring Cloud. Married to an Arikara woman. Made Reno Hill. Had been on Reno recon. Did not cross LBH. Joined on ridge top the six scouts who had captured Sioux ponies. Left the battlefield.

White Cloud (*Machpeya-ska; Mach-pe-as-ka*) — b. 1855. Married to an Arikara woman. Made Reno Hill, but did not cross LBH. Met up with the Ree, Red Bear, and they rode on together to try to join the pony-stealers. Met the three Crows along the way, and then went back to Reno Hill [Libby, *The Arikara Narrative*, pp. 129–130]. Joined on the ridge-top with the six scouts who had captured Sioux ponies. Had been on Reno recon. Left the battlefield.

Whole Buffalo (aka Bear Running in the Timber; also possibly Buffalo Ancestor, Buffalo Body, Round Wooden Cloud, Ring Cloud [see *Ma-tok-sha*, above] which is *Mahpiya Changleska*; and *Pta-a-te; Tonhechi Tu*. If he was indeed Ring Cloud — and his date of birth is more correct for his age than *Ma-tok-sha*, above, he took on the English name of "Adam Carrier" [Hardorff, *On The LBH With Walter Camp*, p. 85, footnote 5]) — b. Dakota Territory, 1834 or 1836–d. unknown. Black eyes, black hair, copper complexion; 5' 8" tall. Blackfeet Sioux [Williams claims Yanktonais], married to an Arikara woman. Helped drive the ponies when Reno charged down the valley. Made Reno Hill. Had been on Reno recon. Left the battlefield. In Camp/Hammer, *Custer in '76*, p. 183, footnote 2, Hammer claims he was also known as *Watoksha*. Either this is incorrect or the Indian name for the Arikara, Rushing Bull, is incorrect. This is further confused because Hammer includes the name Spotted Horn Cloud — another name for Rushing Bull — along with Ring Cloud (see *Ma-tok-sha*, above). It would seem logical that "Spotted Horn Cloud" would be this fellow and not Rushing Bull, but until I have further evidence, I shall keep the names the way I have them. In Camp/Hammer, p. 184, the comment was made that someone saw Whole Buffalo coming down the valley. That would indicate he is *not* the same person alluded to in the footnote above. In footnote 5, p. 190 of the Soldier interview, Whole Buffalo's names are listed. In the main text alluding to the footnote, Soldier uses *Watoksha* as a separate person, seemingly clinching it.

Other Campaign Indians

These were not at the Little Bighorn and all are considered Arikara.

Baker, William (half-breed Ree; *aka*, William James Bailey; *Choka Wo*) — b. Alexandria, VA, 24 Apr 1850–d. St. Cloud, FL, 14 Oct 1933. Had been on Reno recon. Claimed he was in valley fight and on the hilltop, but Varnum, Gerard, and others say he was left at Yellowstone Depot. Even Gray, who places him on Reno's skirmish line, admits to only guessing. Willert claims it was Tall Bear rather than Baker, who accompanied Reno on his scout [*Little Big Horn Diary*, p. 119]. Camp carries him at the battlefield for the entire fight, but this appears to be incorrect [Camp/Hammer, *Custer in '76*, p. 283]. Camp asked Young Hawk if it was Young Hawk and Baker who went out and met LT Bradley on 27 Jun 1876. Young Hawk responded, no, it was himself and his father, Forked Horn. This is more proof Baker was nowhere around [Camp/Hammer, *Custer in '76*, p. 193].

Barking Wolf (aka Scabby Wolf) — b. 1855. Black eyes, black hair; copper complexion; 5'7" tall. Had returned to FAL with the Dakota scout, Left Hand (*Chat-ka*), during the snowstorm of 1–2 Jun 1876. Unlike Left Hand, he must have returned to the column for he was reported sick at Yellowstone Depot. Carried messages. Not listed in Varnum's muster roll.

Black Porcupine (*Sawi-catit*) — b. 1855–d. unknown. Black eyes, black hair, copper complexion; 5'8" tall. Detached service at FAL. At Yellowstone Depot 25 June.

Climbs the Bluff (aka Charging up the Hill) — b. 1845–d. FAL, lung disease, 9 Mar 1880. Black eyes, black hair, copper complexion; 5'9" tall. Detached service at FAL. Carried messages. At Yellowstone Depot around 24 June.

Crow Bear — Sent out from PRD with mail to General Terry. Not certain even if he was a Ree.

Foolish Bear (aka Bear; Crooked Foot; *Coonough*) — b. Dakota Territory, circa 1847–d. unknown. Black eyes, black hair, dark complexion; 5'6" tall. Originally thought by Hammer to have been on Reno's skirmish line in the valley and in the retreat to hilltop. This has since been corrected by Smalley who claims he was only used to carry messages. Listed by Willert as one of four Rees (Curley Head, Howling Wolf, and Running Wolf) who left Terry's camp on the Rosebud, 22 Jun 1876, to deliver dispatches to MAJ Moore at PRD. They supposedly arrived on 24 Jun 1876 [*Little Big Horn Diary*, p. 483]). Red Star, however, claimed he was left behind at PRD [Libby, *The Arikara Narrative*, p. 74]. Liddic claimed he was sick at the PRD on the day of the battle and there is no reason to doubt this [Liddic/Harbaugh, *Camp on Custer*, p. 130, footnote 270].

Horns in Front — b. 1834–d. unknown. Black eyes, black hair, copper complexion; 5'10" tall. Young Hawk's father, though there is plenty of confusion with Forked Horn. Carried messages from Yellowstone Depot. His presence there was confirmed by Little Sioux, Red Star, and Young Hawk [Libby, *The Arikara Narrative*, pp. 73–74; 114]. Running Wolf said he was sick [p. 139].

Jackson, Robert (Bobby) — b. Fort Benton, M.T., 27 Aug 1856 (also seen as 1854)–d. Amethyst, CO, some time around 1916. Brown eyes, black hair, dark complexion; 5'8" tall. Quarter-blood Pikuni Blackfoot and William Jackson's brother. Hammer originally had listed him on detached service at FAL, but Smalley says he was on detached service at the Yellowstone Depot and was discharged there. He then carried mail back to FAL, but was not at the fort during the battle. What is even stranger is that Stewart in his *Custer's Luck*, p. 398, suggests that the "half breed" LT Mathey mentions as being the only person the pack train ran into (*not* Kanipe) was Robert Jackson. The Camp/Hammer book, *Custer in '76*, indicates Jackson had enlisted on 25 Dec 1875, meaning his enlistment would have ended on the day of the battle. Hammer concedes he may have reenlisted and gotten back to the PRD.

There is additional information that Robert Jackson may have been at the battle. In the *Little Big Horn Diary*, page 392, Willert claims Billy Jackson, leaving the timber with three others on the night of 25 Jun 1876, worried that his brother may be among the dead they were passing. Willert cites Dustin, *Custer Tragedy*, page 123. Varnum also claims he took Bob Jackson with him up the Rosebud [*I, Varnum*, p. 59]. Varnum mentions "the two Jacksons" were with him on the Rosebud on 24 Jun 1876 when Custer sent him off to find a trail he had missed [Hammer, *Custer in '76,* p. 59; letter dated 14 Apr 1909 from Boise, ID, from Varnum to Walter Camp]. In an e-mail dated 27 Jun 2006, Vern Smalley writes, "Custer allowed the men to write one last letter to home, and a courier took them the next morning. I think that the courier was Bob Jackson. He left on the morning of June 23 and was at the Yellowstone Depot on June 25 in time to be discharged and seen by Private Harvey Fox (D) who was known to be at the YD [Yellowstone Depot, i.e., PRD]." PVT George Glenn (H) believed Robert Jackson was sent back from the mouth of the Rosebud camp. Glenn saw him there, but did not recall seeing him after [Camp/Hammer, *Custer in '76,* p. 135]. Herendeen said Jackson was *not* at the LBH on 25 June or 26 June, but back at the PRD [Camp/Hammer, *Custer in '76,* p. 222]. PVT Stanislaus Roy "always heard that Bob Jackson and Billy Cross never forded at Ford A. No one remembers seeing them in the valley fight or on west side of river at all" [Camp/Hammer, *Custer in '76,* p. 111]. Young Hawk claimed Robert Jackson was in the camp at the mouth of the Powder after the battle, but was not *in* the battle [Camp/Hammer, *Custer in '76,* p. 193].

Laying Down (aka Lying Down, Wolf, or *Cha-ra-ta*)—b. 1857–d. unknown. Black eyes, black hair, copper complexion; 5'2" tall. Sick at Yellowstone Depot. His presence there was confirmed by Little Sioux in the *Arikara Narrative* excerpt contained in Graham, *The Custer Myth,* p. 44. Red Star also

claimed he was left behind at PRD [Libby, *The Arikara Narrative,* p. 74]. Confirmed by Running Wolf [p. 139].

Long Bear (aka Tall Bear, High Bear)—b. 1831–d. unknown, but after 1899. Black eyes, black hair, copper complexion; 5'7" tall. Detached service at Yellowstone Depot, carrying mail. Willert claimed he was one of the four Rees on the Reno scout, rather than William Baker [*Little Big Horn Diary,* p. 119]. Jim Donovan wrote that he had a fight with Reno and Reno threatened to kill him. Reno told him he couldn't go on the scout because his horse was too weak and the Indian objected. Bloody Knife jumped between the two men and Reno relented [*A Terrible Glory,* p. 163]. This is confirmed in *The Arikara Narrative,* pages 73–74, footnote 38, which may be where Donovan got it. Red Star, however, claimed he was one of those left behind at PRD.

The Shield—b. circa 1848–d. somewhere along the Missouri River, ND or SD, 17 Jul 1919. Black eyes, black hair, copper complexion; 5'9½" tall. Enlisted 11 Dec 1875. Discharged 11 Jun 1876 at FAL.

Sticking Out—b. circa 1853–d. unknown. Black eyes, black hair, copper complexion; 5'9" tall. Enlisted 11 Dec 1875. Discharged 11 Jun 1876 at FAL.

Wagon—b. 1856–d. unknown. Black eyes, black hair, copper complexion; 5'6" tall. Detached service at FAL. At the Powder River Depot some time around 24 Jun 1876.

SECTION III

Indians Present and Estimates of Their Strength[*]

The following lists some 1,488 Indians of various tribes, known or believed to have been present in the Indian village along the Little Big Horn River on June 25, 1876. Of those listed, some 1,274 are men or male children and 214 are women or female children. A total of *at least* 63 of those listed are believed — through documentation or oral history — to have been killed during the battle. In addition, Richard G. Hardorff, a highly-respected historian of the battle of the Little Big Horn, believes an additional six women and four children were killed by Arikara scouts as Major Reno's command rode down the valley toward the great village. Two of these women and at least one child were believed to have been the wives and child of the Hunkpapa warrior-chief, Gall.

Some notes to remember: all entries marked with the symbol — — are known historic figures, but it is *uncertain* if they were at the Little Big Horn. *With one exception, they are not carried in the strength totals, above.*

According to Stephen W. Myers in his article, "Roster of Known Hostile Indians at the Battle of the Little Big Horn," *Research Review,* Summer 1991, Vol. 5, No. 2, and others, an Indian usually had three names: "...the one given by his parents (which was formal and bad luck resulted from its use), the name he

called himself, and the name others called him, which was usually the one he was known by. We use his recognized name in English."

The word "Sioux" is a truncation of *Nadouessioux,* which is a French form of the Chippewa (the *New York Times,* in a September 21, 1998, article, said Ojibwa, but they are the same tribe), "*nadoue-is-iw,*" meaning "little snake"; in other words, "enemy." (The 1990 census numbered 103,255 Sioux in the U.S.) They called themselves Dakota, meaning "allies," and had three main branches, all three speaking in the Siouan linguistic family. This family of languages furnished twelve tribes, the largest grouping on the Plains.

While the Sioux had no "dates," as such, they did refer to the monthly seasons with some measure of specificity [Neihardt, *Black Elk Speaks*]:

- *"Moon of Frost in the Tepee"* (January)
- *"Moon of the Dark Red Calves"* (February)
- *"Moon of the Snowblind"* (March)
- *"Moon of the Red Grass Appearing"* (April)
- *"Moon When the Ponies Shed"* (May)
- *"Moon of Making Fat"* (June)
- *"Moon of Red* [or, *Ripe*] *Cherries"* (July)
- *"Moon When the Cherries Turn Black"* (August)

[*]For estimates of strength see page 196.

- *"Moon When the Calf Grows Hair"* or *"Moon of the Black Calf"*; also, *"Moon When the Plums Are Scarlet"* (September)
- *"Moon of the Changing Season"* (October)
- *"Moon of Falling Leaves"* (November)
- *"Moon [Time] of the Popping Trees"* (December)
- *"Bitten moon is delayed"* (last quarter).

It should also be remembered that the hierarchical structure within the tribes was rather loose and while there was a recognized form of seniority, it was not as clearly defined as we may think. "Even Rain was never made a chief, but he *did* have all the *influence* of one, but not the *power*. The word 'Chief' is too loosely used by whites. Leaders or heads of bands were called Chiefs, *by whites* who were ignorant of the fact that these men were *officers* of the military orders and *as such* were chiefs. English rendition of word more comprehensive than Indian" [Frank H. Huston, Graham, *The Custer Myth*, pp. 80–81].

Dakota or Santee Sioux

The "Dakota" or "Santee" Sioux were the Eastern Sioux, or *Isanti* grouping. They were also known as Waist and Skirt Indians. Myers lists the Teton as well as the Santee Sioux as a sub-group of the Dakota, but this link may be tenuous. The Sioux were the largest single tribe in the Siouan family grouping and were considered the "mother" nation [Smalley, *More Little Bighorn Mysteries,* p. 11–16]. The Dakota were one of two groups primarily *east* of the Missouri River, mainly Iowa, Minnesota — west of the Red River — with some members as far east as Wisconsin. They spoke the Eastern or "D" dialect of the parent language: Santee-Sisseton Dakota.

There were four divisions:

- *Sisseton*
- *Wahpeton* ("village in the leaves")
- *Mdwekanton* or *Mdewkanton*
- *Wahpekute* (smallest of the four, never to-

taling more than 550 people [Donovan, *A Terrible Glory,* p. 69]). Known as the "Red Tops" because of the red cloth they tied around the tops of their spears.

The Santee always camped beside the Hunkpapa, quite possibly for protection, because there were so few of them. Evan Connell [*Son of the Morning Star*] claimed the Santee were the only tribe that habitually practiced decapitation instead of scalping. Wooden Leg, the Northern Cheyenne warrior, however, describes at least two incidents when he was younger, of Cheyenne warriors decapitating their Indian victims [Marquis, *Wooden Leg*, pp. 12 and 22]. Cutting a victim's throat was usually a Sioux practice, left over from when they habitually chopped off their enemies' heads. By the time of the Custer fight, only the Santee still practiced the ghoulish art. According to the Oglala warrior, He Dog, there were only about 30 to 40 Santee lodges at the Little Big Horn [Camp/Hammer, *Custer in '76,* p. 206]. James Donovan wrote that there were thirty Dakota and Nakota lodges, combined, in the village [*A Terrible Glory,* p. 148; probably from Campbell].

James Willert, in his *Little Big Horn Diary,* p. 35, wrote that Frank Grouard, a scout for General Crook during the campaign, "knew that 'after dark,' or just 'before dawn,'" was when the Sioux were most likely to attack. Colonel John Gibbon's Chief-of-Scouts, Lieutenant James Bradley, wrote in his diary: "Indian attacks usually occur just before day" [*The March of the Montana Column*].

Sioux lodges, in general, were constructed tall, but fairly narrow at the base, with a large ventilating flap at the top. Santee lodges were constructed with the poles upside down, their thicker end up. These tepees were also smaller than standard Sioux or Cheyenne lodges. Prior to the 19th century and the widespread use of horses, tepee rings averaged twelve to seventeen feet across, but the introduction of horses enabled Indians to transport heavier loads, so they began using larger lodges. Hunting parties, however, continued to use smaller tepees, about twelve feet in diameter. Family lodges were larger; one source claiming an 18-foot diameter was about average, while others claim 22 feet was the norm.

Connell claims the Sioux did not use tomahawks, though they did use axes, hatchets, and clubs — one guesses there is a fine point to such an observation! First Sergeant John Ryan of Company M, Seventh Cavalry, described Indian lances — he did not specifically mention Sioux or another tribe — as having a blade about two feet long, two inches wide, and sharpened on both sides. The pole was about five feet long, an inch in diameter, usually with a small hole at the non–lethal end where a rawhide thong could be tied and then looped over a warrior's wrist [Barnard, *Ten Years with Custer,* p. 28]. Other than the *Wahpekute*, Sioux warriors rarely carried lances or spears. The Cheyenne warrior Wooden Leg claimed the Sioux were the only Indians he knew of who made regular use of the stone war club. Also carried were "knife sticks," a long shaft with three blades set into slots and protruding about three or four inches [Marquis, *Wooden Leg,* p. 74; also, for a good picture of this brutal weapon, see Scott, *et al., Archaeological Perspectives on the Battle of the Little Bighorn,* p. 103].

Sioux tradition allowed four coups on a dead enemy:

- The first to touch could wear a golden eagle feather upright.
- The second wore an eagle feather tilted to the left.
- The third wore a feather horizontally.
- The fourth might wear a buzzard feather dangling behind his head.

Unlike the Cheyenne, the Sioux often buried their dead on scaffolds.

Nakota or Yankton, Upper and Lower Yanktonnais

The "Nakota" or "Yankton" Sioux were considered the Central Sioux. This was another group *east* of the Missouri River, primarily between the Missouri and Red Rivers, but like so many other tribal nations, some of the Yanktonnais split off from the main group, forming the Assiniboine tribe [Smalley, *More Little Bighorn Mysteries,* p. 11–17]. This group was originally thought to have been the Central or "N" dialect. It appears, however, the Yankton and Yanktonnai spoke *Dakota* and the term is "Yankton-" or "Yanktonnai dakota." "In the twentieth century these three sounds (lakota, dakota, nakota) were generally, but incorrectly assumed to define three dialects, and Yankton-Yanktonnai was mistakenly identified as an 'N' dialect" [*Handbook of North American Indian,* Volume 13, p. 97]. There were two dialects: "Yankton-Yanktonnai Dakota" (Western Dakota) and "Assiniboine-Stoney Nakota" (or Nakoda). This grouping probably had some thirty lodges — combined with the Dakotas — at the Little Big Horn.

Lakota or Teton Sioux

The Lakota or Teton Sioux were the Western grouping, and the largest single group within the Sioux network. As noted above, Stephen Myers lists the Teton and the Santee Sioux as a sub-group of the Dakota, with the Teton Sioux calling themselves Lakota (this latter part is certainly correct). The tribe began to move west from Minnesota during the second half of the 18th century. In the second half of the 19th century, they were living primarily west of the Missouri, and north of the Platte, in the Dakotas, Wyoming, and Montana. Theirs was the Western or "L" dialect of the parent language.

There were seven divisions within the Lakota-Teton grouping:

- Hunkpapa — northernmost of the tribes along with the Blackfeet and Sans Arcs. Also written as *Unkpapa* or Missouri Sioux: "those who dwell by themselves." This tribe usually camped by the village entrance. As with most tribes, they were organized into bands. The following bands were with Sitting Bull in Canada [Dickson/Josephine F. Waggoner]: *Tinazipe-sica* [Bad Bows] (sub-band: *Icira*): Sitting Bull, Four Horns, Red Horn, and Black Moon [Bray/Dickson]; *Talonapin*: Charging Thunder; *Kangiska* (possibly translates to "White Crow"): Gall; *Cankahuran*: Cross Bear and Running Antelope. The Hunkpapa were the largest — by far — of the Sioux tribes, as well as the wealthiest, having avoided warfare for a number of years. They were also the fiercest and most belligerent of the tribes.
- Blackfeet — the northernmost of the tribes along with the Sans Arcs and Hunkpapa. *Sihasapa*; "black moccasins" or Rocky Mountain Sioux. Not the same as the *Blackfoot* tribe or *Siksika*, who are related to the eastern Algonquians. The Blackfoot lived farther north and west. *The Oxford Companion to Military History,* however, claims, "The Canada border-area hostile Algonquian-speaking Blackfoot tribe is included among the Teton Sioux" (obviously a linguistic error). Vern Smalley writes that the Blackfoot tribe, *per se,* is *not* Lakota [*Little Bighorn Mysteries,* p. 2–11]. Smalley is correct here. Also, the Black*feet* are never referred to as Black*foot*.
- Sans Arcs — i.e., Without Bows; *Itazipacola* or *Itazipdro*. Northernmost of the tribes along with the Blackfeet and Hunkpapa.
- Minneconjoux [plural] — "Those who plant crops beside water."
- Two Kettle — *Oohenunpa*; "Two Cookings."
- Oglala — southernmost of the tribes along with the Cu Brulé. "To scatter one's own" [Dickson]; also seen as, "wanders in the mountains." "John Gray suggested ... that the total Oglala population in 1876 was probably about 4,180 people, an estimate consistent with Kingsley Bray's analysis. Gray calculated that of this total, about 2,336 Oglala (53 percent) were residing at the Red Cloud Agency in northwestern Nebraska while an estimated 1,844 people (roughly 264 lodges) were 'in the north.' Of these, Gray suggested that perhaps 240 Oglala lodges were at the Little Bighorn" [Dickson, "Reconstructing the Little Bighorn Village: The Big Road Roster and the Oglala Tribal Circle," p. 3]. There were three main bands within the Oglala grouping: the *Oyuhpe,* the True Oglala, and the *Kiyaksa.* Both the *Oyuhpe* and the True Oglala had so-called Northern Bands and Agency Bands, while the *Kiyaksa* had only the Agency Bands. The Northern Bands were all at the Little Big Horn, while the Agency Bands filtered warriors in and out during the summer of 1876. It was this Agency grouping that inflated the village size and has made it almost impossible to determine precisely who or how many Oglala warriors were at the battle. If we accept Gray's figure of 240 Oglala lodges at the Little Big Horn, we can figure on approximately 1,680 people in the Oglala circles. To this number we must add "agency" Oglala who spent the summer with the "northern" bands.
- Cu Brulé — southernmost of the tribes along with the Oglala. Burnt Thigh or Rear-end; *Sicanju* or Rosebud Sioux.

All of these divisions were represented at the Little Big Horn.

Cheyenne (Ohmeseheso)

In 1825–1826, the Cheyenne divided into northern and southern bands when some bands moved south. Unlike other tribes whose leaders did not get along, this split was amicable. It was also around this time when the Cheyenne allied with the Sioux. Like the Sioux, the Cheyenne came from Minnesota and had lived along the Missouri River. They were also long-term allies with the Arapaho. The Black Hills — called "the Cedars" by the Cheyenne — were sacred to them, as well as to the Sioux. By 1830 the Cheyenne were fully horse-mobile.

The name Cheyenne probably derives from *Sha-hi-ye-na*— red talkers — those who spoke an alien language (this is what the Sioux called them (that or, *Shahiyela; Shyelas*). The Cheyenne called themselves *Tsistsistas*, meaning, people who were alike or similarly bred, i.e., us [Connell; also, Kraft, "Ned Wynkoop's Lonely Walk Between the Races," *Custer and His Times, Book Five,* p. 89]. The Cheyenne belonged to the *Algonquian* linguistic family, one of six such tribes on the prairie, and along with the Arapaho, in the Western Division. They were also known as Kites, usually thought to refer to the fact that their tents could be seen from fairly far away, thereby resembling kites in the distance.

Cheyenne lodges were shorter than those of the Sioux, and had a larger circumference and a smaller ventilating flap at the top. They were usually made with fifteen to seventeen buffalo skins, the average lodge being twelve to fifteen feet in diameter. Generally, the height was the same as the diameter. Their camp circles were pitched in the shape of a crescent moon, with the opening toward the east. Their tepees also opened toward the rising sun. The camp circle of the Northern Cheyenne tribe when it was fully assembled enclosed a space of ¼ or ⅓ of a mile in diameter [Marquis, *Wooden Leg,* p. 78]. In the mid–1870s — but certainly before the Little Big Horn battle — Cheyenne villages ranged from thirty to forty lodges to more than two hundred [Marquis, *Wooden Leg,* p. 156].

After the 1825–1826 migration southward, the Cheyenne had essentially two divisions. The Northern Cheyenne were mainly in Wyoming and Montana. "The men of the

northern Cheyenne ... were the tallest people in the world in the late 19th century; well nourished on bison and berries, and wandering clear of disease on the high plains, they averaged nearly five feet ten" [*The New Yorker,* April 5, 2004]. The Southern Cheyenne were primarily in Colorado, Kansas, Oklahoma, and Texas.

Their tribal government, while deceivingly complicated in theory, was paradoxically loose in practice. They were one of several tribes using military "societies" for their warriors. In the 1860's, Little Wolf was the most important "old man chief" of the Cheyenne. Crazy Head was next, and Crazy Mule was their great medicine man [Marquis, *Wooden Leg,* pp. 14–15].

• *Hotamitanio* or *Hotamitaniu,* or Dog Soldiers (Southern Cheyenne): Dog Soldiers were the most militant and elite of the Cheyenne warrior societies and they filled both social and military purposes, especially as camp police. Their power as a society was broken at the Battle of Summit Springs, July 11, 1869.
• There were also warrior societies — maybe only three identifiable in the 1870s.
  ○ The *Elkhorn Scrapers* or *Elk Soldiers* [*Himoweyuuhki*].
  ○ The *Kit Fox Men* [*Wohksehetaniu*], commonly called "Fox Soldiers," and also known as "Coyote."
  ○ The *Crazy Dogs* [*Hotamimassau*], also known as "Foolish Dogs."
• There was a "chief" of each society, and then generally nine headmen.
• Every ten years the entire tribe would assemble and "elect" forty "big chiefs."
• These forty would then select four "old man chiefs."
• The general order of seniority or "command" was (1) the "old man chiefs"; (2) the forty tribal "big chiefs"; (3) the three "warrior chiefs"; then (4) the twenty-seven "little warrior chiefs."

- The "warrior chiefs" had authority only in their societies.
- When a society was chosen for a particular event, i.e., policing a move or a hunt, that organization ruled [this is generally from Marquis, *Wooden Leg,* pp. 56–57] and woe betide those who moved in front or challenged the "ruling" society's authority.

Stephen Myers writes that there were three or four Cheyenne societies at the Little Big Horn. It appears he places the "Dog Soldiers" alongside the other three. Richard Hardorff said there were three, each with sixty members [Hardorff, "The John Stands in Timber Interview," *Cheyenne Memoirs of the Custer Fight,* p. 168].

Cheyenne warriors generally turned their dead victims face down, fearing it was bad luck to leave an enemy facing the sky. They did not bury their dead on scaffolds like the Sioux did, but rather put the dead body on a platform on tree branches. Mostly, however, they were placed in caves, if available, or placed on the ground out of the way of usual travel, wrapped in blankets or skins, and covered with stones [Marquis, *Wooden Leg,* p. 92].

The warriors carried lances, as opposed to the Sioux, who usually did not, though Kill Eagle — a Blackfeet Sioux — claimed a number of Sioux warriors had lances [Graham, *The Custer Myth,* p. 52]. As a distinguishing feature, Cheyenne warriors used the "barred" feathers of wild turkeys on their arrows and they rarely carried stone war clubs, instead preferring a hatchet or a small ax [Marquis, *Wooden Leg,* p. 73]. Their women and old men used saddles, while the young men always rode bareback. Cheyenne tradition allowed only three coups on a dead enemy. The first could paint his face black with ashes and buffalo blood, the second could unbraid his hair, though he could not wear facial paint. A third coup was allowed for the man who pulled the enemy's scalp.

According to Wooden Leg, almost all the Northern Cheyenne were at the camp along the Little Big Horn River. Two of the four "old men chiefs" were there: Old Bear and Dirty Moccasin. Two were missing: Little Wolf and Rabbit (or Dull Knife). All thirty chiefs of the warrior societies were there except Little Wolf, the leading chief of the Elk warriors. He arrived late in the day of June 25, after the Custer fight was over.

Arapaho

The Arapaho had a limited presence at the Little Big Horn, fielding only five warriors, but the tribe in general was as antagonistic towards the white soldiers as its more numerous cousins. Another of the *Algonquian* linguistic family, one of the six such tribes on the Prairie, along with the Cheyenne, in the Western Division. They were found mainly in Wyoming, Montana, Colorado, Kansas, Oklahoma, and Texas. The Sioux referred to them as "Blue Clouds." The five Arapaho warriors at the battle slipped out of the agency at Fort Robinson (Nebraska), planning on spending the summer scouting and hunting. They met a party of Lakota near the sundance site and went to the village to "have a good time." The Sioux did not trust them, figuring they were scouts for the soldiers, and took their weapons. The Cheyenne chief, Two Moon, got the situation straightened out and their arms were returned. Supposedly, they had little choice but to fight with the Sioux and Cheyenne.

Indians Who Were Present at the Little Big Horn, June 25, 1876

Abandoned One (also, Fled and Abandoned; *Ihpeya Nanpapi*; later named Crow Foot) — (Hunkpapa Lakota-Teton Sioux) — b. March 1876–d. 15 Dec 1890, during the Wounded Knee unrest. An infant twin son of Sitting Bull and Four Robes. Brother of Fled With.

Afraid of Bear—(Lakota-Teton Sioux)—Known to have been in the fighting. Still living at the Standing Rock Agency, Bullhead, SD, 1926 [courtesy of Dickson].

Afraid of Eagle[s] (Scared Eagle; *Wanbli Koki-papi*)—(Hunkpapa Lakota-Teton Sioux)—b. circa 1828?–d. circa 1894? [Dickson]—A sub chief. Associated with Bear Ribs' band, but with Kill Eagle at the Little Big Horn. Brother of Bear Rib [Graham, *The Custer Myth,* p. 56]. Presence confirmed by Myers.

Afraid of Hawk (also, "Mark" Afraid of Hawk)—(Oglala Lakota-Teton Sioux)—Known to have been in the fight at the Little Big Horn. Still living at the Standing Rock Agency, Shields, ND, 1926 [courtesy of Dickson].

Afraid of Nothing (*Takuni Kokipesni*)—(Oglala Lakota-Teton Sioux)—b. circa 1824–d. 1909).

Afraid of Nothing Bear (aka Fools Bear)—(Minneconjou Lakota-Teton Sioux).

All See Him (aka John Bighead Man)—(Northern Cheyenne). Wooden Leg called him very brave in the Custer battle.

American Horse ("George" *Ve-ho-evo-ha*)—(Northern Cheyenne)—b. circa 1842–d. 1911. Greene has incorrectly identified this particular man as the Oglala who was at the Red Cloud Agency during the summer of 1876, missing the battle. Northern *Suhtai*. A "Council of the 44" chief. The only Cheyenne council chief to take part in the fighting against Reno. Did not cross the LBH after Reno, but proceeded downriver where he was one of the first to return to the Cheyenne camp. He saw Custer's column there "almost at the river." In the fight at MTC [CBHMA]. Presence confirmed by Myers.

American Horse (aka Iron Shield; Iron Shirt; Iron Plume)—(Minneconjou Lakota-Teton Sioux)—d. Slim Buttes, 9 Sep 1876. This could be the man who fought both Reno and Custer. One of several Indians named American Horse, this particular fellow being called that by Frank Grouard [Dickson]. Died from wounds suffered at Slim Buttes in the fight with CPT Anson Mills' (3C) troops. Claimed to have killed CPT Fetterman by stabbing him [Stewart, *Custer's Luck,* p. 44]. Some battle participants—notably, Lone Bear (Oglala), Lights (Minneconjou), and Two Eagles (Brulé), plus "Julia" Face (Oglala)—in interviews conducted by Samuel B. Weston (in 1908–1909)—claimed American Horse was not at the battle. Others claim he was. The fact that he was in the Slim Buttes fighting,

along with many others who were at the Little Big Horn, causes me to list him as present.

American Horse—(Lakota-Teton Sioux)—This man was listed in the Crazy Horse surrender register, May 1877, but little or nothing else is known of him [Dickson]. He is possibly an Oglala and because of that and that he was known to be with Crazy Horse, he is carried separately and at the battle. In the surrender ledger, he was listed as "head-of-household," along with Asshole and Old. Their lodge consisted of four adult females and one male child; a total of eight people.

American Horse (*Wasicu Tasunke*)—(Oglala Lakota-Teton Sioux)—b. circa 1840–d. 1908. Son of Sitting Bear. *There is considerable confusion about the several "American Horses" listed as being at the battle. Some sources claim this man was there, but the most reliable has him at the Red Cloud Agency during the summer of 1876* [Dickson; e-mail, 18 Mar 2009]. Presence at the Little Big Horn is confirmed by Myers, though in all likelihood, he is incorrect.

American Man (aka "John Conroy," sometimes seen as John Con-Roy, though this may be a misidentification as noted below; also, Little White Man; American Boy)—(Oglala Lakota—Teton Sioux)—b. circa 1860–d. 12 Sep 1950. Mixed blood. Member of the *Wagluhe* Band. One of 12 Sioux sharpshooters who prevented Reno's troopers from going for water [LBHA]. Misidentified as John Corn Ray in the 1926 LBH re-union list [Dickson]. The Earl Brininstool photograph of twelve Lakota warriors at the 1926 re-union identifies one as "Frank" Conroy [Hardorff, *Hokahey!...,* p. 92].

Amputated Finger—(Oglala Lakota-Teton Sioux).

Antelope (aka "Kate" Bighead or Big Head; Big Head Woman; Howling Woman; Woman Yells) (F)—b. near the North Platte River, 1847 or 1848–d. 1929. Associated with Southern Cheyenne during most of her childhood. With her two brothers, White Bull and White Moon, she joined the Northern Cheyenne in 1870 while they were in the Black Hills country. Noisy Walking's aunt; cousin of *Me-o-tzi.* Her story was given to Dr. Thomas B. Marquis in 1927, and formed the basis for the Indian narrative in the 1991 movie *Son of the Morning Star.* Bruce Liddic refers to a "Howling Woman" as being Noisy Walking's aunt and the one who placed him on a travois, bringing him back to the village, where he died that night [*Vanishing Victory,* p. 160].

Ephriam Dickson, in a 10 Aug 2006 e-mail, wrote, "I noticed in your list of Indians at the Little Bighorn, under the Northern Cheyenne, you have a note about Kate Big Head. You wonder if she was also known as Howling Woman, a name that appears in Liddic's book. Just wanted to confirm for you that this is the same person. Kate Big Head (c. 1848–1929) appears in the early Tongue River Reservation census records as Woman Yells or Howling Woman; later she is listed as Kate Big Head, wife of Samuel Big Head. That this is the same woman is confirmed by "John" Two Moons in 1923 who noted that Big Head was married to Kate 'but the Indians call her Howling Woman. She is blind....'"

Antelope—(Lakota-Teton Sioux)—Known to have been in the fighting and probably not the female Antelope from the Cheyenne tribe, above. Still living at the Standing Rock Agency, Bullhead, SD, 1926 [courtesy of Dickson].

Apache—(Northern Cheyenne). Tall—maybe around 6'2"—and heavy-set. An extremely fast runner. Member of the Elkhorn Scrapers society.

Appearance (*Tanin win*) (F)—(Hunkpapa Lakota-Teton Sioux)—b. circa 1865. Daughter of Charging Thunder and White Glass.

Appearing Bear—(Hunkpapa Lakota-Teton Sioux)—At the Rosebud fight.

Appearing Elk—(Hunkpapa Lakota-Teton Sioux)—Not certain he is a Hunkpapa or even Sioux for that matter, but Rain-in-the-Face reported he was slightly wounded in a charge on Custer Hill. In all likelihood, that would mean he is from this tribe.

Approaching White Buffalo (*Pte sanhinape win*) (F)—(Hunkpapa Lakota-Teton Sioux)—b. circa 1821. Listed in the Sitting Bull Surrender Ledger.

Approaching Woman (*Hinape win*) (F)—(Hunkpapa Lakota-Teton Sioux)—b. circa 1840. Daughter of Fire Cloud and Pretty Woman.

Arapaho Chief—(Northern Cheyenne)—At the Little Big Horn with his family.

Arapaho Chief "Laura" (F)—(Northern Cheyenne)—She was so scared when the attack began that she reputedly fainted.

Arapaho Chief "Lenora" (F)—(Northern Cheyenne)—A young girl at the time of the battle.

Arapaho Chief "Maud" (F)—(Northern Cheyenne)—There is some evidence that she was camped with her family on the so-called "north" side of the LBH when the attack occurred. The "north" said has traditionally been considered the actual east side of the river.

Around the Quiver—(Oglala Lakota–Teton Sioux)—Listed in the Crazy Horse surrender reg-ister, 1877. Along with Duck Belly and Sleeps There, listed as "head-of-household." Lodge consisted of one adult female; total of four people. Not absolutely certain he was at the LBH, though being listed in the ledger with two other adult males makes it a better than even chance he was there.

Ashes—(Sans Arc Lakota-Teton Sioux)—Head of the family. Part of Spotted Eagle's band [Dickson].

Asks for Water (*Mni-okin-ci-win*, probably translated as Water Beggar; aka Walks in the House) (F)—(Oglala Lakota-Teton Sioux)—d. before 1901. Wife of Club Man, sister of Crazy Horse.

Ass Hole (or Asshole)—(Oglala Lakota-Teton Sioux)—Listed in the Crazy Horse surrender register, 1877. Listed as "head-of-household," along with American Horse and Old. Their lodge consisted of four adult females and one male child; a total of eight people.

At the End—(Oglala Lakota-Teton Sioux)—Listed in the Crazy Horse surrender register, 1877. Along with Horned Horse and Sees the Cow, listed as "head-of-household." Lodge consisted of three adult females and one male child; total of seven people.

Attacking Bear (*Mato wata kpe*)—(Hunkpapa Lakota-Teton Sioux)—b. circa 1842. Listed in the Sitting Bull Surrender Ledger. Married to Princess.

Bad Bear—(Hunkpapa Lakota-Teton Sioux)—Fought Custer with Turning Hawk.

Bad Hand—(Hunkpapa Lakota-Teton Sioux)—Seven lodges (40 people), Sep 1876, at Standing Rock [Dickson].

Bad Hand—(Oglala Lakota-Teton Sioux)—Listed in the Crazy Horse surrender register, 1877. Listed as "head-of-household." Lodge consisted of two adult females, one male child, and one female child; total of five people.

Bad Heart Bull ("Amos" Bad Heart Bull; *Tatanka Cante Sica*; aka Eagle Bonnet; *Wanbli Wapaha,* as a young man, circa 1876)—(Oglala Lakota-Teton Sioux)—b. 1868–d. 1913. The son of Bad Heart Bull. He later became the artist for the Bad Heart Bull manuscript published by Blish with drawings of the Little Big Horn battle. There were more than four hundred drawings in his pictograph.

Bad Heart Bull (*Tatanka Cante Sica*)—(Oglala Lakota-Teton Sioux)—b. circa 1840 to 1846–d. 1913. One of three Lakota warriors to meet Reno's advance down the valley (Hard to Hit and Kicking Bear). This is the father of "Amos" Bad Heart Bull and brother of He Dog. Member of He Dog's Sore-back Band. Married to Red Blanket [Dickson].

Bad Horse—(Northern Cheyenne). Was at 1926 re-union.

Bad Lake—(Lakota — Teton Sioux)— In the village at the time of the Rosebud fight, 17 Jun 1876 [LBHA].

Bad Light Hair (aka Bad Yellow Hair)—(Oglala Lakota — Teton Sioux)— d. 25 Jun 1876, killed at the Little Big Horn fighting Custer's column. Body location unknown.

Bad Minneconjou—(Oglala Lakota — Teton Sioux)— Listed in the Crazy Horse surrender register, 1877. Along with Plenty Dogs, listed as "head-of-household." Lodge consisted of three adult females and two female children; a total of seven people. In the battle.

Bad Partisan—(Oglala Lakota — Teton Sioux)— Listed in the Crazy Horse surrender register, 1877. Along with Plenty Shells, Lone Elk, and Crazy Head, listed as "head-of-household." Lodge consisted of four adult females, two male children, and one female child; total of eleven people.

Bad Soup (aka Bad Juice)—(Hunkpapa Lakota — Teton Sioux)— Cousin of White Bull (the Minneconjou). May have been one of only a couple of warriors who rode with Gall during the Custer fight. Had been at Fort Lincoln and claimed to have recognized Custer. Presence confirmed by Myers, though he only lists him as a Teton Sioux. White Bull, in his 1930 interview with Walter Campbell, claimed Bad Soup was a brother-in-law of Sitting Bull.

Bad Sucker—(Oglala Lakota — Teton Sioux)— Listed in the Crazy Horse surrender register, 1877. Listed as "head-of-household." Lodge consisted of three adult females, two male children, and one female child; total of seven people.

Bad Warrior—(Lakota — Teton Sioux)— Still living, at the Cheyenne River Agency, 1926 [LBHA and CBHMA]. On Crazy Horse surrender ledger, 1877. Along with Wood Root, listed as "head-of-household." Lodge consisted of one female adult and one male child; four people, total.

Bad White Man—(Cheyenne)— He was listed in the Crazy Horse surrender ledger, 1877. Probably only a child at the time of the battle.

Badger (aka "John" Issues; or just, Issues)—(Northern Cheyenne). Presence confirmed by Myers. Still alive in 1926 and living at Lame Deer, Montana.

Badger (*Hoka*) (F)—(Oglala Lakota-Teton Sioux)— b. circa 1845. Wife of Running Eagle and mother of One Who Breaks.

Bald Bear—(Northern Cheyenne). A "Council of the 44" chief.

Bald Eagle—(Northern Cheyenne). Helped the boys bring in horses before going into battle. Presence confirmed by Myers.

Ball of the Foot—(Lakota-Teton Sioux).

Bank (*Maya*)—(Oglala Lakota-Teton Sioux)— Father of Respects Nothing [Dickson].

Beans (*Omni ca*) (F)—(Hunkpapa Lakota-Teton Sioux)— b. circa 1846. Wife of Wears the Fur Coat. Listed in the Sitting Bull Surrender Ledger.

Bear Bird—(Oglala Lakota-Teton Sioux)— Listed in the Crazy Horse surrender ledger, 1877. Along with Wrinkler, he was listed as "head-of-household." There were three adult females, two male children, and one female child in his lodge, a total of eight people.

Bear Bonnet—(Hunkpapa Lakota-Teton Sioux)

Bear Chasing—(Lakota-Teton Sioux)— At Cheyenne River Agency, 1926.

Bear Comes Out—(Hunkpapa Lakota-Teton Sioux)— In the Rosebud fight as well as the Little Big Horn. Still living at the Standing Rock Agency, Bullhead, SD, 1926 [courtesy of Dickson].

Bear Ears—(Hunkpapa Lakota-Teton Sioux)— Fought alongside Kill Eagle. Presence confirmed by Myers, though he only lists him as a Teton Sioux.

Bear Ghost—(Hunkpapa Lakota-Teton Sioux)— Apparently fought against Reno, saying Dorman was shot in the chest. LBHA lists him as a Blackfeet Sioux; I will keep him here.

Bear Horn (aka Bear with Horns; *Mato He Kici; Mato-heton*)—(Hunkpapa Lakota-Teton Sioux)— d. 25 Jun 1876, killed at the Little Big Horn. There may have been a Sans Arc named Bear with Horns (Hardorff lists one such man), who is sometimes cited as a Hunkpapa. Killed while chasing soldiers on Battle Ridge. Mortally wounded along west slope of Custer Ridge. It is possible he lasted a few days, dying on June 29. Myers has him listed as being killed in the valley fight. As a Hunkpapa, this is entirely possible, but it is strongly contradicted by the accounts of Standing Bear who claimed to have witnessed this part of the fighting [DeMallie, *The Sixth Grandfather*, p. 186]. Listed on the Sioux memorial.

Bear Horse—(Oglala Lakota-Teton Sioux)— At the 1926 reunion [LBHA].

Bear Jaw—(Oglala Lakota-Teton Sioux)— Listed in the Crazy Horse surrender ledger [CBHMA].

Bear King—(Lakota-Teton Sioux)—Fought alongside Kill Eagle. Presence confirmed by Myers, though he only lists him as a Teton Sioux.

Bear Lays Down ("Benjamin" Bear Lays Down; Bear Lying Down, or, Bear Down; Bear Comes to Lay Down; *Mato Gli Yunka*)—(Oglala Lakota-Teton Sioux)—b. circa 1850–d. 1936. Told of wild firing by Custer's troops [LBHA and CBHMA]. Interviewed by Walter Camp in 1914. [Dickson]

Bear Lice—(Minneconjou Lakota-Teton Sioux)—Counted coup in the Custer fight. Presence confirmed by Myers.

Bear Looking Back (also Bear Looking Behind; Bear Looks Back; *Mato haki kta*)—(Oglala Lakota-Teton Sioux)—b. circa 1848–d. 1901. Part of Big Road's band.

Bear Looking Back (also Looking Back Bear; *Mato haki kta*)—(Hunkpapa Lakota-Teton Sioux)—b. circa 1822. Listed in the Sitting Bull Surrender Ledger. Wife was White Buffalo Cow.

Bear Man—(Cheyenne).

Bear Paw—(Lakota-Teton Sioux)—Listed in the Crazy Horse surrender ledger, 1877. Listed as "head-of-household." Lodge consisted of himself and one adult female; two people, total.

Bear Rib—(Hunkpapa Lakota-Teton Sioux)—A sub-chief [Graham, *The Custer Myth*, p. 56]. Brother of Afraid of Eagles.

Bear Shield—(Hunkpapa Lakota-Teton Sioux). Still living at the Standing Rock Agency, Kenel, SD, in 1926 [courtesy of Dickson]. Participated in the battle.

Bear Sings—(Oglala Lakota-Teton Sioux)—An old man. Not certain he was at the battle.

Bear Soldier—(Hunkpapa Lakota-Teton Sioux)—Still living at Standing Rock Agency, Little Eagle, SD, in 1929. Known to have been in the camp during the battle, but he was not involved in the fighting.

Bear Star—(Oglala Lakota-Teton Sioux)—Listed in the Crazy Horse surrender ledger. Listed as "head-of-household." One female in his lodge, for a total of two people.

Bear Stop—(Minneconjou Lakota-Teton Sioux)—b. circa 1864. Because of the age it is highly doubtful there was any relationship between Bear Stop and the Oglala warrior listed below.

Bear Stops (*Mato Kinajan*)—(Oglala Lakota-Teton Sioux)—b. circa 1848–d. circa 1890s. Member of Big Road's band. There is the possibility that Bear Stops is the same man as Bear Looking Back, above. Because of the date of death, however, they are carried separately until further confirmed.

Bear Tail—(Northern Cheyenne). He and a Sioux killed a soldier who almost got away [LBHA].

Bear Thunder (aka Henry Bear Thunder—(Lakota-Teton Sioux)—At the Cheyenne River Agency, 1926.

Bear Walks on a Ridge (also Ridge Bear; Ridge Walker; Bear That Walks; Bear Who Walks on a Ridge)—(Northern Cheyenne). A headman of the Kit Foxes warrior society, or as Wooden Leg called him, one of the nine "little chiefs" [Marquis, *Wooden Leg*, p. 212]. He was in the village at the Bighorn Mountains that COL Reynolds attacked in early 1876, fighting there together with Two Moon, another Kit Fox little chief. Like all the other warrior society headman of the Northern Cheyenne, Ridge Bear was present at the LBH on 25 Jun 1876. Since the Kit Fox society provided the camp guards on the 25th, he *may* have fought at Ford B. In spring 1877 he was among those Cheyenne surrendering to General Miles at the Yellowstone. Presence confirmed by Myers.

Bear Whirlwind (*Mato Wamniyomni*)—(Oglala Lakota-Teton Sioux)—b. circa 1853. A grandson of Human Fingers and a member of Little Hawk's band.

Beard (aka Dewey Beard; Iron Hail)-(Minneconjou Lakota-Teton Sioux)—b. 1859–d. 3 Nov 1955. Seventeen years old at the battle. Standing Bear's brother. Last Indian survivor of the battle. Never made it to the Reno fight, but turned around to head downstream when he heard shooting at the lower end of the village. Took his Christian name from Admiral George Dewey. Presence confirmed by Myers, though he only lists him as a Teton Sioux.

Bearded Man—(Cheyenne)—d. 25 Jun 1876, killed at the Little Big Horn. Verified by Steven W. Myers, "Roster of Known Hostile Indians at the Battle of the Little Big Horn," *Research Review*, 1991, Vol. 5, No. 2. Ran in among Custer's troops and was killed. Later scalped by a Sioux who mistook him for a Ree.

Bear's Cap—(Hunkpapa Lakota-Teton Sioux)—Fought against Custer. Presence confirmed by Myers, though he only lists him as a Teton Sioux.

Bear('s) Face (*Mato Ite*; also possibly known as Bear's Head)—(Hunkpapa Lakota-Teton Sioux)—A brother of Rain-in-the-Face. If this is Bear's Head, he accompanied Sitting Bull into Canada.

Beautiful White Cow (F)—(Hunkpapa Lakota-Teton Sioux)—Sister of White Eyebrows.

Beaver Claws—(Northern Cheyenne)—b. 1818–d. 1905, a half-brother of Two Moon, father of Young Two Moons. A headman of the Crazy Dog warrior society or as Wooden Leg said, one of the nine "little chiefs" [Marquis, *Wooden Leg,* p. 212]. Presence confirmed by Myers.

Beaver Heart—(Northern Cheyenne). Fought in the valley fight [Myers, "Roster of Known Hostile Indians at the Battle of the Little Big Horn," *Research Review,* 1991, Vol. 5, No. 2]. Presence confirmed by Myers. At 1926 reunion [LBHA].

Belly—(Oglala Lakota-Teton Sioux)—Listed in the Crazy Horse surrender ledger, 1877. Along with Neck Prick, listed as "head-of-household." Lodge consisted of two adult females, three male children, and one female child; eight people, total.

Belly Fat (*Tejikjice*)—(Hunkpapa Lakota-Teton Sioux)—Six lodges (40 people), Sep 1876, at Standing Rock [Dickson].

Belly Full—(Oglala Lakota-Teton Sioux)—Listed in the Crazy Horse surrender ledger, 1877. Listed as "head-of-household." Lodge consisted of two adult females and three male children; six people in total.

Belly Inside—(Oglala Lakota-Teton Sioux)—Listed in the Crazy Horse surrender ledger, 1877. Listed as "head-of-household," his lodge consisting of two female adults, two male children, and three female children; a total of eight people.

Better Woman (*Awaste win*) (F)—(Hunkpapa Lakota-Teton Sioux)—b. circa 1861. Daughter of Spotted Eagle and Her Pretty Road.

Better Woman (*Wi waste ka*)—(Hunkpapa Lakota-Teton Sioux)—b. circa 1840. Son-in-law of Red Thunder and Ripe. Listed in the Sitting Bull Surrender Ledger.

Big Ankle(s)—(Minneconjou Lakota-Teton Sioux)—Lame Deer's nephew. One of the Indian sharpshooters on Sharpshooter's Ridge during the hilltop fight.

Big Beaver—(Northern Cheyenne). Seventeen years old at the time of the battle. Captured a gun from a dead soldier in the Keogh Sector, probably the soldier killed and represented by Marker 174 along the eastern fence of the park boundary. "A soldier got up and mounted his horse (this was one of Keogh's men, or Sorrel Horse Troop), and rode as fast as he could towards the east. This is the lone marker next to the fence to the east of the Keogh position. Two Cheyenne Indians cut him off and killed him. They then scalped him and hung the scalp on the sagebrush. I went over there and got the gun and some other things, and that was the

first gun I ever owned" [Hardorff, *The Custer Battle Casualties, II,* p. 131]. Presence confirmed by Myers. Attended the 1926 reunion.

Big Belly Mule—(Oglala Lakota-Teton Sioux)—Listed in the Crazy Horse surrender ledger. Along with Top Lodge, Iroquois Imitation, and Yellow Left, listed as "head-of-household." Lodge consisted of two female adults, one male child, and three female children; total of ten people.

Big Bend (*Kamni Tanka*)—(Oglala Lakota-Teton Sioux)—b. circa 1846. Older brother of Bird Man. Listed in the Crazy Horse surrender ledger, 1877. Along with Snake Creek, listed as "head-of-household." Lodge consisted of two adult females, two male children, and one female child; total of seven people. Present at the LBH.

Big Crow—(Northern Cheyenne)—d. 8 Jan 1877. A member of Little Wolf's band. He and Black White Man had spotted Custer's column camped on the Rosebud (near present-day Busby) on 24 June 1876. They didn't know who the soldiers were. One of three Indians — spotted by SGT Curtiss — rifling the hardtack box back on the soldiers' trail (Black Horse and Red Cherries were the other two). Member of the Crooked Lance Society. Presence confirmed by Myers.

Big Design—(Oglala Lakota-Teton Sioux)—d. 25 Jun 1876, killed at the Little Big Horn in the valley fight.

Big Eater—(Oglala Lakota-Teton Sioux)—Listed in the Crazy Horse surrender ledger. Along with White Bear and White Hair, he was listed as "head-of-household." There were four adult females, one male child, and two female children in his lodge, a total of ten people.

Big Elk—(Oglala Lakota-Teton Sioux)—Claimed Custer shot himself in the head [LBHA]. Presence confirmed by Myers.

Big Foot—(Northern Cheyenne). Cousin of Wolf Tooth. Riding east with Wolf Tooth and about 50 other warriors when the firing erupted from Reno's column. It may have been Wolf Tooth's band that Keogh's column was firing on from atop the Nye-Cartwright complex. One of the sharpshooters on Sharpshooters' Ridge firing on Reno's command. Presence confirmed by Myers.

Big Hawk—(Sans Arc Lakota-Teton Sioux)—Head of the family. Part of Spotted Eagle's band [Dickson].

Big Leg (*Hutanka*)—(Hunkpapa Lakota-Teton Sioux)—b. circa 1831. Listed in the Sitting Bull Surrender Ledger. Wife was Ticket.

Big Leggings (or Big Leggins)—(Lakota-Teton Sioux)—A half-blood who could read numerals. Told the Indians they had been fighting the 7th Cavalry. Presence confirmed by Myers, though he only lists him as a Teton Sioux.

Big Lodge Chimney—(Oglala Lakota-Teton Sioux)—Listed in the Crazy Horse surrender ledger, 1877. Listed as "head-of-household." Lodge consisted of one adult female, two male children, and two female children; a total of six people.

Big Man—(Oglala Lakota-Teton Sioux)—A leader during the battle. Presence confirmed by Myers.

Big Nose—(Lakota-Teton Sioux)—Presence confirmed by Myers, though he only lists him as a Teton Sioux.

Big Nose—(Northern Cheyenne). One of the few warriors at Ford B when Custer's column arrived there. A camp guard; one of five young men on the first night's watch. According to Pretty Shield, the wife of the Crow scout Goes Ahead, this is the man who shot Custer at Ford B. This is also in Stewart, *Custer's Luck,* p. 444. Along with Horse Road, Little Shield, Wooden Leg, and Yellow Horse, one of five camp guards designated while people slept on the night of the 25th–26th [Marquis, *Wooden Leg,* p. 257]. Presence confirmed by Myers. At 1926 reunion.

Big Owl—(Oglala Lakota-Teton Sioux)—Listed in the Crazy Horse surrender ledger, 1877. Along with Contrary and Mountain, listed as "head-of-household." Lodge consisted of two adult females, two male children, and one female child; total of eight people.

Big Road (*Canku Tanka*; also Wide Road; may also have been known as Bad Road)—(Oglala Lakota-Teton Sioux)—b. circa 1834–d. 1897. Considered a "Northern" Oglala and the leader of the True *Oyuhpe* band. A principal chief who fought Reno. Presence confirmed by Myers. If he is the same as Bad Road, he was one of the leaders who surrendered with Crazy Horse at Camp Robinson.

Big Thigh (also "John" Big Thigh)—(Northern Cheyenne). Living at Lame Deer in 1921 [LBHA].

Bird Man (*Zintkala Wicasa*)—(Oglala Lakota-Teton Sioux)—b. circa 1859. Member of Low Dog's band. Younger brother of Big Bend.

Black Bear (also "William" Black Bear)—(Oglala Lakota-Teton Sioux)—Early in the morning of 25 Jun 1876, he was east of the LBH with Dirt Kettle and Fast Horn—near the divide—looking for horses, when he spotted soldiers. He was heading back to the agency. Specifically mentioned by Standing Bear as one of those returning to warn

the village of the approaching soldiers. Hesitant to admit being in the battle, but known to have participated, admitting it years later. Still living at Standing Rock Agency, Little Eagle, SD, in 1929.

Black Bear—(Cheyenne)—d. killed at the Little Big Horn, 25 Jun 1876, probably during the Custer fighting, though Hardorff felt this man was an unidentified Cheyenne seen by White Bull and killed during the Reno fighting [*Lakota Recollections,* p. 123, footnote 38].

Black Bird—(Northern Cheyenne)—b. circa 1864 or 1865. Watched the fighting from the ridges.

Black Bird (*Zitka la sapa*)—(Hunkpapa Lakota-Teton Sioux)—b. circa 1844–d. at Wounded Knee, 15 Dec 1890 at Wounded Knee. Three lodges (20 people), Sep 1876, at Standing Rock. Listed in the Sitting Bull Surrender Ledger. Wife was Left Handed Woman [Dickson].

Black Body—(Lakota-Teton Sioux)—At Cheyenne River Agency in 1926.

Black Bull—(Brulé Lakota-Teton Sioux)—d. 1897. Wounded in the leg.

Black Bull—(Lakota-Teton Sioux)—He was a young boy at the time of the battle and was still living at the Cheyenne River Agency in 1926.

Black Cloud—(Cheyenne)—d. 25 Jun 1876, killed at the Little Big Horn fighting the Custer companies. Verified by Steven W. Myers, "Roster of Known Hostile Indians," *Research Review,* 1991, vol. 5, no. 2.

Black Coyote—(Northern Cheyenne)—d. Jun 1879; hanged. Husband of Buffalo Calf Road Woman. Ostracized and outcast by the Cheyenne for killing an old man, then hanged by the soldiers—along with Whetstone—for killing a sergeant who had given them food [Marquis, *Wooden Leg,* pp. 328–330].

Black Coyote (*Sungamanitsa*)—(Northern Cheyenne)—d. 25 Jun 1876, killed at the Little Big Horn. There is confusion with this name, as seen just above. Myers claims he was killed at the LBH, so it is just possible there were two men of the same name. I will carry them both, giving more credence to Wooden Leg's claim of the other one being Buffalo Calf Road Woman's husband.

Black Crane—(Northern Cheyenne). A "Council of the 44" chief. There is a "Black Grain" listed below. There is a possibility this might be the same man, but until there is further clarification they are carried as two different people.

Black Deer—(Oglala Lakota-Teton Sioux)—In the Rosebud fight.

Black Dog—(Sans Arc Lakota-Teton Sioux)— Head of the family. Part of Spotted Eagle's band [Dickson].

Black Eagle—(Northern Cheyenne). An old man at the time of the battle. A "Council of the 44" chief. Head chief of the Northern Scabby.

Black Eagle—(Sans Arc Lakota-Teton Sioux)—A tribal leader or "chief," as COL Nelson Miles referred to him in his October 28, 1876, dispatch. One of the five "hostages" designated by Miles during the surrender of 400–600 lodges and their return to the Cheyenne River Agency, October-December 1876. The others were Sun Rise, Red Skirt, White Bull, and Foolish Thunder.

Black Elk (also "Nicholas" Black Elk; *Heh*aka *Sapa)*—(Oglala Lakota-Teton Sioux)—b. 1863–d. Manderson, SD, 17 or 19 Aug 1950. Thirteen at the time of the battle. Son of Black Elk and White Cow Sees. In Reno fight; took two scalps. When he was on the hills to loot the dead soldiers, the warriors began to ride toward Weir Peak. On Crazy Horse surrender ledger. Went on to become a respected tribe holy man, and eventually a Roman Catholic. Presence confirmed by Myers as well as many others.

Black Elk—(Cheyenne). Probably joined the main village in early Jun 1876 with 10 lodges.

Black Elk (*Heh*aka *Sapa)*—(Minneconjou Lakota-Teton Sioux)—b. circa 1857. Member of Hump's band. Listed in the Crazy Horse surrender ledger, 1877. Listed as "head-of-household." Lodge consisted of one female adult and three male children, total of five. [Note—It is not certain which "Black Elk" is which, and this ledger entry may refer to "Nicholas" Black Hawk's father and family, above. If so, then this Minneconjou Black Hawk was also listed in the Crazy Horse ledger, but shared "head-of-household" with Feather Moon and Warms His Blanket. See those entries.]

Black Elk—(Oglala Lakota-Teton Sioux)—b. circa 1827–d. circa 1890. Father of "Nicholas" Black Elk. Medicine man and cousin of Crazy Horse (their grandfathers were brothers). Husband of White Cow Sees. Member of Low Dog's band. Listed in the Crazy Horse surrender ledger, 1877.

Black Eye Lid (also Black Eyelid)—(Oglala Lakota-Teton Sioux)—Listed in the Crazy Horse surrender ledger. Listed as "head-of-household." Also in his lodge were one adult female, one male child, and three female children, a total of six people.

Black Fox—(Oglala Lakota-Teton Sioux)—d. 25 Jun 1876, killed at the Little Big Horn. Father of the younger Black Fox.

Black Fox—(Oglala Lakota-Teton Sioux)—Son of the Black Fox who was killed. Presence confirmed by Myers. Still living at the Standing Rock Agency, Little Eagle, SD, in 1926 [courtesy of Dickson]. Known to have participated in the fighting.

Black Grain—(Northern Cheyenne). Surrendered to Miles in 1877. At the 1926 reunion [LBHA]. See "Black Crane," above.

Black Hawk—(Lakota-Teton Sioux)—Known to have been in the fighting at the Little Big Horn. Still living at the Standing Rock Agency, Wakpala, SD, 1926 [courtesy of Dickson].

Black Horse—(Northern Cheyenne). A member of Little Wolf's band. One of the three Cheyenne warriors seen by SGT Curtiss at the box of hardtack on the soldiers' trail (Big Crow and Red Cherries) [LBHA]. Presence confirmed by Myers.

Black Horse—(Sans Arc Lakota-Teton Sioux)— Head of the family. Part of Spotted Eagle's band [Dickson].

Black Kills—(Northern Cheyenne). Listed in the Crazy Horse surrender ledger [CBHMA].

Black Knife—(Northern Cheyenne). A headman of the Crazy Dogs warrior society, or as Wooden Leg said, one of the nine "little chiefs" [Marquis, *Wooden Leg,* p. 212]. Presence confirmed by Myers.

Black Legs—(Oglala Lakota-Teton Sioux).

Black Moccasin (aka Limber Lance; also seen as Dirty Moccasin[s]; also, Iron)—(Northern Cheyenne). Father of White Bull. A "Headman Chief," or Old Man Chief. There is confusion whether or not this is the same man as Dirty Moccasin, also listed by Myers as an Old Man Chief. For the time being, until more information is available, I list them separately. A "Council of the 44" chief. A principal chief of the Cheyenne. Myers claims he was the head of 170 lodges. Presence confirmed by Myers.

Black Moon (aka Old Black Moon)—(Hunkpapa Lakota-Teton Sioux)—Father of Young Black Moon. Surrendered at Standing Rock in 1881.

Black Moon—(Blackfeet Lakota-Teton Sioux)— May have been the head chief of this tribe at the Little Big Horn [Camp/Hammer, *Custer in '76,* p. 201].

Black Moon—(Hunkpapa Lakota-Teton Sioux)— d. 25 Jun 1876, killed at the Little Big Horn. A war leader of the Sioux "Fox Warrior Society," listed separately from the two other Hunkpapa Lakota-Teton Sioux Black Moons [Myers, "Roster of Known Hostile Indians at the Battle of the Little Big Horn," *Research Review,* Summer 1991, Vol. 5,

No. 2]. Fought Reno, then Custer. He was killed just after crossing the "Middle Ford" (Ford B).

Black Moon [No. 2] (*Wi Sapa*)-(Hunkpapa Lakota-Teton Sioux)— b. c. 1849 — Carried as Young Black Moon's brother who assumed the name upon the brother's death. A young man showed up in both the 1881 and 1885 Standing Rock census and it is just possible he was Young Black Moon's brother [Dickson]. Listed as a band leader in 1885 Standing Rock census.

Black Prairie Dog—(Lakota-Teton Sioux)— Living at Standing Rock Agency, Cannon Ball, ND, in 1929. Known to have been in the fighting at the Little Big Horn.

Black Quail (*Siyo sapa*)—(Hunkpapa Lakota-Teton Sioux)— b. circa 1851. Listed in the Sitting Bull Surrender Ledger. Brother of White Dog.

Black Ree—(Northern Cheyenne). Attended the 1908 gathering of Cheyenne at the battlefield [LBHA].

Black Road (*Canku Sapa*)—(Oglala Lakota-Teton Sioux)— b. circa 1836–d. 1910. An old medicine man. Member of He Dog's band.

Black Shawl Woman (also seen as just Black Shawl) (F)—(Oglala Lakota-Teton Sioux)— Sister of Red Feather and one of Crazy Horse's wives.

Black Shield—(Northern Cheyenne). Presence confirmed by Myers.

Black Shield (*Waha-chauka-sapa*)—(Minneconjou Lakota-Teton Sioux)— A "Sioux headman," probably one of the leading Sioux chiefs. He led the Minneconjou in the Fetterman fight. Presence confirmed by Myers.

Black Stone (also Black Whetstone)—(Northern Cheyenne). At the 1926 reunion. Friend of White Shield.

Black Sun—(Cheyenne). Killed in the Rosebud fight, 17 Jun 1876 [Marquis, *Wooden Leg,* p. 202].

Black Tongue (also "Frank" Black Tongue)— (Lakota-Teton Sioux)— At the Little Big Horn, but probably not in the fighting. Still living at the Standing Rock Agency, Fort Yates, ND, 1926 [courtesy of Dickson].

Black Tongue—(Lakota-Teton Sioux)— At Cheyenne River Agency in 1926.

Black Twin—(Oglala Lakota-Teton Sioux)— According to He Dog, someone named Black Twins had died in 1875. This is *not* the same person [Camp/Hammer, *Custer in '76* and CBHMA].

Black White Man (also "Thomas" Black White Man)—(Northern Cheyenne). Still alive in 1921 and living at Lame Deer, Montana. A member of Little Wolf's band. He and Big Crow had spotted Custer's column camped on the Rosebud (near present-day Busby) on 24 June. They didn't know who the soldiers were.

Black White Man—(Northern Cheyenne). A medicine man. This man is uncertain, but there was a medicine man of the same name who put Wooden Leg through a "medicine experience" in 1875. He is carried as separate from the man above.

Black White Man (*Wasichu Sapa*; Black *Wasichu*)—(Oglala Lakota-Teton Sioux)— d. 27 Jun 1876, of wounds suffered at the Little Big Horn. Mortally wounded on west slope of Custer Hill, though one source says he was found in the Deep Ravine/Cemetery Ravine area around Custer Hill. Died 27 Jun 1876 on Wood Lice Creek. Chase in the Morning's brother; Black Elk's cousin.

Black Wolf—(Northern Cheyenne). Befriended the late-arriving Arapaho, protecting them from the Sioux. A "Council of the 44" chief. Presence confirmed by Myers.

Blackbird—(Oglala Lakota-Teton Sioux)— Listed in the Crazy Horse surrender ledger, 1877. Listed as "head-of-household." Lodge consisted of one female adult, one male child, and three female children; six people, total.

Blind ("Silas" Blind)—(Oglala Lakota-Teton Sioux)— At the 1926 reunion.

Blind Water—(Lakota-Teton Sioux)— Appears in a 1926 photo of 12 veterans of the battle.

Blind Woman (# 1) (F)—(Lakota-Teton Sioux)— Listed in the Crazy Horse surrender ledger, 1877. Listed as "head-of-household." Lodge consisted of one other adult female and one female child; total of three people.

Blind Woman (# 2) (F)—(Lakota-Teton Sioux)— Listed in the Crazy Horse surrender ledger, 1877. Listed as "head-of-household." Lodge consisted of one other adult female; total of two people.

Bloody Knife—(Oglala Lakota-Teton Sioux)— Listed in the Crazy Horse surrender ledger, 1877. Along with the Shield, listed as "head-of-household." Lodge consisted of six adult females, three male children, and five female children; total of sixteen people.

Blue Cloud (also Blue Cloud Man)—(Oglala Lakota-Teton Sioux)— With Black Bear's party, watching the troops at the divide. Probably a member of Iron Crow's band.

Blue Cloud (*Mah pi yato*)—(Hunkpapa Lakota-Teton Sioux)— b. circa 1850. Left Standing Rock with Kill Eagle's band. Presence confirmed by Myers, though he only lists him as a Teton Sioux. Listed in the Sitting Bull Surrender Register.

Blue Coat—(Sans Arc Lakota-Teton Sioux)—Identified as a Sans Arc tribal leader.

Blue Hawk (*Cetan Tola*)—(Oglala Lakota-Teton Sioux)—b. circa 1825 [Dickson].

Blue Hawk (*Cetan Tola*)—(Oglala Lakota-Teton Sioux)—b. circa 1833. Member of Little Hawk's band. Father of Sacred Crow [Dickson].

Blue Horse (# 1)—(Lakota-Teton Sioux)—Existence assumed.

Blue Horse (also referenced as Blue Horse # 2, indicating another man of the same name)—(Oglala Lakota-Teton Sioux)—Listed in the Crazy Horse surrender ledger, 1877. Listed as "head-of-household." Lodge consisted of one adult female and one female child; three people, total.

Blue Mountain—(Hunkpapa Lakota-Teton Sioux)—b. circa 1870–d. early 1900s. Deaf-mute; just a child. Sitting Bull's adopted son and brother of Little Soldier. Son of Seen by the Nation.

Blue Thunder Woman (*Wakin yanto win*) (F)—(Hunkpapa Lakota-Teton Sioux)—b. circa 1821–d. 12 Dec 1881. Wife of Four Horns.

Bluff—(Oglala Lakota-Teton Sioux)—Listed in the Crazy Horse surrender ledger, 1877. Along with Four Crows, listed as "head-of-household." Lodge consisted of two adult females and one male child; total of five people.

Blunt Horn—(Oglala Lakota-Teton Sioux)—d. 1918.

Bob-tail Bear (also "Maurice" Bob-tail Bear)—(Lakota-Teton Sioux)—In the fighting at the Little Big Horn. Still living at the Standing Rock Agency, Bullhead, SD, 1926 [courtesy of Dickson].

Bob-tail Bull—(Hunkpapa Lakota-Teton Sioux)—Apparently identified 1SG Butler, saying he made every shot count. Still living at the Standing Rock Agency in 1929.

Bob-tail Hawk [Graham, *The Custer Myth*, p. 74]—(Lakota-Teton Sioux).

Bob-tail Horse—(Cheyenne)—b. 1850. One of the few warriors at Ford B when Custer's column arrived there. According to Myers, he was one of the first three Cheyenne to cross the river at Ford B to meet Custer and one of the first 10 to open fire on Custer's command. Captured two horses from the Gray Horse troop, bringing them back to the village [Myers, "Roster of Known Hostile Indians," *Research Review*, 1991, vol. 5, no. 2]. A

prominent warrior in the Elk Scraper Society or Elk Horn Society. Still alive in 1921 and living at Lame Deer, Montana. Attended the 1926 reunion. Presence confirmed by Myers.

Bone Club (F)—(Lakota-Teton Sioux)—In the camp at the Little Big Horn. Still living at the Standing Rock Agency, Wakpala, SD, 1926 [courtesy of Dickson].

Bone Tomahawk (*Huhu Canhpi*; also, Bone Club)—(Hunkpapa Lakota-Teton Sioux)—b. circa 1843. Prominent in Sitting Bull's band and listed in the Sitting Bull Surrender Ledger [Dickson]. Husband of Foot. Still living at the Standing Rock Agency, Wakpala, SD, 1926 [courtesy of Dickson]. Known to have been in the fighting at the Little Big Horn.

Box Elder (aka Dog Stands on a Ridge; known as Brave Wolf when he was a young man)—(Northern Cheyenne). Old and blind. Father of Brave Wolf. Head chief of the Northern *Suhtai*. A "Council of the 44" chief. His father had been named Horn, and like his father, he was a holy man and a prophet who warned of Custer's coming.

Boy (*Hoksi la*)—(Hunkpapa Lakota-Teton Sioux)—b. circa 1862. Son of Reaching Cloud and Red Woman.

Braided Locks (aka Wrapped Braids or Wrapped Hair; Braid; also "Arthur Brady")—(Northern Cheyenne)—b. circa 1842. A headman of the Kit Foxes warrior society, or as Wooden Leg called him, one of the nine "little chiefs" [Marquis, *Wooden Leg*, p. 212]. He was in the Powder River fight against Reynolds, 17 Mar 1876. Wounded in the cheek. Wounded in the Custer fight. Since the Kit Fox society were the camp guards on the 25th, he *may* have fought at Ford B. Wore a war bonnet. Presence confirmed by Myers. Living at Lame Deer, Montana, 1921. Still alive and at the Cheyenne River Agency in 1931.

Brave—(Oglala Lakota-Teton Sioux)—At the Cheyenne River Agency in 1926.

Brave Bear (*Mato ohitika*)—(Hunkpapa Lakota-Teton Sioux)—b. circa 1853. Listed in Sitting Bull's Surrender Ledger. Wife was named Fire. [See the Oglala Brave Bear entry.]

Brave Bear—(Oglala Lakota-Teton Sioux). This may have been one of the Indians wanted for murdering the Delorme family on July 5, 1873, near Pembina, DT. It was known that he was with Sitting Bull in Canada and surrendered with him. Brave Bear was hanged in 1881 for these crimes. [See the Hunkpapa Brave Bear entry.]

Brave Bear—(Southern Cheyenne). Fought against both Reno and Custer and considered the bravest man in the Reno fight, counting coup. Has an "honorary" distinction as the Indian who killed Custer [Stewart, *Custer's Luck,* p. 487]. Shot an officer riding a sorrel horse during the Custer fight. Presence confirmed by Myers.

Brave Bird—(Brulé Lakota-Teton Sioux)— Told of his part in the battle during an interview in 1941.

Brave Cow—(Lakota-Teton Sioux)— Counted coup in the Custer fight.

Brave Crow—(Lakota-Teton Sioux)— Sometimes confused with Brave Cow, above. Counted coup in the Custer fight. Presence confirmed by Myers, though he only lists him as a Teton Sioux.

Brave Hawk (aka Belly Fat)—(Lakota-Teton Sioux)— Fought alongside Kill Eagle. Presence confirmed by Myers, though he only lists him as a Teton Sioux.

Brave Heart—(Lakota-Teton Sioux)— d. 1934.

Brave Thunder (*Wakinyan Ohitika*)—(Hunkpapa Lakota-Teton Sioux)— b. circa 1845–d. 15 Dec 1890 at Wounded Knee. Wife was Tall Woman. Listed in the Sitting Bull Surrender Ledger.

Brave Wolf (aka Old Brave Wolf)— A fighting chief of the Northern Cheyenne. Son of Box Elder. He was a "Contrary," and as such "lived according to special rules and was thought to have special powers. His actions or speech might directly contradict what he was asked or what he wished" [Michno]. Fought Reno until the soldiers' panicked out of the timber. "…[I]nsisted that Custer's men came down close to the stream but did not succeed in crossing" [Stewart/Pennington]. Also, that there was some sharp fighting at the ford, that lasted quite a bit of time. Presence confirmed by Myers. There is some confusion here, however. The LBHA lists him dying in 1910, yet saying he was alive in 1926. They also list him as the second Cheyenne to enlist as a scout with Nelson Miles.

Brave Wolf—(Oglala Lakota-Teton Sioux)— d. circa 1879. Listed in the Crazy Horse surrender ledger, 1877. Along with Bad Horse (High White Man) and Red Shirt, listed as "head-of-household." Lodge consisted of three adult females, five male children, and three female children; total of fourteen people. Killed a couple of years later in Canada by Crow Indians.

Bread (*Aguyapi la*) (F)—(Hunkpapa Lakota-Teton Sioux)— b. circa 1868. Niece of Big Leg and Ticket. Listed in the Sitting Bull Surrender Ledger.

Breech Cloth (*Chegnaka Satapa*)—(Minneconjou Lakota-Teton Sioux)— b. circa 1861–d. 25 Jun 1876, killed at the Little Big Horn fighting on Reno

Hill, on the east side during an attempt to make a run against the soldiers' line. His horse threw him and when he tried to get up he was shot. This occurred after the remnants of the regiment had retreated off Weir Peaks and was back in its defensive positions on Reno Hill. Breech Cloth was between 13 and 15 years old at the time of his death.

Bridge Woman (F)—(Northern Cheyenne)— Remained in the village during most of the fighting.

Brings Home Yellow Horse (*Hinzi agli win*) (F)— (Hunkpapa Lakota-Teton Sioux)— b. circa 1868. Young girl at the time of the battle. Daughter of Bear Looking Back and White Buffalo Cow.

Brings News (F)—(Lakota-Teton Sioux)— Listed in the Crazy Horse surrender ledger, 1877, as "head-of-household," her lodge consisting of two other adult females, two male children, and one female child; six people, total.

Brings Plenty—(Hunkpapa Lakota-Teton Sioux) — In the end of the Custer fight. All likelihood a Hunkpapa (recognized by Iron Hawk/Runs in Circle). Killed one of the last two soldiers trying to escape. Possible confusion with the Oglala listed below.

Brings Plenty (*Ota Agli*; also Brings Back Plenty; "John" Brings Plenty)—(Oglala Lakota-Teton Sioux)— b. circa 1847–d. 1928. Part of Big Road's band. Killed a soldier with a war club. Presence confirmed by Myers, though he only lists him as a Teton Sioux.

Broad Tail—(Hunkpapa Lakota-Teton Sioux)— A chief and a leading warrior. May have been at the battle.

Broken Bear Rib (*Mato Cuwiyuksa*)—(Hunkpapa Lakota-Teton Sioux)— Possibly also known just as Bear's Rib. Four lodges (30 people), Sep 1876, at Standing Rock [LBHA/Dickson].

Broken Dish (aka Calfskin Shirt)—(Northern Cheyenne). A "Council of the 44" chief.

Broken Jaw—(Northern Cheyenne). A headman of the Elkhorn Scraper warrior society, or as Wooden Leg called him, one of the nine "little chiefs" [Marquis, *Wooden Leg,* p. 211]. Presence confirmed by Myers.

Brought (also "Pius" Brought)—(Lakota-Teton Sioux)— Known to have been in the fighting at the Little Big Horn. Still living at the Standing Rock Agency, Bullhead, SD, 1926 [courtesy of Dickson].

Brown Ass (aka Red End; Brown Back; *Ozogila*)— (*Wahpekute*/Dakota-Santee Sioux)— One of those who discovered the troops at the divide, returning to give warning. Presence confirmed by Myers.

Brown Bird—(Northern Cheyenne).

Brown Eagle—(Hunkpapa Lakota-Teton Sioux)—One of those alarming the camp.

Brown Wolf (also "Joseph" Brown Wolf)—(Minneconjou Lakota-Teton Sioux)—b. circa 1870–d. 1902. Only six years old at the time of the battle. Son of Owl King and Touch on Head.

Brown Wolf—(Lakota-Teton Sioux)—Still living at the Cheyenne River Agency in 1926.

Brughier, John—(*Wahpekute*/Dakota-Santee Sioux)—A half-breed Santee, he was "a fugitive from Standing Rock Agency as a result of an outstanding arrest warrant for a murder which took place in December 1875…" [Liddic, *Vanishing Victory*, p. 171]. He was in the Hunkpapa circle, though his wife denied that he actually took part in the fighting.

Brulé Woman (aka "Mary" Fine Weather) (F)—(Lakota-Teton Sioux)—Wife of Fine Weather.

The Bud—(Oglala Lakota-Teton Sioux)—Listed in the Crazy Horse surrender ledger. Along with Whistler, listed as "head-of-household." Lodge consisted of three adult females and two female children, seven people in total.

Buffalo Bull—(Minneconjou Lakota-Teton Sioux)—A minor war chief.

Buffalo Calf (also seen listed as Calf)—(Northern Cheyenne). One of the few warriors at Ford B when Custer's column arrived there. Member of the Crazy Dog warrior society. Presence confirmed by Myers, although he also lists a warrior named Calf, another source claiming they are the same person. They are listed here separately. Still alive in 1926.

Buffalo Calf Pipe—(Hunkpapa Lakota-Teton Sioux)—Medicine man. Presence confirmed by Myers.

Buffalo Calf Road Woman (aka Brave Woman) (F)—(Northern Cheyenne)—d. 1879. Wife of Black Coyote; she fought with him. Sister of Comes in Sight. Presence confirmed by Myers. She died while her husband—Black Coyote—was in jail for killing an army sergeant [Marquis, *Wooden Leg*, p. 330].

Buffalo Horse—(Brulé Lakota-Teton Sioux)—Followed the soldiers for two days, then cut across to the LBH to join Sitting Bull.

Buffalo Paunch—(Cheyenne).

The Bugger—(Oglala Lakota-Teton Sioux)—Listed in the Crazy Horse surrender ledger, 1877. Listed as "head-of-household." Lodge consisted of one adult female and three male children; total of five people.

Bull—(Minneconjou Lakota-Teton Sioux)—Fought alongside Kill Eagle. Member of Bad Hand's band. Presence confirmed by Myers, though he only lists him as a Teton Sioux.

The Bull—(Oglala Lakota-Teton Sioux)—Listed in the Crazy Horse surrender ledger, 1877. Along with Shits on His Hand, listed as "head-of-household." Lodge consisted of one other person, a female adult; three people, total.

Bull Bear—(Southern Cheyenne). Chief of Dog Soldiers. In both the Reno and Custer fights. Presence confirmed by Myers.

Bull Dog [Graham, *The Custer Myth,* p. 74]—(Brulé Lakota-Teton Sioux).

Bull Eagle-(Minneconjou Lakota-Teton Sioux)—d. 16 Dec 1876 or Apr 1877. Killed attempting to surrender to Nelson Miles. One of the leaders meeting with Miles in October 1876 to discuss terms of surrender.

Bull Hawk—(Teton-Sioux)—The only reference found is in the *Army and Navy Journal,* dated 12 May 1877, but apparently one of five Sioux leaders to have surrendered with Crazy Horse to Lieutenant Philo Clark at Camp Robinson.

Bull Head—(Hunkpapa Lakota-Teton Sioux)—d. 18 Dec 1890. Fought with Sitting Bull at LBH.

Bull Head—(Southern Cheyenne). Supposedly removed a compass from Custer's pocket [LBHA].

Bull Hump (also Hump; he may have also been known as Buffalo Hump)—(Northern Cheyenne). He claimed Two Moons was the chief warrior of the Cheyenne during the battle due to the absence of other chiefs. May have been part of Little Wolf's band out of the Red Cloud Agency in Nebraska.

Bull Man—(Oglala Lakota-Teton Sioux)—Listed in the Crazy Horse surrender ledger. Along with the Last, Sitting Horse, and White Rabbit, he is listed as "head-of-household." In addition, his lodge had one adult female, three male children, and three female children; eleven people in all.

Bull Proof (F)—(Lakota-Teton Sioux)—Listed in the Crazy Horse surrender ledger, 1877. Listed as "head-of-household." Lodge consisted of two other adult females, one male child, and one female child; five people, total.

Bull Tail ("Clara" Bull Tail) (F) [LBHA]—(Cheyenne).

Bull Thigh ("John" Bull Thigh)—(Cheyenne). Still alive in 1921 and living at Lame Deer, Montana.

Bull Wallowing—(Northern Cheyenne). Had fought Fetterman, Crook, and Custer before ultimately becoming an agency policeman.

Bull's Ghost [Graham, *The Custer Myth,* p. 74]—(Lakota-Teton Sioux).

Bullet Proof (aka Bullets Not Harm Him)—(Northern Cheyenne). Wore White Shield's war shirt in the battle [LBHA]. Presence confirmed by Myers.

Bulls Keep ("Martin" Bulls Keep)—(Cheyenne). Still alive in 1921 and living at Lame Deer, Montana.

Burst Thunder—(Lakota-Teton Sioux)—Told some Sioux that a dead Ree should be scalped. The dead man turned out to be Lame White Man, the Cheyenne chief. Certainly in the Custer fighting.

Butt Horn—(Oglala Lakota-Teton Sioux)—Listed in the Crazy Horse surrender ledger, 1877. Along with Ear Ring Prick, listed as "head-of-household." Lodge consisted of one adult female and one female child; total of four people.

Calf—(Cheyenne). Presence confirmed by Myers, although he also lists a warrior named Buffalo Calf, another source claiming they are the same person. I list them separately. Also like Buffalo Calf, a member of the Crazy Dog Warrior Society. Like Buffalo Calf, one of the warriors who initially defended at Ford B.

Callous Leg—(Lakota-Teton Sioux)—Known to have been in the fighting at the Little Big Horn. Still living at the Standing Rock Agency, Fort Yates, ND, 1926 [courtesy of Dickson]. There is also a Scar Leg, sometimes referred to as Callous Leg, but they are not the same man.

Camps as He Comes—(Sans Arc Lakota-Teton Sioux)—Head of the family. Part of Spotted Eagle's band [Dickson].

Cannonball Woman (aka "Hattie Lawrence") (F)—(Hunkpapa Lakota-Teton Sioux)—b. circa 1866. Eventually, the wife of Kill Assiniboine.

Carries the Badger—(Oglala Lakota-Teton Sioux). Probably a member of Low Dog's band.

Catch the Bear-(Hunkpapa Lakota-Teton Sioux)—d. 15 Dec 1890 at Wounded Knee.

Cedar Woman (*Hante win*) (F)—(Hunkpapa Lakota-Teton Sioux)—b. circa 1844. Wife of Killed by Thunder.

Center Feather (*Wiyaka Cokanya*)—(Oglala Lakota-Teton Sioux)—b. circa 1859. Member of Low Dog's band. His mother was Red Shell. He was listed as a member of Little Hawk's band in the 1881 annuity list [Dickson].

Charcoal Bear (aka Coal Bear)—(Cheyenne). Holy man and keeper of *Esevone,* the sacred buffalo hat. Joined the main band of Indians at their first camp on the Rosebud. He brought a lot of other Cheyenne with him [Marquis, *Wooden Leg,* p. 187]. Presence confirmed by Myers.

Charge the Tiger—(Hunkpapa Lakota-Teton Sioux).

Charger ("Samuel" Charger)—(Minneconjou Lakota-Teton Sioux)—Was at Slim Buttes, so probably the LBH as well.

Charger—(Two Kettles Lakota-Teton Sioux).

Charging Hawk—(Minneconjou Lakota-Teton Sioux)—Beard watched as Charging Hawk killed a tall, buckskin-clad soldier who Beard thought might be the "soldier leader, " right near the end of the battle [*Lakota Noon*]. (See "Hawk," a Cheyenne.) The LBHA carries him as a Brulé, but this appears to be incorrect. Listed in the Crazy Horse surrender ledger, 1877. Along with Red Tail, listed as "head-of-household." Lodge consisted of four adult females and three male children; total of nine people.

Charging Hawk—(Oglala Lakota-Teton Sioux)—b. circa 1828 [Dickson]. These are different men, by birth date. Both were listed in the Sitting Bull Surrender Ledger.

Charging Hawk—(Oglala Lakota-Teton Sioux)—b. circa 1836 [Dickson]. These are different men, by birth date. Both were listed in the Sitting Bull Surrender Ledger.

Charging Hawk—(Oglala Lakota-Teton Sioux; also seen listed as a Brulé)—b. circa 1868. Listed in the Crazy Horse surrender ledger, 1877. Eight years old at the battle. Related a story about seeing a bulldog on the battlefield.

Charging Shield—(Oglala Lakota-Teton Sioux).

Charging Thunder (also Attacking Thunder; Chase the Thunder; *Wakinyan wata kpe*)—(Hunkpapa Lakota-Teton Sioux)—b. circa 1837. His band of warriors was called Fresh Meat Necklace (*Talonapin*). He may not have been chief of this band until after 1880. Wife was White Glass. Listed in the Sitting Bull Surrender Ledger.

Chase in the Morning—(Oglala Lakota-Teton Sioux)—Black White Man's brother.

Chase Them Wounded (*Wanapa Wakuwa*; also seen as Chasing Them Wounded; Chase Wounded; Chasing with an Arrow; Chase with Arrows)-(Assiniboine/Hunkpapa Lakota-Teton Sioux)—b. circa 1868–d. 15 Dec 1890; killed at Standing Rock with his father (Little Assiniboine) and his "adopted uncle," Crow Feet. Often mistaken as Sitting Bull's son, but he was actually the son of Jumping Bull, an Assiniboine, who was adopted by Sitting Bull after his parents were killed. Technically, that would make him Sitting Bull's "grandson." Married to Chooses, probably around 1890. They had a son, born in 1890 and named Little Shield [Dickson]. Both Chase Them Wounded and Jumping Bull were killed during the attempt to arrest Sitting Bull in 1890 on the Standing Rock Reservation.

Chased by Owls (or Chase by Owl and other variations)—(Two Kettles Lakota-Teton Sioux)—d. 25 Jun 1876, killed at the Little Big Horn during Reno's retreat from the timber.

Chasing (*Waku wa la*)—(Hunkpapa Lakota-Teton Sioux)—b. circa 1867. A young boy at the time of the battle. Son of Charging Thunder and White Glass.

Chasing Alone (aka Hunting Alone; *Isnawa kuwa*)—(Hunkpapa Lakota-Teton Sioux)—b. circa 1841. Wife was Whirlwind. Listed in the Sitting Bull Surrender Ledger.

Chasing Eagle—(Hunkpapa Lakota-Teton Sioux)—In the Rosebud fight.

Chasing Hawk (*Cetan Wakuwa*; possibly also known as Chief Boy)—(Oglala Lakota-Teton Sioux)—b. circa 1846–d. prior to 1886. His mother was Comes Above. Member of Low Dog's band [Dickson]. It is unknown if this is the same person as Chief Man, below. They are carried separately.

Chat-ka (aka Left Hand)—(Hunkpapa Lakota-Teton Sioux)—d. 25 Jun 1876, killed at the Little Big Horn. Had been an army scout at Fort Lincoln before the battle. Body found in an abandoned tepee in the valley. He was Sioux, but specific tribe unknown. He enlisted as a soldier scout on 9 Dec 1875. These enlistments lasted six months, so he was mustered out, probably on 9 Jun 1876, but he was on the campaign and was sent back to FAL during the snowstorm of 1–2 Jun 1876. After mustering out, he joined his own people and his horse and body were discovered in the Sioux village after the battle [Camp/Hammer, *Custer in '76,* pages 194 and 284].

Cheyenne Woman (F)—(Minneconjou Lakota-Teton Sioux)—Married to White Swan, probably around 1863. She was his second wife or possibly wife # 2.

Cheyenne Woman (*Sahun win la*) (F)—(Hunkpapa Lakota-Teton Sioux)—b. circa 1831. Mother of Red Hair Woman and the second wife of Bone Tomahawk. Listed in the Sitting Bull Surrender Ledger.

The Chief—(Oglala Lakota-Teton Sioux)—Listed in the Crazy Horse surrender ledger, 1877. Listed as "head-of-household." Lodge consisted of two adult females, one male child, and one female child; five people, total.

Chief Going up a Hill—(Cheyenne)

Chief Man—(Oglala Lakota-Teton Sioux)—Listed in the Crazy Horse surrender ledger, 1877. Listed as "head-of-household." Lodge consisted of two adult females and one female child; total of four people. Present at the LBH.

Circle Bear [Graham, *The Custer Myth,* p. 74]—(Lakota-Teton Sioux).

Circled Lodge (F)—(Lakota-Teton Sioux)—Listed in the Crazy Horse surrender ledger, 1877. Listed as "head-of-household." Lodge consisted of herself and one other adult female; two people, total.

Circling Bear (*Mato Kawinge*)—(Hunkpapa Lakota-Teton Sioux).

Circling Hawk (aka Turning Hawk)—(Hunkpapa Lakota-Teton Sioux)—Still living in the Standing Rock Agency, Little Eagle, SD, in 1929. Know to have fought in the battle.

Circling Hawk—(Oglala Lakota-Teton Sioux).

Climbing Tent (*Tiali*)—(Hunkpapa Lakota-Teton Sioux)—b. 1867. Young boy at time of battle. Son of Takes the Gun.

Closed Hand (aka Black Bear or Fist or Crippled Hand. Also possibly Young Bear)—(Northern Cheyenne)—d. 25 Jun 1876, killed at the Little Big Horn. A "suicide warrior," pledged to sacrifice his life for his tribe. Killed on the north slope of Custer Hill. Son of Long Roach. Wooden Leg claimed he was twenty years old at the battle [Marquis, *Wooden Leg,* p. 268]. "[O]ne of the Indians seen by Varnum on the divide ... killed early in the fight as he ran up a steep slope on the north side" [Myers, "Roster of Known Hostile Indians at the Battle of the Little Big Horn," *Research Review,* Summer 1991, Vol. 5, No. 2, p. 5].

Cloud Man (*Mahepiye-wichorta*)—(Sans Arc Lakota-Teton Sioux)—d. 25 Jun 1876, killed at the Little Big Horn. Body location unknown, but killed fighting Custer's column.

Clown (# 1)—(Oglala Lakota-Teton Sioux)—Listed in the Crazy Horse surrender ledger, 1877. Along with Saddle, listed as "head-of-household." Lodge consisted of two adult females, two male children, and one female child; totaling seven people.

Clown (# 2)—(Lakota-Teton Sioux)—Listed in the Crazy Horse surrender ledger, 1877. Along with

He Dog, the Lights, Wound in Back, and one other whose name appeared illegible, listed as "head-of-household." Lodge consisted of three adult women and three male children; total of eleven people.

Clown—(Lakota-Teton Sioux)—Only a young boy at the time of the battle. Still living at the Cheyenne River Agency in 1926.

Club Man (*Cannaska Yuha;* also seen as War Club; Has a War Club; Keep the War Club; and Owns the War Club)—(Oglala Lakota-Teton Sioux)—b. circa 1835–d. early 1880's, probably between 1882 and 1886 [Dickson, *LBHA Newsletter,* April 2008]. Rumored to have played a major part in Custer's defeat. Visited the battlefield with Phil Sheridan in 1877. Older brother of Little Killer. A brother-in-law of Crazy Horse. Married Crazy Horse's older sister—*Mni-okin-ci-win,* probably translated as Water Beggar or Asks for Water—some time before 1864. Father of Eagle Horse (a son), and two daughters, Recognizing Horse and Wounded Twice. Said that five soldiers broke from the hill and all were killed [LBHA]. Hardorff misidentified him as a Minneconjou [Dickson, *LBHA Newsletter,* "Warrior Club Man was Relative of Crazy Horse," April 2008]. Listed in the Crazy Horse surrender ledger, 1877. Along with Owns Arrow [Little Killer], listed as "head-of-household." Lodge consisted of two female adults, two male children, and three female children; total of nine people.

Clumsy Legs (*Inahpa*)—(Hunkpapa Lakota-Teton Sioux)—b. 1873. Only a small child at the time of the battle. Son of Spotted Eagle and Her Pretty Road.

Cockeyed Woman (F)—(Lakota-Teton Sioux)—Listed in the Crazy Horse surrender ledger, 1877. Listed as "head-of-household." Lodge consisted of one other adult female, two male children, and one female child; five people, total.

Coffee—d. late Jun or early July 1876; accident. Considered a Northern Cheyenne, though he was originally a Southern Cheyenne. Accidentally killed by his own rifle while dismounting a few days after the battle. A helper to the medicine chief. An old man; not married.

Combing—(Lakota-Teton Sioux)—At Cheyenne River Agency in 1926.

Combs (also "Leo" Combs)—(Lakota-Teton Sioux)—Still living at the Standing Rock Agency, Bullhead, SD, in 1926 [courtesy of Dickson]. He was involved in the fighting.

Comes Above (F)—(Oglala Lakota-Teton Sioux)—Mother of Chasing Hawk.

Comes Again—(Oglala Lakota-Teton Sioux)—Lived to at least 86 years old [Stewart, *Custer's Luck,* opposite p. 145]. Listed in the Crazy Horse surrender ledger [CBHMA]. In the battle; presence confirmed by Myers, though he only lists him as a Teton Sioux.

Comes Among Others (*Egna Ku win*) (F)—(Oglala Lakota-Teton Sioux)—b. 1869. Daughter of High White Man.

Comes Among the Camps (*Tiegnaku win*) (F)—(Hunkpapa Lakota-Teton Sioux)—b. circa 1836. Married to Crazy Dog.

Comes Back Holy (F)—(Minneconjou Lakota-Teton Sioux)—Wife of "Joe" Owl King; mother of "Phillip" Brown Wolf. There is some confusion between this person and another woman named Touch on Head. They may be the same person, though the names are always reported separately. If two different women, then both were wives of Owl King. The "mother" of Brown Wolf only adds to the confusion.

Comes Back with Growling (*Hna kula*)—(Hunkpapa Lakota-Teton Sioux)—b. circa 1868. Only eight at the time of the battle. Listed in the Sitting Bull Surrender Ledger. Younger brother of Kills in Lodge.

Comes Flying (*Kinyanhiyiye*)—(Minneconjou Lakota-Teton Sioux)—Presence confirmed by Myers.

Comes from War—(Oglala Lakota-Teton Sioux)—Listed in the Crazy Horse surrender ledger, 1877. Along with Four Bullets and Wood Boat, listed as "head-of-household." Lodge consisted of three adult females, one male child, and four female children; total of eleven people.

Comes in Sight (aka Coming Up; Chief Comes in Sight; Chief Coming Up)—(Northern Cheyenne). Living in Oklahoma at the age of 66. Made a "brave" run at C Company troopers. Wore a war bonnet. His sister was Buffalo Calf Road Woman. Presence confirmed by Myers.

Comes out with Words (*Iahi nape win*) (F)—(Hunkpapa Lakota-Teton Sioux)—b. circa 1864. Daughter of Bear Looking Back and White Buffalo Cow.

Comes the Day (also seen as Comes in Day)—(Oglala Lakota-Teton Sioux)—Listed in the Crazy Horse surrender ledger, 1877. Along with Grandfather, listed as "head-of-household." Lodge consisted of two adult females, four male children, and one female child; total of nine people.

Contrary—(Oglala Lakota-Teton Sioux)—Listed in the Crazy Horse surrender ledger, 1877. Along with Big Owl and Mountain, listed as "head-of-household." Lodge consisted of two adult females, two male children, and one female child; total of eight people.

Contrary Belly (aka Buffalo Bull Wallowing)—(Northern Cheyenne). In the charge that stampeded some horses in Custer's column. Presence confirmed by Myers.

Corn (also "Charlie" Corn)—(Northern Cheyenne). At the 1926 reunion.

Corn—(Oglala Lakota-Teton Sioux). There is some evidence—tenuous—that there was another Corn, an Oglala, in addition to the Cheyenne, above. Bruce Liddic claimed there was an Oglala named Corn [*Vanishing Victory*, p. 107].

Cotton Man—(Lakota-Teton Sioux)—Fought Custer's troops, taking a soldier's carbine [LBHA].

Count (also "Fredolin" Count)—(Lakota-Teton Sioux)—Living at the Standing Rock Agency, Little Eagle, SD, in 1926 [courtesy of Dickson]. At the camp, but he was either too young to participate in the fighting or he simply did not get into the battle.

Cow Walking—(Minneconjou Lakota-Teton Sioux)—Son of Horned Horse and brother of White Eagle. Retrieved his brother's body from the Reno field.

Crab—(Oglala Lakota-Teton Sioux)—A young man and friend of Black Elk.

Crane Woman (aka Buffalo Cow) (F)—(Southern Cheyenne)—Lame White Man's daughter with Twin Woman.

Crawler—(Oglala Lakota-Teton Sioux)—Listed in the Crazy Horse surrender ledger [CBHMA].

Crazy Bear—(Oglala Lakota-Teton Sioux)—Listed in the Crazy Horse surrender ledger, 1877. Along with Skunk Guts, listed as "head-of-household." Lodge consisted of one female adult, one male child, and three female children; a total of seven people.

Crazy Brain (*Manla Witko*; aka "Joseph" Eagle Hawk; also known as Shot from House; *Ti Tanhan Opi*)—(Oglala Lakota-Teton Sioux)—b. circa 1869 to 1873. Son of Eagle Hawk. Often seen shown as a "son" of He Dog, he was actually a nephew [Dickson].

Crazy Dog (also Mad Dog; sometimes mistranslated as Crazy Horse; *Sungna ikinyan*)—(Hunkpapa Lakota-Teton Sioux)—b. circa 1836. Listed in the Sitting Bull Surrender Ledger. Married to Comes Among the Camps.

Crazy Hawk—(Lakota-Teton Sioux)—Living at the Standing Rock Agency in 1929.

Crazy Head—(Northern Cheyenne). Father was a Cheyenne, his mother a captured Crow. Listed as a Cheyenne war chief in the LBHA's Summer 2001 *Research Review*. A "Council of the 44" chief. Considered the third-ranking Cheyenne in the battle [CBHMA]. Wooden Leg called him "the most important tribal big chief" [Marquis, *Wooden Leg*, p. 211]. Fought Custer's column. Wore a war bonnet. Presence confirmed by Myers.

Crazy Head—(Oglala Lakota-Teton Sioux)—Listed in the Crazy Horse surrender ledger, 1877. Along with Plenty Shells, Lone Elk, and Bad Partisan, listed as "head-of-household." Lodge consisted of four adult females, two male children, and one female child; total of eleven people.

Crazy Heart—(Minneconjou Lakota-Teton Sioux)—One of Lame Deer's sons. A "shirt wearer." Presence confirmed by Myers.

Crazy Heart—(Oglala Lakota-Teton Sioux)—Listed in the Crazy Horse surrender ledger. Along with Living Bear and Hoarse, listed as "head-of-household." Lodge consisted of five adult females and three male children, eleven people in total.

Crazy Horse (or *Tashunca-uitco;* birth name was Light Hair; then Curly)-(Oglala Lakota-Teton Sioux)—b. near Bear Butte (near present-day Sturgis, SD), 1839 or late fall, 1840–d. Fort Robinson, Nebraska, around midnight, 5 Sep 1877, or into the early hours of 6 Sep 1877; dying possibly as late as 7 Sep 1877, though this is highly doubtful. Small, fair-skinned, with narrow face, 5'6" to 5'7" tall, lithe and sinewy. Some say he had sandy-colored hair. No photographs of Crazy Horse are known to exist. Photographers Maude and Langdon Clay of Sumner, MS, have a painting thought to be the only one ever done of Crazy Horse [Beth Ann Fennelly, "If These Walls Could Talk," *Oprah At Home*, Summer 2008, pp. 127–128]. Father was named Worm—originally also Crazy Horse—an Oglala holy man; and his mother was Rattle Blanket Woman, thought to be a Brulé, though some say a Minneconjou of the Cheyenne River Sioux (whose chief was Touch the Clouds). His mother committed suicide when Crazy Horse was four, though Black Elk refers to "his mother" and father taking his body away after he died. This was clearly his stepmother.

"Among the Sioux, Horse ... ranked as senior ... of the four principal chiefs of an organization equivalent to the Medicine Lances of the Cheyennes. That is to say, he was of equal rank with the late Roman Nose, Red Cloud, Spotted Tail and others. He wore the long white 'stole' over his shoulders as insignia, and also to tie himself to his planted lance in a fight to the death" [Frank H.

Huston, Graham, *The Custer Myth,* p. 80]. Presence confirmed by Myers. Crazy Horse surrendered at the Red Cloud Agency in May 1877, along with 899 of his followers [1877 Report of the Secretary of the Interior]. At the time, his household consisted of Tall Bull — an adult male — and three adult females and two male children, a total of seven people.

His remains were buried, secretly, by his father, somewhere in northern Nebraska or southern South Dakota.

Crazy Mule—(Northern Cheyenne). A headman of the Crazy Dogs warrior society, or as Wooden Leg said, one of the nine "little chiefs" [Marquis, *Wooden Leg,* p. 212]. This is *not* the same man who was in the Fetterman fight.

Crazy Thunder [Graham, *The Custer Myth,* p. 74] —(Lakota-Teton Sioux).

Crazy Wolf—(Cheyenne). Presence confirmed by Myers.

Crooked Mouth (F)—(Lakota-Teton Sioux)— Listed in the Crazy Horse surrender ledger, 1877. Listed as "head-of-household." Lodge consisted of one other adult female, two people total.

Crooked Nose (F)—(Northern Cheyenne)—d. 1877. Wooden Leg's older sister. Killed herself while in captivity.

Crooked Nose—(Northern Cheyenne). He was in the valley fight, infiltrating the woods. Some of his shots — along with those of Turkey Leg and Old Man — may have hit and killed Company M's Klotzbucher and Lorentz. Wore a war bonnet in the battle. Presence confirmed by Myers.

Cross Bear—(Lakota-Teton Sioux)— Living at the Standing Rock Agency in 1929.

Cross Bear (*Mato Ocinsica*)—(Hunkpapa Lakota-Teton Sioux)—*Cankahuran* band, along with Running Antelope [Dickson/Bray].

Cross Prick—(Oglala Lakota-Teton Sioux)— Listed in the Crazy Horse surrender ledger, 1877 [CBHMA].

Crossed Eagle Quills (F)—(Sans Arc Lakota-Teton Sioux)— b. circa 1865. Her parents were Red Bear and *Tasunke Topa Naun kewin.* Went to Canada with Sitting Bull.

Crossways—(Oglala Lakota-Teton Sioux)— Listed in the Crazy Horse surrender ledger. Listed as "head-of-household," his lodge consisting of one female adult and one male child; three people, total.

Crow—(Hunkpapa Lakota-Teton Sioux)— Said to have given the first war cry at the battle. With Sitting Bull in Canada in 1877.

Crow, "John"—(Lakota-Teton Sioux)— At the Cheyenne River Agency, 1926.

Crow Bear—(Lakota-Teton Sioux)— Said the battle lasted as long as it takes to walk a mile [LBHA].

Crow Bow—(Minneconjou Lakota-Teton Sioux).

Crow Boy—(Sans Arc Lakota-Teton Sioux)— Fought Custer's column. Presence confirmed by Myers, though he only lists him as a Teton Sioux.

Crow Dog—(Oglala Lakota-Teton Sioux)— d. 1910. Fought on Custer Hill and caught three horses. His wife was One Who Walks with the Stars. One source had him listed as a Brulé, but enough evidence exists to carry him as an Oglala. Presence confirmed by Myers, who also has him as an Oglala.

Crow Feet (*Kangi siha*; also seen as Crow Foot)— (Hunkpapa Lakota-Teton Sioux)— b. circa 1874– d. killed at Standing Rock with his father, Sitting Bull, Dec 1890. Only an infant at the time of the battle.

Crow King (aka Patriarch Crow; *Kangi Yatapi* or *Kangi-yatipika*)—(Hunkpapa Lakota-Teton Sioux) –d. at the Standing Rock Agency, 1884. Participated in the Reno battle and was partly responsible for preventing the Indians from further chasing Reno's troops up the bluffs. Led about eighty warriors in attacks against Calhoun (Finley) Ridge and Calhoun Hill, coming in from the south. Also fought along Custer/Battle Ridge. Lost two brothers, Swift Bear and White Bull, in the Reno fight. Presence confirmed by Myers.

Crow Necklace—(Northern Cheyenne). Wore a war bonnet in the battle. A headman of the Crazy Dogs warrior society, or as Wooden Leg said, one of the nine "little chiefs" [Marquis, *Wooden Leg,* p. 212]. Fought Custer's column. Presence confirmed by Myers.

Crow Split His Nose (also A Crow Cut His Nose) —(Northern Cheyenne)— d. 25 Nov 1876. A headman of the Elkhorn Scraper warrior society, or as Wooden Leg called him, one of the nine "little chiefs" [Marquis, *Wooden Leg,* p. 211]. Presence confirmed by Myers.

Cut Belly (aka Open Belly)—(Northern Cheyenne)— d. circa 27 Jun 1876; died of wounds suffered at the Little Big Horn. A "suicide warrior." Note the difference: "warrior," not "boy." There appears to be much confusion when referring to these Cheyenne "suicide" Indians [Myers, "Roster of Known Hostile Indians at the Battle of the Little Big Horn," Research Review, Summer 1991, Vol. 5, No. 2]. Mortally wounded in the Deep Ravine/Cemetery Ravine area around Custer Hill, near the present cemetery grounds. Died a few days later. Son of Roman Nose. Wooden Leg claimed he was 30 years old and died of his wounds after the battle. "...our man who died after we arrived east of Powder river, was hit by a soldier bullet when he was riding across the bench where the stone house ... now is standing" [Marquis, Wooden Leg, p. 268].

Cut Foot—(Northern Cheyenne). A "Council of the 44" chief.

Cuts to Pieces—(Oglala Lakota-Teton Sioux)— Had at least two children, a boy and a girl. May have been at the Little Big Horn.

Dancing Arrow—(Oglala Lakota-Teton Sioux)— Listed in the Crazy Horse surrender ledger, 1877. Along with Sitting Bear, listed as "head-of-household." Lodge consisted of three adult females, two male children, and two female children; nine people, total. He was definitely at the Little Big Horn.

Day (*Anpetu*) (F)—(Hunkpapa Lakota-Teton Sioux) —b. circa 1849. Sister of Bear Looking Back. Listed in the Sitting Bull Surrender Ledger.

Deaf (*Nochan win*) (F)—(Oglala Lakota-Teton Sioux)—b. circa 1811. Member of Low Dog's band. She and her son and grandson were listed in the Sitting Bull Surrender Census, though they are unidentifiable in later data [Dickson].

Deaf Woman (*Nuh can win*) (F)—(Hunkpapa Lakota-Teton Sioux)—b. circa 1851. Listed in the Sitting Bull Surrender Ledger. Mother of Standing in Sight and One They Call out For.

Deed (aka Act; *Wichoka*)—(Sans Arc Lakota-Teton Sioux)—d. 25 Jun 1876, killed at the Little Big Horn. Died in the fighting as Reno retreated from the timber [Myers, "Roster of Known Hostile Indians at the Battle of the Little Big Horn," *Research Review*, Summer 1991, Vol. 5, No. 2].

Deeds (*Wicohan*; aka Two Bear(s); One Hawk or Lone Hawk [probably his formal name]; Thunder Earth or Noisy Walking; also, depending on the researcher, Plenty Trouble or Business)—(Hunkpapa or Sans Arc Lakota-Teton Sioux)—d. 25 Jun 1876; killed at the Little Big Horn, probably the first Indian to die. As much confusion reigns with this young man as with any other individual or aspect of the Little Big Horn. A young boy; brother of Moving Robe and Little Voice; grandson of Four Horns. Out with Brown Back and the hunting party that was also looking for horses. Standing Black Bear claimed to have been with them and

there are other stories of him, as well. Also, Drags the Rope. Black Bear tells of the story in Camp/Hammer, *Custer in '76*, pp. 203–204. The story is consistent with one told by Feather Earring to General Hugh Scott in Sep 1919 [Graham, *The Custer Myth*, p. 97]. Killed near where Reno crossed the Little Big Horn initially, though even this is problematic as there is some historical testimony that he was killed on the west side of the river. A number of years after the battle Crow Indians recalled that the scout, Goes Ahead, killed a young Sioux before the Reno column reached Ford A. Apparently, yet another warrior named Deed or Act is listed as a Sans Arc and was killed during Reno's retreat. Hardorff, however, claimed Deeds was the Sans Arc and was out with his father, Little Bear (*Mato Cikala*) when they were spotted by Varnum and his scouts from atop the Crow's Nest hill [*On the Little Bighorn with Walter Camp*, p. 57, footnote 4; also see, *Hokahey! A Good Day to Die*, p. 19]. Also, the father was identified further by Walter Camp as Brown Back, Brown Ass, or Pants—probably all nicknames—again, depending on who was doing the interpreting. Unless proved otherwise incorrect, Deeds and Deed are carried as two separate individuals.

The Hunkpapa (or Oglala) warrior, Iron Hawk, gave us an interesting version of the Deeds killing: "A boy was out with the party that went hunting and when they were coming back they stopped at Spring Creek. After they got there his horse played out and he was riding home double with someone. Then when he returned, his father told him and another boy to go and get his horse, and this was the last of the boy" [DeMallie, *The Sixth Grandfather*, p. 190]. Other stories revert to the Brown Back /Brown Ass-Deeds relationship as father and son.

Deer (*Tahca*) (F)—(Hunkpapa Lakota-Teton Sioux)—b. circa 1821. Mother of Yellow Dog. Listed in the Sitting Bull Surrender Ledger.

Did Not Butcher—(Lakota-Teton Sioux)— Known to have been in the fighting at the Little Big Horn. Still living at the Standing Rock Agency, Wakpala, SD, 1926 [courtesy of Dickson].

Did Not Go Home (aka "John" Ghost Dog)— (Northern Cheyenne). At the 1926 reunion. Counted coup in the fight with Custer's column.

Did Not Go Home—(Sans Arc Lakota-Teton Sioux)—Fought the Custer battalions. Presence confirmed by Myers. White Bull, in his 1930 interview with Walter S. Campbell, alluded to this man as being one of those who chased two fleeing soldiers as the Custer fight was winding down. These two soldiers were, in all likelihood, 1SG James Butler (L) and CPL John Foley (C).

Dirt Kettle—(Oglala Lakota-Teton Sioux)—Had been east of the LBH with Black Bear and Fast Horn, up near the Divide, looking for horses early on 25 Jun 1876 and had spotted soldiers; heading back to the agency.

Dirty Moccasins—(Northern Cheyenne). An "Old Man Chief." Joined the main body of Indians with 10 lodges in mid–May 1876. Presence confirmed by Myers, though some sources say this is the same man as Black Moccasin. They are carried separately.

Dives Backward—(Northern Cheyenne). A young boy. Nephew of White Shield.

Dog—(Lakota-Teton Sioux)—Fought alongside Kill Eagle. Presence confirmed by Myers, though he only lists him as a Teton Sioux.

Dog Chief—(Oglala Lakota-Teton Sioux)— Friend of Black Elk.

Dog Eagle (also "John" Dog Eagle)—(Lakota-Teton Sioux)—Known to have participated in the fighting at the Little Big Horn. Still living at the Standing Rock Agency, Little Eagle, SD, in 1926 [courtesy of Dickson].

Dog Ear—(Oglala Lakota-Teton Sioux)—Listed in the Crazy Horse surrender ledger, 1877. Along with Melter, listed as "head-of-household." Lodge consisted of one adult female, three male children, and two female children; total of eight people.

Dog Friend (also Dog)—(Northern Cheyenne). Presence confirmed by Myers. At the 1926 reunion.

Dog Growing Up—(Cheyenne). Had a wife and a small boy.

Dog Nothing—(Oglala Lakota-Teton Sioux)— Listed in the Crazy Horse surrender ledger, 1877. Along with Singing Prick and Stinking Tie, listed as "head-of-household." Lodge consisted of three adult females and four female children; total of ten people.

Dog with Horns (*Shunka-heton*)—(Minneconjou Lakota-Teton Sioux)—d. 25 Jun 1876, killed at the Little Big Horn. Feather Earring's brother. Killed in front of Reno's skirmish line.

Dog Woman (*Sunka win*) (F)—(Hunkpapa Lakota-Teton Sioux)—b. circa 1791. Listed as Fighting Bear's mother, but because of the age, this is highly unlikely. Possibly Fighting Bear's grand-mother, though even that may be iffy. Probably his great-grandmother. Listed in Sitting Bull's Surren-der Ledger [Dickson].

Dog's Back Bone (or Dog's Backbone; Dog Back-bone; *Shunka-chay-koha*)—(Minneconjou Lakota-Teton Sioux)—d. 25 or 26 Jun 1876. Killed at the Little Big Horn in the hilltop fight. Shot in the head [Liddic, *Vanishing Victory,* p. 170]. Verified by Myers, "Roster of Known Hostile Indians at the Battle of the Little Big Horn," *Research Review,* Summer 1991, Vol. 5, No. 2. Father of Kingman and brother of Takes the Horses. Friend of White Bull.

Don't Amount to Anything—(Oglala Lakota-Teton Sioux)—Listed in the Crazy Horse surrender ledger, 1877. Along with Spread Pine and Looks Like a Dog, listed as "head-of-household." Lodge consisted of three adult females, four male children, and four female children; total of fourteen people.

Don't Get out of the Way—(Oglala Lakota-Teton Sioux)—Listed in the Crazy Horse surrender ledger. Along with Fat Rump (# 1) and Dry Lake, he was listed as "head-of-household." There was one adult female, two male children, and one female child in his lodge, a total of seven people.

Don't Go out [Graham, *The Custer Myth,* p. 74]— (Lakota-Teton Sioux).

Don't Paint His Face—(Hunkpapa Lakota-Teton Sioux)—A sub-chief.

Drags the Rope—(Oglala Lakota-Teton Sioux)— With a group of Indians when Deeds was killed [LBHA].

Dried Prick—(Oglala Lakota-Teton Sioux)— Listed in the Crazy Horse surrender ledger, 1877. Listed as "head-of-household." Lodge consisted of two adult females and three male children; total of six people.

Drifting Clouds (*Mahpiya kicamna win*) (F)— (Hunkpapa Lakota-Teton Sioux)—b. circa 1801. Listed in the Sitting Bull Surrender Ledger and listed as the mother of Kills in Lodge and Comes Back with Growling. Her age, however, seems to prohibit that and we should probably assume she was their grandmother.

Driver (also "Garfield" Driver)—(Lakota-Teton Sioux)—Still living at the Standing Rock Agency, Little Eagle, SD, in 1926 [courtesy of Dickson]. At the camp, but he was either too young to participate in the fighting or he simply did not get into the battle.

Dry Hide—(Cheyenne).

Dry Lake—(Oglala Lakota-Teton Sioux)—Listed in the Crazy Horse surrender ledger. Along with Fat Rump (# 1) and Don't Get out of the Way, he was listed as "head-of-household." There was one adult female, two male children, and one female child in his lodge, a total of seven people.

Duck—(Cheyenne)—Listed in the Crazy Horse surrender ledger, 1877.

Duck Belly—(Oglala Lakota-Teton Sioux)—Listed in the Crazy Horse surrender ledger, 1877. Along with Around the Quiver and Sleeps There, listed as "head-of-household." Lodge consisted of one adult female; total of four people.

Dull Knife (aka Rabbit; also, Morning Star)—(Northern Cheyenne). Father of Goose Feathers. Probably the same chief as the one involved in the treaties of the 1860's [Stewart, *Custer's Luck,* p. 38]. According to Wooden Leg, he was not at the battle [Marquis, *Wooden Leg,* p. 205]. Joined after all the tribes had separated; probably some time in July 1876 [p. 282].

Eagle Bear—(Oglala Lakota-Teton Sioux)—b. circa 1860–d. Dec 1938. Sixteen years old at the battle. At the reunion in 1926. Brother of Fool's Crow. Presence at battle verified in Windolph/Hunt, *I Fought with Custer.* Watched or participated in both the Reno valley fight and the Custer battle.

Eagle Boy (also "Grover" Eagle Boy)—(Hunkpapa Lakota-Teton Sioux)—b. circa 1862. Fled the village with the women.

Eagle Chase—(Lakota-Teton Sioux)—At the 1926 reunion.

Eagle Chasing (aka "Joseph" Eagle Chasing)—(Northern Cheyenne). At the 1926 reunion.

Eagle Chasing (aka "Roy" Eagle Chasing)—(Northern Cheyenne). Attended 1926 reunion.

Eagle Clothing—(Oglala Lakota-Teton Sioux)—Probably a member of Low Dog's band.

Eagle Dog (*Sunka Wanbli*; also seen as Dog Eagle)—(Oglala Lakota-Teton Sioux)—b. circa 1829–d. 1890s. Member of Big Road's band.

Eagle Elk—(Oglala Lakota-Teton Sioux)—b. near the confluence of the White and Missouri rivers, circa 1851, making him twenty-five years old at time of the battle. The son of Long Whirlwind and Pretty Feather Woman. Used a Winchester repeater. Known to have been in both the valley fight and the Custer battle. Presence confirmed by Myers. Reputed to have been a cousin of Crazy Horse [Hardorff, *Hokahey!,* p. 47]. Belonged to the Last Child Society (*Hoksi Hakakta*), a 40-member military society whose members were the last-born sons of prominent families [Hardorff, *Lakota Recollections of the Custer Fight,* p. 99, footnote 1].

Eagle Feather (*Wanbli sun*) (F)—(Hunkpapa Lakota-Teton Sioux)—b. 1863. Daughter of White Dog and Pretty Woman.

Eagle Feather (*Wanbli upi la*) (F)—(Hunkpapa Lakota-Teton Sioux)—b. circa 1857. Daughter of Reaching Cloud and Red Woman. Note: name translates differently from that of White Dog's daughter, above.

Eagle Feather on the Forehead (F)—(Northern Cheyenne). Wooden Leg's mother.

Eagle Feather Woman (*Wanbli upi win*) (F)—(Hunkpapa Lakota-Teton Sioux)—b. circa 1862. Daughter of Bear Looking Back and White Buffalo Cow.

Eagle Hat (*Wambli-waposta*)—(Sans Arc Lakota-Teton Sioux)—d. 26 Jun 1876, killed at the Little Big Horn, on Reno Hill, near Benteen's line. Sometimes confused with Long Robe who was also killed there. Myers has them listed separately [Myers, "Roster of Known Hostile Indians at the Battle of the Little Big Horn," *Research Review,* Summer 1991, Vol. 5, No. 2].

Eagle Hawk (*Cetan Wanbli*)—(Oglala Lakota-Teton Sioux)—b. circa 1832 to 1835–d. 1904. Member of He Dog's Soreback Band. A brother of He Dog and father of "Joseph" Eagle Hawk.

Eagle Horn—(Lakota-Teton Sioux)—In the camp at the Little Big Horn, but not known to have been in the fighting. May have been too young. Still living at the Standing Rock Agency, Wakpala, SD, 1926 [courtesy of Dickson].

Eagle Man—(Lakota-Teton Sioux)—Fought alongside Kill Eagle. Presence confirmed by Myers, though he only lists him as a Teton Sioux.

Eagle Ring—(Oglala Lakota-Teton Sioux)—b. circa 1865–d. some time after 1906. After the battle he went on the field with the women to strip the bodies of the troopers.

Eagle Tail Feather—(Northern Cheyenne). In the valley fight against Reno. He and two other Cheyenne warriors—Sun Bear and Little Sun—chased three soldiers south along the west bank of the LBH. While unclear, this is probably during the valley fight [Marquis, *Wooden Leg,* p. 222]. Presence confirmed by Myers.

Eagle Thunder—(Lakota-Teton Sioux)—At Cheyenne River Agency in 1926.

Ear Ring Prick—(Oglala Lakota-Teton Sioux)—Listed in the Crazy Horse surrender ledger, 1877. Along with Butt Horn, listed as "head-of-household." Lodge consisted of one adult female and one female child; total of four people.

Earthly Nation (*Maka oyate win*) (F)—(Hunkpapa Lakota-Teton Sioux)—b. circa 1861. Sister-in-law of Bone Tomahawk.

Elk Bear (sometimes name seen reversed as Bear Elk; *Mato-hehcahca*)—(Sans Arc Lakota-Teton Sioux)—d. 25 Jun 1876, killed at the Little Big Horn. Body location unknown, but killed fighting Custer's column.

Elk Boy (*Unpan Hoksila*; aka Huron Elk Boy)—(Oglala Lakota-Teton Sioux)—b. circa 1849–d. 1927. Member of Iron Crow's band. Told the photographer Edward Curtis about his exploits and mentioned that he had fought the white soldiers only once [Dickson].

Elk Head (also Young Elk Head; "Elias" Elk Head)—(Sans Arc Lakota-Teton Sioux)—b. circa 1861–d. at the Cheyenne River Agency, 2 Jun 1941. Son of Elk Head.

Elk Head—(Sans Arc Lakota-Teton Sioux)—b. 1825–d. Green Grass, Cheyenne River Reservation, 14 Dec 1914. One of two Sans Arc (Red Hair being the other) entrusted with protecting the sacred Buffalo Calf Pipe [Dickson]. Father of Young Elk Head and "Martha" Red Eagle.

Elk Heart—(Hunkpapa Lakota-Teton Sioux)—Slightly wounded in the valley fight.

Elk Horn (*Heha kahe*)—(Hunkpapa Lakota-Teton Sioux)—b. circa 1801. Listed in the Sitting Bull Surrender Ledger. Husband of Lady.

Elk Nation (also "Louis" Elk Nation)—(Hunkpapa Lakota-Teton Sioux)—Saved his friend, Little Bear, when he was wounded near the very end of the Custer battle. Still lived at the Standing Rock Agency, Bullhead, SD, in 1929. Presence confirmed by Myers, though he only lists him as a Teton Sioux.

Elk Nation—(Lakota-Teton Sioux)—Still living at the Standing Rock Agency, Bullhead, SD, 1926 [courtesy of Dickson]. This is not the same man listed above, despite the name and whereabouts in 1926. This Elk Nation was also known to have been in the fighting at the Little Big Horn.

Elk Stands Alone (also Elk Stands on Top, Elk Stands Above; Elk Standing Alone; *Heha*ka *Wankata Najin* or *Hehcahca-waykal-nozin*)—(Sans Arc Lakota-Teton Sioux)—d. 25 Jun 1876, killed at the Little Big Horn as he chased a couple of Rees—Bob-tail Bull and Little Brave — on the east side of the Little Big Horn during Reno's retreat. Headman of a military lodge. May have been killed by the Ree scout, Little Brave.

Elk Woman (aka Wolf Traveling) (F)—(Northern Cheyenne)—Wife of Strong Left Hand. Reputed to have been one of the Indian women mutilating the soldiers after the battle.

Enemy—(Oglala Lakota-Teton Sioux)—Listed in the Crazy Horse surrender ledger, 1877. Along with One Teat, listed as "head-of-household." Lodge consisted of two adult females; total of four people.

Exhausted Elk—(Northern Cheyenne).

Face (also more commonly seen as "Julia" Face) (F)—(Oglala Lakota-Teton Sioux)—b. circa 1858. Daughter of the Oglala "head soldier," Face; one wife of the Brulé Thunder Hawk (there were Oglala, Brulé, Sans Arc, and Hunkpapa "Thunder Hawk's"). She later claimed, "None of the warriors reached the high ridge [Battle Ridge/Last Stand Hill] ahead of Custer" [Liddic, *Vanishing Victory*, p. 146]. She was with the Oglala at the time of the battle, traditional for a mixed-tribe marriage.

Face—(Oglala Lakota-Teton Sioux).

Face Turner—(Oglala Lakota-Teton Sioux)—Listed in the Crazy Horse surrender ledger, 1877. Listed as "head-of-household." Lodge consisted of four female adults; five people, total.

Faithful (*Wacin yanpi win*) (F)—(Hunkpapa Lakota-Teton Sioux)—b. circa 1870. Daughter of Bone Tomahawk and Foot. Only a child at the time of the battle.

Fast Bear—(Sans Arc Lakota-Teton Sioux).

Fast Bull—(Minneconjou Lakota-Teton Sioux)—Listed as a Dakota chief in the LBHA's Summer 2001 *Research Review*. Along with Hump and High Backbone, a leader of the Minneconjou [LBHA]. Presence confirmed by Myers.

Fast Eagle—(Oglala Lakota-Teton Sioux)—Claims he held Custer's arms as Walking Blanket Woman (Moving Robe Woman [H]) stabbed him in the back [LBHA].

Fast Elk (*Her*aka *Oranko*)—(Oglala Lakota-Teton Sioux)—b. circa 1837–d. after 1910. Member of Low Dog's band.

Fast Horn—(Oglala Lakota-Teton Sioux)—Had been east of the LBH with Black Bear and Dirt Kettle, up near the Divide, looking for horses early on 25 Jun 1876 and had spotted soldiers. They were heading back to the agency, but of the three only Fast Horn returned to give warning. He Dog confirms that Fast Horn warned the village.

Fast Thunder—(Oglala Lakota-Teton Sioux)—Fought with Crazy Horse [LBHA].

Fast Walker—(Northern Cheyenne). Presence confirmed by Myers. At the Cheyenne River Agency in 1926.

Fast Wolf—(Oglala Lakota-Teton Sioux)—Brother of Stands First and Old Shield.

Fat Bear—(Lakota-Teton Sioux)—Ran 15 miles to warn the camp. Presence confirmed by Myers, though he only lists him as a Teton Sioux.

Fat Clown, "Paul"—(Lakota-Teton Sioux)—At the Cheyenne River Agency, 1926.

Fat on the Beef (also Fat Hide)-(Minneconjou Lakota-Teton Sioux)—d. 16 Dec 1876 or Apr 1877. Killed attempting to surrender to Nelson Miles.

Fat Rump (# 1)—(Oglala Lakota-Teton Sioux)—Listed in the Crazy Horse surrender ledger, 1877. Along with Dry Lake and Don't Get out of the Way, he was listed as "head-of-household." There was one adult female, two male children, and one female child in his lodge, a total of seven people.

Fat Rump (# 2)—(Lakota-Teton Sioux)—Listed in the Crazy Horse surrender ledger, 1877. Along with Lays Laughing and Short Brulé, he was listed as "head-of-household." Lodge consisted of four adult females and one female child; a total of eight people.

Fearless (also "Francis" Fearless)—(Lakota-Teton Sioux)—Known to have been in the fighting at the Little Big Horn. Still living at the Standing Rock Agency, Wakpala, SD, 1926 [courtesy of Dickson].

Fears Nothing (aka Respects Nothing; also, Fearless; *Takuni Oholasni*; previously known as End [*Ihankeya*])-(Oglala Lakota-Teton Sioux)—b. circa 1854–d. 22 May 1923. Member of the *Oyuhpe Oglala* (Big Road's band) [Dickson]. His father was Bank (*Maya*); his wife was White Cow Robe. His horse was downriver and by the time he got him, Respects Nothing reached the Reno fighting when the troops were already in the timber. Claims to have seen the arrival of the pack train on Reno Hill, but Michno thinks it was the advance elements of Benteen's battalion, since the packs did not arrive for at least 37 minutes [Pennington] or one hour later [everybody else]. Also claimed the action with Custer's troops began with C Company, a critical observation in understanding how the Custer fighting developed. Apparently, after being in the group of warriors who drove Reno across the Little Big Horn, Fears Nothing then rode down stream, crossed the river at the Ford B area, and participated in the fighting at the north side of the ridge —probably against Keogh's command—then on Custer/Last Stand Hill.

Fears Nothing—(Oglala Lakota-Teton Sioux)—Not the same man listed above. Probably a member of the Low Dog band.

Feather Earring (or Feather Earrings)—(Minneconjou Lakota-Teton Sioux)—[See Graham, *The Custer Myth*, p. 97.] Brother of Dog with Horns.

Participated in the Reno fight, being one of the first to pass word from the scouts that the soldiers were coming [Michno, *The Mystery of E Troop*]. "When Reno reached the hill, word came that more soldiers below were attacking the village" [p. 82]. Also in the Custer Fight. Claimed there were 5,000 warriors fighting Custer. Presence confirmed by Myers. Still living at the Standing Rock Agency, Kenel, SD, in 1926.

Feather Moon—(Oglala Lakota-Teton Sioux)—Listed in the Crazy Horse surrender ledger, 1877. Along with one of the Black Elks and Warms His Blanket, listed as "head-of-household." Lodge consisted of six adult females and one male child; total of ten people.

Feather on Head (*Wiyaka Aopazan*)—(Oglala Lakota-Teton Sioux)—b. circa 1831–d. 1905. Member of Big Road's band.

Feathered Sun—(Northern Cheyenne). In the Rosebud fight as well.

Feathers, "Frank"—(Lakota-Teton Sioux)—Northeast of the river watching the ponies when he received word that the soldiers were coming [LBHA].

Few Tails—(Oglala Lakota-Teton Sioux)—An old medicine man. Not certain if he was at the battle, but since it seems he was part of Black Elk's tribe I list him as being present.

Fighting Bear (*Mato wica kiza*)—(Hunkpapa Lakota-Teton Sioux)—b. circa 1863. Listed in the Sitting Bull Surrender Ledger.

Fights Thunder—(Sans Arc Lakota-Teton Sioux) —Head of the family. Part of Spotted Eagle's band [Dickson].

Fills the Pipe—(Oglala Lakota-Teton Sioux)—Listed in the Crazy Horse surrender ledger, 1877. Listed as "head-of-household." Lodge consisted of one adult female and three female children; total of five people.

Fills Up—(Oglala Lakota-Teton Sioux)—Listed in the Crazy Horse surrender ledger, 1877. Listed as "head-of-household." Lodge consisted of two adult females and one female child; total of four people.

Fine Shield (*Wahacanka Waste*)—(Oglala Lakota-Teton Sioux)—b. circa 1834. Member of Low Dog's band, though Dickson says he cannot be positively identified.

Fine Weather—(Lakota-Teton Sioux)—At the Cheyenne River Agency in 1926.

Fingers Woman (F)—(Northern Cheyenne). Wooden Leg's sister.

Fire (*Apena*) (F)—(Hunkpapa Lakota-Teton Sioux)—b. circa 1862. Wife of Brave Bear. Listed in the Sitting Bull Surrender Ledger.

Fire Cloud (*Mahpi yapeta*)—(Hunkpapa Lakota-Teton Sioux)—b. circa 1823. Listed in Sitting Bull Surrender Ledger. Wife was Pretty Woman.

Fire Thunder—(Oglala Lakota-Teton Sioux)—b. circa 1849–1850. At the Fetterman fight in 1866. Friend of Black Elk (in latter years). Still alive in 1932.

Fire Wolf—(Cheyenne).

First Cloud (*Mahpiya Toke win*) (F)—(Oglala Lakota-Teton Sioux)—b. circa 1833. Head of Blue Cloud family and a member of Low Dog's band [Dickson].

First Eagle—(Lakota-Teton Sioux)—At the Cheyenne River Agency in 1926.

Fishing Woman (F)—(Northern Cheyenne)—Fled when the soldiers attacked the village. Supposed to have spotted troopers near Ford D.

Flapping Horn—(Northern Cheyenne). Listed in the Crazy Horse surrender ledger, 1877 [CBHMA]. Present at the LBH.

Flat Hip—(Hunkpapa Lakota-Teton Sioux)—One of many claiming to have killed Custer. Presence confirmed by Myers.

Flat Iron—(Cheyenne). Last surviving Cheyenne chief. In 1915, he claimed there were 14,000 people in the 1876 camp, including 8,000 warriors. Presence confirmed by Myers.

Fled With (also "William" Sitting Bull; *Yuha Nanpapi*)—(Hunkpapa Lakota-Teton Sioux)—b. March 1876–d. near Pass Creek, February 1910—An infant; twin son of Sitting Bull and Four Robes. His brother was Abandoned One. The story goes that when Reno attacked, Four Robes panicked and fled with only this one infant. Realizing her mistake, she handed the baby off to a friend and went back to retrieve the other child. Thus, their names.

Fleece—(Northern Cheyenne). Listed in the Crazy Horse surrender ledger [CBHMA]. Probably present at the LBH.

Flying Bird—(Minneconjou Lakota-Teton Sioux)—With Sitting Bull in Canada. Probably at the Little Big Horn.

Flying By (also "George" Flying By)—(Lakota-Teton Sioux)—Known to have been in the fighting at the Little Big Horn. Still living at the Standing Rock Agency, Wakpala, SD, 1926 [courtesy of Dickson].

Flying By (*Keya Heyi*)-(Minneconjou Lakota-Teton Sioux)—b. 1850–d. 25 Jun 1876, killed at the Little Big Horn. Twenty-six-year old second son of Lame Deer. Brother of Foolish Heart. Got into valley fight late and had his horse shot from under him, so he missed most of that battle. After securing another horse, he made the Custer fight. Captured some of Custer's horses, took them to the village and was killed after returning to the battle [Myers, "Roster of Known Hostile Indians at the Battle of the Little Big Horn," *Research Review,* Summer 1991, Vol. 5, No. 2].

Flying By—(Oglala Lakota-Teton Sioux)—An old man during the LBH battle, involved in the Custer fight. He kept encouraging the younger men to move forward and keep fighting. Red Feather claimed he was the only "old man" to be out in front of the younger warriors [Hardorff, *Lakota Recollections of the Custer Fight,* p. 87, footnote 16].

Flying By (*Tahiy-wichash* or *Kin-yan-hiyaye*)—(Cheyenne)—d. 25 Jun 1876, killed at the Little Big Horn while fighting the Custer battalions [Myers, "Roster of Known Hostile Indians at the Battle of the Little Big Horn," *Research Review,* Summer 1991, Vol. 5, No. 2].

Flying Chaser (*Wakuya-kingan*)—(Brulé Lakota-Teton Sioux)—A "headman." Listed as a *Dakota* chief in the LBHA's Summer 2001 *Research Review.* Presence confirmed by Myers, though he only lists him as a Teton Sioux.

Flying Hand—(Oglala Lakota-Teton Sioux).

Flying Hawk (also "Moses" Flying Hawk)—(Oglala Lakota-Teton Sioux)—b. 1852 in the Black Hills, near what is now Rapid City, SD–d. 21 or 24 Dec 1931. Son of Black Fox and Cedar Woman. Another nephew of Sitting Bull and possibly a cousin of Crazy Horse, who was a good friend. Brother of Kicking Bear. The first fighting he was involved in was when Reno's troops made their mad dash out of the timber. From Reno, he crossed the LBH with Crazy Horse and moved up Deep Coulee. He fought on Calhoun Hill and along Battle Ridge, then finally to Custer Hill. In an interview with Judge Eli S. Ricker at the Pine Ridge Reservation in 1907, Flying Hawk said Crazy Horse started crossing the LBH into Deep Coulee before Custer left the second ridge (Nye-Cartwright). Claimed there were only 1,200 warriors and only 1,000 fought Custer, since the rest were out hunting. Presence confirmed by Myers.

Flying Horse (*Tasunke kin yan hu*) (F)—(Hunkpapa Lakota-Teton Sioux)—b. circa 1866. Daughter of Red Thunder and Ripe. A young girl at the time of the battle.

Fool Bull—(Brulé Lakota-Teton Sioux)—b. 1844. Medicine man. Presence confirmed by Myers, though he only lists him as a Teton Sioux. Married to Red Cane.

Fool Heart [Graham, *The Custer Myth*, p. 74]—(Lakota-Teton Sioux).

Fool Horse—(Sans Arc Lakota-Teton Sioux)—Head of the family. Part of Spotted Eagle's band [Dickson].

Fool Soldier—(Sans Arc Lakota-Teton Sioux)—Head of the family. Part of Spotted Eagle's band [Dickson].

Foolish Elk—(Oglala Lakota-Teton Sioux)—b. 1854; twenty-two years old at time of battle. In the fight against Crook and didn't arrive at the LBH camp until 24 June. Fought with Crazy Horse this day. Claimed Custer's troops made two charges, one at Calhoun Hill (probably the C Company move off Battle Ridge) and one at the monument. An intelligent man, well regarded, with a reputation for honesty and truthfulness [Camp/Hammer, *Custer in '76*, p. 197]. In later years was the chief of police at the Rosebud Agency. Presence confirmed by Myers, though he only lists him as a Teton Sioux.

Foolish Heart—(Minneconjou Lakota-Teton Sioux)—First son of Lame Deer; older brother of Flying By. He may have taken his younger brother's name some time after the battle, for interviews with Walter Camp show up with Flying By's name [Hardorff, *On the Little Bighorn with Walter Camp*, p. 158, footnote 3].

Foolish Thunder—(Sans Arc Lakota-Teton Sioux)—Referred to as a "head-warrior" by COL Nelson Miles in an October 28, 1876, dispatch. One of the five "hostages" designated by Miles during the surrender of 400 to 600 lodges and their return to the Cheyenne River Agency, October-December 1876. The others were Sunrise, Red Skirt, White Bull, and Black Eagle.

Fools Crow—(Blackfeet Lakota-Teton Sioux)—Claimed there were 5,000 warriors at the battle. He also claimed the village was more than three miles long [Liddic, *Vanishing Victory*, pp. 102–103].

Fool's Crow—(Cheyenne).

Fool's Crow—(Oglala Lakota-Teton Sioux)—b. circa 1865. Younger brother of Eagle Bear. Eleven years old at the time of the battle. Was in the camp, but not in any of the fighting.

Foot (*Siha win*) (F)—(Hunkpapa Lakota-Teton Sioux)—b. circa 1849. Wife of Bone Tomahawk. Probably one of two or more wives.

Four (*Topa win*) (F)—(Hunkpapa Lakota-Teton Sioux)—b. circa 1862. Daughter of Charging Thunder and White Glass.

Four Bullets—(Oglala Lakota-Teton Sioux)—Listed in the Crazy Horse surrender ledger, 1877. Along with Comes from War and Wood Boat, listed as "head-of-household." Lodge consisted of three adult females, one male child, and four female children; total of eleven people.

Four Crows (*Kangi Topa*)—(Oglala Lakota-Teton Sioux)—b. circa 1832. Listed in the Crazy Horse surrender ledger, 1877. Along with Bluff, listed as "head-of-household." Lodge consisted of two adult females and one male child; total of five people. Member of He Dog's Soreback Band. Probably fought with Crazy Horse.

Four Horns (*He Topa*; aka Moccasin Top)-(Hunkpapa Lakota-Teton Sioux)—b. circa 1823–d. 1887. Deeds' grandfather. Presence confirmed by Myers, though he only lists him as a Teton Sioux.

Four Horns (*He Topa*)—(Hunkpapa Lakota-Teton Sioux)—b. circa 1855. Son of Four Horns.

Four Horses—(Hunkpapa Lakota-Teton Sioux).

Four Robes (also seen as Four Robes Woman and Four Blankets Woman) (F)—(Hunkpapa Lakota-Teton Sioux)—One of Sitting Bull's two wives, the other being her sister, Seen by the Nation. She had infant twin sons, one of whom was named Abandoned One, the other, Fled With.

Four Times Woman (F)—(Hunkpapa Lakota-Teton Sioux)—She was a sister of White Bull.

Four Woman (*Winyan topa win*) (F)—(Hunkpapa Lakota-Teton Sioux)—b. circa 1867. Sister of Killed While Standing. Swimming in the river when the alarm was raised that soldiers were coming.

Fox Belly—(Oglala Lakota-Teton Sioux)—An old medicine man. May have been at the Little Big Horn.

Frog—(Minneconjou Lakota-Teton Sioux)—Leader of a small family unit. One of four sons of Lone Horn (d. 1875). The others were Touch the Clouds, Roman Nose, and Spotted Elk.

Frog—(Northern Cheyenne). Father-in-law of White Bull.

Full Stomach—(Lakota-Teton Sioux)—At the Cheyenne River Agency in 1926.

Gain Victory in Battle (*Akicin yin kte*)—(Hunkpapa Lakota-Teton Sioux)—b. circa 1871. Son of Elk Horn and Lady. A toddler at the time of the battle.

Gall (*Pi-zi* or *Co-kam-I-ya-ya;* aka Red Walker; The Man Who Goes in the Middle; Comes in Center)-(Hunkpapa Lakota-Teton Sioux)— b. somewhere along the Moreau River in SD, 1838 or 1840–d. Oak Creek, SD, 5 Dec 1893 [Hardorff, *Lakota Recollections,* p. 42, footnote 14], 1894, or 1895 [this latter date is from Graham, *The Custer Myth,* p. 132]. In Taylor the date of death is listed as 1896. These are probably wrong and 1895 seems to be the correct year. Short, squat, extremely powerful; 12 years after LBH, he stepped on a scale and weighed 260 lbs. Chief of a warrior society; above average skills and leadership abilities. *Kangiska* band [LBHA/Dickson/Bray]. Listed as the #2 Dakota war chief in the LBHA's Summer 2001 *Research Review.* Did not care for Sitting Bull. Liddic writes that Gall was with some Cheyenne looking for horses when Custer made his observations from Sharpshooters' Ridge [*Vanishing Victory,* p. 85]. As Reno began his firing, Gall rode in the opposite direction, north, beyond the Cheyenne camp, to round up his horses. He circled back to the Hunkpapa camp and there, as he readied to mount a charge against Reno's men in the timber, he heard women calling from the hills across the river. Iron Cedar reached him and warned of Custer's column heading for the Cheyenne camp (Gall's timing was around two hours after noon, tying in with Pennington). He went up to the bluffs to see for himself and sat on a knoll south of MTC watching Custer's approach. Gall never got into the Reno fight and was late in getting into the Custer fight. In fact, chances are *he led no one* during the entire fight. After leaving the bluffs, rather than go straight to Ford B, he went looking for his family. He was seen with Sitting Bull and One Bull. He found his two wives and three children all dead. Michno says he mourned for a short time, then rode for the river crossing. In all likelihood his family was killed by the Ree scouts — Little Sioux, Boy Chief, Red Star, and Strikes Two — who were after Sioux ponies and found the women and children running through the timber along the right bank of the LBH. Eventually captured at Poplar River in January 1881, by COL Guido Ilges, Fifth Infantry. Edward Godfrey seemed particularly impressed and fond of Gall [See Graham, *The Custer Myth,* pp. 131–132]. Presence confirmed by Myers.

Gets Married (F)—(Lakota-Teton Sioux)— Listed as "head-of-household" in the Crazy Horse surrender ledger, 1877. Lodge consisted of two female adults, two male children, and one female child; five people, total.

Gets Together—(Oglala Lakota-Teton Sioux)— Listed in the Crazy Horse surrender ledger, 1877. Listed as "head-of-household," his lodge consisting of one female adult, two male children, and two female children; a total of six people.

Ghost Hide (also just Ghost)—(Northern Cheyenne). Listed in the Crazy Horse surrender ledger, 1877.

Girl (*Win cincala*) (F)—(Hunkpapa Lakota-Teton Sioux)— b. 1873. A small child at the battle. Daughter of Black Bird and Left Handed Woman.

Gives Out—(Oglala Lakota-Teton Sioux)— Listed in the Crazy Horse surrender ledger [CBHMA].

Goes After Other Buffalo—(Northern Cheyenne). A headman of the Elkhorn Scraper warrior society, or as Wooden Leg called him, one of the nine "little chiefs" [Marquis, *Wooden Leg,* p. 211]. Presence confirmed by Myers.

Gone Again—(Lakota-Teton Sioux)— Listed in the Crazy Horse surrender ledger, 1877. Listed as "head-of-household." Lodge consisted of one female adult and one female child; total of three people.

Good Bear (aka Pretty Bear)—(Hunkpapa Lakota-Teton Sioux)— Father of Good Bear Boy. Leader of a small group of Indians. One of the leaders meeting with Miles in October 1876 to discuss terms of surrender.

Good Bear Boy (aka Pretty Bear, Good Bear)— (Hunkpapa Lakota-Teton Sioux)— Good Bear's son. Wounded during the valley fight — probably in front of Reno's skirmish line — and saved by Lone Bull/One Bull, the Hunkpapa. Presence confirmed by Myers, though he only lists him as a Teton Sioux. Recovered from his wounds and died many years later, living at the Standing Rock Agency.

Good Bed Woman (F)—(Brulé Lakota-Teton Sioux) — Wife of Hollow Horn Bear.

Good Boy—(Oglala Lakota-Teton Sioux)— Listed in the Crazy Horse surrender ledger, 1877. Along with Red Hawk, listed as "head-of-household." Lodge consisted of one adult female and four female children; seven people, total.

Good Dog—(Lakota-Teton Sioux)— Living at the Standing Rock Agency, Little Eagle, SD, in 1929. Known to have fought in the battle.

Good Feather Woman (F)—(Minneconjou Lakota-Teton Sioux)— White Bull's mother.

Good Fox—(Minneconjou Lakota-Teton Sioux)— Fought Custer's column. Presence confirmed by Myers.

Good Hand—(tribe unknown)— Knew how to repair jammed guns discarded by the soldiers [LBHA].

Good Thunder—(Oglala Lakota-Teton Sioux).

Good Voice Elk (also seen as Good Voiced Elk)—(Hunkpapa Lakota-Teton Sioux)—Interviewed by Walter Camp in 1909, telling Camp that some 25 to 30 soldiers died in a gully [usually interpreted as Deep Ravine].

Good Weasel—(Oglala Lakota-Teton Sioux).

Goose Feathers—(Northern Cheyenne). Dull Knife's son. In the Rosebud fight [LBHA].

Gopher—(Oglala Lakota-Teton Sioux)—Listed in the Crazy Horse surrender ledger, 1877. Along with Little Back, listed as "head-of-household." Lodge consisted of three adult females, two male children, and one female child; total of eight people.

Grace (*Waun sila win*) (F)—(Hunkpapa Lakota-Teton Sioux)—b. circa 1864. Daughter of Elk Horn and Lady.

Grandfather—(Oglala Lakota-Teton Sioux)—Listed in the Crazy Horse surrender ledger, 1877. Along with Comes the Day, listed as "head-of-household." Lodge consisted of two adult females, four male children, and one female child; total of nine people.

Grass Prick—(Lakota-Teton Sioux)—Listed in the Crazy Horse surrender ledger, 1877. Along with Iron White Man, listed as "head-of-household." Lodge consisted of four adult females, two male children, and one female child; total of nine people.

Grass Rope-(Brulé Lakota-Teton Sioux)

Grasshopper ("Isaac" Grasshopper)—(Northern Cheyenne). Still alive in 1921 and living at Lame Deer, Montana [LBHA].

Gray Bull—(Hunkpapa Lakota-Teton Sioux)—In the Rosebud fight.

Gray Eagle (*Wanbli Rita*; also "Judge" Gray Eagle)—(Hunkpapa Lakota-Teton Sioux)—One of Sitting Bull's bodyguards. Brother of Sitting Bull's two wives, Four Robes and Seen by the Nation. Still living at the Standing Rock Agency, Bullhead, SD, in 1929. Known to have been involved in the fighting.

Gray Earth Track (aka Tracking White Earth)—(*Wahpekute*/Dakota-Santee Sioux)—A son of *Inkpaduta*, and a twin brother of Sounds the Ground as He Walks. Reputed to have Custer's horse Vic after the battle. He may have gotten Vic with Sounds the Ground as He Walks. LT Edgerly told Walter Camp that Vic was killed.

Gray Head (also seen spelled Grey Head) (F)—(Lakota-Teton Sioux)—Listed in the Crazy Horse surrender ledger, 1877. Listed as the "head-of-household." Her lodge consisted solely of her.

Gray Whirlwind (aka Sunken Ass)—(Hunkpapa Lakota-Teton Sioux)—Reported that Sitting Bull's horse was wounded at the beginning of the valley fight.

Greases His Arm—(Oglala Lakota-Teton Sioux)—Listed in the Crazy Horse surrender ledger, 1877. Along with Two Face, listed as "head-of-household." Lodge consisted of two adult females, one male child, and two female children; total of seven people.

Greasy Dog (F)—(Northern Cheyenne)—b. circa 1868. Only a small girl at the time of the battle.

Green Blanket (F)—(Lakota-Teton Sioux)—Listed in the Crazy Horse surrender ledger, 1877. Listed as "head-of-household." Lodge consisted of her and one female child; two people, total.

Grey (*Hote win*) (F)—(Oglala Lakota-Teton Sioux)—b. circa 1838. Wife of Four Crows; mother of One Who Kills [Dickson].

Grind Stone (*Izuzu*; also "John" Grind Stone; or Grindstone)—(Lakota-Teton Sioux)—Still living at the Standing Rock Agency, Little Eagle, SD, in 1926 [courtesy of Dickson]. At the camp, but he was either too young to participate in the fighting or he simply did not get into the battle. Probably a Hunkpapa and brother of "Stanton" Grind Stone.

Grind Stone (*Izuzu*; also "Stanton" Grind Stone; or Grindstone)—(Hunkpapa Lakota-Teton Sioux). Still living at the Standing Rock Agency, Little Eagle, SD, in 1926 [courtesy of Dickson]. At the camp, but he was either too young to participate in the fighting or he simply did not get into the battle. Probably a brother of "John" Grind Stone.

Hail Bear—(Hunkpapa Lakota-Teton Sioux)—In the Rosebud fight [LBHA].

Hail Stones in Her Stomach (F)—(Lakota-Teton Sioux)—Wife of Long Feather.

Hair Lip (*Pute-ishma*)—(Cheyenne)—d. 25 Jun 1876, killed at the Little Big Horn [Myers, "Roster of Known Hostile Indians at the Battle of the Little Big Horn," *Research Review*, Summer 1991, Vol. 5, No. 2].

Hairy (also **Hair**)—(Oglala Lakota-Teton Sioux)—This could be the same man mentioned by Liddic, *Vanishing Victory*, p. 103. Bruce Liddic called him Hair. Listed in the Crazy Horse surrender ledger, 1877. Listed as "head-of-household." Lodge consisted of two adult females and two female children; total of five people.

Hairy Chin-(Lakota-Teton Sioux)—d. Jul 1889. Medicine man.

Hairy Hand ("Henry" Hairy Hand)—(Northern Cheyenne). Still alive in 1921 and living at Lame Deer, Montana [LBHA].

The Hand—(Oglala Lakota-Teton Sioux)—Listed in the Crazy Horse surrender ledger, 1877. Listed as "head-of-household." Lodge consisted of two adult females and two male children; five people, total.

Hanging Wolf—(Northern Cheyenne). Crossed the LBH and fired at Custer's column as it approached Ford B [LBHA].

Hangs His Head—(Oglala Lakota-Teton Sioux)— Listed in the Crazy Horse surrender ledger, 1877. Along with Ree, One Glass, and Soldier, listed as "head-of-household." Lodge consisted of three adult females, one male child, and four female children; total of twelve people.

Hard to Hit—(Oglala Lakota-Teton Sioux)—d. circa 1879. One of three Lakota to meet Reno's advance in the valley (Bad Heart Bull being another). Cousin of Black Elk. Killed in Canada by Crows.

Hard to Kill (also "William" Hard to Kill)—(Minneconjou Lakota-Teton Sioux)—b. circa 1865–d. 23 Jun 1926. Son of Owl King and Touch on Head.

Has Horn(s)—(Hunkpapa Lakota-Teton Sioux)— Fought against Custer's column. Presence confirmed by Myers, though he only lists him as a Teton Sioux.

Hawk (*Tce-tan*)—(Cheyenne). Rain-in-the-Face claimed it was this man who actually killed Custer [Stewart, *Custer's Luck*, p. 486]. There is a Minneconjou named Charging Hawk who Michno says may have been the one to have killed Custer.

Hawk Bear—(Sans Arc Lakota-Teton Sioux)— Head of the family. Part of Spotted Eagle's band [Dickson].

Hawk Bear, "Moses"—(Lakota-Teton Sioux)—At the Cheyenne River Agency, 1926.

Hawk Man (*Cetan Wicasa*)—(Sans Arc Lakota-Teton Sioux)—d. 25 Jun 1876, killed at the Little Big Horn, in the valley fight leading a charge into the timber. He was probably killed in front of Reno's skirmish line. A Hunkpapa, also known as Hawk Man, was killed fighting Custer [Myers, "Roster of Known Hostile Indians at the Battle of the Little Big Horn," *Research Review,* Summer 1991, Vol. 5, No. 2].

Hawk Man—(Hunkpapa Lakota-Teton Sioux)— d. 25 Jun 1876, killed at the Little Big Horn while fighting the Custer battalions [Myers, "Roster of Known Hostile Indians at the Battle of the Little Big Horn," *Research Review,* Summer 1991, Vol. 5, No. 2]. A Sans Arcs, also known as Hawk Man, was killed fighting in front of Reno's skirmish line.

Hawk Stays Up—(Hunkpapa Lakota-Teton Sioux)—Claimed to have counted coup in the Custer fight. Presence confirmed by Myers.

He Dog—(Northern Cheyenne).

He Dog (*Sunka Bloka*; also seen as Male Dog*)*— (Oglala Lakota-Teton Sioux)—b. near Bear Butte, SD, 1840–d. possibly 1931, but more likely 1936. He was the son of a prominent Oglala headman named Black Stone (or Black Rock); his mother's name was Blue Day. Uncle of "Amos" Bad Heart Bull. Leader of the Soreback Band (*Cankahuhan*) [Dickson]. His wife's name was Stone. Interviewed by Walter Camp in 1910. Elected a "Shirt Wearer." Fought both the Reno and Custer columns. Camp asked him if 28 bodies were in Deep Ravine and he said that was correct. Michno feels this was a typical leading question, one answered in the affirmative only because the Indian thought that was what the interviewer wanted. Also in the Rosebud fight against Crook, 17 Jun 1876. General Hugh L. Scott also interviewed He Dog in 1920. He told Scott he first attacked "Custer" near the dry creek (MTC) and that Custer never got near the river. In this interview, He Dog never mentioned any 28 men in a deep ravine. Listed as a Dakota chief in the LBHA's Summer 2001 *Research Review.* Listed in the Crazy Horse surrender ledger, May 6, 1877, at Fort Robinson. Along with Clown (# 2), the Lights, Wound in Back, and one other whose name appeared illegible, listed as "head-of-household." Lodge consisted of three adult women and three male children; total of eleven people. Presence confirmed by Myers and many others.

He That Knocks Down (*Waka hihpe ya*)—(Hunkpapa Lakota-Teton Sioux)—b. circa 1875. Only an infant at the time of the battle. Son of Reaching Cloud and Red Woman.

Head Swift (also "Charles" Head Swift)—(Northern Cheyenne)—Swimming in the Little Big Horn when the alarm was raised. According to John Stands in Timber's *Cheyenne Memories,* he was swimming with Wandering Medicine and Yellow Robe [p. 195].

Heap Bear Lays Down—(Oglala Lakota-Teton Sioux)—Listed in the Crazy Horse surrender ledger. Along with One Kills at Eight Steps, listed as "head-of-household." Lodge consisted of three adult females, five people in total.

Her Four Blankets (*Tasina topa win*; also probably Four Robes) (F)—(Hunkpapa Lakota-Teton Sioux)—b. circa 1855. Sitting Bull's wife.

Her Holy Door (aka Lost Woman; Pretty Door; *Nuni win*) (F)—(Hunkpapa Lakota-Teton Sioux)—b. circa 1816–d. 1884. Sitting Bull's mother.

Her Horse (*Tasunke*) (F)—(Hunkpapa Lakota-Teton Sioux)—b. circa 1871. Daughter of Red Thunder and Ripe. Only five years old at the time of the battle.

Her Looking Horse (*Tasunke wakita win*) (F)—(Hunkpapa Lakota-Teton Sioux)—b. 1874. A baby at the time of the battle. Daughter of Brave Thunder and Tall Woman.

Her Mysterious Pipe (*Tacan nupa wakan win*) (F)—(Hunkpapa Lakota-Teton Sioux)—b. circa 1867. Daughter of Chasing Alone and Whirlwind.

Her Nation (F)—(Lakota-Teton Sioux)—Still living at the Standing Rock Agency, Kenel, SD, in 1926 [courtesy of Dickson]. Participation in the battle is doubtful.

Her Neck (*Witahu*) (F)—(Hunkpapa Lakota-Teton Sioux)—b. circa 1867. Niece of Mosquito.

Her Plenty Horses (*Tasunke ota win*) (F)—(Hunkpapa Lakota-Teton Sioux)—b. circa 1864. Sitting Bull's daughter.

Her Plenty Horses (*Tasunke ota win*) (F)—(Hunkpapa Lakota-Teton Sioux)—b. circa 1865. Not related to Sitting Bull's daughter. Sister of Fighting Bear. Listed in the Sitting Bull Surrender Ledger.

Her Pony (*Tasunke*) (F)—(Hunkpapa Lakota-Teton Sioux)—b. circa 1864. Daughter of Killed by Thunder and Cedar Woman.

Her Pretty Road (*Tacan ku waste win*) (F)—(Hunkpapa Lakota-Teton Sioux)—b. circa 1833. Wife of the Hunkpapa warrior, Spotted Eagle.

Her Sacred Spirit (*Niya wakan win*) (F)—(Hunkpapa Lakota-Teton Sioux)—b. circa 1862. Sister-in-law of Shooting Bear.

High Backbone (or High Back)—(Minneconjou Lakota-Teton Sioux)—Listed as a Dakota chief in the LBHA's Summer 2001 *Research Review*. Presence confirmed by Myers.

High Bear (aka Tall Bear)-(Sans Arc Lakota-Teton Sioux)—d. 1910. A sub-chief. Presence confirmed by Myers.

High Bear (aka Tall Bear; White Antelope)—(Northern Cheyenne)—d. 7 Jul 1876, killed during the Sibley scout. Found the roster of a first sergeant and filled it with drawings of the battle. Fought against the Custer battalions. Presence confirmed by Myers and mentioned in Hardorff, *Lakota Recollections,* pages 29–30, footnote 15.

High Bear (*Mato Wakantuya*)-(Hunkpapa Lakota-Teton Sioux)—d. before 1884. Brother of Crow King.

High Bull (*Tatanka wankantuya*)—(Hunkpapa Lakota-Teton Sioux)—b. circa 1850. Listed in the Sitting Bull Surrender Ledger. Married to Left Hand Woman.

High Cat (F)—(Lakota-Teton Sioux)—At the Little Big Horn, but not involved in the fighting. Still living at the Standing Rock Agency, Fort Yates, ND, 1926 [courtesy of Dickson].

High Eagle—(Lakota-Teton Sioux)—d. 25 Jun 1876, killed at the Little Big Horn fighting Reno. Listed on the Sioux memorial. A Sioux chief. Known only as a Teton Sioux.

High Eagle (*Wanbli Wakantuya*)-(Oglala Lakota-Teton Sioux)—b. 1865–d. 1953. Lived to at least 88 [Stewart, *Custer's Luck,* opposite p. 145]. Also seen listed as a Hunkpapa. Presence confirmed by Myers, though he only lists him as a Teton Sioux.

High Elk—(Sans Arc Lakota-Teton Sioux)—d. 25 Jun 1876, killed at the Little Big Horn fighting Reno [Graham, *The Custer Myth,* p. 47; quoting Kill Eagle]. PVT W.O. Taylor (A) saw him after the fighting and described him: "In a little depression there lay outstretched a stalwart Sioux warrior, stark narked with the exception of a breech clout and moccasins. He lay with his head up the hill, his right arm extended in the direction the fatal shot had come, a look of grim defiance on his face, which was not disfigured with the streaks of yellow, green, and crimson, so common to many…. He had been scalped by some soldier, the greatest misfortune that could happen, for thereby his soul was annihilated…. Never had I seen a more perfect specimen of physical manhood, he must have been about thirty years old, nearly if not quite six feet in height and of splendid proportions. He looked like a bronze statue that had been thrown to the ground. It was such a form that MacMonnies might have had for a model when he sculptured 'The Last Arrow.' I could not help a feeling of sorrow as I stood gazing upon him. He was within a few hundred rods of his home and family which we had attempted to destroy and he had died to defend. The home of his slayer was perhaps a thousand miles away. In a few days the wolves and buzzards would have his remains torn asunder and scattered, for the soldiers had no disposition to bury a dead Indian, and his family and tribe were even then in full retreat.

"I have since learned that his name was High Elk. His medicine bag, which was all the property he had left on him I brought away as a souvenir of a very brave man in a memorable battle. It was carried on a belt and was made from the leather of a bootleg, fashioned in shape and size like a pistol cartridge box, and sewed together with fine wire, the flap studded with brass tacks. Among its contents were three little parcels of different colored dry paint, each done up in a piece of soft buckskin, a piece of dry flagroot, part of a coarse comb, a few matches and some thread and needles" [Taylor/ Martin, *With Custer on the Little Bighorn*, pp. 62–63].

High Hawk—(Northern Cheyenne)—d. some time after 1936. Only a young boy at the time of the battle. Watched the fighting from a distance. Attended the 60th reunion of the battle.

High Horse (also His High Horse)—(Sans Arc Lakota-Teton Sioux)—Identified by White Bull as a Sans Arc tribal leader.

High Horse—(Minneconjou Lakota-Teton Sioux)—d. 25 Jun 1876, killed at the Little Big Horn in the valley fight. Supposed to have helped kill a Ree [Myers, "Roster of Known Hostile Indians at the Battle of the Little Big Horn," *Research Review*, Summer 1991, Vol. 5, No. 2]. Killed in the fight against Custer's column.

High Walking ("Frank" High Walking)—(Northern Cheyenne). Son of One Horn. Presence confirmed by Myers. Still alive in 1921 and living at Lame Deer, Montana.

High White Man (also Tall White Man; *Wasicu Wankatuya*; aka Bad Horse; *Tasunke Sica*)—(Oglala Lakota-Teton Sioux)—b. circa 1829 or 1830–d. 1909. Listed in the Crazy Horse surrender register, 1877. Along with Brave Wolf and Red Shirt, listed as "head-of-household." Lodge consisted of three adult females, five male children, and three female children; total of fourteen people. Member of He Dog's Soreback Band. Husband of both Slow and To Scare with Feet [Dickson].

The Hill—(Oglala Lakota-Teton Sioux)—Listed in the Crazy Horse surrender ledger, 1877. Listed as "head-of-household." Lodge consisted of himself and one adult female; two people, total.

His Eagle Blanket—(Hunkpapa Lakota-Teton Sioux)—b. circa 1870. Only a young boy at the time of the battle. Son of Chasing Alone and Whirlwind.

His Fight (*Okicize Tawa*)—(Oglala Lakota-Teton Sioux)—b. circa 1831. Member of Low Dog's band.

His Good Horse (*Tasunke Waste*)—(Oglala Lakota-Teton Sioux)—b. circa 1846. Member of Iron Crow's band.

His Gray Horse (*Tasunke hinto*)—(Hunkpapa Lakota-Teton Sioux)—b. circa 1874. Only an infant at the time of the battle. Son of One Who Buys (F) and brother of One Who Takes Down.

His Holy Pipe—(Lakota-Teton Sioux)—Said to have wounded Isaiah Dorman [LBHA].

His Plenty Old Man (*Tawica hca ota*)—(Hunkpapa Lakota-Teton Sioux)—b. circa 1811–d. circa 1881, probably. Listed in the Sitting Bull Surrender Ledger. Wife was Pawnee Woman.

(Mrs.) His White Horse (F)—(Lakota-Teton Sioux)—Wife of White Horse (aka His White Horse).

Hoarse—(Oglala Lakota-Teton Sioux)—Listed in the Crazy Horse surrender ledger. Along with Living Bear and Crazy Heart, listed as "head-of-household." Lodge consisted of five adult females and three male children, eleven people in total.

Hole in Face—(Oglala Lakota-Teton Sioux)—Listed in the Crazy Horse surrender ledger, 1877. Listed as "head-of-household." Lodge consisted of one female adult and two male children; four people, total.

Hollow Horn Bear (*Mato Heli Dogeca*)—(Brulé Lakota-Teton Sioux)—b. circa 1850–d. 1913. Son of Iron Shell, though the LBHA lists him as the *father*, which is incorrect. Twenty-six years old at the time of the battle. His wife was Good Bed Woman. He was a summer roamer out of the Spotted Tail Agency. He and about twenty Two Kettle Lakota were out searching for lost ponies in May 1876, when they spotted Terry's column moving along the Heart River. They followed for a few days, then bypassed them and joined Sitting Bull's band. He claimed to have fought both Reno and Custer.

Hollow Horn Eagle—(Brulé Lakota-Teton Sioux)—Spoke of his part in the battle in a 1941 interview.

Hollow Horns-(Sans Arc Lakota-Teton Sioux)—d. 16 Dec 1876 or Apr 1877. Killed trying to surrender to Nelson Miles.

Hollow Sunflower—(Oglala Lakota-Teton Sioux)—Listed in the Crazy Horse surrender ledger, 1877. Listed as "head-of-household." Lodge consisted of two adult females and one female child; four people, total.

Hollow Wood—(Northern Cheyenne). At the 1926 reunion. Surrendered to Nelson Miles. Served as a scout.

Hollow Wood, "Minnie" (F)—(Lakota-Teton Sioux)—Her husband was Hollow Wood, but the only person with that name was a Cheyenne. She won the right to wear a war bonnet because of her participation in the battle.

Holy Black Tail Deer—(Oglala Lakota-Teton Sioux)—b. circa 1857–d. some time after 1932. A friend of Black Elk.

Holy Bull (also Holy Buffalo)—(Oglala Lakota-Teton Sioux)—In the Reno fight [LBHA].

Holy Cloud—(Nakota-Yankton Sioux)—Reputed to have fought alongside of Gray Whirlwind and Iron Bear.

Holy Face Bear—(Hunkpapa Lakota-Teton Sioux)—Said the soldiers fired too high [LBHA].

Holy Lodge (F)—(Sans Arc Lakota-Teton Sioux)—d. 1894. Married to White Bull, a Minneconjou, circa 1871. Iron White Man's daughter.

Holy Rock (also "Johnson" Holy Rock)—(Oglala Lakota-Teton Sioux)—b. circa 1866. His family was part of the Badger Band (band, *tiospaye*).

Holy Skin (*Ha Wakan*)—(Oglala Lakota-Teton Sioux)—b. circa 1850–d. circa 1918. Member of the Iron Crow band.

Holy Woman (F)—(Blackfeet Lakota-Teton Sioux)—Kill Eagle's daughter [Graham, *The Custer Myth,* p. 53].

Hona (also known as "Adam" Hona; also possibly *Hola* or Little Voice)—(If *Hona* rather than *Hola,* possibly Nakota-Yanktonnais Sioux, otherwise, Lakota-Teton Sioux)—Living at the Standing Rock Agency, Kenel, SD, 1929. Hardorff computed him to be Deeds' brother, but this is doubtful as that would add a third person to the Deeds-Brown Back incident and there is no historical support for that. If the notations in Hardorff are not incorrect, *Hona* may have been a very young uncle of Little Bear, Deeds' father [see *Hokahey!...,* p. 19].

Horn Chips (aka Encouraging Bear; also just Chips or Chipps)—(Oglala Lakota-Teton Sioux)—d. 4 Jan 1916. Holy man and Crazy Horse's medicine man. Claimed only 32 Indians were killed. Hardorff claimed Horn Chips was *not* present at the Little Big Horn, but as a "spiritual advisor" to Crazy Horse, there is evidence that Hardorff may be wrong. Helped Crazy Horse's father bury the famous warrior.

Horn Cloud (also "Joseph" Horn Cloud)—(Lakota-Teton Sioux)—Only a young boy at the time of the battle.

Horned Horse (also Horny Horse; Horn Horse; *Tasunke Heton*)—(Oglala Lakota-Teton Sioux)—b. circa 1822–d. 1897. A spokesman for Crazy Horse in 1877. It is not certain he was at the battle, though Liddic quotes him as if he were [*Vanishing Victory,* p. 159], and Dickson clearly believes he was there ["The Horned Horse Map," *Little Big Horn Associates Newsletter,* Vol. XVIII, No. 7, September 2009]. His son, White Eagle (or Lone Eagle), was killed in the Reno-valley fighting. Surrendered in April 1877, at the Red Cloud Agency, where he discussed the battle with First Lieutenant John Gregory Bourke, an aide to Crook during the campaign. He has also been listed as a Minneconjou, but he may have been confused with the Horned Horse below. Listed in the Crazy Horse surrender ledger, 1877. Along with At the End and Sees the Cow, listed as "head-of-household." Lodge consisted of three adult females and one male child; total of seven people.

Horned Horse (*Sunka kan heton*)—(Oglala Lakota-Teton Sioux; possibly originally a Minneconjou)—b. circa 1849. Possibly a member of Low Dog's band.

Horny Horse—(Hunkpapa Lakota-Teton Sioux)—Fought Custer's column. Presence confirmed by Myers.

Horse Bear—(Oglala Lakota-Teton Sioux)—Listed in the Crazy Horse surrender ledger, 1877. Along with Little Bull, listed as "head-of-household." Lodge consisted of four adult females, two male children, and three female children; a total of eleven people.

Horse Road(s) (aka Chicken Hawk)—(Northern Cheyenne). Father of Limber Bones or Limber Hand. Along with Big Nose, Little Shield, Wooden Leg, and Yellow Horse, one of five camp guards designated while people slept on the night of the 25th–26th [Marquis, *Wooden Leg,* p. 257]. Presence confirmed by Myers.

Horse Runs Ahead—(tribe unknown)—Wounded in the heel at the Rosebud fight. At the LBH fight, but did not get in it [LBHA].

Horse Stands (F)—(Oglala Lakota-Teton Sioux)—Married Shell Boy (about 1857). Mother of Right-in-the-Camp.

Horseshoe—(Lakota-Teton Sioux)—At the Cheyenne River Agency, 1926.

Howling Eagle—(Cheyenne).

Howling Wolf—(Northern Cheyenne). Wore a war bonnet in the battle. Known to have fought the Custer column. Presence confirmed by Myers.

Human Fingers (*Wicanaspuhu*)—(Oglala Lakota-Teton Sioux)—b. circa 1799–d. circa 1891. Probably a member of Iron Crow's band.

Hump (aka Hump Nose; *Etokeah*)-(Minneconjou Lakota-Teton Sioux)— b. 1842 or 1848–d. 1908. Iron Thunder's older brother (by one year). Also the brother of Little Crow. One of the most hostile of the non-treaty Lakota. Had a leading part in the Fetterman Massacre in 1866. He also claimed that it was noon when Reno attacked; fought Reno, then Custer. In the forefront of the attack on Calhoun Hill, where he was badly wounded in the leg. Sometimes confused with High Backbone. Also listed as an Oglala and a Sans Arc. I carry him here, only. "Every able-bodied Indian there took part in the fight, as far as I could tell. Those that did not join in the fight it was because they could not find room to get in" [Willert, *Little Big Horn Diary*, p. 352, quoting Graham, *The Custer Myth*]. Presence confirmed by Myers.

Hump Nose—(Sans Arc Lakota-Teton Sioux)— Presence confirmed by Myers.

Humped Little Crow—(Minneconjou Lakota-Teton Sioux)— He claimed *Inkpaduta's* son got Custer's horse [LBHA].

Hunts the Enemy (aka Owns Sword)—(Oglala Lakota-Teton Sioux)— Member of the Bad Face band [LBHA].

Ice (aka White Bull; Ice Bear; *Ho-tu-a-hwa-ko-mas*)—(Northern Cheyenne)— b. 1837–d. 1921. A holy man and warrior chief. Paraded around wearing a captured guidon. Married to Wool Woman. Older brother of Antelope and father of Noisy Walking. Son of Black Moccasin [see Marquis, *Wooden Leg*, p. 249]. Did not participate directly in the fighting. Listed as a Cheyenne war chief in the LBHA's Summer 2001 *Research Review.* Tall Bull claimed Ice was one of the three Cheyenne head chiefs at the battle (along with Two Moons and Lame White Man) [Camp/Hammer, *Custer in '76*, p. 212]. Presence confirmed by Myers, although he carries "Ice Bear" and "White Bull" separately. I have chosen not to do so, for they were both chiefs leading me to believe they were the same person. Too many apparent duplications in Myers.

Inkpaduta (aka Scarlet Top, Red Point, Red Top, Red Tip, Scarlet Point)—(*Wahpekute*/Dakota-Santee Sioux)-b. around 1815–d. near Batoche, Saskatchewan in 1878 or, more likely 1879. The son of Black Eagle (*Wamdesapa*; d. 1846). Had scars from smallpox. Had a large family: daughters as well as about 12 sons. He was apparently a kind and decent man and even had some white friends. He was continually provoked, however— including the killing of his brother and family and his mother— and finally went on a rampage that the army was never able to stop. He was the most feared Indian

of the time—1850's and 1860's. Good friends with Sitting Bull. Evan Connell wrote that no one hated the whites as much as *Inkpaduta*. James Donovan and Greg Michno also say *Inkpaduta* led the Santee at the LBH. Edgar Stewart called him a gangster. He was responsible for the Spirit Lake (Iowa) Massacre in June 1857 [*Custer's Luck*, p. 18]. A "Red Top" is listed as a Dakota war chief in the LBHA's Summer 2001 *Research Review.* "…[T]he only major Sioux chieftain never to make peace with, never to surrender to, and never to be captured by the United States government" [Donovan, *A Terrible Glory*, p. 341]. Presence at the LBH confirmed by Myers.

Iron Bear—(Nakota-Yankton Sioux)— Fought alongside Gray Whirlwind and Holy Cloud. Traveled with Thunder Bear from old Fort Peck.

Iron Bull—(Oglala Lakota-Teton Sioux)— Claimed there were about 6,000 people in the village.

Iron Cedar—(Hunkpapa Lakota-Teton Sioux)— During the valley fight, he was up on the bluffs east of the river. Brought word to warriors in valley fight of additional soldiers in the coulees. Presence confirmed by Myers.

Iron Child (*Maza Cincala*)—(Oglala Lakota-Teton Sioux)— b. circa 1848–d. circa 1914. Member of Little Hawk's band.

Iron Crow (*Kangi Maza*)—(Oglala Lakota-Teton Sioux)— b. circa 1828. Headman of a small family camp.

Iron Dog—(Hunkpapa Lakota-Teton Sioux). In his November 2, 1876, dispatch to COL Nelson Miles (5I), COL W. B. Hazen (6I) referred to Iron Dog as Sitting Bull's brother-in-law. He had been at Fort Peck, Montana, with about 100 lodges, but left in a hurry as Hazen's command approached. With Sitting Bull in Canada in 1877.

Iron Elk—(Hunkpapa Lakota-Teton Sioux)— One of Sitting Bull's bodyguards.

Iron Hail (*Wasu maza win*) (F)—(Hunkpapa Lakota-Teton Sioux)— b. 1875. An infant at the time of the battle. Daughter of Wears the Fir Coat and Beans.

Iron Hawk (*Cetan Maza*)—(Oglala Lakota-Teton Sioux)— b. circa 1834–d. 1908. Member of He Dog's Soreback Band. Interviewed by Judge Ricker in 1907 [Dickson]. "Homer's" father (see entry for Runs in Circle, aka "Homer" Iron Hawk). Dickson believes he was an Oglala, while both Michno and Hardorff carry him as Hunkpapa. Edgar I. Stewart, in his book, *Custer's Luck*, claimed he lived to at least 99, but this is incorrect [opposite p. 145]. Wounded at the Little Big Horn.

Iron Heart (*Maza canteya*) — (Hunkpapa Lakota-Teton Sioux) — b. circa 1841. Son of Elk Horn and Lady. Listed in the Sitting Bull Surrender Ledger.

Iron Horn (also Iron Horse and possibly Iron Heart; *Hesan nimaza*) — (Hunkpapa Lakota-Teton Sioux) — b. circa 1816. Three lodges (twenty people), Sep 1876, at Standing Rock. A brother of Rain-in-the-Face.

Iron Horse — (Oglala Lakota-Teton Sioux) — At the 1926 reunion.

Iron Lightning — (Lakota-Teton Sioux) — Fought Custer's column. It is possible this is the Minneconjou also named Iron Thunder. Presence confirmed by Myers, though he only lists him as a Teton Sioux.

Iron Magpie — (Oglala Lakota-Teton Sioux) — Listed in the Crazy Horse surrender ledger. Along with Pretty Legs, he was listed as "head-of-household." There were four adult females and five female children in his lodge, a total of eleven people.

Iron People — (Lakota-Teton Sioux) — Living at the Cheyenne River Agency, 1926.

Iron Shell — (Brulé Lakota-Teton Sioux) — Hollow Horn Bear's father. Signed the 1868 treaty [Stewart, *Custer's Luck,* p. 50].

Iron Shirt ("Fred" Iron Shirt) — (Northern Cheyenne). Still alive in 1921 and living at Lame Deer, Montana. A headman of the Crazy Dogs warrior society, or as Wooden Leg said, one of the nine "little chiefs" [Marquis, *Wooden Leg,* p. 212]. Presence confirmed by Myers.

Iron Star — (Hunkpapa Lakota-Teton Sioux) — A relative of No Neck [Dickson].

Iron Star — (Minneconjou Lakota-Teton Sioux) — d. 7 May 1877. Warrior chief. Presence confirmed by Myers.

Iron Tail — (Oglala Lakota-Teton Sioux) — In Canada after Crazy Horse's death [Neihardt, *Black Elk Speaks,* p. 149].

Iron Thunder (possibly also Iron Lightning)- (Minneconjou Lakota-Teton Sioux) — b. 1843 or 1848. Twenty-eight-year-old brother of Hump and Little Crow (LBHA claims he was 33 at time of battle, but this wrong; he was 33 at the time of the 1881 interview [Graham, *The Custer Myth,* p. 79]). One of five or six Indians — three or four Sioux and two Cheyenne — who rode along the bluffs with White Bull to Weir Point, watching Keogh's column move across Luce Ridge. Fought both Reno and Custer. Presence confirmed by Myers.

Iron White Man (*Maza Wicasa*; also, "Joseph" Iron White Man) — (Oglala Lakota-Teton Sioux) — b. circa 1859 – d. 1930. Listed in the Crazy Horse surrender ledger, 1877. Along with Grass Prick, listed as "head-of-household." Lodge consisted of four adult females, two male children, and one female child; total of nine people. Member of Little Hawk's band.

Iron White Man — (Sans Arc Lakota-Teton Sioux) — Father of Holy Lodge. Part of Spotted Eagle's band [Dickson].

Iroquois Imitation — (Oglala Lakota-Teton Sioux) — Listed in the Crazy Horse surrender ledger. Along with Top Lodge, Big Belly Mule, and Yellow Left, listed as "head-of-household." Lodge consisted of two female adults, one male child, and three female children; total of ten people.

Jack Rabbit — (Lakota-Teton Sioux) — Followed Sitting Bull to Canada [LBHA].

Jealous Bear — (Northern Cheyenne). Listed in the Crazy Horse surrender ledger [CBHMA]. Probably present at the LBH.

Jumping Horse — (Oglala Lakota-Teton Sioux) — A young man and friend of Black Elk.

Just Walks — (Northern Cheyenne). At the 1926 reunion. Surrendered to Nelson Miles. Served as a scout.

Kansu (also Young *Kansu*) — (Hunkpapa Lakota-Teton Sioux) — Charged Reno with One Bull and others as the soldiers fell back toward the timber [LBHA].

Kicking Bear (F) — (Oglala Lakota-Teton Sioux) — Wife of Crazy Horse.

Kicking Bear (*Mato Wanar tako*) — (Oglala Lakota-Teton Sioux) — b. in an Oglala village, 1848 – d. 1904. Brother of Flying Hawk; son of Black Fox and Iron Cedar Woman. The first fighting he was involved in was when Reno's troops made their mad dash out of the timber. Along with Kicking Bear, he supposedly killed one of the Ree scouts in the Reno fight. If the scout, Little Brave, had been finished off near Reno Hill, the one Red Feather and Kicking Bear claimed to have killed had to have been Bob-tail Bull. Red Feather shot his horse, Kicking Bear then shot him twice, and Red Feather finished him off with a knife. Close ally of Crazy Horse and with Crazy Horse in the Custer fight. Presence confirmed by Myers and Hardorff.

Kill Assiniboine — (Hunkpapa Lakota-Teton Sioux) — Hattie Lawrence's husband [Liddic, *Vanishing Victory,* p. 104].

Kill Eagle (or Kills Eagle; *Wan-bli-kte*)—(Blackfeet Lakota-Teton Sioux)—Fifty-six years old at time of battle. Out of the Standing Rock Agency. A chief with 26 lodges. CPT J. S. Poland's report says "some 20 lodges" [CPT J. S. Poland's report; Graham, *The Custer Myth,* p. 46]. "[S]aid the soldiers didn't come within 60 yards of the ford [he is referring to Ford D; probably Sioux Ford on the McElfresh map, but there is a remote possibility it could also be Gibbon's Ford] before they drove them off and up the hill" [Liddic, *Vanishing Victory,* p. 147]. Described a move beyond Cemetery Ridge by the soldiers, northwest to another ford on the LBH [Ford D], then a move back to where the present cemetery location. Presence confirmed by Myers, though he only lists him as a Teton Sioux. Hardorff claimed he was an agency Indian [*Hoka-hey!...,* p. 122]. On 18 Sep 1876, a dispatch from Phil Sheridan dated the previous day, was received by General R. C. Drum in Chicago. In it, Sheridan informed Drum that, "Col. Carlin reports that Kill Eagle and Little Wound, with a hundred people, all their arms, ammunition and about a hundred ponies, surrendered to him at Standing Rock Agency on the 15th. Twenty-nine men surrendered, all of whom were in the fight on the Little Big Horn" [Hutchins, *The Army and Navy Journal,* p. 100; the 23 Sep 1876 edition of the *Journal*].

Kill the [?] [possibly, Brave Thunder]—(Sans Arc Lakota-Teton Sioux)—Head of the family. Part of Spotted Eagle's band [Dickson].

Kill the Bear—(Sans Arc Lakota-Teton Sioux)—Head of the family. Part of Spotted Eagle's band [Dickson].

Kill the Bear [# 2]—(Sans Arc Lakota-Teton Sioux)—Head of the family. Part of Spotted Eagle's band [Dickson].

Kill with Anger (*Ocinsica Kte*)—(Hunkpapa Lakota-Teton Sioux).

Killed by Night (*Hankepi wicakte*)—(Oglala Lakota-Teton Sioux)—b. circa 1859. Son of Iron Hawk and Showing Breath; brother of Runs in Circle ("Homer" Iron Hawk). Member of He Dog's Soreback Band.

Killed by Thunder (*Wakin yankte pi*; also, later, Red Thunder)—(Hunkpapa Lakota-Teton Sioux)—b. circa 1843. Listed in the Sitting Bull Surrender Ledger. Wife was Cedar Woman.

Killed While Standing (*Najin han wica kte*)—(Hunkpapa Lakota-Teton Sioux)—b. circa 1864.

Kills Alive (also "Henry" Kills Alive)—(Lakota-Teton Sioux)—Said only twenty-one Indians were killed [LBHA]. Still living at the Standing Rock

Agency, Little Eagle, SD, in 1926 [courtesy of Dickson]. At the camp, but he was either too young to participate in the fighting or he simply did not get into the battle.

Kills Alive (*Niyake kte*)—(Hunkpapa Lakota-Teton Sioux)—b. circa 1870. Young boy at the time of the battle. Son of Shooting Bear and Pretty Woman.

Kills an Enemy (*Sugn ole he kte*)—(Oglala Lakota-Teton Sioux)—b. 1875. Only a year old at the battle. Son of Little Bull and Little Calf.

Kills at Night (also Kills in the Night)—(Oglala Lakota-Teton Sioux)—Listed in the Crazy Horse surrender ledger, 1877. Along with Undone, listed as "head-of-household." Lodge consisted of one adult female, one male child, and one female child; total of five people. In the battle.

Kills at Night—(Lakota-Teton Sioux)—This individual was at the camp, but did not participate in the fighting, making him a different individual from the Kills At Night listed above. May have been a son, the male child shown above. Still living at the Standing Rock Agency, Little Eagle, SD, in 1926.

Kills Crow (also "Anselm" Kills Crow)—(Lakota-Teton Sioux)—Still living at the Standing Rock Agency, Little Eagle, SD, in 1926 [courtesy of Dickson]. At the camp, but he was either too young to participate in the fighting or he simply did not get into the battle.

Kills Enemy in Winter—(Oglala Lakota-Teton Sioux)—With Black Bear's party watching Custer at the divide [LBHA].

Kills Hawk (also "Robert" Kills Hawk)—(Lakota-Teton Sioux)—Living at the Standing Rock Agency, Bullhead, SD, 1929. Fought in the battle.

Kills Her Own (*Ki kte win*) (F)—(Hunkpapa Lakota-Teton Sioux)—b. circa 1872. Daughter of Slow White Buffalo and One Who Judges. Only a small child at the time of the battle.

Kills Him (also Killed)—(Sans Arc Lakota-Teton Sioux)—d. 25 Jun 1876, killed at the Little Big Horn fighting Custer's column. Body location unknown.

Kills in Lodge (*Tiyo wica kte*)—(Hunkpapa Lakota-Teton Sioux)—b. circa 1864. Listed in the Sitting Bull Surrender Ledger. Only twelve at the time of the battle. Brother of Comes Back with Growling.

Kills in the Night (or Kills Night)—(Northern Cheyenne). At the 1926 reunion. One of those who chased a lone soldier on a sorrel horse near the very end of the fight. Old Bear was another. Apparently, Turtle Rib, the Minneconjou, was a third. Presence confirmed by Myers.

Kills Many—(Northern Cheyenne). Listed in the Crazy Horse surrender ledger [CBHMA]. Probably present at the LBH.

Kills Standing—(Minneconjou Lakota-Teton Sioux)—Brother of (Lazy) White Bull.

Kills the Hawk—(Lakota-Teton Sioux)—Not the same man listed above as "Robert" Kills Hawk. Like Robert, however, this man was also still living at the Standing Rock Agency, Bullhead, SD, 1926 [courtesy of Dickson]. Known to have been in the fighting at the Little Big Horn.

Kills the Married—(Oglala Lakota-Teton Sioux) —Listed in the Crazy Horse surrender ledger, 1877. Listed as "head-of-household." Lodge consisted of two adult females; three people, total.

Kills Twice—(Lakota-Teton Sioux)—b. circa 1868. As a young boy he did not get into the fighting, but he held horses for many of the warriors.

Kills with Difficulty (*Tehiya Wica Kte*)—(Oglala Lakota-Teton Sioux)—b. circa 1825–d. before 1886. Member of Little Hawk's band [Dickson].

King Man (also seen as Kingman)—(Sans Arc Lakota-Teton Sioux)—Head of the family. Part of Spotted Eagle's band [Dickson].

Kingman (also "Harry" Kingman; probably also King Man)—(Sans Arc Lakota-Teton Sioux)—b. circa 1866–d. 1956. Son of King Man. Did not get into the fighting, merely watched the battle.

Kingman—(Minneconjou Lakota-Teton Sioux)— Son of Dog's Back Bone.

Knife—(Oglala Lakota-Teton Sioux)—With Black Bear's party watching Custer at the divide [LBHA]. Listed in the Crazy Horse surrender ledger [CBHMA].

Knife Chief—(Oglala Lakota-Teton Sioux)— Listed as the #3 Dakota war chief in the LBHA's Summer 2001 *Research Review*. The *Review* carried him as a Hunkpapa, but the LBHA and CBHMA carry him as an Oglala, which is how he is listed here, especially since Red Hawk also said he was Oglala. Wounded in the body, the shot breaking both arms. Probably shot during the valley fight, but possibly during the Reno hilltop fight instead. Presence confirmed by Myers who also has him listed as an Oglala. Father of Steals Horses. Listed in the Crazy Horse surrender ledger, 1877. Listed as "head-of-household." Lodge consisted of three adult females, seven male children, and eight female children; nineteen people, total. Knife

Chief's was the largest lodge in the surrender ledger.

Knife King—(Hunkpapa Lakota-Teton Sioux)— Wounded while recalling warriors from the firing line near Reno Hill, 26 Jun 1876.

Knocked Down by Hail (*Wasu kato*)—(Hunkpapa Lakota-Teton Sioux)—b. circa 1874. Baby at the time of the battle. Son of *Zu-Me* and Old Bear Woman.

Lady (*Wiko ske*) (F)—(Hunkpapa Lakota-Teton Sioux)—b. circa 1823. Wife of Elk Horn.

Lame Deer (*Ta-ak-cha-ooshta*)-(Minneconjou Lakota-Teton Sioux)—d. 7 May 1877. Along with Spotted Elk, one of the two main Minneconjou chiefs. One of the primary leaders of the battle. Father of Flying by and Crazy Heart. Killed on 7 May 1877 by Nelson Miles' soldiers. Presence confirmed by Myers.

Lame Red Shirt-(Minneconjou Lakota-Teton Sioux)—d. 16 Dec 1876 or Apr 1877. Killed while attempting to surrender to Nelson Miles.

Lame Sioux—(Northern Cheyenne). Hunting with Wooden Leg when they spotted Crook on the Rosebud.

Lame White Bull—Southern Cheyenne. A warrior in the Crazy Dog Warrior Society. Fought Custer's column. Presence confirmed by Myers.

Lame White Man (aka White Man Cripple, Mad Wolf, Mad Hearted Wolf, Rabid Wolf, Dull Knife. There may be some confusion with these names, *possibly* adding up to more than the usual three. The Sioux called him Bearded Man or Moustache, possibly confusing him with another Cheyenne of the same name, also killed at the LBH)—(Southern Cheyenne)—b. circa 1839–d. 25 Jun 1876, killed at the Little Big Horn. Presence verified by Steven W. Myers, "Roster of Known Hostile Indians," *Research Review*, 1991, Vol. 5, No. 2. Myers carries "Bearded Man" as a different individual, which is done here, as well. More than one source claim he was probably the leading Cheyenne chief, although some dispute that claim. Wooden Leg stated Lame White Man was the head Cheyenne warrior chief, not Two Moons [Graham, *The Custer Myth*, p. 104; also, Marquis, *Wooden Leg*]. Tall Bull claimed he was one of the three Cheyenne head chiefs at the battle, along with White Bull [Ice] and Two Moons [Camp/Hammer, *Custer in '76*, p. 212]. Considered one of the bravest and wisest men in the Cheyenne tribe. Wooden Leg said he was regarded as the most capable warrior chief among the Cheyenne. Head soldier of his tribe's Elk Society [Liddic], also known as the Elkhorn Scrapers society. Thirty-seven years old at the time of the battle. Joined the main body of Indians with ten lodges at the end of Apr 1876. According to Greg Michno, he was killed in the Deep Ravine-Cemetery Ravine area on the way to Custer Hill, "a few hundred yards down Custer Ridge from Last Stand Hill." While this is close, it does not fit the description provided by Hardorff. In *Hokahey!...*, p. 65, Hardorff refers to him as Bearded Man, claiming the warrior, Little Crow, was inadvertently lifting the dead Cheyenne's scalp, mistaking him for a Crow or Shoshone scout. This occurred "on the west slope of Custer [Battle] Ridge, just below the crest," and a "few hundred yards farther north" of the Custer/Battle Ridge mid-way point.

Michno's description of where the body was found does not agree with the description given by Wooden Leg. Early on in the Wooden Leg story, he tells of crossing the LBH at what is Ford B, moving up Deep Coulee, then into a gulch leading toward Calhoun Coulee. His description of the 40 soldiers coming off the hill and advancing to the ridge where the Indians were comes entirely too early in the narrative to be anything other than Calhoun Coulee and the C Company charge (*not* the charge off Last Stand Hill by E Company). This is the area where Lame White Man led his charge into the soldiers. Wooden Leg's narrative from this point on is very clear and has him moving to the north side of the field, via the eastern ridges and gullies and the Keogh Sector. After the battle, Wooden Leg tells of going back and finding Noisy Walking and Lame White Man. His description of Noisy Walking also calls into question whether or not he was a so-called "suicide boy." Wooden Leg was 18 at the time of the fight and he claimed Noisy Walking was the same age. That would seem to eliminate him as a "suicide boy."

Had been with the Northern Cheyenne for so long, he and his family were considered part of that branch. Wife was Twin Woman. Children were Crane Woman and Red Hat. Brother-in-law to Tall Bull. His maternal grandson was John Stands in Timber.

"Larrabee, Lucilee" (F)—(Lakota-Teton Sioux)— b. circa 1872. Still alive in 1962. She was in the village as a small child when the fighting broke out (source: Little Big Horn Photo Registry, numbers 0941–0942).

The Last—(Oglala Lakota-Teton Sioux)—Listed in the Crazy Horse surrender ledger. Along with Sitting Horse, Bull Man, and White Rabbit, he is listed as "head-of-household." In addition, his lodge had one adult female, three male children, and three female children; eleven people in all.

Last Bear (*Mato Ehake*)—(Oglala Lakota-Teton Sioux)—b. circa 1849. Member of Low Dog's band.

Last Bull—(Northern Cheyenne). A headman of the Kit Foxes warrior society. Wooden Leg called him the "leading chief" of the society. Wooden Leg said he was held in particularly high esteem as a "warrior chief" [Marquis, *Wooden Leg*, p. 211]. Since the Kit Fox society was the camp guards on the 25th, he *may* have fought at Ford B. Had a wife and two daughters, probably all at the LBH. Presence confirmed by Myers.

Last Woman (*Ehake inyanke*)—(Hunkpapa Lakota-Teton Sioux)—b. circa 1874. Small child at the time of the battle. Son of White Dog and Pretty Woman.

Laughter (F)—(Lakota-Teton Sioux)—Listed in the Crazy Horse surrender ledger, 1877. Listed as "head-of-household." Lodge consisted of one male child and one female child; total of three people.

Lays Laughing—(Oglala Lakota-Teton Sioux)—Listed in the Crazy Horse surrender ledger, 1877. Along with Fat Rump (# 2) and Short Brulé, he was listed as "head-of-household." Lodge consisted of four adult females and one female child; a total of eight people.

Lean Crow—(Lakota-Teton Sioux)—Followed Sitting Bull to Canada.

Leaper—(Lakota-Teton Sioux)—Known only to be a Sioux. Uncertain if he was at the battle, though circumstantial comments place him there.

Left Hand (aka Long Horn)—(Cheyenne)—d. 25 Jun 1876, killed at the Little Big Horn. Little Wolf's cousin and father of Red Bird. Son of Ice and Wool Woman; nephew of Antelope (Kate Bighead and/or possibly Howling Woman, if she isn't the same person). Killed fighting the Custer battalions [Myers, "Roster of Known Hostile Indians at the Battle of the Little Big Horn," *Research Review*, Summer 1991, Vol. 5, No. 2].

Left Hand—(Arapaho)—Born in the Powder River country, the son of a man called Cherry. He was part Blackfoot and part Cheyenne, but was affiliated with the Arapaho for most of his life. Mistook a Lakota for a Crow and killed him using a lance [Graham, *The Custer Myth*, p. 110]. In 1920, he and Waterman were the only two Arapaho surviving from the LBH fight.

Left Hand Shooter (or Left Handed Shooter)—(Northern Cheyenne). A headman of the Elkhorn Scraper warrior society, or as Wooden Leg called him, one of the nine "little chiefs" [Marquis, *Wooden Leg*, p. 211]. Presence confirmed by Myers.

Left Hand Woman (*Catka win*) (F)—(Hunkpapa Lakota-Teton Sioux)—b. circa 1852. Married to High Bull.

Left Handed Ice—(Lakota-Teton Sioux)—d. 25 Jun 1876, killed at the Little Big Horn. There was a Sioux who had been an army scout during the campaign, but who had left and joined the hostiles. This was *Chat-ka*, aka Left Hand, a Hunkpapa Sioux. These two may be the same, but Myers makes no allusion to him, only that this fellow was a Teton and was killed some time during the fighting [Myers, "Roster of Known Hostile Indians at the Battle of the Little Big Horn," *Research Review*, Summer 1991, Vol. 5, No. 2, p. 8].

Left Handed Woman (*Catka win la*) (F)—(Hunkpapa Lakota-Teton Sioux)—b. circa 1847. Wife of Black Bird. Listed in the Sitting Bull Surrender Ledger.

Leggings—(Oglala Lakota-Teton Sioux)—Listed in the Crazy Horse surrender ledger, 1877. Listed as "head-of-household." Lodge consisted of two adult females, three male children, and one female child; total of seven people.

Lightning ("Frank" Lightning)—(Northern Cheyenne). Told John Stands in Timber about the battle.

Lightning Killer—(Oglala Lakota-Teton Sioux)—Listed in the Crazy Horse surrender ledger, 1877. Listed as "head-of-household." Lodge consisted of two adult females and one female child; four people, total.

Lights (also The Lights; *Cragre* or Chases Red Clouds, Runs After the Clouds; *Mahpiyah luwa isaye*)-(Minneconjou Lakota-Teton Sioux)—b. circa 1853; twenty-three years old at time of the battle. Interviewed in 1909 by Sewell B. Weston. Fought under Spotted Elk. In the fights with Crook (17 Jun 1876) and Reno. Got in the Custer fight in time to see Custer's men moving along Nye-Cartwright. The soldiers got to within only a quarter-mile of the river, then moved — in good order — to Greasy Grass Ridge (this is probably Calhoun or Finley-Finckle Ridge). They then proceeded to Calhoun Hill. Lights himself, was just northeast of Calhoun Hill at the time. Listed in the Crazy Horse surrender ledger, 1877. Along with He Dog, Clown (# 2), Wound in Back, and one other whose name appeared illegible, listed as "head-of-household." Lodge consisted of three adult women and three male children; total of eleven people.

The Lights—(Oglala Lakota-Teton Sioux)—Listed in the Crazy Horse surrender ledger [CBHMA]. Probably present at the LBH.

Likes to Fight—(Oglala Lakota-Teton Sioux)—Listed in the Crazy Horse surrender ledger. Listed as "head-of-household." His lodge had two female adults and two female children, for a total of five people.

Limber Bones (aka Limber Hand, Limber Lance)—(Northern Cheyenne)—b. circa 1862–d. 25 Jun 1876, killed at the Little Big Horn. One of the "suicide warrior" [Myers, "Roster of Known Hostile Indians at the Battle of the Little Big Horn," *Research Review*, Summer 1991, Vol. 5, No. 2]. Unmarried; twenty years old. Killed on the north slope of Custer Hill. Son of Horse Roads. Buried in the hills west of the camp.

Limber Hand (also Limberhand)—(Northern Cheyenne)—b. 1876. Only an infant at the time of the battle. A cousin of Limber Bones.

Limping Black Elk—(Lakota-Teton Sioux)—Presence confirmed by Myers, though he only lists him as a Teton Sioux.

Limpy—(Northern Cheyenne). Surrendered to Miles, then served as a scout. At the 1926 reunion.

(Mrs.) Limpy (F)—(Northern Cheyenne)—Wounded in the breast during the fighting.

Lips Wears Salt—(Brulé Lakota-Teton Sioux)—Eventually settled at Pine Ridge.

Little Assiniboine (*Hohe Cikala*; aka Jumping Bull; *Tatanka Psica*)-(Assiniboine/Hunkpapa Lakota-Teton Sioux)—b. circa 1844–d. 15 Dec 1890 at Wounded Knee. His parents were killed about 1855 and Sitting Bull later adopted him. By 1868 he was married and had children, among them a boy named Chase Them Wounded, theoretically making the boy a grandson of the Hunkpapa warrior. Known to be at the Little Big Horn. He went to Canada with Sitting Bull and was later listed in Crawler's Band when they were transferred to the Standing Rock Agency in 1881 [Dickson]. Along with this son, Little Assiniboine was killed at the Standing Rock Reservation in the attempt to arrest Sitting Bull.

Little Back—(Oglala Lakota-Teton Sioux)—Listed in the Crazy Horse surrender ledger, 1877. Along with Gopher, listed as "head-of-household." Lodge consisted of three adult females, two male children, and one female child; total of eight people.

Little Bear (*Mato Cikala;* quite possibly the same man as Brown Pants, Brown Back, Brown Ass, or Pants, though newer research is making that problematic; but certainly, if this man was Deeds's father, then also known as Crawler)—(Hunkpapa or

Sans Arc Lakota-Teton Sioux)—Deeds' father; also the father of Moving Robe Woman. Wounded while charging Custer Hill. Friend of Elk Nation, who saved him when wounded. Presence confirmed by Myers. Hardorff claimed he was the father of Deeds and they were the two spotted by Varnum and his scouts when they were at the Crow's Nest. He also claims they were Sans Arc [*On the Little Bighorn with Walter Camp*, p. 57, footnote 4]. One of those who discovered Custer's column at or near the divide, returning to warn the camp. He had been east of the village with others—including his son Deeds who was killed—hunting and looking for stray horses, when they spotted the soldiers. This took place near where Reno crossed the LBH. One of those who spread the alarm. May have been "old." Black Bear tells of the story in Camp/Hammer, *Custer in '76*, pages 203–204.

Much of the confusion with names may come from the fact that Deeds and Little Bear/Crawler were out together on the morning of the 25th. They returned and Little Bear sent his son out again. The boy then was riding with Brown Back when he was killed by Reno's Ree or Crow scouts.

Little Bear—(Northern Cheyenne). Listed in the Crazy Horse surrender ledger [CBHMA]. Fought the Custer column.

Little Big Man—(Northern Cheyenne)—b. circa 1850.

Little Big Man—(Oglala Lakota-Teton Sioux)—b. circa 1840–d. 1887. Fought against both Reno and Custer. Made a drawing of the battle. Listed in the Crazy Horse surrender ledger, 1877. Listed as "head-of-household." Lodge consisted of one adult female and one female child; total of three people. Little Big Man was reputed to have been the Indian trying to subdue Crazy Horse as the latter pulled a knife on some soldiers, just before being bayoneted in 1877. Crazy Horse died that evening or early the following morning.

Little Bird (also Littlebird; "Peter" Littlebird)—(Northern Cheyenne)—d. 1946. Too young to get in the fighting. Possibly the son of the Cheyenne warrior, Little Bird. He claimed women rounded up the stray horses after the fighting was over.

Little Bird—(Northern Cheyenne). Wounded in the thigh during a chase in the valley fight against Reno. Wore a trailing war bonnet. Presence confirmed by Myers.

Little Boy—(Oglala Lakota-Teton Sioux)—Listed in the Crazy Horse surrender ledger, 1877. Along with Thick Face, listed as "head-of-household." Lodge consisted of one male child and one female child; four people, total.

Little Buck—(Oglala Lakota-Teton Sioux)—Listed in the Crazy Horse surrender ledger.

Little Buck Elk—(Hunkpapa Lakota-Teton Sioux)—Claimed Indians were as "thick as bees" in the fight, "…and in such great numbers that all of them could not participate" [Hutchins, *The Army and Navy Journal*, p. 106, in a 21 Oct 1876 edition of the *Journal*, citing a 25 Sep 1876 letter from Indian Agent Mitchell from Fort Peck, M.T.]. Claimed he was in the fight against Custer.

Little Buffalo—(Hunkpapa Lakota-Teton Sioux)—Hit a soldier with his bridle, then took the soldier's horse [LBHA].

Little Bull (*Tatanka Ciqala*)—(Oglala Lakota-Teton Sioux)—b. circa 1846. Husband of Little Calf and father of One Who Goes out and Kills an Enemy. Member of He Dog's Soreback Band in 1881, but probably Low Dog's band at the time of the battle. Listed in the Crazy Horse surrender ledger, 1877. Along with Horse Bear, listed as "head-of-household." Lodge consisted of four adult females, two male children, and three female children; a total of eleven people.

Little Calf (*Tajila*) (F)—(Oglala Lakota-Teton Sioux)—Wife of Little Bull.

Little Chief—(Lakota-Teton Sioux)—b. circa 1872.

Little Chief—(Northern Cheyenne). A "Council of the 44" chief.

Little Chief—(Southern Cheyenne). Fishing in the river with White Shield, not far from Ash (Reno) Creek when they spotted the soldiers [LBHA].

Little Coyote—(Northern Cheyenne).

Little Creek—(Northern Cheyenne). A headman of the Crazy Dogs warrior society, or as Wooden Leg said, one of the nine "little chiefs" [Marquis, *Wooden Leg*, p. 212]. Presence confirmed by Myers.

Little Crow—(Hunkpapa Lakota-Teton Sioux).

Little Crow (*Inkpa-huta*)—(Minneconjou Lakota-Teton Sioux)—He was thought to be the man who accidentally scalped either Bearded Man or Lame White Man depending on the source. He mistook him for an army Ree scout. Brother of Hump and Iron Thunder. Myers claims his father was Red Top, though this may not be the famous *Inkpaduta*/Red Top. Said to have caught Custer's horse. Presence confirmed by Myers.

Little Crow—(*Wahpekute*/Dakota-Santee Sioux)—Led the Santee Sioux in the 1862 "Minnesota massacres" [Stewart, *Custer's Luck*, p. 19]. It is doubtful—though not certain—that he was at the Little Big Horn and he is listed here primarily as a historical figure.

Little Current—(Sioux)—With Sitting Bull in Canada. At the Little Big Horn battle.

Little Dog—(Lakota-Teton Sioux)—At the Cheyenne River Agency in 1926.

Little Eagle (*Wanbli Cika*)—(Oglala Lakota-Teton Sioux)—b. circa 1836. Fought alongside Kill Eagle. Presence confirmed by Myers, though he only lists him as a Teton Sioux. Part of Low Dog's band. Quite possibly the Little Eagle still living at the Standing Rock Agency, Bullhead, SD, in 1926, though he would have been 90 years of age.

Little Face—(Southern Cheyenne)—b. 1864–d. 1961. Interviewed by Father Peter J. Powell. Son of Roman Nose, brother of Cut Belly. While he was only twelve at the time of the battle, he was a source for much Cheyenne tradition and passed on a significant amount of oral history before he died. Described a move by the soldiers beyond Cemetery Ridge, northwest to another ford on the LBH, then a move back into the area of the present cemetery.

Little Ghost—(*Wahpekute*/Dakota-Santee Sioux)—b. circa 1872. A son of *Inkpaduta*. Said to have been fishing in the river with his father when Reno attacked.

Little Gun—(Northern Cheyenne). Still alive in 1921 and living at Lame Deer, Montana [LBHA].

Little Hawk—(Brulé Lakota-Teton Sioux).

Little Hawk (*Cetan Cikala*)—(Oglala Lakota-Teton Sioux)—b. circa 1835–d. circa 1898. Headman of his own band, the *Hunkpatila*. There is a Brulé by the same name. Listed in the Crazy Horse surrender ledger, 1877. Along with Snatch Stealer, listed as "head-of-household." Lodge consisted of three adult females, two male children, and three female children; a total of ten people. He was clearly in the battle. Presence confirmed by Myers, though he only lists him as a Teton Sioux. An uncle of Crazy Horse.

Little Hawk—(Northern Cheyenne). Still living in 1908. In the valley fight. Drank some soldier's captured whiskey. A tribe strongman; good wrestler. Presence confirmed by Myers.

Little Horse—(Lakota-Teton Sioux)—Appears in a 1926 photo of twelve veterans of the battle.

Little Horse—(Northern Cheyenne). Listed as a Cheyenne war chief in the LBHA's Summer 2001 *Research Review*. Had a wife, two daughters, and a son. A headman of the Kit Fox warrior society, or as Wooden Leg called him, one of the nine "little chiefs" [Marquis, *Wooden Leg*, p. 212]. Wore a war

bonnet in the battle. Since the Kit Fox society was the camp guards on the 25th, he *may* have fought at Ford B. Known to have fought the Custer column. Presence confirmed by Myers, who claims he may have been the warrior who stripped Tom Custer's body.

Little Killer (*Cika Wicakte* or *Cikala kte*; also seen as Owns Arrow)—(Oglala Lakota-Teton Sioux)—b. circa 1849–d. 1939. Younger brother of Club Man. Listed in the Crazy Horse surrender ledger, 1877. Along with War Club [Club Man], listed as "head-of-household." Lodge consisted of two female adults, two male children, and three female children; total of nine people. Member of Low Dog's band.

Little Knife—(Hunkpapa Lakota-Teton Sioux)—Told of the torture of a soldier in the camp. Presence confirmed by Myers. With Sitting Bull in Canada in 1877.

Little Moon—(Hunkpapa Lakota-Teton Sioux)—At LBH reunion in 1926. Still living at the Standing Rock Agency, Wakpala, SD, 1926 [courtesy of Dickson]. May have been too young to have been in the fighting, though he was at the Little Big Horn.

Little Owl—(Oglala Lakota-Teton Sioux)—Probably a member of Iron Crow's band.

Little Prick—(Oglala Lakota-Teton Sioux)—Listed in the Crazy Horse surrender ledger, 1877. Along with Sits up Above and the Rump, listed as "head-of-household." Lodge consisted of three adult females, two male children, and two female children; total of ten people.

Little Robe—(Southern Cheyenne). A warrior in the Crazy Dog Society. Fought Custer's column. Presence confirmed by Myers.

Little Shabby (*Nahco win ciqa*) (F)—(Oglala Lakota-Teton Sioux)—b. 1858. One of Eagle Hawk's two wives.

Little Shield—(Northern Cheyenne). Wore a war bonnet in the battle. Along with Big Nose, Horse Road, Wooden Leg, and Yellow Horse, one of five camp guards designated while people slept on the night of the 25th and the 26th [Marquis, *Wooden Leg*, p. 257]. Known to have fought the Custer column. Presence confirmed by Myers.

Little Shield—(Oglala Lakota-Teton Sioux)—Younger brother of He Dog.

Little Shield—(Sans Arc Lakota-Teton Sioux)—Head of the family. Part of Spotted Eagle's band [Dickson].

Little Soldier (also "Eugene" Little Soldier)—(Lakota-Teton Sioux)—b. 1863. Fought with bow and arrows against Reno.

Little Soldier (also "Louis" Sitting Bull)—(Hunk-papa Lakota-Teton Sioux)—A stepson of Sitting Bull. In 1936, he was interviewed by Joseph G. Masters and at that time claimed about sixty-four Indians had been killed during the fighting [Hardorff, *Hokahey!,* p. 129].

Little Soldier—(Oglala Lakota-Teton Sioux)—At the Wounded Knee fight. There is also a Hunkpapa named Little Soldier. Still living at the Standing Rock Agency, Fort Yates, ND, 1926. He was at the Little Big Horn, but may have been too young to get into the fighting.

Little Sun—(Cheyenne). In the valley fight against Reno. He and two other Cheyenne warriors—Sun Bear and Eagle Tail Feather—chased three soldiers south along the west bank of the LBH. While un-clear, this is probably during the valley fight [Marquis, *Wooden Leg,* p. 222]. May have been the "Lit-tle Sun" who moved back and forth between the Custer fight and Reno's men on the hill, watching to make sure Reno didn't help the others. Presence confirmed by Myers. At the reunion in 1926.

Little Voice—(Hunkpapa Lakota-Teton Sioux)—Brother of Deeds.

Little Warrior—(Oglala Lakota-Teton Sioux)—Lived to the age of 80. Still living at the Standing Rock Agency in 1929. Stepson of Sitting Bull. Pres-ence confirmed by Myers, though he only lists him as a Teton Sioux.

Little White Man—(Northern Cheyenne)—d. 1931. Living at Lame Deer, Montana, 1921.

Little Wolf (also referred to as *Chief* Little Wolf, without the official honor; aka Thorny Tree, as a child)—(Cheyenne)—b. 1851–d. 1927. Not the same man as the Northern Cheyenne one; younger [Marquis, *Wooden Leg,* p. 356]. A cousin of Wooden Leg; brother-in-law of Two Moon. He was Little Wolf's nephew and was given his adult name by his uncle after displayed particular courage against some Shoshones. At the Little Big Horn. While his uncle arrived shortly after the Custer fight, this nephew was there for the entire battle. After the band was moved to the Tongue reserva-tion, he was chosen as a chief of the entire tribe and a few years later made the principal "old man chief" [Marquis, *Wooden Leg,* p. 356]. Reference is made to his presence at the battle by the Cheyenne, Weasel Bear, who was in the Reno fight [Windolph/Hunt, *I Fought with Custer,* p. 217].

Little Wolf—(Hunkpapa Lakota-Teton Sioux).

Little Wolf—(Northern Cheyenne)—b. 1821–d. 1904. An "Old Man Chief." Northern *Suhtai* and "Sweet Medicine Chief." Listed as a Cheyenne war chief in the LBHA's Summer 2001 *Research Review.* Head chief of the Elkhorn Scrapers warrior society. Father of Pawnee. Red Bird's so-called "uncle," a cousin of Long Horn (or Left Hand). Apparently, Little Wolf bestowed his name on his nephew. Little Wolf's party of seven lodges had left the Red Cloud Agency in Nebraska to join the Sioux. "… Little Wolf, '…with 1,000 of his people, including 200 warriors…' [*sic*] departed Red Cloud Agency for the northwest" [Willert, quoting Walter Camp/Hammer, *Little Big Horn Diary,* p. 146]. This is the interview with Tall Bull, 22Jul1910, *Custer in '76,* p. 212, footnote 2. *This number is completely wrong.* [See Marquis, *Wooden Leg,* p. 250; also, Hardorff, *Hokahey!,* p. 26.] More likely a band of about 40 people in seven lodges. Trailed the soldiers to the Little Big Horn area and arrived on June 25, but after the Custer fighting ended [see Marquis, *Wooden Leg,* pp. 248–249]. Presence confirmed by Myers. Eventually, he wound up disgracing himself among his own people by killing a Cheyenne scout named Famished Elk while drunk. He paid for it by smashing his pipe, giving up his horses, and quitting whatever positions he was entitled to as an "old man chief." Considered by some as one of the great Cheyenne leaders.

Little Wound—(Hunkpapa Lakota-Teton Sioux)—Known to have left the Standing Rock Agency in Dec 1875 to join Sitting Bull. Number of lodges unknown [Stewart, *Custer's Luck,* p. 78]. His son (name unknown) was killed at the battle [Graham, *The Custer Myth,* p. 48]. On 18 Sep 1876, a dispatch from Phil Sheridan dated the previous day, was re-ceived by General R. C. Drum in Chicago. In it, Sheridan informed Drum that, "Col. Carlin reports that Kill Eagle and Little Wound, with a hundred people, all their arms, ammunition and about a hundred ponies, surrendered to him at Standing Rock Agency on the 15th. Twenty-nine men sur-rendered, all of whom were in the fight on the Little Big Horn" [Hutchins, *The Army and Navy Journal,* p. 100; the 23 Sep 1876 edition of the *Journal*]. In all likelihood, this is the Little Wound referred to in the dispatch.

Little Wound—(Oglala Lakota-Teton Sioux)—Chief of the *Kuinyan* Band. (See Red Cloud.) There is some evidence—far from strong, however—that he was at the Little Big Horn encampment. His band, the *Kuinyan* band of the *Kiyaksa Tiyospaye,* an Agency Band, was not at the battle, though this is not definitive proof Little Wound himself was not there [primarily from Dickson].

Lives Out—(Lakota-Teton Sioux)—Listed in the Crazy Horse surrender ledger, 1877. Along with Man on Top, listed as "head-of-household." Lodge consisted of two adult females and one male child; total, five people.

Living Bear—(Oglala Lakota-Teton Sioux)—Listed in the Crazy Horse surrender ledger. Along with Crazy Heart and Hoarse, listed as "head-of-household." Lodge consisted of five adult females and three male children, eleven people in total.

Loafer—(Oglala Lakota-Teton Sioux)—Listed in the Crazy Horse surrender ledger, 1877. Along with Singing Bear, listed as "head-of-household." Lodge consisted of one adult female, one male child, and two female children; total of six people.

Lone Bear *(Mato Wajila)*—(Oglala Lakota-Teton Sioux)—b. circa 1847; 29 years old at time of battle. Follower of Crazy Horse. Barely made it into the Reno fight, but thought it lasted from about 9 am to 11 am. Thought the Custer fight lasted from about noon to 4 pm. Interviewed by Sewell B. Weston in 1909.

Lone Bear—(Northern Cheyenne). Claimed six Cheyenne were killed and buried in the hills west of the Little Big Horn River.

Lone Bull—(Minneconjou Lakota-Teton Sioux)—A "headman."

Lone Dog (also seen as Long Dog)—(Sans Arc Lakota-Teton Sioux)—d. 25 Jun 1876, killed at the Little Big Horn. One of those warriors who had ridden into the camp warning of the approaching soldiers. Had been with Deeds. Body location unknown, but killed fighting Custer's column.

Lone Eagle—(Lakota-Teton Sioux)—At the Cheyenne River Agency, 1926.

Lone Eagle—(Sans Arc Lakota-Teton Sioux)—Head of the family. Part of Spotted Eagle's band [Dickson].

Lone Elk (also seen listed as Long Elk [Myers])—(Oglala Lakota-Teton Sioux)—Listed in the Crazy Horse surrender ledger, 1877. Along with Plenty Shells, Bad Partisan, and Crazy Head, listed as "head-of-household." Lodge consisted of four adult females, two male children, and one female child; total of eleven people. In the battle and wounded in the valley fight. Presence confirmed by Myers.

Lone Horn—(Minneconjou Lakota-Teton Sioux)—A "headman." Presence confirmed by Myers.

Lone Man (aka One Man)—(Hunkpapa Lakota-Teton Sioux).

Lone Man (*Wicasa Isnala*; also One Man; aka "John"; *Ishnawichah*)—(Oglala Lakota-Teton Sioux)—b. circa 1850–d. 1934. Member of He Dog's Soreback Band. Saw a dead Lakota in a gully whose body was mistakenly mutilated by Indians [LBHA]. Presence confirmed by Myers, though he only lists him as a Teton Sioux.

Lone Wolf—(Lakota-Teton Sioux)—One of the lesser chiefs and headmen at the battle.

Lone Woman—(Sans Arc Lakota-Teton Sioux)—Head of the family. Part of Spotted Eagle's band [Dickson].

Lone Woman (*Wi Isnala*) (F)—(Oglala Lakota-Teton Sioux)—b. circa 1816. She was a widow with four children at the time of the surrender. Part of Low Dog's band.

Long Bear—(Oglala Lakota-Teton Sioux)—Wounded during the Wounded Knee battles. Uncertain if he was at the Little Big Horn.

Long Bull (also "Paul" Longbull or Long Bull)—(Lakota-Teton Sioux). Still living at the Standing Rock Agency, Little Eagle, SD, in 1926 [courtesy of Dickson]. At the camp, but he was either too young to participate in the fighting or he simply did not get into the battle.

Long Dog—(Hunkpapa Lakota-Teton Sioux)—Fought Custer's column. Donovan refers to him as a chief [*A Terrible Glory*, p. 341]. In his November 2, 1876, dispatch to COL Nelson A. Miles (5I), COL W. B. Hazen (6I) said there was a Long Dog "with the Yanktonnais" at Fort Peck, Montana. In a 25 Oct 1876 dispatch, Miles also referred to him as one of Sitting Bull's chiefs and called Long Dog "one of the worst men in the tribe." In early September, 1876, he was reported to be at the head of some 150 warriors trying to procure ammunition from an of agency agent.

Long Dung—(Oglala Lakota-Teton Sioux)—Medicine man. Presence confirmed by Myers.

Long Elk—(Minneconjou Lakota-Teton Sioux)—Shot in the face while he was somewhere west of the Custer Ridge complex of hills. Uncertain if he survived the battle. He is also mentioned by Standing Bear [DeMallie, *The Sixth Grandfather,* p. 185].

Long Feather—(Lakota-Teton Sioux)—Apparently identified in a picture as a warrior who took part in the battle [LBHA]. Husband of Hail Stones in Her Stomach.

Long Forehead—(Cheyenne). May have been part of Little Wolf's band out of the Red Cloud Agency in Nebraska.

Long Handle—(Oglala Lakota-Teton Sioux)—Listed in the Crazy Horse surrender ledger, 1877.

Along with Water Snake and Tanned Nuts, listed as "head-of-household." Lodge consisted of two adult females; total of five people.

Long Horn—(Hunkpapa Lakota-Teton Sioux)—Chief of the Holy Band.

Long Mandan—(Sans Arc Lakota-Teton Sioux)—Head of the family. Part of Spotted Eagle's band [Dickson].

Long Name—(Oglala Lakota-Teton Sioux)—Listed in the Crazy Horse surrender ledger, 1877. Listed as "head-of-household." His lodge consisted of two adult females, a total of three people.

Long Roach—(Northern Cheyenne). Father of Closed Hand. The LBHA also claims he was the father of Roman Nose (unless Closed Hand had yet *another* name, Roman Nose, as well; this would make three of those guys).

Long Road (aka *Cankuhanska*; also seen as Long Robe, though this is in all likelihood more a typo than a fact; supposedly known as Thunder Shield among the Cheyenne)—(Sans Arc Lakota-Teton Sioux)—d. 26 Jun 1876, killed at the Little Big Horn, counting coup on a dead soldier on Benteen's line on 26 June. This is verified by Liddic, *Vanishing Victory,* p. 178, and Hardorff, *On the Little Big Horn with Walter Camp,* p. 13, footnote 4. The current memorial marker at the battlefield places him at the southern end of the Benteen battlefield-side of Reno Hill. Sometimes confused with Eagle Hat who was also killed there. Myers has them listed separately [Myers, "Roster of Known Hostile Indians at the Battle of the Little Big Horn," *Research Review,* Summer 1991, Vol. 5, No. 2]. Hardorff claims—as he does with several Indians—that Long Road was also known as Eagle Hat and that the two are in fact, one. In the Standing Bear account, he seems to compress time somewhat and relates this shooting as though it occurred on the 25th, after the Reno excursion to Weir Peaks [see DeMallie, *The Sixth Grandfather,* p. 187]. If nothing else, Standing Bear's account confirms—or is the genesis for—Long Road's death.

Long Soldier (*Akicita Hanska*)—(Hunkpapa Lakota-Teton Sioux)—Four lodges (25 people), Sep 1876, at Standing Rock [Dickson].

Long Tree—(Nakota-Yankton Sioux)—Traveled with Thunder Bear from old Fort Peck.

Long Visitor—(Oglala Lakota-Teton Sioux)—Listed in the Crazy Horse surrender ledger, 1877. Along with Spunker, listed as "head-of-household." Lodge consisted of two adult females, two male children, and five female children; total of eleven people.

Long Wolf—(Lakota-Teton Sioux)—d. West Brompton, England, June 1892. He became a member of Buffalo Bill Cody's "Wild West Show" in 1886. Died in June 1892. Buried in West Brompton Cemetery, England. The attending physician, Dr. Maitland Coffin, described him as "a complete mass of gunshot wounds and sabre cuts" [Maddra, *Hostiles? The Lakota Ghost Dance and Buffalo Bill's Wild West,* p. 161].

Looking Back—(Lakota-Teton Sioux)—Known to have taken part in the battle of the Little Big Horn. Still living at the Standing Rock Agency, Wakpala, SD, 1926 [courtesy of Dickson].

Looking Cloud (*Mahpiya Wakta*)—(Oglala Lakota-Teton Sioux)—b. circa 1852–d. circa 1918). Member of the Iron Crow band.

Looking Elk (aka "Oliver"; *Hehakawaketo*)-(Minneconjou Lakota-Teton Sioux)—b. 1845. Presence confirmed by Myers, though he only lists him as a Teton Sioux. There is a Hunkpapa with the same name, but they seem to be different men.

Looking Elk—(Hunkpapa Lakota-Teton Sioux)—Known to have fought at the Little Big Horn. Refused to take Good Bear Boy off the battlefield while under fire. Still living at the Standing Rock Agency, Little Eagle, SD, in 1926 [courtesy of Dickson].

Looking Woman (*Waki te win*) (F)—(Hunkpapa Lakota-Teton Sioux)—b. circa 1841. Daughter of Fire Cloud and Pretty Woman.

Looks Like a Dog—(Oglala Lakota-Teton Sioux)—Listed in the Crazy Horse surrender ledger, 1877. Along with Don't Amount to Anything and Spread Pine, listed as "head-of-household." Lodge consisted of three adult females, four male children, and four female children; total of fourteen people.

Looks White—(Oglala Lakota-Teton Sioux)—Listed in the Crazy Horse surrender ledger, 1877. Along with Slow White Cow, listed as "head-of-household." Lodge consisted of two adult females and two female children; six people, total.

Looks Yellow—(Oglala Lakota-Teton Sioux)—Listed in the Crazy Horse surrender ledger, 1877. Listed as "head-of-household." Lodge consisted of two female adults; total of three people.

Lost Leg—(Northern Cheyenne). He returned to the battlefield several days later looking for horses, but the odor was so strong, his band could not even get close [LBHA].

Low Dog—(Brulé Lakota-Teton Sioux)—There is an Oglala by the same name and one of the two Low Dogs moved back and forth between the

Custer fight and Reno's men on the hill, watching to make sure Reno didn't help the others. One of them is listed as a Dakota chief in the LBHA's Summer 2001 *Research Review*. It is unclear which is which. Since the Oglala Low Dog died in 1894, this was probably the one living at the Standing Rock Agency, Kenel, SD, in 1926.

Low Dog (*Sunka Kucigala*)—(Oglala Lakota-Teton Sioux)—b. circa 1846 or 1847–d. 1894. [There is also a Brulé by the same name.] Tall, straight, regular features, with small hands and feet [Graham, *The Custer Myth*, p. 76]. Low Dog moved back and forth between the Custer fight and Reno's men on the hill, watching to make sure Reno did not help the others. Also fought on Custer Ridge. Claimed 38 Indians were killed. One of the Indians killed and put in a lodge found in the camp after the battle was Low Dog's full-brother. Listed as a Dakota chief in the LBHA's Summer 2001 *Research Review*. Presence confirmed by Myers, who lists this fellow as an Oglala.

Mad Wolf (aka Wolf That Has No Sense; *Hahk-o-ni* or *Miv-a-wo-nih*)—(Northern Cheyenne)—b. 1825–d. 1905. An old man at the time of the battle. One of the few warriors at Ford B when Custer's column arrived there; wore a war bonnet there. A Dog Soldier. Presence confirmed by Myers.

Magpie—(Oglala Lakota-Teton Sioux)—One of those warning the camp of the soldiers' approach; brought horses with him.

Magpie Eagle (also seen as just Magpie)—(Southern Cheyenne). Still living in 1904. Some sources claim he was Northern Cheyenne. A "Council of the 44" chief. Joined the village on 24 Jun 1876 with fifteen to twenty lodges. Wounded in the Rosebud fight, but still fought at the LBH. Presence confirmed by Myers.

Mahwissa (F)—(Southern Cheyenne). The sister of Black Kettle, the Cheyenne chief killed at the Washita in 1868. There is a story in Michno's *Lakota Noon*, p. 293—probably apocryphal—that it was *Mahwissa* who stuck the awl into Custer's ears. She was visiting Northern Cheyenne relatives.

Makes Dirt (Dirt; Dung with Dirt)—(Oglala Lakota-Teton Sioux)—Part of He Dog's band, but nothing else is known of the family [Dickson].

Makes Enemy—(Oglala Lakota-Teton Sioux)—Probably part of Iron Crow's band. Attended the 1926 reunion.

Makes Enemy (*Toka Kanga*; "Henry" Makes Enemy)—(Oglala Lakota-Teton Sioux)—b. circa 1857–d. 1928. Member of Little Hawk's band. Married to Little hawk's daughter, Shell Woman.

Makes Room (or Make Room; also They Make Room for Him)-(Minneconjou Lakota-Teton Sioux)—b. circa 1826–d. 1905. Listed as a Dakota chief in the LBHA's Summer 2001 *Research Review*. White Bull's father. Chief of his band. Presence confirmed by Myers. White Bull said his father was not involved in the actual fighting, though he was at the battle.

Makes Trouble Ahead (*Kokab Wosica*)—(Oglala Lakota-Teton Sioux)—b. circa 1823–d. circa 1893. Member of He Dog's *Cankahuhan* band.

Makes Widows Cry—(Oglala Lakota-Teton Sioux)—Listed in the Crazy Horse surrender ledger, 1877. Listed as "head-of-household." Lodge consisted of himself and one adult female, two people, total.

Male Bear—(Lakota-Teton Sioux)—Apparently identified in a picture as a warrior who took part in the battle [LBHA]. Still living at the Standing Rock Agency, Little Eagle, SD, in 1926 [courtesy of Dickson]. Known to have participated in the fighting.

Man Afraid of His Horses—(Oglala Lakota-Teton Sioux)—A chief during the 1860s, prominent in discussions of the 1866 treaty and he signed the 1868 treaty [Stewart, *Custer's Luck*, pp. 33 and 50]. It is not clear if he was at the Little Big Horn.

Man on Top—(Oglala Lakota-Teton Sioux)—Listed in the Crazy Horse surrender ledger, 1877. Along with Lives Out, listed as "head-of-household." Lodge consisted of two adult females and one male child; total, five people.

Man That Smells His Hand—(Hunkpapa Lakota-Teton Sioux).

Man Whose Breast Is Dobbed with Mud [Graham, *The Custer Myth*, p. 48]—(Lakota-Teton Sioux)—d. 25 Jun 1876, killed at the Little Big Horn.

The Man Who Walks with His Dogs—(Lakota-Teton Sioux)—Fought alongside Kill Eagle. Presence confirmed by Myers, though he only lists him as a Teton Sioux.

Many Claws—(Lakota-Teton Sioux)—Claimed Custer's soldiers "did a lot of bugling" toward the end of the battle, with two different calls being repeated [LBHA].

Many Colored Braids—(Cheyenne). Had a wife, two daughters, and a son.

Many Elk—(Lakota-Teton Sioux)—Living at the Standing Rock Agency, Little Eagle, SD, in 1926 [courtesy of Dickson]. At the camp, but he was either too young to participate in the fighting or he simply did not get into the battle.

Many Horses (F)—(Hunkpapa Lakota-Teton Sioux)—A daughter of Sitting Bull.

Many Lice (also Plenty Lice)—(Oglala Lakota-Teton Sioux)—d. 25 Jun 1876, killed at the Little Big Horn, fighting the Custer columns. Reputed to have been wounded in the Crook fight on the Rosebud, 17 Jun 1876, but participated in the LBH battle as well. Body location unknown.

Maple Tree—(Cheyenne).

The Marmot—(Sioux)—With Sitting Bull in Canada. At the Little Big Horn battle.

Meat—(Cheyenne).

Medicine Bear—(Northern Cheyenne). Attended 1926 reunion. Claimed Custer was killed early in fight. A "Council of the 44" chief. Presence confirmed by Myers.

Medicine Bird—(Oglala Lakota-Teton Sioux)—With Black Bear's party watching Custer at the divide [LBHA].

Medicine Bull—(Northern Cheyenne). Among a group of Cheyenne under Little Wolf, on their way from the agency to the camp, they came upon Custer's troops before they left the valley of the Rosebud. Scouts from this group (Big Crow, Black Horse, and Red Cherries) discovered the lost pack from one of Custer's mules. This is the pack that SGT Curtiss went back to retrieve. Fought on second day of battle. Presence confirmed by Myers.

Medicine Cloud—(Nakota-Yankton Sioux)—Traveled with the others from old Fort Peck.

Medicine Man [Dickson]—(Hunkpapa Lakota-Teton Sioux)—Seven lodges (forty-six people), Sep 1876, at Standing Rock.

Medicine Turns Around—(Lakota-Teton Sioux)—He was with Sitting Bull in Canada in 1877.

Medicine Wolf (aka Red Horse)—(Northern Cheyenne). This may be the same man as "George" Red Horse. A "Council of the 44" chief.

Medicine Wolf (also "Augusta" Medicine Wolf) (F)—(Northern Cheyenne)—A little girl at the time of the battle. Not a bad assumption that she was the daughter of the chief, above. Her parents apparently hid her in the bushes as the fighting began.

Melter—(Oglala Lakota-Teton Sioux)—Listed in the Crazy Horse surrender ledger, 1877. Along with Dog Ear, listed as "head-of-household." Lodge consisted of one adult female, three male children, and two female children; total of eight people.

Moccasin Hide—(Oglala Lakota-Teton Sioux)—Listed in the Crazy Horse surrender ledger, 1877. Along with Pisses in the Horn, listed as "head-of-household," his lodge consisted of three adult females and two male children; a total of seven people.

Monahsetah (in Sioux, *Meotzi;* The New Grass That Shoots in the Spring; Mary [Isaac]) (F)—Originally from the southern branch, but now living with the Northern Cheyenne. One source says her father was the chief Black Kettle who was killed at the Washita, 27 Nov 1868. Gail Kelly-Custer claims she was half-white, her father being Chief Little Rock and her mother being a doctor of Irish descent ["My Heritage, My Search," *Custer and His Times, Book Five,* p. 277]. According to Kelly-Custer, she eventually married a white man named John Isaac. She had a seven-year-old son—Yellow Bird or Yellow Hair—born out of wedlock and rumored to be the son of Custer. Meotzi, however, was already seven months pregnant when she met Custer, and the child was born a full-blood Indian, despite light streaks in his hair. There was speculation of a second child, but no evidence [Michno]. According to Kelly-Custer the child was given to and raised by George Custer's half-brother, Brice Custer. In Pennington, Joseph White Cow Bull confirms the story of a romance with Custer and the birth of the son, Yellow Bird. Much of this appears apocryphal, however. White Cow Bull's yarns are barely believable under the best of circumstances, and Gail Kelly-Custer's claims to be a direct descendant of George Custer are met with vehemence unrivaled even in this contentious arena.

Mosquito (*Caponka*)—(Hunkpapa Lakota-Teton Sioux)—b. circa 1852. Listed in the Sitting Bull Surrender Ledger.

Mosquito—(Northern Cheyenne). A headman of the Kit Foxes warrior society, or as Wooden Leg called him, one of the nine "little chiefs" [Marquis, *Wooden Leg,* p. 212]. Since the Kit Fox society was the camp guards on the 25th, he *may* have fought at Ford B. Presence confirmed by Myers.

Mountain—(Oglala Lakota-Teton Sioux)—Listed in the Crazy Horse surrender ledger, 1877. Along with Contrary and Big Owl, listed as "head-of-household." Lodge consisted of two adult females, two male children, and one female child; total of eight people.

Moving Robe or **Moving Robe Woman** (or Eagle Robe; Her Eagle Robe; She Walks with Her Shawl; Walking Blanket Woman; *Tasinamani Win* or *Tashenamani;* aka "Mary" Crawler) (F)—(Hunkpapa Lakota-Teton Sioux)—b. near Grand River, SD, circa 1854–d. post–1937. Daughter of Crawler, sister of Deeds. An account in Michno (Eagle Elk's) says this woman killed a "dark-skinned man ... sitting on the ground." This could have been Isaiah Dorman whose horse had been shot from under him, pinning him to the ground or it could have been LT McIntosh who was part Indian. Presence confirmed by Myers, though he lists her as an Oglala. Still living at the Standing Rock Agency, Bullhead, SD, 1937.

Mustache—(Lakota-Teton Sioux)—d. 25 Jun 1876, killed at the Little Big Horn. Myers only has him listed as a Teton Sioux killed at the battle [Myers, "Roster of Known Hostile Indians at the Battle of the Little Big Horn," *Research Review*, Summer 1991, Vol. 5, No. 2, p. 8].

Nation (F)—(Lakota-Teton Sioux)—Wife number three of White Swan. They were married, circa 1868. Mother of "Edward" Swan.

Neat Prick (or Neck Prick)—(Oglala Lakota-Teton Sioux)—Listed in the Crazy Horse surrender ledger, 1877. Along with Belly, listed as "head-of-household." Lodge consisted of two adult females, three male children, and one female child; eight people, total.

Nine—(Nakota-Yankton Sioux)—With Sitting Bull in Canada. Probably at the Little Big Horn.

No Flesh—(Brulé Lakota-Teton Sioux)—Killed a guidon bearer and took the flag.

No Neck—(Oglala Lakota-Teton Sioux)—Listed in the Crazy Horse surrender ledger, 1877. Listed as "head-of-household." Lodge consisted of one adult female, three male children, and one female child; total of six people. He was in the battle.

No Neck (*Tahu Wanica*)-(Hunkpapa Lakota-Teton Sioux)—d. early to mid–1885. Presence confirmed by Myers, though he only lists him as a Teton Sioux.

No Two Horns-(Hunkpapa Lakota-Teton Sioux)—d. 1942. Credited with several kills in the battle. Still living at the Standing Rock Agency, Shields, ND, in 1929. He was one of Sitting Bull's closest companions and accompanied him to Canada.

No Water (aka Water All Gone)—(Oglala Lakota-Teton Sioux)—Possibly killed at Wounded Knee.

Noisy (also "Paul" Noisy)—(Brulé Lakota-Teton Sioux)—Claimed the soldiers were shooting in every direction.

Noisy Arrow—(Northern Cheyenne). Listed in the Crazy Horse surrender ledger [CBHMA]. Probably present at the LBH.

Noisy Walking (aka Left Hand; also Thunder Walking)—(Northern Cheyenne)—d. 25 Jun 1876, killed at the Little Big Horn. Fifteen or eighteen years old, he was one of the "suicide warriors." Son of White Bull [Myers, "Roster of Known Hostile Indians at the Battle of the Little Big Horn," *Research Review*, Summer 1991, Vol. 5, No. 2]. Mortally wounded in the Deep Ravine/Cemetery Ravine area around Custer Hill. He was found in upper Deep Ravine, about 150 feet south of the present-day marker set for Lame White Man. He was still alive, but died in the village later that night. This could be disputed. Wooden Leg claimed Noisy Walking was lying in the "gulch" that C Company charged into: "...down in the gulch where the band of soldiers nearest the river had been killed in the earlier part of the battle." I also question whether he was a so-called "suicide boy," since Wooden Leg claimed they were the same age, eighteen [Marquis, *Wooden Leg*, p. 241]. Wooden Leg reiterates after he found the body of Lame White Man, "Two Sioux had been killed in this same first charge upon the soldiers," [p. 243] leading one to believe Noisy Walking was also mortally wounded in this area.

Nose in Sight—(Oglala Lakota-Teton Sioux)—Listed in the Crazy Horse surrender ledger, 1877. Listed as "head-of-household." Lodge consisted of two adult females, two male children, and two female children; total of seven people.

Old—(Oglala Lakota-Teton Sioux)—Listed in the Crazy Horse surrender ledger, 1877. Listed as "head-of-household," along with American Horse and Ass Hole. Their lodge consisted of four adult females and one male child; a total of eight people.

Old Bear—(Hunkpapa Lakota-Teton Sioux).

Old Bear—(Northern Cheyenne). An old man at the time of the battle. An *Omisis*, an "Old Man Chief." One of those who chased a lone soldier on a sorrel horse near the very end of the fight. Kills in the Night was another. Apparently, Turtle Rib, the Minneconjou, was a third. Presence confirmed by Myers.

Old Bear Woman (*Mato winuhca*) (F)—(Hunkpapa Lakota-Teton Sioux)—b. circa 1852. Wife of *Zu-Me*.

(Old) Black Moon (or just Black Moon; also Black Sun)-(Hunkpapa Lakota-Teton Sioux)—b. 1814 or 1815–d. 1888. Was with Sitting Bull in huge village of some 2,000 lodges on the Little Missouri, 1865 [Stewart, *Custer's Luck*, p. 29]. Appears in the 1885 Standing Rock Agency census.

Old Buffalo Hair (*Pte hin pahpe*)—(Hunkpapa Lakota-Teton Sioux)—b. circa 1851. Brother of Charging Thunder. Listed in the Sitting Bull Surrender Ledger.

Old Bull—(Hunkpapa Lakota-Teton Sioux)—b. 1850–d. 1949. Still living at the Standing Rock Agency, Bullhead, SD, in 1929. In the fighting at the Little Big Horn.

Old Bull—(Northern Cheyenne)—A young boy at the time of the battle. His father was in the fighting.

Old Crow—(Northern Cheyenne). A "Council of 44" chief.

Old Eagle—(Sans Arc Lakota-Teton Sioux)—Along with Two Bears, prepared the burial site for Old She Bear at the "lone tepee" [LBHA].

Old Hollow Horn—(Oglala Lakota-Teton Sioux)—A powerful "bear medicine man." At Wounded Knee.

Old Man—(Cheyenne)—d. 25 Jun 1876, killed at the Little Big Horn. Son of Black Crane. In the valley fight, infiltrating the woods. Some of his shots—along with those of Crooked Nose and Turkey Leg—may have hit and killed Company M's Klotzbucher and Lorentz. Killed during Reno's retreat [Myers, "Roster of Known Hostile Indians at the Battle of the Little Big Horn," *Research Review,* Summer 1991, Vol. 5, No. 2].

Old Man Coyote (aka Old Man)—(Northern Cheyenne). A headman of the Crazy Dogs warrior society. Wooden Leg said he was the leading chief of the Crazy Dog warriors [Marquis, *Wooden Leg,* p. 212]. Wooden Leg said he was held in particularly high esteem as a "warrior chief" [Marquis, *Wooden Leg,* p. 211]. Presence confirmed by Myers.

Old Red War Bonnet—(Northern Cheyenne). In the Rosebud fight [LBHA].

Old Shield—(Oglala Lakota-Teton Sioux)—Brother of Stands First and Fast Wolf.

Old Wolf—(Northern Cheyenne). A "Council of the 44" chief.

One Brings Shit Far Away—(Oglala Lakota-Teton Sioux)—Listed in the Crazy Horse surrender ledger. Listed as "head-of-household." Also in his lodge were three adult females, two male children, and three female children, a total of nine people.

One Bull (also Lone Bull; *Tatanka wanji na*; "Henry Oscar" One Bull)—(Minneconjou Lakota-Teton Sioux)—b. near Bear Butte, SD, circa 1852 to 1854–d. 23 Jun 1947. Claimed to be twenty-three at the time of the battle. Adopted at the age of four by Sitting Bull, his uncle. Married the Hunkpapa girl Red Whirlwind Woman (Scarlet Whirlwind). One of Sitting Bull's bodyguards. There is considerable confusion here with another Minneconjou of the same name. This man was Lazy White Bull's brother and the one who rescued Good Bear Boy on Reno's skirmish line. Also, there is no dispute that Lazy White Bull was a Minneconjou. It is just possible that there are two with the same name and the confusion has to do with the battle incident and the sibling relationship. One of the first warriors to ride towards Reno; had instructions from Sitting Bull to try to parley with soldiers. Failing that, he was one of those leading the charge against Reno. Claims to have seen the arrival of the pack train on Reno Hill, but Michno thinks it was the advance elements of Benteen's battalion, since the packs did not arrive for at least thirty-seven minutes [Pennington] or one hour later [everybody else]. After following on the Reno chase and killing three soldiers, he recrossed the LBH, met with Sitting Bull, then rode towards the Hunkpapa village, and then recrossed to the east bank. He was not involved in the Custer fight. Claimed the soldiers running down from the ridge discarded their rifles and used revolvers. Presence confirmed further by Myers. Again, if this is the correct man, he did several interviews with Walter Camp and Stanley Vestal, among others [Dickson; Hardorff]. One of them was still living at the Standing Rock Agency, Bullhead, SD, 1926 [courtesy of Dickson]. (See below.)

One Bull (also Lone Bull; *Tatanka Winjila*)—(Minneconjou or Hunkpapa Lakota-Teton Sioux)—A half-brother of Sitting Bull. Presence confirmed by Myers. Listed in the Sitting Bull Surrender Census and married to One Who Kills Assiniboine. (See above.)

One Dog—(Sans Arc Lakota-Teton Sioux).

One Elk—(Lakota-Teton Sioux)—Living at the Standing Rock Agency, 1929. Said that eight soldiers trying to escape from Custer Hill were mounted. Known to have been involved in the fighting.

One Ghost—(Sans Arc Lakota-Teton Sioux)—Head of the family. Part of Spotted Eagle's band [Dickson].

One Grass (also seen as One Glass)—(Oglala Lakota-Teton Sioux)—Listed in the Crazy Horse surrender ledger 1877. Along with Hangs His Head, Ree, and Soldier, listed as "head-of-household." Lodge consisted of three adult females, one male child, and four female children; total of twelve people.

One Hand (*Namsan nila*)—(Hunkpapa Lakota-Teton Sioux)—b. circa 1821. Brother of One Who Breaks Arrow. Listed in the Sitting Bull Surrender Ledger.

One Horn—(Minneconjou Lakota-Teton Sioux)—Presence confirmed by Myers.

One Horn—(Northern Cheyenne). Father of "Frank" High Walking.

One Kills at Eight Steps—(Oglala Lakota-Teton Sioux)—Listed in the Crazy Horse surrender ledger. Along with Heap Bear Lays Down, listed as "head-of-household." Lodge consisted of three adult females, five people in total.

One Side—(Oglala Lakota-Teton Sioux)—Friend of Black Elk.

One Side of the Tent (*Tio koton win*) (F)—(Hunkpapa Lakota-Teton Sioux)—b. circa 1859. Daughter of White Dog and Pretty Woman.

One Stab—(Oglala Lakota-Teton Sioux)—Known to be a Sioux chief in the 1860s. During the Black Hills Expedition of 1874, One Stab was the chief of a small band of Oglala that Custer's column came upon. The small Indian encampment consisted of 5 lodges and 27 people [Barnard, *Ten Years with Custer,* pp. 227–228].

One Teat (also seen spelled "Teet")—(Oglala Lakota-Teton Sioux)—Listed in the Crazy Horse surrender ledger, 1877. Along with Enemy, listed as "head-of-household." Lodge consisted of two adult females; total of four people.

The One That Runs the Ree (also possibly known as The Race Runner)—(*Wahpekute*/Dakota-Santee Sioux)—With Sitting Bull in Canada in 1877.

One That Searches (F)—(Lakota-Teton Sioux)—Listed in the Crazy Horse surrender ledger, 1877. Listed as "head-of-household." Lodge consisted of two other adult females and one female child; four people, total.

One That Sees (*Wanyake la*) (F)—(Hunkpapa Lakota-Teton Sioux)—b. circa 1869. A child at the time of the battle. Daughter of Big Leg and Ticket.

One That Steals—(Oglala Lakota-Teton Sioux)—Listed in the Crazy Horse surrender ledger, 1877. Listed as "head-of-household." Lodge consisted of two adult females, one male child, and three female children; total of seven people.

One They Call Out For (*Kipanpi win*) (F)—(Hunkpapa Lakota-Teton Sioux)—b. circa 1873. Only a baby at the time of the battle. Daughter of Deaf Woman; sister of Standing in Sight.

One They Look At (*Wanye kapila*) (F)—(Hunkpapa Lakota-Teton Sioux)—b. circa 1869. Daughter of Red Thunder and Ripe. A young girl at the time of the battle.

One They Plundered of (*Waki pi win*) (F)—(Hunkpapa Lakota-Teton Sioux)—b. circa 1873. Only a small child at the battle of the LBH. Daughter of Bear Looking Back and White Buffalo Cow.

One Who Breaks (*Wabobleca*; aka "Wallace" Running Eagle)—(Oglala Lakota-Teton Sioux)—b. 1874. Son of Running Eagle and Badger. Only two years old at the time of the battle.

One Who Breaks Arrow (*Wanna wega*)—(Hunkpapa Lakota-Teton Sioux)—b. circa 1825. Listed in the Sitting Bull Surrender Ledger. Husband of Reed Woman and brother of One Hand.

One Who Buys (*Ope ton win*) (F)—(Hunkpapa Lakota-Teton Sioux)—b. circa 1849. Mother of One Who Takes Down and His Gray Horse.

One Who Goes out (*Tankal Yela*)—(Oglala Lakota-Teton Sioux)—b. 1871. Son of Little Bull and Little Calf. Only five years old at the time of the battle.

One Who Judges (*Waki cun za win*) (F)—(Hunkpapa Lakota-Teton Sioux)—b. circa 1851. Wife of Slow White Buffalo.

One Who Kills (*Kte ka*)—(Oglala Lakota-Teton Sioux)—b. circa 1863. Son of Four Crows and Grey. Thirteen years old at the time of the battle.

One Who Kills Assiniboines (*Hohe kte win*) (F)—(Hunkpapa Lakota-Teton Sioux)—b. circa 1861. Wife of Lone Bull/One Bull.

One Who Saves Life (*Wanikiya*) (F)—(Oglala Lakota-Teton Sioux)—b. 1873. Daughter of Bad Heart Bull and Red Blanket. Only three years old at time of battle [Dickson].

One Who Speaks Bad (*Sica Yata Keya*; possibly, Tongue [Dickson])—(Oglala Lakota-Teton Sioux)—b. circa 1820. Probably a member of Low Dog's band.

One Who Takes Down (*Waca ju kpa*)—(Hunkpapa Lakota-Teton Sioux)—b. circa 1873. A small child at the time of the battle. Listed as head of household despite his age. Son of One Who Buys (F); brother of His Gray Horse. Listed in the Sitting Bull Surrender Ledger.

One Who Takes Part with Others (*Wanaki ksin*; became known as "Henry" Little Soldier)—(Hunkpapa Lakota-Teton Sioux) b. circa 1868–d. 1940s. Sitting Bull's adopted son. Son of Seen by the Nation and brother of Blue Mountain. Just a child at the battle.

One Who Walks with the Stars (F)—(Oglala Lakota-Teton Sioux)—Wife of Crow Dog. Supposedly killed two soldiers in the water from the riverbank. Presence confirmed by Myers. Myers does not mention that this person is a woman, though he also leaves out his usual "warrior" caveat.

One Whose Club They're Afraid of (*Tacanhpi kokipapi*)—(Hunkpapa Lakota-Teton Sioux)—b. circa 1842. Son of Fire Cloud and Pretty Woman. Listed in the Sitting Bull Surrender Ledger.

Otter Robe (also "Joe" Otterrobe)—(Hunkpapa Lakota-Teton Sioux)—May not have participated in the fighting, but was in the camp. Still living at the Standing Rock Agency, Bullhead, SD, in 1926 [courtesy of Dickson].

Owl Bull—(Oglala Lakota-Teton Sioux)—With Black Bear's party watching Custer at the divide [LBHA].

Owl King (also "Joe" Owl King)—(Minneconjou Lakota-Teton Sioux)—Husband of Touch on Head and father of Brown Wolf and Hard to Kill. His second wife was Wind. As noted in their entries, Touch on Head and Comes Back Holy may have been the same woman. If not, then Owl King seemed to have a third wife.

Owl Man (*Hinhan wicasa*)—(Hunkpapa Lakota-Teton Sioux)—b. 1875. An infant at time of battle. Son of Takes the Gun.

Own[s] Bob-tail Horse—(Lakota-Teton Sioux)—One of three Sioux scouts who saw Custer coming, 22 Jun 1876.

Owns an Animal with Horns—(Oglala Lakota-Teton Sioux)—Part of the Iron Crow band.

Owns Red Horse (also seen as just Red Horse; *Shunkisha-yuha*)—(Northern Cheyenne)—d. 25 Jun 1876, killed at the Little Big Horn, fighting the Custer battalions [Myers, "Roster of Known Hostile Indians at the Battle of the Little Big Horn," *Research Review,* Summer 1991, Vol. 5, No. 2]. Myers lists a Teton Sioux of the same name, also killed during the fighting.

Owns Red Horse—(Lakota-Teton Sioux)—d. 25 Jun 1876, killed at the Little Big Horn. Myers lists him only as a Teton Sioux, while also showing a Cheyenne of the same named killed during the battle. For consistency's sake, both are carried here [Myers, "Roster of Known Hostile Indians at the Battle of the Little Big Horn," *Research Review,* Summer 1991, Vol. 5, No. 2, p. 8].

Owns (the) Horn (also seen as Owns Horn or Own Horn)—(Minneconjou Lakota-Teton Sioux)—Fought against Custer's column. One of three or four Sioux and two Cheyenne who rode along the bluffs with White Bull to Weir Point, watching Keogh's column move across Luce Ridge. Presence confirmed by Myers, though he only lists him as a Teton Sioux.

Painted Brown (also Paints Brown)—(Oglala Lakota-Teton Sioux)—One of the first warriors to mount, fighting both Reno's and Custer's columns [LBHA]. Still living at the Standing Rock Agency, Wakpala, SD, 1926 [courtesy of Dickson].

Painted Horse—(tribe unknown)—Among several Indians who left the battlefield and twelve days later were involved in the Sibley fight [LBHA].

Painted Rock (*Inyan Owapi*)—(Oglala Lakota-Teton Sioux)—b. circa 1830. Member of Little Hawk's band.

Pawnee—(Northern Cheyenne). Son of Little Wolf. Camp guard. If true, he was a member of the Kit Fox warrior society. This could mean he was at Ford B when Custer's column approached. Presence confirmed by Myers.

Pawnee Woman (*Pala ni win*) (F)—(Hunkpapa Lakota-Teton Sioux)—b. circa 1821. Wife of His Plenty Old Man.

Pemmican—(Oglala Lakota-Teton Sioux)—Lived to at least 85 [Stewart, *Custer's Luck,* opposite p. 145]. Presence confirmed by Myers, though he only lists him as a Teton Sioux.

Pig—(Northern Cheyenne). Little warrior chief of the Elkhorn Scraper Society or as Wooden Leg called him, one of the nine "little chiefs" [Marquis, *Wooden Leg,* p. 211]. Presence confirmed by Myers.

Pine (also "Robert" Pine)—(Lakota-Teton Sioux)—At the battle but was not involved in the fighting. May have been too young. Still living at the Standing Rock Agency, Bullhead, SD, 1926 [courtesy of Dickson].

Pine—(Northern Cheyenne). Attended the 1926 reunion. Fought against both Reno and Custer. Presence confirmed by Myers.

Pisses in the Horn—(Oglala Lakota-Teton Sioux)—Listed in the Crazy Horse surrender ledger, 1877. Along with Moccasin Hide, listed as "head-of-household," his lodge consisting of three adult females and two male children; a total of seven people.

Plenty Bears—(Northern Cheyenne). A headman of the Elkhorn Scraper warrior society, or as Wooden Leg called him, one of the nine "little chiefs" [Marquis, *Wooden Leg,* p. 211]. Presence confirmed by Myers.

Plenty Crows—(Northern Cheyenne). Supposed to have been captured by the Rees. The Ree scout, Soldier, told a story to Camp that a number of Sioux warriors followed Soldier and a party of Rees who were driving stolen Sioux ponies toward the Rosebud. The hostiles pressed hard, trying to get the horses back. One warrior had his face painted red and rode a bay horse with a bald face and a yellow ribbon in his hair. The Rees wounded him and he turned back. Soldier said a Sioux named "Plenty Crow" from the Cheyenne River reservation told him this warrior was a Cheyenne and he was indeed wounded.

Plenty Dogs—(Oglala Lakota-Teton Sioux)— Listed in the Crazy Horse surrender ledger, 1877. Along with Bad Minneconjou, listed as "head-of-household." Lodge consisted of three adult females and two female children; a total of seven people.

Plenty of Buffalo Bull Meat—(Northern Cheyenne). A headman of the Kit Foxes warrior society, or as Wooden Leg called him, one of the nine "little chiefs" [Marquis, *Wooden Leg,* p. 212]. Since the Kit Fox society was the camp guards on the 25th, he *may* have fought at Ford B. Presence confirmed by Myers.

Plenty of Meat (aka Plenty of Trouble; *Obcayata*)—(*Wahpekute*/Dakota-Santee Sioux)—One of those who spotted Custer at the divide. Presence confirmed by Myers.

Plenty Shells—(Oglala Lakota-Teton Sioux)— Listed in the Crazy Horse surrender ledger, 1877. Along with Bad Partisan, Lone Elk, and Crazy Head, listed as "head-of-household." Lodge consisted of four adult females, two male children, and one female child; total of eleven people.

Plum Man—(Northern Cheyenne). A "Council of the 44" chief.

Plum Tree—(Northern Cheyenne). Father of Sun Bear and Two Feathers. In the village with his family. Had three wives, all sisters.

Poor (*Wachpanne*)—(Oglala Lakota-Teton Sioux) —Uncertain if he was at the Little Big Horn, but since he was with Black Elk's people the likelihood he was there is strong.

Poor Bear—(Oglala Lakota-Teton Sioux)—Listed in the Crazy Horse surrender ledger, 1877. Listed as "head-of-household." Lodge consisted of one adult female, one male child, and one female child; total of four people.

Poor Bear—(Sans Arc Lakota-Teton Sioux)— Head of the family. Part of Spotted Eagle's band [Dickson].

Poor Dog—(Oglala Lakota-Teton Sioux)—Listed in the Crazy Horse surrender ledger, 1877. Along with Soaring Bear, listed as "head-of-household." Lodge consisted of one adult female, two male children, and two female children; total of seven people.

Poor Elk—(Sans Arc Lakota-Teton Sioux)—Head of the family. Part of Spotted Eagle's band [Dickson].

Porcupine—(Northern Cheyenne)—d. 1921 or some time after 1926 reunion. Son of White Shield. Attended the 1926 reunion.

Powder Face—(Northern Cheyenne). Attended 1926 reunion. Surrendered to Miles in 1877.

Powder Side—(Hunkpapa Lakota-Teton Sioux)— Wounded north of the Reno Hill entrenchments, 25Jun1876. He recovered from his wounds.

Prairie Chicken (*Siyo*)—(Oglala Lakota-Teton Sioux)—b. 1862. Son of High White Man. Member of Iron Crow's band.

Pray to Him (also "Lawrence" Pray to Him)— (Lakota-Teton Sioux)—Living at the Standing Rock Agency, Little Eagle, SD, in 1926 [courtesy of Dickson]. At the camp, but he was either too young to participate in the fighting or he simply did not get into the battle.

Pretends Eagle (aka Sleeps from Home)— (Hunkpapa Lakota-Teton Sioux)—Still living at the Standing Rock Agency, Kenel, SD, in 1929. May have been too young to have been in the battle.

Pretty Bird (*Zitka la waste*)—(Hunkpapa Lakota-Teton Sioux)—b. circa 1866. Son of White Dog and Pretty Woman.

Pretty Crimson Woman (*Waluta waste win*) (F)— (Hunkpapa Lakota-Teton Sioux)—b. 1869. Daughter of Black Bird and Left Handed Woman.

Pretty Feather Woman (*Wiyaka waste win*; also, Good Feather and Good Feather Woman) (F)— (Hunkpapa Lakota-Teton Sioux)—b. circa 1829. Mother of Killed While Standing. There is some confusion regarding this woman. Some sources list her as a Minneconjou, but that could be because she married into the tribe (Makes Room, her husband, was a Minneconjou). If the Hunkpapa version and the Minneconjou version are the same person, then she was also the mother of Lazy White Bull (White Bull).

Pretty Legs—(Oglala Lakota-Teton Sioux)— Listed in the Crazy Horse surrender ledger. Along with Iron Magpie, he was listed as "head-of-household." There were four adult females and five female children in his lodge, a total of eleven people.

Pretty Track Woman (*Oye waste win*) (F)—(Hunkpapa Lakota-Teton Sioux)—b. circa 1875. An infant at the time of the battle. Daughter of Big Leg and Ticket.

Pretty Weasel (*Hintunkasan Waste*)—(Oglala Lakota-Teton Sioux)—b. circa 1851 or 1857–d. 1927. Often rode with Crazy Horse. A member of He Dog's Soreback Band [Dickson]. Brother of Red Hawk.

Pretty White Buffalo (also seen as Pretty White Buffalo Woman; Beautiful White Cow; *Tatanka-he-gle-ska*. After her husband was killed at Wounded Knee on 15 Dec 1890, she was given the name *Pte-San-Waste-Win,* meaning Beautiful White Cow) (F)-(Hunkpapa Lakota-Teton Sioux)—b. circa 1843. Married to Spotted Horn Bull. A cousin of Sitting Bull. Seems to have been about 33 years old at the time of the battle and apparently watched the fighting from the west banks of the Little Big Horn. About 65 years old when she retold her story of the battle to the Standing Rock Indian agent, James McLaughlin, in 1908.

Pretty Woman (*Winyan waste*) (F)—(Hunkpapa Lakota-Teton)—b. circa 1825. Wife of Fire Cloud.

Pretty Woman (*Winyan waste*) (F)—(Hunkpapa Lakota-Teton Sioux)—b. circa 1843. Wife of White Dog.

Pretty Woman (*Winyan waste*) (F)—(Hunkpapa Lakota-Teton Sioux)—b. circa 1845. Wife of Shooting Bear.

Princess (*Han can win*) (F)—(Hunkpapa Lakota-Teton Sioux)—b. circa 1846. Wife of Attacking Bear. Listed in the Sitting Bull Surrender Ledger.

Protector—(Oglala Lakota-Teton Sioux)—An old man by the time of Wounded Knee.

Puffed Cheek—(Cheyenne). At the Powder River fight, 17 Mar 1876.

Pulls Out—(Oglala Lakota-Teton Sioux)—Listed in the Crazy Horse surrender ledger, 1877. Listed as "head-of-household." Lodge consisted of two adult females, two male children, and three female children; total of eight people.

Pumpkin Hill—(Oglala Lakota-Teton Sioux)—Listed in the Crazy Horse surrender ledger, 1877. Listed as "head-of-household." Lodge consisted of two adult females, three male children, and one female child; seven people, total.

Puts on His Shoes—(Lakota-Teton Sioux)—At the Cheyenne River Agency, 1926.

Quill Dress (aka "Sadie" Whiteman or "Sadie" White Man) (F)—(Northern Cheyenne)—b. circa 1863–d. 1950. She was among the women who stripped the bodies on the Custer battlefield. Claimed to have taken the soldiers' watches, spurs, weapons, hiding some of the loot in rattlesnake holes.

Rain-in-the-Face (or *Tok'-i'-tcu-wa*, meaning He-Who-Takes-the-Enemy; also *Itiomagju*; also seen referred to as Big Rain)-(Hunkpapa Lakota-Teton Sioux)—b. about 1835 near the forks of the Cheyenne River, SD–d. at Standing Rock Agency, 12 or 14 Sep 1905. A big, powerful man. Connell says at the age of 60 he weighed almost 200 pounds and had a 46" chest. Utterly fearless and reputed to be able to withstand horrible pain. Had been arrested by a detachment of troops led by CPT George Yates and 1LT Tom Custer, 14 Dec 1874, for the killing of Dr. John Honsinger, the Seventh Cavalry's veterinary surgeon, and the sutler, Mr. Augustus Baliran during the Yellowstone Expedition, 1873. Did not get into the Reno fight, but instead went north when Custer's column was spotted. Presence confirmed by Myers, though the Oglala, Red Hawk said Rain-in-the-Face was not in the battle, but away. It is unclear where.

According to an article appearing in the Toronto *Globe,* Oct 1876, some Indians claim "Big Rain" killed the man they later discovered as Custer, Big Rain shooting him in the head. Because of the way he was dressed, they did not think Custer was a soldier, but rather someone who just fell in with the troops.

Raised Him—(Lakota-Teton Sioux)—Still living in 1926.

Rattler—(Lakota-Teton Sioux)—His son was wounded during the fight [Graham, *The Custer Myth,* p. 54].

Rattlesnake Nose—(Northern Cheyenne). A headman of the Kit Foxes warrior society, or as Wooden Leg called him, one of the nine "little chiefs" [Marquis, *Wooden Leg,* p. 212]. Since the Kit Fox society was the camp guards on the 25 June he *may* have fought at Ford B. Presence confirmed by Myers.

Rattling Hawk—(Oglala Lakota-Teton Sioux)—Wounded during the Rosebud fight; stayed in village watching the battle, though one account claims he did some fighting. Black Elk claimed he was not able to fight. Listed in the Crazy Horse surrender ledger.

Reaching Cloud (also High in the Clouds; Against the Cloud; *Mahpi ya eya pato*)—(Hunkpapa Lakota-Teton Sioux)—b. circa 1832. Listed in the Sitting Bull Surrender Ledger. Wife was Red Woman.

Reaching to Something (*Iyagle win*) (F)—(Oglala Lakota-Teton Sioux)—Mother of Little Bull.

Real Hawk (*Cetan hca*)—(Oglala Lakota-Teton Sioux)—b. circa 1851–d. 1903). Member of Big Road's band.

Rectum (Guts or Open Belly)—(Hunkpapa Lakota-Teton Sioux)—d. 25 Jun 1876, killed at the Little Big Horn. Body location unknown. Myers claimed he was killed fighting Custer, but he may have been killed in the valley, primarily because he was a Hunkpapa [Myers, "Roster of Known Hostile Indians at the Battle of the Little Big Horn," *Research Review,* Summer 1991, Vol. 5, No. 2, p. 8]. Hardorff disagrees and lists him among those killed fighting Custer.

Red Arm(s)—(Northern Cheyenne). In the village with his family. Probably the same chief as the one involved in the treaties of the 1860's [Stewart, *Custer's Luck,* p. 38]. Had three wives, all sisters.

Red Bear (also "George" Red Bear)—(Sans Arc Lakota-Teton Sioux)—A sub-chief. Reputed to have led the Sans Arcs [Graham, *The Custer Myth,* p. 63]. Presence confirmed by Dickson and Myers. Head of the family. Part of Spotted Eagle's band [Dickson]. Fled to Canada with his family when Sitting Bull refused to surrender.

Red Bird (aka Young Little Wolf; eventually took the name Little Wolf from his famous uncle)—(Northern Cheyenne). This could also be "William" Red Bird.

Red Bird—(Hunkpapa Lakota-Teton Sioux)—Living at the Cheyenne River Agency in 1926.

Red Bird—(Lakota-Teton Sioux)—Known to have been in the fighting at the Little Big Horn. Still living at the Standing Rock Agency, Wakpala, SD, 1926 [courtesy of Dickson].

Red Blanket (*Tasina Luta win*) (F)—(Oglala Teton-Sioux)—b. circa 1847. Wife of Bad Heart Bull (the elder) [Dickson].

Red Bull—(Sans Arc Lakota-Teton Sioux)—Head of the family. Part of Spotted Eagle's band [Dickson].

Red Calf Woman (*Taji luta win*) (F)—(Hunkpapa Lakota-Teton Sioux)—b. circa 1869. Only a child at the battle. Daughter of Blue Cloud and Shooting Wood.

Red Cane (F)—(Brulé Lakota-Teton Sioux)—Wife of Fool Bull.

Red Cherries—(Northern Cheyenne). A group of Cheyenne under Little Wolf, on their way from the agency to the camp, came upon Custer's troops before they left the valley of the Rosebud. Scouts from this group discovered the lost pack from one of Custer's mules. This is the pack that SGT Curtiss went back to retrieve. One of the three scouts seen by SGT Curtiss (Big Crow and Black Horse). In the hilltop fight, 26 Jun 1876.

Red Cloud (aka "Jack" Red Cloud)—(Oglala Lakota-Teton Sioux)—Son of the old Oglala chief Red Cloud. A young man when the battle occurred. Also at Rosebud fight. At the 1926 reunion.

Red Cloud—(Cheyenne).

Red Cloud (*Magpi Luta*)—(Oglala Lakota-Teton Sioux)—b. circa 1833–d. 1918. Claimed there were only 4,000 Indians in the whole camp [Liddic]. There is a Red Cloud on the 1900 Pine Ridge census. He is listed as sixty-seven at that time, making him thirty-five at the time of the 1868 treaty and forty-three at the time of the LBH battle. He would have been eighty-five when he died. Donovan claims he was not at the battle, but this seems to be incorrect [*A Terrible Glory,* p. 185]. "Among the Sioux, Horse ... ranked as senior ... of the four principal chiefs of an organization equivalent to the Medicine Lances of the Cheyennes. That is to say, he was of equal rank with the late Roman Nose, Red Cloud, Spotted Tail and others. He wore the long white 'stole' over his shoulders as insignia, and also to tie himself to his planted lance in a fight to the death" [Frank H. Huston, Graham, *The Custer Myth,* p. 80]. "Bull ... I think was a 'Water Pourer': only seven of them at a time among all the Lakotah Nation—equivalent to Cardinals of the Church of Rome. *Magpi Luta* (i.e. Red Cloud) also took that degree and became a sort of Richelieu" [Frank H. Huston, in a March 1925, letter to W. A. Graham. [Graham, *The Custer Myth,* p. 80]. Dickson names Red Cloud as among three Oglala leaders—Little Wound and Young Man Afraid of His Horses—as men who "largely avoided becoming involved" ["... Soreback Band...," p. 1] in conflicts between whites and the Indians. This does not mean, however, that these men were not at the Little Big Horn during the fighting.

Surrounded by and surrendered to Crook's command, October 1876.

Red Crane—(Oglala Lakota-Teton Sioux)—Listed in the Crazy Horse surrender ledger, 1877. Along with Torn Belly and White Bull, listed as "head-of-household." Lodge consisted of two female adults and one female child; total of six people.

Red Crow (*Kangi Luta*)—(Oglala Lakota-Teton Sioux)—b. circa 1835–d. 1890s. Member of Low Dog's band.

Red Dog—(Oglala Lakota-Teton Sioux)—In 1877, he told General Crook that there were 1,800 lodges at the LBH.

Red Dog—(Sans Arc Lakota-Teton Sioux)—Head of the family. Part of Spotted Eagle's band [Dickson].

Red Eagle (also "Martha" Red Eagle) (F)—(Sans Arc Lakota-Teton Sioux)—b. 1 Jan 1854–d. 26 Oct 1936. Daughter of Elk Head and sister of Young Elk Head.

Red Earth (*Makasa*) (F)—(Oglala Lakota-Teton Sioux)—b. circa 1844. Probably a member of Low Dog's band. Her family was probably known as Red Earth Woman [Dickson].

Red Face—(Hunkpapa Lakota-Teton Sioux)—d. 25 Jun 1876, killed at the Little Big Horn. Body location unknown, but killed fighting Custer's column.

Red Feather—(Oglala Lakota-Teton Sioux)—Part of Big Road's band of Northern Oglala. Friend of Eagle Elk. Brother of Black Shawl Woman, a wife of Crazy Horse (m. 1870). Along with Kicking Bear, he supposedly killed one of the Ree scouts in the Reno fight. If Little Brave had been finished off near Reno Hill, this one had to have been Bob-tail Bull. Red Feather shot his horse, Kicking Bear then shot him twice, and Red Feather finished him off. Claims to have seen the arrival of the pack train on Reno Hill, but Michno thinks it was the advance elements of Benteen's battalion, since the packs did not arrive for at least 37 minutes [Pennington] or one hour later [everybody else]. Also charged Calhoun Hill. Also seen listed as a Brulé. In later years he became a member of the Pine Ridge Police, but a leg amputation put an end to that service. He had also become a very devout Catholic.

Red Fire Woman (*Apesa win*) (F)—(Hunkpapa Lakota-Teton Sioux)—b. circa 1868. Daughter of Shooting Bear and Pretty Woman.

Red Fish—(Lakota-Teton Sioux)—A prominent and highly respected chief. Presence confirmed by Myers, though he only lists him as a Teton Sioux.

Red Flute Woman (F)—(Oglala Lakota-Teton Sioux)—Probably a member of Iron Crow's band.

Red Fox—(Northern Cheyenne). On Custer Hill after the battle.

Red Fox—(Oglala Lakota-Teton Sioux).

Red Fox—(Oglala Lakota-Teton Sioux)—b. circa 1870. Even as a child he remembered hearing the firing during the battle. May have been the son of the Red Fox listed above.

Red Hail—(Hunkpapa Lakota-Teton Sioux).

Red Hair—(Sans Arc Lakota-Teton Sioux)—One of two Sans Arc (Elk Head being the other) entrusted with protecting the sacred Buffalo Calf Pipe [Dickson].

Red Hair Woman (*Hinsa win*) (F)—(Hunkpapa Lakota-Teton Sioux)—b. circa 1867. Daughter of Cheyenne Woman and—it appears—Bone Tomahawk, since Cheyenne Woman was his second wife [Dickson]. Listed in the Sitting Bull Surrender Ledger.

Red Haired Bear—(Northern Cheyenne). Medicine man.

Red Hat (also Red Hood)—(Southern Cheyenne). Lame White Man's son. His mother was Twin Woman.

Red Hawk (also "Austin" Red Hawk)—(Oglala Lakota-Teton Sioux)—b. 1854. Sub-chief. Fought in the valley against Reno, but didn't cross the LBH. Continued to fight with Crazy Horse's band. According to Michno, "Red Hawk said that only after making a desperate fight on Custer Hill, did the remaining soldiers retreat downhill" ["Myth-Busting at the Little Bighorn, *Custer and His Times, Book Five,* p. 181]. Listed in the Crazy Horse surrender ledger. Along with Good Boy, listed as "head-of-household." Lodge consisted of one adult female and four female children; seven people, total. This is the man in the famous Edward S. Curtis photograph of 1905, "An Oasis in the Badlands." At the 1926 reunion. Presence confirmed by Myers.

Red Hill—(Brulé Lakota-Teton Sioux)

Red Horn—(Hunkpapa Lakota-Teton Sioux)—Chief of a Soreback Band.

Red Horn Buffalo—(Hunkpapa Lakota-Teton Sioux)—d. 25 Jun 1876, killed at the Little Big Horn. Wounded, probably mortally, in the Deep Ravine-Cemetery Ravine area around Custer Hill while charging Custer Hill. LBHA and CBHMA list him merely as wounded, but offer nothing else. Iron Hawk/Runs in Circle claimed he was killed [DeMallie, *The Sixth Grandfather,* p. 191].

Red Horn Buffalo (probably also known as Red Horn Bull; *Tatanka Heluta*)—(Oglala Lakota-Teton Sioux)—b. circa 1851–d. at the Pine Ridge Reservation, 1920. Wounded in the jaw during Reno's retreat from the valley. Presence confirmed by Myers. If he was Red Horn Bull, he was probably a member of Big Road's band [Dickson].

Red Horn Bull—(Minneconjou Lakota-Teton Sioux)—Led the charge against Reno's troops in the valley. Famous as a runner. Presence confirmed by Myers, though he carries him as an Oglala.

Red Horse ("George" Red Horse)—(Northern Cheyenne). Attended 1926 reunion. This may be the same man as Medicine Wolf.

Red Horse—(Hunkpapa Lakota-Teton Sioux)— Ten lodges (65 people), Sep 1876, at Standing Rock [Dickson]. There is a Minneconjou chief with the same name.

Red Horse—(Minneconjou Lakota-Teton Sioux) —A head chief in the council lodge. One mile from the village when Reno struck; digging turnips with the women. Claimed the soldiers made five brave stands. There is a Hunkpapa chief by the same name. Presence confirmed by Myers. Famous for his pictographs of the battle and for his verbal description of the fighting.

Red Horse—(*Wahpekute*/Dakota-Santee Sioux)— A son of *Inkpaduta*. Said by some to have been the Indian who actually killed Custer [Stewart, *Custer's Luck*, p. 486]. CPT J. S. Poland's report claimed that the last soldier killed was killed by Red Top's two sons [Graham, *The Custer Myth*, p. 46].

Red Leaf—(Lakota-Teton Sioux)—Surrendered with Red Cloud, October 1876.

Red Nose—(Northern Cheyenne)—b. 23 Jun 1876. A two-day-old infant at the time of the battle. Son of Wolf Medicine.

Red Owl—(Northern Cheyenne). A headman of the Crazy Dogs warrior society, or as Wooden Leg said, one of the nine "little chiefs" [Marquis, *Wooden Leg*, p. 212]. Presence confirmed by Myers.

Red Owl—(Oglala Lakota-Teton Sioux)—At the 1926 reunion.

Red Robe—(Northern Cheyenne). Father of the Roman Nose.

Red Rock—(Oglala Lakota-Teton Sioux)—Listed in the Crazy Horse surrender ledger, 1877. Listed as "head-of-household." Lodge consisted of one adult female and one male child; total of three people.

Red Shell (*Panke ska Luta win*) (F)—(Oglala Lakota-Teton Sioux)—b. circa 1832. Mother of Center Feather in Low Dog's band.

Red Shirt—(Oglala Lakota-Teton Sioux)—He was an Oglala soldier at the Red Cloud Agency in 1871. He was considered an agency Indian. In 1880 he traveled with Red Cloud to Washington D. C. and seven years later joined the Buffalo Bill Wild West Show, touring Europe. He was still alive in 1909. While there is considerable speculation about his presence at the Little Big Horn, he was listed in the Crazy Horse surrender ledger in 1877, making it fairly likely that he was present at the Little Big Horn. Along with Brave Wolf and Bad Horse (High White Man), listed as "head-of-household." Lodge consisted of three adult females, five male children, and three female children; total of fourteen people.

Red Skirt—(Minneconjou Lakota-Teton Sioux)— The principal chief of the Minneconjou, at least according to COL Nelson A. Miles (5I) in an October 28, 1876, dispatch. Miles also claimed he was related to Bull Eagle. One of the five "hostages" designated by Miles during the surrender of 400–600 lodges and their return to the Cheyenne River Agency, October-December 1876. The others were Sunrise, Foolish Thunder, White Bull, and Black Eagle.

Red Star—(Sans Arc Lakota-Teton Sioux)—Head of the family. Part of Spotted Eagle's band [Dickson].

Red Tail—(Oglala Lakota-Teton Sioux)—Listed in the Crazy Horse surrender ledger, 1877. Along with Charging Hawk, listed as "head-of-household." Lodge consisted of four adult females and three male children; total of nine people.

Red Tent Woman (*Tipi luta win*) (F)—(Hunkpapa Lakota-Teton Sioux)—b. 1869. Daughter of Brave Thunder and Tall Woman.

Red Thunder (*Wakin yan luta*)—(Hunkpapa Lakota-Teton Sioux)—b. circa 1841. Wife was Ripe. Listed in the Sitting Bull Surrender Ledger.

Red Tomahawk-(Hunkpapa Lakota-Teton Sioux)—d. 1931. One who spotted Custer in the soldiers' second camp on the Rosebud. Was at the LBH reunion, 1926. Also seen as a Northern Cheyenne.

Red Top Knot (also Red Topknot)—(Cheyenne)—Listed in the Crazy Horse surrender ledger, 1877.

Red Whirlwind Woman (also Scarlet Whirlwind; Scarlet Woman) (F)—(Hunkpapa Lakota-Teton Sioux)—Married to One Bull, a Minneconjou.

Red White Buffalo Cow (*Pte san duta win*) (F)—(Hunkpapa Lakota-Teton Sioux)—b. circa 1861. Daughter of Four Horns.

Red Willow—(Oglala Lakota-Teton Sioux)—At Wounded Knee, but uncertain if he was at the Little Big Horn.

Red Woman (*Winyan luta win*) (F)—(Hunkpapa Lakota-Teton Sioux)—b. circa 1835. Wife of Reaching Cloud.

Ree (F)—(Lakota-Teton Sioux)—Listed in the Crazy Horse surrender ledger, 1877. Listed as "head-of-household." Lodge consisted of one male child and one female child; total of three people.

Ree—(Oglala Lakota-Teton Sioux)—Listed in the Crazy Horse surrender ledger, 1877. Along with Hangs His Head, One Glass, and Soldier, listed as "head-of-household." Lodge consisted of three adult females, one male child, and four female children; total of twelve people. Present at the LBH.

Reed Woman (*Psa win*) (F)—(Hunkpapa Lakota-Teton Sioux)—b. circa 1833. Wife of One Who Breaks Arrow.

Remaining Woman (*Owanji yanke win*) (F)—(Hunkpapa Lakota-Teton Sioux)—b. circa 1873. Only a baby at the time of the battle. Daughter of Bone Tomahawk and Foot.

Returns from Scout (*Tonweya Gli*)—(Oglala Lakota-Teton Sioux)—b. circa 1841–d. 1918. Probably a member of the Low Dog band. Married to Shell.

Rib Man—(Oglala Lakota-Teton Sioux)—Husband of Shouts At. Known to have been in the battle.

Rich Walker ("Ethel" Rich Walker) (F)—(Cheyenne).

Rider—(Oglala Lakota-Teton Sioux)—Listed in the Crazy Horse surrender ledger, 1877. Along with Short, listed as "head-of-household." Lodge consisted of two adult females; total, four people.

Ridge Bear ("Zac" Ridgebear)—(Cheyenne). Still alive in 1921 and living at Lame Deer, Montana.

Ridge Walker (also just known as "Mrs." Ridge Walker; "Meneha" Ridge Walker)—(Northern Cheyenne)—A small girl at the time of the battle.

Ridiculous [Graham, *The Custer Myth*, p. 51]—(Oglala Lakota-Teton Sioux).

Right in the Camp (aka "Joshua" Shell Boy)—(Oglala Lakota-Teton Sioux)—b. 1866. Son of Shell Boy.

Ripe (*Wasu ton*) (F)—(Hunkpapa Lakota-Teton Sioux)—b. circa 1839. Wife of Red Thunder.

Rising Eagle (*Wanbli Inape win*) (F)—(Oglala Lakota-Teton Sioux)—b. 1858. Daughter of High White Man.

Rising Fire—(Northern Cheyenne).

Rising Sun—(Northern Cheyenne). May have also been one of the first Cheyenne warriors to confront Custer's column at Ford B. Took a watch from a dead soldier; could have been Henry Harrington's.

(Some have discredited the Harrington-watch story.) Presence confirmed by Myers.

River (*Wa kpa*) (F)—(Hunkpapa Lakota-Teton Sioux)—b. circa 1846. Listed in the Sitting Bull Surrender Ledger. Sister of Mosquito.

Roan Bear (aka White Man Bear)—(Northern Cheyenne). Belonged to the Fox warrior society. One of the warriors at Ford B when Custer's column arrived there. Presence confirmed by Myers.

Robe Hair Outside—(Oglala Lakota-Teton Sioux)—Listed in the Crazy Horse surrender ledger, 1877. Listed as "head-of-household." Lodge consisted of one adult woman and two female children; total of four people.

Roman Nose (aka Crooked Nose)—(Southern Cheyenne). Member of the Dog Men Warrior Society. Presence confirmed by Myers. This was not the famous Roman Nose who was killed in 1868.

Roman Nose (aka Hump Nose or just Hump)—(Northern Cheyenne)—d. 25 Jun 1876, killed at the Little Big Horn, another of the "suicide warriors" [Myers, "Roster of Known Hostile Indians at the Battle of the Little Big Horn," *Research Review*, Summer 1991, Vol. 5, No. 2]. Killed during the Reno fight, on the west bank of the river. Son of Long Roach or Red Robe. Wooden Leg claimed he was sixteen years old at the battle [Marquis, *Wooden Leg*, p. 268]. If it is true that he was killed during the Reno fight, it may preclude this particular individual from being one of the suicide warriors. They are generally believed to have fought only the Custer columns.

Roman Nose-(Hunkpapa Lakota-Teton Sioux)—d. certainly by 1925. "Among the Sioux, Horse ... ranked as senior ... of the four principal chiefs of an organization equivalent to the Medicine Lances of the Cheyennes. That is to say, he was of equal rank with the late Roman Nose, Red Cloud, Spotted Tail and others. He wore the long white 'stole' over his shoulders as insignia, and also to tie himself to his planted lance in a fight to the death" [Frank H. Huston, Graham, *The Custer Myth*, p. 80]. [It is not sure if Huston was referring to this man or the great Cheyenne warrior of the same name. That Cheyenne was dead by the time of the LBH.] Not certain he was at the battle, but since he was so prominent, he is carried as a participant. It is also uncertain whether it was this man or the Minneconjou, below, who was attacked at Slim Buttes along with the Minneconjou chief, American Horse.

Roman Nose—(Lakota-Teton Sioux)—This entry is questionable, though a Roman Nose was known to be alive and living at the Standing Rock Agency, Little Eagle, SD, in 1926. He was at the camp, but he was either too young to participate in the fighting or he simply did not get into the battle. That profile fits none of the other known "Roman Noses," so he is carried as a separate individual.

Roman Nose—(Minneconjou Lakota-Teton Sioux)—A sub–chief. Presence confirmed by Myers. It is uncertain whether it was this man or the Hunkpapa Roman Nose, above, who was attacked at Slim Buttes along with the Minneconjou chief, American Horse. A son of Lone Horn (d. 1875) and brother of Spotted Elk, Touch the Clouds, and Frog.

Rose Bud (also "Joseph" Rose Bud)—(Lakota-Teton Sioux)— May have been too young to have been in the fighting at the Little Big Horn, but he was in the camp. Still living at the Standing Rock Agency, Bullhead, SD, 1926 [courtesy of Dickson].

Round Fool (aka Round Fool's Impersonation)— (Oglala Lakota-Teton Sioux)—Apparently spotted a soldier hiding in the bushes below Reno Hill on 26 Jun 1876. The soldier was subsequently killed.

Round Stone ("Louis" Roundstone)—(Northern Cheyenne). Still alive in 1921 and living at Lame Deer, Montana.

The Rump—(Oglala Lakota-Teton Sioux)—Listed in the Crazy Horse surrender ledger, 1877. Along with Sits up Above and Little Prick, listed as "head-of-household." Lodge consisted of three adult females, two male children, and two female children; total of ten people.

Runner—(Oglala Lakota-Teton Sioux)—Listed in the Crazy Horse surrender ledger, 1877. Listed as "head-of-household." Lodge consisted of one adult female, one male child, and one female child; four people, total.

Running Antelope (*Tatoka Iyanke*)—(Hunkpapa Lakota-Teton Sioux)—Soreback Band (*Chankaohan*), along with Cross Bear [Dickson/Bray]. Thirteen lodges (75 people), Sep76, at Standing Rock [Dickson].

Running Eagle (*Wanbli Inyanke*)—(Oglala Lakota-Teton Sioux)—b. circa 1842–d. circa 1899. Son of Red Cloud's sister. Husband of Badger; father of One Who Breaks. Member of He Dog's Soreback band [Dickson]. Said to have killed or certainly shot the Ree scout, Bob-tail Bull. At the time of the battle he may have been with Iron Crow's band.

Running Elk—(Oglala Lakota-Teton Sioux)— Standing Bear's uncle. May have been at the Little Big Horn.

Running Horse (*Tasunke Inyanke*)—(Oglala Lakota-Teton Sioux)—b. circa 1836. Black Elk's uncle. (There was another Indian named Horse Runs Ahead who was wounded in the heel at the Rosebud fight. He was also at the LBH fight, though didn't get in it. There is no tribe listed and this may be a duplication; however, they are carried separately until further clarification.) Part of Iron Crow's band.

Runs Close to Camp—(Oglala Lakota-Teton Sioux)—Listed in the Crazy Horse surrender ledger, 1877. Listed as "head-of-household." Lodge consisted of two adult females and two female children; total of five people.

Runs Fearless—(Oglala Lakota-Teton Sioux)— May have counted coup on Ree scout, Bob-tail Bull.

Runs in Circle (*Oksan Inyanka*; aka Iron Hawk; "Homer" Iron Hawk; also Runs Around)—(Oglala or Hunkpapa Lakota-Teton Sioux)—b. Montana, 1862, 1864, or 1867–d. 1950. Dickson says he was an Oglala, while Michno and Hardorff claim both the father and son were Hunkpapa. Often confused with the father of the same, later name. Thirteen or nine years old at the battle, probably thirteen. A big young man. Told his story to John Neihardt in 1931, but it seems he claimed a lot of what his father did there as his own story. Slept late that day and the sun was barely overhead when scouts yelled out that soldiers were coming. He was eating his first meal of the day. Did not get into the Reno fight, but joined others who were heading off to fight Custer: "it took me a long time to put an eagle feather on my head! I painted my face a dark red. About the time I got through dressing for the war the Reno troop was through fighting so I did not get to fight any" [DeMallie, *The Sixth Grandfather*, p. 190]. Killed a soldier with his bow and arrow. Presence confirmed by Myers, who also carries him as a Hunkpapa. In *Black Elk Speaks*, Iron Hawk claimed to be a Hunkpapa [Neihardt, p. 100], but there is the possibility of a change in tribal affiliation as Dickson's work is definitive, even challenging tribal claims. A lot of what this man claimed could pertain to his father — Iron Hawk — rather than Runs in Circle, himself. Claimed to have been wounded in the fighting, going as far as to show Judge Ricker the scar [Hardorff, *Lakota Recollections...*, p. 67].

Runs in Sight (F)—(Lakota-Teton Sioux)—Listed in the Crazy Horse surrender ledger, 1877. Listed as "head-of-household." Lodge consisted of two other adult females and two male children; total of five people.

Runs on Top (also seen as Runs On)—(Oglala Lakota-Teton Sioux)— Listed in the Crazy Horse surrender ledger, 1877. Along with Spotted Hand, listed as "head-of-household." Lodge consisted of six adult females, two male children, and one female child; total of eleven people.

Runs the Enemy (also Enemy Runs Him; *Tok kahin hpe ya*)—(Two Kettles Lakota-Teton Sioux) — b. circa 1846; 30 years old; LBHA and CBHMA claim he was 15 at the time of the battle. In the group pressuring Reno's left flank in the valley fight. Still alive in 1926.

Sacred Crow (*Kangi Wakan*)—(Oglala Lakota-Teton Sioux)— b. circa 1851. Member of Little Hawk's band. He was the son of Blue Hawk.

Saddle—(Oglala Lakota-Teton Sioux)— Listed in the Crazy Horse surrender ledger, 1877. Along with Clown, listed as "head-of-household." Lodge consisted of two adult females, two male children, and one female child; total of seven people.

Sand Crane—(Northern Cheyenne). Swimming in the LBH when he heard the firing [LBHA].

Sandstone—(Northern Cheyenne). Sharpshooter on Sharpshooter Ridge during hilltop fight.

Save Himself—(Lakota-Teton Sioux)— d. 25 Jun 1876, killed at the Little Big Horn, but nothing else is known about him. Listed in Kicking Bear's casualty list.

Saves Bear (*Mato Ninyanpi*)—(Oglala Lakota-Teton Sioux)— b. circa 1838. Head of the Bear Spares Him family, a name by which he may also have been known. Member of Low Dog's band.

Saw Her as They Go by (*Wanyag mani pi win*) (F)—(Hunkpapa Lakota-Teton Sioux)— b. circa 1867. Sitting Bull's daughter.

Scabby—(Northern Cheyenne)— d. Nov 1876. Fought Reno and rode his horse across the front of the soldiers five times and was never hit. Presence confirmed by Myers.

Scabby Eyelid—(Northern Cheyenne). In Rosebud fight.

Scabby Face—(Oglala Lakota-Teton Sioux)— Listed in the Crazy Horse surrender ledger, 1877. Listed as "head-of-household." Lodge consisted of three female adults and three female children; seven people, total.

Scabby Head (Scabby Face)—(Blackfeet Lakota-Teton Sioux)— Reputed to have been the head chief [Graham, *The Custer Myth*, p. 63]. Presence confirmed by Myers, though he only lists him as a Teton Sioux.

Scabby Place—(Oglala Lakota-Teton Sioux)— Listed in the Crazy Horse surrender ledger, 1877. Listed as "head-of-household." Lodge consisted of two adult females and two female children; total of five people.

Scar Leg (also possibly known as Callous Leg ["Last Stand Magazine," Vol. 1, April 2009: "Custer's Foes in Reunion"]—(Lakota-Teton Sioux) — At the Cheyenne River Agency, 1926.

Scaring Bear—(Oglala Lakota-Teton Sioux)— Listed in the Crazy Horse surrender ledger [CBHMA]. Probably present at the LBH.

Scarlet Bear (aka Two Heart)—(Lakota-Teton Sioux)— Fought alongside Kill Eagle. Presence confirmed by Myers, though he only lists him as a Teton Sioux.

Scarlet Eagle (aka Sitting Crow)—(Lakota-Teton Sioux)— Fought alongside Kill Eagle. Presence confirmed by Myers, though he only lists him as a Teton Sioux.

Scarlet Thunder (aka Iron Horn)—(Minneconjou Lakota-Teton Sioux)— Fought alongside Kill Eagle. Presence confirmed by Myers, though he only lists him as a Teton Sioux.

Scattering Bear (*Mato Wayuhi*; also The Man That Scatters the Bear)—(Hunkpapa Lakota-Teton Sioux)— He was with Sitting Bull in Canada in 1877. Husband of Speaks Once.

Seen by the Nation (also Nation That Sees Her; Seen by Her Nation; *Oyate wanya kepi win*) (F)— (Hunkpapa Lakota-Teton Sioux)— b. circa 1851. One of Sitting Bull's two wives, the other being her sister, Four Robes. She was also his ex-sister-in-law.

Sees the Cow—(Oglala Lakota-Teton Sioux)— Listed in the Crazy Horse surrender ledger, 1877. Along with Horned Horse and At the End, listed as "head-of-household." Lodge consisted of three adult females and one male child; total of seven people.

Seminole, Jules — A southern mixed-blood married to a Northern Cheyenne woman.

Shabby (*Nahco win*) (F)—(Oglala Lakota-Teton Sioux)— b. circa 1845. One of Eagle hawk's two wives.

Shadow Comes in Sight—(Northern Cheyenne)— Son of Left Hand Shooter. After the battle, he left with Ice (White Bull), traveling with Crazy Horse.

Sharp Nose—(Cheyenne)— Was at the battle, but did not engage in any fighting. Listed in the Crazy Horse surrender ledger, 1877.

Sharp Pointed (*Pestola Yuha*)—(Oglala Lakota-Teton Sioux)—b. circa 1856–d. after 1910. Probably a member of Low Dog's band.

Shave Elk (*Hehaka Tasla*; *Eccoca Taskla*; aka "Thomas" Disputed)—(Oglala Lakota-Teton Sioux)—b. 1854–1855 or possibly 1858–d. probably between late-1911 and early-1912 [Dickson]. Interview by Walter Camp around 1910–1911. Shave Elk was his name at the time of the fighting. A member of Big Road's Northern band, which would put him in the *Oyuhpe Oglala* [Dickson]. He was in the Rosebud fight. He missed the Reno fight, but rode up MTC with either one or four other Lakota when he spotted Custer's column. They turned around and hurried back to the ford, shouting warnings to the village. This is verified in Liddic, *Vanishing Victory*, pages 101–102 and in Liddic/Harbaugh, *Camp on Custer*, p. 122, in a Walter Camp interview of Shave Elk. Probably surrendered at the Red Cloud Agency in May 1877 with Crazy Horse, though his name does not appear on the ledger [Dickson]. He fled with Big Road in late 1877, early 1878, and wound up in Canada [Dickson]. In 1887 he had just married Gall's daughter.

Shave Head—(Hunkpapa Lakota-Teton Sioux)—A brother of Rain-in-the-Face.

Shell (aka "Agnes" Returns from Scout) (F)—(Oglala Lakota-Teton Sioux). Married to Returns from Scout. According to Dickson, she said she saw her dead relatives during the Ghost Dance.

Shell Boy (also seen as "Shield Boy," but this is an error; *Pakiska Hoksila*)—(Oglala Lakota-Teton Sioux)—b. circa 1836 or Jan 1837 [Dickson]. Member of the *Oyuhpe* band of the Oglala (Big Road's band). Married to Horse Stands (about 1857). Father of Right-In-The-Camp.

Shell Boy—(Brulé Lakota-Teton Sioux)—b. circa 1841. A member of Bull Dog's band [Dickson].

Shell Ear Ring—(Lakota-Teton Sioux)—Counted coup on two soldiers [LBHA].

Shell Necklace—(Lakota-Teton Sioux)—At the Cheyenne River Agency, 1926.

Shell Necklace—(Sans Arc Lakota-Teton Sioux)—Head of the family. Part of Spotted Eagle's band [Dickson].

Shell Woman (F)—(Minneconjou Lakota-Teton Sioux)—Sister of Lazy White Bull; daughter of Makes Room and Good Feather (Pretty Feather Woman).

Shell Woman (*Panke ska win*) (F)—(Hunkpapa Lakota-Teton Sioux)—b. circa 1873. Only a small

child at the time of the battle. Daughter of Chasing Alone and Whirlwind.

The Shield—(Oglala Lakota-Teton Sioux)—Listed in the Crazy Horse surrender ledger, 1877. Listed as "head-of-household." Lodge consisted of six adult females, three male children, and five female children; total of sixteen people.

Shits on His Head (as improbable as this may seem, he has also been seen as Shits on His Hand)—(Oglala Lakota-Teton Sioux)—Listed in the Crazy Horse surrender ledger, 1877. Along with the Bull, listed as "head-of-household." Lodge consisted of one other person, a female adult; three people, total.

Shits on the Eagle—(Oglala Lakota-Teton Sioux)—Listed in the Crazy Horse surrender ledger, 1877. Listed as "head-of-household." Lodge consisted of one adult female, two male children, and two female children; six people, total.

Shooter—(Sans Arc Lakota-Teton Sioux)—Head of the family. Part of Spotted Eagle's band [Dickson].

Shooting Bear (*Mato kute pi*)—(Hunkpapa Lakota-Teton Sioux)—b. circa 1845. Listed in the Sitting Bull Surrender Ledger. Married to another Pretty Woman.

Shooting Wood (*Cano win*) (F)—(Hunkpapa Lakota-Teton Sioux)—b. circa 1852. Wife of Blue Cloud.

Shoots Bear as He Runs (also seen as Shooting Bear as He Runs)-(Minneconjou Lakota-Teton Sioux)—d. 1879. One of three or four Sioux and two Cheyenne who rode along the bluffs with White Bull to Weir Point, watching Keogh's column move across Luce Ridge. Also fought Custer's column. Presence confirmed by Myers, though he only lists him as a Teton Sioux.

Shoots Walking (aka "H. W." Shoots Walking)—(Hunkpapa Lakota-Teton Sioux)—A young boy at the time of the battle, but despite his mother's and sister's pleas, he managed to ride into the fighting. Told of Custer's men being drunk or acting erratic. Known to have taken part in the fighting. At the 1926 reunion and still living at the Standing Rock Agency, Little Eagle, SD, in 1926.

Short—(Oglala Lakota-Teton Sioux)—Listed in the Crazy Horse surrender ledger, 1877. Along with Rider, listed as "head-of-household." Lodge consisted of two adult females; total, four people.

Short Brulé—(Oglala Lakota-Teton Sioux)—Listed in the Crazy Horse surrender ledger, 1877. Along with Lays Laughing and Fat Rump (# 2), he was listed as "head-of-household." Lodge consisted of four adult females and one female child; a total of eight people.

Short Bull (aka Short Buffalo; *Tatanka pte cela*; also, "Grant" Short Bull*)*—(Oglala Lakota-Teton Sioux)—b. circa 1851–d. 30 Aug 1935. In his early twenties; youngest brother of He Dog and a nephew of Red Cloud. In the valley fight. Presence confirmed by Myers, though he lists him incorrectly as a Brulé. Rode with Crazy Horse.

Short Woman (F)—(Cheyenne)—Listed in the Crazy Horse surrender ledger, 1877.

Short Woman (*Wi pte cela*) (F)—(Oglala Lakota-Teton Sioux)—b. 1853. Niece of Eagle Hawk.

Shot At (aka Blue Cloud; "Samuel" Shot At)—(Northern Cheyenne). Attended the 1926 reunion.

Shot Close (*Kiyela Imyapi*)—(Oglala Lakota-Teton Sioux)—b. circa 1854 to 1857–d. circa 1915. Member of He Dog's Soreback band.

Shot in the Face (also possibly known as Shot in the Eye)—(Oglala Lakota-Teton Sioux)—Said there were about 6,000 people in the village.

Shout At—(Lakota-Teton Sioux)

Shouts At (*Ash'api*) (F)—(Oglala Lakota-Teton Sioux)—b. circa 1842–d. 1927. Wife of Rib Man. According to her reminiscences (Westerns Brand Book, March 1962), she was in the village at the Little Big Horn at the time the soldiers attacked. She had just given birth to a baby ten days earlier and was not able to ride a horse or run. Rather than fleeing with the other women and children she had to remain behind in the village during the attack.

Showing Breath (*Niyalanm win*) (F)—(Oglala Lakota-Teton Sioux)—b. circa 1836. Wife of Iron Hawk and mother of Killed by Night and Runs in Circle ("Homer" Iron Hawk).

Side Rib—(Oglala Lakota-Teton Sioux)—Listed in the Crazy Horse surrender ledger, 1877. Listed as "head-of-household." Lodge consisted of one adult female and two male children; total of four people.

Singing Bear—(Oglala Lakota-Teton Sioux)—Listed in the Crazy Horse surrender ledger, 1877. Along with Loafer, listed as "head-of-household." Lodge consisted of one adult female, one male child, and two female children; total of six people.

Singing Prick—(Oglala Lakota-Teton Sioux)—Listed in the Crazy Horse surrender ledger, 1877. Along with Dog Nothing and Stinking Tie, listed as "head-of-household." Lodge consisted of three adult females and four female children; total of ten people.

Sits Beside His Medicine—(Northern Cheyenne). A headman of the Kit Foxes warrior society, or as Wooden Leg called him, one of the nine "little chiefs" [Marquis, *Wooden Leg,* p. 212]. Since the Kit Fox society was the camp guards on the 25 June 1876, he *may* have fought at Ford B. Presence confirmed by Myers.

Sits Up Above—(Oglala Lakota-Teton Sioux)—Listed in the Crazy Horse surrender ledger, 1877. Along with Little Prick and the Rump, listed as "head-of-household." Lodge consisted of three adult females, two male children, and two female children; total of ten people.

Sitting Bear—(Oglala Lakota-Teton Sioux)—Listed in the Crazy Horse surrender ledger, 1877. Along with Dancing Arrow, listed as "head-of-household." Lodge consisted of three adult females, two male children, and two female children; nine people, total.

Sitting Bull—A Southern Cheyenne Dog Soldier.

Sitting Bull (aka "John" Sitting Bull)-(Hunkpapa Lakota-Teton Sioux)—d. 1955. Stepson of Sitting Bull. Lived to at least 90 [Stewart, *Custer's Luck,* opposite p. 145]. Presence confirmed by Myers.

Sitting Bull (or *Ta-tan-kah-yo-tan-kah*; or, *Tatanka Iyotake*; Jumping Badger [at birth]; later, Slow)-(Hunkpapa Lakota-Teton Sioux)—b. between 1830 and 1837, probably alongside a tributary of the Missouri in SD (Donovan says "about 1831" [*A Terrible Glory*, p. 74])–d. killed, 15 Dec 1890 at Wounded Knee, SD, probably by Indian police. Powerfully built, "heavy-set, muscular man, about five feet eight inches in stature...." [Godfrey, *Custer's Last Battle 1876,* p. 13] Donovan has him listed as 5'10" [*A Terrible Glory,* p. 75]. Kill Eagle described him "as a heavy, muscular man, with large head and light hair hanging to his shoulders." [Graham, *The Custer Myth,* p. 47] Also, "About five feet ten inches; he is very heavy and muscular and big around in the breast; he has a very large head; his hair is not long, it only comes down to his shoulders" [p. 55]. He was an "old-man chief," the highest rank possible in his own tribe. Highly regarded among the Sioux. "In council his views had great weight, because he was known as a great medicine man. He was a chief, but not a warrior chief" [Godfrey, *Custer's Last Battle 1876,* p. 13]. Michno says he was 42 at the time of the battle, which would put his birth date at 1834. Dickson uses 43 years of age. Michno's best scenario for Sitting Bull's whereabouts during the battle is that he reached the LBH during the Reno chase and there met his bodyguard and adopted son, One Bull, probably on the west bank of the river. It seems Sitting Bull then returned to the camp through the valley. Reports that he climbed the bluffs on the east side of the river to view the movements downstream are probably wrong. Sitting Bull then gathered other warriors to protect women and children and viewed the Custer fight from the west side of the river. He stayed there from "noon to almost sundown." If this is correct, it clearly points out that there were so many warriors; many never even got into the fight because they were late for the Reno battle, then remained in or near camp to protect those people who did not flee. "Bull ... I think was a 'Water Pourer': only seven of them at a time among all the Lakotah Nation — equivalent to Cardinals of the Church of Rome. *Magpi Luta* (i.e. Red Cloud) also took that degree and became a sort of Richelieu." [Frank H. Huston, in a March 1925, letter to W. A. Graham, *The Custer Myth*, p. 80]. Married to Her Four Blankets and Seen by Her Nation. As near as Sitting Bull could estimate, there were "5,200 guns, including warriors and armed boys and squaws who were supposed to fight if emergency required" [Liddic/Harbaugh, *Camp on Custer*, p. 63]. Many years later, Sitting Bull would claim "many Indians talked of the battle without knowing anything about it in particular and some had surely misstated facts" [p. 64. In footnote 127, Liddic wrote that the old-time Sioux used to say, "There are too many tongues."].

After Sitting Bull had returned from his self-imposed exile in Canada and had agreed to surrender, he arrived at the Standing Rock Agency on August 1, 1881. After he was there a while, there was thought to be some discontent and the army figured it was better to send him away. He objected, but to no avail and was ordered to Fort Randall where he stayed until May 1883. He was permitted to return to Standing Rock after that.

On September 2, 1876, an article recounted a legend about Sitting Bull. It appeared in the *Army and Navy Journal* and was written by an unnamed correspondent of the Richmond *Dispatch*. It was another of those fantastic tales ascribed to Sitting Bull that only fed the anti–Indian frenzy of the day. The story went: "There may be all truth in the story that Sitting Bull and 'Bison' McLean are one. 'Bison' McLean was a cadet at West Point from Missouri from 1844 to 1848, and stood well intellectually in a large and bright class. His diploma was refused him when his class graduated in 1848, he having been convicted before a court-martial of dishonorable conduct.... He had joined the Gila Apache Indians ... and had with him a wife or two.... [H]e declared to me that he would never forget or forgive the injustice and injuries he conceived he had received from his classmates and the

academic authorities at West Point.... His nature is untamed and licentious, his courage superb and his physical qualities almost Herculean, except in size. He is fair complexioned, light-colored hair, very full-bearded and hairy-bodied man, with a large head and bold, irregular, full face. His height is about five feet ten or eleven inches.... When a cadet there was no disguise he would not assume and no hazard he would not venture for the gratification of his appetites. He never used strong drink ... [he] was brought to grief by the testimony of his own classmates, against whose watchfulness he had, perhaps, taken no precaution. Such a man, after thirty years' experience among the savages, might well fill the position of Sitting Bull. There are many contemporaries of 'Bison' McLean, when at the Military Academy, and some still in the Army, who will corroborate the above" [Hutchins, *The Army and Navy Journal*, pp. 88–89].

Sitting Elk—(Oglala Lakota-Teton Sioux).

Sitting Hawk—(Oglala Lakota-Teton Sioux)—At the 1926 reunion.

Sitting Horse—(Oglala Lakota-Teton Sioux)—Listed in the Crazy Horse surrender ledger. Along with the Last, Bull Man, and White Rabbit, he is listed as "head-of-household." In addition, his lodge had one adult female, three male children, and three female children; eleven people in all.

Sitting Man ("Chales" or "Charles" Sitting Man; aka Wolf Necklace)—(Northern Cheyenne)—b. circa 1867–d. 1961. He was eight or ten at the time of the battle. The last witness—not a participant—of the battle to die.

Skunk Guts—(Oglala Lakota-Teton Sioux)—Listed in the Crazy Horse surrender ledger, 1877. Along with Crazy Bear, listed as "head-of-household." Lodge consisted of one female adult, one male child, and three female children; a total of seven people.

Skunk Head—(Oglala Lakota-Teton Sioux)—Listed in the Crazy Horse surrender ledger. Listed as "head-of-household." Lodge consisted of two adult females and one female child; four people, total.

Sleeping Rabbit—(Northern Cheyenne). He was a sharpshooter on Sharpshooter Ridge during the hilltop fight.

Sleeps from Home (F)—(Lakota-Teton Sioux)—Present at the battle, though only a child. Still living at the Standing Rock Agency, Kenel, SD, in 1926 [courtesy of Dickson].

Sleeps There—(Oglala Lakota-Teton Sioux)—Listed in the Crazy Horse surrender ledger, 1877.

Along with Duck Belly and Around the Quiver, listed as "head-of-household." Lodge consisted of one adult female; total of four people.

Slow (*Hanhi win*) (F)—(Oglala Lakota-Teton Sioux)—b. circa 1838. One of High White Man's two wives.

Slow Bull—(Oglala Lakota-Teton Sioux)—b. 1844. Photographed by Edward Sheriff Curtis [*Visions of a Vanishing Race,* p. 31–34].

Slow White Buffalo (aka Feeble White Buffalo; Slow White Bull; *Pte san hunke sni*)—(Hunkpapa Lakota-Teton Sioux)—b. circa 1848 to 1851–d. 1947. Listed in the Sitting Bull Surrender Ledger. Wife was One Who Judges.

Slow White Cow—(Oglala Lakota-Teton Sioux)—Listed in the Crazy Horse surrender ledger, 1877. Along with Looks White, listed as "head-of-household." Lodge consisted of two adult females and two female children; six people, total.

Small Bear—(Minneconjou Lakota-Teton Sioux)—Son of White Bull. In an October 28, 1876, dispatch COL Nelson Miles claimed Small Bear was taking some 50 lodges into the Cheyenne River Agency to surrender. Uncertain of his tribal affiliation, but thought to be Minneconjou.

Smells the Bear—(Lakota-Teton Sioux)—Known to have been in the fighting at the Little Big Horn. Still living at the Standing Rock Agency, Wakpala, SD, 1926 [courtesy of Dickson].

Smoky Woman (*Sote win*) (F)—(Hunkpapa Lakota-Teton Sioux)—b. circa 1814. Listed in the Sitting Bull Surrender Ledger as the only person in the household. Nothing else known of her.

Snake Creek—(Oglala Lakota-Teton Sioux)—Counted coup on two soldiers [LBHA]. Listed in the Crazy Horse surrender ledger, 1877. Along with Big Bend, listed as "head-of-household." Lodge consisted of two adult females, two male children, and one female child; total of seven people. Present at the LBH.

Snatch Loser—(Oglala Lakota-Teton Sioux)—Listed in the Crazy Horse surrender ledger, 1877. Along with Yellow Robe, listed as "head-of-household." Lodge consisted of one adult female and two male children; total of five people.

Snatch Stealer—(Oglala Lakota-Teton Sioux)—Listed in the Crazy Horse surrender ledger, 1877. Along with Little Hawk, listed as "head-of-household." Lodge consisted of three adult females, two male children, and three female children; a total of ten people.

Snow Bird (aka White Bird)—(Northern Cheyenne). A headman of the Crazy Dogs warrior society, or as Wooden Leg said, one of the nine "little chiefs" [Marquis, *Wooden Leg,* p. 212]. Presence confirmed by Myers.

Soaring Bear—(Lakota-Teton Sioux)—Listed in the Crazy Horse surrender ledger, 1877. Along with Poor Dog, listed as "head-of-household." Lodge consisted of one adult female, two male children, and two female children; total of seven people.

Soft Prick—(Oglala Lakota-Teton Sioux)—Listed in the Crazy Horse surrender ledger, 1877. Listed as "head-of-household." Lodge consisted of three adult females and two male children; total of six people.

Soldier—(Oglala Lakota-Teton Sioux)—Listed in the Crazy Horse surrender ledger, 1877. Along with Hangs His Head, One Glass, and Ree, listed as "head-of-household." Lodge consisted of three adult females, one male child, and four female children; total of twelve people.

Soldier Hawk—(Oglala Lakota-Teton Sioux)—In the valley fight.

Soldier Wolf—(Northern Cheyenne)-b. circa 1859, making him about seventeen years old at the time of the battle. Still living in 1897. Did not fight in the "front lines of the battle" [Michno]. Fought Reno and Custer, killing a soldier. Presence confirmed by Myers. Described Indian women and children fleeing across Ford B and mounting the bluffs and seeing additional troops approaching—Custer's column. It may have been some of these people who drew the troops' fire from Luce Ridge. Also, see the Cheyenne, Tall Bull.

Sore Face (*Ite han han*)—(Hunkpapa Lakota-Teton Sioux)—b. circa 1868. Young boy at the time of the battle. Son of Wears the Fur Coat and Beans.

Sounds the Ground as He Walks (also Sound the Ground as He Walks; aka Walks Under the Ground; Noisy Walking)—(*Wahpekute*/Dakota-Santee Sioux)—A son of *Inkpaduta,* and twin brother of Tracking White Earth. He was at the battle. The LBHA has him listed again under his second name, but this must be an error, especially in light of the fact their comment points out he insisted he was the one who killed the "head man," i.e., Custer. There may actually be some validity in that statement because of the business about Custer's horse, Vic. Michno quoted more than one story about him getting Custer's horse, Vic. The LBHA alludes to this, as well, and it is recorded in Walter S. Campbell's interviews with White Bull [see Hardorff, *Lakota Recollections,* p. 121, footnote

35]. Maybe Sounds the Ground and Gray Earth Track got the horse together. LT Edgerly told Walter Mason Camp that Vic was killed. CPT J. S. Poland's report claimed the last soldier killed was killed by Red Top's two sons [Graham, *The Custer Myth*, p. 46].

Speaks Once (also The One That Speaks Once) (F)—(Hunkpapa Lakota-Teton Sioux)—Wife of Scatters the Bear. with Sitting Bull in Canada in 1877.

Spider—(Lakota-Teton Sioux).

Spotted Bear—(Hunkpapa Lakota-Teton Sioux) —Said that Gray Earth Track got Custer's horse [LBHA]. Still living at the Standing Rock Agency, Little Eagle, SD, in 1926 [courtesy of Dickson]. At the camp, but he was either too young to participate in the fighting or he simply did not get into the battle.

Spotted Blackbird—(Northern Cheyenne). Still alive in 1921 and living at Lame Deer, Montana. Reputed to have said, "If we could have seen where each bullet landed we might have known [who killed Custer]. But hundreds of bullets were flying that day" [Liddic/Harbaugh, *Camp on Custer*, p. 62, footnote 120].

Spotted Eagle (aka Two Eagle[s])—(Sans Arc Lakota-Teton Sioux)—Listed as a Dakota chief in the LBHA's Summer 2001 *Research Review*. Presence confirmed by Dickson and Myers. Went to Canada with Sitting Bull. Surrendered in 1880 at Fort Keogh. Transferred to the Standing Rock Agency in the summer of 1881. Later that year he moved his "families" to the Cheyenne River Agency [Dickson]. Still living at the Cheyenne River Agency in 1926.

Spotted Eagle—(Sans Arc Lakota-Teton Sioux)— Head of the family. Son of Spotted Eagle. Part of Spotted Eagle's band [Dickson].

Spotted Eagle (*Wanbli gle ska*)—(Hunkpapa Lakota-Teton Sioux)—b. circa 1823. Listed in the Sitting Bull Surrender Ledger. Husband of Her Pretty Road.

Spotted Elk (*Hehaka gleska*)—(Oglala Lakota-Teton Sioux)—b. circa 1847. Member of the Low Dog band.

Spotted Elk (later known as Big Foot)—(Minneconjou Lakota-Teton Sioux)—b. circa 1826–d. Wounded Knee, SD, 29 Dec 1890. One of four sons of Lone Horn (d. 1875; the others were Roman Nose, Frog, and Touch the Clouds). Along with Lame Deer, one of the two main Minneconjou chiefs, though there is some dispute to that claim. Presence confirmed by Myers.

Spotted Elk—(Northern Cheyenne). A sharpshooter on Sharpshooter Ridge.

Spotted Half—(Lakota-Teton Sioux)—Listed in the Crazy Horse surrender ledger, 1877, though name appeared to be partially illegible. Listed as "head-of-household." Lodge consisted of two adult females and two female children; total of five people.

Spotted Hand—(Oglala Lakota-Teton Sioux)— Listed in the Crazy Horse surrender ledger, 1877. Along with Runs on Top, listed as "head-of-household." Lodge consisted of six adult females, two male children, and one female child; total of eleven people.

Spotted Hawk—(Northern Cheyenne)—b. circa 1869. Spoke of Indians parading around in soldiers' uniforms the night of the battle.

Spotted Hoop—(Hunkpapa Lakota-Teton Sioux).

Spotted Horn Bull (*Tatanka He Gleska*)-(Hunkpapa Lakota-Teton Sioux)—d. killed, 15 Dec 1890 at Wounded Knee. Married to Pretty White Buffalo. Joined Buffalo Bill's Wild West Show. In 1883, he said there were about 5,000 warriors and chiefs at the battle.

Spotted Horse (also "James" Spotted Horse)— (Lakota-Teton Sioux)—Living at the Standing Rock Agency, Little Eagle, SD, in 1926 [courtesy of Dickson]. At the camp, but he was either too young to participate in the fighting or he simply did not get into the battle.

Spotted Horse (also "Ludlow" Spotted Horse)— (Lakota-Teton Sioux)—Living at the Standing Rock Agency, Little Eagle, SD, in 1926 [courtesy of Dickson]. At the camp, but he was either too young to participate in the fighting or he simply did not get into the battle.

Spotted Rabbit—(Minneconjou Lakota-Teton Sioux)—Fought against Custer's column. In the last stages of the Custer fight. Presence confirmed by Myers, though he only lists him as a Teton Sioux.

Spotted Rabbit—(Northern Cheyenne). Attended 1926 reunion.

Spotted Skunk (*Maka Gleska*)—(Oglala Lakota-Teton Sioux)—b. circa 1857. Member of Low Dog's band. Son of White Hair.

Spotted Tail—(Brulé Lakota-Teton Sioux)—b. in what is today South Dakota: on the White River, west of the Missouri River, circa 1823–d. South Dakota, near the Rosebud Agency, 5 Aug 1881, killed by fellow tribesman Crow Dog. A prominent chief during the 1860s. Signed the 1868 treaty and was considered extremely intelligent and sagacious [Stewart, *Custer's Luck,* pp. 50 and 55]. He could read and write English. Not certain if he was at the LBH; Donovan says he was not [*A Terrible Glory,* p. 185], as does Bruce Liddic [*Camp on Custer,* p. 117]. He became chief of the Lower Brulé in the late 1860s. "Among the Sioux, Horse … ranked as senior … of the four principal chiefs of an organization equivalent to the Medicine Lances of the Cheyennes. That is to say, he was of equal rank with the late Roman Nose, Red Cloud, Spotted Tail and others. He wore the long white 'stole' over his shoulders as insignia, and also to tie himself to his planted lance in a fight to the death" [Frank H. Huston, Graham, *The Custer Myth,* p. 80].

Spotted Wolf (probably also known as Young Spotted Wolf)—(Northern Cheyenne). If he was also "Young Spotted Wolf," then he was a "Council of the 44" chief. If not, then this was another Spotted Wolf. He and White Elk captured a soldier's revolver which they kept until they were old men [LBHA]. Listed in the Crazy Horse surrender ledger [CBHMA].

Spread Pine (also seen as Spreaded Pine)—(Oglala Lakota-Teton Sioux)—Listed in the Crazy Horse surrender ledger, 1877. Along with Don't Amount to Anything and Looks Like a Dog, listed as "head-of-household." Lodge consisted of three adult females, four male children, and four female children; total of fourteen people.

Spunker—(Oglala Lakota-Teton Sioux)—Listed in the Crazy Horse surrender ledger, 1877. Along with Long Visitor, listed as "head-of-household." Lodge consisted of two adult females, two male children, and five female children; total of eleven people.

Squint Eyes—(Northern Cheyenne). Attended 1926 reunion.

Stand and Look Backward—(Brulé Lakota-Teton Sioux).

Standing Bear (also "Emily" Standing Bear) (F)—(Brulé Lakota-Teton Sioux)—b. circa 1868. Some sources list her as an Oglala. She was swimming in the river with some friends when Reno attacked.

Standing Bear (also "Luther" Standing Bear)—(Brulé Lakota-Teton Sioux)—b. 1863–d. 1936. Member of Lips Wears Salt's band. Wrote several books on the Sioux.

Standing Bear—(Brulé Lakota-Teton Sioux)—d. 1898. Father of "Luther." A mixed-blood Brulé who re-married within the Oglala in 1865.

Standing Bear—(Lakota-Teton Sioux)—This entry is problematic, at best. COL Nelson A. Miles

(5I) mentions a Standing Bear in a 25 Oct 1876 dispatch, referring to him as one of the leaders meeting with Miles in October 1876 to discuss terms of surrender. No other Standing Bear fits the description, and as such was in all likelihood either a Hunkpapa or Minneconjou sub-chief.

Standing Bear (*Mato Najun*; aka "Sam Howard")-(Minneconjou Lakota-Teton Sioux)—b. on the Tongue River, MT, circa 1859–1860–d. 1934. Sixteen years old at time of battle. Younger brother of Beard. Friends with Black Elk. Spotted Custer's column as it made its turn and started up the bluffs for Reno Hill. He was clearly on the hills on the east side of the river. Known to have been in the Custer battle, but while he watched the Reno battle, he did not participate in the valley fighting. Took a buckskin shirt from a dead soldier and knocked another soldier from his horse. He was apparently one of the Indians involved in the death of the D Company farrier, Vincent Charley, after the troops left Weir Peak for Reno Hill [Liddic, *Vanishing Victory,* p. 135]. Was at the 1926 battle reunion. Did not take part in the Rosebud battle against Crook, but showed up at the battleground the following day. Presence confirmed by Myers. Still living at the Standing Rock Agency, Wakpala, SD, 1926 [courtesy of Dickson].

Standing Bear (*Mato Najin*)—(Oglala Lakota-Teton Sioux)—One of these four last Standing Bear's was a member of Little Hawk's band [Dickson].

Standing Bear (*Mato Najin*)—(Oglala Lakota-Teton Sioux) [Dickson].

Standing Bear (*Mato Najin*)—(Oglala Lakota-Teton Sioux) [Dickson].

Standing Bear (*Mato Najin*)—(Oglala Lakota-Teton Sioux) [Dickson].

Standing Black Bear—(Lakota-Teton Sioux)—Claimed to have been with Deeds on the morning of 25 Jun 1876.

Standing Bull (*Tatanka Najin*)—(Oglala Lakota-Teton Sioux)—b. circa 1835–d. circa 1900). Member of Little Hawk's band.

(Mrs.) Standing Cloud (F)—(Lakota-Teton Sioux)—At the battle, but not a participant in the fighting. Still living at the Standing Rock Agency, Kenel, SD, in 1926 [courtesy of Dickson].

Standing Elk—(Brulé Lakota-Teton Sioux)—There was a Brulé chief in 1866 and 1868 by this name [Stewart, *Custer's Luck,* pp. 36 and 50]. Uncertain if he was at the Little Big Horn.

Standing Elk—(Cheyenne)—Along with Dull Knife, surrendered to Gen. George Crook at Camp

Robinson, 21 Apr 1877. By the time they surrendered, some 780 Cheyenne had given themselves up to military authority since 1 Jan 1877.

Standing Elk—(Lakota-Teton Sioux)—At the Cheyenne River Agency in 1926. There was also a Sans Arc named Standing Elk.

Standing Elk—(Sans Arc Lakota-Teton Sioux)—d. 25 Jun 1876, killed at the Little Big Horn in the valley fight [Myers, "Roster of Known Hostile Indians at the Battle of the Little Big Horn," *Research Review,* Summer 1991, Vol. 5, No. 2, p. 8].

Standing Holy (F)—(Hunkpapa Lakota-Teton Sioux)—b. 1875–d. 1926. Baby daughter of Sitting Bull and Seen by the Nation.

Standing in Sight (*Tan inyan najin*)—(Hunkpapa Lakota-Teton Sioux)—b. circa 1871. Listed in the Sitting Bull Surrender Ledger. Head of household despite his age. Son of Deaf Woman.

Stands First (*Concu-luta-win*; "Nancy" Stands First) (F)—(Oglala Lakota-Teton Sioux)—b. circa 1859. Wife of Stands First; mother of "Alexander" Stands First. Also had another son and a daughter, both born after the battle of the Little Big Horn. Lived with her husband on the Red Cloud/Pine Ridge Reservation. Known to be alive still in 1900.

Stands First (known as "Alexander" Stands First; *Tokeya Najin*)—(Oglala Lakota-Teton Sioux)—b. circa 1875–d. circa 1897)—Son of Stand First. Only an infant when the battle occurred.

Stands First (*Tokeya Najin*; also Standing First; Walk Ahead; Long Holy; *Wakan Hanska*)—(Southern Oglala Lakota-Teton Sioux)—b. circa 1849–d. January 1917. Brother of Old Shield and Fast Wolf; father of "Alexander" Stands First [from Dickson]. Said to have captured Custer's personal flag. Finally lived at the Red Cloud/Pine Ridge Agency. Photographed by Edward Sheriff Curtis.

Stands Straddle—(Lakota-Teton Sioux)—At the Cheyenne River Agency in 1926.

Star—(Northern Cheyenne). Cousin of Wooden Leg. In the Rosebud fight. Listed in the Crazy Horse surrender ledger [CBHMA].

Steals Horses (aka Rattlesnake)—(Hunkpapa Lakota-Teton Sioux)—b. circa 1864–d. 1941.

Steals Horses—(Oglala Lakota-Teton Sioux)—Son of Knife Chief. In the valley fight. Presence confirmed by Hardorff.

Stinking Bear—(Oglala Lakota-Teton Sioux)—Saw a warrior knocked down by the barrel of a soldier's gun [LBHA].

Stinking Tie—(Oglala Lakota-Teton Sioux)—Listed in the Crazy Horse surrender ledger, 1877.

Along with Singing Prick and Dog Nothing, listed as "head-of-household." Lodge consisted of three adult females and four female children; total of ten people.

Stone (aka Rock; *Inyan*) (F)—(Oglala Lakota-Teton Sioux)—b. circa 1840. Wife of He Dog. There is a chance she was pregnant at the time of the battle [Dickson].

Straight Head, "Moses"—(Lakota-Teton Sioux)—At the Cheyenne River Agency, 1926.

Strong—(Lakota-Teton Sioux)—Fought alongside Kill Eagle. Presence confirmed by Myers, though he only lists him as a Teton Sioux.

Strong Dog—(Hunkpapa Lakota-Teton Sioux).

Strong Elk—(Oglala Lakota-Teton Sioux).

Strong Fox—(Oglala Lakota-Teton Sioux)—Listed in the Crazy Horse surrender ledger, 1877. Listed as "head-of-household." Lodge consisted of two adult females and one male child; total of four people.

Strong Left Hand (also Strong Left Arm)—(Northern Cheyenne). A headman of the Crazy Dogs warrior society, or as Wooden Leg said, one of the nine "little chiefs" [Marquis, *Wooden Leg,* p. 212]. Presence confirmed by Myers. He was married to Elk Woman (Wolf Traveling).

Strong Wolf (aka Big Wolf)—(Northern Cheyenne). A "Council of the 44" chief.

Struck by Crow (*Kangi Apagi*; also known as White Tail)—(Oglala Lakota-Teton Sioux)—b. 1846–d. 1927. Fought in the Fetterman battle, the Rosebud battle, and the LBH. Member of Low Dog's band until 1881, when he moved to Big Road's band.

Struck Plenty (*Oape Ota*)—(Hunkpapa Lakota-Teton Sioux).

Stumbling Bear—(Minneconjou Lakota-Teton Sioux).

Stump Horn ("Frank" Stumphorn)—(Northern Cheyenne). Still alive in 1921 and living at Lame Deer, Montana.

Sudden Brave (also seen as Suddenbrave)—(Lakota-Teton Sioux)—Known to have taken part in the fighting. Still living at the Standing Rock Agency, Little Eagle, SD, in 1926 [courtesy of Dickson].

Sun Bear—(Northern Cheyenne)—b. 1843. Son of Plum Tree; brother of Two Feathers. In the valley fight against Reno, where he was wounded. Charged Custer and was wounded again. Sun Bear and two other Cheyenne warriors — Eagle Tail Feather and Little Sun — chased three soldiers south along the west bank of the LBH. While unclear, this is probably during the valley fight [Marquis, *Wooden Leg*, p. 222]. Wore a war bonnet. Attended 1926 reunion. Presence confirmed by Myers.

Sunrise (also Sun Rise) — (Sans Arc Lakota-Teton Sioux) — Mentioned by COL Nelson Miles as a "chief" of the Sans Arc, in Miles' October 28, 1862, dispatch, referring to surrendering Indians. One of the five "hostages" designated by Miles during the surrender of 400–600 lodges and their return to the Cheyenne River Agency, October-December 1876. The others were Foolish Thunder, Red Skirt, White Bull, and Black Eagle.

Swan "Edward" — (Minneconjou Lakota-Teton Sioux) — b. 1874. Son of White Swan and Nation; half-brother of Walter Swan.

Swan "Walter" — (Minneconjou Lakota-Teton Sioux) — b. 1868. Son of White Swan and Cheyenne Woman; half-brother of Edward Swan.

Sweat — (Oglala Lakota-Teton Sioux).

Swift Bear — (Lakota-Teton Sioux) — At the Cheyenne River Agency in 1926.

Swift Bear (*Matao Luzahan* or *Mato-oheonke*) — (Hunkpapa Lakota-Teton Sioux) — d. 25 Jun 1876, killed at the Little Big Horn — One of Crow King's brothers. Another brother, White Bull, was also killed during Reno's retreat. Killed in the valley fight as Reno's troops were retreating from the timber. Another account has him being killed while charging with five other warriors including One Bull and Good Bear Boy. The Minneconjou warrior, White Bull (who survived the battle), said Swift Bear was shot by one of the Ree scouts [see Hardorff, *Lakota Recollections*, p. 110, and footnote 9, same page], quite possibly Young Hawk.

Swift Cloud (*Hcahcipiya* or *Mahepiya-cheouka*) — (Cheyenne) — d. 25 Jun 1876, killed at the Little Big Horn while fighting the Custer battalions [Myers, "Roster of Known Hostile Indians at the Battle of the Little Big Horn," *Research Review*, Summer 1991, Vol. 5, No. 2]. Myers also lists a Teton Sioux by the same name as being killed during the fighting [see p. 8].

Swift Cloud — (Lakota-Teton Sioux) — d. 25 Jun 1876, killed at the Little Big Horn. Listed by Myers only as a Teton Sioux killed in the fighting [Myers, "Roster of Known Hostile Indians at the Battle of the Little Big Horn," *Research Review*, Summer 1991, Vol. 5, No. 2, p. 8].

Swift Dog — (Lakota-Teton Sioux) — Still living at the Cheyenne River Agency in 1926. He became a famous Lakota artist.

Sword [LBHA] — (Oglala Lakota-Teton Sioux).

Take(s) the Horses — (Minneconjou Lakota-Teton Sioux) — Brother of Dog's Back Bone.

Takes the Gun (aka One Who Disarms; *Maza kan wicaki*) — (Hunkpapa Lakota-Teton Sioux) — b. circa 1844. Listed in the Sitting Bull Surrender Ledger. Still living at the Standing Rock Agency, Little Eagle, SD, in 1926 [courtesy of Dickson]. Known to have participated in the fighting.

Takes the Horses — (Minneconjou Lakota-Teton Sioux) — Brother of Dog's Back Bone.

Tall Bull (*Hotuga Kastatche* or *Hotoa qa ihoois* or *Hotuya-kostache;* also Jacob) — (Northern Cheyenne) — b. 1853–d. at Lame Deer, probably around 1920–1922. Twenty-two years old at the battle. Fought Crook on 17 Jun 1876. When the Crook battle occurred, the Cheyenne were camped at the "lone tepee" site [Camp/Hammer, *Custer in '76,* p. 212]. Brother-in-law of Lame White Man, brother of Twin Woman. In the valley fight against Reno, but did not pursue Reno's men across the LBH. Rode north to meet the new threat. Lost his horse in the battle. Interviewed by Walter Camp in 1910. One of his more interesting comments was that a number of women, trying to escape Reno, went *east,* crossed the Little Big Horn and climbed the bluffs. These women were who discovered Custer's approaching column (Michno, in *The Mystery of E Troop,* says that a number of Grinnell's informants said the same thing). Also, see Soldier Wolf.

About the same height as Wooden Leg, 6′ 2″. Presence confirmed by Myers.

Tall Bull-(Minneconjou Lakota-Teton Sioux) — d. 16 Dec 1876 or Apr 1877. Killed while attempting to surrender to Nelson Miles.

Tall Bull — (Oglala Lakota-Teton Sioux) — Listed in the Crazy Horse surrender ledger, 1877. A member of Crazy Horse's family and listed as a "head-of-household," along with Crazy Horse. Their lodge consisted of three adult females and two male children; total of seven people.

Tall Sioux (aka Long Sioux) — (Northern Cheyenne). In sweat lodge when Reno attacked village. A friend of Lame White Man.

Tall White Man ("Joseph" Tall White Man) — (Northern Cheyenne). A headman of the Elkhorn Scraper warrior society, or as Wooden Leg called him, one of the nine "little chiefs" [Marquis, *Wooden Leg,* p. 211]. Presence confirmed by Myers.

Tall Woman (*Winyan hanska*) (F) — (Hunkpapa Lakota-Teton Sioux) — b. circa 1849. Wife of Brave Thunder.

Tangled Yellow Hair ("James" Tangled Yellow Hair)—(Northern Cheyenne)—b. circa 1866–d. 1935.

Tanglehorn Elk (also seen as Tangled Horn Elk)—(Northern Cheyenne). Captured an army carbine; Myers says it was Custer's. Presence confirmed by Myers.

Tanned Nuts—(Oglala Lakota-Teton Sioux)—Listed in the Crazy Horse surrender ledger, 1877. Along with Water Snake and Long Handle, listed as "head-of-household." Lodge consisted of two adult females; total of five people.

Thick Face—(Oglala Lakota-Teton Sioux)—Listed in the Crazy Horse surrender ledger, 1877. Along with Little Boy, listed as "head-of-household." Lodge consisted of one male child and one female child; four people, total.

Thief (also "Martin" Thief)—(Lakota-Teton Sioux)—Known to have been in the fighting at the Little Big Horn. Still living at the Standing Rock Agency, Bullhead, SD, 1926 [courtesy of Dickson].

Thin Elk—(Lakota-Teton Sioux)—Presence confirmed by Myers, though he only lists him as a Teton Sioux.

Three Bear (or Three Bears; interestingly, also known as Two Bear; Two Bears; *Mato Numpa*)—(Minneconjou or, less probable, Hunkpapa Lakota-Teton Sioux)—d. 27 or 28 Jun 1876, of wounds suffered at the Little Big Horn. According to the Friends of the Little Bighorn Battlefield newsletter of 25 Oct 2006, he was a Hunkpapa—Myers lists him as a Minneconjou as here—and was shot on 25 Jun 1876 on the Reno-Benteen battlefield. Probably received a mortal wound, dying on June 27 or 28 [Myers, "Roster of Known Hostile Indians at the Battle of the Little Big Horn," *Research Review,* Summer 1991, Vol. 5, No. 2, p. 8]. An old man and one of the first to die or be mortally wounded. The fact that he was old and a Hunkpapa are supported by 1SG John Ryan's memoirs [Barnard, *Ten Years with Custer,* p. 246]. Black Elk mentions him as dying after the battle and at a place called Wood Louse or Lice Creek [Neihardt, *Black Elk Speaks,* p. 129; also, Hardorff, *Lakota Recollections,* p. 29, footnote 14].

Three Hawks—(Oglala Lakota-Teton Sioux)—Listed in the Crazy Horse surrender ledger, 1877. Listed as "head-of-household." Lodge consisted of two adult females and one male child; four people, total.

Thunder Bear—(Nakota-Yankton Sioux)—In both the Reno and Custer fights.

Thunder Hawk—(Brulé Lakota-Teton Sioux)—d. Hot Springs, SD, committed suicide while in prison; circa 1900. Wounded in the leg during the Battle of the Rosebud with George Crook. Stayed in camp while his wives attended to him.

Thunder Hawk (*Cetan Wakiyan*)—(Hunkpapa Lakota-Teton Sioux)—Fifteen lodges (95 people), Sep 1876, at Standing Rock [LBHA/Dickson].

Thunder Hawk—(Oglala Lakota-Teton Sioux)—Listed in the Crazy Horse surrender ledger. At the battle. He is listed as "head-of-household" in the surrender ledger, his lodge consisting of one female adult and one male child; three people, total.

Thunder Hawk—(Sans Arc Lakota-Teton Sioux)—Head of the family. Part of Spotted Eagle's band [Dickson].

Thunder Tail—(Oglala Lakota-Teton Sioux)—Listed in the Crazy Horse surrender ledger. Along with White Twin, he is listed as one of two "heads-of-household." His lodge consisted of White Twin, plus five adult females, and one male child; total of eight people.

Ticket (*Kansu la*) (F)—(Hunkpapa Lakota-Teton Sioux)—b. circa 1844. Wife of Big Leg.

Ties His Hair—(Northern Cheyenne). Listed in the Crazy Horse surrender ledger, 1877 [CBHMA]. Probably present at the LBH.

Tiopa—(Hunkpapa Lakota-Teton Sioux)—A younger cousin of Sitting Bull. At the battle, but not engaged in the fighting. Probably too young. Fled to Canada with Sitting Bull.

To Growl At (*Ahna*)—(Hunkpapa Lakota-Teton Sioux)—b. circa 1871. Only a child at the time of the battle. Son of Charging Thunder and White Glass.

To Scare with Feet (*Nahapa*) (F)—(Oglala Lakota-Teton Sioux)—b. circa 1840. One of High White Man's two wives.

To Whoop At (*Iyasa*)—(Hunkpapa Lakota-Teton Sioux)—b. circa 1874. Only a baby at the time of the battle. Son of Charging Thunder and White Glass.

Tobacco—(Oglala Lakota-Teton Sioux)—Listed in the Crazy Horse surrender ledger, 1877. Listed as "head-of-household." Lodge consisted of one adult female, four male children, and two female children; total of eight people.

Too Young (*Pa incela sni*)—(Hunkpapa Lakota-Teton Sioux)—b. circa 1860. Son of Bear Looking Back and White Buffalo Cow. Listed in the Sitting Bull Surrender Ledger.

Top Lodge—(Oglala Lakota-Teton Sioux)—Listed in the Crazy Horse surrender ledger. Along with

Big Belly Mule, Iroquois Imitation, and Yellow Left, listed as "head-of-household." Lodge consisted of two female adults, one male child, and three female children; total of ten people.

Torn Belly—(Oglala Lakota-Teton Sioux)—Listed in the Crazy Horse surrender ledger, 1877. Along with Red Crane and White Bull, listed as "head-of-household." Lodge consisted of two female adults and one female child; total of six people.

Touch on Head (also Press on Head) (F)—(Minneconjou Lakota-Teton Sioux)—Wife of Owl King and mother of Hard to Kill and Brown Wolf. There is some confusion between this person and another woman named Comes Back Holy. They may be the same person, though the names are always reported separately. If two different women, then both were wives of Owl King. The "mother" of Brown Wolf only adds to the confusion.

Touch the Clouds (aka Tall Sioux)-(Minneconjou Lakota-Teton Sioux)—d. 1905. Fairly tall, as his name may indicate. One of four sons of Lone Horn (d. 1875). Listed as a Dakota chief in the LBHA's Summer 2001 *Research Review*. [See Crazy Horse.] Donovan says he remained at the Cheyenne River Agency and was not at the LBH [*A Terrible Glory*, p. 185]—as do several other well-respected historians—but Myers and very strong Sioux oral tradition confirm his presence at the battle. A moderate leader (which might support his being at the agency rather than the Little Big Horn). His three brothers, however, were at the battle: Frog, Spotted Elk, and Roman Nose, and his tribal importance cannot be understated. Unless definitive proof arises, Touch the Clouds must be carried as "at the battle."

Touches His Grub—(Northern Cheyenne). Listed in the Crazy Horse surrender ledger [CBHMA]. Probably present at the LBH.

Tripe—(Northern Cheyenne). Listed in the Crazy Horse surrender ledger [CBHMA]. Probably present at the LBH.

Tripe Fold—(Oglala Lakota-Teton Sioux)—Listed in the Crazy Horse surrender ledger, 1877. Listed as "head-of-household." Lodge consisted of three adult females and one male child; total of five people.

Turkey Leg(s) (aka Thomas Flying)—(Northern Cheyenne). Attended the 1926 reunion. In the valley fight, infiltrating the woods. Some of his shots—along with those of Crooked Nose and Old Man—may have hit and killed Company M's Klotzbucher and Lorentz. Presence confirmed by Myers. He also lists a "Young Turkey Leg," who

also "charged the timber." They are listed separately here.

Turning Bear—(Lakota-Teton Sioux)—Know only as a Sioux. Brother of Old She Bear. This may be confusing because a warrior named Old She Bear was a Cheyenne killed in the Crook fight.

Turning Hawk—(Hunkpapa Lakota-Teton Sioux).

Turtle Rib—(Minneconjou Lakota-Teton Sioux)—b. 1848. Twenty-eight years old at the battle. Not in the Rosebud fight. Arrived at the camp on 24 Jun 1876. Fought under Lame Deer. The soldiers actually followed their trail. Was in the Reno fight, but very late because he was asleep when Reno charged down the valley. Helped kill one of the Rees and saw others getting away with some ponies. Did not see any fighting at Medicine Tail Ford (Ford B). The soldiers were already on the high ground east of the river. When he got there he saw a running battle with soldiers on foot. Presence confirmed by Myers.

Turtle Road—(Cheyenne). In the camp with Two Crows. Their tepee contained six men and eight women [LBHA].

Twin (*Cekpa win*) (F)—(Oglala Lakota-Teton Sioux)—b. circa 1814. Mother of Eagle Hawk.

Twin ("Fred" Twin)—(Lakota-Teton Sioux)—b. circa 1869. Helped the herding of the younger children to safety when the troops hit.

Twin—(Northern Cheyenne). A "Council of the 44" chief.

Twin—(Northern Cheyenne). Wooden Leg's younger brother (too young to be the same person as above).

Twin Bear [Graham, *The Custer Myth*, p. 74]—(Lakota-Teton Sioux).

Twin Woman (F)—(Southern Cheyenne)—Lame White Man's wife. Originally Southern Cheyenne. Tall Bull's sister.

Two Band—(Sans Arc Lakota-Teton Sioux)—Head of the family. Part of Spotted Eagle's band [Dickson].

Two Bear—(Sans Arc Lakota-Teton Sioux)—d. 25 Jun 1876, killed at the Little Big Horn by Custer's scouts on the "charge" toward the village [Myers, "Roster of Known Hostile Indians at the Battle of the Little Big Horn," *Research Review*, Summer 1991, Vol. 5, No. 2, p. 8]. There may be some confusion here between this man and a Three Bear Minneconjou. They are listed separately, one a Minneconjou and the other, this man, a Sans Arc.

Two Birds—(Northern Cheyenne). With Little Wolf's band. Presence confirmed by Myers.

Two Bull(s)—(Hunkpapa Lakota-Teton Sioux)—Estimated that there were 600 to 800 warriors at the battle.

Two Bulls—(Nakota-Yankton Sioux)—Claimed Custer's soldiers fought like boys, not men.

Two Crows—(Cheyenne).

Two Eagles—(also possibly known as Spotted Eagle)—(Sans Arc Lakota-Teton Sioux)—Head of the family. Part of Spotted Eagle's band [Dickson] and a Sans Arc tribal leader.

Two Eagles—(Cu Brulé Lakota-Teton Sioux)—b. 1858. Interviewed by Sewell B. Weston in 1908 while living on the Rosebud Reservation. Said Custer's column split in two columns, one moving down MTC, the other across Nye-Cartwright. Fought both Reno and Custer.

Two Face—(Oglala Lakota-Teton Sioux)—Listed in the Crazy Horse surrender ledger, 1877. Along with Greases His Arm, listed as "head-of-household." Lodge consisted of two adult females, one male child, and two female children; total of seven people.

Two Feathers—(Northern Cheyenne). At the battle. Son of Plum Tree; brother of Sun Bear. Helped Wooden Leg provide the names of the warrior society chiefs to Thomas B. Marquis. Presence confirmed by Myers.

Two Furs—(Lakota-Teton Sioux)—In the Little Big Horn fighting. Still living at the Standing Rock Agency, Bullhead, SD, 1926 [courtesy of Dickson].

Two Moon (frequently seen as Two Moons [plural]; later, Old Two Moon[s]; *Ish hayu Nishus;* also spelled *Ishe-heyu-nishis*)—(Northern Cheyenne)—b. in the Shoshone territory of western Wyoming in 1842–d. near the Rosebud, 1917. He was the son of a captive Arikara—Carries the Otter—who married into the Northern Cheyenne tribe. Probably the same chief as the one involved in the treaties of the 1860's [Stewart, *Custer's Luck*, p. 38]. Dark and short; known to be a "big-mouth." Had been a government scout for a while. A headman of the Kit Foxes warrior society, or as Wooden Leg called him, one of the nine "little chiefs" [Marquis, *Wooden Leg*, p. 212]. He was in the Powder River fight against Reynolds, 17 Mar 1876. Led a group of Cheyenne in the valley fight. Waterman, an Arapaho, claimed that Two Moon led the Cheyenne after Lame White Man was killed. LBHA, *Research Review,* Summer 2001, confirms this. Described a move by the soldiers beyond Cemetery Ridge, northwest to another ford on the Little Big Horn, then a move back to where the present cemetery is. Also fought on the hilltop. Tall Bull claimed he was one of the three Cheyenne head chiefs at the battle, along with White Bull [Ice] and Lame White Man [Camp/Hammer, *Custer in '76,* p. 212]. A writer named Hamlin Garland published an interview with Two Moon in the September 1898 edition of *McClure's Magazine.* It gave his story of the battle [Bruun, Erik and Crosby, Jay, eds., *Our Nation's Archive,* p. 413].

Two Runs (aka Mrs. Little Horse; "Constance" Two Runs) (F)—(Sans Arc Lakota-Teton Sioux)—b. 1860–d. 8 Jan 1942. Daughter of Elk Head. Living at the Standing Rock Agency, Kenel, SD, in 1926. At the battle but not a participant.

Two Strikes (aka Knock Off Two)—(Brulé Lakota-Teton Sioux)—b. circa 1819–1921–d. 1914 or 1915. Killed two soldiers who were riding on one horse. Presence confirmed by Myers.

Undone—(Oglala Lakota-Teton Sioux)—Listed in the Crazy Horse surrender ledger, 1877. Along with Kills At Night, listed as "head-of-household." Lodge consisted of one adult female, one male child, and one female child; total of five people.

Useful Heart—(Lakota-Teton Sioux)—At the Cheyenne River Agency in 1926.

Uses Her Own Words (F)—(Minneconjou Lakota-Teton Sioux)—Sister of White Bull.

Uses His Arrows—(Lakota-Teton Sioux)—Living at the Standing Rock Agency, Little Eagle, SD, in 1926 [courtesy of Dickson]. At the camp, but he was either too young to participate in the fighting or he simply did not get into the battle.

Uses His Knife—(Sans Arc Lakota-Teton Sioux)—Head of the family. Part of Spotted Eagle's band [Dickson].

Walking Bear—(Sans Arc Lakota-Teton Sioux)—Head of the family. Part of Spotted Eagle's band [Dickson].

(Mrs.) Walking Elk (F)—(Lakota-Teton Sioux)—At the camp during the battle. Still living at the Standing Rock Agency, Kenel, SD, in 1926 [courtesy of Dickson].

Walking Hunter—(Hunkpapa Lakota-Teton Sioux).

Walking Medicine—(Northern Cheyenne). Listed in the Crazy Horse surrender ledger [CBHMA]. Probably present at the LBH.

Walking White Cow (also seen as White Cow Walking)—(Oglala Lakota-Teton Sioux)—Brother of White Eagle and son of Horned Horse. Still living at the Standing Rock Agency, Cannon Ball, ND, 1926 [courtesy of Dickson]. Known to have been in the fighting at the Little Big Horn.

Walking White Man—(Cheyenne)—d. 25 Jun 1876, killed at the Little Big Horn. A "chief" of sorts [Myers, "Roster of Known Hostile Indians at the Battle of the Little Big Horn," *Research Review,* Summer 1991, Vol. 5, No. 2].

Walks at Night—(Cheyenne)—b. 1863. Swimming in the LBH when Reno's troops attacked.

Walks at Night—(Lakota-Teton Sioux).

Walks in Mud—(Oglala Lakota-Teton Sioux)— Listed in the Crazy Horse surrender ledger, 1877. Listed as "head-of-household." Lodge consisted of one adult female and one male child; total of three people.

Walks Last—(Northern Cheyenne). Attended 1926 reunion. His pony was killed on a run past Custer's soldiers; he crawled away. Presence confirmed by Myers.

Wandering Medicine—(Northern Cheyenne)— Swimming with Yellow Robe and Swift Head when Reno struck.

War Shanty—(Oglala Lakota-Teton Sioux)— Listed in the Crazy Horse surrender ledger. Along with White Face, he was listed as "head-of-household." There were two adult females and one female child in his lodge, a total of five people.

Warms His Blanket—(Oglala Lakota-Teton Sioux)—Listed in the Crazy Horse surrender ledger, 1877. Along with one of the Black Elks and Feather Moon, listed as "head-of-household." Lodge consisted of six adult females and one male child; total of ten people.

Warrior (aka "Joseph" Warrior)—(Lakota-Teton Sioux)—At the Cheyenne River Agency, 1926.

Water (in later years, "Alex" Water; *Mni*) [Dickson]-(Oglala Lakota-Teton Sioux)—b. circa 1865–d. 1935. *Tapisleca* Band [Dickson]. At the 1926 reunion.

Water Snake—(Oglala Lakota-Teton Sioux)— Listed in the Crazy Horse surrender ledger, 1877. Along with Long Handle and Tanned Nuts, listed as "head-of-household." Lodge consisted of two adult females; total of five people.

Waterman—(Arapaho)—Twenty-two years old. The Sioux accused him of being "a spy," but several of the Cheyenne took the Arapaho under their wings to protect them (see the Cheyenne, Black Wolf). He and Left Hand were the only two of the

five still alive when he was interviewed by Col. Tim McCoy in 1920. Waterman was another of those Indians who said the battle began at the upper end of the village (Reno's charge) as early as 9 am. of course he also said that only one Indian was killed there, but that may only indicate what he, personally, saw.

Waters (also "Isadore" Waters)—(Lakota-Teton Sioux)—Still living at the Standing Rock Agency, Little Eagle, SD, in 1926 [courtesy of Dickson]. At the camp, but he was either too young to participate in the fighting or he simply did not get into the battle.

Wawokiya (also "William" *Wawokiya*)—(Lakota-Teton Sioux)—Still living at the Standing Rock Agency, Little Eagle, SD, in 1926 [courtesy of Dickson]. At the camp, but he was either too young to participate in the fighting or he simply did not get into the battle.

Wears the Fur Coat (also Wears Fur Coat; *Ogli hinsma un*)—(Hunkpapa Lakota-Teton Sioux)— b. circa 1840. Listed in the Sitting Bull Surrender Ledger. Married to Beans.

Weasel Bear ("Frank" Weasel Bear)—(Northern Cheyenne). This is a different man from the Northern Cheyenne Weasel Bear because he was only fourteen or fifteen years old at the time of the battle [Stewart, *Custer's Luck,* p. 459, footnote 158; see also, Windolph, *I Fought with Custer,* picture facing p. 214]. Fought both Reno and Custer. He claimed it was Cheyenne warriors who actually killed George Custer.

Weasel Bear—(Hunkpapa Lakota-Teton Sioux). There is an Oglala by the same name.

Weasel Bear—(Northern Cheyenne). A headman of the Kit Foxes warrior society, or as Wooden Leg called him, one of the nine "little chiefs" [Marquis, *Wooden Leg,* p. 212]. Since the Kit Fox society was the camp guards on 25 June, he *may* have fought at Ford B. Presence confirmed by Myers.

Web (*Taho mni*) (F)—(Hunkpapa Lakota-Teton Sioux)—b. circa 1859. Niece of Yellow Dog. Listed in the Sitting Bull Surrender Ledger.

Well-Knowing One (aka Green Grass)— (Southern Arapaho)—d. before 1920.

Whetstone—(Cheyenne)—d. Jun 1879 (hanged). Hanged — along with Black Coyote — for killing a sergeant a couple years after the battle.

Whirling—(Oglala Lakota-Teton Sioux)—At Standing Rock in 1920 [LBHA].

Whirlwind (aka Little Whirlwind or Swift Cloud)—(Northern Cheyenne)—d. 25 Jun 1876, killed at the Little Big Horn. Supposed to have been only sixteen years old [Myers, "Roster of Known Hostile Indians at the Battle of the Little Big Horn," *Research Review*, Summer 1991, Vol. 5, No. 2]. Shot fighting a Ree up on the flats of the east bank of the LBH as Reno's retreat continued.

Whirlwind (*Wamni yomni*) (F)—(Hunkpapa Lakota-Teton Sioux)—b. circa 1851. Wife of Chasing Alone. Listed in the Sitting Bull Surrender Ledger.

Whirlwind Bear—(Lakota-Teton Sioux)—All that is known of this man is that he was with Sitting Bull in Canada in 1877.

Whistler (*Jolowan* or *Jola*)—(Oglala Lakota—Teton Sioux)—b. circa 1833–d. circa 1899. Listed in the Crazy Horse surrender ledger, 1877. Member of Low Dog's band. Present at the LBH. Along with The Bud, listed as "head-of-household." Seven people in his lodge: two heads-of-household; four adult females; and one female child.

Whistler—(Oglala Lakota—Teton Sioux)—Listed in the Crazy Horse surrender ledger. [CBHMA]. Probably present at the LBH. Lodge consisted of head-of-household, four adult females, and one female child; six people, total.

White Bear (*Mato Ska*)—(Oglala Lakota-Teton Sioux)—b. circa 1843. Ten people in his lodge, and along with White Hair and Big Eater, he was listed as "head-of-household." There were four adult women, one male child, and two female children in the lodge. Listed in the Crazy Horse surrender ledger, 1877. Listed as "head-of-household." Lodge consisted of two adult females, one male child, and one female child; total of five people. Either or both of the White Bear/Oglala entries were members of Low Dog's band.

White Bear (*Mato Ska*)—(Oglala Lakota-Teton Sioux)—Five people in his lodge. Listed in the Crazy Horse surrender ledger. Present at the LBH. Either or both of the White Bear/Oglala entries were members of Low Dog's band.

White Bear—(Sans Arc Lakota-Teton Sioux)—Head of the family. Part of Spotted Eagle's band [Dickson].

White Beard—(Lakota-Teton Sioux)—Camp guard. Gave his horse to a fleeing woman and child [LBHA]. Presence confirmed by Myers, though he only lists him as a Teton Sioux.

White Bird—(Lakota-Teton Sioux).

White Bird—(Northern Cheyenne). Wounded in the leg during the Custer fight. Presence confirmed by Myers.

White Body—(Northern Cheyenne). Wore a war bonnet. Known to have fought the Custer column. Presence confirmed by Myers.

White Buffalo (also White Buffalo Bull; White Bull)—(Hunkpapa Lakota-Teton Sioux)—d. 25 Jun 1876, killed at the Little Big Horn. One of Crow King's brothers. Another brother, Swift Bear, was also killed. Killed in the valley fight as Reno's troops retreated from the timber.

White Buffalo (*Pte san win*) (F)—(Hunkpapa Lakota-Teton Sioux)—b. circa 1866. Sister of Fighting Bear.

White Buffalo (*Tatanka Ska*; also White Bull)—(Oglala Lakota-Teton Sioux)—b. circa 1858–d. 1937. Mother was an Arikara. Part of Big Road's band. Tribal historian who listed Indians killed by Custer. Presence confirmed by Myers, though he only lists him as a Teton Sioux.

White Buffalo Bull—(Sans Arc Lakota-Teton Sioux)—Head of the family. Part of Spotted Eagle's band [Dickson].

White Buffalo Cow (*Pte ska win*) (F)—(Hunkpapa Lakota-Teton Sioux)—b. circa 1823. Wife of Bear Looking Back.

White Buffalo Cow (*Pte ska win*) (F)—(Oglala Lakota-Teton Sioux)—b. 1865. Niece of Eagle Hawk.

White Buffalo Shaking off the Dust (aka Many Bullet Wounds)—(Northern Cheyenne). Wooden Leg's father.

White Bull (aka Lazy White Buffalo; Lazy White Bull; "Joseph" White Bull; *Pte-san-hunka*)-(Minneconjou Lakota-Teton Sioux)—b. Apr 1849–d. 21 Jul 1947. Nephew of Sitting Bull (even though the tribes are different). Twenty-six years old at the battle. His father was Makes Room and his mother, Good Feather (Pretty Feather Woman). Married to Holy Lodge (d. 1894), a Sans Arc, and lived within their circle, the tradition. One of three or four Sioux and two Cheyenne who rode along the bluffs to Weir Point, watching Keogh's column move across Luce Ridge. In interviews with Stanley Vestal [Michno, *The Mystery of E Troop*, p. 80] it seems Custer's column was well along toward—or even *at*—the Calhoun Hill area, as White Bull watched from north of Reno Hill and east of the LBH. Described a move by the soldiers beyond Cemetery Ridge, northwest to another ford on the LBH, then a move back to where the present cemetery is. Fought in the valley, on Reno Hill, and on Custer Ridge. Wounded in the ankle. Claimed there were only about 2,500 warriors who actually fought in the battle. Still living at the Standing Rock Agency in 1929. Presence confirmed by Myers. Apparently, some time after years went by, he tried to minimize the role played by Crazy Horse [see Hardorff, *Lakota Recollections of the Custer Fight,* pages 87–88, footnote 17]. Reputed to have had 15 wives, and four times he tried to have two wives at once.

As with many other characters involved in the Little Big Horn battle, White Bull is the subject of considerable controversy. In his 1930 narrative with Walter S. Campbell, White Bull referred to striking a soldier who "had on a coat." The event sequencing in a very confusing narrative would place White Bull in the vicinity of Last Stand/Custer Hill. This led Campbell to the conclusion that White Bull had slain Custer, himself, of course like any other contention associated with this battle, Campbell was challenged immediately by none other than the Custer scholar Edgar I. Stewart. The fray was joined from there. A further reading of White Bull's interviews, however, indicated the soldier with the coat had no mustache. George Custer, while he had cut short his golden hair, sported a large, droopy mustachio, putting to rest Campbell's claim of having found Custer's killer.

White Bull—(Minneconjou Lakota-Teton Sioux) — Referred to by COL Nelson Miles as the father of Small Bear, probably Minneconjou. In an October 28, 1876, dispatch, Miles claimed the son would be taking 50 lodges into the Cheyenne River Agency to surrender. One of the five "hostages" designated by Miles during the surrender of 400 to 600 lodges and their return to the Cheyenne River Agency, October-December 1876. The others were Sun Rise, Red Skirt, Foolish Thunder, and Black Eagle.

White Bull (*Tantonka-ska*)—(Hunkpapa Lakota-Teton Sioux)—d. 25 Jun 1876. Killed at the Little Big Horn in the valley fight.

White Calf (*Pte hincala ska win*) (F)—(Hunkpapa Lakota-Teton Sioux)—b. circa 1856. Daughter of Bear Looking Back and White Buffalo Cow.

White Cloud—(Oglala Lakota-Teton Sioux)—Listed in the Crazy Horse surrender ledger, 1877. Listed as "head-of-household." Lodge consisted of four adult females, one male child, and two female children; total of eight people.

White Cow Bull (*Ptebloka Ska*)—(Oglala Lakota-Teton Sioux)—d. 1942. Unmarried; 27 years old. Visiting with the Cheyenne woman, *Meotzi,* when Reno hit. One of the few warriors at Ford B when Custer's column arrived there. Supposedly was also a sharpshooter who fired at Reno's troops on the hill, killing "several." Presence confirmed by Myers.

White Cow Robe (F)—(Oglala Lakota-Teton Sioux)—Wife of Fears Nothing.

White Cow Sees (F)—(Oglala Lakota-Teton Sioux)—Wife of Black Elk and mother of (Nicholas) Black Elk.

White Cow Walking—(Oglala Lakota-Teton Sioux)—Still living at the Standing Rock Agency in 1929.

White Cross Eye—(Northern Cheyenne). Listed in the Crazy Horse surrender ledger [CBHMA]. May have been present at the LBH.

(Mrs.) White Deer (F)—(Lakota-Teton Sioux)—At the battle, but probably only a child. Still living at the Standing Rock Agency, Kenel, SD, in 1926 [courtesy of Dickson].

White Dirt (aka Powder)—(Northern Cheyenne). A "Council of the 44" chief.

White Dog (*Sunka ska*)—(Hunkpapa Lakota-Teton Sioux)—b. circa 1832. Listed in the Sitting Bull Surrender Ledger. Married to another woman named Pretty Woman. Slipped away from military control in Jun 1882 and nothing further is known of him [Dickson].

White Dress—(Oglala Lakota-Teton Sioux)—Showed John Stands in Timber where a Sioux warrior was killed in the valley fight [LBHA].

White Eagle—(Cheyenne).

White Eagle—(Nakota-Yankton Sioux)—Listed as a Dakota war chief in the LBHA's Summer 2001 *Research Review.* Chief of about 40 warriors.

White Eagle (*Wambli Ska* [*sha*]; also seen listed as Lone Eagle)—(Oglala Lakota-Teton Sioux)—d. 25 Jun 1876, killed at the Little Big Horn. Son of Horned Horse and brother of Cow Walking. Killed in the valley fight. Also seen listed as a Minneconjou. Hardorff claimed he was the only Oglala killed during the valley fight and that he was killed on the east side of the LBH [*Hokahey!...*, p. 51]. The former claim is probably incorrect, for there is evidence that an Oglala named Big Design was also killed in the Reno fighting.

White Elk (aka Wandering Buffalo Bull)—(Northern Cheyenne)—b. circa 1848–d. 1914. In his late 20s at the time of the battle. Wore a war bonnet in the battle. Known to have fought the Custer column. At the Fetterman fight [Stewart, *Custer's Luck,* p. 44]. Captured a cavalry horse. Presence confirmed by Myers.

White Eye [LBHA/Dickson]—(Hunkpapa Lakota-Teton Sioux)—Four lodges (26 people), Sep 76, at Standing Rock [LBHA/Dickson].

White Eyebrows—(Hunkpapa Lakota-Teton Sioux)—Brother of Beautiful White Cow.

White Face (*Itehin san*) (F)—(Hunkpapa Lakota-Teton Sioux)—b. circa 1852. Wife of Yellow Dog.

White Face—(Oglala Lakota-Teton Sioux)—Listed in the Crazy Horse surrender ledger. Along with War Shanty, he was listed as "head-of-household." There were two adult females and one female child in his lodge, a total of five people.

White Face Bear—(Lakota-Teton Sioux)—Living at the Standing Rock Agency, Fort Yates, ND, in 1929.

White Feathered Woman (*Wiyaka ska win*) (F)—(Hunkpapa Lakota-Teton Sioux)—b. circa 1869. Sister of Fighting Bear.

White Foot Print (also White Footprint)—(*Wahpekute*/Dakota-Santee Sioux)—In the group with *Inkpaduta* that came south from Manitoba, joining the Teton Sioux in the fall of 1875. He was the uncle of Dr. Charles Eastman, who later became the reservation physician at Pine Ridge and who wrote a book about the battle of the Little Big Horn.

White Frog—(Northern Cheyenne). Presence confirmed by Myers.

White Ghost—(Hunkpapa Lakota-Teton Sioux)—Sub-chief [LBHA].

White Glass (*Panke ska*) (F)—(Hunkpapa Lakota-Teton Sioux)—b. circa 1838. Wife of Charging Thunder.

White Gut—(Hunkpapa Lakota-Teton Sioux).

White Hair (*Pehin San*)—(Oglala Lakota-Teton Sioux)—b. circa 1821–d. circa 1890s. Listed in the Crazy Horse surrender ledger. Present at the LBH. Along with White Bear and Big Eater, he was listed as "head-of-household." There were four adult females, one male child, and two female children in his lodge, a total of ten people.

White Hair on Face—(Hunkpapa Lakota-Teton Sioux)—Twenty years old at LBH. Fought on foot.

White Hand Bear (also "Pius" White Hand Bear)—(Lakota-Teton Sioux)—In the fighting at the Little Big Horn. Still living at the Standing Rock Agency, Bullhead, SD, 1926 [courtesy of Dickson].

White Hawk—(Lakota-Teton Sioux)—Living at the Cheyenne River Agency in 1926.

White Hawk—(Northern Cheyenne). Still living in 1908. A headman of the Elkhorn Scraper warrior society, or as Wooden Leg called him, one of the nine "little chiefs" [Marquis, *Wooden Leg*, p. 211]. Presence confirmed by Myers.

White Head (aka Gray Head)—(Northern Cheyenne). A "Council of the 44" chief.

White Hollow Horn—(Minneconjou Lakota-Teton Sioux)—Presence confirmed by Myers.

White Horse (also His White Horse)—(Lakota-Teton Sioux)—Living at the Standing Rock Agency, Little Eagle, SD, in 1935. Warrior in the Dog Men Warrior Society [CBHMA]. Fought Custer's column.

White Horse (also "Thomas" White Horse)—(Lakota-Teton Sioux)—Still living at the Standing Rock Agency, Little Eagle, SD, in 1926 [courtesy of Dickson]. At the camp, but he was either too young to participate in the fighting or he simply did not get into the battle.

White Horse—Southern Cheyenne Dog Soldier. Presence confirmed by Myers. Attended the 1926 reunion.

White Lodge—(Nakota-Yankton Sioux)—Longtime ally of *Inkpaduta*.

White Man ("Sadie" Whiteman) (F)—(Cheyenne).

White Moon—(Northern Cheyenne). Brother of Antelope Woman. Attended the 1926 reunion.

White Necklace (F)—(Northern Cheyenne)—Wife of Wolf Chief. Reputed to have decapitated a dead soldier.

White Plume (*Wiyaka Ska*)—(Oglala Lakota-Teton Sioux)—b. circa 1854. Member of Low Dog's band, then Big Road's.

White Princess (*Hunka ska win*) (F)—(Hunkpapa Lakota-Teton Sioux)—b. circa 1856. Daughter of Spotted Eagle—the Hunkpapa—and Her Pretty Road.

White Rabbit—(Oglala Lakota-Teton Sioux)—Listed in the Crazy Horse surrender ledger. Along with the Last, Bull Man, and Sitting Horse, he is listed as "head-of-household." In addition, his lodge had one adult female, three male children, and three female children; eleven people in all.

White Shell (*Panke ska win*) (F)—(Hunkpapa Lakota-Teton Sioux)—b. circa 1858. Daughter of Bear Looking Back and White Buffalo Cow.

White Shield (aka Young Black Bird)—(Southern Cheyenne [CBHMA]; Northern Cheyenne [Myers]). Still alive in 1908. Father of Porcupine; son of Spotted Wolf, one of the bravest of the old-time Cheyenne warriors. When Custer's column arrived at Ford B, it was confronted by only a handful of Cheyenne warriors, with possibly a couple Sioux. White Shield showed up moments later. Presence confirmed by Myers.

White Shirt (*Ogle ska*) (F)—(Hunkpapa Lakota-Teton Sioux)—b. circa 1871. A child at the time of the battle. Daughter of Big Leg and Ticket.

White Star—(Oglala Lakota-Teton Sioux)—Listed in the Crazy Horse surrender ledger [CBHMA]. Probably present at the LBH.

White Swan—(Minneconjou Lakota-Teton Sioux)—d. 1900. Presence confirmed by Myers. Had at least three wives, one of them being the younger-listed Cheyenne Woman. She was the mother of Walter Swan. Apparently married some time around 1863. Wife number three was named Nation (they were married some time around 1868) and she was the mother of Edward Swan.

White Thunder—(Cheyenne).

White Twin—(Oglala Lakota-Teton Sioux)—Listed in the Crazy Horse surrender ledger. Along with Thunder Tail, listed as a "head-of-household." Five females and one male child were also in the lodge.

White Wolf (aka Shot in the Head)—(Northern Cheyenne)—b. circa 1847. Supposed to have been about eleven years older than Wooden Leg. Used a repeating rifle. Had accidentally wounded himself in the thigh at the Rosebud fight and was forced to stay in bed at the LBH fight. Presence confirmed by Myers. Got the name "Shot in the Head" when he was wounded as an army scout fighting the Nez Percé. Still alive in 1930.

White Woman (*Wasicu ska win*) (F)—(Hunkpapa Lakota-Teton Sioux)—b. 1873. A baby at the time of the battle. Daughter of Brave Thunder and Tall Woman.

The Whore—(Oglala Lakota-Teton Sioux)—Listed in the Crazy Horse surrender ledger, 1877. Listed as "head-of-household." Lodge consisted of one adult female and three male children; total of five people.

Widow [# 1] (F)—(Lakota-Teton Sioux)—Listed in the Crazy Horse surrender ledger, 1877. "Head-of-household" with no adult males. Lodge consisted of two male children and one female child; four people, total.

Widow [# 2] (F)—(Lakota-Teton Sioux)—Listed in the Crazy Horse surrender ledger, 1877. "Head-of-household" with no adult males. Lodge consisted of one other adult female and two male children; four people, total.

Wife of the Bear Scatterer (F)—(Sioux)—In Canada with Sitting Bull.

Wild Hog—(Southern Cheyenne). A headman of the Elkhorn Scraper warrior society. He is not listed by Wooden Leg.

Wild Horse [LBHA]—(Oglala Lakota-Teton Sioux).

Wind (F)—(Minneconjou Lakota-Teton Sioux)—One of Owl King's wives.

Winter (*Wani yetu*)—(Hunkpapa Lakota-Teton Sioux)—b. circa 1868. Son of White Dog and Pretty Woman.

With Horns—(Minneconjou Lakota-Teton Sioux)—White Bull's (above) friend; removed him from the battlefield. Fought against Custer's column. If not a Minneconjou then probably a Hunkpapa. Presence confirmed by Myers, though he only lists him as a Teton Sioux.

Without Weapon (F)—(Northern Cheyenne)—Stands in Timber's grandmother. Apparently loaned White Elk a horse during the fighting.

Wolf Chief—(Northern Cheyenne). Still alive in 1921 and living at Lame Deer, Montana. Gave Marquis a number of important points about the battle [LBHA]. He was married to White Necklace.

Wolf Medicine—(Northern Cheyenne). A headman of the Elkhorn Scraper warrior society, or as Wooden Leg called him, one of the nine "little chiefs" [Marquis, *Wooden Leg*, p. 211]. Wore a war bonnet in the battle. Known to have fought the Custer column. Presence confirmed by Myers. His two-day old infant, Red Nose, was in his lodge when the fighting broke out.

Wolf Name (also "William" Wolf Name or Wolfname)—(Northern Cheyenne). At the 1926 reunion. Living at Lame Deer, Montana, 1921.

Wolf Necklace—(Cheyenne). Interviewed by Father Peter J. Powell.

Wolf Tooth—(Northern Cheyenne). Cousin of Big Foot. Riding east with Big Foot and about fifty other warriors when the firing erupted from Reno's column. It may have been Wolf Tooth's band that Keogh's column was firing on from atop the Nye-Cartwright complex. Presence confirmed by Myers. "All I could see were tomahawks, hatchets and guns raised above the heads of the warriors through the dust. There wasn't much [rifle] smoke for no one had time to reload. Soon the field was covered with bodies" [Myers, quoting from Father P. J. Powell, *People of the Sacred Mountain*, p. 1028].

Wolf Voice—(Cheyenne).

Woman (*Winyan*) (F)—(Hunkpapa Lakota-Teton Sioux)—b. circa 1829. Mother of Takes the Gun.

Woman Bone—(Oglala Lakota-Teton Sioux)—Listed in the Crazy Horse surrender ledger, 1877. Listed as "head-of-household." Lodge consisted of two adult females, four male children, and four female children; eleven people, total.

Woman's Breast—(Minneconjou Lakota-Sioux)

Wood Boat—(Oglala Lakota-Teton Sioux)—Listed in the Crazy Horse surrender ledger, 1877. Along with Comes from War and Four Bullets, listed as "head-of-household." Lodge consisted of three adult females, one male child, and four female children; total of eleven people.

Wood Root—(Oglala Lakota-Teton Sioux)—Listed in the Crazy Horse surrender ledger, 1877. Along with Bad Warrior, listed as "head-of-household." Lodge consisted of one female adult and one male child; four people, total.

Wooden Leg (aka Eats from His Hand [as a boy; name changed when he was eighteen, just a day or two after the LBH battle]; *Kum mok quiv vi ok ta*)—(Northern Cheyenne)—b. near Cheyenne River, in the Black Hills, 1858–d. 1940. 6'2" tall, 235 lbs. (measured by Thomas B. Marquis in 1920). Yellow Hair's younger brother. He was a warrior of the Elkhorn Scrapers Society. Wooden Leg called it the Elk warriors [Marquis, *Wooden Leg*, p. 40]. In the Powder River fight against Reynolds in 1876. Participated in the valley fight against Reno. Claims to have killed a Ree on the hills east of the river during Reno's retreat. If true, it had to have been Little Brave or Bob-tail Bull. Not at the Ford B fighting. He estimated about three hundred Cheyenne lodges and the circles of *each* of the Sioux circles, larger. He also estimated about seven people per lodge and two to three warriors per lodge. That would make 600 to 900 Cheyenne warriors at the LBH, probably an inflated number.

"The idea of full dress in preparation for a battle comes not from a belief that it will add to the fighting ability. The preparation is for death.... Every Indian wants to look his best when he goes to meet the Great Spirit, so the dressing up is done whether the imminent danger is an oncoming battle or a sickness or injury at times of peace.... When any [Sioux or Cheyenne] ... got into a fight not expected, with no opportunity to dress properly, they usually ran away and avoided close contact and its consequent risks. Enemy people not understanding their ways might suppose them to be cowards because of such flight" [Marquis, *Wooden Leg*, pp. 83–84].

A boy became a warrior around sixteen or seventeen and it ended around thirty-five or forty. "The fathers and the older men ordinarily stayed in the background, to help or to shield the women and children.... Even in a surprise attack upon us, it was expected the seniors should run away ... while the more lively and supposedly more ambitious young men met the attack" [Marquis, *Wooden Leg*, pp. 118–119].

"...[W]hen any battle actually began it was a case of every man for himself. There were no ordered groupings, no systematic movements in concert, no compulsory goings and comings ... every individual went where and when he chose, every one looked out for himself only, or each helped a friend if such help were needed and if the able one's personal inclination just then was toward friendly helpfulness" [Marquis, *Wooden Leg*, pp. 119–120].

Crossed while chasing Reno's retreating men. Recrossed west, then again went east of the river. Was on the hills to the north of Reno's position when he heard someone shout that more soldiers were downriver [pp. 225–226]. Along with Big Nose, Horse Road, Little Shield, and Yellow Horse, one of 5 camp guards designated while people slept on the night of June 25–26 [Marquis, *Wooden Leg*, p. 257]. Presence confirmed by Myers.

Wooden Sword—(Lakota-Teton Sioux)—Known only as a Sioux and it is uncertain if he was at the battle.

Wooden Thigh—(Northern Cheyenne). Son of Little Wolf. A camp guard and in the battle. If true, he was a member of the Kit Fox warrior society. Presence confirmed by Myers.

Wool Woman (F)—(Northern Cheyenne). Wife of Ice and mother of Noisy Walking.

Worm (*Waglula*)—(Oglala Lakota-Teton Sioux)—d. circa 1881. Crazy Horse's father. Presence confirmed by Myers, though he lists him only as a Teton Sioux and he makes no reference to him being Crazy Horse's father.

Wounded Eye—(Northern Cheyenne).

Wounded from Tent (*Titanhan Opi*)—(Oglala Lakota-Teton Sioux)—b. 1868. Son of Eagle Hawk.

Wounded Hand—(Minneconjou Lakota-Teton Sioux).

Wounded in Back (or Wound in Back)—(Oglala Lakota-Teton Sioux)—Listed in the Crazy Horse surrender ledger, 1877. Along with He Dog, the Lights, Clown (# 2), and one other whose name appeared illegible, listed as "head-of-household."

Lodge consisted of three adult women and three male children; total of eleven people.

Wounded Lice—(Minneconjou Lakota-Teton Sioux)—On a scout with Lazy White Bull when they encountered the Montana column.

Wrinkled Face—(Oglala Lakota-Teton Sioux)—Listed in the Crazy Horse surrender ledger, 1877. Listed as "head-of-household." Lodge consisted of him and one adult female, only two people.

Wrinkler—(Oglala Lakota-Teton Sioux)—Listed in the Crazy Horse surrender ledger. Along with Bear Bird, he was listed as "head-of-household." There were three adult females, two male children, and one female child in his lodge, a total of eight people.

Yellow (*Zi win*) (F)—(Hunkpapa Lakota-Teton Sioux)—b. circa 1845. Sister-in-law of Brave Thunder. Listed in the Sitting Bull Surrender Ledger.

Yellow Bear—(Lakota-Teton Sioux).

Yellow Bird (aka Yellow Hair)—(Southern Cheyenne). Son of *Monahsetah*; rumored to have been the child of Custer. Probably no more than seven years old at the time of the battle.

Yellow Bird—(Oglala Lakota-Teton Sioux)—d. killed at Wounded Knee, 29 Dec 1890.

Yellow Breast—(Oglala Lakota-Teton Sioux).

Yellow Cloud—(Sans Arc Lakota-Teton Sioux)—Reputed to have been a Sans Arc chief, though Hardorff claimed he has never been properly identified [see Two Eagles interview, *Lakota Recollections*, p. 151, and footnote 9, same page].

Yellow Dog—(Northern Cheyenne). In the Rosebud fight, as well. Indicated many warriors wore buffalo horn caps [LBHA].

Yellow Dog (*Sun kagi*)—(Hunkpapa Lakota-Teton Sioux)—b. circa 1846. With Sitting Bull in Canada in 1877. Listed in the Sitting Bull Surrender Ledger. Wife was White Face.

Yellow Eagle—(Arapaho)—d. before 1920.

Yellow Eagle—(Cheyenne). In the Rosebud fight.

Yellow Eyes—(Hunkpapa Lakota-Teton Sioux)—b. circa 1828–d. at the Standing Rock Agency, 1908. In the camp when Reno attacked. Fled to Canada with Sitting Bull.

Yellow Fat (aka "Joseph" Yellow Fat)—(Lakota-Teton Sioux)—Probably too young to have participated in the fighting, but he claimed to have been in the village. Still living at the Standing Rock Agency, Kenel, SD, in 1926 [courtesy of Dickson].

Yellow Flower (F)—(Cheyenne)—b. 1869–d. 1961. Seven years old at the time of the battle. Smalley writes that she remembered Custer's command arriving east of the Cheyenne camp [*Little Bighorn Mysteries*, p. 5–3].

Yellow Fly—(Arapaho)—d. before 1920.

Yellow Hair—(Northern Cheyenne). Wooden Leg's older brother. Fought both Reno and Custer. Presence confirmed by Myers.

Yellow Hair Woman (F)—(Northern Cheyenne)—Told of women singing victory songs after the fighting was over.

Yellow Hair Woman (*Hinzi win la*) (F)—(Hunkpapa Lakota-Teton Sioux)—b. 1872. Daughter of Takes the Gun.

Yellow Hoop (*Cangle ska gi win*) (F)—(Hunkpapa Lakota-Teton Sioux)—b. circa 1847. Listed in the Sitting Bull Surrender Ledger as a daughter of Red Thunder and Pipe. Her age, however, precludes this unless the age listed is incorrect. If her age is correct, then she was probably the wife of Better Woman, listed as Red Thunder's son-in-law.

Yellow Horse—(Northern Cheyenne). In the battle. Along with Big Nose, Horse Road, Little Shield, and Wooden Leg, one of five camp guards designated while people slept on the night of June 25–26 [Marquis, *Wooden Leg,* p. 257]. Presence confirmed by Myers.

Yellow Horse—(Oglala Lakota-Teton Sioux)—Said that eighty-three Indians were killed and others were dying from their wounds [LBHA].

Yellow Horse—(Southern Cheyenne). Wooden Leg said Yellow Horse was an old man.

Yellow Left—(Oglala Lakota-Teton Sioux)—Listed in the Crazy Horse surrender ledger. Along with Top Lodge, Iroquois Imitation, and Big Belly Mule, listed as "head-of-household." Lodge consisted of two female adults, one male child, and three female children; total of ten people.

Yellow Nose (*Sapawicasa*)-(Ute/Southern Cheyenne)—b. circa 1849. Still alive and living in Oklahoma in 1915, though he was blind by that time. When he was nine he was captured by the Cheyenne, Lean Bear, and remained with that tribe for the rest of his life. Married to a Northern Cheyenne woman. Lived with the Southern Cheyenne in Indian Territory (Oklahoma), but was visiting his wife's relatives in the Northern Cheyenne tribe during the time of the battle. Did not participate in the Reno fight. Bathing in the river about noon when the fighting began. According to Michno, Yellow Nose and some others crossed the LBH at MTC and proceeded up a small promontory where they spotted Custer's column. They shouted and waved blankets to warn the Indians fighting Reno of Custer's northern approach. This promontory was Butler Ridge. Famous for snatching a company guidon. Greg Michno claimed it was Yates' F Company pennant while the command was in MTC and behind Company E (which was closer to the river). Some accounts say this event occurred on Calhoun Hill, while others claim it was the Yates guidon alright, but it was snatched when Custer and Yates were on Last Stand Hill. Edgar I. Stewart wrote that the flag in question was Custer's personal flag carried by SGT Robert Hughes (K Company) [*Custer's Luck,* p. 472], though there is little evidence to support this theory. What is more likely than any of these stories is that Yellow Nose captured the C Company guidon during the rout on Finley Ridge [see Brust, Pohanka, Barnard, *Where Custer Fell,* p. 92]. Most Indian testimony seems to bear this out. Yellow Nose's famous story appeared in the *Chicago Record-Herald* in September 1905, and in *The Indian School Journal* of November 1905. It has never been seriously questioned. George Bird Grinnell, Father Peter Powell, and John Stands in Timber variously interviewed him. Presence confirmed by Myers and many others.

Yellow Robe—(Oglala Lakota-Teton Sioux)—Listed in the Crazy Horse surrender ledger, 1877. Along with Snatch Loser, listed as "head-of-household." Lodge consisted of one adult female and two male children; total of five people.

Yellow Robe ("William" Yellow Robe)—(Northern Cheyenne)—d. Mar 1957. Swimming with Wandering Medicine and Head Swift when Reno attacked.

Yellow Shirt—(Oglala Lakota-Teton Sioux)—Killed some time after the battle as he was watching one of the steamboats on the Yellowstone.

Yellow Weasel—(Northern Cheyenne). Captured a bugle. Presence confirmed by Myers.

Yellow Wolf (*Sungmanitu Gi*)—(Oglala Lakota-Teton Sioux)—b. circa 1830–d. 1904. Member of Little Hawk's band.

Yells at Daybreak (aka Rooster)—(Lakota-Teton Sioux)—In the Rosebud fight, 17 Jun 1876 [LBHA].

Young Bear—(Lakota-Teton Sioux)—d. 25 Jun 1876, killed at the Little Big Horn fighting Custer's column. Myers lists him only as a Teton Sioux.

Young Bear (*Mato-chinchala*)—(Cheyenne)—d. 25 Jun 1876, killed at the Little Big Horn while fighting the Custer column [Myers, "Roster of Known Hostile Indians at the Battle of the Little Big Horn," *Research Review,* Summer 1991, Vol. 5, No. 2].

Young Black Moon (aka Flying Charge)—(Hunkpapa Lakota-Teton Sioux)—d. 25 Jun 1876, killed at the Little Big Horn in the valley fight against Reno, in front of the timber, though both the LBHA and CBHMA show him as being killed fighting Custer's column. The LBHA's *Research Review,* Summer 2001, lists him as a chief. War leader of the Fox Warrior Society, a Cheyenne society. The name Flying Charge is also seen listed as a Blackfeet Sioux [CBHMA].

Young Eagle—(Hunkpapa Lakota-Teton Sioux)—Seventeen years old at time of battle. Living at Standing Rock Agency in 1929.

Young Hawk (also "Eli" Young Hawk)—(Hunkpapa Lakota-Teton Sioux)—Made the 1926 reunion. Still living at the Standing Rock Agency, Wakpala, SD, 1926 [courtesy of Dickson].

Young Little Wolf (aka *Laban* Little Wolf; Red Bird)—(Northern Cheyenne)—d. 1927. First saw Custer at Medicine Tail Coulee. Presence confirmed by Myers.

Young Man Afraid of His Horses—(Oglala Lakota-Teton Sioux). It is not certain he was at the battle and Dickson makes a case for him as one of the Oglala leaders who strove to avoid conflicts. (See Red Cloud.)

(Young) Sitting Bull (aka Drumpacker)-(Oglala Lakota-Teton Sioux)—d. 16 Dec 1876 or Apr 1877. Killed attempting to surrender to Nelson Miles. This is probably the same man Stewart refers to as an Oglala who signed the 1868 peace treaty [*Custer's Luck,* p. 50]. Probably present at the LBH.

Young Skunk (aka Standing Rabbit)—(Oglala Lakota-Teton Sioux)—d. 25 Jun 1876, killed at the Little Big Horn. Body location unknown, but killed fighting Custer's column. Indian accounts indicate Young Skunk was the warrior who actually killed the Arikara scout, Bob-tail Bull.

Young Spotted Elk—(Northern Cheyenne)—Told of watching young Lakota and Cheyenne boys/men take the suicide vows.

Young Turkey Leg—(Northern Cheyenne). Fought in the valley fight and charged the timber. Presence confirmed by Myers.

Young Two Moon (aka "John" Two Moons)—(Northern Cheyenne). Twenty-one-year old nephew of Two Moon. CBHMA has him listed as the son of Two Moons, but this is incorrect. His father was Beaver Claws (b. 1818–d. 1905), a half-brother of Two Moon. One of those who stayed back from most of the fighting, watching some of it. Did not see the Reno fight. Watched as Custer's column left Nye-Cartwright Ridge. The cavalry was moving at a lope, paying little attention to any pursuing Indians.

Zu-me—(Hunkpapa Lakota-Teton Sioux)—b. circa 1850. Listed in the Sitting Bull Surrender Ledger. Wife was Old Bear Woman.

Estimates of Indian Strength

It will never be known for sure how many Indians were in the village that day and estimates range from "not-so-many" to "an-awful-lot." Even with eyewitness testimony and unimpassioned, quasi-empirical legwork, some refuse to accept the more evident, preferring to rely on their own prejudgments or prejudiced theories. The old passions of cover-up and self-serving justification always seem to replace the obvious. For those with a more open mind, we offer the following, remembering that according to documents from 1881, tribes like the Oglala Sioux averaged approximately 4.6 people per lodge [Dickson, "Reconstructing the Indian Village at the Little Bighorn: The *Cankahuhan* or Soreback Band, Oglala," *Greasy Grass*, May 2006, Vol. 22, p. 14]: Over 2,000—

1. CPT Frederick William Benteen — In the July 4, 1F876 letter to his wife, Benteen wrote that there were 3,000 warriors there [Graham, *The Custer Myth*, p. 300]. "Captain Benteen stated later that there were 'picnic parties' of Indians as large as a regiment standing around the river bottom looking on, and that fully 2,000 hostiles were idling about, waiting for a place from which to shoot. He declared ... there was not a foot of unoccupied land anywhere and that there were Indians everywhere ... the command was surrounded by from eight to nine thousand hostiles" [Stewart, *Custer's Luck*, p. 422].

2. COL William S. Brackett —12,000–15,000 Indians, with about 1/3 of them (4,000–5,000) warriors [*Contributions to the Historical Society of Montana, IV*, p. 263].

3. LT James H. Bradley (7th Infantry; Gibbon's Chief-of-Scouts)— Bradley never gave a specific amount, but from the comments he made in his memoirs, it appears he felt there were at least 2,000 or more warriors. "...[T]here were Indians enough in the timber [to Bradley's front when Terry halted the command in the LBH valley on the evening of 26 June] and on the hills before them, in chosen positions of great strength, to have cut them all to pieces and driven them back in ruinous disorder. From subsequent examination of the ground I am convinced that there were not less than a thousand of these ambushed savages, with plenty more to co-operate with them, and not only would they have easily defeated the cavalry, but they would have given our whole command a desperate fight had we advanced that evening another mile" [Bradley, *The March of the Montana Column*, p. 161].

4. CPT Philo Clark (Second Cavalry)— On June 17, the day of the Rosebud fight with Crook, the Indians had about 1,200 standing lodges and 400 wickiups, about 3,500 warriors [Graham, *The Custer Myth*, p. 116].

5. Lewis Crawford — 2,000 to 2,500, but the country could not have sustained that number if they stayed together for very long.

6. Crazy Horse —1,800 lodges and 400 wickiups. At least 7,000 warriors, *plus* any number of transients and hangers-on [South Dakota Historical *Collections, vol. VI*, p. 227].

7. LT Carlo DeRudio — 3,000 to 4,000 warriors, but he admitted that at the time of the battle he would have guessed at a higher number [RCOI].

8. Fred Dustin —10,000 to 12,000 people, of whom 3,000 to 3,500 were war-

riors. No more than 2,500 warriors, however, participated in the battle [*The Custer Tragedy*, p. 106].

9. Feather Earring — In response to the question from General Scott: "How many lodges were there?"

"A: There were very many; three or four young men in a lodge. We gave each man a willow stick in order to count them. I know we counted over 5,000, and they were not all there; many were over on Arrow Creek stealing horses from the Crows" [Graham, *The Custer Myth*, p. 98].

10. LT Winfield Scott Edgerly — 20,000 horses, 6 to 8 ponies per man = 2,500 to 3,300 warriors. On 18 Aug 1881, in a statement made at Fort Yates and carried in the *Leavenworth Times*, Edgerly said, based on knowing the size of and seeing Terry's command coming up the valley — 500 men — he estimated the size of the Indian force to be about 7,000 warriors. In a speech quoted in a New Hampshire newspaper around 1896 to 1897, Edgerly said the command had "proof positive" that there were no more than 600 Indians, but in his opinion there turned out to be "not less ... than 3,000" [Clark, *Scalp Dance*, p. 70].

11. Flat Iron — [the last surviving Cheyenne chief who took part in the battle] 14,000 Indians in the camp, of whom 8,000 were fighting men [*Helena Independent*, October 15, 1915].

12. COL John Gibbon — 1,200–2,500 warriors [*Contributions to the Historical Society of Montana, IV, 1903*, p. 285]. [Note: carried below, as well.]

13. LT Edward Settle Godfrey — Godfrey's estimate of the number of warriors was at least 3,000 to cover the ground he saw [Nichols, *RCOI*, p. 494].

14. PVT Theodore W. Goldin — Estimated the warrior strength to be between 4,000 and 5,000 men [Graham, *The Custer Myth*, p. 271].

15. George Bird Grinnell — at least 200

Cheyenne lodges. Two Moon claimed his band consisted of 50 lodges and it was only one of several Cheyenne bands at the battle [Thrall, "The Sioux War," Kansas State Historical *Collections, Vol. XVI*, p. 573]. There were 6 Sioux villages, each as large or larger than the Cheyenne. The Cheyenne told Grinnell there would be as many as three to four fighting men per lodge. That would have meant between 4,500 to 6,000 warriors present [*The Fighting Cheyennes*, pp. 343–344].

16. LT Luther Hare — counted where 40 tepees had stood and from that estimated there were about 1,500 lodges plus 400 wickiups. Based on that, a *low* estimate of the Indian fighting force would be around 4,000 [RCOI; *Official Transcript*, p. 389]. Estimated there were between 20,000 to 25,000 ponies.

17. George Herendeen — this was the largest camp he had ever seen, but he felt the Indians had moved the camp the morning the troops arrived (*this is highly unlikely*). Just after the battle, he estimated the village contained about 6,000 people, half of who were warriors (3,000) [Graham, *The Custer Myth*, p. 260]. Later, at the RCOI, he told the court there were about 1,800 lodges and 3,500 fighting men [*Official Transcript*, p. 334; *Army & Navy Journal, July 15, 1876*; RCOI]. In his 1911 interview with Walter Camp, Herendeen claimed there were 1,800 lodges and 3,500 warriors. Herendeen felt there were between 400–500 in the surrounding hills.

18. Orin Grant Libby — 2,500 to 3,000 [*The Arikara Narrative*, p.24].

19. Little Buck Elk (Hunkpapa) claimed there was so many Indians not all could participate in the fighting.

20. Dr. Thomas B. Marquis — Wooden Leg told Marquis that the Cheyenne circle was about 300 lodges — some 1,600 people — and that the Blackfeet was about the same. The Sans Arcs was larger; the Oglala

and Minneconjou circles were larger than the Sans Arcs; the Hunkpapa circle about twice the size of the Cheyenne. Based on this, Marquis estimated a camp of some 12,000 people, which could easily have meant 3,000 or more warriors [Graham, *The Custer Myth*, p. 106]. Most of the tepees were family lodges.

Actually, the above is misleading. What Marquis wrote was, "At the Northern Cheyenne fair at Lame Deer in 1927, I estimated the encampment at about 1,100. Wooden Leg and some older men were asked to compare this camp with the one on the Little Big Horn ... it was generally agreed that there must have been 1,600 or more Cheyennes in their camp when the Custer soldiers came" [Marquis, *Wooden Leg*, p. 206, footnote].

21. 1LT John F. McBlain (Ninth Cavalry)—"With Gibbon's command was an odometer cart, and the instrument registered the camp as four and three-quarters miles long; now let anyone familiar with Indian ways of camping picture to himself the fighting strength of that camp. I never did and do not now believe that there was a soul less than 6,000 fighting men" [McBlain, "With Gibbon on the Sioux Campaign of 1876"].

22. "Major" James McLaughlin—the Hunkpapa circle did not contain over 400 lodges [*My Friend, the Indian*, pp. 136–137]. McLaughlin was the U. S. Indian Agent at Devil's Lake Agency, D. T., from 1870 to 1881. The title "Major" is courtesy and custom for Indian agents. From 1881 to 1892, McLaughlin made a great effort to determine the number of Indians at the LBH. Edward Godfrey wrote, "...about one-third of the whole Sioux nation, including the northern Cheyennes and Arapahoes, were present at the battle; he estimates the number present as between twelve and fifteen thousand; that one out of four is a low estimate in determining the number of war-

riors present; every male over fourteen years of age may be considered a warrior in a general fight ... considering the extra hazards of the hunt and expected battle, fewer squaws would accompany the recruits from the agencies. The minimum strength of their fighting men may then be put down as between 2,500 and 3,000. Information was dispatched from General Sheridan that from one agency alone about 1,800 lodges had set out to join the hostile camp; but that information did not reach General Terry until several days after the battle" [*Custer's Last Battle 1876*, p. 14].

23. CPT Anson Mills (CO, M/3C, with Crook's command)—Custer attacked a village of some 15,000 to 20,000 people, with 4,000 to 5,000 warriors. About half that number had been in the Rosebud fight against Crook [*My Story*, p. 409].

24. CPT Myles Moylan—3,500–4,000 warriors. There was a separate and distinct camp of wickiups [RCOI; *Official Transcript*, p. 308]. Moylan put the number at 900 to 1,000 around the command [Stewart, *Custer's Luck*, pp. 422–423].

25. CPT J. S. Payne (5th Cavalry)—Payne felt—based on speaking to various sources—that there were about 2,500 warriors in the battle [Nichols, *RCOI*, p.275].

26. CPT John Scroggs Poland (bvt LTC; Sixth Infantry; Post Commanding Officer at Standing Rock)—Some time after the battle he wrote that at the Standing Rock Agency there averaged about seven Indians per lodge and four per wickiup [Smalley, *Little Bighorn Mysteries*, p. 6–4]. If there were 1,900 lodges, that would mean 13,300 Indians plus 1,600 for the wickiups, or close to 15,000 total. He also said not all the Indians in the village were engaged at any one time [CPT J. S. Poland's report; Graham, *The Custer Myth*, p. 46].

27. MAJ Marcus A. Reno—"The lowest computation puts the Indian strength at about 2,500, and some think there were

5,000 warriors present" [Graham, *The Custer Myth,* p. 229; quoting from Reno's statement to the *New York Herald*].

28. Nicholas Ruleau — a fur trader who had lived at the Pine Ridge Agency since 1879 and who spoke the Sioux tongue and knew a number of Indians who fought at the Little Big Horn: [Hardorff, *Lakota Recollections,* p. 38; in a 1906 interview with Judge Eli S. Ricker]

- Oglala: 350 warriors, led by Crazy Horse.
- Hunkpapa: 1,000 warriors, led by Sitting Bull.
- Minneconjou: 700 warriors, led by Buffalo Bull.
- Sans Arc: 300 warriors, led by Spotted Eagle.
- Brulé (also called Rosebud Sioux): 80 warriors, led by Flying Chaser.
- Santee: 40 warriors, led by Red Top.
- Yankton Sioux: 40 warriors.
- Cheyenne: 45 warriors, led by Little Coyote.
- Total Indians: about 6,000 in camp. Ruleau said about one-third of the total number were single men, accounting for the lower total as compared to the number of warriors.
- Total warriors: 2,555.

29. 1SG John Ryan (Company M, Seventh Cavalry) — In his book, Ryan claims there were usually five or six warriors to a lodge: " ... the ordinary rate...." [Barnard, *Ten Years with Custer,* p. 252] (seems a bit excessive). Ryan estimated the Indian strength at the Pompey's Pillar fight during the Stanley Expedition of 1873 at 1,500 warriors [p. 270]. Ryan also makes the point that in 1873, "...Sitting Bull was not at that time joined by any very formidable force of agency Indians" [p. 271]. "...I have seen the Cheyennes, Arapahoes, Kiowas, Apaches and Comanches move together in the Indian Territory and in Kansas years before, while campaigning there under General Custer, and I should say there was double

the amount move out from this camp" [p. 301].

30. GEN Hugh Scott — a year after the battle he attempted to count the rings and reached 1,500 without counting them all. From this, he estimated closer to 7,000 Indians were in the camp [*Some Memories of a Soldier,* p. 49].

31. LTC Michael V. Sheridan — On 6 Jun 1876, Col. Michael V. Sheridan — LG Philip Sheridan's brother — dispatched a message to Terry: "'Courier from Red Cloud Agency reported ... [on 5 Jun 1876] that Yellow Robe ... says that 1,800 lodges were on the Rosebud and about to leave for Powder River ... and says they will fight and have about 3,000 warriors.'" This now clearly indicated the military expected a large number of Indians, willing to fight. Terry received this message *after* the LBH fight [Willert, *Little Big Horn Diary,* p. 97].

32. LTG P. H. Sheridan — At least 2,000 Indians from the Missouri River agencies — men, women, and children — surrendered to Nelson Miles on 27 Oct 1876. This did not count either Sitting Bull's band or Crazy Horse's and it also did not include any of the Northern Cheyenne. It also did not include any of those taken in by Mackenzie. There were still more Indians out and being hunted down by Crook, Merritt, and Mackenzie [Sheridan's report, dated 25 Nov 1876; Carroll, ... *The Federal View,* p. 78].

33. Vern Smalley — Estimates of 1,000 warriors attacking Reno is reasonable [*Little Bighorn Mysteries,* p. 6–5]. "After the fact, we know there were roughly 3,500 warriors who would have slaughtered [Reno] just as they did Custer" [*More Little Bighorn Mysteries,* p. 13–5].

34. Spotted Horn Bull — In an 1883 interview — with his wife, Pretty White Buffalo, telling most of the story — he said 5,000 would cover the warriors and chiefs [Graham, *The Custer Myth,* p. 84].

35. Edgar I. Stewart wrote that if Vestal,

Grinnell, and McLaughlin are in general agreement, the matter should be settled. They were [*Custer's Luck,* footnote 15, pp. 311–312]. After the battle, Terry learned from General Sheridan that about 1,800 additional lodges had set out to join the hostiles. Stewart believed about 3,000 warriors were there and they were in a generally higher proportion than would be the case. Stewart felt there might have been "thousands" of Indians in the vicinity this day.

36. BG Alfred H. Terry — In his 27 June 1876 battle dispatch, said both Benteen and Reno estimated not less than 2,500 warriors, but other officers thought the number of Indians engaged was much more [O'Neil, … *Official Report … Terry,* p. 15].

37. PVT Peter Thompson — 2,800 warriors ["The Experience of a Private Soldier in the Custer Massacre," p. 79].

38. LT Charles Varnum — the wickiups were very thick along the edge of the timber, along the stream, and at the south end of the village [RCOI]. LT Charles Varnum — Four thousand [Graham, *The Custer Myth,* p. 343]. Varnum felt there were as many as 4,000 Indians, many of whom were never engaged. The men on the hill could see large masses of them a good ways off.

39. Stanley Vestal [aka Walter Campbell] — quotes White Bull, saying there were about 2,500 warriors "fit to bear arms." He put the number of lodges at over 2,000 with from one to three warriors per lodge, more than half of them seasoned warriors. Vestal also said, "the top estimate of the effective manpower of the Western Sioux when all together" was 3,000 [*Sitting Bull,* p. 157, also p. 147; *Warpath: True Story of the Fighting Sioux,* p. 80; *Warpath and Council Fire,* p. 235]. Vestal agreed with Grinnell, though Grinnell's numbers appear considerably higher than Vestal's.

40. White Man Runs Him — 4,000 to 5,000 warriors [Graham, *The Custer Myth,* p. 16].

41. PVT Charles A. Windolph — "Altogether there may have been as many as one third of all the Sioux tribesmen here — possibly close to 10,000 out of 30,000. That would figure out somewhere between 2,000 to 3,000 warriors." [Windolph, *I Fought with Custer,* pp. 91–92.]

1,500–2,000 —

1. Barron Brown — no more than 2,000 warriors, only one-half of whom had modern firearms [*Comanche,* p. 27].

2. COL John Gibbon — 1,200–2,500 warriors [*Contributions to the Historical Society of Montana, IV, 1903,* p. 285]. [Note: Gibbon's estimate is carried above, as well.]

3. Frazier Hunt — 1,800 to 2,000 warriors [*Custer, the Last of the Cavaliers,* p. 174].

4. Runs the Enemy — 2,000 warriors took part in the battle [Dixon, *The Vanishing Race,* p. 179].

1,500 or less —

1. Dr. Charles Eastman — no more than 5,000 Indians, total. Hunkpapa: 224 lodges; Sans Arcs: 85; Santee: 15; Cu Brulé: 140; Minneconjoux: 190; Oglala: 240; Cheyenne: 55 [total: 949]. He said that at 5 per lodge, this equals 4,945. With 25% warriors (too high a percentage, he said) plus 200 attached from various agencies (too low, he said), Custer only had 1,411 warriors confronting him, less than he actually anticipated. Dropping old men and boys would reduce the number to 800 or 900 ["The Story of the Little Big Horn," *Chautauquan, Vol. XXXI, July, 1900,* p. 354]. Eastman went on to say that it was not the numbers Custer under- or overestimated, but the military ability of the Indians. "I reiterate that there were not 12,000 to 15,000 Indians at that camp as has been represented; nor were there over 1,000 warriors in the fight. It is not necessary to exaggerate the number of the Indians engaged in this notable battle.

The simple truth is that Custer met the combined forces of the hostiles, which were greater than his own, and that he had not so much underestimated their numbers as their ability" ["The Sioux Narrative," *Chautauquan Magazine,* 1900].

2. Flying Hawk—1,200 warriors in the entire village, but only about 1,000 took part in the battle. The others were out hunting [*Flying Hawk's Tales,* p. 40].

3. Gregory F. Michno—Maybe 1,500 warriors. "Refocusing our myopic vision to other years and regions, we can find at least one dozen villages larger than the one on the Little Bighorn, and on-field geographical and spatial considerations illustrate the impossibility of the exaggerated size estimations. The village was about one and one-half miles long, and contained about 1,200 lodges and perhaps 1,500 warriors" ["Myth-Busting at the Little Bighorn," *Custer and His Times, Book Five,* p. 156].

Unsure—

1. Gall—Could not tell how many were in the camp. His own following consisted of some 60 lodges [Joseph Henry Taylor, "Bloody Knife and Gall," *North Dakota Historical Quarterly,* vol. IV, April 1930, p. 165; "Major" James McLaughlin, *My Friend, the Indian,* p. 134].

2. George E. Hyde—Fifty lodges of the "wildest of the Northern Cheyennes" were the only ones at the battle [*Red Cloud's Folk,* p. 182].

3. Red Cloud—4,000 Indians in the camp [Joseph K. Dixon, *The Vanishing Race,* p. 170]. Unclear if he meant warriors or total people.

Appendix A.
Unit Rosters and Strength Summaries

Headquarters

LTC George A. Custer
MAJ Marcus A. Reno
1LT William W. Cooke
1LT (Dr.) George E. Lord
Dr. James M. DeWolf
Dr. Henry R. Porter
SGM William H. Sharrow
CTMP Voss, Henry

HQ Notes

- 6 officers, 2 EM in battle.
- 1 officer (VET SURG), 2 EM left at PRD.
- 3 officers on detached service.
- 1 officer with Terry's HQ
- HQ strength: assigned at FAL: 10 officers, 4 EM (3 officers on detached service; 1 officer detached to Terry's staff).
- Leaving FAL: 7 officers, 4 EM, 2 civilians (1 officer, 2 EM left at PRD)
- At LBH: 6 officers, 2 EM, 2 civilians, plus attachments.
- Bodies of HQ staff found only on Custer Hill (along with 2 civilians), although TMP Henry Dose's (orderly attached from G Co.) body was found in MTC vicinity.
- Length of Service, EM: at PRD: 5+ years: 2. At LBH: 5+ years: 2.

Company A

CPT Myles Moylan
1LT Charles DeRudio

2LT Charles A. Varnum
1SG Heyn, William
SGT Culbertson, Ferdinand
SGT Easley, John T.
SGT Fehler, Henry
SGT McDermott, George M.
CPL Dalious, James
CPL King, George H.
CPL Roy, Stanislaus
TMP Hardy, William G.
TMP McVeigh, David
BSM Hamilton, Andrew
FAR Bringes, John
SAD Muering, John
PVT Aller, Charles
PVT Armstrong, John E.
PVT Bancroft, Neil
PVT Baumgartner, Louis
PVT Blair, Wilbur F.
PVT Blake, Thomas
PVT Bott, George A.
PVT Connor, Andrew
PVT Cowley, Cornelius
PVT Deihle, Jacob
PVT Drinan, James
PVT Durselew, Otto
PVT Foster, Samuel J.
PVT Franklin, John W.
PVT Gilbert, John M.
PVT Harris, David W.
PVT Holmstead, Frederick
PVT Hook, Stanton
PVT Ionson (Jonson), Emil
PVT Johnson, Samuel
PVT McClurg, William
PVT McDonald, James
PVT Moodie, William
PVT Nugent, William D.
PVT Proctor, George W.

PVT Reeves, Francis M.
PVT Rollins, Richard
PVT Seayers, Thomas
PVT Seibelder, Anton
PVT Strode, Elijah T.
PVT Sullivan, John
PVT Sweetser, Thomas P.
PVT Taylor, William O.
PVT Weaver, Howard H.

Co. A Notes

3 officers, 47 EM in battle. Rode dark bay horses; in 1868, when Custer first "colored" his regiment, they were considered "brown" bays.

- 8 EM KIA, all on bottoms.
- 6 WIA, 1 of whom DOW.
- Strengths: assigned at FAL, 17 May 1876: 3 officers, 56 EM (5 EM did not accompany).
- Leaving FAL: 3 officers, 51 EM (4 EM left at PRD).
- Length of Service, at PRD: 2 to 5 years: 4. At LBH: 6 mos to 1 year: 9; 1 to 2 years: 7; 2 to 5 years: 23; 5+ years: 8.
- EM born in a foreign country: 21 (44.7 percent); Germany/Prussia: 8; Ireland: 7; Scotland: 2; Canada: 1; France: 1; Denmark: 1; Sweden: 1. Total non–English speaking: 11 (23.9 percent).
- American-born EM: 26 (55.3 percent).

Company B

CPT Thomas M. McDougall
2LT Benjamin Hodgson
1SG Hill, James
SGT Criswell, Benjamin C.
SGT Hutchinson, Rufus D.
SGT Murray, Thomas
CPL Cunningham, Charles
CPL Dougherty, James
CPL Smith, William M.
CPL Wetzel, Adam
BSM Crump, John
FAR Moore, James F.
SAD Bailey, John A.
PVT Barsantee, James F.
PVT Boam, William
PVT Boren, Ansgarius
PVT Callan, Thomas J.
PVT Campbell, Charles A.
PVT Carey, John J.
PVT Carmody, Thomas
PVT Clark, Frank
PVT Coleman, Thomas W.
PVT Criswell, Harry
PVT Crowe, Michael
PVT Crowley, Patrick
PVT Davenport, William
PVT DeVoto, Augustus
PVT Dorn, Richard B.
PVT Frank, William
PVT Martin, William
PVT Mask, George B.
PVT McCabe, John
PVT McLaughlin, Terrence
PVT McMasters, William
PVT O'Neill, John
PVT Pym, James
PVT Randall, George F.
PVT Ryan, Stephen L.
PVT Sager, Hiram W.
PVT Shea, Daniel
PVT Spinner, Philipp
PVT Stout, Edward
PVT Stowers, Thomas J.
PVT Trumble, William
PVT Wallace, Richard A.
PVT Woods, Aaron L.

Co. B Notes

2 officers, 44 EM in battle. Rode light bays.

- Rode on Reno's recon.
- 1 officer, 2 EM KIA; 5 WIA.
- Strength: assigned at FAL, 17 May 1876: 3 officers, 71 EM (1 officer, 6 EM did not ac-company; 2 EM assigned to Dep't duty).
- Leaving FAL with company: 2 officers, 63 EM (19 EM left at PRD).
- Length of Service, at PRD: < 6 mos: 17; 2 to 5 years: 1; 5+ years: 1. At LBH: less than 6 mos: 6; 6 mos to 1 year: 1; 1 to 2 years: 7; 2 to 5 years: 16; 5+ years: 14.
- EM born in a foreign country: 17 (38.6 percent); Ireland: 7; Germany/Prussia: 3; England: 3; Scotland: 2; Sweden: 1; Italy: 1. Total non–English speaking: 5 (11.4 percent).
- American-born EM: 27 (61.4 percent).

Company C

CPT Thomas Ward Custer
2LT Henry M. Harrington
1SG Bobo, L. Edwin
SGT Finckle, George A.
SGT Finley, Jeremiah
SGT Hanley, Richard P.
SGT Kanipe, Daniel A.
CPL Foley, John
CPL French, Henry E.
CPL Ryan, Daniel
TMP Bucknell, Thomas J.
TMP Kramer, William
FAR Fitzgerald, John
BSM King, John
SAD Howell, George
PVT Allan, Alfred
PVT Bennett, James C.
PVT Brennan, John
PVT Brightfield, John
PVT Criddle, Christopher
PVT Eiseman, George
PVT Engle, Gustave
PVT Farrand, James
PVT Farrar, Morris M.
PVT Fowler, Isaac
PVT Griffin, Patrick
PVT Hathersall, James
PVT Jordan, John
PVT Lewis, John
PVT Mahoney, John J.
PVT McGuire, John B., Jr.
PVT Meyer, August
PVT Meyer, Frederick
PVT Mullin, Martin
PVT Phillips, Edgar
PVT Rauter, John
PVT Rix, Edward
PVT Russell, James H.
PVT St. John, Ludwick
PVT Shade, Samuel S.
PVT Shea, Jeremiah
PVT Short, Nathan
PVT Stuart, Alpheus
PVT Stungewitz, Ygnatz
PVT Thadus, John
PVT Thompson, Peter
PVT Van Allen, Garrett H.
PVT Warner, Oscar T.
PVT Watson, James
PVT Whitaker, Alfred
PVT Wright, Willis B.
PVT Wyman, Henry

Co. C Notes

2 officers, 50 EM in battle. Rode light sorrels; in 1868, sorrels.

- Rode on Reno's recon.
- Only Co. C's dead were found on Finley *Ridge*. Its dead were also found in the Keogh Sector and on LSH.
- No Co. C troopers were identified in Deep Ravine.
- 2 officers, 36 EM KIA; 4 WIA, with 1 DOW.
- Strength: assigned at FAL, 17 May 1876: 3 officers, 66 EM (6 EM did not accompany).
- Leaving FAL: 2 officers, 60 EM (9 EM left at PRD, including 1 EM deserting and 1 EM sick; 1 EM left at Rosebud/Yellowstone camp).
- Length of Service, at PRD or other: 6 mos to 1 year: 3; 2 to 5 years: 4; 5+ years: 4. At LBH: 6 mos to 1 year: 18; 2 to 5 years: 20; 5+ years: 12.
- EM born in a foreign country: 19 (38.0 percent); England: 5; Ireland: 5; Germany/Prussia: 4; Switzerland: 2; Australia: 1; Russia: 1; Scotland: 1. Total non–English speaking: 7 (14.3 percent).
- American-born EM: 31 (62.0 percent).

Company D

CPT Thomas B. Weir
2LT Winfield S. Edgerly

1SG Martin, Michael
SGT Flannagan, James
SGT Harrison, Thomas W.
SGT Russell, Thomas
CPL Wylie, George W.
TMP Bohner, Aloys
BSM Deetline, Frederick
FAR Charley, Vincent
SAD Meyers, John
PVT Alberts, James H.
PVT Ascough, John B.
PVT Brant, Abram B.
PVT Cox, Thomas
PVT Dann, George
PVT Dawsey, David E.
PVT Fay, John J.
PVT Fox, John
PVT Golden, Patrick M.
PVT Green, Joseph H.
PVT Hager, John
PVT Hall, John Curtis
PVT Hardden, William
PVT Harris, James
PVT Harris, William M.
PVT Hetler, Jacob
PVT Holden, Henry
PVT Horn, George
PVT Houghtaling, Charles
PVT Housen, Edward
PVT Hunt, George
PVT Hurd, James
PVT Kavanagh, John
PVT Keller, John J.
PVT Kipp, Fremont
PVT Kretchmer, Joseph
PVT Manning, David
PVT Marshall, William A.
PVT McDonnell, Patrick
PVT Meadwell, John R.
PVT O'Mann, William
PVT Randall, William J.
PVT Reid, Elwyn S.
PVT Sanders, Charles
PVT Scott, George D.
PVT Smith, Henry G.
PVT Smith, William E.
PVT Stivers, Thomas W.
PVT Tolan, Frank
PVT Welch, Charles H.
PVT Wynn, James

Co. D Notes

2 officers, 50 EM in battle. Black Horse Troop.

- 3 EM KIA; 3 WIA.
- Strength: assigned at FAL, 17 May 1876: 3 officers, 65 EM (1 officer, 4 EM did not accompany).
- Leaving FAL with the company: 2 officers, 61 EM (11 EM left at PRD).
- Length of Service, at PRD: 6 mos to 1 year: 4; 1 to 2 years: 1; 2 to 5 years: 4; 5+ years: 2. At LBH: 6 mos to 1 year: 10; 2 to 5 years: 25; 5+ years: 15.
- EM born in a foreign country: 19 (38.0 percent); Ireland: 9; Germany/Prussia: 6; England: 1; Canada: 1; Switzerland: 1; Spain: 1. Total non–English speaking: 8 (16.0 percent).
- American-born EM: 31 (62.0 percent).

Company E

1LT Algernon E. Smith
2LT James (Jack) G. Sturgis
1SG Hohmeyer, Frederick
SGT James, William B.
SGT Ogden, John S.
SGT Riley, James T.
CPL Brown, George C.
CPL Eagan, Thomas P.
CPL Mason, Henry S.
CPL Meyer, Albert H.
TMP McElroy, Thomas
TMP Moonie, George A.
BSM Miller, Henry
SAD Shields, William M.
FAR Spencer, Abel B.
PVT Abbotts, Harry
PVT Baker, William H.
PVT Barth, Robert
PVT Berwald, Frank
PVT Boyle, Owen
PVT Brogan, James
PVT Connor, Edward
PVT Darris, John
PVT Davis, William
PVT Farrell, Richard
PVT Forbes, John Stuart
PVT Heim, John
PVT Henderson, John
PVT Henderson, Sykes
PVT Huber, William
PVT James, John
PVT Kimm, John G.
PVT Knecht, Andrew
PVT Lange, Henry A.
PVT Liddiard, Herod T.

PVT McKenna, John
PVT O'Connor, Patrick E.
PVT Pendtle, Christopher
PVT Rees, William Henry
PVT Reese, William
PVT Rood, Edward
PVT Schele, Henry
PVT Smallwood, William
PVT Smith, Albert A.
PVT Smith, James (1st)
PVT Smith, James (2nd)
PVT Stafford, Benjamin F.
PVT Stella, Alexander
PVT Torrey, William A.
PVT Van Sant, Cornelius
PVT Walker, George P.

Co. E Notes

2 officers, 49 EM in battle. Gray Horse Troop.

- Rode on Reno's recon
- LT Smith's body was the only one from Co. E found on Custer Hill. Rest of dead found on the South Skirmish Line and in Deep Ravine. None were found in Keogh or Calhoun sectors.
- At least 8 bodies identified in Deep Ravine.
- 2 officers, 37 EM KIA (includes 36 EM with Custer and 1 EM attached to Reno with packs); 7 NCOs killed; 2 WIA.
- Strength: assigned at FAL, 17 May 1876: 3 officers, 61 EM (1 officer, 8 EM did not accompany).
- Leaving FAL: 2 officers, 53 EM (3 EM left at PRD; 1 EM sick).
- Length of Service, at PRD or other: < 6 mos: 1; 2 to 5 years: 3; 5+ years: 1. At LBH: 6 mos to 1 year: 2; 1 to 2 years: 9; 2 to 5 years: 24; 5+ years: 14.
- EM born in a foreign country: 22 (44.9 percent); Ireland: 9; Germany/Prussia: 7; England: 2; Wales: 1; Italy: 1; Greece: 1; Poland: 1. Total non–English speaking: 10 (20.4 percent).
- American-born EM: 27 (55.1 percent).

Company F

CPT George W. M. Yates
2LT William VanWyck Reily
1SG Kenney, Michael
SGT Curtiss, William A.
SGT Nursey, Frederick
SGT Vickory-Groesbeck, J.
SGT Wilkinson, John R.
CPL Briody, John
CPL Coleman, Charles
CPL Teeman, William
TMP Way, Thomas N.
BSM Manning, James R.
FAR Brandon, Benjamin
PVT Atcheson, Thomas
PVT Brady, William
PVT Brown, Benjamin F.
PVT Brown, William A.
PVT Bruce, Patrick
PVT Burnham, Lucien
PVT Carney, James
PVT Cather, Armantheus D.
PVT Davern, Edward
PVT Dohman, Anton
PVT Donnelly, Timothy
PVT Gardner, John
PVT Gregg, William J.
PVT Hammon, George W.
PVT Howard, Frank
PVT Hunter, Frank
PVT Kelly, John P.
PVT Klein, Gustav
PVT Knauth, Herman
PVT Lefler, Meig
PVT Lerock, William H.
PVT Liemann, Werner L.
PVT Lossee, William A.
PVT Lyons, Bernard
PVT Madsen, Christian
PVT Milton, Francis E.
PVT Monroe, Joseph
PVT Myers, Frank
PVT Omling, Sebastian
PVT Pickard, Edwin H.
PVT Reiley, Michael
PVT Rooney, James M.
PVT Rudden, Patrick
PVT Saunders, Richard D.
PVT Sicfous, Francis W.
PVT Sweeney, John W.
PVT Warren, George A.

Co. F Notes

2 officers, 48 EM in battle. "Band Box Troop"; rode light bays.

- Rode on Reno's recon.

- Co. F's dead were found on LSH; 2 in Deep Ravine.
- 2 officers, 36 EM KIA.
- Strength: assigned at FAL, 17 May 1876: 3 officers, 68 EM (2 officers, 8 EM did not accompany; 4 EM were detached to Department HQ for various functions).
- Leaving FAL with company: 2 officers, 57 EM (8 EM left at PRD, 1 also serving extra duty; 1 EM detached, aboard *Far West* to care for Custer's luggage).
- Length of Service, at PRD: 6 mos to 1 year: 1; 2 to 5 years: 2; 5+ years: 5. At LBH: 6 mos to 1 year: 12; 2 to 5 years: 16; 5+ years: 20.
- EM born in a foreign country: 23 (47.9 percent); Germany/Prussia: 8; Ireland: 7; Canada: 3; England: 2; Denmark: 2; France: 1. Total non–English speaking: 11 (22.9 percent).
- American-born EM: 25 (52.1 percent).

Company G

1LT Donald McIntosh
2LT George "Nick" Wallace
Acting 1SG Botzer, Edward
SGT Brown, Alexander
SGT Considine, Martin
SGT Northeg, Olans H.
CPL Akers, James
CPL Hagemann, Otto
CPL Hammon, John E.
CPL Martin, James
TMP Dose, Henry C.
BSM Taylor, Walter O.
FAR Wells, Benjamin J.
SAD Selby, Crawford
PVT Boyle, James P.
PVT Brinkerhoff, Henry M.
PVT Campbell, Charles W.
PVT Dwyer, Edmond P.
PVT Goldin, Theodore W.
PVT Graham, Thomas E.
PVT Grayson, Edward
PVT Hackett, John
PVT Johnson, Benjamin
PVT Lattman, John
PVT Loyd, George
PVT McCormick, Samuel J.

PVT McDonnell, John
PVT McEagan, John
PVT McGinniss, John J.
PVT McGonigle, Hugh
PVT McVay, John
PVT Moore, Andrew J.
PVT Morrison, John
PVT O'Neill, Thomas F.
PVT Petring, Henry
PVT Rapp, John
PVT Reed, John A.
PVT Robb, Eldorado J.
PVT Rogers, Benjamin F.
PVT Seafferman, Henry
PVT Small, John R.
PVT Stanley, Edward
PVT Stevenson, Thomas W.
PVT Wallace, John W.
PVT Weiss, Markus

Co. G Notes

2 officers, 43 EM in battle. Rode mixed horses and sorrels. In 1868, mostly chestnuts and mixed.

- 1 officer, 13 EM KIA; 6 EM WIA.
- Strength: assigned at FAL, 17 May 1876: 3 officers, 66 EM (1 officer, 7 EM did not accompany).
- Leaving FAL: 2 officers, 59 EM (16 EM left at PRD).
- Length of Service, at PRD: < 6 mos: 12; 6 mos to 1 year: 1; 1 to 2 years: 3. At LBH: < 6 mos: 3; 6 mos to 1 year: 2; 1 to 2 years: 7; 2 to 5 years: 18; 5+ years: 13.
- EM born in a foreign country: 21 (48.8 percent); Ireland: 11; Germany/Prussia: 6; Scotland: 1; Norway: 1; Switzerland: 1; Hungary: 1. Total non–English speaking: 9 (21.4 percent).
- American-born EM: 21 (48.8 percent).
- Unknown: 1 (2.3 percent).

Company H

CPT Frederick W. Benteen
1LT Francis M. Gibson
1SG McCurry, Joseph
SGT Connelly, Patrick
SGT Geiger, George H.
SGT Maroney, Matthew

SGT McLaughlin, Thomas
SGT Pahl, John
CPL Bishop, Alexander B.
CPL Lell, George
CPL Nealon, Daniel
TMP Martin (Martini), John (Giovanni)
TMP Ramell, William
BSM Mechlin, Henry W. B.
SAD Voit, Otto
PVT Adams, Jacob
PVT Bishley, P. Henry
PVT Bishop, Charles H.
PVT Black, Henry
PVT Channell, William
PVT Cooper, John H.
PVT Day, John H.
PVT Dewey, George W.
PVT Diamond, Edward
PVT Farley, William
PVT George, William M.
PVT Glenn, George W.
PVT Haack, Henry
PVT Haley, Timothy
PVT Hughes, Thomas
PVT Hunt, John
PVT Jones, Julien D.
PVT Kelley, George
PVT Kelly, James
PVT Lawhorn, Thomas
PVT McDermott, Thomas
PVT McNamara, James
PVT Meador, Thomas
PVT Moller, Jan
PVT Nees, Edler
PVT Nicholas, Joshua S.
PVT O'Ryan, William
PVT Phillips, John J.
PVT Pinkston, John S.
PVT Severs, Samuel
PVT Williams, William C.
PVT Windolph, Charles A.

Co. H Notes

2 officers, 45 EM in battle. Rode "blood" bays and light bays.

- 3 EM KIA, all on Reno Hill; 20 WIA, 1 of whom DOW.
- Strength: assigned at FAL, 17 May 1876: 3 officers, 55 EM (1 officer, 8 EM did not accompany).
- Leaving FAL: 2 officers, 47 EM (2 EM left at PRD).
- Length of Service, at PRD: 5+ years: 2. At LBH: 6 mos to 1 year: 6; 1 to 2 years: 4; 2 to 5 years: 22; 5+ years: 13.
- EM born in a foreign country: 16 (35.6 percent); Ireland: 9; Germany/Prussia: 4; England: 1; Italy: 1; Denmark: 1. Total non–English speaking: 6 (13.6 percent).
- American-born EM: 29 (64.4 percent).

Company I

CPT Myles W. Keogh
1LT James E. Porter
1SG Varden, Frank E.
SGT Bustard, James
SGT DeLacy, Milton J.
CPL Morris, George C.
CPL Staples, Samuel F.
CPL Wild, John
TMP McGucker, John
TMP Patton, John W.
BSM Bailey, Henry A.
PVT Barry, John D.
PVT Braun, Franz C.
PVT Broadhurst, Joseph F.
PVT Connors, Thomas
PVT Cooney, David
PVT Downing, Thomas P.
PVT Driscoll, Edward C.
PVT Gillette, David C.
PVT Gross, George H.
PVT Hetesimer, Adam
PVT Holcomb, Edward P.
PVT Horn, Marion E.
PVT Jones, Henry P.
PVT Kelly, Patrick
PVT Kennedy, Francis J.
PVT Korn, Gustave
PVT Lehman, Frederick
PVT Lehmann, Henry
PVT Lloyd, Edward W.
PVT McIlhargey, Archibald
PVT McNally, James P.
PVT McShane, John
PVT Mitchell, John E.
PVT Noshang, Jacob
PVT O'Bryan, John
PVT Owens, Eugene
PVT Parker, John
PVT Pitter, Felix J.
PVT Post, George
PVT Quinn, James
PVT Ramsey, Charles
PVT Reed, William
PVT Rossbury, John W.

PVT Symms, Darwin L.
PVT Troy, James E.
PVT Van Bramer, Charles
PVT Whaley, William B.

Co. I Notes

2 officers, 46 EM in battle. The "Wild I," after Keogh, though this nickname may be apocryphal for 1876. After the battle, CPL John Wild's body was identified and a wooden stake was erected with "Wild I" written on it, the "I" referring to his unit. There is, however, evidence of the use of the sobriquet while Keogh was doing service for the Vatican. Rode light bays; in 1868, bays and sorrels.

- Rode on Reno's recon.
- Co. I dead were found in the Keogh Sector and on LSH.
- No Co. I personnel were found in Deep Ravine.
- 2 officers, 36 EM KIA. Only 2 SGTs were involved in the battle and killed; 1 WIA became a DOW.
- Strength: assigned at FAL, 17 May 1876: 3 officers, 65 EM (1 officer, 11 EM did not accompany; 3 EM with Dep't HQ in field).
- Leaving FAL: 2 officers, 51 EM (4 EM left at PRD; 1 EM sick).
- Length of Service, at PRD: 6 mos to 1 year: 1; 2 to 5 years: 4. At LBH: 6 mos to 1 year: 5; 1 to 2 years: 1; 2 to 5 years: 33; 5+ years: 7.
- EM born in a foreign country: 21 (45.6 percent); Ireland: 11; Germany/Prussia: 4 England: 3; Canada: 2; Switzerland: 1. Total non–English speaking: 5 (10.9 percent).
- American-born EM: 25 (54.3 percent)

Company K

1LT Edward Settle Godfrey
2LT Luther R. Hare
1SG Winney, DeWitt
SGT Fredericks, Andrew
SGT Rafter, John J.

SGT Rott, Louis
CPL Callahan, John J.
CPL Hose, George
TMP Helmer, Julius
TMP Penwell, George B.
BSM Burke, Edmund H.
FAR Steinker, John R.
SAD Madden, Michael P.
PVT Blunt, George
PVT Boisen, Christian C.
PVT Bresnahan, Cornelius
PVT Brown, Joseph
PVT Burkhardt, Charles
PVT Clear, Elihu F.
PVT Coakley, Patrick
PVT Corcoran, Patrick
PVT Creighton, John C.
PVT Donohue, John F.
PVT Foley, John
PVT Gibbs, William
PVT Gordon, Thomas A.
PVT Jennys, Alonzo
PVT Lasley, William W.
PVT McConnell, Wilson
PVT McCue, Martin
PVT Mielke, Max
PVT Murphy, Michael
PVT Murphy, Thomas
PVT Raichel, Henry W.
PVT Robers, Jonathan
PVT Schlafer, Christian
PVT Schwerer, John
PVT Shauer, John
PVT Siefert, August B.
PVT Wasmus, Ernest
PVT Whitlow, William

Co. K Notes

2 officers, 41 EM for battle. Rode sorrels.

- 5 EM KIA, including 2 with Custer; 2 WIA.
- Strength: assigned at FAL, 17 May 1876: 3 officers, 69 EM (1 officer, 7 EM did not accompany).
- Leaving FAL: 2 officers, 62 EM (21 EM left at PRD).
- Length of Service, at PRD: < 6 mos service: 6; 6 mos to 1 year: 3; 1 to 2 years: 4; 2 to 5 years: 5; 5+ years: 3. At LBH: 1 to 2 years: 3; 2 to 5 years: 18; 5+ years: 20.
- EM born in a foreign country: 22 (53.7 percent); Germany/

Prussia: 10; Ireland: 8; England: 2; Canada: 1; Denmark: 1. Total non–English speaking: 11 (26.8 percent).
- American-born EM: 19 (46.3 percent).

Company L

1LT James Calhoun
2LT John J. Crittenden
1SG Butler, James
SGT Cashan, William
SGT Mullen, John
SGT Warren, Amos B.
CPL Gilbert, William H.
CPL Harrison, William H.
CPL Seiler, John
TMP Walsh, Frederick
BSM Siemon, Charles
FAR Heath, William H.
SAD Perkins, Charles
PVT Abrams, William G.
PVT Adams, George E.
PVT Andrews, William
PVT Assadaly, Anthony
PVT Babcock, Elmer
PVT Banks, Charles
PVT Brown, Nathan T.
PVT Burkman, John W.
PVT Cheever, Ami
PVT Crisfield, William B.
PVT Duggan, John F.
PVT Dye, William
PVT Etzler, William
PVT Galvan, James J.
PVT Graham, Charles
PVT Hamilton, Henry
PVT Harrington, Weston
PVT Hauggi, Louis
PVT Hughes, Francis T.
PVT Kavanaugh, Thomas G.
PVT Lobering, Louis
PVT Logue, William J.
PVT Mahoney, Bartholomew
PVT Marshall, Jasper
PVT Maxwell, Thomas E.
PVT McCarthy, Charles
PVT McGue, Peter
PVT McHugh, Philip
PVT Miller, John
PVT Moore, Lansing A.
PVT O'Connell, David J.
PVT Pardee, Oscar F.
PVT Reibold, Christian
PVT Roberts, Henry
PVT Rogers, Walter B.

PVT Rose, Peter E.
PVT Schmidt, Charles
PVT Scott, Charles
PVT Siemonson, Bent
PVT Snow, Andrew
PVT Stoffel, Henry
PVT Sullivan, Timothy
PVT Tarbox, Byron L.
PVT Tessier, Edmond D.
PVT Tweed, Thomas S.
PVT Vetter, Johann M.

Co. L Notes

2 officers, 57 EM in battle. Rode bays and light bays.

- Rode on Reno's recon.
- Co. L dead were the only ones found on Calhoun Hill. Some found in Keogh Sector and LSH Hill; 1 found in Deep Ravine.
- 2 officers, 44 EM KIA; 1 WIA.
- Strength: assigned at FAL, 17 May 1876: 5 officers, 67 EM (3 officers, 4 EM did not accompany; 1 officer from 20th Inf.).
- Leaving FAL: 2 officers, 63 EM (6 EM left at PRD).
- Length of Service, at PRD: 2 to 5 years: 4; 5+ years: 2. At LBH: 6 mos to 1 year: 12; 1 to 2 years: 1; 2 to 5 years: 21; 5+ years: 23.
- EM born in a foreign country: 22 (38.6 percent); Ireland: 7; Germany/Prussia: 7; England: 4; Canada: 2; Denmark: 1; Scotland: 1. Total non–English speaking: 8 (14.0 percent).
- American-born EM: 35 (61.4 percent).

Company M

CPT Thomas H. French
1LT Edward G. Mathey
1SG Ryan, John
SGT Carey, Patrick
SGT McGlone, John
SGT O'Harra, Miles F.
SGT Weihe, Henry C.
CPL Lalor, William
CPL Scollin, Henry M.
CPL Stressinger, Frederick
TMP Fischer, Charles

TMP Weaver, Henry C.
SAD Donahoe, John
PVT Bates, Joseph
PVT Braun, Frank
PVT Cain, Morris
PVT Davis, Henry Harrison
PVT Gallenne, Jean Baptiste
PVT Gebhart — Tanner, Jacob
PVT Golden, Bernard
PVT Gordon, Henry
PVT Heid, George
PVT Kavanaugh, Charles
PVT Klotzbucher, Henry
PVT Lorentz, George
PVT Mahoney, Daniel
PVT Meier, John H.
PVT Meyer, William D.
PVT Moore, Hugh N.
PVT Morris, William E.
PVT Neely, Frank
PVT Newell, Daniel J.
PVT Pigford, Edward D.
PVT Rutten, Roman
PVT Ryder, Hobart
PVT Rye, William W.
PVT Seamans, John
PVT Senn, Robert
PVT Severs, James W.
PVT Sivertson, John
PVT Slaper, William C.
PVT Smith, George E.
PVT Sniffen, Frank W.
PVT Stratton, Frank
PVT Summers, David
PVT Thornberry, Levi
PVT Thorpe, Rollins L.
PVT Turley, Henry J.
PVT Varner, Thomas B.
PVT Voight, Henry C.
PVT Weaver, George
PVT Weeks, James
PVT Whisten, John V.
PVT Wiedman, Charles T.
PVT Wilber — Darcy, James
PVT Williams, Charles H.

Co. M Notes

2 officers, 54 EM in battle. Rode light bays.
- 12 EM KIA; 11 WIA, 1 of whom DOW.
- Strength: assigned at FAL, 17 May 1876: 3 officers, 63 EM (2 EM did not accompany).
- Leaving FAL: 2 officers, 61 EM (6 EM left at PRD; 1 EM was detached).

- Length of Service, at PRD and Yellowstone: 2 to 5 years: 4; 5+ years: 2. At LBH: 6 mos to 1 year: 19; 2 to 5 years: 22; 5+ years: 13.
- EM born in a foreign country: 22 (40.7 percent); Germany/Prussia: 8; Ireland: 7; England: 2; Switzerland: 2; France: 1; Canada: 1; Norway: 1. Total non–English speaking: 12 (22.2 percent).
- American-born EM: 32 (59.3 percent).

Strength Summary

The authorized strength for the Seventh Cavalry in 1876 was 43 officers and 845 enlisted personnel, 888 men total. These twelve regimental companies were authorized three officers and 70 enlisted men each, and a headquarters staff of seven officers and five EM. No band, *per se,* was authorized.

The make-up of a cavalry regiment was as follows:

1 colonel
1 lieutenant colonel
3 majors
12 captains
1 adjutant (lieutenant)
1 quartermaster lieutenant
12 first lieutenants
12 second lieutenants
1 sergeant major
1 quartermaster sergeant
1 saddler sergeant
1 chief trumpeter
1 chief musician
12 first sergeants
60 sergeants
48 corporals
24 trumpeters
24 farriers/blacksmiths
12 saddlers
12 wagoners
648 privates

Each post — or place of "subsistence supplies" — was author-

ized one Commissary Sergeant, separate from, but attached to the regiments. One veterinary surgeon (at $75/month) was authorized for each cavalry regiment (Congressional Acts of June 16, 1874, and June 23, 1874, and March 2, 1875, and March 3, 1875). When the Seventh Cavalry departed Fort Abraham Lincoln on May 17, 1876, there were 32 officers and 706 EM (738 total) with the regiment. In addition, there were one officer and eight enlisted men from the regiment assigned to General Terry's headquarters.

Detached, not on campaign: There were fifteen officers and seventy-nine enlisted men — ninety-four, total — who were detached for one reason or another, and did not accompany the regiment on the campaign. Some of these men were on extended leaves-of-absence. Of those leaving Fort Lincoln, some were left behind to guard the Powder River depot: one officer (the veterinary surgeon), and 124 EM, including 14 men from the band. Two Ree scouts remained behind at the Powder River Depot (William Baker and Robert Jackson). One enlisted man was inadvertently left behind on the Rosebud (possibly Private Morris Farrar of Company C), but he eventually managed to join Reno on the hilltop. There were also six men who were on the campaign, but who were sick, or deserted, or were further assigned. In addition, Private Dennis Lynch, Company F, was sent by Custer to the steamer *Far West* — on June 22 — to maintain the colonel's luggage.

In the battle there was a total of 31 officers (includes contract surgeons, Porter and DeWolf) plus 576 EM. The total, including scouts, interpreters, civilians, and quartermaster employees at the Little Big Horn, was 655 men.

On August 19, 1876, *The Army*

and Navy Journal reported that on 17 Aug 1876, Congress had authorized an increase in the number of men in a cavalry company to 100, thus raising an additional 2,500 men to aid in fighting the Indians. In addition, the height and weight requirements for a cavalryman were changed to a minimum height of 5'3" from 5'5", and to 175 pounds from 155 pounds.

Seventh Cavalry, from Fort Lincoln to the Little Big Horn

Unit	Assigned 17 May 76 O	EM	Temporary Duty O	EM	Dept. or Detached Duty O	EM	Leaving Fort A. Lincoln O	EM	Left at Powder River Depot O	EM	AWOL/Sick/Det EM	Picked Up, 22 Jun	At the Little Bighorn O	EM	Killed in Action O	EM	DOW O	EM	With Custer O	EM
H Q	10	4	3	0	1		7	4	1	2			6	2	4	2			3	2
Company A	3	56	0	5			3	51		4			3	47		8		1		
Company B	3	71	1	6			2	63		19			2	44	1	2				
Company C	3	66	0	6		2	2	60		8	2		2	50	2	36		1	2	36
Company D	3	65	1	4			2	61		11			2	50		3				
Company E	3	61	1	8			2	53		3	1		2	49	2	37			2	36
Company F	3	68	2	8			2	57		8	1		2	48	2	36			2	36
Company G	3	66	1	7			2	59		16			2	43	1	13				1
Company H	3	55	1	8		3	2	47		2			2	45		3		1		
Company I	3	65	1	11			2	51		4	1		2	46	2	36		1	2	36
Company K	3	69	1	7			2	62		21			2	41		5				2
Company L	5	67	3	4			2	63		6			2	57	2	44			2	44
Company M	3	63	0	2			2	61		6	1		2	54		12		1		
Band	0	17	0	3			0	14		14			0	0						
Totals	**48**	**793**	**15**	**79**	**1**	**8**	**32**	**706**	**1**	**124**	**6**		**31**	**576**	**16**	**237**		**5**	**13**	**193**
civilians		2						2						2		2				2
QM employees		5						5		4	7	2		7		5				2
Ree scouts		42				4		38			1			24		2				
Dakota scouts		5						5						4						
Crow scouts												6		6						
civilian packers												6		5		1				
Grand Total	**895**		**94**		**9**		**788**		Total: PRD/"Far West"		**143**	**14**	Total at LBH: **655**		Total Killed: **263**		**268**		Total Killed with Custer: **210**	

Seventh Cavalry, Battalion Dispositions, 25 June 1876

Battalion Dispositions	Off. 25 Jun	EM 25 Jun	Off. Att. (+)	EM Att. (+)	Off. Det. (-)	EM Det. (-)	EM w/ Packs (-)	Officer Totals	EM Totals	Strag. 25 Jun (-)	Mess. 25 Jun (-)	Battle Strength	KIA/ DOW w/Unit	WIA	Made Reno Hill	Fit for Duty 27 Jun
LTC G.A. Custer:																
CPT Keogh: Company C	2	50					8	2	42	5	1 Kanipe	38	38		4	0
Company I ‡	2	46					9	2	37	1		38	38		1	0
Company L	2	57					13	2	44			46	46			0
CPT Yates: Company E	2	49				2	9	2	38	2		38	38		2	0
Company F	2	48				1	10	2	37	1		38	38		1	0
Custer: HQ†	5	2		4	2			3	6		1 **Martin**	8	8			0
QM: Boyer & Boston Custer		2							2			2	2			0
Crow scouts		4							4	4		0	0			0
Kellogg & H. Reed		2							2			2	2			0
Totals	15	260	0	4	2	3	49	13	212	13	2	210	210	0	8	0
MAJ M. Reno:																
Company A	3	47			1	1	7	2	39			41	9	6	35	26
Company G	2	43				1	7	2	35			37	13	5	26	19
Company M	2	54			1		8	1	46			47	13	10	38	24
Bn HQ*	1	0	5	7				6	7			13	3	2	9	8
Soldiers, sub-total:	8	144	5	7	2	2	22	11	127			138	38	23	108	77
QM Interpreters ffi		2							2			2	1		1	1
QM scouts		3							3			3	2		1	1
Rees		21							21	13		8	2	1	5	2
Dakotas		4							4	4		0	0		0	0
Crows		2							2			2	0	1	2	1
Totals	8	176	5	7	2	2	22	11	159	17		153	43	25	117	83
CPT F. Benteen:																
Company H	2	45				1	7	2	37		add: 1 **Martin**	40	4	17	40	19
Company D	2	50					7	2	43			45	3	3	45	39
Company K	2	41			1	4	6	1	31			32	3	3	31	26
Ree scouts (Stab)		1							1	1		0	0	0	0	0
Totals	6	137	0	0	1	5	20	5	112	1	1	117	10	23	116	84

Battalion Dispositions	Off. 25 Jun	EM 25 Jun	Off. Att. (+)	EM Att. (+)	Off. Det. (−)	EM Det. (−)	EM w/ Packs (−)	Officer Totals	EM Totals	Strag. 25 Jun (−)	Mess. 25 Jun (−)	Battle Strength	KIA/ DOW w/Unit	WIA	Made Reno Hill	Fit for Duty 27 Jun
CPT T. McDougall:						Trumble										
Company B	2	44			1 (Hodgson)	1		1	43			44	2	4	44	38
LT Mathey: Packs			1 (Mathey)					1	0			1			1	1
Company A									7			7			7	7
Company C									8		add: 1 (Kanipe)	9	1	2	14	11
Company D									7			7			7	7
Company E									9			9	1		11	10
Company F									10			10		1	11	11
Company G									7			7			7	6
Company H									7			7		1	7	7
Company I									9			9			10	9
Company K									6			6			6	6
Company L									13			13		1	13	12
Company M					1 (Mathey)				8			8			8	8
civilian packers		5							5			5			5	3
Ree scouts (Good Face & Billy Cross)		2							2	1		1	1	1	1	1
Totals	2	51	1		2	1		2	141	1		143	5	10	152	137
Stragglers leaving the battlefield												25				
Totals	31	624						31	624			655	268	58	385	304
Totals		655							655			655				

*Attachments to Reno's battalion HQ: 6 officers (Reno; 2 from Regimental HQ, the contract surgeons, Porter & DeWolf; Varnum [A]; Hare[K]; Hodgson, ADJ [B]) & 6 EM (Strode [A], Abbotts & Pendle [E], Davern [F], Penwell & Clear [K]).

†Attachments to Regimental HQ: SGT Hughes (K), TMP Martini (H), TMP Dose (G), CPL Callahan (K)

‡PVTs McIlhargey (I) and Mitchell (I) were originally attached to MAJ Reno as a striker and a cook, but were ordered back to the Custer column with messages from the major. They remained with their unit, Company I, and met their fate with Keogh. They are therefore carried with that original unit. In addition, the QM Ree interpreter, Fred Gerard, was dispatched with a verbal message to LT Cooke. Gerard returned to Reno and is simply carried as part of the "QM Interpreters" row.

Appendix B.
Lists of Scouts:
Williams, Graham, and Camp

Roger L. Williams' List of Varnum's Scouts (55)

1. Baker, William
2. Barking Wolf
3. Bear, aka Foolish Angry Bear, Foolish Bear
4. Bear Running in the Timber, aka Buffalo Ancestor, Buffalo Body, Whole Buffalo, *Pta-a-te*
5. Bear Eyes, aka Wolf Stands in the Cold, Wolf in the Blizzard
6. Black Calf, aka Boy Chief, *Anikadil*
7. Black Fox
8. Black Porcupine
9. Bloody Knife
10. Bobtailed Bull
11. Broken Penis
12. Bull
13. Bull in the Water, aka Bull Stands in the Water
14. Bush, aka Brush, Red Brush, Red Wolf
15. Cards
16. *Caroo*, aka Bear Come Out, Comes the Bear; Old Caddoo
17. Climbs the Bluff, aka Charging Up the Hill, Scabby Wolf
18. Cross, William, aka *E-esk*
19. Curley
20. Curly Head, aka Curly Hair
21. Foolish Bear, aka Red Foolish Bear, Red Bear
22. Forked Horn, aka Crooked Horn
23. Goes Ahead, aka One Ahead, Comes Leading
24. Good Elk, aka Handsome Elk, Red Bear
25. Good Face, aka Pretty Face, *Skare'*
26. Goose
27. Hairy Moccasin
28. Half Yellow Face, aka Big Belly
29. Howling Wolf, aka *Chara'-ta*, Wolf
30. Horns in Front
31. Howling Wolf, aka Wolf
32. Laying Down
33. Left Hand, aka Left Handed
34. Little Brave
35. Little Sioux, aka Sioux
36. Long Bear, aka High Bear, Tall Bear
37. *Ma-tok-sha*, aka Bear Waiting, Round Wooden Cloud, Ring Cloud, Carrier, *Watokshu, Watoksha*
38. One Feather
39. One Horn
40. Owl
41. Red Star, aka Strike Bear, Strikes the Bear, White Calf, Red Star
42. Rushing Bull, aka Charging Bull, Little Crow
43. The Shield
44. Soldier
45. Stab, aka Stabbed
46. Sticking Out
47. Strikes the Lodge
48. Strikes Two
49. Wagon
50. White Cloud
51. White Eagle
52. White Man Runs Him, aka Crow Who Talks Gros Ventre
53. White Swan, aka Strikes Enemy
54. Wolf Runs, aka Running Wolf
55. Young Hawk

W. A. Graham (41/43*)

1. Baker, William
2. Barking Wolf
3. Bear
4. Bear Come Out
5. Bears Eyes
6. Bear Running in the Timber
7. Black Calf
8. Black Fox
9. Black Porcupine
10. Bull
11. Bull in the Water

12. Bush
13. Climbs the Bluff
14. Cross, William
15. Curly Head
16. Foolish Bear
17. Forked Horn
18. Good Elk
19. Good Face
20. Goose
21. Horns in Front
22. Howling Wolf
23. Jackson, William
24. Laying Down
25. Long Bear
26. One Feather
27. One Horn
28. Owl
29. Rushing Bull
30. Round Wooden Cloud
31. Sioux
32. Soldier
33. Stab
34. Strike Bear
35. Strike the Lodge
36. Strikes Two
37. Wagon
38. White Cloud
39. White Eagle

40. Wolf Runs
41. Young Hawk

Graham also lists * Bloody Knife and * Bob-tail Bull as part of a "separate detachment."

Walter Camp (43/44)*

1. Baker, William
2. Barking Wolf
3. Bears Eyes
4. Black Fox
5. Black Porcupine
6. Bob-tail Bull
7. Boy Chief
8. Broken Penis
9. Bull (Bellow)
10. Bull Stands in Water
11. Cards
12. Climbs the Bluff
13. Cross, Billy
14. Curly Head
15. Foolish Bear
16. Forked Horn
17. Good Face
18. Goose
19. Horns in Front
20. Howling Wolf

21. Jackson, Robert
22. Jackson, William
23. Laying Down
24. Little Brave
25. Little Sioux
26. Long Bear
27. One Feather
28. One Horn
29. Owl
30. Red Bear
31. Red Foolish Bear
32. Red Star
33. Red Wolf
34. Running Wolf
35. Rushing Bull
36. The Shield
37. Soldier
38. Stab
39. Sticking Out
40. Strikes the Lodge
41. Strikes Two White Eagle
42. Young Hawk
43. Wagon

* Bloody Knife is not on this list, but Bob-tail Bull is included.

Appendix C.
Demographics and Length of Service

Douglas Scott's work, using enlistment and birth dates — both notoriously unreliable — puts the average age of enlisted personnel at the battle in the range of 24 to 25 years, while some researchers claim it was closer to twenty-two. Greg Michno, in *The Mystery of E Troop*, page 17, lists the average height at 5'7" and the average weight at 140 pounds. Slightly more reliable, a study of birthplaces for the 576 enlisted personnel at the battle show there were some 247 foreign births (42.9 percent of the regiment). Of these, 104 (18.1 percent ... almost one in five enlisted men) were born in a country where English was not the native tongue, while 143 (24.8 percent, just about one in four) were members of the English-speaking British Empire. There were 328 U.S. births (56.9 percent). If we add all the English-speaking men together, they would total 472 or 81.9 percent of the command. And of course, there is the usual problem associated with the Little Big Horn fight: it is unknown where John R. Small of G Company (0.2 percent) came from.

The total number of European- and other foreign-born troopers represented 42.9 percent of the enlisted personnel of the Seventh Cavalry. These men came from:

Ireland	97 (16.84%)	Sweden	2 (0.4%)
Prussia/Germany	76 (13.2%)	Norway	2 (0.4%)
England	26 (4.5%)	Wales	1 (0.2%)
Canada	11 (1.9%)	Australia	1 (0.2%)
Scotland	7 (1.2%)	Spain	1 (0.2%)
Switzerland	7 (1.2%)	Russia	1 (0.2%)
Denmark	6 (1.1%)	Poland	1 (0.2%)
France	3 (0.5%)	Greece	1 (0.2%)
Italy	3 (0.5%)	Hungary	1 (0.2%)

In addition, there were 328 American-born troopers, hailing from 29 states:

New York	68 (11.8%) of total enlisted personnel	New Jersey	5 (0.9%)
		Vermont	4 (0.7%)
Pennsylvania	63 (10.9%)	Wisconsin	3 (0.5%)
Massachusetts	36 (6.3%)	Iowa	3 (0.5%)
Ohio	35 (6.1%)	Connecticut	2 (0.3%)
Indiana	19 (3.3%)	West Virginia	2 (0.3%)
Kentucky	15 (2.6%)	Georgia	2 (0.3%)
Illinois	13 (2.3%)	North Carolina	2 (0.3%)
Maryland	10 (1.7%)	Louisiana	2 (0.3%)
Missouri	9 (1.6%)	Tennessee	2 (0.3%)
Rhode Island	7 (1.2%)	District of Columbia	1 (0.2%)
Virginia	6 (1.0%)	Delaware	1 (0.2%)
Maine	5 (0.9%)	South Carolina	1 (0.2%)
Michigan	5 (0.9%)	Kansas	1 (0.2%)
New Hampshire	5 (0.9%)	Texas	1 (0.2%)

Some writers and historians claim the Seventh Cavalry was loaded with "green" troops, raw recruits, untested, improperly trained, hardly "horse-broken," and brand new to the service. The following tables disprove that contention, especially since the majority of those we can classify as recruits were left behind at the Powder River/Yellowstone Depot. The first table shows the length of service for enlisted personnel at the battle:

Company	0–6 mos.	6 mos–1 yr	(total < 1 yr)	1–5 yrs	+5 yrs
HQ (2)	0 (0%)	0 (0%)	0 (0%)	0 (0%)	2 (100%)
A (47)	0 (0%)	9 (19.1%)	9 (19.1%)	30 (63.8%)	8 (17.0%)
B (44)	6 (13.6%)	1 (2.3%)	7 (15.9%)	23 (52.3%)	14 (31.8%)
C (50)	0 (0%)	18 (36.0%)	18 (36.0%)	20 (40.0%)	12 (24.0%)
D (50)	0 (0%)	10 (20.0%)	10 (20.0%)	25 (50.0%)	15 (30.0%)
E (49)	0 (0%)	2 (4.1%)	2 (4.1%)	33 (67.3%)	14 (28.6%)
F (48)	0 (0%)	12 (25%)	12 (25%)	16 (33.3%)	20 (41.7%)
G (43)	3 (7.0%)	2 (4.7%)	5 (11.6%)	25 (58.1%)	13 (30.2%)
H (45)	0 (0%)	6 (13.3%)	6 (13.3%)	26 (57.8%)	13 (28.9%)
I (46)	0 (0%)	5 (10.9%)	5 (10.9%)	34 (73.9%)	7 (15.2%)
K (41)	0 (0%)	0 (0%)	0 (0%)	21 (51.2%)	20 (48.8%)
L (57)	0 (0%)	12 (21.1%)	12 (21.1%)	22 (38.6%)	23 (40.4%)
M (54)	0 (0%)	19 (35.2%)	19 (35.2%)	22 (40.7%)	13 (24.1%)
Total: 576	9 (1.6%)	96 (16.7%)	105 (18.2%)	297 (51.6%)	174 (30.2%)

This second table shows the length of service for those enlisted personnel who remained behind at the Powder River Depot, or who were on some sort of detached service while the remainder of the regiment marched up the Yellowstone and Rosebud, to their fateful meeting with destiny ... not to mention a lot of Sioux and Cheyenne warriors! This table includes those who were on extra duty, those too sick to continue on, and a couple of deserters.

Unit	< 6 mos	6m–1 yr	(total < 1 yr)	1–5 yrs	+5 yrs
HQ† (2)	0	0	0	0	2
A (4)	0	0	0	4	0
B (19)	17	0	17	1	1
C (10)	0	3	3	4*	3
D (11)	0	4	4	5	2
E (3)	1	0	1	1	1
F (8)	0	1	1	2	5
G (16)	12	1	13	3	0
H (2)	0	0	0	0	2
I (5)	0	1‡	1	4	0
K (21)	6	3	9	9	3
L (6)	0	0	0	4	2
M (6)	0	0	0	4	2
Total: 113	36 (31.9%)	13 (11.5%)	49 (43.4%)	41 (36.3%)	23 (20.4%)

*— This total includes PVT Ottocar Nitsche who was left behind at the Yellowstone/Rosebud Camp and PVT William Kane who had heart disease and was left at PRD, then shipped by steamer to FAL.

†— Does not include attachments or the Vet. Surgeon.

‡— Includes PVT Mark E. Lee who was sick aboard the steamer *Far West*.

The percentage of the *entire* regiment left at the PRD represented by each category:

6.3%	2.3%	8.5%	7.1%	4.0%

The percentage of each category left at the Powder River Depot:
- **80.0 percent** of those with less than 6 months service were left at PRD.
- **11.9 percent** of those with 6 months to 1-year service were left at PRD.
- 31.8 percent of those with less than 1 year service were left at PRD.
- **12.1 percent** of those with 1 to 5 years service were left at PRD.
- **11.8 percent** of those with more than 5 years service were left at PRD.

Regimental totals for enlisted personnel, only:

	< 6 mos	6m–1 yr	(total < 1 yr)	1–5 yrs	+5 yrs
689 EM:	45 (6.5%)	109 (15.8%)	154 (22.4%)	338 (49.1%)	197 (28.6%)

Appendix D.
Regimental Duty Stations

Fort Abraham Lincoln (1872–1891)

The following is from Hebard, Grace Raymond and E. A. Brininstool, *The Bozeman Trail*, Volumes I and II, Cleveland OH: The Arthur H. Clark Company, 1922; and Sheridan, Phillip H., *Outline Descriptions of the Posts of the Military Division of the Missouri, Commanded by Lieutenant General Phillip H. Sheridan*, Bellevue, NE, The Old Army Press, 1969.

Established in August 1872 as Fort McKeen, the name was changed to Fort Abraham Lincoln on 19 Nov 1872. Latitude 46 degrees, 46'17", Longitude, 100 degrees 50'37". Located on the right bank (west side) of the Missouri River opposite Bismarck, D.T. Post office and telegraph office located at the post. Quarters for six companies; cavalry barracks, 7 officer's quarters, 6 cavalry stables, guardhouse, granary, QM storehouse, hospital, laundress quarters, log scouts' quarters, bakery, etc. Water hauled from Missouri River in wagons. Wood supplied by contract. Mean temperature, 43 degrees; average rainfall, 13 inches. The nearest Indians were on their reservation at Standing Rock Agency 50–60 miles south of the post. Estimated at 6,000, composed of Upper and Lower Yanktonnais, Hunkpapa, and Blackfeet Sioux. Fort Berthold Agency for Rees, Gros Ventre, and Mandan; population estimated at 1,920 and located 122 miles to the northwest by river. Today, it is Fort Abraham Lincoln State Park, Mandan, ND; four miles south of Mandan/Bismarck via ND HWY 1806, I-90 exits 155 and 153.

"Fort Abraham Lincoln ... was built as a temporary camp on 14 June 1872, and named Fort McKeen. It was built on the west bank of the Missouri River near the present site of Bismarck, to protect the construction crews of the Northern Pacific Rail Road. On 15 August 1872, the post was moved to a new site five miles away, and on 19 November 1872, it was renamed Fort Abraham Lincoln" [footnote in *I, Varnum*, p. 49]. Lieutenant Godfrey claimed there were thirty-nine widows (from the battle) at Fort Lincoln [Graham, *The Custer Myth*, p. 148]. There were seven houses on Officers' Row. Custer's original house burned down in Feb 1874, but a new one was built almost immediately. Captain William McCaskey, 20th Infantry, was in charge of the post while the Seventh Cavalry was out campaigning.

Pre-Campaign Dispositions, Permanent Posting to February 1876, to May 1876

(Note — Five to six companies were normally stationed at Fort Abraham Lincoln — A, C, D, F, and I, in early 1876. In 1875, three companies of the regiment had been sent south to hunt down what were called "White Leaguers." These were B and G, to Shreveport, LA; and K, to McComb City, MS. Since returning from "Re-Construction" duty, companies H and M had been stationed at Fort Rice permanently. In his memoirs, however, John Ryan wrote that three companies left Rice for the campaign, but other than H and M, he does not note the third [Barnard, *Ten Years with Custer*, p. 265]. He was probably alluding to Company K, but K had been transferred to Mississippi, and made its way to Fort Lincoln for the campaign, directly from McComb City. Companies E and L had been stationed at Fort Totten.)

Company A — At Fort Abraham Lincoln, Feb 1876–May 1876.

Company B — At Department of the Gulf, Feb–Mar 1876. Left Shreveport, LA, 19 Apr 1876, arrived Fort Lincoln, 1 May 1876.

Company C — At Fort Lincoln, Feb 1876–May

1876. (Hammer says C Company was at Fort Seward and did not leave for Fort Lincoln until 17 Apr 1876). Fort Seward was where Lieutenant Harrington arrived from his leave of absence in Highland Falls, NY. It was located near Jamestown, ND, due south of Fort Totten and mid-way between Fargo (to the east) and Bismarck to the west. At the end of the Stanley Expedition in Sep 1873, C Company was assigned to Fort Rice, and according to First Sergeant John Ryan, C Company was still at Rice in the early part of 1876 [Barnard, *Ten Years with Custer*, p. 260].

Company D — At Fort Lincoln, Feb 1876–May 1876.

Company E — At Fort Totten, Feb 1876, located about 160 miles northeast of Bismarck, ND (by road), about mid-way between Minot, ND (to the west), and Grand Forks, ND (to the east), near Devil's Lake. Departed Fort Totten, 10 Mar 1876, arrived at Fort Lincoln, 17 Apr 1876.

Fort Totten, ND (1867–1890). Established in 1867. Quarters for *four companies*; officers quarters, barracks, hospital, guardhouse, magazine, bakery, offices, storehouses, cavalry two stables, etc. Nearest telegraph and railroad located at Jamestown, D.T., one hundred miles southeast. Water hauled by wagons is obtained from nearby springs. Wood supplied by contract; climate healthy and very dry. Winters are generally severe with temperatures falling to -40 degrees below zero; high winds and snowstorms, with wind blowing with considerable form all seasons. Winter usually sets in with November and continues through March. Decommissioned in 1890, becoming the property of the Bureau of Indian Affairs. Subsequently used as a school and a health care facility. The nearest Indians were Sisseton and Wahpeton Sioux numbering about 1,000, under charge of Indian Agent. Fort Totten State Historic Site is located on the southeastern edge of Fort Totten, ND, off U.S. 2 and ND Highway 57 [Hebard/Brininstool, *The Bozeman Trail*, and Klockner, *The Officer Corps of Custer's Seventh Cavalry*, p. 121].

Company F — At Fort Lincoln, Feb 1876–May 1876.

Company G — At Department of the Gulf, Feb–Mar 1876. Left Shreveport, LA, 19 Apr 1876, arrived Fort Lincoln, 1 May 1876.

Company H — At Fort Rice, located about 30 miles south of Abraham Lincoln, on the west bank of the Missouri River, just to the north of the present-day town of Cannon Ball. Departed Fort Rice, 5 May 1876, arrived Fort Lincoln, 6 May 1876.

Fort Rice, ND (1864–1878). Established in 1864. Latitude 46 degrees 30", longitude, 100 degrees 34'. Located on the right bank (west side) of the Missouri River. Post office, quarters for *four companies*, officers quarters, company barracks, hospital, guardhouse, library, commissary storehouses, two cavalry stables, quartermaster stables, two blockhouses, stockade, etc. Nearest telegraph and railroad located at Bismarck, D.T. Climate generally dry, average temperature 42 degrees, summer short and hot, 90 to 110, winter frequently -40 below zero. Water obtained by wagons from Missouri River. Decommissioned in 1878, abandoned in 1879. The nearest Indians were located at Standing Rock Agency (Sioux) and Fort Berthold Agency (Arikara, Mandan and Gros Ventre). Fort Rice State Historic Site is approximately twenty miles south of Fort Lincoln State Park, ND via ND Highway 1806 [Hebard/Brininstool, *The Bozeman Trail*, and Klockner, *The Officer Corps of Custer's Seventh Cavalry*, p. 120].

Company I — At Fort Lincoln, Feb 1876–May 1876.

Company K — At the completion of the Black Hills Expedition — Aug 1874 — Company K was stationed at Fort Rice. Some time after this the company was transferred south, Department of the Gulf, Feb 1876–Mar 1876. Left McComb City, MS, 18 Apr 1876, arrived Fort Lincoln, 1 May 1876.

Company L — At Fort Totten, Feb 1876. Left Fort Totten, 10 Mar 1876, arrived Fort Lincoln, 17 Apr 1876.

Company M — Permanent duty station was Fort Rice, arriving there in early half of 1873 from Reconstruction duty in South Carolina and Mississippi and returning there after the completion of the Stanley Expedition in Sep 1873. Left Fort Rice, 5 May 1876, arrived Fort Lincoln, 6 May 1876.

Appendix E.
Horses, Uniforms and
Weapons, and Tactics

Horses

Bays — Various shades of red-brown ranging from tan to dark mahogany, distinguished by black legs below the knee and a black mane and tail. Many of the mixed-color breeds could be classified as bays.

Blacks

Buckskins — Yellow-tan in color, with black points, including mane and tail. Also pretty much the same thing as a "clay-bank" sorrel.

Chestnuts — Red-brown; also, sorrels.

Claybanks (see buckskins) — Light copper with mane and tail of a darker copper. Much the same as a "buckskin."

Duns — Dull gray-brown.

Grays — Gray is a term for white horses. All white horses are technically "grays" unless they are albino then they are white. This is a horse that is born dark, and whose haircoat gradually changes to white. It is more properly termed "graying" or "aging gray," but if you see a white horse (with dark skin), he is really a gray. The term is shortened and gives no thought to the original darker color. There are some terms for stages of the graying process: steel-gray if they are a dark blue; rose-gray if a bay or chestnut is graying out and is mixed red and white hairs; dapple-gray if the lighter color dapples appear in the coat. There are also flea-bitten grays (white with darker, usually red, hairs sprinkled throughout) and almost pure-white (the advanced-stage) grays. [Courtesy of Ms. Linda Terrell.] The Scots Grays were white horses. Grays are the most difficult to see from a distance [Stewart, *Custer's Luck,* p. 145]. The Viennese Lipizzaner is born jet black and turns white with age.

Roans — Could be chestnut, sorrel, or bay sprinkled with gray to yellow-white markings.

Sorrels — Ran from a light yellow-brown to a light red-brown. A common horse color usually used to refer to a copper-red shade of chestnut horse. The mane and tail would be of the same or similar color, possibly even a shade lighter. The color generally ranges from a reddish-gold to a deep burgundy or chocolate. Some insist that chestnut and sorrel are two distinct colors, arguing that "sorrel" should be used to describe only lighter shades or shades with a clear reddish tint, while "chestnut" should denote the darker shades with more brown.

Vern Smalley, in his books, *Little Bighorn Mysteries* and *More Little Bighorn Mysteries,* lists several variations within each company. This is confirmed by First Sergeant John Ryan [Barnard, *Ten Years with Custer,* p. 68]:

- A — dark bays; dark sorrels, liver chestnut, dark chestnut seal brown.
- B, H, and M — light bays; duns and buckskins.
- C — light sorrel; bright sorrel, blond sorrel, light chestnut, palomino.
- D — black; ravens and coals.
- E — grays; possibly some whites.
- F, I, and L — standard bays; mahogany bays, blood bays, standard chestnuts, standard browns.
- G — mixed; copper duns, grulla, red roan, blue roan, rose gray, claybank, young gray, paint, other combinations not fitting elsewhere.
- K — standard sorrel; chestnut sorrel, bright chestnut, dusty chestnut.

An article in the *New York Times,* op-ed section, October 22, 2005, by author John Thorn: "When spectator sports began in this country in the 1820's, it was ... horse racing that symbolized the age. The purse in a stakes match went to the horse that won two of three heats, all run on the same day (the steadfast steed Eclipse was the sports hero of the day). Endurance was what mattered..." Greg Michno, making a comparison with Vagrant, the Kentucky Derby winner of 1876 — who ran the 1½ mile track in 2+ minutes — feels the "loaded, tired cavalry horses ... would certainly have galloped the mile and a half in four or five minutes," referring to Reno's retreat from the timber. This would be some eighteen to twenty-two miles per hour, considerably less than Vagrant's time.

Lieutenant Edward Godfrey wrote: "The bridles were different from the present pattern; the carbine socket was a small sack about twenty inches long in which was carried about twelve pounds of oats, strapped on the cantle; there was no hood on the stirrup used by the men" [Godfrey/Graham, *The Custer Myth*, p. 346]. Custer ordered the removal of the stirrup-hood. The guidon bearers, however, were probably exempt from the order because the guidon socket was riveted to the hood of the left stirrup [Scott, Fox, Connor, *Archaeological Perspectives on the Battle of the Little Bighorn*, p. 207].

- Army regulations required horseshoes to be replaced monthly.

James Willert quoted correspondent John Finnerty, riding with Crook's column: "Finerty was impressed — especially by the hardy *foot troops* advancing far ahead. He paid them tribute: '...We used to joke about the infantry and call them by their Indian nickname of "walk-a-heaps," but before the campaign was over we recognized that man is a hardier animal than the horse, and that shank's mare is the very best kind of charger'" [*Little Big Horn Diary*, p. 87].

Uniforms and Weapons

Note — Lieutenant Godfrey wrote, "Nearly all the men wore the blue, but many, perhaps most of them, had their trousers reinforced with white canvas on the seat and on the legs from the knees half way up. Nearly every one wore the short top boot (that was then uniform) not high like those now worn, although a few of the officers wore the Wellington boot and had white canvas leggings" [Godfrey, Graham, *The Custer Myth*, p. 346].

Blouse — uniform jacket, officers and EM:

- 1872 — style officers had 4 gilt buttons and frogging on each side.
- 1874 — style fatigue blouse (flannel) was current for EM.

- ○ 5 buttons.
- ○ Yellow cord edging on collar and cuffs.
- EM also wore three other types of blouse: (1) the 1872, nine — button plaited fatigue blouse; (2) the long, nine — button frock coat (1858–1872) — in many cases, modified by being made shorter; and, (3) the long-standing cavalry shell jacket which became obsolete in 1872.
  - ○ At least one frock or 1872-fatigue blouse was worn at the battle. A nine — button array was discovered by archaeologists on Reno Hill in 1985.
- 1875 — style added another button.
- Sack coat — slightly longer, straight-sided jacket for both officers (with frogging) and enlisted personnel.
- Single-breasted frock coat — officer's uniform jacket.
  - ○ Company grade (1851–1872–style) were single-breasted, 9 gilt buttons.
  - ○ Field grade were usually double-breasted.

Beneath the blue uniform jackets, the troops wore coarse, pullover, flannel or knit, shirts.

- Standard in 1876 was gray.
- Some wore dark blue, newly issued on experimental basis.
- Some still wore the white shirts left over from the Civil War.
- Others probably wore a civilian-type, checkered "hickory" style, pink or blue.
- Officers almost always wore the "fireman-style" blue shirt, with no rank insignia: double-breasted, trimmed in white tape, usually with a set of cross-sabers and "7" embroidered in white or yellow silk on the points of the collar.

Overcoat —

- Light blue kersey with long cape.
- Double-breasted.
- Only some time after 1876 was the inside of the cape lined with the branch of service color.

Trousers — EM's were sky-blue kersey.

- After the Civil War, the officers' trousers were changed from dark-blue (the same as their uniform coats) to the same light-blue color as the EM, though of a much finer quality material.
- Many — officers and EM — reinforced their trousers with white canvas on the seat and inside legs.
- 1861 — style officers' trousers were sky blue with a ⅛" yellow (cavalry) "welt" (stripe).
- Only officers, sergeants, and corporals were authorized to wear a trouser stripe, each of a different width. Corporal: ½"; sergeant: 1"; officers: 1½".

- Double yellow stripes on trumpeters' trousers, though not authorized until 1883, were not uncommon in the Seventh Cavalry and were "authorized" by Custer.
- Suspenders were not of general issue until 1883, however, the archaeological excavation of 1984 uncovered a commercially-made suspender grip indicating at least some troops used them [Scott and Fox, *Archaeological Insights into the Custer Battle*, pp. 86–87].

Summer-weight cotton drawers — underwear.
Boots — not quite knee-high.

- By regulation, the trousers were supposed to *cover* the boot, but many ignored this on campaign.
- Coarse leather, very poor quality.
- Soldiers rubbed soap on their feet and socks to avoid blisters.

Brogans — shoes.
Hats — standard issue hats were black felt.

- High crowns.
- Wide, "snap-brims," meaning sides could hook up.
- Trimmed with yellow (cavalry) worsted band and tassels.
- Many troops wore similar — and dissimilar — civilian hats because of the poor quality of the military-issue.
- Many C Company troopers wore gray hats.

Carbine sling — the carbine was carried on the right side, suspended on a broad leather strap resting on the left shoulder. Muzzle was carried down and when a soldier was mounted, the barrel was loosely held by a leather socket near the saddle stirrup.

Troops used a .45-caliber (.45/55-grain carbine load, or .45/70-grain infantry load), Model 1873 Springfield carbine (single-shot) and 6-shot, .45-caliber Colt, single-action revolver:

- The carbine had a 1,000+ yards maximum range and a 250 yards maximum effective range.
- A trained soldier could get off about 17 rounds per minute.
- Weapon weighed approximately 7.5 pounds.
- The National Armory of Springfield, MA, manufactured the carbine.
- One hundred rounds of carbine ammunition and 24 rounds of pistol ammo were issued to each man.

Note — Military ammunition used in 1876 was not headstamped, but did have a distinctive style of crimping near the base of the cartridge.

Officers' Uniforms on the Little Big Horn

Note — Godfrey wrote: "All of the officers wore the dark blue shirt with rather wide falling collar [then known colloquially as the "fireman's" shirt], which when the blouse was worn, was over the blouse collar; most of them had cross-sabers and 7, like the old cap ornament, worked in white or yellow silk on the points of the collar" [Godfrey/Graham, *The Custer Myth*, p. 345]. Sergeant Daniel Kanipe tells us, "...[T]he officers who were killed, or most all of them, wore regular soldier's uniform and I don't think that any of the officers had shoulder straps on any of their blouses. As to the wool hats I will say that 'C' Troop and 'E' and 'L' all wore white hats. The other companies of the Regiment wore black hats" [Hardorff, *On the Little Bighorn with Walter Camp*, p. 12].

1. Frederick Benteen: wore the dark blue shirt with a wide falling collar. Probably wore blue regulation trousers.
2. James Calhoun: buckskin blouse; blue "fireman's" shirt; blue regulation trousers.
3. William Cooke: buckskin blouse; blue "fireman's" shirt; blue regulation trousers; white felt hat. DeRudio claimed he was wearing his blue shirt and buckskin pants.
4. Jack Crittenden: wore the dark blue shirt with a wide falling collar. Probably wore blue regulation trousers.
5. George Custer: buckskin suit; blue "fireman's," bib-type shirt, piped in white; wide-brimmed, low-crowned, whitish-gray felt hat; red scarf. Probably had the buckskin jacket stowed on his horse because of the heat.

- According to PVT Giovanni Martini (H), Custer wore a "blue-gray flannel shirt, buckskin trousers, and long boots ... a regular company hat" [Stewart, *Custer's Luck*, p. 274].
- PVT Peter Thompson (C): Custer "was in shirt sleeves; his buckskin pants were tucked into his boots; his buckskin shirt fastened to the rear of his saddle; and a broad-brimmed, cream colored hat ... the brim of which was turned up on the right side and fastened by a small hook and eye to the crown" [Willert, *Little Big Horn Diary*, p. 254].
- LT DeRudio claimed Custer and Cooke, "'were the only ones who had blue shirts and no jackets and buckskin pants...'" [Nichols, *RCOI*, p. 332].
- "Custer carried a Remington Sporting rifle, octagonal barrel; two Bulldog self-cocking, English, white-handled pistols, with a ring in the butt for a lanyard; a hunting knife, in a

beaded fringed scabbard; and a canvas cartridge belt. He wore a whitish gray hat, with broad brim and rather low crown, very similar to the Cowboy hat; buck skin suit, with a fringed welt in outer seams of trousers and arms of blouse; the blouse with double-breasted military buttons, lapels generally open; turn-down collar, and fringe on bottom of shirt" [Godfrey/Graham, *The Custer Myth*, p. 345].

• 1SG John Ryan (M) confirmed most of Godfrey's observations. "General Custer wore a broad brimmed slouch hat, buckskin shirt and pants, and high top cavalry boots. He was armed with a Remington Sporting Rifle that used a brass shell. He also carried in his belt two pistols, one a .45-caliber Colts [*sic*] and the other a French Navy, and a hunting knife" [Ryan/Barnard, *Ten Years with Custer*, pp. 303–304].

6. Tom Custer: buckskin suit; blue "fireman's" shirt; white felt hat. Also known to wear a buckskin shirt. Dressed generally the same as brother George [Godfrey/Graham, *The Custer Myth*, p. 345].

• "...Thomas W., wore a broad brimmed slouch hat, a buckskin shirt and carried a .45-caliber Colt pistol, and I think a Springfield sporting rifle, caliber .45" [Ryan/Graham, *The Custer Myth*, p. 347].
• SGT Kanipe claimed Tom Custer wore regulation blue pants, but with a sergeant's stripe, not an officer's [Hardorff, *On the Little Bighorn with Walter Camp*, p. 11].

7. Carlo DeRudio: wore the dark blue shirt with a wide falling collar. Probably wore blue regulation trousers.

8. Dr. James DeWolf: indications are that he wore the blue "fireman's" shirt.

9. Winfield Edgerly: blue "fireman's" shirt; black snap-brim campaign hat. Probably wore blue regulation trousers.

10. Tom French: deerskin jacket and a large-brimmed hat. Probably wore the dark blue shirt with a wide falling collar under the jacket. Probably wore blue regulation trousers.

11. Frank Gibson: wore the dark blue shirt with a wide falling collar. Probably wore blue regulation trousers.

12. Ed Godfrey: wore the dark blue shirt with a wide falling collar. Probably wore blue regulation trousers, although there is some indication he wore white canvas pants. His men may have been similarly attired, as K Company was known as the "Dude Company."

13. Luke Hare: wore the dark blue shirt with a wide falling collar. Probably wore blue regulation trousers.

14. Henry Harrington: blue regulation blouse; white canvas trousers with fringe on the outer seams.

15. Benny Hodgson: was wearing a vest. SGT Culbertson in his RCOI testimony mentioned that while Hodgson's watch and chain were gone, the gold bar inside his vest was still there [Nichols, *RCOI*, p. 371]. Wore the dark blue shirt with a wide falling collar. Probably wore blue regulation trousers.

16. Myles Keogh: buckskin blouse; blue "fireman's" shirt; blue regulation trousers; apparently wearing shoes rather than boots on 25 Jun 1876. SGT Caddle (I Company), quoted in *Conquest of the Missouri*, p. 379, claimed he found one of Keogh's shoes when he went with the reburial party in 1877.

17. Dr. George Lord: blue regulation shirt and blue regulation trousers. Also, wore glasses.

18. Ed Mathey: wore the dark blue shirt with a wide falling collar ("fireman's" shirt). Probably wore blue regulation trousers.

19. Tom McDougall: wore the dark blue shirt with a wide falling collar. Probably wore blue regulation trousers.

20. Donald McIntosh: Reported to have been wearing a buckskin shirt when he was killed and his body found. If this is true, the buckskin shirt was worn over a calico shirt with gutta-percha buttons. Probably wore blue regulation trousers. Also known to wear a buckskin coat and blue "fireman's" shirt.

21. Myles Moylan: wore the dark blue shirt with a wide falling collar. Probably wore blue regulation trousers.

22. Dr. Henry Porter: buckskin blouse.

23. James Porter: buckskin blouse; blue "fireman's" shirt; blue regulation trousers. "I found Porter's buckskin blouse in the village ... and from the shot holes in it, he must have had it on and must have been shot from the rear, left side, the bullet coming out on the left breast near the heart" [Godfrey/Graham, *The Custer Myth*, p. 346].

24. William Van Wyke Reily: blue "fireman's" shirt; blue regulation trousers.

25. Marcus Reno: regulation blue undress coat (a sack or "sacque" coat); blue regulation trousers; straw hat.

26. Algernon Smith: buckskin blouse; blue "fireman's" shirt; blue regulation trousers; white felt hat. Often preferred shoes with white gaiters to boots.

27. Jack Sturgis: blue "fireman's" shirt; blue regulation trousers. Lieutenants DeRudio and McClernand claimed to have seen a buckskin shirt with Sturgis' name on it in the Indian village. Godfrey remembered him wearing his blue army coat.

From this, it seems he wore the regulation coat over his "fireman's" shirt, then removed the jacket in the heat. The buckskin shirt could easily have been tied to his saddle or with his gear.

28. Charles Varnum: blue "fireman's" shirt; straw hat. Probably wore blue regulation trousers.

29. George Wallace: wore the dark blue shirt with a wide falling collar ("fireman's" shirt). Probably wore blue regulation trousers.

30. Tom Weir: wore the dark blue shirt with a wide falling collar. Probably wore blue regulation trousers.

31. George Yates: buckskin blouse; blue "fireman's" shirt; blue regulation trousers.

Tactics

(See Fox, *Archaeology, History, and Custer's Last Battle.*)

Emory Upton's 1874 manual on tactics and formations established a unified system within the U.S. Army.

- Two other systems on tactics were used as well.
- Poinsett
- BG Philip St. George Cooke's, *Cavalry Tactics: or, Regulations for the Instruction, Formations, and Movements of the Cavalry of the Army and Volunteers of the United States,* Philadelphia, J. B. Lippincott, 1862.

The introduction of a "set of fours" as the basic unit affected tactical maneuverability, simplifying operations, i.e., a squad.

- Increased speed.
- Eliminated cumbersome maneuvers.

In 1876, the primary, i.e., minimum, tactical unit was still the platoon, not the squad. At the battle of the Little Big Horn, there was no evidence found of any platoon-type operations, only company-size operations.

Regardless of organization, the primary mode of engaging the enemy was skirmishing:

- Prescribed intervals between skirmishers. Normal interval was fifteen feet between men.
- Formation structures.
- Deployment procedures.
- Composition of units.
- Skirmish tactics for cavalry: dispersal of men on a combat or firing line.
- On a march, skirmishers cleared the way for the main body. Skirmishers could be mounted or on foot.
- Late 19th-century cavalry did not often employ mounted skirmishing; operated more as mounted infantry.
- Tactics prescribed normal interval of five yards between skirmishers on line, with intervals of fifteen yards between squads.
- These intervals, as wide as they are, provide for the dispersal necessary to counteract effects of newer, more accurate weapons.
- Skirmishers usually aligned in a linear formation.
- 1876 cavalry used a single-shot carbine:
  ° Odd-numbered skirmishers fired first
  ° Then re-loaded as even-numbered fired
  ° Then all continued to fire.

Appendix F.
Indian Encampments Leading
to the Little Big Horn

Line of March from Powder River Country, Spring, 1876

[From Marquis, *Wooden Leg*]

1. Cheyenne [p. 179]
2. Oglala
3. Minneconjoux
4. Hunkpapa

The Sans Arcs joined the encampment on a tributary of the Powder; the Blackfeet Sioux were the next to join. The Santee joined and moved with the Cheyenne [pp. 180–182].

Rosebud Indian Camps, Then Beyond

1. About seven or eight miles up from the Yellowstone, probably around May 22.
2. About May 25, they stayed in camp # 2, about twelve miles farther up the river from the first. Only one night at this camp.
3. Teat Butte camp. Probably around May 26. Only one night.
4. Greenleaf Creek camp. Around May 27. Stayed five or six nights.
5. Sundance camp. Probably reached it around June 2.
6. Mouth-of-Davis Creek/Busby camp. Probably reached by June 8 or 9. May have stayed only one night.
7. Davis Creek/East-of-the-divide camp. Probably around June 10. Stayed only one night. The camp extended "northward up a broad coulee full of plum thickets" [Marquis, *Wooden Leg*, p. 197].
8. Great Medicine Creek/Reno Creek camp.

The center of the camp was "where the present road crosses a bridge at the fork of the creek" [Marquis, *Wooden Leg*, p. 198].

9. Upper LBH camp; June 18, for sure.
10. Lower LBH camp; reached here on June 24. [Note — This date is disputed by Runs In Circle/Iron Hawk who claimed the village was set up a day earlier, i.e., June 23. Runs In Circle made this claim in an interview with Judge Eli S. Ricker, May 13, 1907. The claim was supported by an Oglala named Knife who married and "eloped" with his wife on that same day. See Hardorff, *Lakota Recollections of the Custer Fight*, p. 64, footnote 2.]

Indian Camps in the Little Big Horn Valley

"The Cheyenne location was about two miles north from the present railroad station at Garryowen, Montana [1920s–1930s]. We were near the mouth of a small creek flowing from the southwestward into the river. Across the river east of us and a little upstream from us was a broad coulee, or little valley, having now the name Medicine Tail coulee" [Marquis, *Wooden Leg,* p. 206]. Wooden Leg claimed there were only six main Indian circles: Cheyenne, Minneconjou, Oglala, Sans Arc, Hunkpapa, and Blackfeet Sioux. The Brulé, Assiniboine, and Waist and Skirts (Santee) stayed in their own groups, but close to another circle [pp. 208–209]. The rest were set up as follows:

• Santee: next to the Hunkpapa.
• Brulé: part by the Oglala, part by the Blackfeet.
• The general order was Cheyenne, Sans Arcs,

Minneconjoux, Hunkpapa along the river. The Oglala were away from the river and southwest of the Cheyenne and Sans Arcs. The Blackfeet were also set back from the river and between the Oglala and Hunkpapa, nearer the latter [p. 209].

- All the camps were east of the 1930 highway and the railroad, an important fact in determining village size.
- Wooden Leg said there were no whites or mixed breeds [p. 209].

The Sioux warrior, Black Elk, said the village configuration was:

- Hunkpapa, farthest south, then...
- Oglala
- Minneconjou
- Sans Arc
- Blackfeet
- Cheyenne
- Santee and Yanktonnais, farthest north [Neihardt, *Black Elk Speaks,* p. 106]. Standing Bear, a Minneconjou, did not agree with this placement of the Santee, but he did not address it specifically. He merely alluded to the fact that Muskrat Creek (Medicine Tail Coulee) was below the Santee camp [see p. 114].

Dr. John Gray said the village was about 3 miles long, but this is clearly wrong. Greg Michno wrote that the village was only about 1½ miles long,

stretching from the Medicine Tail Coulee ford (Ford B) to just beyond Shoulder Blade Creek (probably from where it comes out of the hills and not where it flows into the Little Big Horn) and the western edge of Garryowen Loop. This is the general area of the village as it is depicted on the McElfresh map and by measuring that distance it proves to be about 7,325 feet or 1.39 miles long. Neither Michno nor McElfresh take into account Wooden Leg's claim that the Cheyenne village extended a little farther north, and Wooden Leg should not be discounted:

> The Cheyenne location was about 2 miles north from the present railroad station at Garryowen, Montana. We were near the mouth of a small creek flowing from the southwestward into the river. Across the river east of us and a little upstream from us was a broad coulee, or little valley, having now the name Medicine Tail coulee [Marquis, *Wooden Leg,* p. 206].

The only creek near this location would have been Onion Creek. That would make the length of the village somewhere around 1¾ miles and it would fit perfectly with Wooden Leg's description, especially when compared to Ford B's location and Wooden Leg's description. The McElfresh map has Onion emptying into the Little Big Horn too far downstream, but a topographical map shows intermittent branches farther upstream and closer to Ford B. These little branches could have easily flowed into the river in 1876.

Appendix G.
Indian Dispositions and Weapons, June 25, 1876

Note—The following abbreviations are used to denote the various tribal designations:

A — Arapaho
B — Blackfeet Sioux
C — Cheyenne (Northern or Southern unknown)
CB — Cu Brulé Sioux
C/U — Cheyenne/Ute
H — Hunkpapa Sioux
L — Lakota Sioux (specific tribe unknown)
M — Minneconjou Sioux
NC — Northern Cheyenne
N-S — Nakota Santee
O — Oglala Sioux
S — Santee Sioux
SA — Sans Arc Sioux
T — Teton-Sioux
2K — Two Kettle Sioux

Indians Believed to Have Been at the Ford B Fight

According to Wooden Leg, if the village were attacked, the camp guards would rally to its defense. It would therefore make sense that any camp guards remaining in the Cheyenne camp would have rallied at Ford B. The Kit Fox warrior society provided the Cheyenne camp guards on June 25.

Cheyenne (seven to ten; possibly a few more):

- Bob-tail Horse
- Roan Bear
- Buffalo Calf
- Big Nose
- Mad Wolf
- White Shield — not there initially, but joined them a few minutes later.
- Rising Sun
- Hanging Wolf
- Young Little Wolf— he first saw Custer in MTC, which should put him near the ford.
- American Horse — the Cheyenne chief, returning from the Reno fight where he was not one of those crossing the Little Big Horn.
- Possibly Pawnee, Wooden Thigh, Yellow Horse, and Horse Road, who were camp guards.

Sioux (maybe four or five):

- White Cow Bull (Oglala)
- *Shave Elk* (Oglala): *Possibly* at Ford B. A member of Big Road's Northern band of Oglala Sioux, Shave Elk and four others were riding up Medicine Tail Coulee when they saw Custer's column coming at them. They rode back down, crossed at Ford B, and it is not unreasonable — though not certain — that one or more of them stayed to help defend the ford. If they all stayed — and that is equally unlikely — then it would explain the various commentaries about four or five Sioux being at the ford. If Shave Elk's band remained at Ford B to oppose the on-coming soldiers, it could mean as many as twenty Indians fought Custer's column at the crossing. This, of course, would include the four Cheyenne camp guards, above. Yellow Nose, a Ute/Cheyenne, may have been another.

Cheyenne Who Found Curtiss' Pack (Little Wolf's Band)

- Black Horse
- Big Crow
- Red Cherries

Indians Believed to Have Been Near the Divide on the Morning of 25 June

- Black Bear (O)
- Dirt Kettle (O)
- Fast Horn (O)
- Blue Cloud (O)
- Kills Enemy in Winter (O)
- Knife (O)
- Medicine Bird (O)
- Owl Bull (O)

- Plenty of Meat (S)
- Brown Back (aka Brown Pants) (H)
- Deeds (H)
- Drags the Rope (O)
- Lone Dog (SA)
- Standing Black Bear (L)
- Two Bears (SA) — killed back toward Reno Hill.

Known to be Part of Wolf Tooth's Band

1. Wolf Tooth (C)
2. Big Foot (C)

Indians Believed to Have Been on the East Side of the LBH

In a July 13, 1910, interview with Walter Camp, the Oglala warrior, He Dog, said there were 15 or 20 "Sioux" on east side of the river [Hammer, *Custer in '76*, p. 207].

1. Elk Stands Alone (SA) — killed there.
2. Eagle Elk (O)
3. Gall (H)
4. He Dog (O) — after the Reno fighting began, he crossed the river.
5. Iron Cedar (H)
6. Iron Thunder (M)
7. Kicking Bear (O)
8. Owns the Horn (M)
9. Red Feather (O)
10. Red Horse (M)
11. Running Eagle (O) — certainly during the Reno chase.
12. Shoots Bear as He Runs (M)
13. Standing Bear (M) — at least initially and long enough to see the Custer column. He was probably on "Black Butte," now known as Weir Peaks.
14. Whirlwind (C) — killed there, either by Little Brave or Bob-tail Bull, the Ree scouts.
15. White Bull/Lazy White Buffalo (M)
16. White Eagle (O) — certainly during the Reno chase. Killed.
17. White Shield (C)

18. Wooden Leg (C) — crossed while chasing Reno's retreating men. Re-crossed west, then again went east of the river. Was on the hills to the north of Reno's position when he heard someone shout that more soldiers were down-river.
19. Yellow Nose (C/U)
20. Young Skunk (O) — certainly during the Reno chase. Killed later.
21. Unknown (C)
22. Unknown (C)
23. *Mrs. Spotted Horn Bull* (H)

Indians Believed or Known to Have Fought in the Reno Valley Fight

Note: *Italics* indicate female.

1. American Horse (C)
2. American Horse/Iron Plume (M)
3. Bad Heart Bull (O)
4. Bear Ghost (H)
5. Beaver Heart (C)
6. Big Design (O) — killed.
7. Big Road (O)
8. Black Bear (C) — killed.
9. Black Elk (O)
10. Black Moon (H)
11. Brave Bear (C)
12. Brave Wolf (C)
13. Bull Bear (C)
14. Chased by Owls (2K) — killed.
15. Crazy Horse (O)
16. Crooked Nose (C)
17. Crow (L)
18. Crow King (H)
19. Crow Walking (M)
20. Deed [Act] (SA) — killed.
21. Dog with Horns (M) — killed.
22. Eagle Bear (O)
23. Eagle Elk (O)
24. Eagle Tail Feather (C)
25. Elk Heart (H) — wounded.
26. Elk Stands Alone (SA) — killed.
27. Fast Thunder (O)
28. Fears Nothing (O)

29. Feather Earring (M)
30. Flying By (M)
31. Flying Hawk (O)
32. Foolish Elk (O)
33. Good Bear Boy (H)
34. Gray Whirlwind (H)
35. Hard to Hit (O)
36. Hawk Man (SA) — killed.
37. He Dog (O)
38. High Eagle (T) — killed.
39. High Elk (SA) — killed.
40. High Horse (M)
41. His Holy Pipe (L)
42. Hollow Horn Bear (CB)
43. Holy Bull (O)
44. Holy Cloud (N-S)
45. Hump (M)
46. Iron Bear (N-S)
47. Iron Cedar (H)
48. Iron Thunder (M)
49. Kansu (H)
50. Kicking Bear (O)
51. Knife Chief (O) — wounded.
52. Little Bear/Crawler (H)
53. Little Big Man (O)
54. Little Bird (C)
55. Little Hawk (C)
56. Little Soldier (L)
57. Little Sun (C)
58. Lone Bear (O)
59. Lone Bull (H)
60. Long Elk [Lone Elk] (O) — wounded.
61. Looking Elk (H)
62. Low Dog (O)
63. *Moving Robe Woman* (H)
64. Old Man (C) — killed.
65. One Bull (M)
66. *One Who Walks with the Stars* (O)
67. Painted Brown (O)
68. Pine (C)
69. Plenty Crows (C)
70. Rectum (H)
71. Red Feather (O)
72. Red Hawk (O)
73. Red Horn Buffalo (O)
74. Red Horn Bull (M)
75. Respects Nothing (O)
76. Roman Nose (C) — killed.
77. Running Eagle (O)
78. Runs Fearless (O)
79. Runs the Enemy (2K)

80. Scabby (C)
81. Short Bull (O)
82. Soldier Hawk (O)
83. Soldier Wolf (C)
84. Standing Elk (SA) — killed.
85. Steals Horses (O)
86. Sun Bear (C)
87. Swift Bear (H) — killed.
88. Tall Bull (C)
89. Thunder Bear (N-S)
90. Turkey Leg (C)
91. Turtle Rib (M)
92. Two Bear (SA) — killed.
93. Two Eagles (CB)
94. Three Bears (M) — killed.
95. Two Moon (C)
96. Weasel Bear (NC)
97. Whirlwind (C) — killed.
98. White Buffalo (H) — killed.
99. White Bull (H) — killed.
100. White Bull (M)
101. White Eagle (O) — killed.
102. Wooden Leg (C)
103. Yellow Hair (C)
104. Young Black Moon (H) — killed.
105. Young Skunk (O)
106. Young Turkey Leg (C)

Indians Believed or Known to Have Fought Custer's Column

1. Afraid of Eagles (H)
2. All See Him (C)
3. American Horse/Iron Plume (M)
4. American Horse (C)
5. Appearing Elk (H)
6. Bad Bear (H)
7. Bad Light Hair (O) — killed.
8. Bear Ears (H)
9. Bear Horn (H) — killed.
10. Bear King (L)
11. Bear Lays Down (O)
12. Bear Lice (M)
13. Bear Tail (C)
14. Bear's Cap (H)
15. Beard (M)
16. Bearded Man (C) — killed.
17. Big Beaver (C)
18. Big Elk (O)
19. Big Foot (C)
20. Big Nose (C)
21. Black Bear (C) — killed.
22. Black Cloud (C) — killed.
23. Black Moon (H) — killed.
24. Black White Man (O) — killed.
25. Bob-tail Horse (C)
26. Braided Locks (C)
27. Brave Bear (C)
28. Brave Cow (L)
29. Brave Crow (L)
30. Brave Hawk (L)
31. Brave Wolf (C)
32. Brings Plenty (H)
33. Buffalo Calf (C)
34. Bull (M)
35. Bull Bear (C)
36. Bull Head (C)
37. Burst Thunder (L)
38. Charging Hawk (M)
39. Closed Hand (C) — killed.
40. Cloud Man (SA) — killed.
41. Club Man (O)
42. Comes in Sight (C)
43. Contrary Belly (C)
44. Cotton Man (L)
45. Crazy Head (C)
46. Crazy Horse (O)
47. Crow Bear (L)
48. Crow Boy (SA)
49. Crow Dog (O)
50. Crow King (H)
51. Crow Necklace (C)
52. Cut [Open] Belly (C) — killed.
53. Did Not Go Home (SA)
54. Did Not Go Home (C)
55. Dog (L)
56. Eagle Bear (O)
57. Eagle Elk (O)
58. Eagle Man (L)
59. Elk Bear (SA) — killed.
60. Elk Nation (H)
61. Fast Eagle (O)
62. Fast Thunder (O)
63. Fears Nothing (O)
64. Feather Earring (M)
65. Flat Hip (H)
66. Flying By (O)
67. Flying By (M) — killed.
68. Flying By (C) — killed.
69. Flying Hawk (O)
70. Foolish Elk (O)
71. Gall (H)
72. Good Fox (M)
73. Gray Earth Track (S)
74. Hanging Wolf (C)
75. Has Horns (H)
76. Hawk (C)
77. Hawk Man (H) — killed.
78. Hawk Stays Up (H)
79. He Dog (O)
80. High Bear (C)
81. High Horse (M) — killed.
82. Hollow Horn Bear (CB)
83. Horny Horse (H)
84. Howling Wolf (C)
85. Hump (M)
86. Iron Hawk (H or O)
87. Iron Lightning (L)
88. Iron Thunder (M)
89. Kicking Bear (O)
90. Kill Eagle (B)
91. Kills Him (SA) — killed.
92. Kills in the Night (C)
93. Lame White Man (C) — killed.
94. Left Hand (A)
95. Left Hand (C) — killed.
96. Lights (M)
97. Limber Bones (C) — killed.
98. Little Bear/Crawler (H)
99. Little Bear (C)
100. Little Big Man (O)
101. Little Buck Elk (H)
102. Little Crow (M)
103. Little Eagle (L)
104. Little Face (C)
105. Little Horse (C)
106. Little Robe (C)
107. Little Shield (C)
108. Little Sun (C)
109. Little Whirlwind (C) — killed.
110. Lone Bear (O)
111. Lone Dog (SA) — killed.
112. Long Dog (H)
113. Long Elk (M)
114. Low Dog (O)
115. Mad Wolf (C)

116. The Man Who Walks with His Dogs (L)
117. Many Claws (L)
118. Many Lice (O) — killed.
119. Medicine Bear (C)
120. *Moving Robe Woman* (H)
121. No Flesh (CB)
122. Noisy Walking (C) — killed.
123. Old Bear (C)
124. One Elk (L)
125. Owns Red Horse (C) — killed.
126. Owns the Horn (M)
127. Painted Brown (O)
128. Pine (C)
129. Rain-in-the-Face (H)
130. Rattling Hawk (O)
131. Rectum (H) — killed.
132. Red Face (H) — killed.
133. Red Feather (O)
134. Red Fox (C)
135. Red Hawk (O)
136. Red Horn Buffalo (H) — killed.
137. Red Horse (D-S)
138. Respects Nothing (O)
139. Rising Sun (C)
140. Roan Bear (C)
141. Runs in Circle (H or O)
142. Scarlet Bear (L)
143. Scarlet Eagle (L)
144. Scarlet Thunder (M)
145. Shave Elk (O)
146. Shoots Bear as He Runs (M)
147. Shoots Walking (H)
148. Short Bull (O)
149. Soldier Wolf (C)
150. Sounds the Ground as He Walks (D-S)
151. Spotted Elk (M)
152. Spotted Rabbit (M)
153. Standing Bear (M)
154. Stands First (O)
155. Strong (L)
156. Sun Bear (C)
157. Swift Cloud (C) — killed.
158. Tall Bull (C)
159. Thunder Bear (N-S)
160. Turtle Rib (M)
161. Two Bulls (N-S)
162. Two Eagles (CB)

163. Two Moon (C)
164. Walks Last (C)
165. Waterman (A)
166. Weasel Bear (NC)
167. White Bird (C)
168. White Body (C)
169. White Bull (M)
170. White Cow Bull (O)
171. White Elk (C)
172. White Horse (L)
173. White Shield (C)
174. With Horns (M)
175. Wolf Medicine (C)
176. Wolf Tooth (C)
177. Wooden Leg (C)
178. Wooden Thigh (C)
179. Yellow Hair (C)
180. Yellow Horse (C)
181. Yellow Nose (C/U)
182. Young Bear (C) — killed.
183. Young Bear (L) — killed.
184. Young Little Wolf (C) — killed.
185. Young Skunk (O) — killed.

Indians Known or Thought to Have Fought with Crazy Horse

Note: Most of the warriors listed on the Crazy Horse surrender ledger are *believed* to have been part of this group. Only a few are *known* for sure to have fought with the great chieftain. They are marked as such. The rest are listed only as possibilities.

1. American Horse
2. Around the Quiver
3. Ass Hole
4. At the End
5. Bad Hand
6. Bad Minneconjou
7. Bad Partisan
8. Bad Sucker
9. Bad Warrior
10. Bear Bird
11. Bear Jaw
12. Bear Star
13. Belly
14. Belly Full
15. Belly Inside
16. Big Belly Mule
17. Big Bend

18. Big Eater
19. Big Lodge Chimney
20. Big Owl
21. Black Elk — for Reno fight.
22. Black Eye Lid
23. Black Kills (NC)
24. Blackbird
25. Bloody Knife
26. Blue Horse
27. Bluff
28. Brave Wolf
29. The Bud
30. The Bugger
31. The Bull
32. Bull Man
33. Butt Horn
34. The Chief
35. Chief Man
36. Clown (# 1)
37. Club Man
38. Comes Again
39. Comes from War
40. Comes the Day
41. Contrary
42. Crawler (O)
43. Crazy Bear
44. Crazy Head
45. Crazy Heart
46. Cross Prick
47. Crossways
48. Dancing Arrow
49. Dog Ear
50. Dog Nothing
51. Don't Amount to Anything
52. Don't Get Out of the Way
53. Dried Prick
54. Dry Lake
55. Duck Belly
56. Ear Ring Prick
57. Enemy
58. Face Turner
59. Fast Thunder (O) — known.
60. Fat Rump (# 1)
61. Feather Moon
62. Fills the Pipe
63. Fills Up
64. Flapping Horn
65. Fleece (NC) — not certain
66. Flying Hawk (O) — known.
67. Foolish Elk (O) — known.

68. Four Bullets
69. Four Crows (O)—known.
70. Gets Together
71. Ghost Hide
72. Gives Out
73. Good Boy
74. Gopher
75. Grandfather
76. Greases His Arm
77. Hairy
78. The Hand
79. Hangs His Head
80. He Dog (O)—known. Leader of the Soreback band.
81. Heap Bear Lays Down
82. High White Man
83. The Hill
84. Hoarse
85. Hole in Face
86. Hollow Sunflower
87. Horse Bear
88. Iron Magpie
89. Iron Tail
90. Iroquois Imitation
91. Jealous Bear
92. Kicking Bear (O)—known.
93. Kills at Night
94. Kills Many
95. Kills the Married
96. Knife
97. The Last
98. Lays Laughing
99. Leggings
100. Lightning Killer
101. The Lights
102. Likes to Fight
103. Little Back
104. Little Bear (NC)
105. Little Big Man
106. Little Boy
107. Little Buck
108. Little Bull
109. Little Hawk
110. Little Killer—member of Low Dog's band.
111. Little Prick
112. Living Bear
113. Loafer
114. Lone Bear (O)—known.
115. Lone Elk
116. Long Handle
117. Long Name
118. Long Visitor
119. Looks Like a Dog
120. Looks White
121. Looks Yellow
122. Makes Widows Cry
123. Man on Top
124. Melter
125. Moccasin Hide
126. Mountain
127. Neat Prick
128. No Neck
129. Noisy Arrow
130. Nose in Sight
131. Old
132. One Brings Shit Far Away
133. One Grass
134. One Kills at Eight Steps
135. One Teat
136. Pisses in the Horn
137. Plenty Dogs
138. Plenty Shells
139. Poor Bear
140. Poor Dog
141. Pretty Legs
142. Pretty Weasel (O)—known.
143. Pulls Out
144. Pumpkin Hill
145. Red Crane
146. Red Feather (O)—known.
147. Red Hawk (O)—known.
148. Red Rock
149. Red Tail
150. Ree
151. Rider
152. Robe Hair Outside
153. The Rump
154. Runner
155. Runs Close to Camp
156. Runs on Top
157. Scabby Face
158. Scabby Place
159. Scaring Bear
160. Sees the Cow
161. The Shield
162. Shits on His Head
163. Shits on the Eagle
164. Short
165. Short Brulé
166. Short Bull (O)—known.
167. Side Rib
168. Singing Bear
169. Singing Prick
170. Sits Up Above
171. Sitting Bear
172. Sitting Horse
173. Skunk Guts
174. Skunk Head
175. Sleeps There
176. Slow White Cow
177. Snake Creek
178. Snatch Loser
179. Snatch Stealer
180. Soft Prick
181. Soldier
182. Spotted Hand
183. Spotted Wolf (NC)
184. Spread Pine
185. Spunker
186. Star
187. Stinking Tie
188. Strong Fox
189. Tall Bull
190. Tanned Nuts
191. Thick Face
192. Three Hawks
193. Thunder Hawk
194. Thunder Tail
195. Ties His Hair
196. Tobacco
197. Top Lodge
198. Torn Belly
199. Touches His Grub
200. Tripe
201. Tripe Fold
202. Two Face
203. Undone
204. Walking Medicine
205. Walks in Mud
206. War Shanty
207. Warms His Blanket
208. Water Snake
209. Whistler—member of Low Dog's band.
210. Whistler (# 2)
211. White Bear (# 1)
212. White Bear (# 2)
213. White Bull (M)—joined the band once it was behind Keogh's battalion.
214. White Cloud
215. White Cross Eye
216. White Face
217. White Hair
218. White Rabbit
219. White Star
220. White Twin
221. The Whore
222. Woman Bone
223. Wood Boat
224. Wood Root

225. Wounded in Back
226. Wrinkled Face
227. Wrinkler
228. Yellow Left
229. Yellow Robe
230. Young Skunk — killed.

Indians Known to Have Fought with Kill Eagle

1. Afraid of Eagles (H)
2. Bear Ears (H)
3. Bear King (L)
4. Brave Hawk (L)
5. Bull (M)
6. Dog (L)
7. Eagle Man (L)
8. Little Eagle (L)
9. Scarlet Bear (L)
10. Scarlet Eagle (L)
11. Scarlet Thunder (M)
12. Strong (L)
13. The Man Who Walks with His Dogs (L)

The Cheyenne Suicide "Boys" or Suicide "Warriors"

• Little Whirlwind — *questionable.*
• Cut Belly — 30 years old.
• Closed Hand — 20 years old.
• Noisy Walking — 15 or 18 years old.
• Limber Bones — 20 years old.
• Roman Nose — 16 years old.
• Liddic claims there were 5 Cheyenne suicide boys, all less than 20 years of age [*Vanishing Victory,* p. 158].
• Note: The night before the battle — and   unrelated — a dance was held honoring those young men who had vowed to sacrifice their lives in the event of a fight. Most were young Cheyenne men or boys, but there were Sioux as well, primarily Oglala.
• The suicide boys/warriors were among the last warriors to enter the fight. There is some evidence — probably speculative — that the suicide boys were the ones that overran the E Company position on Cemetery Ridge, forcing George Custer

to move his troops to Last Stand Hill where the final minutes of the fight were played out.

Greg Michno talks about the "suicide boys" as being a point of contention with modern writers. "The idea that families would let their young sons take a suicide vow is questioned by contemporary authors.... Yet, self-sacrifice was not all unknown.... In Hassrick, *The Sioux,* 32, 74, 100, 294, we are told that it was a Lakota maxim that it was better to die in battle than live to be old, that war demanded sacrifice, that sacrifice of life could be worth the price, and that even self-destruction was a proven method of securing recognition from one's fellow men as well as from the gods. Perhaps 'suicide boys' was just a poor translation of a Native American concept whites could not easily understand."

In his article, "Lingering Clouds at the Greasy Grass" [*Research Review,* Vol. 19, No. 2, Summer, 2005, p. 5], Cesare Marino claimed there were at least twenty young men, Lakota and Cheyenne, involved as the so-called "suicide boys."

Indian Sharpshooters Believed to be on Sharpshooters' Ridge

1. Big Ankles (M)
2. Big Foot (C)
3. Sandstone (C)
4. Sleeping Rabbit (C)
5. Spotted Elk (C)
6. White Cow Bull (O)

Known Sioux and Cheyenne Firearms at the Battle of the Little Bighorn

(Primarily from Fox, *Archaeology, History, and Custer's Last Battle*; Scott and Fox, *Archaeological Insights into the Custer Battle*; and Scott, Fox, and Connor, *Archaeological Perspectives on the Battle of the Little Bighorn.*)

1. Forehand and Wadsworth [Ethan Allen] .32-caliber
2. Forehand and Wadsworth [Ethan Allen] .42-caliber
3. Colt .36-caliber
4. Colt .38-caliber
5. Sharps .40-caliber
6. Smith and Wesson .44-caliber
7. Evans Old Model .44-caliber
8. Henry .44-caliber
9. Winchester Model 1873 .44-caliber
10. Winchester 66, "Yellow Boy," .44-caliber Henry rimfire
11. Colt conversion .44-caliber
12. Colt Model 1860 .44-caliber
13. Colt Model 1871 .44-caliber
14. Colt Model 1872 .44-caliber
15. Remington New Model Army 1858 .44-caliber percussion revolver
16. Remington Model 1858 conversion .44-caliber
17. Ballard .44-caliber
18. Colt Model 1873 pistol .45-caliber (Army-issue)
19. Springfield Model 1873 carbine .45-caliber (Army-issue)
20. Sharps Sporting Rifle .45-caliber
21. Sharps .45-caliber
22. Sharps .50-caliber
23. Maynard .50-caliber
24. Smith .50-caliber
25. Springfield .50-caliber
26. Starr .54-caliber
27. Spencer .56/56
28. Spencer .56/50
29. Enfield .577-caliber
30. At least eight other unknown .40-, .44-, .45-, and .50-caliber weapons
31. Shotgun of unknown type
32. .44-caliber center-fire Old Model Colt Boxer primed
33. .58-caliber muzzleloaders
34. .44-caliber rimfire Long F. Wesson rifle

Bibliography

Books

Axelrod, Alan. *Art of the Golden West*. New York: Abbeville Press, 1990.

Barnard, Sandy (ed.). *Ten Years with Custer: A 7th Cavalryman's Memoirs*. Terre Haute, IN: AST Press, 2001.

Bradley, Lieutenant James H., and Edgar I. Stewart (ed.). *The March of the Montana Column*. Norman: University of Oklahoma Press, 2001.

Bray, Kingsley M. *Crazy Horse*. Norman: University of Oklahoma Press, 2006.

Brininstool, E. A. *A Trooper with Custer and Other Historic Incidents of the Battle of the Little Big Horn*. Columbus, OH: The Hunter — Trader — Trapper Co., 1925.

Brust, James S., Brian C. Pohanka, and Sandy Barnard. *Where Custer Fell*. Norman: University of Oklahoma Press, 2005.

Callwell, Colonel C. E. *Small Wars: Their Principles & Practice*. Lincoln, NE: Bison Books/University of Nebraska Press, 1996.

Camp, Walter Mason, and Kenneth Hammer (ed.). *Custer in '76*. Norman: University of Oklahoma Press, 1990.

Camp, Walter M., Richard G. Hardorff (ed.). *On the Little Bighorn with Walter Camp*. El Segundo, CA: Upton & Sons, 2002.

Carell, Paul. *Foxes of the Desert*. Atglen, PA: Schiffer Military History, 1994.

Carroll, John M. *The Benteen-Goldin Letters on Custer and His Last Battle*. New York: Liveright, 1974.

_____. (ed.). *General Custer and the Battle of the Little Big Horn: The Federal View*. Bryan, TX, and Mattituck, NY: J. M. Carroll, 1986.

Chorne, Laudie J. *Following the Custer Trail of 1876*. Bismarck, ND: Printing Plus, 1997.

Clark, George. *Scalp Dance: The Edgerly Papers on the Battle of the Little Big Horn*. Oswego, NY: Heritage Press, 1985.

Connell, Evan. *Son of the Morning Star*. New York: HarperCollins, 1984.

Cross, Walt. *Custer's Lost Officer*. Stillwater, OK: Cross Publications, 2006.

Curtis, Edward Sheriff. Florence Curtis Graybill, and Victor Boesen, (eds.). *Visions of a Vanishing Race*. Edison, NJ: Promontory Press, 1994.

Darling, Roger. *Benteen's Scout*. El Segundo, CA: Upton & Sons, 2000.

DeMallie, Raymond J. (ed.) *The Sixth Grandfather*. Lincoln: University of Nebraska Press, 1985.

Donahue, Michael N. *Drawing Battle Lines: The Map Testimony of Custer's Last Fight*. El Segundo, CA: Upton and Sons, 2008.

Donovan, James. *A Terrible Glory*. New York: Little, Brown, 2008.

Dustin, Fred. *The Custer Tragedy*. Glendale, CA: Arthur H. Clark, 1965.

Fox, Richard Allan, Jr. *Archaeology, History, and Custer's Last Battle*. Norman: University of Oklahoma Press, 1993.

Graham, Colonel William A. *The Custer Myth*. Mechanicsburg, PA: Stackpole Books, 2000.

Gray, John S. *Custer's Last Campaign*. Lincoln: University of Nebraska Press, 1993.

Greene, Jerome A. *Evidence and the Custer Enigma*. Silverthorne, CO: Vistabooks, 1995.

Hardorff, Richard G. *The Custer Battle Casualties*. El Segundo, CA: Upton and Sons, 2002.

_____. *The Custer Battle Casualties, II*. El Segundo, CA: Upton and Sons, 1999.

_____. *Hokahey! A Good Day to Die!* Lincoln: Bison/University of Nebraska Press, 1999.

Hart, John P. (ed.) *Custer and His Times, Book Five*, Cordova, TN: The Little Big Horn Associates, 2008.

Heitman, Francis B. *Historical Register and Dictionary of the United States Army*. Washington, D.C.: Government Printing Office, 1903.

Holmes, Richard (ed.). *The Oxford Companion to Military History*. New York: Oxford University Press, 2001.

Hutchins, James S. (ed.). *The Army and Navy Journal on the Battle of the Little Bighorn and Related Matters, 1876–1881*. El Segundo, CA: Upton and Sons, 2003.

Kershaw, Robert J. *Red Sabbath*. Hersham, Surrey, UK: Ian Allan, 2005.

King, W. Kent. *Massacre: The Custer Cover-Up.* El Segundo, CA: Upton, 1989.

Klokner, James B. *The Officer Corps of Custer's Seventh Cavalry.* Atglen, PA: Schiffer Military History, 2007.

Kuhlman, Charles A. *Legend into History.* Harrisburg, PA: Stackpole, 1952.

Libby, Orin G. (ed.). *The Arikara Narrative of Custer's Campaign and the Battle of the Little Bighorn.* Norman: University of Oklahoma Press, 1998.

Liddic, Bruce R. *Vanishing Victory.* El Segundo, CA: Upton, 2004.

_____, and Paul Harbaugh. *Camp on Custer.* Spokane, WA: Arthur H. Clark, 1995.

Maddra, Sam A. *Hostiles? The Lakota Ghost Dance and Buffalo Bill's Wild West.* Norman: University of Oklahoma Press, 2006.

Marquis, Thomas B., Int. *Wooden Leg: A Warrior Who Fought Custer.* Lincoln: University of Nebraska Press, 1931 [1965].

Michno, Gregory F. *Lakota Noon.* Missoula, MT: Mountain Press, 1997.

_____. *The Mystery of E Troop.* Missoula, MT: Mountain Press, 1994.

Neihardt, John G. (ed.). *Black Elk Speaks.* Lincoln: University of Nebraska Press, 1988.

Nichols, Ronald H., ed. *Men with Custer.* Hardin, MT: Custer Battlefield Historical & Museum Association, 2000.

_____. *Reno Court of Inquiry.* Hardin, MT: Custer Battlefield Historical & Museum Association, 1996.

O'Neil, Tom, compiler. *The Field Diary and Official Report of General Alfred H. Terry.* Brooklyn, NY: Arrow and Trooper, date unknown.

Overfield, Loyd J., II. *The Little Big Horn, 1876.* Lincoln: University of Nebraska Press, 1990.

Pennington, Jack. *The Battle of the Little Bighorn.* El Segundo, CA: Upton, 2001.

Schoenberger, Dale T. *End of Custer.* Blaine, WA: Hancock House, 1995.

Scott, Douglas D., and Richard A. Fox, Jr. *Archaeological Insights into the Custer Battle.* Norman: University of Oklahoma Press, 1987.

Scott, Douglas D., and Richard A. Fox, Jr., and Melissa A. Connor. *Archaeological Perspectives on the Battle of the Little Bighorn.* Norman: University of Oklahoma Press, 1989.

Scott, Douglas D., P. Willey, Melissa A. Connor. *They Died with Custer.* Norman: University of Oklahoma Press, 1998.

Smalley, Vern. *Little Bighorn Mysteries.* Bozeman, MT: Little Buffalo Press, 2005.

_____. *More Little Bighorn Mysteries.* Bozeman, MT: Little Buffalo Press, 2005.

Stewart, Edgar I. *Custer's Luck.* Norman: University of Oklahoma Press, 1955.

Sturtevant, William C. (gen. ed.), and Raymond J. DeMallie (ed.). *Handbook of North American Indians.* Vol. 13. Washington D.C.: Smithsonian Institute, 2001.

Swanson, Glenwood J. *G. A. Custer, His Life and Times.* Agua Dulce, CA: Swanson Productions, 2004.

Taylor, William O., with Greg Martin. *With Custer on the Little Bighorn.* New York: Viking Press, 1996.

Varnum, Charles A., John Carroll (ed.). *I, Varnum.* Mattituck, NY: J. M. Carroll, 1982.

Viola, Herman J. *Little Bighorn Remembered.* New York: Rivilo Books; Times Books, Random House, 1999.

Welch, James, and Paul Stekler. *Killing Custer.* New York: W. W. Norton, 1994.

Willert, James. *Little Big Horn Diary.* El Segundo, CA: Upton and Sons, 1997.

Williams, Roger L. *Military Register of Custer's Last Command.* Norman, OK: Arthur H. Clark, 2009.

Windolph, Charles A., Frazier Hunt, Hunt Robert (eds.). *I Fought with Custer.* Lincoln: University of Nebraska Press, 1987.

Articles, Journals, and Periodicals

Abrams, Marc (ed.). *Last Stand Magazine.* Brooklyn, NY. Vol. 1 (April 2009).

_____. *Last Stand Magazine.* Brooklyn, NY. Vol. 2 (August 2009).

Boyes, William W., Jr. "Custer's Battle Plan for 25 June 1876." *Research Review,* Vol. 22, No. 1 (Winter 2008).

Dickson, Ephriam D., III. *Reconstructing the Indian Village at the Little Bighorn: The Cankahuhan or Soreback Band, Oglala.*

_____. *Reconstructing the Little Bighorn Village: The Big Road Roster and the Oglala Tribal Circle.*

_____. *The Sitting Bull Surrender Census.* 21st Annual Symposium Custer Battlefield Historical & Museum, Association, Inc., June 22, 2007.

_____. Standing Rock Agency Letter and List of Little Bighorn Participants, April 7, 1926.

Godfrey, E. S. "Custer's Last Battle." *Century Magazine,* January 1892. Reprint by OUTBOOKS, Olympic Valley, CA, 1976.

Hillyer, Raymond C. "Which They Had Captured All." *Research Review,* Vol. 21, No. 1 (Winter 2007).

Mangum, Neil C. "The Little Bighorn Campaign." *Blue & Gray,* Vol. XXIII, No. 2 (2006).

Marino, Cesare. "Lingering Clouds at the Greasy Grass." *Research Review,* Vol. 19, No. 2 (Summer 2005).

Montana Historical Society. *Montana: The Magazine of Western History.* Summer 1960.

Myers, Stephen W. "Roster of Known Hostile Indians at the Battle of the Little Big Horn." *Research Review,* Vol. 5, No. 2 (June 1991).

The New Yorker, April 5, 2004.

Nunnally, Michael. "Seventh U.S. Cavalry Trooper Grave Found?" *LBHA Newsletter,* Vol. XLIII, No. 3 (April 2009).

Saum, Lewis O. "Private John F. O'Donohue's Reflections on the LBH." *Montana Magazine,* Vol. 50, No. 4 (Winter 2000).

Sklenar, Larry. "Too Soon Discredited?" *Research Review*, Vol. 9, No. 1 (January 1995).

Thompson, Peter. *The Experience of a Private Soldier in the Custer Massacre*. State Historical Society of North Dakota and the *Belle Fourche Bee*, 1914.

Thorn, John. Op-Ed, *New York Times*, October 22, 2005.

Wagner, Frederic C., III. "Frederic Francis Gerard, a Questionable Cause and an Unforeseen Effect." *Research Review*, Vol. 21, No. 1 (Winter 2007).

Archives and Documents

Camp, Walter. Field Notes, Folder 94, Brigham Young University Library.

Georgetown University Archives: *Catalogue of the Officers and Students, 1852–1853.*

Georgetown University Archives: *Catalogue of the Officers and Students, 1865–1866.*

Georgetown University Archives: *Catalogue of the Officers and Students, 1866–1867.*

Georgetown University Archives: *Catalogue of the Officers and Students, 1867–1868.*

Georgetown University Archives: *Catalogue of the Officers and Students, 1871–1872.*

Georgetown University Archives: *College Journal*, Georgetown College, Aug–Oct 1876, Vol. V, No. 1.

Georgetown University Archives: Entrance Book, 1850–1895.

United States Army Command and General Staff College. Various.

United States Census, 1900, Cheyenne River Agency, South Dakota

United States Census, 1900, Pine Ridge Agency, South Dakota.

United States Census, 1900, Standing Rock Agency, North Dakota.

United States Census, 1900, Standing Rock Agency, South Dakota.

United States National Archives, Regimental Returns for the Seventh U.S. Cavalry, 1876.

Index